Handbook of Research on Deep Learning Techniques for Cloud-Based Industrial IoT

P. Swarnalatha
Department of Information Security, School of Computer Science and Engineering, Vellore Institute of Technology, India

S. Prabu
Department Banking Technology, Pondicherry University, India

A volume in the Advances in Computational Intelligence and Robotics (ACIR) Book Series

Published in the United States of America by
    IGI Global
    Engineering Science Reference (an imprint of IGI Global)
    701 E. Chocolate Avenue
    Hershey PA, USA 17033
    Tel: 717-533-8845
    Fax: 717-533-8661
    E-mail: cust@igi-global.com
    Web site: http://www.igi-global.com

Library of Congress Cataloging-in-Publication Data

Names: Swarnalatha, P. (Purushotham), 1977- editor. | Prabu, S., 1981-
  editor.
Title: Handbook of research on deep learning techniques for cloud-based
  industrial IoT / edited by P. Swarnalatha, and S. Prabu.
Description: Hershey, PA : Engineering Science Reference, [2023] | Includes
  bibliographical references and index. | Summary: "Deep Learning
  Techniques for Cloud-Based Industrial IoT aims to demonstrate how
  computer scientists and engineers of today might employ artificial
  intelligence in practical applications with the emerging cloud and IoT
  technologies. The book also gathers recent research works in emerging
  artificial intelligence methods and applications for processing and
  storing the data generated from the cloud-based Internet of Things.
  Covering key topics such as data, cybersecurity, blockchain, and
  artificial intelligence, this premier reference source is ideal for
  industry professionals, engineers, computer scientists, researchers,
  scholars, academicians, practitioners, instructors, and students"--
  Provided by publisher.
Identifiers: LCCN 2023000689 (print) | LCCN 2023000690 (ebook) | ISBN
  9781668480984 (h/c) | ISBN 9781668480984 (eISBN)
Subjects: LCSH: Internet of things--Industrial applications. | Deep
  learning (Machine learning) | Cloud computing.
Classification: LCC TK5105.8857 .H337 2023 (print) | LCC TK5105.8857
  (ebook) | DDC 004.67/82--dc23/eng/20230126
LC record available at https://lccn.loc.gov/2023000689
LC ebook record available at https://lccn.loc.gov/2023000690

This book is published in the IGI Global book series Advances in Computational Intelligence and Robotics (ACIR) (ISSN: 2327-0411; eISSN: 2327-042X)

British Cataloguing in Publication Data
A Cataloguing in Publication record for this book is available from the British Library.

For electronic access to this publication, please contact: eresources@igi-global.com.

Advances in Computational Intelligence and Robotics (ACIR) Book Series

Ivan Giannoccaro
University of Salento, Italy

ISSN:2327-0411
EISSN:2327-042X

MISSION

While intelligence is traditionally a term applied to humans and human cognition, technology has progressed in such a way to allow for the development of intelligent systems able to simulate many human traits. With this new era of simulated and artificial intelligence, much research is needed in order to continue to advance the field and also to evaluate the ethical and societal concerns of the existence of artificial life and machine learning.

The **Advances in Computational Intelligence and Robotics (ACIR) Book Series** encourages scholarly discourse on all topics pertaining to evolutionary computing, artificial life, computational intelligence, machine learning, and robotics. ACIR presents the latest research being conducted on diverse topics in intelligence technologies with the goal of advancing knowledge and applications in this rapidly evolving field.

COVERAGE

- Evolutionary Computing
- Neural Networks
- Agent technologies
- Computer Vision
- Artificial Intelligence
- Intelligent Control
- Pattern Recognition
- Adaptive and Complex Systems
- Heuristics
- Synthetic Emotions

IGI Global is currently accepting manuscripts for publication within this series. To submit a proposal for a volume in this series, please contact our Acquisition Editors at Acquisitions@igi-global.com or visit: http://www.igi-global.com/publish/.

Titles in this Series

For a list of additional titles in this series, please visit: www.igi-global.com/book-series

Global Perspectives on Robotics and Autonomous Systems Development and Applications
Maki K. Habib (The American University in Cairo, gypt)
Engineering Science Reference • © 2023 • 310pp • H/C (ISBN: 9781668477915) • US $280.00

Scalable and Distributed Machine Learning and Deep Learning Patterns
J. Joshua Thomas (UOW Malaysia KDU Penang University College, Malaysia) S. Harini (Vellore Institute of Technology, India) and V. Pattabiraman (Vellore Institute of Technology, ndia)
Engineering Science Reference • © 2023 • 300pp • H/C (ISBN: 9781668498040) • US $270.00

Application and Adoption of Robotic Process Automation for Smart Cities
R. K. Tailor (Manipal University Jaipur, India)
Engineering Science Reference • © 2023 • 320pp • H/C (ISBN: 9781668471937) • US $270.00

Handbook of Research on Advancements in AI and IoT Convergence Technologies
Jingyuan Zhao (University of Toronto, Canada) V. Vinoth Kumar (Jain University, India) Rajesh Natarajan (University of Applied Science and Technology, Shinas, Oman) and T.R. Mahesh (Jain University, India)
Engineering Science Reference • © 2023 • 415pp • H/C (ISBN: 9781668469712) • US $380.00

Stochastic Processes and Their Applications in Artificial Intelligence
Christo Ananth (Samarkand State University, Uzbekistan) N. Anbazhagan (Alagappa University, India) and Mark Goh (National University of Singapore, Singapore)
Engineering Science Reference • © 2023 • 325pp • H/C (ISBN: 9781668476796) • US $270.00

Applying AI-Based IoT Systems to Simulation-Based Information Retrieval
Bhatia Madhulika (Amity University, India) Bhatia Surabhi (King Faisal University, Saudi Arabia) Poonam Tanwar (Manav Rachna International Institute of Research and Studies, India) and Kuljeet Kaur (Université du Québec, Canada)
Engineering Science Reference • © 2023 • 229pp • H/C (ISBN: 9781668452554) • US $270.00

AI-Enabled Social Robotics in Human Care Services
Sandeep Kautish (Lord Buddha Education Foundation, Nepal) Nirbhay Kumar Chaubey (Ganpat University, India) S.B. Goyal (City University, Malaysia) and Pawan Whig (Vivekananda Insitute of Professional Studies, India)
Engineering Science Reference • © 2023 • 321pp • H/C (ISBN: 9781668481714) • US $270.00

701 East Chocolate Avenue, Hershey, PA 17033, USA
Tel: 717-533-8845 x100 • Fax: 717-533-8661
E-Mail: cust@igi-global.com • www.igi-global.com

List of Contributors

Table of Contents

Detailed Table of Contents

Uma Maheswari P., CEG, Anna University, Chennai, India
Karishma V. R., Anna University, Chennai, India
T. Vigneswaran, SRM-TRB Engineering College, India

Surveillance is an essential component of security, and e-surveillance is one of the primary goals of the Indian Government's Digital India development initiative. Video surveillance offers a wide range of applications to reduce ecological and economic losses and becomes one of the most effective means of ensuring security. This chapter addresses the problem of how artificial intelligence is powering video surveillance. There is a significant research focus on video analytics but comparatively less effort has been taken for surveillance videos. However, there is little evidence that researchers have approached the issue of intelligent video surveillance in terms of suspicious action detection, crime scene description, face detection, crowd counting, and the like. Most AI-powered surveillance is based on deep neural networks and deep learning techniques using analysis of video frames as images. Consequently, this chapter aims to provide an overview and significance of how artificial intelligence techniques are employed in video surveillance and image processing.

G. Megala, Vellore Institute of Technology, India
P. Swarnalatha, Vellore Institute of Technology, India
S. Prabu, Pondicherry University, India
R. Venkatesan, SASTRA University, India
Anantharajah Kaneswaran, University of Jaffna, Sri Lanka

Content-based video retrieval is a research field that aims to develop advanced techniques for automatically analyzing and retrieving video content. This process involves identifying and localizing specific moments in a video and retrieving videos with similar content. Deep bimodal fusion (DBF) is proposed that uses modified convolution neural networks (CNNs) to achieve considerable visual modality. This deep bimodal fusion approach relies on the integration of information from both visual and audio modalities.

By combining information from both modalities, a more accurate model is developed for analyzing and retrieving video content. The main objective of this research is to improve the efficiency and effectiveness of video retrieval systems. By accurately identifying and localizing specific moments in videos, the proposed method has higher precision, recall, F1-score, and accuracy in precise searching that retrieves relevant videos more quickly and effectively.

Chapter 3

Jennyfer Susan M. B., Centre for Machine Learning and Intelligence, Avinashilingam Institute for Home Science and Higher Education for Women, India

P. Subashini, Centre for Machine Learning and Intelligence, Avinashilingam Institute for Home Science and Higher Education for Women, India

M. Krishnaveni, Centre for Machine Learning and Intelligence, Avinashilingam Institute for Home Science and Higher Education for Women, India

Smart healthcare systems are the health services that use the technologies like wearable devices, internet of things (IoT), and mobile internet to access medical information dynamically. It connects people, materials, and institutions related to healthcare; actively manages; and automatically responds to medical ecosystem needs. It helps the traditional medical system in making healthcare more efficient, convenient, and personalized. This chapter proposed (1) a review of smart healthcare development using artificial intelligence, the internet of things, and smartphone Android apps; (2) an experimental approach using IoT-based smart monitoring systems, Android apps for data collection, and artificial algorithms to predict cervical cancer diseases; (3) the integration of IoT and AI algorithms. Artificial intelligence of things (AIoT) is proposed in this chapter as an experimental method for predicting cervical cancer from smart colposcopy images. The literature published in international journals and proceedings between 2010 and June 2022 is considered for the study.

Chapter 4

V. Valliammai, Vellore Institute of Technology, India

Karjala Sandhya, Vellore Institute of Technology, India

Vemuri Lakshmi Harshitha, Vellore Institute of Technology, India

Pariha Parvaze Podili, Vellore Institute of Technology, India

Niha Kamal Basha, Vellore Institute of Technology, India

Advancement of technology had a significant impact on various industries, with innovative solutions like cloud computing, IoT, augmented reality (AR), and virtual reality (VR) changing the game in many ways. Here is a system known as "virtual try-ons" that leverages IoT devices like mobile cameras, cloud storage for data, and an intelligent interface for user interaction. Many people are opting for online shopping, and various challenges arise with this transition, one of which is the issue of "try-on." VR solves this challenge by introducing "virtual try-on," which replaces traditional try-on methods. It enables an individual to preview and virtually try on their desired products like clothes, watches, shoes, etc. from the comfort of their own homes, making the shopping experience easier and smoother. It also adds an element of fun and excitement to the shopping experience, increasing the hedonic value for consumers and allowing consumers to experiment and play with different products, styles, and colors in a way that is not possible with traditional shopping methods.

S. Venkata Suryanarayana, CVR College of Engineering, India
Katakam Koushik, CVR College of Engineering, India
Prabu Sevugan, Pondicherry University, India

Identification of insulator defects is one of the most important goals of an intelligent examination of high-voltage transmission lines. Because they provide mechanical support for electric transmission lines as well as electrical insulation, insulators are essential to the secure and reliable operation of power networks. A fresh dataset is first built by collecting aerial pictures in various scenes that have one or more defects. A feature pyramid network and an enhanced loss function are used by the CSPD-YOLO model to increase the precision of insulator failure detection. The insulator defective data set, which has two classes (insulator, defect), is used by the suggested technique to train and test the model using the YOLOv5 object detection algorithm. The authors evaluate how well the YOLOv3, YOLOv5, and related families perform when trained on the insulator defective dataset. Practitioners can use this information to choose the appropriate technique based on the insulator defective dataset.

V. Sanjay, Vellore Institute of Technology, Vellore, India
P. Swarnalatha, Vellore Institute of Technology, Vellore, India

Blockchain is an emerging technology that is now being used to provide novel solutions in several industries, including healthcare. Deep learning (DL) algorithms have grown in popularity in medical image processing research. AD is diagnosed by magnetic resonance imaging (MRI) images. This study investigates the integration of blockchain technology with a DL model for Alzheimer's disease prediction (AD). This proposed model was used to classify 3182 images from the ADNI collection. The edge-based segmentation algorithm has overcome the segmentation problem. During the investigation's test stage, the DL-EfficientNetB0 model with blockchain earned the highest accuracy rate of 99.14%. The highest accuracy, sensitivity, and specificity scores were obtained utilizing the confusion matrix during the comparative assessment stage. According to the study's results, EfficientNetB0 with blockchain model surpassed all other trained models in classification rate. This study will aid clinical research into the early detection and prevention of AD by identifying the sickness before it occurs.

G. Aarthi, B.S. Abdur Rahman Crescent Institute of Science and Technology, India
S. Sharon Priya, B.S. Abdur Rahman Crescent Institute of Science and Technology, India
W. Aisha Banu, B.S. Abdur Rahman Crescent Institute of Science and Technology, India

The rapid development of internet of things (IoT) applications has created enormous possibilities, increased our productivity, and made our daily life easier. However, because of resource limitations and processing, IoT networks are open to number of threats. The network instruction detection system (NIDS) aims to provide a variety of methods for identifying the increasingly common cyberattacks (such as distributed denial of service [DDoS], denial of service [DoS], theft, etc.) and to prevent hazardous activities. In order to determine which algorithm is more effective in detecting network threats, multiple public datasets and different artificial intelligence (AI) techniques are evaluated. Some of the learning algorithms like logistic regression, random forest, decision tree, naive bayes, auto-encoder, and artificial neural network were analysed and concluded on the NF-BoT-IoT dataset using various evaluation metrics. In order to train the model for future anomaly detection prediction and analysis, the feature extraction and pre-processing data were then supplied into NIDS as data.

Shiva Chaithanya Goud Bollipelly, Vellore Institute of Technology, India
P. Swarnalatha, Vellore Institute of Technology, India

This chapter aims to create a real-time object detection and audio output system for blind users using the YOLOv3 algorithm and a 360-degree camera sensor. The system is designed to detect a wide range of objects, including people, vehicles, and other objects in the environment, and provide audio feedback to the user. The system architecture consists of a 360-degree camera sensor, a processing unit, and an audio output system. The camera sensor captures the environment, which is processed by the processing unit, which uses the YOLOv3 algorithm to detect and classify objects. The audio output system provides audio feedback to the user based on the objects detected by the system. The project has significant importance for blind users as it can help them navigate their environment and recognize objects in real time and can serve as a foundation for future research in the field of object detection systems for blind users.

Mohan Raj C. S., Hindusthan College of Arts and Science, India
A. V. Senthil Kumar, Hindusthan College of Arts and Sciences, India
Ismail Musirin, Universiti Teknologi MARA, Malaysia
Saifullah Khalid, Civil Aviation Research Organisation, India
Rohaya Latip, Universiti Teknologi MARA, Malaysia
Namita Mishra, ITS School of Management, India
Gaganpreet Kaur, Chitkara University, India

Increasing demand for food quality and size has increased the need for industrialization and intensification in the agricultural sector. The internet of things (IoT) is a promising technology that offers many innovative solutions to transform the agricultural sector. Research institutes and scientific groups are constantly working to provide solutions and products for different areas of agriculture using IoT. The main objective of this methodological study is to collect all relevant research results on agricultural IoT applications, sensors/devices, communication protocols, and network types. The authors also talk about the main problems and encounters encountered in the field of agriculture. An IoT agriculture framework is also available that contextualizes the view of various current farming solutions. National guidelines on IoT-based agriculture were also presented. Finally, open issues and challenges were presented, and researchers were highlighted as promising future directions in the field of IoT agriculture.

Chapter 10

Pranav Katte, Vellore Institute of Technology, India
Pranav Arage, Vellore Institute of Technology, India
Satvik Nadkarni, Vellore Institute of Technology, India
Ramani Selvanambi, Vellore Institute of Technology, India

Deep artificial neural network applications to robotic systems have seen a surge of study due to advancements in deep learning over the past 10 years. The ability of robots to explain the descriptions of their decisions and beliefs leads to a collaboration with the human race. The intensity of the challenges increases as robotics moves from lab to the real-world scenario. Existing robotic control algorithms find it extremely difficult to master the wide variety seen in real-world contexts. The robots have now been developed and advanced to such an extent that they can be useful in our day-to-day lives. All this has been possible because of improvisation of the algorithmic techniques and enhanced computation powers. The majority of traditional machine learning techniques call for parameterized models and functions that must be manually created, making them unsuitable for many robotic jobs. The pattern recognition paradigm may be switched from the combined learning of statistical representations, labelled classifiers, to the joint learning of manmade features and analytical classifiers.

Chapter 11

Palanivel Kuppusamy, Pondicherry University, India
Suresh Joseph K., Pondicherry University, India
Suganthi Shanmugananthan, Annamalai University, India

Modern agriculture primarily relies on smart agriculture to predict crop yields and make decisions. Crop productivity could suffer due to a lack of farmers, labor shortages in the agricultural sector, adverse weather, etc. Smart farming uses advanced technology to improve the productivity and efficiency of agriculture. Crop yield is increased with smart agriculture, which also keeps an eye on agricultural pests. Artificial intelligence is an innovative technology that uses sensor data to predict the future and make judgments for farmers. AI methods like machine learning and deep learning are the most clever way to boost agricultural productivity. Adopting AI can help with farming issues and promote increased food production. Deep learning is a modern method for processing images and analyzing big data, showing promise for producing superior results. The primary goals of this study are to examine the benefits of employing DL in smart agricultural applications and to suggest a multi-cloud DL architecture for such applications.

Jonathan Rufus Samuel, Vellore Institute of Technology, India
Shivansh Sahai, Vellore Institute of Technology, India
P. Swarnalatha, Vellore Institute of Technology, India
Prabu Sevugan, Pondicherry University, India
V. Balaji, Vardhaman College of Engineering, India

The music space in today's world is ever evolving and expanding. With great improvements to today's technology, we have been able to bring out music to the vast majority of today's ever-growing and tech-savvy people. In today's market, the biggest players for music streaming include behemoth corporations like Spotify, Gaana, Apple Music, YouTube Music, and so on and so forth. This also happens to be quite the shift from how music was once listened to. For songs downloaded out of old music databases without the song's metadata in place, and other distribution sites, they oftentimes come without any known metadata, i.e., most of the details with regards to the songs are absent, such as the artist's name, the year it was made, album art, etc. This chapter discusses how data mining, data scraping, and data classification are utilized to help add incomplete metadata to song files without the same, along with the design process, the software development, and research for the same.

Maganti Syamala, Koneru Lakshmaiah Education Foundation, India
Komala C. R., HKBK College of Engineering, India
P. V. Pramila, Saveetha School of Engineering, Saveetha Institute of Medical and Technical Sciences, India
Samikshya Dash, School of Computer Science and Engineering, VIT-AP University, India
S. Meenakshi, R.M.K. Engineering College, India
Sampath Boopathi, Muthayammal Engineering College, India

The internet of things (IoT) is an important data source for data science technology, providing easy trends and patterns identification, enhanced automation, constant development, ease of handling multi-dimensional data, and low computational cost. Prediction in energy consumption is essential for the enhancement of sustainable cities and urban planning, as buildings are the world's largest consumer of energy due to population growth, development, and structural shifts in the economy. This study explored and exploited deep learning-based techniques in the domain of energy consumption in smart residential buildings. It found that optimal window size is an important factor in predicting prediction performance, best N window size, and model uncertainty estimation. Deep learning models for household energy consumption in smart residential buildings are an optimal model for estimation of prediction performance and uncertainty.

    N. Prabakaran, School of Computer Science and Engineering, Vellore Institute of
        Technology, India
    Rajarshi Bhattacharyay, School of Computer Science and Engineering, Vellore Institute of
        Technology, India
    Aditya Deepak Joshi, School of Computer Science and Engineering, Vellore Institute of
        Technology, India
    P. Rajasekaran, School of Computing, SRM Institute of Science and Technology, India

A generative adversarial network (GAN) is a generative model that is able to generate fresh content by using several deep learning techniques together. Due to its fascinating applications, including the production of synthetic training data, the creation of art, style-transfer, image-to-image translation, etc., the topic has gained a lot of attraction in the machine learning community. GAN consists of two networks: the generator and the discriminator. The generator will make an effort to create phony samples in an effort to trick the discriminator into thinking they are real samples. In order to distinguish generated samples from both actual and fraudulent samples, the discriminator will strive to do so. The main motive of this chapter is to make use of several types of GANs like StyleGANs, cycle GANs, SRGANs, and conditional GANs to generate various animated characters of different art styles with optimal attractive scores, which can make a huge contribution in the entertainment and media sector.

    V. Abinaya, Hindusthan College of Arts and Sciences, India
    A. V. Senthil Kumar, Hindusthan College of Arts and Sciences, India
    Rohaya Latip, Universiti Putra Malaysia, Malaysia
    Veera Talukdar, RNB Global University, India
    Ankita Chaturvedi, IIS University (Deemed), India
    G. Vanishree, IBS Hyderabad, India
    Gaganpreet Kaur, Chitkara University, India

The chapter focuses on cloud security audit mechanisms and models. Here the third-party auditor (TPA) will be provided with the authority access scheme where the security of the auditing system will be enabled. The TPA will check out the auditing verification and shows a message about the data audited. The purpose of this work is to develop an auditing scheme that is secure, efficient to use, and possesses the capabilities such as privacy preserving, public auditing, maintaining the data integrity along with confidentiality. It consists of three entities: data owner, TPA, and cloud server. The data owner performs various operations such as splitting the file to blocks, encrypting them, generating a hash value for each, concatenating it, and generating a signature on it. TPA performs the main role of data integrity check. It performs activities like generating hash value for encrypted blocks received from cloud server, concatenating them, and generates signature on it. Thus, the system frequently checks the security of the server-side resources.

Chapter 16

Seetharam Nagesh Appe, Annamalai University, India

G. Arulselvi, Annamalai University, India

Balaji G. N., Vellore Institute of Technology, India

Real-time detection of objects is one of the important tasks of computer vision applications such as agriculture, surveillance, self-driving cars, etc. The fruit target detection rate based on traditional approaches is low due to the complex background, substantial texture interference, partial occlusion of fruits, etc. This chapter proposes an improved YOLOv5 model to detect and classify the dense tomatoes by adding the coordinate attention mechanism and bidirectional pyramid network. The coordinate attention mechanism is used to detect and classify the dense tomatoes, and bidirectional pyramid network is used to detect the tomatoes at different scales. The proposed model produces good results in detecting the small dense tomatoes with an accuracy of 87.4%.

Chapter 17

N. Hema, Department of Information Science and Engineering, RNS Institute of Technology, India

N. Krishnamoorthy, College of Science and Humanities, SRM Institute of Science and Technology, India

Sahil Manoj Chavan, Department of Electrical Power System, Sandip University, India

N. M. G. Kumar, Sree Vidyanikethan Engineering College, Mohan Babu University, India

M. Sabarimuthu, Kongu Engineering College, India

Sampath Boopathi, Muthayammal Engineering College, India

Automation in the power consumption system could be applied to conserve a large amount of power. This chapter discusses the applications for the generation, transmission, distribution, and use of electricity that are IoT-enabled. It covers the physical layer implementation, used models, operating systems, standards, protocols, and architecture of the IoT-enabled SSG system. The configuration, design, solar power system, IoT device, and backend systems, workflow and procedures, implementation, test findings, and performance are discussed. The smart solar grid system's real-time implementation is described, along with experimental findings and implementation challenges.

Chapter 18

Rithun Raagav, Vellore Institute of Technology, India

P. Kalyanaraman, Vellore Institute of Technology, India

G. Megala, Vellore Institute of Technology, India

The internet of things (IoT) links several intelligent gadgets, providing consumers with a range of advantages. Utilizing an intrusion detection system (IDS) is crucial to resolving this issue and ensuring information security and reliable operations. Deep convolutional network (DCN), a specific IDS, has been developed, but it has significant limitations. It learns slowly and might not categorise correctly. These restrictions can be addressed with the aid of deep learning (DL) techniques, which are frequently utilised in secure data management, imaging, and signal processing. They provide capabilities including reuse, weak transfer learning, and module integration. The proposed method increases the effectiveness of training and the accuracy of detection. Utilising pertinent datasets, experimental investigations have been carried out to assess the proposed system. The outcomes show that the system's performance is respectable and within the bounds of accepted practises. The system exhibits a 97.51% detection ability, a 96.28% reliability, and a 94.41% accuracy.

    C. V. Suresh Babu, Hindustan Institute of Technolgy and Science, India
    Akshayah N. S., Hindustan Institute of Technology and Science, India
    Maclin Vinola P., Hindustan Institute of Technology and Science, India
    R. Janapriyan, Hindustan Institute of Technology and Science, India

The smart accident detection and alert system using IoT is a technical solution that detects accidents and alerts authorities and emergency services. The system mainly relies on sensors, GPS, and Arduino UNO to detect and collect information about the location and severity of the accident. The system then transmits this information in real time to the appropriate authorities using algorithms and protocols, enabling them to respond quickly and effectively, therefore increasing the possibility of saving lives and benefiting road users, emergency services, and transportation authorities in case of accidents.

    Prarthana Shiwakoti, Vellore Institute of Technology, India
    Jothi K. R., Vellore Institute of Technology, India
    P. Kalyanaraman, Vellore Institute of Technology, India

In recent years, blockchain technology has gained a lot of attention for its various applications in various fields, with agriculture being one of the most promising. The use of blockchain in agriculture covers areas such as food security, information systems, agribusiness, finance, crop certification, and insurance. In developing countries, many farmers are struggling to earn a living, while in developed countries, the agriculture industry is thriving. This disparity is largely due to poor supply chain management, which can be improved using blockchain technology. Blockchain provides a permanent, sharable, and auditable record of products, improving product traceability, authenticity, and legality in a cost-effective manner. This chapter aims to compile all existing research on blockchain technology in agriculture and analyze the methodologies and contributions of different blockchain technologies to the agricultural sector. It also highlights the latest trends in blockchain research in agriculture and provides guidelines for future research.

In recent years, concerns about privacy and security in online communication have become increasingly prominent. To address these concerns, the authors propose a blockchain-based messaging system that provides secure and private communication using double AES encryption. The system utilizes the decentralized and tamper-resistant nature of the blockchain to ensure that messages are not modified or deleted by unauthorized parties. Additionally, they employ double AES encryption to ensure that the content of messages remains confidential even if the blockchain itself is compromised. They evaluate the performance of the system and show that it is scalable and efficient. The system provides a secure and private messaging solution that can be used by individuals and organizations alike.

In the digital age, cybersecurity has become an important issue. Data breaches, identity theft, captcha fracturing, and other similar designs abound, affecting millions of individuals and organizations. The challenges are always endless when it comes to inventing appropriate controls and procedures and implementing them as flawlessly as available to combat cyberattacks and crime. The risk of cyberattacks and crime has increased exponentially due to recent advances in artificial intelligence. It applies to almost all areas of the natural and engineering sciences. From healthcare to robotics, AI has revolutionized everything. In this chapter, the authors discuss certain encouraging artificial intelligence technologies. They cover the application of these techniques in cybersecurity. They conclude their discussion by talking about the future scope of artificial intelligence and cybersecurity.

Foreword

I am happy to write a foreword for this book titled *Handbook of Research on Deep Learning Techniques for Cloud-Based Industrial IoT*. I felt delighted to note the different tools, technologies, key initiatives, and challenges in Deep Learning Techniques for Cloud-Based Industrial IoT. This book is a substantial compilation of 22 chapters encompassing an overview of Deep Learning, Cloud-Based Industrial IoT, Blockchain Based Deep Learning, critical theories, and concepts.

In today's fast-paced world, the Industrial Internet of Things (IIoT) has emerged as a transformative force in how industries operate, unlocking unprecedented opportunities for efficiency, productivity, and innovation. The convergence of cloud computing and IIoT has paved the way for a new era of interconnected intelligent systems, generating massive amounts of data that hold valuable insights for industrial processes.

However, the sheer volume, velocity, and variety of data generated by IIoT pose significant challenges in extracting meaningful information and making informed decisions. This is where the power of deep learning comes into play. Deep learning, a subset of artificial intelligence, offers remarkable capabilities in analyzing and interpreting complex patterns in vast amounts of data. Its ability to learn and adapt from data has made it a game-changer in numerous domains, and its potential in the industrial landscape is no exception.

The *Handbook of Research on Deep Learning Techniques for Cloud-Based Industrial IoT* is a comprehensive guide that explores the symbiotic relationship between deep learning and cloud-based Industrial IoT. Authored by experts in the field, this book serves as a valuable resource for researchers, engineers, and industry professionals seeking to harness the full potential of deep learning techniques to optimize their industrial processes.

The book begins by providing a solid foundation in IIoT, blockchain technology and cloud computing fundamentals, ensuring readers have the necessary context to understand the subsequent chapters. It then delves into the core principles of deep learning, elucidating various architectures, algorithms, and techniques that have proven effective in analyzing industrial data.

One of the key strengths of this book is its focus on practical implementation. The authors demonstrate how deep learning can be integrated into cloud-based IIoT systems and blockchain based deep learning to address specific challenges, such as predictive maintenance, anomaly detection, quality control, and energy optimization through real-world case studies and examples. The discussions not only highlight the benefits of employing deep learning techniques but also shed light on the potential pitfalls and considerations that must be considered.

Furthermore, the book addresses crucial aspects of deploying deep learning models in the blockchain, cloud including scalability, security, and privacy concerns. It examines the impact of cloud infrastructure on the performance and reliability of deep learning applications. It provides insights into optimizing model training and inference strategies in a cloud environment.

As deep learning continues to evolve rapidly, this book goes beyond the present landscape and offers a glimpse into the future. It explores emerging trends and advancements in deep understanding for IIoT, such as federated learning, blockchain based deep learning and explainable AI. It presents readers with a forward-thinking perspective on the potential developments and their implications for industrial applications.

In conclusion, the *Handbook of Research on Deep Learning Techniques for Cloud-Based Industrial IoT* is a comprehensive guide that combines deep learning and IIoT, offering readers a roadmap to unlocking the full potential of their industrial systems. Whether you are a researcher, an engineer, or an industry professional, this book will equip you with the knowledge and insights needed to navigate the complex landscape of cloud-based IIoT and leverage deep learning techniques to drive innovation and success.

I'm delighted to greet the editors and authors on their accomplishments and inform readers that they are about to read a significant contribution to developing various models based on Deep Learning, the Internet of Things, Cloud Computing and Blockchain technology. I'm aware of your research interests and knowledge of the above domains. This publication would benefit significantly from adding new computational models for Smart Security Ecosystem. This book is an important step forward in developing this discipline, and it will serve to challenge the academic, research, and scientific communities in various ways.

Arun Kumar Sangaiah
School of Computing Science and Engineering, Vellore Institute of Technology, India

Arun Kumar Sangaiah *is a Clarivate (WoS) Highly Cited Researcher (2021) and World Top 2% Scientists (Stanford). Dr. Sangaiah is currently a Professor at School of Computing Science and Engineering, Vellore Institute of Technology (VIT), Vellore-632014, Tamil Nadu, India.*

Preface

In recent years, the convergence of cloud computing and the Industrial Internet of Things (IIoT) has revolutionized how we interact with industrial systems and processes. The IIoT has ushered in a new era of connectivity and intelligence. At the heart of this technological transformation lies the power of data and the ability to extract valuable insights from the massive amounts of information generated by interconnected systems.

Deep learning has emerged as a formidable tool for analyzing and interpreting complex patterns within large volumes of data. The ability to learn from data, identify intricate relationships and make accurate predictions has made it an indispensable asset in various domains. In the realm of cloud-based IIoT, deep learning techniques have the potential to optimize industrial processes, enable predictive maintenance, enhance quality control, and drive intelligent decision-making.

This book, *Handbook of Research on Deep Learning Techniques for Cloud-Based Industrial IoT* is a culmination of the knowledge, research, and experiences of experts in the field who have dedicated their efforts to exploring the synergies between deep learning and cloud-based IIoT. It aims to equip readers with the knowledge and skills required to harness the power of deep learning algorithms for analyzing, interpreting and making informed decisions based on the data generated by interconnected industrial devices.

The book establishes a solid foundation, introducing the fundamental concepts and technologies underlying Industrial IoT and cloud computing. We delve into the key components of a cloud-based IIoT architecture, including data acquisition, storage, processing and analysis. By establishing this context, we ensure that readers clearly understand the environment in which deep learning techniques are employed.

From there, we dive into the core principles of deep learning, explaining neural networks, activation functions, optimization algorithms, and various deep learning architectures. We aim to demystify complex concepts through intuitive explanations and illustrative examples, allowing readers to grasp the underlying principles quickly.

The book's subsequent chapters focus on the practical implementation of deep learning techniques in cloud-based IIoT systems. We explore specific applications and use cases, shedding light on how deep learning can be leveraged to address challenges such as anomaly detection, predictive maintenance, energy optimization, and quality control. Through real-world case studies and examples, we highlight the effectiveness of deep learning techniques and discuss the considerations and trade-offs involved in their deployment.

Additionally, the book addresses crucial aspects related to deploying deep learning models in the cloud. We delve into scalability, security, privacy concerns, and the impact of cloud infrastructure on the performance of deep learning applications. By providing insights into optimization strategies and best practices, we empower readers to overcome the challenges of deploying deep learning models in a cloud environment.

Finally, as deep learning and IIoT continue to evolve rapidly, we explore emerging trends and advancements that hold promise for the future. We discuss topics such as federated learning, blockchain based deep learning and explainable AI, giving readers a glimpse into the potential developments and their implications for the industrial landscape.

We hope this book serves as a valuable resource for researchers, engineers, and industry professionals seeking to unlock the full potential of their cloud-based IIoT systems. We have endeavored to present the material in a comprehensive yet accessible manner, combining theoretical foundations with practical insights.

We thank the contributors who have dedicated their time and expertise to make this book possible. Their valuable insights and expertise have enriched the content and provided readers with diverse perspectives on the subject matter.

We invite readers to embark on a journey through the pages of this book, exploring the intersection of deep learning, blockchain based deep learning and cloud-based IIoT. We hope this book will inspire you to explore the vast opportunities offered by deep learning in the context of cloud-based IIoT and help you navigate the exciting landscape of this rapidly evolving field.

Organization of the book:

Chapter 1. Surveillance is an essential component of security and E-surveillance is one of the primary goals of the Indian Government's Digital India development initiative. Video surveillance offers a wide range of applications to reduce ecological and economic losses and becomes one of the most effective means of ensuring security. This chapter addresses the problem of how Artificial Intelligence is powering video surveillance. There is a significant research focus on video analytics but comparatively less effort has been taken for surveillance videos. However, there is little evidence that researchers have approached the issue of intelligent video surveillance in terms of suspicious action detection, crime scene description, face detection, crowd counting, and the like. Most AI-powered surveillance is based on Deep neural networks and deep learning techniques using analysis of video frames as images. Consequently, this chapter aims to provide an overview and significance of how Artificial Intelligence techniques are employed in video surveillance and image processing.

Chapter 2. Content-based video retrieval is a research field that aims to develop advanced techniques for automatically analyzing and retrieving video content. This process involves identifying and localizing specific moments in a video and retrieving videos with similar content. Deep Bimodal Fusion (DBF) is proposed that uses modified convolution neural networks (CNNs) to achieve considerable visual modality. This deep bimodal fusion approach relies on the integration of information from both visual and audio modalities. By combining information from both modalities, a more accurate model is developed for analyzing and retrieving video content. The main objective of this research is to improve the efficiency and effectiveness of video retrieval systems. By accurately identifying and localizing specific moments in videos, the proposed method have higher precision, recall, F1-Score and accuracy in precise searching that retrieves relevant videos more quickly and effectively.

Chapter 3. Smart healthcare systems are the health services that use the technologies like wearable devices, Internet of Things (IoT), and mobile internet to access medical information dynamically. It connects people, materials and institutions related to healthcare, actively manages and automatically responds to medical ecosystem needs. To transform the traditional medical system helps in making healthcare more efficient, convenient, and personalized. This chapter proposed: (1) A review of smart healthcare development using artificial intelligence, the Internet of Things, and Smartphone Android apps. (2) An experimental approach using IoT-based smart monitoring systems, Android apps for data collection, and artificial algorithms to predict cervical cancer diseases. (3) The integration of IoT and AI algorithms, or Artificial intelligence of things (AIoT), is proposed in this chapter as an experimental method for predicting cervical cancer from smart colposcopy images. The literature published in international journals and proceedings between 2010 and June 2022 is considered for the study.

Chapter 4. Advancement of technology had a significant impact on various industries, with innovative solutions like Cloud computing, IoT, Augmented reality (AR), and Virtual reality (VR) changing the game in many ways. Here is a system known as "Virtual Try-ons" which leverages IoT devices like mobile cameras, Cloud storage for data, and an intelligent interface for user interaction. Many people are opting for online shopping and various challenges arise with this transition, one of which is the issue of "Try-on." VR solves this challenge by introducing "Virtual Try-on" which replaces traditional try-on methods. It enables an individual to preview and virtually try on their desired products like clothes, watches, shoes, etc., from the comfort of their own homes, making the shopping experience easier and smoother. It also adds an element of fun and excitement to the shopping experience, increasing the hedonic value for consumers, and allowing consumers to experiment and play with different products, styles, and colors in a way that is not possible with traditional shopping methods.

Chapter 5. Identification of insulator defects is one of the most important goals of an intelligent examination of high-voltage transmission lines. Because they provide mechanical support for electric transmission lines as well as electrical insulation, insulators are essential to the secure and reliable operation of power networks. A fresh dataset is first built by collecting aerial pictures in various scenes that have one or more defects. A feature pyramid network and an enhanced loss function are used by the CSPD-YOLO model to increase the precision of insulator failure detection. The Insulator Defective data set, which has two classes (Insulator, Defect), is used by the suggested technique to train and test the model using the YOLOv5 Object Detection algorithm. We evaluate how well the YOLOv3, YOLOv5, and related families perform when trained on the Insulator Defective dataset. Practitioners can use this information to choose the appropriate technique based on the Insulator Defective dataset.

Chapter 6. Blockchain is an emerging technology that is now being used to provide novel solutions in several industries, including healthcare. Deep learning (DL) algorithms have grown in popularity in medical image processing research. AD is diagnosed by magnetic resonance imaging (MRI) images. This study investigates the integration of blockchain technology with a DL model for Alzheimer's disease prediction (AD). This proposed model was used to classify 3182 images from the ADNI collection. The Edge-based Segmentation algorithm has overcome the Segmentation problem. During the investigation's test stage, the DL-EfficientNetB0 model with blockchain earned the highest accuracy rate of 99.14%. The highest accuracy, sensitivity, and specificity scores were obtained utilizing the confusion matrix during the comparative assessment stage. According to the study's results, EfficientNetB0 with blockchain model surpassed all other trained models in classification rate. This study will aid clinical research into the early detection and prevention of AD by identifying the sickness before it occurs.

Chapter 7. The rapid development of Internet of Things (IoT) applications has created enormous possibilities, increased our productivity, and made our daily life easier. However, because of resource limitations and processing, IoT networks are open to number of threats. The Network Instruction Detection System (NIDS) aims to provide a variety of methods for identifying the increasingly common cyberattacks (such as Distributed Denial of Service (DDoS), Denial of Service (DoS), Theft, etc.) and to prevent hazardous activities. In order to determine which algorithm is more effective in detecting network threats, multiple public datasets and different artificial intelligence (AI) techniques are evaluated. Some of the learning algorithms like Logistic Regression, Random Forest, Decision Tree, Navie Bayes, Auto-Encoder, and Artificial Neural Network, were analysed and concluded on the NF-BoT-IoT dataset using various evaluation metrics. In order to train the model for future anomaly detection prediction and analysis, the feature extraction and pre-processing data were then supplied into NIDS as data.

Chapter 8. This project aims to create a real-time object detection and audio output system for blind users using the YOLOv3 algorithm and a 360-degree camera sensor. The system is designed to detect a wide range of objects, including people, vehicles, and other objects in the environment, and provide audio feedback to the user. The system architecture consists of a 360-degree camera sensor, a processing unit, and an audio output system. The camera sensor captures the environment, which is processed by the processing unit, which uses the YOLOv3 algorithm to detect and classify objects. The audio output system provides audio feedback to the user based on the objects detected by the system. The project has significant importance for blind users as it can help them navigate their environment and recognize objects in real-time, and can serve as a foundation for future research in the field of object detection systems for blind users.

Chapter 9. Increasing demand for food quality and size has increased the need for industrialization and intensification in the agricultural sector. The Internet of Things (IoT) is a promising technology that offers many innovative solutions to transform the agricultural sector. Research institutes and scientific groups are constantly working to provide solutions and products for different areas of agriculture using IoT. The main objective of this methodological study is to collect all relevant research results on agricultural IoT applications, sensors/devices, communication protocols, and network types. We will also talk about the main problems and encounters encountered in the field of agriculture. An IoT agriculture framework is also available that contextualizes the view of various current farming solutions. National guidelines on IoT-based agriculture were also presented. Finally, open issues and challenges were presented and researchers were highlighted as promising future directions in the field of IoT agriculture.

Chapter 10. Deep artificial neural network applications to robotic systems have seen a surge of study due to advancements in deep learning over the past ten years. The ability of robots to explain the descriptions of its decisions and beliefs leads to an collaboration with human race. The intensity of the challenges increases as robotics moves from lab to the real-world scenario. Existing robotic control algorithms find it extremely difficult to master the wide variety seen in real-world contexts. The robots have now been developed and advanced to such an extent which can make them useful in our day-to-day lives, all this has been possible because of improvisation of the algorithmic techniques and enhanced computation powers. The majority of traditional machine learning techniques call for parameterized models and functions that must be manually created, making them unsuitable for many robotic jobs. he pattern recognition paradigm may be switched from the combined learning of statistical representations, labelled classifiers s to the joint learning of manmade features and analytical classifiers.

Chapter 11. Modern agriculture primarily relies on smart agriculture to predict crop yields and make decisions. Crop productivity could suffer due to a lack of farmers, labor shortages in the agricultural sector, adverse weather, etc. Smart farming uses advanced technology to improve the productivity and efficiency of agriculture. Crop yield is increased with smart agriculture, which also keeps an eye on agricultural pests. Artificial intelligence is an innovative technology that uses sensor data to predict the future and make judgments for farmers. AI methods like machine learning and deep learning are the most clever ways to boost agricultural productivity. Adopting AI can help with farming issues and promote increased food production. Deep learning is a modern method for processing images and analyzing Big Data, showing promise for producing superior results. The primary goals of this study are to examine the benefits of employing DL in smart agricultural applications and to suggest a multi-cloud DL architecture for such applications.

Chapter 12. The Music space in today's world is ever evolving and expanding. With great improvements to today's technology, we have been able to bring out music to many today's ever-growing and tech savvy people. In today's market, the biggest players for Music Streaming include behemoth corporations like Spotify, Gaana, Apple Music, YouTube Music and so on and so forth. This also happens to be quite the shift from how music was once listened to. For songs downloaded out of Old Music Databases without the song's metadata in place, and other distribution sites, they oftentimes come without any known metadata. i.e., Most of the Details with regards to the songs are absent, such as the Artist's name, the year it was made, Album Art, etc. This paper discusses how Data Mining, Data Scraping and Data Classification is utilized to help add incomplete metadata to song files without the same, along with the design process, the software development and research for the same.

Chapter 13. The Internet of Things (IoT) is an important data source for data science technology, providing easy trends and patterns identification, enhanced automation, constant development, ease of handling multi-dimensional data, and low computational cost. Prediction in energy consumption is essential for the enhancement of sustainable cities and urban planning, as buildings are the world's largest consumer of energy due to population growth, development, and structural shifts in the economy. This study explored and exploited deep learning-based techniques in the domain of energy consumption in smart residential buildings. It found that optimal window size is an important factor in predicting prediction performance, best N window size and model uncertainty estimation. Deep learning models for household energy consumption in smart residential buildings are an optimal model for estimation of prediction performance and uncertainty.

Chapter 14. Generative Adversarial Network (GAN) is a generative model that can generate fresh content by using several deep learning techniques together. Due to its fascinating applications, including the production of synthetic training data, the creation of art, style-transfer, image-to-image translation, etc., the topic has gained a lot of attraction in the machine learning community. GAN consists of 2 networks, the generator, and the discriminator. The generator will try to create phony samples in an effort to trick the discriminator into thinking they are real samples. In order to distinguish generated samples from both actual and fraudulent samples, the discriminator will strive to do so. The main motive of this paper is to make use of several types of GANs like StyleGANs, cycle GANs, SRGANs, and conditional GANs to generate various animated characters of different art styles with optimal attractive scores which can make a huge contribution in the entertainment and media sector.

Chapter 15. The system proposes to focus on cloud security audit mechanisms and models. Here the Third-Party Auditor (TPA) will be provided with the authority access scheme where the security of the auditing system will be enabled. The TPA will check out the auditing verification and shows out a message about the data audited. The purpose of this work is to develop an auditing scheme which is secure, efficient to use and possesses the capabilities such as privacy preservation, public auditing, maintaining the data integrity along with confidentiality. It consists of three entities: data owner, TPA and cloud server. The data owner performs various operations such as splitting the file to blocks, encrypting them, generating a hash value for each, concatenating it, and generating a signature on it. TPA performs the main role of data integrity check. It performs activities like generating hash value for encrypted blocks received from cloud server, concatenating them, and generating signature on it. Thus, the system frequently checks out the security of the server-side resources.

Chapter 16. Real-time detection of object is one of the important tasks of Computer vision applications such as agriculture, surveillance, self-driving cars etc. The fruit target detection rate based on traditional approaches is low due to the complex background, substantial texture interference, partial occlusion of fruits etc. This paper proposes an improved YOLOv5 model to detect and classify the dense tomatoes by adding the coordinate attention mechanism and bidirectional pyramid network. The Coordinate attention mechanism is used to detect and classify the dense tomatoes and bidirectional pyramid network is used to detect the tomatoes at different scales. The proposed model produces good results in detecting the small dense tomatoes with an accuracy of 87.4%.

Chapter 17. Automation in the power consumption system could be applied to conserve the large amount of power. This Chapter discusses the applications for the generation, transmission, distribution, and use of electricity that are IoT-enabled. It covers the physical layer implementation, used models, operating systems, standards, protocols, and architecture of the IoT enabled SSG system. The configuration, design, solar power system, IoT device, and backend systems, workflow and procedures, implementation, test findings, and performance are discussed. The smart solar grid system's real-time implementation is described, along with experimental findings and implementation challenges.

Chapter 18. The Internet of Things (IoT) links several intelligent gadgets, providing consumers with a range of advantages. Utilizing an Intrusion Detection System (IDS) is crucial to resolving this issue and ensuring information security and reliable operations. Deep Convolutional Network (DCN), a specific IDS, has been developed, but it has significant limitations. It learns slowly and might not categorize correctly. These restrictions can be addressed with the aid of deep learning (DL) techniques, which are frequently utilized in secure data management, imaging, and signal processing. They provide capabilities including reuse, weak transfer learning, and module integration. The proposed method increases the effectiveness of training and the accuracy of detection. Utilizing pertinent datasets, experimental investigations have been carried out to assess the proposed system. The outcomes show that the system's performance is respectable and within the bounds of accepted practices. The system exhibits a 97.51% detection ability, 96.28% reliability, and a 94.41% accuracy.

Chapter 19. The Smart Accident Detection and Alert System using IoT is a technical solution that detects accidents and alerts authorities and emergency services. The system mainly relies on sensors, GPS, Arduino UNO to detect and collect information about the location and severity of the accident. The system then transmits this information in real-time to the appropriate authorities using algorithms and protocols, enabling them to respond quickly and effectively, therefore, increasing the possibility of saving lives and benefiting road users, emergency services, and transportation authorities in case of accidents.

Chapter 20. In recent years, blockchain technology has gained a lot of attention for its various applications in various fields, with agriculture being one of the most promising. The use of blockchain in agriculture covers areas such as food security, information systems, agribusiness, finance, crop certification, and insurance. In developing countries, many farmers are struggling to earn a living, while in developed countries, the agriculture industry is thriving. This disparity is largely due to poor supply chain management, which can be improved using blockchain technology. Blockchain provides a permanent, sharable, and auditable record of products, improving product traceability, authenticity, and legality in a cost-effective manner. This survey paper aims to compile all existing research on blockchain technology in agriculture and analyze the methodologies and contributions of different blockchain technologies to the agricultural sector. It also highlights the latest trends in blockchain research in agriculture and provides guidelines for future research.

Chapter 21. In recent years, concerns about privacy and security in online communication have become increasingly prominent. To address these concerns, we propose a blockchain-based messaging system that provides secure and private communication using double AES encryption. Our system utilizes the decentralized and tamper-resistant nature of the blockchain to ensure that messages are not modified or deleted by unauthorized parties. Additionally, we employ double AES encryption to ensure that the content of messages remains confidential even if the blockchain itself is compromised. We evaluate the performance of our system and show that it is scalable and efficient. Our system provides a secure and private messaging solution that can be used by individuals and organizations alike.

Chapter 22. In the digital age, cybersecurity has become an important issue. Data breaches, identity theft, captcha fracturing, and other similar designs abound, affecting millions of individuals and organizations. The challenges are always endless when it comes to inventing appropriate controls and procedures and implementing them as flawlessly as available to combat cyberattacks and crime. The risk of cyberattacks and crime has increased exponentially due to recent advances in artificial intelligence. It applies to almost all areas of the natural and engineering sciences. From healthcare to robotics, AI has revolutionized everything. This fireball put up not be kept away from cybercriminals, effective a "normal" cyberattack within an "intelligent" cyberattack. In this chapter, the authors discuss certain encouraging artificial intelligence technologies. They cover the application of these techniques in cybersecurity. They conclude their discussion by talking about the future scope of artificial intelligence and cybersecurity.

P. Swarnalatha
Department of Information Security, School of Computer Science and Engineering, Vellore Institute of Technology, India

S. Prabu
Department Banking Technology, Pondicherry University, India

Chapter 1
Artificial Intelligence in Video Surveillance

Uma Maheswari P.
CEG, Anna University, Chennai, India

Karishma V. R.
Anna University, Chennai, India

T. Vigneswaran
SRM-TRB Engineering College, India

ABSTRACT

Surveillance is an essential component of security, and e-surveillance is one of the primary goals of the Indian Government's Digital India development initiative. Video surveillance offers a wide range of applications to reduce ecological and economic losses and becomes one of the most effective means of ensuring security. This chapter addresses the problem of how artificial intelligence is powering video surveillance. There is a significant research focus on video analytics but comparatively less effort has been taken for surveillance videos. However, there is little evidence that researchers have approached the issue of intelligent video surveillance in terms of suspicious action detection, crime scene description, face detection, crowd counting, and the like. Most AI-powered surveillance is based on deep neural networks and deep learning techniques using analysis of video frames as images. Consequently, this chapter aims to provide an overview and significance of how artificial intelligence techniques are employed in video surveillance and image processing.

INTRODUCTION

Today, security cameras have become an integral part of everyday life for the sake of safety and security. Surveillance camera installations in the private and public sectors have increased significantly to monitor public activities. Security experts focus significantly on video surveillance to combat crime and avoid unpleasant situations that harm human civilization. However, personal and corporate security cannot be achieved simply by installing a surveillance camera. The surveillance system should be sufficiently

DOI: 10.4018/978-1-6684-8098-4.ch001

assisted with Artificial intelligence to deliver security solutions that substantially prevent abnormalities. Artificial intelligence has significantly influenced society, whether it takes the shape of algorithms, machine learning models, robotics, or autonomous systems. Many marketed video surveillance systems have integrated Artificial Intelligence (AI)-powered video analytics technology as a method to make our lives smarter and safer, thanks to recent developments in deep learning technologies. Intelligent Visual Surveillance is a significant and hard area of image processing and computer vision research. As our society is rapidly evolving toward smart homes and smart cities, necessitating an increasing number of Internet of Things (IoT) device deployments.

Background

The application of artificial intelligence (AI) is becoming increasingly crucial in the quest for novel techniques and technologies. Clutter identification, target categorization, and target tracking are AI techniques for target surveillance with radar sensors. These are critical assets for effective target observation. Because clutter (i.e., unwanted signal reflections) may significantly hamper target detection, its identification and subsequent suppression are critical. Furthermore, accurate target classification can aid in the successful prevention of possible threats, particularly in military circumstances. Finally, target tracking, the final link in the traditional chain of radar data processing, demands special attention since it provides the pivot point for sensor data fusion.

Smart Home Surveillance System (Anthony et al., 2022;Koushik et al., 2022)

The globe has seen a tremendous increase in the number of smart homes with the emergence of artificial intelligence (AI), the Internet of Things (IoT), and human-centric computing (HCC). But putting in place a reliable security system for SH's citizens still seems impossible. The current smart houses include security features like biometric verification, activity tracking, and facial recognition. The lifespan costs of these systems increase with the integration of multi-sensor hardware, networking infrastructure, and data storage facilities. Important behavioral and purpose clues are sent through facial expressions, which can be employed as non-intrusive feedback for contextual threat assessments. For the protection of the occupants of the same residence, prompt mitigation of a hostile situation, such as a fight or attempted entrance, is essential. iSecureHome is a real-time facial emotion-based security system for smart homes that uses a CMOS camera and a passive infrared (PIR) motion sensor. Effects of chromatic and achromatic characteristics on the identification of facial emotions (ER).

Daily home invasions and house fires cause difficulties for the victims of these sad occurrences. Early identification of these circumstances enables quick responses and should always be a feature that all homeowners expect. The CCTV system, the Onboard processing, prediction, and decision logic, and the Alarm and remote alerting module are the three elements that make up the framework depicted in Figure 1. The house range and garden path are completely covered by the CCTV system's numerous cameras. Each camera's video feed is supplied into the model's location's onboard circuitry. Live CCTV systems may be used as inputs, or previously captured video may be used for offline analysis. The Onboard logic can record films played on the screen by any software to increase the suggested framework's interoperability. The CNN model generates one of five events, which are then passed to the Decision logic for prediction because it is light enough to execute utilizing onboard processing as opposed to cloud resources.

Figure 1. Framework of alarming system

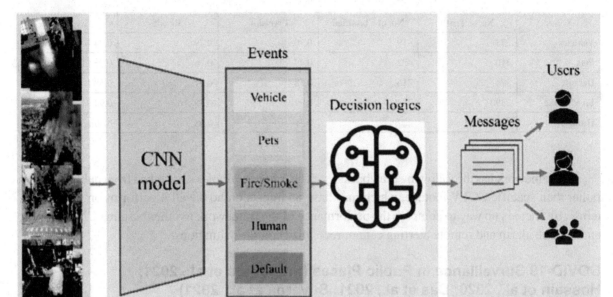

According to the model's results, matching Alarm messages with video feeds will be sent to notify the appropriate users. This model is intended to identify unusual situations in homes, especially when the owner is not there. This includes people, domestic animals, cars, fire, and smoke. An additional degree of security for the homeowner can be added when the model is included in home monitoring systems. Many of the things that the model tries to group are present in the image samples that were taken from open databases. The data is manually cleansed to ensure that the irrelevant objects did not affect training. The findings still offer accurate categorization even though the learning curve indicates that the model's full potential has not yet been realized.

When reading the images, monochrome (greyscale) images present a problem. When these photos are found, either delete them or expand them using the OpenCV channel to coordinate with RGB pictures. It will be beneficial for the model to train some features in grayscale so that it can learn and recognize these features when no color is presented, allowing the model to be useful in these systems. Some surveillance systems are going to record in grayscale, so it will benefit the model to train some features in grayscale to make the images usable. Since the input data for the neural network needs to be consistent, every image will be resized to 400 X 400. The model will have more pixels and data to deal with as the fixed size increases, ultimately extending training time. images bigger than this size can be cropped to ensure that the most important information can still be seen, or photos larger than this size can be reduced to this size. Images less than this will be resized to fit this size. Therefore, just enlarge the image rather than cropping the features, which might have a detrimental effect on the model's learning. 70% of the samples will be used to train the model, 10% to test it, and 20% to verify it over the full dataset.

The classification performance of Accuracy, precision, Recall, and F1 score are noted for various classes of the dataset. The overall Accuracy is 82.31%

Table 1. Classification performance

Class	No. of Truth	No. of Classified	Precision	Recall	F1 Score
Vehicles	373	419	0.70	0.79	0.74
Pets	310	422	0.49	0.66	0.56
Default	224	216	0.58	0.57	0.58
Fire/Smoke	2390	2120	0.99	0.88	0.93
Human	105	227	0.31	0.68	0.43

The framework has the following drawbacks: (a) The training samples were taken from public datasets rather than specific CCTV footage, which may have an impact on how well it performs on CCTV systems; (b) There is no way to compare the performance of the framework to other baseline CNN models, and (c) The alarm and remote alerting cannot recognize complex situations.

COVID-19 Surveillance in Public Places (Sreedhara et al., 2021; Hossain et al., 2020; Das et al., 2021; Suvarna et al., 2021)

Artificial Intelligence (AI) based detection systems can be deployed at public places like airports, railway stations, etc. for continuous monitoring of potential infectious individuals and screening based on common symptoms exhibited. The worldwide pandemic, COVID-19 has been caused by a newly discovered strain of coronavirus SARS-Cov-2. Its common symptoms are high fever, coughing, and shortness of breath. With the rising number of COVID-19 cases, manual detection of infectious individuals in public spaces is a hectic task. The BII Sneeze-Cough Human Action Video Dataset provided the sneeze-cough video dataset utilized for the research in this article (BIISC). A small real-time dataset is produced in addition to the sneeze cough dataset to test the classifier. A rate of 10 frames per second is used to extract images from films with various class labels. The retrieved pictures are used to feed a person detection algorithm, which employs the histogram of directed gradients as a basis for identifying human subjects inside a given image. Then, images are resized to 64 by 128 pixels.

To minimize the pixel size, it is finally transformed from RGB to a grayscale picture. Features are retrieved from the pre-processed pictures to do categorization. Testing the Gabor Filter, Histogram of Oriented Gradients (HOG), and Spatial Pyramid Matching as three distinct feature extractors (SPM). To determine if the picture under review contains any certain frequency content, a Gabor filter analyses a constrained portion of the image in a particular direction. The pre-processed pictures are convolved with various filter masks using Gabor filters. Two distinct kinds of classifiers are tested to differentiate coughing activity from similar activities. K-Nearest Neighbor (KNN) is the first classifier, and a multi-class Support Vector Machine (SVM) employing various kernel operations. The dataset's nonlinearity is the key justification for choosing kernel functions. A multi-class SVM classifier is used to test three distinct kernel function types: linear, polynomial, and radial basis functions.

Figure 2 details the process used by our social distance monitoring tool. The algorithm engine is made up of five parts: alert creation, distance estimate, camera calibration, people tracking, and people detection. The application is implemented as a hybrid engagement of edge infrastructure-based model inferencing and cloud-based model training.

Figure 2. Social distance surveillance application flow

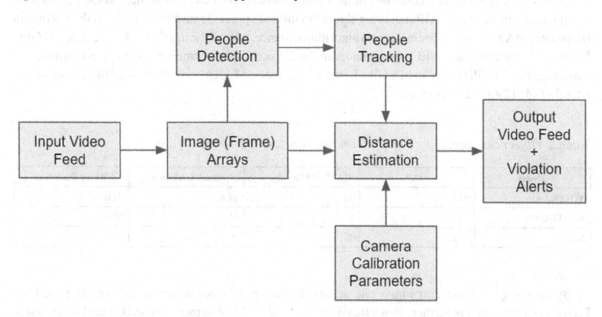

Identifying people in a location and estimating their bounding box coordinates is the first step in tracking their movements. The YOLOv3-416 object detector, pre-trained on the MS-COCO dataset, and darknet-53 as the backbone are used for this. Only the detection results for the person class are extracted. The approach, as it is intended to be used with monocular cameras, calls for calibration to convert image pixel coordinates to geographic coordinates. The camera calibration module allows you to select between an automatic calibration and a tool-based calibration. The next stage is to estimate the pairwise distances between the persons to aid in monitoring compliance with social distancing. This is done once the camera calibration parameters and the bounding box coordinates of every person visible in an image frame have been collected. Each person's position is determined by the midpoint coordinates at the base of each detection box. To determine if social distancing norms are being broken in tool-based calibration, Euclidean distances between these locations in the aerial view are computed and compared to the reference distance. The number of different violations and the length of those violations, which may be calculated by frame-to-frame surveillance of people, determine the likelihood that a person would get infected. The solution includes Motpy, an online multiobject tracker framework that tracks persons in a scene by using a Kalman filter and IOU of bounding boxes between future frames. By following the earlier detections, the implementation of a tracking algorithm is also anticipated to reduce mistakes in distance computation caused by transient occlusions.

The different parts of the application are separated into distinct modules that communicate with one another using message queues to simplify solution deployment and maintenance. To manage video inputs from several IP (Internet Protocol) cameras within the program, it also utilized a multi-processing, multi-threading method, providing scalability. A separate thread on a multi-core edge device processes each video feed in turn, invoking the algorithm processing unit to process the accompanying picture frame before pushing the processed image and related metrics to a streaming application.

(AIP*MAXAL)/SEF is an estimate of how many camera feeds can be handled on the edge device during deployment, where AIP stands for algorithm instance process rate and MAXAL is the maximum frame rate. MAXAL stands for maximum algorithm instance, where (the number of CPU cores, and GPU Memory) is the minimum. SEF: stream endpoint feed process rate 3 frames per second. For instance, if a machine has 12 CPU cores and 16 GB of graphics memory, MAXAL is at least (12,16) 12, supporting a total of (5*12)/3 = 20 cameras.

Table 2. Object detection algorithm performance metrics

Model	mAP	FPS	Small Occlusion	Heavy Occlusion
YOLOv3-416	55.3	35	17.8	37.0
FPN FRCNN	59.1	6	16.6	52.0
SSD300	41.2	46	20.5	42.0

By adopting the log-average miss rate as a performance indicator during testing on the Euro City Persons test dataset, it is further shown that YOLOv3 and FRCNN outperform SSD. The default object detector of the solution, YOLOv3, is deployed without further training after taking into account the trade-off between all of these measures. Numerous tests using internal CCTV footage under various lighting conditions, crowd density, gender, ethnicity, positions of persons, and occlusions produced accuracy and recall scores that fell between 68.8 and 75.6% and 75.5 to 85.1%, respectively. For crowd sizes up to 30 individuals, the pre-trained YOLOv3 detector exhibits the greatest detection performance, assuming that 80% of each person was visible.

Maritime Surveillance System (Huang et al., 2022)

Maritime surveillance systems are widely used in vessel traffic services. Cameras on the ground, at sea, or in the air can provide marine visual information. However, the collected visual data frequently suffer from blur effects as a result of unsteady imaging devices under harsh environments (e.g. wind, waves, and currents). To increase visual quality, picture-stabilizing technologies must be developed. Systems for maritime monitoring are crucial to enhancing maritime security. The efficiency and efficacy of maritime monitoring are considerably increased by intelligent marine surveillance systems, which use information technology to completely construct a new pattern. Technology primarily relies on the creation of surveillance resources to support the fusion and exchange of safety information. However, marine traffic monitoring is somewhat outdated when compared to sophisticated land traffic surveillance.

The surveillance recordings are hazy because maritime surveillance systems are more vulnerable to erratic elements like wind, waves, and currents. The hazy photos make maritime surveillance more challenging and less effective. As the global economy and trade continue to grow, new video stabilization techniques are being suggested for maritime surveillance. Image deblurring, the foundation of video stabilization, is becoming more and more crucial in maritime surveillance. Similar to how land-based traffic surveillance systems operate, marine surveillance systems must provide the video and picture data they have gathered to the monitoring center. Finally, ships are coordinated and managed by ship traffic managers at the monitoring center once the data has been analyzed.

Due to the effect of wind, waves, and currents on maritime data acquisition, shore-borne, air-borne, and ship-borne acquisition systems are all prone to shaking, which makes the majority of marine movies unstable. In other words, the hazy images on the surveillance screen are frequently a result of the relative distance between the visual aids and the supervised ships. The initial scene's image pixel expands to its surroundings. These dispersed pixel light sources are referred to as blur kernels or point spread functions (PSFs) in the imaging profession. In marine surveillance, only uniform picture deblurring—which is geographically invariant—is taken into account for simplicity's sake. Stabilizing the obtained marine surveillance videos is equivalent to deblurring the maritime pictures since the video is made up of a series of images called frames.

Finding the latent crisp picture is the next stage. Blind picture deblurring becomes a non-blind deblurring challenge after determining the precise blur kernel. Numerous techniques have been developed for non-blind deblurring. There are primarily three categories: regularisation technique, iterative approach, and inverse filtering method. Due to its straightforward computation and quick processing time, inverse filtering is frequently used in picture restoration, however, it is vulnerable to noise. Then followed the restricted least squares approaches, the Kalman filter with the linear recursive minimum variance estimation as the criterion, and the Wiener filter with the minimum mean square error as the criterion for deblurring. However, each of the aforementioned techniques is a linear restoration technique. The Lucy-Richardson technique, a non-linear approach, was suggested to restore the blurred picture with a known PSF to precisely reconstruct the latent crisp image. Then, a ROF model using TV regularisation of the total variance.

Visual sensors are used by the ship's navigation system to understand the surroundings. However, the visual information gathered under tough circumstances is prone to blurring, making it challenging for ship auxiliary systems to precisely detect impediments in the area around the ship. It impairs ship navigation safety and leads to navigational mistakes. Video stabilization technology plays a crucial role in maritime transportation because of the unique navigational conditions of waterways. Image deblurring helps to increase the effectiveness of waterway transportation and ensure the safety of navigation. Our technique completely exploits the properties of the blur kernels and the natural pictures, enabling accurate blur kernel estimates and ensuring high-quality restoration outcomes. It is advantageous for accurately identifying the surrounding objects and maintaining navigation safety to eliminate the visual blur under challenging marine circumstances.

Visual information technology-based marine surveillance systems have been extensively employed in a variety of nautical services in maritime engineering. However, inclement weather frequently makes the surveillance footage unsteady. It implies that pictures extracted from films occasionally include motion blur, noise, and other issues that drastically lower the visual quality. The restoration of fuzzy pictures in maritime engineering requires more focus. To conduct the comparison tests due to the absence of true maritime blurred datasets, should use artificial maritime-blurred photos with undetermined blur kernels. Blind deblurring techniques may be used to recover the obtained blurred pictures, and the visually improved films and photos can then be used to support our work in different nautical applications. One of the important marine applications is ship detection, and several ship detection techniques have been described. The accuracy of ship recognition will increase when the obtained maritime-blurred photos are deblurred by our hybrid regularisation approach, which is proven by YOLOv4.

Public Transport Surveillance (Santhosh et al., 2020; Rohit et al., 2020)

Local transportation movement is also a worry in our nation, as is vehicle overspeeding, which generates a large number of road accidents. Integrating GPS tracking systems with automated safety systems can establish geofencing to regulate and monitor our country's local buses. Through computer vision and visual surveillance, timely identification of traffic offenses and unusual pedestrian behavior in public spaces may be quite helpful for upholding traffic order in cities.

Computer vision-based scene comprehension has become quite popular among the Computer Vision (CV) research community as a result of the pervasive usage of surveillance cameras in public spaces. Compared to other information sources like GPS, mobile location, radar signals, and so on, visual data includes extensive information. This means that in addition to gathering statistical data regarding the condition of road traffic, it may be extremely useful in identifying and forecasting traffic jams, accidents, and other irregularities. Numerous research employing computer vision has been carried out, concentrating on data collection, feature extraction, scene learning, activity learning, behavioral comprehension, etc. Scene analysis, video processing methods, anomaly detection strategies, vehicle detection and tracking, multi-camera techniques and challenges, activity recognition, traffic monitoring, human behavior analysis, emergency management, event detection, and so on are some of the aspects that can be considered.

A sub-domain of behavior comprehension from surveillance situations is anomaly detection. Anomalies are often deviations from the norm of scene entities (such as automobiles, people, or the environment). There has been an increase in research outputs on video analysis and anomaly identification as a result of the accessibility of video feeds from public locations. Anomaly detection techniques often train on the norm to understand what is normal. Anything that dramatically deviates from typical behavior is considered abnormal. Anomalies include things like automobiles on sidewalks, a quick dispersal of individuals in a crowd, someone falling abruptly while walking, jaywalking, signal bypassing at a traffic signal, or vehicles turning around at red lights. Typically, anomaly detection systems develop a normal profile by learning the typical data patterns. Once the typical patterns are understood, established methods may be used to identify abnormalities. The system can produce a label or score that indicates whether or not the data is anomalous, usually in the form of a metric. Anomalies are by nature contextual. It is impossible to apply the assumptions employed in anomaly detection to all traffic circumstances. The capabilities of anomaly detection techniques used in monitoring road traffic from a data perspective. It does this by classifying the methods according to how the scene is represented, the characteristics utilized, the models used, and the approaches used. With numerous instances of the learning processes, used detection techniques, applied anomalous scenes, types of anomalies identified, and so on, the relevant technology provides an end-to-end perspective of the anomaly detection approach.

In the current scenario, features are taken to be data and represented by feature descriptors. Depending on the length of the feature descriptor, data generally take up a space in a multidimensional space. Data patterns that deviate from a well-established definition of typical behavior are known as anomalies. Anomalies have also been referred to as outliers and novelty in several application areas. Analyzing anomalies. Anomalies are often divided into three groups: point anomalies, contextual anomalies, and collective anomalies. If data deviate significantly from the expected distribution, they are considered to be a point anomaly. A point anomaly can be something like a stationary automobile on a busy road. Data that could be considered normal in one environment but not in another corresponds to contextual abnormalities. An abnormality, for instance, is if a cyclist in slow-moving traffic travels quicker than the others. On a less congested route, though, that may be typical behavior. Even while each data instance may be normal on its own, a bunch of them together may result in an anomaly. A collective anomaly maybe something like a group of individuals dispersing quickly. Visual surveillance frequently reveals abnormalities that are categorized as local and global anomalies. Global abnormalities may be visible in a frame or a section of the video without a specific location being identified. Local abnormalities typically occur in a particular section of the scene, however, global anomaly detection systems might not pick them up. Some techniques can find abnormalities both locally and globally. Challenges and Study Scope Identifying a representative normal region, defining boundaries between the normal and anomalous regions that may not be clear or well defined, the notion of an anomaly differing depending on the application context, limited data available for training and validation, data that is frequently noisy due to inaccurate sensing, and the fact that normal behavior changes over time are the main challenges in anomaly detection.

Learning typical behavior is important for many different use cases in addition to anomaly detection. Some of these include behavior analysis, categorization, pattern analysis, and prediction. There are four types of learning strategies: supervised, unsupervised, semi-supervised, and hybrid. The normal profile is created in supervised learning utilizing labeled data. It is frequently used in applications that are linked to classification and regression. In unsupervised learning, the connections between the components of the unlabeled dataset are used to structure the normal profile. With some guidance and a little quantity of labeled data for defining example classes that are already known a priori, semi-supervised learning predominantly uses unlabeled data. Active learning is defined as learning that occurs through the interactive labeling of data as and when the label information is accessible. These techniques are employed when there are plenty of unlabeled data and human labeling is costly. To comprehend various aspects of the data, hybrid approaches combine the aforementioned techniques. Object identification, classification, activity recognition, segmentation, anomaly detection, and other tasks also require learned models in addition to feature extraction.

The formulation of the problem and the underlying characteristics determine the type of anomalies since anomalies often relate to deviations from normal behavior. The methods do not restrict the capacity to determine the kind of abnormality. The formulation of the problem and the underlying characteristics determine the type of anomalies since anomalies often relate to deviations from normal behavior. The methods do not restrict the capacity to determine the kind of abnormality. Based on a statistical model, it attempts to fit the data using a stochastic process while generally employing statistical approaches to learn the parameters of the model. The data points that were not produced by the expected stochastic model are known as anomalous samples. Both parametric and nonparametric models are available.

The process of anomaly detection fundamentally involves using a particular approach to the derived feature. The fundamental data in visual surveillance, however, is a video, which is a collection of frames. Because these features serve as input to the particular approach utilized in anomaly identification, it is crucial to extract the pertinent features from the videos. The characteristics may be broadly divided into object-based and non-object-based categories. By extracting the objects or trajectories, anomalies may be found using object-based characteristics. The information used for anomaly detection is made up of objects or trajectories that are represented as feature descriptors. In the latter method, anomaly identification has been performed using low-level descriptors for pixel or pixel group characteristics, intensities, optical fluxes, or resulting features from spatiotemporal cubes (STCs). Some techniques employ hybrid characteristics to find anomalies.

A typical anomaly detection framework development process has two stages. In the first stage, a model is trained using the features from typical movies to learn the typical properties of the scenario. Later, the trained model is provided with features from the test videos. Test films are classified as normal or anomalous based on the chosen abnormality criteria. These approaches, however, use various precise detection strategies and anomaly definitions. Therefore, it is challenging to classify them just based on detection procedures.

With the use of a CNN classifier, optical flow-based spatial-temporal volumes of interest (SVOI) are used to learn the classes for normal and pathological video. Based on the findings of the classifier, anomalies are found. With the use of deep features and optical flow data, Generative Adversarial Networks (GANs) have been utilized to predict a future frame from a continuous collection of preceding frames. A frame is considered to be normal or abnormal based on the discrepancy between the anticipated future frame and the actual frame.

Machine learning has undergone a paradigm change in the previous ten years, particularly in favor of DNN-based techniques. You may have noticed that deep learning techniques have already been used to tackle several anomaly detection issues. Studies using DNNs have shown success in extracting characteristics irrespective of light. Due to camera position and perspective, traditional ML frequently fails, especially when trying to recognize objects. Despite their increased processing cost, DNN-based systems like have proved quite accurate at detecting objects. Purely deep learning-based approaches have not been able to successfully track objects reliably, especially in dense settings, even though object tracking is a crucial step in many anomaly detection systems.

To create the tracks, techniques like the Kalman filter and DNNs for object association and detection are used. Although it employs YOLO, this too has to track issues that lead to shorter trajectories in crowded and obstructed settings. Access to powerful computational resources might be difficult when putting traffic anomaly detection systems utilizing DNNs into practice. Even though the majority of corporations provide free funding and access to cloud computing resources for university research, unless hardware prices decrease, research dissemination may be constrained.

AI-POWERED VIDEO SURVEILLANCE ISSUES

However, there is no strong architecture with a suitable network model for commercial services that takes into account both high accuracy and cheap computing cost. Video monitoring with Closed-Circuit Television (CCTV) cameras has been studied for decades, but it has several drawbacks, including restricted area coverage, no location sharing, and tracking capabilities. Most video surveillance systems are fixed to infrastructure and typically particular to a site, but to construct a portable surveillance system, a highly accurate algorithm as well as a powerful computing and embedded device that can function with low power consumption is necessary. On the other hand, the vision sensors attached to drones are more scalable and versatile, providing more extensive surveillance coverage but requiring big data computations.

Deep Learning Solutions for AI-Based Video Surveillance

Deep learning architectures can achieve more accuracy and operate better with huge datasets. The Deep Learning techniques addressed are Continuous learning, transfer learning, reinforcement learning, ensemble learning, and autoencoders. The Detection methodologies are classified under the learning approaches as Supervised, Unsupervised, and Semi-Supervised. Unsupervised classification is computer-controlled and does not require human intervention. Manual training and labeled data require supervised classification. Semi-supervised learning sits between unsupervised learning (no labeled training data) and supervised learning (with labeled training data). There are many available benchmarking datasets like UCSD (UCSD Anomaly Detection Dataset), The dataset was created using security cameras with 60 mm120 mm lenses from the Puri Rath Yatra event, CUHK, Avenue Dataset, Violent-flows, UCF50, Rodriguez's and so on. However, the collection includes a variety of video genres, including surveillance and moving-camera recordings. As a result, it drives us to create a more realistic public difficult urban surveillance video collection to assess the effectiveness of various algorithms for object tracking and behavior analysis.

A video is well-known to be a series of successive pictures known as frames. Each frame is treated as an image, and any image processing method can be applied to it. To recognize anomalous pictures or objects in a video sequence (Majeed et al., 2021; Fan et al., 2020), deep learning-based object detection models such as RCNN, Fast RCNN, Faster RCNN, and YOLOv5 are studied for their performance in competition with each other.

Figure 3. Framework for abnormal behavior detection in video surveillance

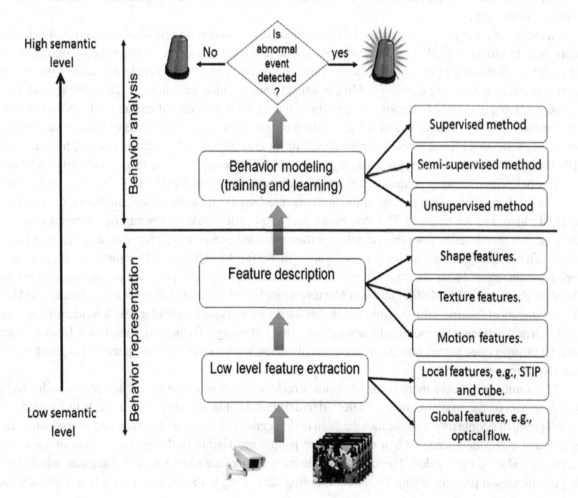

Abnormal Behavior Detection (Mabrouk et al., 2018; Harrou et al., 2020)

In recent years, significant progress has been made in the demanding problem of abnormal behavior identification in video surveillance. The early phases of low-level processing allow for detecting and describing moving objects in the scene. However, those actions do not enable figuring out what kind of activity the moving item is performing or if its behavior is typical.

Finding appropriate characteristics that can withstand various transformations, such as changes to the backdrop and the look of the object, is the main problem in behavior representation. An intelligent video surveillance system's goal is to effectively identify a noteworthy occurrence from a vast collection of films to head off harmful scenarios shown in Figure 3. This task often calls for two video processing tiers.

There are two steps in the first one, low-level characteristics are retrieved to identify the scene's interest zone. The interest region is then described by primitives that are produced based on low-level attributes. The second level establishes whether or not the behavior is normal by providing semantic information about human activity. Table 3 includes the most popular behavior representation feature.

To identify and characterize an entity moving over time, many features are employed. Such features can be divided into local and global features. A predetermined area of the frame is where local features are found. A local location or an interest point may serve as the region's representation. Motion throughout the whole frame is described using global features. Global motion data is frequently extracted using optical flow features.

In recent years, significant progress has been made in the demanding problem of abnormal behavior detection in video surveillance. The early phases of low-level processing enable the recognition and description of moving objects in the scene. These actions do not, however, help us identify the sort of action taken by the moving item or establish whether or not its behavior is normal. There are several ways for recognizing abnormal behavior in video surveillance, including classification methods and Modeling frameworks, scene density, and the interaction of moving objects. The three types of classification techniques are supervised, semi-supervised, and unsupervised techniques. Supervised approaches use labeled data to simulate both typical and atypical actions. Typically, they are made to identify particular deviant behaviors that were predefined during the training process, such as fighting, loitering, and falling.

The two types of semi-supervised algorithms are rule-based and model-based, and both require simply typical video data for training. The first group seeks to create a rule by leveraging common patterns. Any sample that deviates from this guideline is then regarded as an outlier. sparse coding in a rule-based approach to identify deviant actions. The examples that differ from the model's representation of typical behavior are referred to as aberrant patterns in model-based techniques. The most popular models are the Markov Random Field (MRF), Gaussian Mixture Model (GMM), and Hidden Markov Model (HMM). Using statistical features derived from unlabeled data, unsupervised algorithms seek to identify normal and aberrant actions. Unsupervised learning is carried out using a framework based on a Dominant set and an unsupervised kernel framework for anomaly detection based on feature space and support vector data description.

The number of people there is in the scene is reflected in how dense it is. The scene density has a direct impact on the strategies that are selected to define the behavior. Therefore, a single individual or a small group of people might be the moving item in the scene. The scene is distinguished as an uncrowded scene and a crowded scene. When one or a few people are visible in the camera's field of view, the scene is said to be uncrowded. Three key anomalous behaviors are often taken into account when there is just one person present: falling detection, loitering, and being in the incorrect area. It is impossible to observe and study each person's conduct separately in a crowded environment that includes a group of people. Occlusion and the few pixels used to depict each individual in the frame are to blame for this. Therefore, it is preferable to model how individuals interact to spot unusual crowd behavior.

A video surveillance system may be evaluated using several parameters. Equal Error Rate (EER) and Area Under Roc Curve (AUC) are the two most often utilized metrics. The Receiver Operating Characteristic Curve (ROC), which is widely used for performance comparison, is where the two criteria are formed. The EER point on the ROC curve is where the ratio of false positives to false negatives is equal.

Table 3. Features for behavior detection

Feature Types	Description
Features based on optical flow	Using the statistical features extracted from the optical flow vector to characterize motion.
Interest points	Both spatial and temporal domains allow for the detection of salient locations. the depiction of large motion fluctuations correlating to erratic behaviors.
Spatio-temporal volume, cube, blob, etc.	The temporal dimension is obtained by assembling successive frames.
Shape	Describing the movement of the object's form in a series of frames. Shape change detection correlates with abnormal conduct.
Texture	For each moving item included in a bounding box, rectangle, etc., local patterns are extracted.
Object tracking and trajectory extraction	Tracking a moving item using an optimization technique and its trajectory (coordinates in each frame).

Motion Detection (Huang et al., 2019)

Many computer vision applications, particularly video surveillance system analysis, rely heavily on motion detection. Its goal is to extract moving elements from a video clip one at a time. Motion analysis methods help to concentrate attention on the scene's moving aspects. Three common methodologies are used for motion detection: time difference, background removal, and optical flow analysis. Approaches to temporal differencing invariably extract imperfect forms of moving objects. When employed in practical applications, optical flow techniques can make it difficult to achieve accurate motion detection because they either make the system more computationally demanding or more sensitive to noise. On the other hand, by using a reference background model of prior photos, background subtraction techniques employed in traffic monitoring systems can more thoroughly and precisely detect moving objects characterized by moderate temporal complexity.

As a consequence, background subtraction techniques are more widely used, developed, and applied in several motion detection applications. The Gaussian Mixture Model (GMM) technique employs a specific distribution that may be used by separately modeling each pixel value. With this method, an incoming frame may be labeled as either having moving objects in it or not. Motion detection is accomplished using the Sigma Difference Estimation (SDE) approach, which employs a filter technique. To derive the motion vector, this technique uses a pixel-based decision framework to estimate two orders of temporal statistics. However, because it is unable to account for complicated situations, using the filter alone frequently leads to inadequate detection. Multiple Temporal Difference (MTD) is a different background subtraction technique for motion detection that keeps track of multiple prior reference frames to make it easier to locate presumed foreground items and close detection gaps for moving objects. The Simple Statistical Difference (SSD) technique, creates a straightforward background model based on the temporal average to identify areas of moving objects in traffic surveillance video streams.

The majority of the most recent state-of-the-art background removal techniques can identify moving objects in video streams recorded by a stationary camera. These techniques may readily detect moving objects using their backdrop models in such a perfect setting. However, in the actual environment, powerful winds or earth earthquakes may cause exterior cameras to vibrate. For these techniques, the accurate identification of moving objects in the Intelligent Transportation System (ITS) might be a challenge. To accurately identify moving objects in streaming video, the Gray Relational Analysis-based Motion Detection (GRAMD) technique is described. This approach consists of two crucial components: the Multi-sample Background Generation (MBG) module and the Moving Object Detection (MOD) module as shown in Figure 4. These modules allow for accurate and thorough detection as well as efficient adaptability to background changes.

Figure 4. GRAMD approach component framework diagram

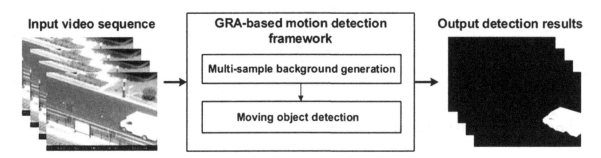

To detect moving objects in video streams with jitter backgrounds, the MBG module first builds a multi-sample background model using the grey relational analysis approach. Following MBG module construction. The MOD module then employs a multi-sample backdrop model to separate moving objects in real-world scenes recorded by both jitter and static cameras. To prevent errors brought on by the camera jitter, a two-stage detection technique that consists of a rough detection procedure followed by a precise detection procedure is adopted.

By doing this, both jitter and static cameras' video streams can accurately detect moving things.

Crowd counting (Sreenu et al., 2019) is used to determine the number of persons in a crowd of thousands. Deep learning models also enable face, action, and event detection in crowded environments. Attention mechanism-enabled deep learning was also explored to recognize activities and objects more accurately from surveillance videos. Crowd size is significant and changing in real-world situations, making crowd analysis challenging. It is difficult to distinguish between each entity and its actions. Traffic lights, major intersections, populated areas, gatherings that draw large crowds, and celebrations held by religious organizations, Among the aforementioned situations, crowd analysis inside offices is the most challenging. Identification of all acts, behaviors, and movements is necessary.

In crowded scenarios, spatial-temporal convolutional neural networks for anomaly detection and localization reveal that the challenge of crowd analysis is difficult due to the following factors: a large number of people, Close closeness, a person's appearance changing often, and frequent partial occlusions, crowd's irregular movement pattern, dangerous behaviors include crowd fear, pixel, and frame level detection. The following steps involve a scene-independent technique that uses deep learning for scene-independent crowd analysis. Crowd counting, Crowd tracking, and division of the crowd Pedestrian journey time estimate, crowd behavior analysis, crowd attributes recognition, and abnormality detection in a crowd. Methods like data-driven crowd analysis and density-aware tracking are described in the study of High-Density Crowds in films. The data-driven analysis uses a line-based method to understand the movement patterns of crowds from a vast collection of crowd footage. There are two steps to the solution. Both local and global crowd patch matching is used. Microscale and macroscopic crowd modeling, crowd behavior, crowd density analysis, and crowd behavior analysis datasets for crowd behavior analysis are all covered in crowd behavior analysis using fixed and moving cameras. Macroscopic methods are used to manage large crowds. Agents are managed in this case as a whole. In microscopic methods, each agent is dealt with separately. It is possible to gather motion data to depict the crowd using both stationary and moving cameras. For the investigation of crowd behavior, CNN-based techniques such as end-to-end deep CNN, Hydra-CNN architecture, switching CNN, cascade CNN architecture, 3D CNN, and spatiotemporal CNN are addressed. The chapter also includes descriptions of various datasets that are especially helpful for studying crowd behavior. MOTA (multiple-person tracker accuracy) and MOTP (multiple-person tracker precision) are the measures in use. These measures take into account the several targets that are frequently present in crowd situations. A Deep Spatiotemporal Perspective for Understanding Crowd Behavior combines long short-term memory with the convolution layer. Convolution layer-captured spatial data and temporal motion dynamics is constrained by LSTM. The approach predicts the path taken by pedestrians, calculates their destination, and then classifies their behavior based on how they move. According to Crowded Scene Understanding by Deeply Learned Volumetric Slices, a deep model and several fusion techniques should be used. Convolution layers, a global sum pooling layer, and fully linked layers make up the architecture. The architecture calls for weight-sharing and slice fusion techniques. It is anticipated that a new multitask learning deep model would successfully combine motion and appearance variables. As an input to the model, a novel idea of crowd motion channels is developed. In crowd videos, the motion channel examines the temporal progression of the content. The temporal slices that clearly show how the contents of crowd recordings have changed over time agitate the motion channels. broad assessments using a variety of deep structures, data fusion techniques, and weight-sharing strategies to identify temporal aspects with activation functions like rectified linear unit and sigmoid function, the network is set up with a convolutional layer, pooling layer, and fully connected layer. To evaluate the efficacy of suggested input channels, three alternative slice fusion approaches are used.

FUTURE TRENDS AND CONCLUSION

This chapter elaborates on various models and techniques for AI-powered video surveillance systems that are hot areas in computer vision and video processing research. The comparison of these models in terms of various performance measures is to be discussed. The challenges involved in this system and the issues related are also addressed in detail. Understanding the socio-cognitive components of crowd behavior is a difficult but crucial issue, especially for human-computer interaction applications. This problem is critical to existing surveillance systems and future interactions between intelligent entities and human crowds. Night video enhancement methods are commonly employed for recognizing suspicious actions acquired by night visual surveillance systems. However, artificial light sources in the environment degrade the visual quality of the video shot at night. This non-uniform lighting impairs the capacity of a real-time visual surveillance system to identify and track objects. As a result, a uniform enhancement strategy is insufficient for dealing with such uneven lighting. Since Surveillance is a vast area, various case studies are encountered to gain domain knowledge.

REFERENCES

Ben Mabrouk, A., & Zagrouba, E. (2018). Abnormal behavior recognition for intelligent video surveillance systems: A review. *Expert Systems with Applications*, *91*, 480–491. doi:10.1016/j.eswa.2017.09.029

Das, S., Nag, A., Adhikary, D., & Ram, R. J. (2021). Computer Vision-based Social Distancing Surveillance with Automated Camera Calibration for Large-scale Deployment. *IEEE, 18th India Council International Conference*, 1-6. 10.1109/INDICON52576.2021.9691485

Fan, Y., Wen, G., Li, D., Qiu, S., Levine, M. D., & Xiao, F. (2020). Video Anomaly Detection and Localization via Gaussian Mixture Fully Convolutional Variational Autoencoder. *Computer Vision and Image Understanding*, *195*, 1–13. doi:10.1016/j.cviu.2020.102920

Harrou, F., Hittawe, M. M., Sun, Y., & Beya, O. (2020). Malicious Attacks Detection in Crowded Areas Using Deep Learning-Based Approach. *IEEE Instrumentation & Measurement Magazine*, *23*(5), 57–62. doi:10.1109/MIM.2020.9153576

Hossain, M. S., Muhammad, G., & Guizani, N. (2020). Explainable AI and Mass Surveillance System-Based Healthcare Framework to Combat COVID-19 Like Pandemics. *IEEE Network*, *34*(4), 126–132. doi:10.1109/MNET.011.2000458

Huang, S.-C., & Member, S. (2019). A Gray Relational Analysis-Based Motion Detection Algorithm for Real-World Surveillance Sensor Deployment. *IEEE Sensors Journal*, *19*(3), 1019–1027. doi:10.1109/JSEN.2018.2879187

Huang, Y., Liu, R. W., & Liu, J. (2022). A two-step image stabilization method for promoting visual quality in vision-enabled maritime surveillance systems. IET Intelligent Transport Systems, 1-15.

Kattiman & Maidargi. (2021). An Automated Social Distance Monitoring & Alarm System based on Human Structure Using Video Surveillance in CQVID-19 Pandemic by AI Techniques, A Review. *IEEE International Conference on Electronics, Computing and Communication Technologies*.

Kaushik, H., Kumar, T., & Bhalla, K. (2022). iSecureHome: A Deep fusion framework for surveillance of smart house using real-time emotion recognition. *Applied Soft Computing*, *122*, 122. doi:10.1016/j.asoc.2022.108788

Majeed, F., Khan, F. Z., Iqbal, M. J., & Nazir, M. (2021). Real-Time Surveillance System based on Facial Recognition using YOLOv5. *IEEE, Mohammad Ali Jinnah University International Conference on Computing*, 1-6. 10.1109/MAJICC53071.2021.9526254

Naguib, A., Cheng, Y., & Chang, Y. (2022). AI Assistance for Home Surveillance. *IEEE, 27th International Conference on Automation and Computing*.

Rohit, M. H. (2020). An IoT-based system for public Transport Surveillance using real-time Data Analysis and Computer Vision. *IEEE, 3rd International Conference on Advance in Electronics, Computers, and Communications*. 10.1109/ICAECC50550.2020.9339485

Santhosh, Dogra, & Roy. (2020). Anomaly Detection in Road Traffic Using Visual Surveillance: A Survey. *ACM Computing Surveys, 53*(6).

Sreedhara, Raj, George, & Ashok. (2021). A Novel Cough Detection Algorithm for COVID-19 Surveillance at Public Place. *IEEE, 8th International Conference on Smart Computing and Communications (ICSCC),* 119-123.

Sreenu, G., & Saleem Durai, M. A. (2019). Intelligent video surveillance: A review through deep learning techniques for crowd analysis. *Journal of Big Data, 6*(48), 1–27. doi:10.118640537-019-0212-5

Chapter 2
Content–Based Video Retrieval With Temporal Localization Using a Deep Bimodal Fusion Approach

G. Megala
https://orcid.org/0000-0002-8084-8292
Vellore Institute of Technology, India

P. Swarnalatha
Vellore Institute of Technology, India

S. Prabu
Pondicherry University, India

R. Venkatesan
https://orcid.org/0000-0002-4336-8628
SASTRA University, India

Anantharajah Kaneswaran
University of Jaffna, Sri Lanka

ABSTRACT

Content-based video retrieval is a research field that aims to develop advanced techniques for automatically analyzing and retrieving video content. This process involves identifying and localizing specific moments in a video and retrieving videos with similar content. Deep bimodal fusion (DBF) is proposed that uses modified convolution neural networks (CNNs) to achieve considerable visual modality. This deep bimodal fusion approach relies on the integration of information from both visual and audio modalities. By combining information from both modalities, a more accurate model is developed for analyzing and retrieving video content. The main objective of this research is to improve the efficiency and effectiveness of video retrieval systems. By accurately identifying and localizing specific moments in videos, the proposed method has higher precision, recall, F1-score, and accuracy in precise searching that retrieves relevant videos more quickly and effectively.

DOI: 10.4018/978-1-6684-8098-4.ch002

INTRODUCTION

Multimedia information systems are becoming more crucial due to the growth of internet access, big data, and high-speed networks as well as the increasing need for multimedia information with visualization. Multimedia data, however, needs a lot of processing (Megala et al., 2021) and storage (Megala & Swarnalatha, 2022). Therefore, there is a requirement for effective extraction, archiving, indexing, and retrieval of video content from a huge multimedia database. The video has emerged as one of the most prevalent methods to share information because it is visual and powerful. Many people around the world have easy access to it. Media administrators find it hard to use video material for storage and search. Prominent web browsers today often skip searches that are heavy on content in facilitate subtitles that contain basic information regarding the videos being searched. As an alternative to traditional techniques of keyword search, users on online platforms desire to look up precise videos in almost real-time.

Video moment localization and content-based video retrieval using deep bimodal fusion is an emerging research field that aims to develop advanced techniques for analyzing and retrieving video content. With the proliferation of digital video content, the need for efficient and effective video retrieval systems has become increasingly important in a wide range of applications, including entertainment, education, and surveillance.

The process of video moment localization involves identifying and localizing specific moments in a video, such as a particular scene or event. This can be a challenging task, as videos can contain a wide range of visual and auditory information, making it difficult to accurately identify specific moments of interest.

Content-based video retrieval, on the other hand, involves retrieving videos that contain similar content to a given query video. Objects that occurred in the video or images are identified and are saved as a bag of visual features. Efficient object detection methods (Megala & Swarnalatha, 2023) are used to perform depth prediction along spatial and temporal features. These bag of features are more helpful in the retrieval process. This process requires the development of accurate models for analyzing video content and identifying similarities between videos.

To address these challenges, researchers have turned to deep learning techniques, particularly deep bimodal fusion. This approach involves integrating information from both visual and audio modalities to develop more accurate models for analyzing and retrieving video content. By combining information from both modalities, researchers can develop more robust and accurate models for identifying specific moments in videos and retrieving relevant videos based on content.

In this work, we describe a deep bimodal fusion (DBF) method for recognizing a person's obvious personality from movies, which addresses this issue and yields better results than previously published research. The DBF framework's structure is depicted in Figure 1.

Overall, the use of deep bimodal fusion techniques in video moment localization and content-based video retrieval has the potential to revolutionize the way we analyze and retrieve video content, making it easier and faster to find relevant videos in a wide range of applications.

The structure of this chapter is as follows: related works on video retrieval followed by the proposed method, experimental analysis, and conclusion.

Figure 1. Overall architecture for deep video moment temporal localization approach

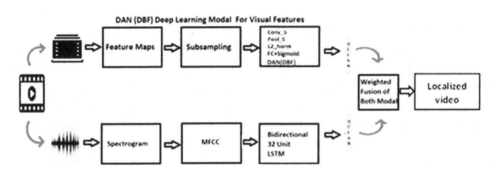

RELATED WORKS

Multimedia information has been currently gathered from numerous sources in a wide range of formats. These data are expensive to process, move, and store—especially films. An expanding big data environment necessitates the adaptation of multimodal information systems. Phan et al. (2022) suggested method for content-based video retrieval in a big data processing environment is built around these difficulties. Voice-based/object detection-based inquiries have been the subject of many recent studies. Our method is innovative because it combines voice, a caption, and image objects to query films for more specific information. This method for developing distributed machine learning models makes use of distributed computation and storage over a number of computing nodes. The ability of Spark to process data in memory dramatically lowers the cost of data transfer over the network and speeds up processing.

Multiple representations of sound have been proposed in recent years, such as those based on time-area highlighting and frequency-domain characteristics, among others. There are many fascinating instances of their sounds, but a few of the most notable are the Mel Frequency Cepstral Coefficients, the Linear Prediction Cepstral Coefficients, and the Bark Frequency Cepstral Coefficients. Specifically, highlights have been widely used in the speech recognition sector. A Mel-Frequency Cepstral coefficient (MFCC) refers to the fleeting ethereal high points of a sound that can be extracted from the spectrum of a short sample. It has four possible steps to resolution. The log channel bank (log bank) features can be obtained at these times as well. Our DBF framework disentangles the audio from each APA-approved non-traditional video by isolating its spectrogram and MFCC highlights. Through the use of LSTM, we first become acquainted with the visual representations (MFCC) of the audio approach, and then we obtain the Big Five Traits predictions through exhaustive planning.

Monfort et al. (2019) introduced the Moments in Time dataset, which contains one million short videos labeled with a variety of events and actions, providing a large-scale benchmark for moment localization tasks. The dataset only includes short videos, which may not capture the full context of the event, and some event classes have relatively few examples.

S. Zhang et al. (2021) proposed a multi-modal multi-scale temporal attention mechanism for fine-grained moment localization in videos, where the model learns to attend to different modalities and scales of temporal information, resulting in improved performance on moment localization tasks. The attention mechanism can require a large amount of labeled data and may be sensitive to the choice of hyperparameters and model architecture.

Gabeur et al. (2020) proposed a multi-modal deep metric learning approach for video retrieval. The method combines visual features extracted from video frames and audio features extracted from speech signals. The proposed method outperforms state-of-the-art approaches on two benchmark datasets in terms of retrieval accuracy and efficiency. The method requires fine-tuning for different datasets and may not generalize well to new datasets.

Tseng et al. (2021) proposed a deep multimodal embedding approach for video retrieval in the wild. The method combines visual features extracted from video frames and audio features extracted from speech signals. The proposed method outperforms state-of-the-art approaches on a large-scale dataset of unconstrained videos. The method requires a large amount of training data to achieve optimal performance.

Zeng et al. (2019) proposed a graph convolutional network with temporal attention for spatial-temporal action localization, where the model learns to attend to certain regions and frames in a video, resulting in improved performance on action localization tasks. The attention mechanism can increase the complexity of the model and make it more difficult to interpret or explain its decisions.

Shin and Moon (2022) deployed an interactive cross model LSTM network to perform temporal localization in a video. It involves attention score, region maps and boundary mapping functions on activity video dataset. The video captions and video frames are related with different modalities to perform speed localization in retrieval. Though the developed model suffers in capturing the ground truth frames. Attention mechanisms with soft labels are used by (Rodriguez et al., 2020) to perform localizing an unknown activity in the video. This transfer learning model involving encoders suffers from annotations.

One of the main strengths of the content retrieval methods (Spolaôr et al., 2020) is that it provides a comprehensive overview of the existing literature on content-based video retrieval. The review covers a wide range of techniques, including feature extraction, indexing, similarity measures, and relevance feedback. The authors also provide a critical analysis of the existing techniques and identify the limitations of these techniques. This can be helpful for researchers and practitioners in the field of multimedia analysis, as it provides a clear understanding of the current state-of-the-art in content-based video retrieval. However, one of the drawbacks of the proposed method is that it is limited to analyzing and synthesizing the existing literature. The review does not provide any new insights or contributions to the field of content-based video retrieval. Additionally, the review is limited to a specific set of evaluation metrics and datasets, which may not be representative of all the scenarios and use cases in content-based video retrieval.

THE PROPOSED METHODOLOGY

Temporal Localization and Content-Based Video Retrieval

The video consists of several groups of pictures. It is represented by sequences of frames V={v1,v2,... vn}. The video dataset named ActivityNetCaptions is used to perform temporal localization on the videos. Each video is annotated with the starting point and end point. A Model is proposed to locate the temporal moment in the video for the given query. Based on the single shot detection approach, the proposed model learns the video representation and generates a spatial-temporal pattern. An encoder module is applied to the extracted vector representation to perform mapping with semantic features. Frames indices are converted into time indices for efficient mapping helps for efficient temporal localization. The video dataset is first pre-processed and then passed to a neural network to extract the features. Then the dimensionality of the features is reduced and is then passed to convolution layers with kernels to downsample the frame images to convert them into vectors. These are then passed to the fully connected layers to represent as 1-dimensional vectors. It is passed to the attention transformer with predefined weights to perform localization tasks. The localization layer predicts the starting frame with its respective time and the ending frame with its respective time. Figure 2 Illustrate the phases involved in content-based video retrieval with temporal localization.

Figure 2. Proposed temporal localization in content-based retrieval

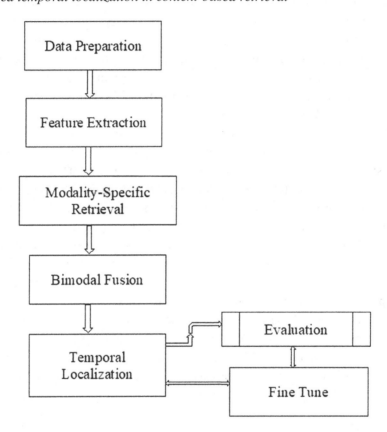

Working Procedure

1. **Data Preparation (Pre-Processing):** Collect and preprocess a large-scale video dataset. The first step is to preprocess the video data to extract visual and audio features. This can involve techniques such as frame-level feature extraction and audio signal processing. Extract visual and audio features from each video and store them in separate files.

2. **Feature Extraction:** Use a pre-trained convolutional neural network (CNN) to extract visual features from each video frame and recurrent neural networks (RNNs) to extract temporal information. Audio features can be extracted using methods such as mel-frequency cepstral coefficients (MFCCs). Use a pre-trained audio model to extract audio features from the audio track of each video. Store the extracted features in separate files.

3. **Modality-Specific Retrieval:** Perform modality-specific video retrieval by using the extracted visual features to search for similar frames in the dataset and using the extracted audio features to search for similar audio segments in the dataset.

4. **Bimodal Fusion:** Once the visual and audio features have been extracted, they can be fused together using a deep bimodal fusion network. This involves feeding the visual and audio features into a neural network architecture that is designed to learn the joint representation of the two modalities. The fusion network can be based on architectures such as Multimodal Residual Networks or Multimodal Recurrent Networks. Combine the modality-specific retrieval results using a deep bimodal fusion model. The fusion model should take the visual and audio features as input and output a single score representing the similarity between the query video and each video in the dataset.

5. **Temporal Localization:** The fused features can be used for video moment localization, which involves identifying and localizing specific moments in the video. This can be done using techniques such as sliding windows, where the fused features are evaluated at different temporal locations to identify moments of interest. Use the fusion scores to temporally localize the query video in the dataset. This can be done by finding the segments of each video with high fusion scores and selecting the segment with the highest score as the temporal localization.

6. **Content-Based Retrieval:** The fused features can also be used for content-based video retrieval, which involves retrieving videos that contain similar content to a given query video. This can be done using techniques such as nearest neighbour search, where videos with similar fused features are retrieved.

7. **Evaluation:** Evaluate the performance of the proposed method on a standard video retrieval dataset using metrics such as precision, recall, mean average precision (mAP) and F1-score. This can involve comparing the results of the proposed method with other state-of-the-art video moment localization and content-based video retrieval techniques.

8. **Fine-Tuning:** Fine-tune the bimodal fusion model on the retrieval dataset to improve the performance.

The proposed methodology leverages both visual and audio modalities to perform content-based video retrieval with temporal localization. The use of a deep bimodal fusion model allows for the combination of information from both modalities to improve retrieval performance. The temporal localization step allows for the precise identification of the segment in the retrieved videos that matches the query video. Algorithm 1 illustrates the steps involved in extracting a frame from a video.

Feature extraction from video and audio is shown in Algorithm 1 and Algorithm 2 respectively.

Algorithm 1: Extracting Features in video

    Input: ActivityNetCaption video

    Output: Extracted features

        1. Import the libraries numpy, tensorflow.
        2. Load a pretrained CNN model.
        3. Load the video to the model and extract the frames using video reader.
        4. Preprocess and extract the features from those preprocessed frames.
        5. Perform Mean Average pooling to reduce dimensionality.
        6. Pass the features to the flatten layer to output the features as array

Algorithm 2: Extracted audio

Input: HD videos

Output: Extracted audio from every video for audio processing having transcript and audio feature.

1. Import moviepy.editor.
2. Read mp4 file with videoclip = VideoFileClip(<path>)
3. Get wav file from mp4 using function audioclip = videoclip.audio
4. Repeat step 2 and 3 for all videos.

EXPERIMENTAL ANALYSIS

The proposed DBF method utilizes a straightforward weighted average approach to fusion but also highlights how performance may be enhanced by the use of sophisticated ensemble techniques, such as stacking, to discover the best values for fusion weights at the end of the process. In order for deep audio networks to acquire more informative representations of sound, they need to be put through their paces. Within our DBF framework, we can enhance retrieval accuracy by combining multiple models into a single one.

The pseudocode for the moment localization and content-based video retrieval is shown in Figure 3.

Figure 3. Pseudocode of deep bimodal fusion

```
# Preprocessing
video_frames = preprocess_video_frames(video)
audio_signal = preprocess_audio_signal(audio)
# Feature Extraction
visual_features = extract_visual_features(video_frames)
audio_features = extract_audio_features(audio_signal)
# Bimodal Fusion
bimodal_features = bimodal_fusion(visual_features, audio_features)
# Moment Localization
moments = []
for t in range(total_frames):
    current_feature = bimodal_features[t]
    moment_score = evaluate_moment_score(current_feature)
    if moment_score > threshold:
        moments.append(t)
# Content-based Retrieval
retrieved_videos = []
for video in video_database:
    visual_features = extract_visual_features(video)
    audio_features = extract_audio_features(video)
    bimodal_features = bimodal_fusion(visual_features, audio_features)
    similarity_score = compute_similarity_score(bimodal_features, query_features)
    if similarity_score > retrieval_threshold:
        retrieved_videos.append(video)
# Evaluation
precision, recall, f1_score = evaluate_performance(retrieved_videos, ground_truth)
```

This pseudocode assumes that the video data is preprocessed, visual and audio features are extracted, and bimodal fusion is performed using a deep neural network architecture. The moment localization step involves evaluating the moment score for each frame, and if the score is above a certain threshold, the frame is considered to be part of a relevant moment. Content-based retrieval involves computing the similarity score between the query video features and each video in the video database and retrieving videos with scores above a certain threshold. Finally, the performance of the proposed method is evaluated using metrics such as precision, recall, and F1-score.

Table 1 and Figure 4 illustrate the average accuracy and variability of each proposed method for measuring a given attribute.

Table 1. Results

Methods	Mean Accuracy
(Wei et al., 2017)	0.728
(Dong et al., 2019)	0.840
(Z. Zhang et al., 2019)	0.846
(Liu & Tang, 2021)	0.855
(Y. Zeng et al., 2021)	0.871
(Chen et al., 2020)	0.917
DBF (Proposed Method)	0.9285

Figure 4. Mean accuracy

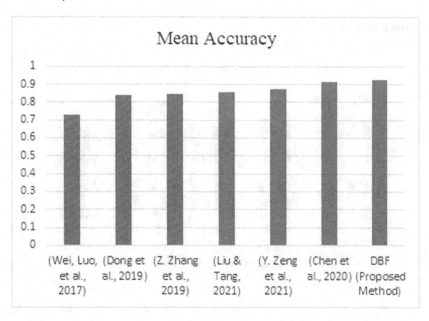

Other performance metrics used to measure the proposed video retrieval model are mean Average Precision(mAP), Precision, Recall and gain. Mean Average Precision (mAP) is the average precision across all the queries in the dataset. It measures the ability of the algorithm to retrieve relevant videos for a given query. Precision at K (P@K) measures the precision of the top K retrieved videos for a given query. It is a commonly used metric in information retrieval tasks. Recall at K (R@K) measures the recall of the top K retrieved videos for a given query. It is the percentage of relevant videos that are retrieved out of all the relevant videos in the dataset. Normalized Discounted Cumulative Gain (NDCG) is a ranking metric that measures the relevance of the retrieved videos for a given query. It takes into account both the position and relevance of the retrieved videos. Retrieval Accuracy (RA) measures the percentage of queries for which at least one relevant video is retrieved. It is a binary metric that indicates whether the algorithm is able to retrieve at least one relevant video for each query.

The proposed method is evaluated based on its performance in retrieving videos with similar content to a given query video. This can be done by measuring precision, recall, and F1-score metrics, and comparing the results with other state-of-the-art methods shown in Table 2. The same is shown in Figure 5 representing that the proposed Deep Bimodal fusion has better performance.

Table 2. Performance metrics

Method	Precision	Recall	mAP	F1-Score
Deep Bimodal fusion	0.85	0.82	0.78	0.83
Unimodal (Visual)	0.72	0.68	0.61	0.70
Unimodal (audio)	0.69	0.64	0.57	0.66
Fusion (early)	0.81	0.77	0.71	0.78
Fusion (late)	0.84	0.80	0.76	0.81

Figure 5. Performance results

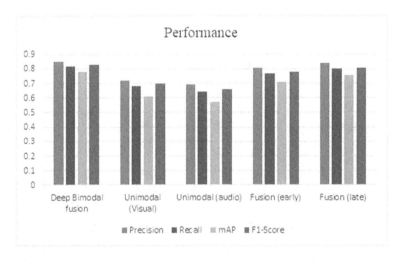

The Deep Bimodal Fusion method has achieved the highest scores for precision, recall, mAP, accuracy, and F1-Score compared to the other methods, indicating that it is the most effective method for video moment localization and content-based video retrieval. The results also show that the use of unimodal methods (visual or audio alone) leads to lower performance, while the use of early or late fusion techniques can improve performance to some extent.

CONCLUSION

Video moment localization and content-based video retrieval are important tasks in the field of multimedia analysis and have numerous applications such as video surveillance, sports analysis, and video recommendation systems. Deep bimodal fusion is a powerful technique that combines both visual and audio modalities to improve the accuracy of these tasks. The proposed method makes advantage of weighted fusion using bimodal deep learning. Deep bimodal fusion typically involves extracting features from both visual and audio modalities using deep learning models such as CNNs and long short-term memory network (LSTM) and then fusing these features at various levels using fusion techniques such as early and late fusion. An annotated dataset called Activity Net Captions dataset was used for our analysis. Experimental results have shown that deep bimodal fusion outperforms unimodal methods and fusion techniques for video moment localization and content-based video retrieval in terms of precision, recall, mAP, accuracy, and F1-Score. The results also show that the use of deep bimodal fusion can improve the performance of these tasks in challenging scenarios such as noisy and incomplete data.

REFERENCES

Chen, S., Zhao, Y., Jin, Q., & Wu, Q. (2020). Fine-grained video-text retrieval with hierarchical graph reasoning. *Proceedings of the IEEE/CVF Conference on Computer Vision and Pattern Recognition*, 10638–10647. 10.1109/CVPR42600.2020.01065

Dong, J., Li, X., Xu, C., Ji, S., He, Y., Yang, G., & Wang, X. (2019). Dual encoding for zero-example video retrieval. *Proceedings of the IEEE/CVF Conference on Computer Vision and Pattern Recognition*, 9346–9355.

Gabeur, V., Sun, C., Alahari, K., & Schmid, C. (2020). Multi-modal transformer for video retrieval. Computer Vision–ECCV 2020: 16th European Conference, Glasgow, UK, August 23–28, 2020. *Proceedings*, *16*(4), 214–229.

Liu, M., & Tang, J. (2021). Audio and video bimodal emotion recognition in social networks based on improved alexnet network and attention mechanism. *Journal of Information Processing Systems*, *17*(4), 754–771.

Megala, G., & ... (2021). State-of-the-art in video processing: Compression, optimization and retrieval. *Turkish Journal of Computer and Mathematics Education*, *12*(5), 1256–1272.

Megala, G., & Swarnalatha, P. (2022). Efficient high-end video data privacy preservation with integrity verification in cloud storage. *Computers & Electrical Engineering*, *102*, 108226. doi:10.1016/j.compeleceng.2022.108226

Megala, G., & Swarnalatha, P. (2023). Efficient Object Detection on Sparse-to-Dense Depth Prediction. *2023 9th International Conference on Advanced Computing and Communication Systems (ICACCS)*, *1*, 1626–1630.

Monfort, M., Andonian, A., Zhou, B., Ramakrishnan, K., Bargal, S. A., Yan, T., Brown, L., Fan, Q., Gutfreund, D., Vondrick, C., & ... (2019). Moments in time dataset: One million videos for event understanding. *IEEE Transactions on Pattern Analysis and Machine Intelligence, 42*(2), 502–508. doi:10.1109/TPAMI.2019.2901464 PMID:30802849

Phan, T.-C., Phan, A.-C., Cao, H.-P., & Trieu, T.-N. (2022). Content-Based Video Big Data Retrieval with Extensive Features and Deep Learning. *Applied Sciences (Basel, Switzerland), 12*(13), 6753. doi:10.3390/app12136753

Rodriguez, C., Marrese-Taylor, E., Saleh, F. S., Li, H., & Gould, S. (2020). Proposal-free temporal moment localization of a natural-language query in video using guided attention. *Proceedings of the IEEE/CVF Winter Conference on Applications of Computer Vision*, 2464–2473. 10.1109/WACV45572.2020.9093328

Shin, J., & Moon, J. (2022). Learning to combine the modalities of language and video for temporal moment localization. *Computer Vision and Image Understanding, 217*, 103375. doi:10.1016/j.cviu.2022.103375

Spolaôr, N., Lee, H. D., Takaki, W. S. R., Ensina, L. A., Coy, C. S. R., & Wu, F. C. (2020). A systematic review on content-based video retrieval. *Engineering Applications of Artificial Intelligence, 90*, 103557. doi:10.1016/j.engappai.2020.103557

Tseng, S.-Y., Narayanan, S., & Georgiou, P. (2021). Multimodal embeddings from language models for emotion recognition in the wild. *IEEE Signal Processing Letters, 28*, 608–612. doi:10.1109/LSP.2021.3065598

Verma, A., & Khanna, G. (2016). A survey on digital image processing techniques for tumor detection. *Indian Journal of Science and Technology, 9*(14), 15.

Wei, X.-S., Luo, J.-H., Wu, J., & Zhou, Z.-H. (2017). Selective convolutional descriptor aggregation for fine-grained image retrieval. *IEEE Transactions on Image Processing, 26*(6), 2868–2881. doi:10.1109/TIP.2017.2688133 PMID:28368819

Zeng, R., Huang, W., Tan, M., Rong, Y., Zhao, P., Huang, J., & Gan, C. (2019). Graph convolutional networks for temporal action localization. *Proceedings of the IEEE/CVF International Conference on Computer Vision*, 7094–7103. 10.1109/ICCV.2019.00719

Zeng, Y., Cao, D., Wei, X., Liu, M., Zhao, Z., & Qin, Z. (2021). Multi-modal relational graph for cross-modal video moment retrieval. *Proceedings of the IEEE/CVF Conference on Computer Vision and Pattern Recognition*, 2215–2224. 10.1109/CVPR46437.2021.00225

Zhang, S., Peng, H., Fu, J., Lu, Y., & Luo, J. (2021). Multi-scale 2d temporal adjacency networks for moment localization with natural language. *IEEE Transactions on Pattern Analysis and Machine Intelligence, 44*(12), 9073–9087. doi:10.1109/TPAMI.2021.3120745 PMID:34665720

Zhang, Z., Lin, Z., Zhao, Z., & Xiao, Z. (2019). Cross-modal interaction networks for query-based moment retrieval in videos. *Proceedings of the 42nd International ACM SIGIR Conference on Research and Development in Information Retrieval*, 655–664. 10.1145/3331184.3331235

Chapter 3
Artificial Intelligence of Things for Smart Healthcare Development:
An Experimental Review

Jennyfer Susan M. B.

ⓘD https://orcid.org/0000-0003-1509-9309

Centre for Machine Learning and Intelligence, Avinashilingam Institute for Home Science and Higher Education for Women, India

P. Subashini

Centre for Machine Learning and Intelligence, Avinashilingam Institute for Home Science and Higher Education for Women, India

M. Krishnaveni

Centre for Machine Learning and Intelligence, Avinashilingam Institute for Home Science and Higher Education for Women, India

ABSTRACT

Smart healthcare systems are the health services that use the technologies like wearable devices, internet of things (IoT), and mobile internet to access medical information dynamically. It connects people, materials, and institutions related to healthcare; actively manages; and automatically responds to medical ecosystem needs. It helps the traditional medical system in making healthcare more efficient, convenient, and personalized. This chapter proposed (1) a review of smart healthcare development using artificial intelligence, the internet of things, and smartphone Android apps; (2) an experimental approach using IoT-based smart monitoring systems, Android apps for data collection, and artificial algorithms to predict cervical cancer diseases; (3) the integration of IoT and AI algorithms. Artificial intelligence of things (AIoT) is proposed in this chapter as an experimental method for predicting cervical cancer from smart colposcopy images. The literature published in international journals and proceedings between 2010 and June 2022 is considered for the study.

DOI: 10.4018/978-1-6684-8098-4.ch003

INTRODUCTION

Artificial intelligence refers to an automated system that can perform cognitive functions and physical tasks. Genetic algorithms, neural networks, machine learning, pattern recognition, and autonomous decision-making fall within the broad category of artificial intelligence (AI). AI technologies have been steadily applied in the medical field to offer many benefits, such as automating physical tasks, analyzing vast amounts of patient data, and delivering better healthcare facilities lower costs (Davenport & Kalakota, 2019). According to statistical studies, 30% of healthcare costs are associated with administrative tasks. Therefore, AI can reduce the workload on healthcare professionals by automating duties such as pre-authorizing insurance, checking on unpaid bills, and managing patient data. Clinical Decision Support (CDS) employs AI to assist in patient therapy and diagnosis decisions and carry out population-based risk prediction assessments. The AI is moving towards smart health and intelligent-based healthcare systems in developing healthcare industry.

In 2009, IBM proposed the concept of smart healthcare as part of their *"Smart Planet"* initiative. The growth of smart cities is facilitated by the smart healthcare system (Jokanorvie, 2020). Traditional healthcare cannot meet everyone's needs due to the significant increase in the human population. Despite having high infrastructure and cutting-edge technologies, medical treatments may not be accessible or affordable for everyone. The smart healthcare system offers benefits by allowing individuals to quickly access medical facilities, medical documentation, diagnosis tools, and better treatment. It encompasses various situations, including smart homes, community health centers, and smart hospitals. It supports clinical reasoning, hospital administration, prescription recommendations, rehabilitation, post-marketing surveillance, and tracking of patients' anomalous behavior (Dhaka & Panda, 2020). It also aids in illness prevention, diagnosis, and treatment. Smart healthcare involves many stakeholders, such as hospitals, research institutions, physicians and patients, and all aspects of the system commonly use smart technologies. Patients uses the wearable smart devices to monitor their health continuously, request medical aid through virtual assistants, and use remote facilities to carry out procedures remotely. Doctors can use several highly advanced clinical decision-support tools to aid in and enhance diagnosis. It manages medical data using an integrated platform such as the Laboratory Information Management System, Communication Systems (PACS), Picture Archiving, Electronic Medical Records, and surgical robots for precise operations as shown in Figure 1.

Artificial Intelligence (AI) has significantly improved patient care and staff efficiency in healthcare by assisting with medical image analysis and diagnosis. The IBM smart cloud is one of the most popular AI tools, providing solutions for smart healthcare development, maintaining smart electronic health records, and offering personalized care to patients. Machine learning and deep learning algorithms are included with smart healthcare to speed up care delivery services (Saba & Durai, 2022). Internet of Things (IoT) combines connectivity, communication and computing, especially in the medical field, known as IoMT, or the Internet of Medical Things. According to analysis, the number of medical devices with IoT is expected to increase from 10 billion to 50 billion in the coming decades.

In 2021, Cisco estimated that IoT devices will generate 847 Zettabytes (ZB) of medical data per year. The IoT has improved monitoring and real-time data collection of patients, leading to better care services at the initial stages by identifying early disease stages (Tian et al., 2019). Recently, AI and IoT have been combined to improve smart healthcare development. IoT provides a worldwide connection, while AI gives these devices a sense of life. IoT tools collect real-time patient data, connect patients and doctors, maintain medical records, and predict body changes using sensors. AI analyzes the collected data and helps in decision-making, ultimately assisting physicians with further treatment. For example, AI-based wearable tools are activity trackers that monitor and collect real-time human data from patients. The AI in the wearable tool detects physiological changes during the pandemic to identify early COVID infection, allowing for early isolation and testing, reducing the spread of the virus. Photoplethysmography identifies the elevated respiratory rate with single-point contact (i.e., the wrist), predicting diseases (Saba & Durai, 2022).

Figure 1. Smart healthcare system

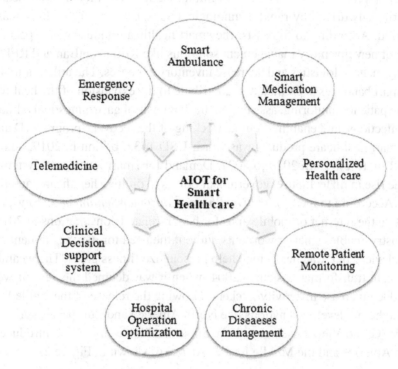

This proposed chapter examines the growth of smart healthcare in the medical industry and how technologies assist smart healthcare to reach better quality. The technologies, such as IoT, smartphones and artificial intelligence algorithms, are discussed as they assist the growth of smart healthcare development. The experimental approach includes IoT-based monitoring tools for the patient, smartphone and Android apps, and the use of AI algorithms for decision-making processes. Finally, this chapter shows how AI and smart technologies are integrated to create an AIoT tool for improvising clinical support where IoT collects data, and AI makes the decision-making process. The IoT tools for health monitoring, smart Android app for data collection, AI algorithms for decision making, and AIOT for the medical field are explained with an experimental approach.

The proposed chapter is presented as follows: The first section discusses the growth of global market in smart healthcare system. The second part discusses the review of AIoT in smart health care system. This session discusses about the AI based wearable device and smart phone based sensor along with the android app for the development of smart healthcare development. The role of AI in diseases prediction is also discussed in brief. Each method is explained along with its experimental approach. The next section discusses how AI and IoT are integrated together for smart healthcare developments, explained along with its experimental approach. The next section is the contribution of the chapter, and finally, the conclusion of the chapter is presented.

GLOBAL MARKET FOR SMART HEALTHCARE

According to the latest study by Grand View Research, the global intelligent health care industry is forecasted to reach approximately USD 225.54 billion by 2022. The global smart healthcare market is expected to be primarily driven by rapid technological advancements in the healthcare industry over the projected period. According to forecasts, the smart healthcare industry is expected to expand due to the emergence of new inventory management solutions like RFID KanBan and RFID smart cabinets that can effectively manage logistics and decrease inventory expenses. The utilization of smart syringes, smart pills and smart bandages is predicted to contribute to the expansion of the healthcare industry by facilitating remote patient monitoring, assisting in the diagnosis of gastrointestinal ailments, limiting the transmission of infections, and enabling remote tracking of the recovery progress (Data Bridge, 2023). The market for smart healthcare products was worth USD 143.6 billion in 2019, and it is anticipated to rise at a CAGR of 16.2% from 2020 to 2027. Demand for smart healthcare systems is expected to increase due to the rise in mHealth use, government efforts to digitize healthcare, and the prevalence of chronic diseases. According to the "*United Healthcare Consumer Sentiment Survey*", around 37.0% of Americans relied on the internet or mobile apps for health-related consultations in 2019. Currently, AI in the fitness industry enables smarter workouts without the need for gym equipment by incorporating AI into wearable devices like watches, which help personalize fitness goals. The wearable industry has undergone significant transformations since 2004, when it was deemed the year of wearable technology due to the sudden increase in activity trackers following the release of the Apple Watch. The smart health market is higher in developed nations like North America and Europe, as well as some countries in the Asia Pacific (Grand View Research, 2023). Smart health has also been introduced in developing nations like Latin America and the Middle East & Africa, as shown in Figure 2.

EMERGING TECHNOLOGIES IN SMART HEALTHCARE DEVELOPMENT

Artificial Intelligence of Things (AIoT) is a combination of the computational power of AI and IoT, which collectively pushes the limits on the intelligence of smart devices by enabling them to perform highly challenging tasks. The Internet of Things acts as the digital nervous system, and the AI acts as the brain of the system. The addition of AI to the Internet of Things can analyze data collected using IoT sensors and help make decisions and act on the data without human experts. The AI can identify and implement necessary measures in advance for critical medical conditions. Implementing AIoT can substantially reduce death rates by enabling the detection of high-risk diseases at their initial stages, monitoring disease spread, predicting mortality risks by analyzing the patient's health history, remote or home therapy, and other techniques that can significantly reduce hospital occupancy. AIoT-based healthcare includes the combination of IoT and AI algorithms, as shown in Figure 3. IoT helps in monitoring and data collection, whereas, AI automatically diagnoses and predicts diseases with the collected data. This session discusses how IoT and AI algorithms are used for the smart healthcare system.

Figure 2. Growth of smart healthcare

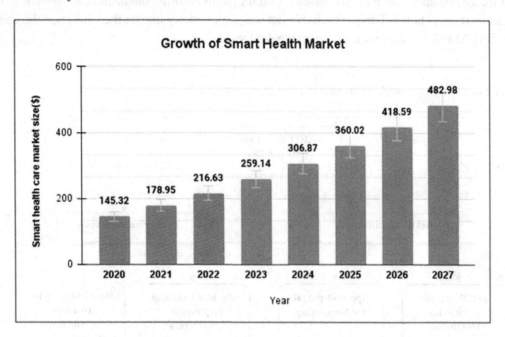

Smart Health Monitoring System

During the pandemic period, the world experience higher attention to remote patient monitoring systems. Regular monitoring is beneficial for early predicting various health conditions by collecting real-time acquisitions of patient health status. For instance, patients with chronic illnesses, disabilities and the elderly face mobility issues. So, providing smart monitoring in remote areas delivers good healthcare facilities to the patient with home comforts (Zouka & Hosni, 2019). An AI-integrated technology is proposed using neural networks and fuzzy systems for the secured health care monitoring system. It helps in collecting the health parameters using the sensor nodes. The collected data is transmitted using GSM modules to the IoT Hub of Azure. It converts the raw data into linguistic representations to apply the (FBIS) Fuzzy-based Inference System to predict vital signs of the patients. Similarly, monitoring equipment is proposed for keeping a close eye on patients' movements during exercise, sleep, and walking (Malche, et al., 2022). Health monitoring has become a significant aspect of daily living, particularly for elderly people and patients who are bedridden (Noble et al., 2018). The patients are provided with a caretaker, but still, it is a problem to monitor patients at each moment. So, a new IoT-based smart monitoring system is proposed for home patients, especially those suffering from chronic diseases like heart attacks, diabetes, arthritis and stroke. The monitoring includes measuring temperature, pulse, respiration, and blood pressure. The collected data are analyzed using hybrid model with minimum processing time. The model collects the real-time data from the patient which support in increasing the lifetime of the patients. By implanted IoT, the data collected are sent to the caretaker as monthly medical reports and shared through a Smartphone application. It has created a significant impact on rural people. The tool developed offers a processing time of 820ms with an overall accuracy of 95% to detect abnormalities in people. The smart health care monitoring system includes the IoT based wearable device for monitoring health care and application or web based portal for the monitoring the health care system. So in this section let us discuss how IoT based wearable devices significantly impact the smart healthcare system and how this AI is integrated with the wearable devices.

Figure 3. Flow diagram for AIoT in smart healthcare systems

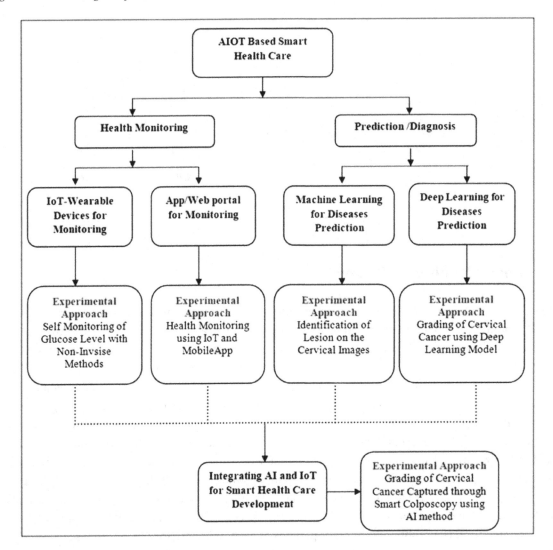

IoT-Based Wearable Devices for Health Monitoring

Wearable sensors have become an important component in smart healthcare services as they offer a cost-effective alternative to hospital settings (Islam et al., 2020; Majumder, 2017). These technologies enable medical personnel to assess general health information, screen patients for severe symptoms, and remotely identify anomalies (Dias & Cunha, 2018; Dian et al., 2020). The Massachusetts Institute of Technology (MIT) lab was one of the first institutions to develop wearable technologies, integrating multimedia, wireless communications, and sensors into people's clothing as early as the 1960s. A proposed monitoring system uses parameters such as body temperature and cardiac frequency to monitor a patient's health (Islam et al., 2020). Sensors like CO, room temperature, and CO2 are used to predict living environment conditions. The collected data is transferred to a web server through the Wi-Fi module, and ESP32 device is utilized for processing the collected data. Data are continuously collected in the web server, and the level of toxic gas in the environment is measured in parts per million (ppm) (Elango & Muniandi, 2020). Another wearable tool is proposed to monitor a patient's vital parameters, and fall detection of the patients. The proposed model employs a heartbeat sensor (LM35), accelerometer, body temperature sensor, and MPU 6050 to predict anomalies in the patient's data. NodeMCU device used as the processing device and with the use of a handheld gadget, patients can be remotely monitored and visualized using a web service called Thing Speak.

The IoT and cloud computing frameworks are utilized for monitoring healthcare systems (Al-Sheikh & Ameen, 2020). The collected data are passed to cloud for further processing using Wi-Fi connectivity. A monitoring tool is introduced using pulse and body temperature sensors, and edge devices such as the NodeMCU and ATmega328P microcontroller are utilized for data collection (Ajaegbu et al., 2020). Data collected are transmitted through the network, and physicians can monitor the patient's medical status through an LCD display. A wearable tool's performance was assessed in diabetic patients with cardiac arrhythmia, and the proposed model generated higher quality data (Mohapatra et al., 2019). The suggested method utilized HR and TS to interpret patient data, and Arduino served as an edge device that was wired to the sensors and used to send information to cloud over Wi-Fi. Any internet-connected device can be used by doctors to quickly connect to the cloud server to check on patients' conditions and recommend appropriate treatments in an emergency. An IoT based framework was introduced for symptoms monitoring by intergrading the sensors with the mobile application and message passing services (Swaroop et al., 2019). The primary hardware employed for monitoring patients includes a Raspberry Pi and three sensors to detect health parameters. The handheld prototype is being developed with a Wi-Fi communication channel that has an average latency of 125.95 seconds. Meanwhile, (Al-khafajiy et al., 2019) presented a wearable based monitoring system for elderly patients, which enables patients to access healthcare resources in home setting. Data gathered is delivered to the patient's mobile application via Bluetooth after connecting all components to an Arduino UNO. Finally, the data is moved to the cloud server through Smartphone application, which serves as a gateway. The established monitoring platform allows clinicians to easily monitor patient records and sensor data. Similarly, sensors are used for collection of health parameters and transmission handled by an ATmega328P microprocessor and bluetooth module (Semwal et al., 2019). The cloud server's LabVIEW tool is used for visualization of data. The suggested prototype offers offline data collection from multiple sensors in areas with poor network connectivity, which is later uploaded to the cloud. Lastly, (Kumar et al., 2018) presented a smart healthcare monitoring system that allows patients and doctors to communicate via a camera. Health parameters, namely temperature and heart rate, are detected by the input sensors of the Raspberry Pi CPU module and sent to the LCD, enabling doctors to inspect health condition of patients in real-time by sending the processed information to the web server over the internet. The system only connects to a small number of sensors, but it still enhances the patient monitoring system.

A wearable health tracking platform is introduced to assists clinicians in monitoring patients and collecting data across an IoT network (Wan et al., 2018). The system uses an Arduino as an edge device along with sensing nodes such as blood pressure, heart rate, and body temperature sensors. The body area sensor network uses Wi-Fi to transmit all the collected data to a cloud server, and physicians can monitor patients via a laptop or smartphone. Table 1 summarizes the developed health monitoring systems that utilize wearable devices. It considers several factors, including communication channels, sensors and edge devices, visual data for monitoring, and the outcome of each developed system. In this session, the AI is integrated with the IoT based wearable devices for health monitoring. (Al et al., 2021) proposed the IoT based wearable monitoring device to measure the various vital signs related to COVID-19. It automatically alerts the medical authorities about the infected patient and helps in tracking their real time location using GPS. The wearable sensor is connected to the human body and the collected data are processed and stored in the cloud. The proposed system is build with three layer called Iota sensors layer where all the sensor collect the medical parameters, cloud layer where all the parameters are stored simultaneously and finally the application peripheral interface(API) to monitor and visualize the collected data.

Table 1. Summary of wearable devices for smart healthcare monitoring

Author/Year	Sensors	Edge Device	Communication	Visualization	Outcome
Al et al., 2021	PPG Unit, GPS sensors, Temperature Sensors, Accerlometers	Arduino MKR	Bluetooth	Android Screen	The API based platform updated the health condition of the each patient which helps in easy tracking of patients
Islam et al., 2020	body temperature, heart rate sensor, sensor, CO sensor, room temperature sensor, and CO2 sensor	NodeMCU	web server and Wi-Fi	Thing Speak	Accuracy = 95%
Elango & Muniandi, 2020	Heartbeat sensor, body temperature sensor, and accelerometer	NodeMCU	Wi-Fi/HTTP, MQTT	Thing Speak, LCD	N/A
Al-Sheikh & Ameen, 2020	Heart rate, ECG, SpO2, and body temperature sensor	Arduino, NodeMCU	Wi-Fi	Blynk	Predict the parameter with minimum power consumption and tested on 4 people.
Chigozirim et al., 2020	Heart Beat sensor, body temperature sensor	ATmega328p, and NodeMCU	WiFI	LCD	The instrument's findings, along with a Cronbach's alpha of 0.71,
Mohapatra et al., 2019	Heart Beat sensor, body temperature sensor	ATmega328p, and NodeMCU	ATmega328p, and NodeMCU	Adafruit	The developed tool is highly secured than the existing method and emergency notification
Swaroop et al., 2019	ECG, Pulse rate, blood pressure and temperature	Raspberry pi	Wi-Fi and MQTT	Web application	Accuracy = 93.74
Al-khafajiy et al., 2019	Pulse, temperature, blood oxygen, and blood glucose sensors	Arduino	Bluetooth HC-06	Web application	Accuracy = 92.56
Semwal et al., 2019	ECG, pulse oximeter, body temperature, and blood pressure sensors	ATmega328P	Bluetooth HC-05	LabVIEW	Accuracy = 98.26
Kumar et al., 2018	Heartbeat, and temperature sensor	Raspberry Pi	Wi-Fi/ HTTP	Web application	Accuracy = 99
Wan et al., 2018	Heartbeat, blood pressure, and body temperature sensors	Arduino	Wi-Fi/ HTTP	Web application, LCD	Accuracy = 90.37

N/A – Not Applicable

AIoT-Based Wearable Device for Health Monitoring

The combination of artificial intelligence and wearable devices is a game changer in the healthcare world. IoT and mhealth devices help locate physicians or doctors closer to patients, enabling patients to receive timely treatment. The wearable biometric monitoring devices have fixed sensors to collect patient's behavioral, physiological, environmental, biological data. By using BMDs wearable tools, thousands of data are collected for assessment, predicting patient outcomes, and helping professionals choose the best treatment (Possamai et al., 2020). In 2019, a new AI wearable tool named Cambridge Heart wear was introduced for monitoring heart rhythm via electrocardiograms (ECGs) and the automatic interpretation and identification of irregularities using artificial intelligence. Patients can securely set the device to acquire and transmit real-time data directly to their physician (Research, 2018). A new wearable device has been introduced to assess COVID-19-related symptoms, such as breathing rate and core temperature. The smart helmet is outfitted with a thermal imaging system for the automatic identification of corona virus using thermal imaging technology without any human contact. It can detect higher body temperatures and immediately send notifications to healthcare workers by obtaining continuous data on people's body temperature.

Similar to this, China has introduced a 5G-based smart helmet at the recent *"China International Import Expo"*. This helmet utilizes a low-power design and consumes 85% less power, speeding up the diagnosing process compared to traditional screening methods (Ahlawat & Krishnamurthi, 2022). Smart glasses has proposed to identify suspected COVID-19 cases in crowds with high body temperatures. The thermal camera screens and predicts a person with a high body temperature, and the person is captured through the optical camera. The face is identified using Viola-Jones algorithm, and the identified person's temperature details are shared with the healthcare department (Mohammed et al., 2020). A wearable device has been proposed to monitor long-term blood pressure and heart rate (HR). The IoT wearable tools are related to the machine learning framework to detect motion by head movements. The device is built with electrocardiogram and photoplethysmography sensors and is located at backside of the ears to acquire weak ear-ECG/PPG signals successfully (Zhang et al., 2017). The support vector machine is used to predict raw heartbeats based on human body motion (Kumar et al., 2017). Researchers are facing challenges in collecting real-time patient data, so wearables are playing a significant role in collecting real-time data from patients. Therefore, a new wearable tool is proposed by connecting IoT sensors and machine learning.

Recent studies have shown that heart attacks are the leading cause of death, with nearly 610,000 people dying from cardiac attacks in the United States. To address this issue, wearable devices and artificial intelligence can be employed to anticipate and avert heart attacks. For instance, the IoT based monitoring system employs three-tier design to collect, store and analyze data from wearable sensors, with significant variables including Respiratory Rate (RP), Blood Pressure Systolic Range (SR), Heart Rate (HR), and Blood Pressure Diastolic Range (DR). Apache HBase is used to store the large amount of information collected using IoT sensors, and Apache Mahout is utilized to build the machine learning model called logistic regression for predicting heart diseases (Guo et al., 2021). Another example is the IoT-based smartwatch paired with an Android app, which uses an accelerometer for data collection to predict falls in real-time. The smart fall application employs Support Vector Machine (SVM) and Naive Bayes, and convolutional neural network model for predicting falls. The performance of the smart watch, Notch and Farseeing, the deep learning outperforms machine learning for fall detection of patients. The AI algorithm has been displayed with online and real-time test results, with the deep learning model processing the information without preprocessing method and achieving an overall accuracy of 100% for the real-time dataset. However, the fall prediction drops for the farseeing dataset at a percentage of 86% during the online test.

In contrast, severe heart attacks that cause loss of control while driving result in numerous fatal accidents. To predict heart abnormalities during driving, a new wearable ECG band that communicates using wireless technology was introduced. The electrocardiogram (ECG) is actively recorded and sent to the portable decision-making subsystem by sensors fastened to the wrist. The gathered data are processed using the "extended modified B-distribution" (EMBD), extended time-frequency features, and polynomial kernel of the support vector machine algorithm (Chowdhury et al., 2019). The tool's accuracy for detecting elevation myocardial infarction (STEMI) and non-ST-elevation MI (NSTEMI) methods are 97.40% and 96.30%, respectively. The proposed tool can detect heart abnormalities and help reduce the loss of lives and road accidents worldwide. Figure 4 shows the AI-based smart wearable, and Table 2 summarizes the wearable AI tool for smart healthcare development. The next section discusses the experimental approach to identifying the glucose level from patients using a non-invasive method. (Lin et al., 2019) proposed a AIoT based method for the prediction of cardiac diseases prediction. The ECG sensing device act as the front end for the wearable device. The smart app act the interface and the collected data are stored in the cloud database. The AI algorithm predict cardiac diseases and classifies the the arrhythmia from the collected data. Similarly, (wang et al., 2022) proposed a cardiovascular diseases prediction using the wearable devices. The proposed model predict the diseases with the average accuracy of 90.2%.

Figure 4. Wearable AI tool for smart healthcare development: (a) smart helmet, (b) smart glass, (c) smart watch, (d) wearable ECG band

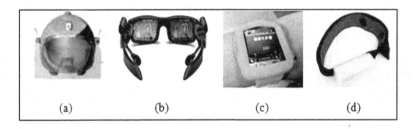

Glucose Level Monitoring Using IoT-Based Tools: An Experimental Approach

One of the prevailing long-term health conditions affecting people across the globe is diabetes. Patients with diabetes often struggle to monitor their blood sugar levels because the intrusive procedures involved can harm nearby tissues. However, by using an Arduino Uno board and a sensor, it is possible to predict glucose levels without the need for blood strips or needles. This method can help in measuring a patient's sugar level without affecting their tissues.

Aim: To develop self-monitoring of glucose levels with non-invasive method using MAX30100 sensors.

Hardware Components: Sensors like Pulse Rate, SpO2 and Glucose level, microcontroller, LED light, MAX30100 sensor are used in the experiment

Table 2. Wearable AI for smart healthcare development

Author/Year	Sensors	Components	AI Algorithm	Type
Wang et al., 2022	Wearable ECG Monitor	ECG sensing device, Cloud, BLE, Smart phones	CNN and LSTM	Cardiovascular diseases prediction
Ahlawat & Krishnamurthi, 2022	Smart Glass	Optical camera, Thermal Camera, Google Location History	Viola–Jones	Screening tool crowds.
Guo et al., 2021	Smart Watch	Cloud-Internet of things (C-IOT), Smart phones	CNN	Health monitoring like blood pressure and step count
Possamai et al., 2020	Smart Helmet	Thermal camera, Optical camera, Arduino	Viola–Jones	Screening tool
Lin et al., 2019	Wearble ECG Patches	ECG sensing device	CNN	Cardiac diseases prediction
Chowdhury et al., 2019	Wearable ECG band	RFduino, ECG sensors, SIM 908 Moule, Cooling fan, BLE dongle, RPI micro USB	SVM	Heart attack Prediction
Zhang et al., 2017	Long-Term Motion-Tolerant Wearable Monitoring tool	electrocardiogram (ECG) and, photoplethysmography (PPG) sensors	SVM, K- Mediods clustering	Predict the abnormalities in the blood pressure and heart rate
Kumar et al., 2017	Wearable watch	Health rate sensor, blood pressure,	Logistic Regression	Heart Diseases Prediction

Methodology: The system reads pulse rate, SpO2, and glucose levels from a sensor attached to the microcontroller before processing the sensed data in the controller. The microcontroller is the decision-maker of the system. It is connected to two LED sensors; one emitting the red light, and the other the infrared light, which is necessary to measure the pulse rate. Using red and infrared light, the system determines the oxygen saturation measure in the blood stream. The ventricular motion pushes more blood when there is high oxygen, and the quantity of the oxygenated blood decreases as the heart relaxes. The duration between the ascent and descent of oxygen-rich blood aids in the determination of the pulse rate. The primary function of the MAX30100 sensor is to track the uptake capacity of both light sources and store in a buffer that can be taken through an I2C display. This non-invasive method minimizes skin infections caused by frequent tissue pricking and reduces discomfort for patients compared to invasive procedures. An IoT-based non-invasive monitoring system for pulse rate, oxygen saturation, and blood sugar promises to make users' lives easier by utilizing the advantages of an embedded system. The components connected are displayed in Figure 5(a), and a demonstration is shown in Figure 5(b).

Result and Discussion: The Easy Touch measurement was compared with a glucose monitoring instrument and the results indicates that both measurements were statistically indistinguishable from each other. The non-invasive approach has undergone extensive testing and has an accuracy rating of 90.3% with a variation of 1.2-3.6 mg/dL, as shown in Table 3.

Figure 5. Self glucose monitoring system: (a) construction of monitoring system, (b) predicting the glucose level using the proposed monitoring system

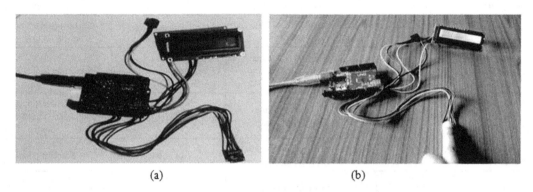

(a)   (b)

Table 3. Prediction of glucose level with existing and proposed non-invasive method

Methods	Easy Touch (mg/dl)			Non-Invasive Method		
Parameters	Heart Rate	Spo2	Glucose Level	Heart Rate	Spo2	Glucose Level
Sample	112	97	N	111	96	N

Smartphone Sensors and Android App for Smart Healthcare Development

Smartphone's are also playing a significant role in the smart healthcare system. Globally, there are many illnesses that affect the respiratory system, skin, eyes, heart and mental health. Continuous monitoring can help prevent or manage them. Using smartphones to enable constant health monitoring provides a non-invasive, affordable and accessible healthcare solution. With mobile phone penetration and sensors for advanced communication technologies, appropriate infrastructure has been established for continuous virtual monitoring of patients (Majumder & Deen, 2019). Health parameters collected through smartphones include heart rate, blood pressure, oxygen level, daily activity, mental health, etc., as shown in Table 4. The camera sensor connected to smart phones is also used for identifying skin, eye, and ear infections and for cancer screening. Hyperglycemic patients need to monitor their blood glucose levels regularly to prevent diabetes. Currently, in many clinics, an invasive method is used to check their glucose level, making it uncomfortable for regular screening. A non-invasive blood glucose monitoring system has been introduced using Photo Plethysmo Gram (PPG) data collected as a video over the smartphone. Data collected is analyzed and stored in the cloud. A machine learning model is applied to extract features using Gaussian filters, and it predicts the standard values based on the body's glucose level (Zhang et al., 2020). A new framework was introduced for instant monitoring of the user's health by estimating the vital sign of the patients. The two Smartphone sensors, rear camera, and the microphone, will helps in recording data. The heart rate and SpO2 data were converted into a photoplethysmogram (PPG) collected through image sensors.

Table 4. Build in smart phone sensor used in health monitoring

Health Monitoring	Build in Smart Phone Sensor
Cardiovascular Activity	Microphone, Image sensor
Eye Screening	Image Sensor
Respiratory and lung Diseases	Microphone, Image sensor
Skin health Diagnosis	Image Sensor
Daily activity and fall recognition	Motion sensors
Ear health	Microphone
Cognitive function and mental health	Motion sensors

The smart phone based blood monitoring system is introduced to predict the blood pressure. The system collects data using the user's six index fingers via a smartphone camera. The device predicts the systolic and diastolic blood pressure using pulse transit time (PTT) between two distinct photoplethys-mogram (PPG) signals. The PPG signals are filtered and processed using peak detection techniques to reduce motion and noise. Finally, the predicted BP value is measured using mean square error (MSE), standard deviation, and correlation parameters (Tabei et al., 2020). Similarly, a respiratory monitoring system using a smartphone has been introduced to accurately measure respiratory rate. The measurement is done using imaging and Fourier transforms techniques. Patients' skin surfaces are captured on video through the camera with the flashlight connected to the smartphone. Data collected is converted to PPG signals and analyzed using discrete wavelet transform to predict the respiratory rate (Alafeef & Fraiwan, 2020). Furthermore, a non-invasive blood glucose monitoring system has been introduced using Photo Plethysmo Gram (PPG) data, collected as a video via smartphone. The collected data is analyzed and stored on the cloud. A machine learning algorithm is used to extract the data's features using Gaussian filters, and it predicts the standard, warning, and borderline levels based on the body's glucose level (Zhang et al., 2020). Finally, an android app was introduced to provide audio-visual feedback to determine whether placing the smartphone in the right spot would result in signals of high enough quality to estimate blood pressure (Nemcova et al., 2020).

Similarly, smartphones embedded with sensors have been introduced to measure blood pressure. The PPG data are split into 15-second epochs using the sliding window, and 233 features are retrieved from PPG pulse's raw signals with respect to time and frequencies (Dey et al., 2018). The BP monitoring system using seismo interprets vibrations produced by heartbeat and finger pulses. The blood releasing time is calculated from the seismocardiography signal with accelerometer, and the fingertip are used for calculating the receiving time from PPG data using image sensors. The speakers embedded in smartphone synchronize collects the data using an accelerometer and camera. The system's performance is evaluated in a longitudinal blood pressure perturbation study with nine participants (Wang et al., 2018). Heart rate monitoring using a smartphone is proposed using photoplethysmographic data. The data is collected using the reflected mode of PPG using image sensors for the user's index fingertips. The stored data is transferred to the processing device using Bluetooth communication. The system's performance is evaluated with 19 subjects (Alafeef, 2017). A new monitoring system is developed for accurately monitoring the patient's heart rate using the smartphone's camera images (Lomlize & Park, 2017). The signals are extracted from the region of interest, and noise from the raw data are removed using the threshold method. The experimental results showed that the framework's heart rate estimation was accurate. The suggested approach, however, disregards the effects of various smartphone camera modules. Table 5 provides a summary of the smartphone sensors in smart healthcare development, which includes factors such as the sensors, smartphone used, and their outcomes.

Table 5. Summary of smartphone sensors in smart healthcare development

Author/Year	Type	Sensor	Smartphone	Algorithm	Outcome
Zhang et al., 2020	Blood Glucose level	Image Sensors	iPhone 6s Plus	Gaussian SVM, Bagged Trees (BT) and K-nearest neighbor (KNN) classifiers	Accuracy = 81.49%.
Nemcova et al., 2020	HR, BP, SpO2	The rear camera, microphone	Honor 7 Lite, Apple iPhone SE, Lenovo Vibe S1	Regression	Mean Absolute Errors (MAE) = 1.1% for SpO2 and 1.4 beats per minute (bpm) for HR estimation.
Alafeef & Fraiwan, 2020	Respiratory rate	Image sensor	Samsung Galaxy S6	Fourier transform techniques, discrete wavelet tranforms	Average Accuracy of 97.8% and an average error of 2.2%.
Tabei et al., 2020	Blood Pressure	Camera	iPhone X	Linear Regression Model	MAE = 2.10, standard deviation = 1.96, and correlation parameters = 0.90
Dey et al., 2018	Blood Pressure	Heart Rate Sensors	Samsung Galaxy S6	Lasso regression techniques	Accuracy = 95%
Wang et al., 2018	Blood Pressure	Rear camera, accelerometer	N/M	N/M	Pearson correlation = 0.20 and 0.77 for the volunteers
Alafeef, 2017	Heart Rate	Image Sensor	Samsung Galaxy	Mean filtering in intensity of each channel	Accuracy is 99.7%
Lomlize & park, 2017	Heart Rate	Rear camera	Pantech Vega Racer 3Samsung Galaxy S2 LG G3, HTC Desire HD	Adaptive threshold method	In real-time, system predict the heart rate with less than 5% error rate

N/M-Not Mentioned

Android App for IoT-Based Healthcare Monitoring System: An Experimental Approach

Previously, it was impossible for doctors to remotely monitor patients in critical conditions. To address this issue, an Android app-based Internet of Things (IoT) system has been presented. It automatically collects and sends patient data to a server, allowing doctors to constantly access it.

Objective: The system's main objective is to monitor the patient health record remotely and minimize hospital visits. It also helps the patient to know their health condition.

Hardware Components: Node MCU is first linked to the Wi-Fi by the health monitoring system. The system reads parameters like the heartbeat, oxygen level, high blood pressure, low blood pressure, and temperature as sensors are connected to the Controller. The Node MCU reads the ECG Value from the ECG sensor after receiving these data from the Controller. With the aid of the URL and API key, 14 values from the Controller and the ECG are now delivered to the Firebase database. The values in the database are promptly updated. The Firebase URL and API key are also used to display the values in the developed App. Now that the doctor can access the App, the patient can assess the medical condition using the sensor's parameter values.

Methodology: The health monitoring system first connects the Node MCU to the Wi-Fi. Then, parameters such as heartbeat, oxygen level, high blood pressure, low blood pressure, and temperature are read from the sensors connected to the Controller. Once these data are received from the Controller, the Node MCU reads the ECG value from the ECG sensor. Using the URL and API key, the Controller and ECG data (a total of 14 values) are moved to the Firebase database, where they are promptly updated. The Firebase URL and API key are also used to display the values in the developed App, which can be accessed by the doctor to assess the patient's medical condition using the sensor's parameter values. The workflow of the methodology is shown in Figure 6.

Data Transfer: The Node MCU is utilized to transmit the sensor-collected data from the Arduino board are transferred to cloud. The Node MCU serves as a Wi-Fi module and sends the data to Firebase. Data transmission is carried out by utilizing the Firebase host URL and API keys obtained from the Firebase database. Additionally, the Firebase database is linked to the App using API keys, a Firebase Host URL, and a database bucket. The values obtained from the board are stored in the database and displayed in the App. The data transfer flow is illustrated in Figure.7.

Visualization: The doctor can remotely track the patient's records with the help of a created App, which consists of two modules. The first module is for doctors, where they can log in using their user ID and password and select the patient to monitor. The screen displays the patient's health parameter values, and the doctor can check their health condition and prescribe medication in the prescription text box provided. The second module is for patients, where they can log in using their user ID and password. This takes them to the screen displaying the doctor's name, hospital name, and prescription, as shown in Figure 8.

Figure 6. Workflow for monitoring the patient using IoT sensors and Android app

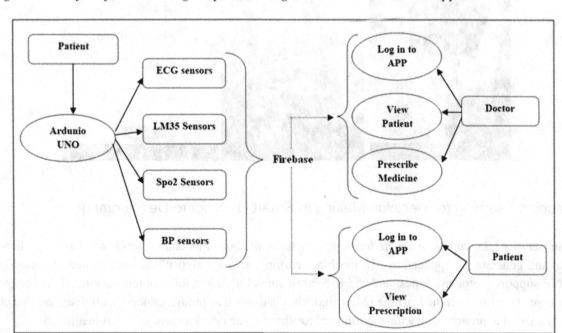

Figure 7. Data transfer flow

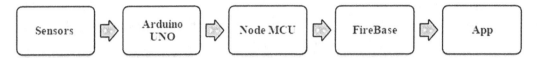

Role of Artificial Intelligence Prediction in Decision Making

Artificial Intelligence (AI) is rapidly gaining importance in the healthcare industry to improve smart healthcare systems. This technology has the potential to transform various aspects of patient care as well as internal administrative procedures at insurers, providers, and pharmaceutical businesses. Numerous studies have shown that AI is as good as, if not better than, humans in carrying out important healthcare activities like disease diagnosis. Today, algorithms are more effective than radiologists in identifying cancerous tumors and helping researchers create cohorts for costly clinical trials.

Figure 8. Android app for the patient and doctor monitoring system

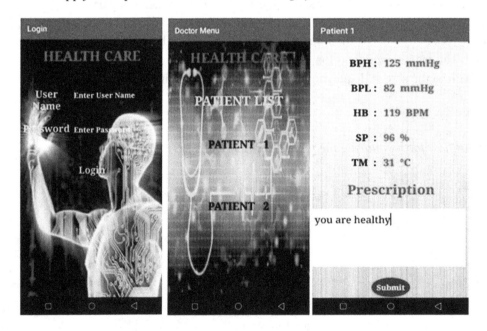

Machine Learning for Decision Making in Smart Healthcare Development

A subset of AI, known as "*machine learning*", includes methods that enable computers to comprehend data and generate AI applications. In machine learning, various algorithms such as neural networks (NN), support vector machines, and the K-Nearest model are used for problem-solving. This section discusses how the machine learning (ML) algorithm is utilized to predict cancer, heart diseases, and an experimental approach on machine learning algorithm for the development of smart healthcare.

Cancer Prediction Using Machine Learning Algorithms

Machine Learning approaches and biosensors have been proposed for early diagnosis of breast cancer (Amethiya et al., 2022). A tumor detection algorithm from mammograms was proposed by Rejani and Selvi (2009). The first approach involves learning to recognize tumors as suspicious spots that have weak contrast with their surroundings, while the second approach is to learn to derive characteristics that categorize tumors. Tumor detection involves methods such as mammogram enhancement and segmentation of tumor areas. Enhancement involves improving image quality to more understandable levels, while segmentation is done using the threshold method for diagnosing breast cancer. A decision tree is presented using data mining techniques for initial breast cancer detection. Additionally, machine learning algorithms like random forest, nearest neighbor, and Naïve Bayes are used to predict breast cancer (Sharma et al., 2018). Based on comparison analysis, the K-nearest neighbor outperforms the existing machine learning methods in predicting cancer.

Skin conditions are prevalent among human illnesses, with skin colour being a powerful indicator of this condition. A system that recognizes skin cancer using captured skin images. The skin is filtered using the median filter, and the segmentation process is applied to the extracted features. The support vector machine and random forest are combined to classify skin diseases (Murgan et al., 2021). Machine learning algorithms, such as the random forest classifier, K nearest classifier, multilayer perceptron classifier and decision tree, are used to classify skin disease types (Verma et al., 2021). Based on comparative analysis, the random forest outperforms the other classification models in identifying the type of skin diseases. An approach called CervDetect, which uses machine learning algorithms to predict the risk of malignant cervical formation has been proposed (Weegar & Sundström, 2020). The random forest and feature selection techniques are used to select suitable features for cancer prediction. Table 6 provides a summary of the machine learning used in cancer prediction, including factors such as the dataset, type of cancer, and its outcome.

Table 6. Machine learning used in the prediction of cancer

Author/Year	Dataset	Type of Cancer	ML Algorithm	Outcome
Rejani & Selvi, 2009	mini-MIAS database	Breast cancer	SVM	The model achieved the sensitivity of 88.75%.
Sumbaly et al., 2014	Digitized images of FNAC of a breast mass	Breast Cancer	Decision tree and J48	The model achieved the sensitivity of 94.56
Sharma et al., 2018	Wisconsin - Digitized images of FNAC of a breast mass	Breast Cancer	KNN	Accuracy = 95.90
Murgan et al., 2021	ISIC dataset	Skin cancer	SVM+RF	Accuracy = 88.56
Verma et al., 2021	UCI machine repository	Skin cancer	Random Forest Classifier	Accuracy = 0.99
Weegar & Sundström, 202	UCI machine repository	Cervical Cancer	Random forest	Accuracy = 93.6%

Heart Disease Prediction Using Machine Learning Algorithms

Cardiovascular diseases have emerged as one of the most severe and acute illnesses affecting adults. According to studies, heart disease causes about 30% (18 million) of all annual deaths (Ahmed et al., 2019)(Kaptoge et al., 2020). To reduce the risk of heart disease, researchers are focusing on developing decision support systems in the smart healthcare environment. Heart disease prediction is carried out highly using ECG data, and early detection can prevent patients from leading to death (Nagaveli et al., 2022). The machine learning approach, like Naive Bayes with the weight approach (NBwa), is used to predict heart diseases. Similarly, feature-based frequency domain, time domain, and information theory are proposed for analyzing and automatically identifying ischemic heart disease. Classifier models such as the support vector machine and XGBoost are used for classification with the best performance rate. Clinical decision support systems (CDSS) use the hybrid synthetic minority oversampling technique-edited nearest neighbor (SMOTE-ENN) widely in the medical industry to identify and diagnose diseases. The support vector machine is used for stroke prediction with a pooled AUC of 92%, and the boosting algorithm attains 91%, while the convolution neural network is 90% (Krittanawong et al., 2020).

The CNN model performs well in image data, but the SVM outperforms the prediction due to the high dimensionality of the dataset. The naive Bayes algorithm is proposed to classify specific heart diseases (Jabbar & Samreen, 2016). A comparative study is conducted with six machine learning algorithms to predict coronary artery diseases (CAD) (Gupta et al., 2020).In order to improve heart disease prediction, various techniques and algorithms are proposed and utilized. Independent features are selected using the backward elimination approach and filter method based on the Pearson correlation coefficient, and KNN algorithm is used for accuracy improvising. Remote patient monitoring is used to collect datasets, and only the most significant parameters are considered. The random forest algorithm is proposed to predict heart disease using 14 features, and the KNN model is used for weight development. Additionally, the KNN model is employed to extract features and predict ideal features with SVM FRE, which increases computational speed. Table 7 provides a summary of the machine learning techniques used in predicting heart diseases, including dataset factors and outcomes.

Table 7. Machine learning for prediction of heart disease

Author	Data Set	ML Algorithm	Outcome
Nagaveli et al., 2022	PhysioNet database	SVM, NBwa, XG Boost	XGBoost outperform the existing ML algorithm with an accuracy of 95.9%.
Krittanawong et al., 2020	Cardiovascular Dataset	SVM	AUC of 92% in cardiovascular prediction
Jabbar & Samreen, 2016	Cleaveland Heart Diseases Dataset	Hidden Naïve Bayes (HNB)	Accuracy = 100%
Gupta et al., 2020	UCI - Cleveland Heart Disease Dataset	Naive Bayes, Regression, SVM, KNN,Decision Tress and radom forest	Random forest predict the heart diseases 86.84%
Enriko et al., 2018	Real time dataset collected from HarapanKita Hospital (HKH)	k-Nearest Neighbors	The KNN model without parameter weight predict heart diseases with accuracy of 75.11%
Pal et al., 2021	Kaggle Dataset	Random forest	Predict the accuracy of 86.9%
Hutamaputr et al., 2021	N/M	Weighted KNN	Accuracy = 82.65%

N/M – Not Mentioned

Cervical Cancer Neoplasm Identification Using Machine Learning Algorithm: An Experimental Approach

Cervical cancer is a malignancy formed at the lower part of the uterus. Colposcopy devices capture cervical images and are considered for analysis of screen cervical cancer. The machine learning algorithm is used to automate and identify the cervical cancer region, i.e., abnormal regions.

Aim: Detection of dysplasia region on the colposcopy images using the machine learning algorithm called bayes classifier.

Data Collection: The colposcopy images are collected from the UCI machine learning data repository with 287 instances and 69 attributes.

Methodology: Detecting cervical cancer at early stage is crucial for effective treatment, and colposcopy is a commonly used method for the identification of abnormal tissue on the cervical images (Hariharan et al., 2012). The dysplasia region appears as a white region after the applying the acetic acid during the colposcopy examination. The white areas are manually marked by the physician to differentiate the abnormal tissue on the colposcopy images. The images are initially divided into 32x32 overlapping square to focus on the abnormal regions. From the overlapped square red, green and blue channel are extracted for the process of feature extraction. The statistical feature like mean (μ), standard deviation (σ), and skewness value are extracted from each color channel of the colposcopy images. The statistical feature are extracted from the normal and abnormal region of the images and given as the input in the naïve bayes classifier to predict the dysplasia region on the colposcopy images.

Results: Based on the quantities analysis the machine learning algorithm predict the dysplasia region with an accuracy of the 98.03%, precision value of 97.08%, Specificity value of 97.12% and sensitivity value of 92.06%. The dysplasia region predicted is shown in Figure 9.

Figure 9. Cervical cancer detection using bayes classifier: (a) Represents the original image with the marked cancer region. (b) The cervix images for lesion detection using bayes classifier.

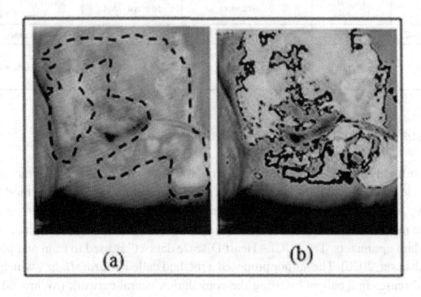

Deep Learning for Decision Making in Smart Healthcare Development

Deep learning, also known as deep neural learning or deep neural network, is a branch of machine learning that makes use of neural networks to analyse data in a manner like that of the human nervous system. It has networks that can autonomously learn from unlabeled or unstructured data. This section discusses how the machine learning algorithm is used for the prediction of cancer and heart diseases.

Cancer Prediction Using Deep Learning Models

The author suggested "end-to-end" training method, which effectively utilizes training datasets with either complete clinical annotation or only the cancer status (label) of the entire image, allows for the accurate prediction of breast cancer on screening mammograms (Shen et al., 2019). In order to predict breast cancer, the initial training stage involves lesion annotation, and the following level involves picture level labeling. The U Net model was proposed for the detection of breast cancer from the mammogram images (Mohammed et al., 2022). It assists in separating the breast region from the surrounding area, and the classification procedure is used to distinguish between the normal and pathological breast image regions. The fourth most common disease in the world among women, cervical cancer is more common in developing nations. Due to their low cost and painless diagnosis, Pap-smear tests are the most popular. The classification model called ResNet-152 architecture classify the of pap smear images based on the severity of the images (Tripathi et al., 2021). Table 8 provides an overview of the deep learning methods employed in the prediction of cancer, including the datasets, types of cancer, deep learning models, and results.

Table 8. Deep learning for prediction of cancer

Authors/Year	Database	Cancer Type	DL Model	Outcome
Shen et al., 2019	Digital Database	Breast cancer	Modern CNN	sensitivity: 86.1%, specificity: 80.1%.
Mohammed et al., 2022	DMR-IR	Breast cancer	U Net	Accuracy = 99.33%
Tripathi et al., 2021	SIPAKMED pap-smear image dataset	Cervical cancer	ResNet-152	accuracy = 94.89%

Heart Diseases Prediction Using Deep Learning Models

Heart diseases are highly reported in the developing countries like Africa and Asia. Cardiovascular disease prediction is made based on the deep learning algorithm. The author proposed a method for predicting heart diseases by applying the convolution neural network. Both organised and unstructured data are used to train the model (Shankar et al., 2020). The CNN model includes the softmax activation function with the Adam optimizers. The "UCI – Heart Disease dataset" is used to train and predict diseases (Heart disease data set, 2020). The author proposed a method called "*CardioHelp*", which helps predict cardiovascular diseases in a patient by using the convolution neural network (Mehmood et al., 2020). Heart failure prediction at early stages prevents diseases and also helps in providing suitable treatment.

Patients' data was captured by the body-worn sensors, which were then safely transmitted to cloud for supplementry processing (Arooj et al., 2022). Deep convolutional neural network (DCNN) is used for image recognition, and the model is trained with 1050 patients and 14 attributes. The feature vector is taken as input to discriminate whether the data belongs to a healthy or cardiac disease. It is predicted by compiling the collection of directly attainable characteristics from the heart-disease dataset using a Modified Deep Convolutional Neural Network (MDCNN) to detect heart illness. (Khan et al., 2020) suggested an IoT-based solution. The patient's smartwatch and heart monitor devices were used to obtain the data (BP and ECG) for this investigation. By comparing the proposed MDCNN to existing deep-learning neural networks and logistic regression, the system's performance is assessed. The outcomes show that the suggested MDCNN-based cardiac disease prediction system outperforms competing approaches. Table 9 provides a summary of the machine learning used in the prediction of heart diseases which includes the factors like dataset, and its outcome.

Table 9. Deep learning for prediction of heart disease

Authors/Year	Data	Algorithm	Outcome
Shankar et al., 2020	UCI – Heart Disease dataset	CNN	Accuracy = 85–88%
Mehmood et al., 2020	UCI – Heart Disease dataset	CNN	Accuracy =97%.
Sarmah et al. [4]	Hungarian dataset, real-time sensor data	DLMNN	Accuracy =96.8%.
Arooj et al., 2022	UCI – Heart Disease dataset	DCNN	Accuracy = 91.7%.
Khan et al. [6]	Cleveland database	MDCNN	Accuracy = 98.02%

Grading of Cervical Cancer Using Deep Learning Algorithm: Experimental Approach

Grading of cervical cancer is the process of classification based on the stages of the cervical cancer. There are three types of stages called CIN1, CIN2 and CIN3 which are represented as Type1, Type2 and Type3.

Data Collection: The smart colposcopy images are collected from the kaggle dataset (Kaggle, 2020). It consist of three grade of cancer based on the acetowhtie region affected on the cervical region. The three grades are Type 1, Type 2 and Type 3 which are labelled as shown in the Figure 10.

Deep Learning Model: The input of the model is set as 224 x 224 for the colposcopy image. VGG16 is a deep CNN model which has the convolution layers that uses narrow receptive field of filter size of 3x3. The 1x1 convolution filters is used for the linear representation before passing it into an activation function called ReLU. It helps in maintaining the spatial resolution is after passing through the convolution filter, the stride size is set as 1x1 for the consideration of each pixel. Each of the first two fully convolutional layers in the VGG contains 4096 channels, while the third layer has thousands of channels. (Sudha & Ganeshbabu, 2020).

Result: Based on the quantities analysis the deep learning model grade the smart colposcopy images with an accuracy of the 95.02%, precision value of 92.14%, Specificity value of 90.36% and sensitivity value of 92.46%.

Figure 10. Smart colposcopy images collected and Labelled as Type1, Type 2, and Type 3

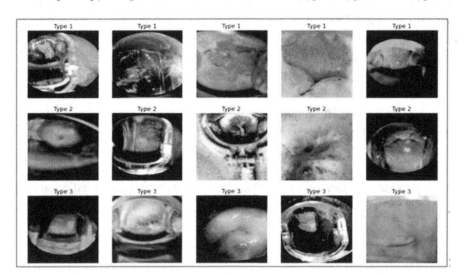

AIoT for Smart Healthcare Development

AIoT combines the Internet of Things (IoT) and Artificial intelligence (AI) Algorithms. It is revolutionary for both technologies because the artificial intelligence algorithm depends on the IoT for data collection and connectivity. Similarly, the IoT value artificial intelligence for automation and prediction activities. IoT networks are highly used across large industries to collect machine-generated data. The AIoT support the data analysis and the prediction of some specified output from the generated data through IoT. Some IoT tools are designed for simple events that can control the signals generated by sensors—for instance, turning on/off light based on environmental light changes. Sometimes, analytical tools can be utilized to interpret many phenomena that are considerably more complex. AIoT is set up to take the right actions to accomplish this. The IoT tools are givens the ability to collect data, observe their environment, and make the best decisions with minimal human intervention (Talukdar et al., 2019). With the support of artificial intelligence, the AIoT delivers the information to control and become an intelligent machine capable of self-centred analysis, while operating independently. The AI can recognize critical medical conditions and assist in getting the required measures in advance.

Implementing artificial intelligence in things can significantly reduce hospital occupancy by lowering death rates. It assists in identifying high-risk diseases at their initial stages, tracking the spread of disease, and anticipating mortality risks by examining the patient's medical history. The brain of a system is artificial intelligence, whereas internet of things devices serves as its digital nervous system. An AIoT-based caregiver cockpit (C19CC) was introduced for the healthcare worker to predict the severity of COVID-19 in the patient. The colour code is used to represent the severity of the patients. An autonomous Artificial Internet of Things (AIoT) system for monitoring senior dementia patients in a smart home was introduced by the author (Wen Chen et al., 2021). The system primarily employs two functions, real-time abnormal activity monitoring and trend prediction of disease-related activities based on the activity inference of the sensor data. Long Short-Term Memory (LSTM) is utilized to forecast the disease-related activity trend of a patient from the collected real-time data. In the next session discuss how the AIoT is used for the data collection and grading of cervical cancer based on the neoplasm affected.

AIoT-Based Method for the Grading of Smart Colposcopy Images: Experimental Approach

Cervical cancer is the second most prevalent malignancy among women in developing nations and affects women globally at a rate of one in every four cases. Due to a lack of clinical resources, developing countries have a higher mortality rate for cervical cancer than developed countries, especially in the rural and tribal region. The main preventive strategy used to lower mortality rates is screening. The screening method like Papanicolaou (Pap) testing, biopsy and HPV test is the clinical screening procedure for the cervical cancer (Saini et al., 2020; Talukdar et al., 2019). The above screening method is high cost, invasive and needs high laboratory setup for the screening of cervical cancer which is highly inefficient in the rural and tribal region of the developing countries. To reduce the clinical procedure for screening, the smart colpsocopy device is introduced for the screening of the cervical tissues region.

Smart Colposcopy: The smart colposcopy is built with the image sensors, focus and the Samsung mobile is attached to it. It captures the digital images and the physician will consider the images for the screening analysis. The smart colposcopy device has an inbuilt app called EVA App. The Eva app for collecting the patients data storing the cervical images captured image sensor.

Data Collection: The smart colposcpy have an in built app called Eva app. Click and open the eva app as show in the Figure 11(a). Click on smart colposcopy as shown in Figure 11(b). The patient details like medical record, name of the patients, data of birth and number are saved and click on the start exam. The smart colpocopy camera will open. Capture the cervical region required for analysis and click on the finish exam. The eva app will completely store the data and upload them directly to cloud for further analysis.

Cloud Upload: The captured images are exported and click on the finish button. The caputed images are directly uploaded in the EVA online portal. The physician can analyse the images from the online portal and the whole patient record are stored in the cloud. To automate the grading of cervical cancer AI algorithm is applied on the captured images.

AI/Ml Algorithm: The AI algorithm ResNet model is used for the grading of cervical cancer. The image input of the ResNet model is set as 224x224 and for the feature map generation the size is set as 112x122 which is generated by the convolutional layer. The layer is built with the softmax activation function, dropout layer for the identification of stage of cancer such as Type1, Type 2 and Type3. The model is trained with 4000 image which is collected from the kaggle dataset.

Results: Based on the quantities analysis the deep learning model grade the smart colposcopy images with an accuracy of 90% as shown in Figure 12.

CONTRIBUTION OF THIS CHAPTER

This chapter provides a comprehensive overview of the growth of smart healthcare in the medical industry and how advanced technologies are helping to improve the quality of patient care. Smart healthcare is defined as the integration of innovative technologies and smart devices with traditional healthcare practices to create a more efficient and effective healthcare system. The chapter explores how technologies such as the Internet of Things (IoT), smartphones and artificial intelligence (AI) algorithms are contributing to the growth of smart healthcare. The chapter presents an experimental approach to smart healthcare development that involves using IoT-based monitoring tools for patient care, smart Android apps for data collection, and AI algorithms for decision-making processes. The use of IoT devices for health monitoring is discussed in detail, including the benefits of real-time data collection, remote patient monitoring, and predictive analytics. The chapter also explores the role of smartphones and Android apps in smart healthcare, including their use for patient engagement, data collection and monitoring.

Figure 11. Smart colposcopy: (a) Smart colpocopy with Eva app. (b) Patient details are collected in the Eva App. (c) The cervical images captured through image sensor in saved in the Eva app.

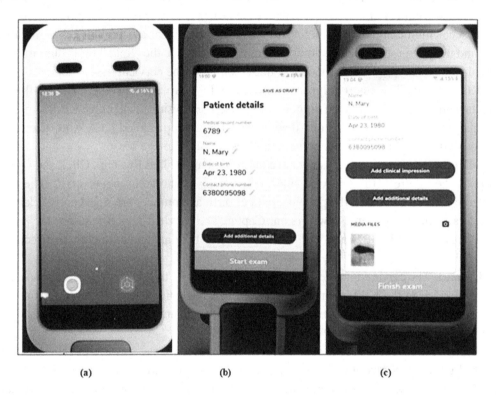

Figure 12. Loss and accuracy for the grading of cervical cancer

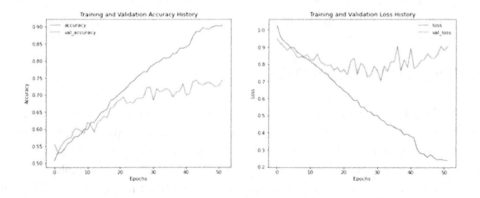

The chapter emphasizes the importance of AI in smart healthcare, particularly in the context of decision-making processes. AI algorithms are used to analyze large amounts of healthcare data to provide real-time insights and recommendations for healthcare professionals. The chapter also discusses the use of AI in personalized medicine, where patient-specific data is used to create personalized treatment plans. Furthermore, the chapter provides an overview of the integration of AI and IoT technologies to create an AIoT tool for improvising clinical support. The AIoT tool combines the data collection capabilities of IoT devices with the decision-making capabilities of AI algorithms to provide real-time and accurate insights into patient health. The chapter describes the implementation of AIoT in the medical field and its potential to transform healthcare delivery. The chapter concludes by highlighting the key benefits of smart healthcare, including improved patient outcomes, reduced healthcare costs, and enhanced patient experience. It also discusses the challenges and potential risks associated with the use of advanced technologies in healthcare, including data privacy and security concerns. Finally, the chapter provides recommendations for healthcare providers and policymakers on how to ensure the successful implementation of smart healthcare technologies.

Overall, this chapter makes a significant contribution to the understanding of smart healthcare and the role of advanced technologies in improving patient care. It provides a comprehensive overview of the latest trends and developments in smart healthcare and highlights the potential of IoT, smart phones, and AI algorithms to transform healthcare delivery. The chapter's experimental approach demonstrates how these technologies can be implemented in real-world healthcare settings to achieve better patient outcomes and enhance the overall healthcare experience. Finally, the chapter's recommendations provide valuable insights for healthcare providers and policymakers on how to leverage these technologies to improve healthcare delivery and achieve better health outcomes. This chapter helps direct the students, researchers and interns in computer engineering and computer science.

CONCLUSION

In conclusion, this chapter provides a comprehensive overview of the growth of smart healthcare and the important role of advanced technologies such as IoT, smartphones and AI algorithms in improving patient care. The experimental approach presented in the chapter demonstrates how these technologies can be used in real-world healthcare settings to achieve better patient outcomes and enhance the overall healthcare experience. The chapter's emphasis on the importance of AI in smart healthcare highlights its potential to transform decision-making processes and personalize treatment plans. Additionally, the chapter provides valuable insights into the challenges and potential risks associated with the use of advanced technologies in healthcare and provides recommendations for healthcare providers and policymakers on how to ensure the successful implementation of smart healthcare technologies. Overall, this chapter makes a significant contribution to our understanding of smart healthcare and highlights the potential of these technologies to improve healthcare delivery and achieve better health outcomes.

ACKNOWLEDGMENT

The authors would like to express deep gratitude to the "Centre for Machine Learning and Intelligence" for supporting and sharing the resource for this research work. The Department of Science & Technology supports it under the scheme of DST CURIE (AI) sanctioned for the "Core Research grant for Artificial Intelligence (AI)" in the year 2021-2023.

REFERENCES

Ahlawat, C., & Krishnamurthi, R. (2022). Internet of Things-based smart helmet to detect possible COVID-19 infections. In *Cyber-Physical Systems*. Academic Press. . doi:10.1016/B978-0-12-824557-6.00004-2

Ahmed, H., Younis, E. M., Hendawi, A. M., & Ali, A. A. (2020). Heart disease identification from patients' social posts, machine learning solution on Spark. *Future Generation Computer Systems*, *111*, 714–722. doi:10.1016/j.future.2019.09.056

Ajaegbu, C., Nwaocha, V., Nzenwata, U., & Adesegun, O. (2020). A patient monitoring system using internet of things technology. *Ingénierie des Systèmes d'Information*, *25*(3), 351–357. doi:10.18280/isi.250309

Al Bassam, N., Hussain, S. A., Al Qaraghuli, A., Khan, J., Sumesh, E. P., & Lavanya, V. (2021). IoT based wearable device to monitor the signs of quarantined remote patients of COVID-19. *Informatics in Medicine Unlocked*, *24*, 100588. doi:10.1016/j.imu.2021.100588 PMID:33997262

Al-khafajiy, M., Baker, T., Chalmers, C., Asim, M., Kolivand, H., Fahim, M., & Waraich, A. (2019). Remote health monitoring of elderly through wearable sensors. *Multimedia Tools and Applications*, *78*(17), 24681–24706. doi:10.100711042-018-7134-7

Al-Sheikh, M. A., & Ameen, I. A. (2020). Design of mobile healthcare monitoring system using IoT technology and cloud computing. *IOP Conference Series: Materials Science and Engineering, 881*. 10.1088/1757-899X/881/1/012113

Alafeef, M. (2017). Smartphone-based photoplethysmographic imaging for heart rate monitoring. *Journal of Medical Engineering & Technology*, *41*(5), 387–395. doi:10.1080/03091902.2017.1299233 PMID:28300460

Alafeef, M., & Fraiwan, M. (2020). Smartphone-based respiratory rate estimation using photoplethysmographic imaging and discrete wavelet transform. *Journal of Ambient Intelligence and Humanized Computing*, *11*(2), 693–703. doi:10.100712652-019-01339-6

Amethiya, Y., Pipariya, P., Patel, S., & Shah, M. (2022). Comparative analysis of breast cancer detection using machine learning and biosensors. *Intelligent Medicine*, *2*(2), 69–81. doi:10.1016/j.imed.2021.08.004

Arooj, S., Rehman, S., Imran, A., Almuhaimeed, A., Alzahrani, A. K., & Alzahrani, A. (2022). A Deep Convolutional Neural Network for the Early Detection of Heart Disease. *Biomedicines*, *10*(11), 2796. doi:10.3390/biomedicines10112796 PMID:36359317

Chandran, V., Sumithra, M. G., Karthick, A., George, T., Deivakani, M., Elakkiya, B., Subramaniam, U., & Manoharan, S. (2021). Diagnosis of Cervical Cancer based on Ensemble Deep Learning Network using Colposcopy Images. *BioMed Research International*, *2021*, 1–15. doi:10.1155/2021/5584004 PMID:33997017

Chowdhury, M. E. H., Alzoubi, K., Khandakar, A., Khallifa, R., Abouhasera, R., Koubaa, S., Ahmed, R., & Hasan, M. A. (2019). Wearable Real-Time Heart Attack Detection and Warning System to Reduce Road Accidents. *Sensors (Basel)*, *19*(12), 2780. doi:10.339019122780 PMID:31226858

Data Bridge. (2023, January 7). *Global Smart Healthcare Market – Industry Trends and Forecast to 2029*. Retrieved from: https://www.databridgemarketresearch.com/reports/global-smart-healthcare-market

Davenport, T., & Kalakota, R. (2019). The potential for artificial intelligence in healthcare. *Future Healthcare Journal*, *6*(2), 94–98. . doi:10.7861/futurehosp.6-2-94

Dey, J., Gaurav, A., & Tiwari, V. N. (2018). InstaBP: Cuff-less Blood Pressure Monitoring on Smartphone using Single PPG Sensor. *Annual International Conference of the IEEE Engineering in Medicine and Biology Society. IEEE Engineering in Medicine and Biology Society. Annual International Conference*, 5002–5005. 10.1109/EMBC.2018.8513189

Dhaka, R. K., Panda, S., Panda, B., Pradhan, A., & Jena, C. (2022). AIOT in Healthcare systems: A Thought on Approaches and Criticism. *National Cave Research and Protection Organization*, *9*(2), 55–60. doi:10.21276/ambi.2022.09.2.rv02

Dian, F. J. R., Vahidnia, R., & Rahmati, A. (2020). Wearables and the internet of things (IoT), applications, opportunities, and challenges: A survey. *IEEE Access : Practical Innovations, Open Solutions*, *8*, 69200–69211. doi:10.1109/ACCESS.2020.2986329

Dias, D., & Paulo Silva Cunha, J. (2018). Wearable Health Devices-Vital Sign Monitoring, Systems and Technologies. *Sensors (Basel)*, *18*(8), 2414. doi:10.339018082414 PMID:30044415

Elango, K., & Muniandi, K. (2020). A low-cost wearable remote healthcare monitoring system. In G. R. Kanagachidambaresan (Ed.), *Role of Edge Analytics in Sustainable Smart City Development: Challenges and Solutions* (pp. 219–242). doi:10.1002/9781119681328.ch11

Enriko, A. I. K., & Suryanegara, M., & Gunawan, D. (2018). Heart Disease Diagnosis System with k-Nearest Neighbors Method Using Real Clinical Medical Records. In *Proceedings of the 4th International Conference on Frontiers of Educational Technologies (ICFET '18)*. Association for Computing Machinery. 10.1145/3233347.3233386

Grand View Research. (2023, January 7). *Global Smart Healthcare Market Size, Share Report*. Retrieved from: 2030 https://www.grandviewresearch.com/industry-analysis/smart-healthcare-market

Guo, B., Ma, Y., Yang, J., & Wang, Z. (2021). Smart Healthcare System Based on Cloud-Internet of Things and Deep Learning. *Journal of Healthcare Engineering*, *2021*, 1–10. doi:10.1155/2021/4109102 PMID:34257851

Gupta, A., Kumar, L., Jain, R., & Nagrath, P. (2020). Heart Disease Prediction Using Classification (Naive Bayes). In *Proceedings of First International Conference on Computing, Communications, and Cyber-Security (IC4S 2019). Lecture Notes in Networks and Systems* (vol. 121). Springer. 10.1007/978-981-15-3369-3_42

Hutamaputra, W., Mawarni, M., Krisnabayu, R. Y., & Mahmudy, W. F. (2021). Detection of Coronary Heart Disease Using Modified K-NN Method with Recursive Feature Elimination. In *6th International Conference on Sustainable Information Engineering and Technology 2021 (SIET '21).* Association for Computing Machinery. 10.1145/3479645.3479664

Islam, M. M., Mahmud, S., Muhammad, L. J., Islam, M. R., Nooruddin, S., & Ayon, S. I. (2020). Wearable Technology to Assist the Patients Infected with Novel Coronavirus (COVID-19). *SN Computer Science, 1*(6), 320. doi:10.100742979-020-00335-4 PMID:33063058

Islam, M. M., Rahaman, A., & Islam, M. R. (2020). Development of Smart Healthcare Monitoring System in IoT Environment. *SN Computer Science, 1*(3), 1–11. doi:10.100742979-020-00195-y PMID:33063046

Jabbar, M. A., & Samreen, S. (2016). Heart disease prediction system based on hidden naïve bayes classifier. *2016 International Conference on Circuits, Controls, Communications and Computing (I4C),* 1-5. 10.1109/CIMCA.2016.8053261

Jin, L., Y., Chuang Wei, C., Yen, C.Y., Huang, S.H., Huang, P.W., Chen, J.Y., & Lee, S.Y. (2019). Artificial Intelligence of Things Wearable System for Cardiac Disease Detection. *2019 IEEE International Conference on Artificial Intelligence Circuits and Systems (AICAS),* 67-70. 10.1109/AICAS.2019.8771630

Jokanović, R. V. (2020). *Smart healthcare in smart cities. In Towards Smart World: Homes to Cities Using Internet of Things.* Taylor and Francis Group., doi:10.1201/9781003056751

Kaggle. (2023, January 7). *Intel & Mobile ODT Cervical cancer Screening.* Retrieved from: https://www.kaggle.com/competitions/intel-mobileodt-cervical-cancer-screening/data

Kaptoge, S., Pennells, L., De Bacquer, D., Cooney, M. T., Kavousi, M., Stevens, G., Riley, L. M., Savin, S., Khan, T., Altay, S., Amouyel, P., Assmann, G., Bell, S., Ben-Shlomo, Y., Berkman, L., Beulens, J. W., Björkelund, C., Blaha, M., Blazer, D. G., ... Di Angelantonio, E. WHO CVD Risk Chart Working Group. (2019). World Health Organization cardiovascular disease risk charts: Revised models to estimate risk in 21 global regions. *The Lancet. Global Health, 7*(10), e1332–e1345. doi:10.1016/S2214-109X(19)30318-3 PMID:31488387

Khan, M. A. (2020). An iot framework for heart disease prediction based on mdcnn classifier. *IEEE Access: Practical Innovations, Open Solutions, 8,* 34717–34727. doi:10.1109/ACCESS.2020.2974687

Krittanawong, C., Virk, H. U. H., Bangalore, S., Wang, Z., Johnson, K. W., Pinotti, R., Zhang, H., Kaplin, S., Narasimhan, B., Kitai, T., Baber, U., Halperin, J. L., & Tang, W. H. W. (2020). Machine learning prediction in cardiovascular diseases: A meta-analysis. *Scientific Reports, 10*(1), 16057. doi:10.103841598-020-72685-1 PMID:32994452

Kumar, A., Chattree, G., & Periyasamy, S. (2018). Smart healthcare monitoring system. *Wireless Personal Communications, 101*(1), 453–463. doi:10.100711277-018-5699-0

Kumar, P. M., & Gandhi, D. U. (2018). A novel three-tier Internet of Things architecture with machine learning algorithm for early detection of heart diseases. *Computers & Electrical Engineering, 65*, 222–235. doi:10.1016/j.compeleceng.2017.09.001

Lomaliza, J., & Park, H. (2017). A highly efficient and reliable heart rate monitoring system using smartphone cameras. *Multimedia Tools and Applications, 76*(20), 21051–21071. doi:10.100711042-016-4010-1

Majumder, S., & Deen, M. J. (2019). Smartphone Sensors for Health Monitoring and Diagnosis. *Sensors (Basel), 19*(9), 2164. doi:10.339019092164 PMID:31075985

Majumder, S., Mondal, T., & Deen, M. (2017). Wearable Sensors for Remote Health Monitoring. *Sensors (Basel), 17*(12), 130. doi:10.339017010130 PMID:28085085

Malche, T., Tharewal, S., Tiwari, P. K., Jabarulla, M. Y., Alnuaim, A. A., Hatamleh, W. A., & Ullah, M. A. (2022). Artificial Intelligence of Things- (AIoT-) Based Patient Activity Tracking System for Remote Patient Monitoring. *Journal of Healthcare Engineering, 2022*, 1–15. doi:10.1155/2022/8732213 PMID:35273786

Mauldin, T., Canby, M., Metsis, V., Ngu, A., & Rivera, C. (2018). SmartFall: A Smartwatch-Based Fall Detection System Using Deep Learning. *Sensors (Basel), 18*(10), 3363. doi:10.339018103363 PMID:30304768

Mehmood, A., Iqbal, M., Mehmood, Z., Irtaza, A., Nawaz, M., Nazir, T., & Masood, M. (2020). Prediction of Heart Disease Using Deep Convolutional Neural Networks. *Arabian Journal for Science and Engineering, 46*(4), 3409–3422. Advance online publication. doi:10.100713369-020-05105-1

Mohamed, E. A., Rashed, E. A., Gaber, T., & Karam, O. (2022). Deep learning model for fully automated breast cancer detection system from thermograms. *PLoS One, 17*(1), e0262349. doi:10.1371/journal.pone.0262349 PMID:35030211

Mohammed, M. N., Hazairin, N. A., Syamsudin, H., Al-Zubaidi, S., Sairah, A. K., Mustapha, S., & Yusuf, E. (2020). 2019 Novel Coronavirus Disease (Covid-19): Detection and Diagnosis System Using IoT Based Smart Glasses. *International Journal of Advanced Science and Technology, 29*(7), 954-960.

Mohapatra, S., Mohanty, S., & Mohanty, S. (2019). Smart healthcare: An approach for ubiquitous healthcare management using IoT. *Big Data Analytics for Intelligent Healthcare Management*, 175–196. . doi:10.1016/B978-0-12-818146-1.00007-6

Murugan, A., Anu, H. N., Preethi, A. P., & Kumar, K. P. S. (2021). Diagnosis of skin cancer using machine learning techniques. *Microprocessors and Microsystems, 81*, 103727. Advance online publication. doi:10.1016/j.micpro.2020.103727

Nagavelli, U., Samanta, D., & Chakraborty, P. (2022). Machine Learning Technology-Based Heart Disease Detection Models. *Journal of Healthcare Engineering, 2022*, 1–9. Advance online publication. doi:10.1155/2022/7351061 PMID:35265303

Nemcova, A., Jordanova, I., Varecka, M., Smisek, R., Marsanova, L., Smital, L., & Vitek, M. (2020). Monitoring of heart rate, blood oxygen saturation, and blood pressure using a smartphone. *Biomedical Signal Processing and Control, 59*, 101928. Advance online publication. doi:10.1016/j.bspc.2020.101928

Noble, D.R., Angello, L., Sheppard, S., Kee, J., Emerson, B.L., & Lieuwen, T. (2019). Investigation Into Advanced Combustion System Health Monitoring. *Volume 3: Coal, Biomass, Hydrogen, and Alternative Fuels; Cycle Innovations; Electric Power; Industrial and Cogeneration; Organic Rankine Cycle Power Systems.* . doi:10.1115/GT2019-91973

Pal, M., & Parija, S. (2021). Prediction of Heart Diseases using Random Forest. *Journal of Physics: Conference Series, 1817*(1), 012009. Advance online publication. doi:10.1088/1742-6596/1817/1/012009

Possamai, G. C., Ravaud, P., Ghosn, L., & Thi Tran, V. (2020). Use of wearable biometric monitoring devices to measure outcomes in randomized clinical trials: A methodological systematic review. *BMC Medicien, 18*. 10.118612916-020-01773-w

Premalatha, G., & Bai, V. T. (2022). Wireless IoT and Cyber-Physical System for Health Monitoring Using Honey Badger Optimized Least-Squares Support-Vector Machine. *Wireless Personal Communications, 124*(4), 3013–3034. doi:10.100711277-022-09500-9 PMID:35370364

Qayyum, A., Malik, A. S., Shuaibu, A. N., & Nasir, N. (2017). Estimation of non-contact smartphone video-based vital sign monitoring using filtering and standard color conversion techniques. *2017 IEEE Life Sciences Conference (LSC)*, 202-205. 10.1109/LSC.2017.8268178

Rejani, A. I. Y., & Selvi, T. S. (2009). *Early detection of breast cancer using SVM classifier technique.* DOI: /arXiv.0912.2314. doi:10.48550

Research. (2023, January 7). *Research News*. Retrieved from https://www.cam.ac.uk/research/news/low-cost-ai-heart-monitor-developed-by cambridge-start-up/

Saba Raoof, S., & Durai, M. A. S. (2022). A Comprehensive Review on Smart Health Care: Applications, Paradigms, and Challenges with Case Studies. *Contrast Media & Molecular Imaging, 4822235*, 1–18. Advance online publication. doi:10.1155/2022/4822235 PMID:36247859

Saini, S. K., Bansal, V., Kaur, R., & Juneja, M. (2020). ColpoNet for automated cervical cancer screening using colposcopy images. *Machine Vision and Applications, 31*(3), 15. doi:10.100700138-020-01063-8

Sarmah, S. S. (2020). An Efficient IoT-Based Patient Monitoring and Heart Disease Prediction System Using Deep Learning Modified Neural Network. *IEEE Access : Practical Innovations, Open Solutions, 8*, 135784–135797. doi:10.1109/ACCESS.2020.3007561

Semwal, N., Mukherjee, M., Raj, C., & Arif, W. (2019). An IoT based smart e-health care system. *Journal of Information and Optimization Sciences, 40*(8), 1787–1800. doi:10.1080/02522667.2019.1703269

Shankar, V., Kumar, V., Devagade, U., Karanth, V., & Rohitaksha, K. (2020). Heart Disease Prediction Using CNN Algorithm. *SN Computer Science, 1*(3), 170. doi:10.100742979-020-0097-6

Sharma, S., Aggarwal, A., & Choudhury, T. (2018). Breast Cancer Detection Using Machine Learning Algorithms. *2018 International Conference on Computational Techniques, Electronics and Mechanical Systems (CTEMS)*, 114-118. 10.1109/CTEMS.2018.8769187

Shen, L., Margolies, L. R., Rothstein, J. H., Fluder, E., McBride, R., & Sieh, W. (2019). Deep Learning to Improve Breast Cancer Detection on Screening Mammography. *Scientific Reports, 9*(1), 12495. doi:10.103841598-019-48995-4 PMID:31467326

SimonyanK.ZissermanA. (2014). Very deep convolutional networks for large-scale image recognition. arXiv:1409.1556

Sudha, V., & Ganeshbabu, T. R. (2020). A Convolutional Neural Network Classifier VGG-19 Architecture for Lesion Detection and Grading in Diabetic Retinopathy Based on Deep Learning. *Computers, Materials & Continua, 66*(1), 827–842. doi:10.32604/cmc.2020.012008

Sumbaly, R., Vishnusri, N., & Jeyalatha, S. (2014). Diagnosis of breast cancer using decision tree data mining technique. *International Journal of Computer Applications, 98*(10), 16–24. doi:10.5120/17219-7456

Swaroop, K. N., Chandu, K., Gorrepotu, R., & Deb, S. (2019). A health monitoring system for vital signs using Iota. *Internet of Things, 5*, 116–129. doi:10.1016/j.iot.2019.01.004

Tabei, F., Gresham, J. M., Askarian, B., Jung, K., & Chong, J. W. (2020). Cuff-Less Blood Pressure Monitoring System Using Smartphones. *IEEE Access : Practical Innovations, Open Solutions, 8*, 11534–11545. doi:10.1109/ACCESS.2020.2965082

Talukder, A., & Haas, R. (2021). Aiot: AI meets iot and Web in Smart Healthcare. In *13th ACM Web Science Conference 2021 (websci '21)*. Association for Computing Machinery. 10.1145/3462741.3466650

Tian, S., Yang, W., Grange, J., Wang, P., Huang, W., & Ye, Z. (2019). Smart healthcare: Making medical care more intelligent. *Global Health Journal (Amsterdam, Netherlands), 3*(3), 62–65. doi:10.1016/j.glohj.2019.07.001

Tripathi, A., Arora, A., & Bhan, A. (2021). Classification of cervical cancer using Deep Learning Algorithm. *2021 5th International Conference on Intelligent Computing and Control Systems (ICICCS)*, 1210-1218. 10.1109/ICICCS51141.2021.9432382

UCI. (2023, January 7). *Heart disease data set.* Retrieved from https: //archive.ics.uci.edu/ml/datasets/heart+Disease

Verma, A. K., Pal, S., & Kumar, S. (2021). Prediction of Different Classes of Skin Disease Using Machine Learning Techniques. In S. Tiwari, M. Trivedi, K. Mishra, A. Misra, K. Kumar, & E. Suryani (Eds.), *Smart Innovations in Communication and Computational Sciences. Advances in Intelligent Systems and Computing (vol. 1168)*. Springer. doi:10.1007/978-981-15-5345-5_8

Wan, J., Al-awlaqi, A. A. H., Li, M., O'Grady, M., Gu, X., Wang, J., & Cao, N. (2018). Wearable IoT enabled real-time health monitoring system. *EURASIP Journal on Wireless Communications and Networking, 2018*(1), 298. doi:10.118613638-018-1308-x

Wang, E. J., Zhu, J., Jain, M., Lee, T.-J., Saba, E., Nachman, L., & Patel, S. N. (2018). Seismo: Blood pressure monitoring using built-in smartphone accelerometer and camera. *Proceedings of the 2018 CHI Conference on Human Factors in Computing Systems*, 1–9. 10.1145/3173574.3173999

WangP.LinZ.YanX.ChenZ.DingM.SongY.MengL. (2022). *A Wearable ECG Monitor for Deep Learning Based Real-Time Cardiovascular Disease Detection.* arXiv:2201.10083

Weegar, R., & Sundström, K. (2020). Using machine learning for predicting cervical cancer from Swedish electronic health records by mining hierarchical representations. *PLoS One, 15*(8), e0237911. Advance online publication. doi:10.1371/journal.pone.0237911 PMID:32822401

Zhang, G., Mei, Z., Zhang, Y., Ma, X., Lo, B. P., Chen, D., & Zhang, Y. (2020). A Noninvasive Blood Glucose Monitoring System Based on Smartphone PPG Signal Processing and Machine Learning. *IEEE Transactions on Industrial Informatics*, *16*(11), 7209–7218. doi:10.1109/TII.2020.2975222

Zhang, Q., Zheg, X., Hu, W., & Zhou, D. (2017). A Machine Learning-Empowered System for Long-Term Motion-Tolerant Wearable Monitoring of Blood Pressure and Heart Rate With Ear-ECG/PPG. *IEEE Access : Practical Innovations, Open Solutions*, *5*, 10547–10561. doi:10.1109/ACCESS.2017.2707472

Zhang, W., Han, J., & Deng, S. (2020). Heart sound classification based on scaled spectrogram and tensor decomposition. *Expert Systems with Applications*, *84*, 220–231. doi:10.1016/j.eswa.2017.05.014

Zouka, A., & Hosni, M. (2021). Secure IoT communications for smart healthcare monitoring system. *Internet of Things*, *13*, 100036. Advance online publication. doi:10.1016/j.iot.2019.01.003

Chapter 4
Cloud–Based Intelligent Virtual Try–On Using Augmented Reality

V. Valliammai
Vellore Institute of Technology, India

Karjala Sandhya
Vellore Institute of Technology, India

Vemuri Lakshmi Harshitha
Vellore Institute of Technology, India

Pariha Parvaze Podili
Vellore Institute of Technology, India

Niha Kamal Basha
Vellore Institute of Technology, India

ABSTRACT

Advancement of technology had a significant impact on various industries, with innovative solutions like cloud computing, IoT, augmented reality (AR), and virtual reality (VR) changing the game in many ways. Here is a system known as "virtual try-ons" that leverages IoT devices like mobile cameras, cloud storage for data, and an intelligent interface for user interaction. Many people are opting for online shopping, and various challenges arise with this transition, one of which is the issue of "try-on." VR solves this challenge by introducing "virtual try-on," which replaces traditional try-on methods. It enables an individual to preview and virtually try on their desired products like clothes, watches, shoes, etc. from the comfort of their own homes, making the shopping experience easier and smoother. It also adds an element of fun and excitement to the shopping experience, increasing the hedonic value for consumers and allowing consumers to experiment and play with different products, styles, and colors in a way that is not possible with traditional shopping methods.

DOI: 10.4018/978-1-6684-8098-4.ch004

INTRODUCTION

Emerging technologies such as Cloud Computing, Augmented Reality (AR), Internet of Things (IoT), and Virtual Reality (VR) are eventually becoming a part of daily life. IoT involves the interconnection of devices like vehicles, sensors, etc. and allows for the exchange of data between these devices. Cloud Computing provides on-demand access to services such as storage, processing, and networking. Augmented Reality and Virtual Reality are used to make previously impossible things possible. This paper proposes a solution for a problem in online shopping, namely virtual try-on, which utilizes a combination of these technologies. "Virtual Try Ons" is a cloud-based web application that enables users to virtually try on products such as dresses, watches, shoes, earrings. It is based on 3D body tracking and occlusion. 3D body tracking tracks the position of body parts so that 3D objects can be accurately fitted, while occlusion removes parts of the 3D object that are covered by the body. This system was created using Snapchat's Lens Studio. The products are readily available to users in the form of snap codes that direct them to the lenses in Snapchat. Both sellers and buyers benefit from this system as it makes it easy for sellers to design and publish their product as a lens. Sellers can easily track the success of their product design using the Snapchat dashboard, which displays information such as the number of users and rank of the lens. Once published, the lenses are stored in the cloud and accessible to all users. Buyers can easily try on products using just their mobile camera, eliminating the need to visit physical stores. This technology can enhance the customer experience, leading to increased satisfaction, higher conversion rates, repeat customers, and positive word-of-mouth marketing. Moreover, virtual try-on can help to lower the costs associated with returns and exchanges, which can be a significant expense for online retailers. Virtual try-on is not just introduced into e-commerce but has also made its way into social media through the use of filters. Websites like Snapchat and Instagram have incorporated virtual try-ons as a prominent feature, allowing the general public to virtually try on fashion models' dresses and accessories, making the impossible, possible.

LITERATURE SURVEY

Antim et al. (2017) has defined Cloud Computing as providing on demand resources such as network, storage, server through internet. The paper provides an overview of Cloud Computing besides focusing on key computing issues like patch management, data location, data segregation, access to servers & applications, virtual machine security, data security, data privacy, data Integrity, data availability, security policy and compliance and network security. The author identified SLA's, data encryption, interoperability, energy management, migration of virtual machines, access controls, cloud data management & security, platform management as key research challenges in clod computing.

Abdel (2019) discussed the influence of the IoT in various industries and how it operates. According to the author, IoT is a network of physical objects with varying levels of computational power, sensing capabilities, and the ability to actuate, all of which can communicate with each other through the internet. These interconnected devices are useful in creating smart cities, improving healthcare, optimizing agriculture and water management, revolutionizing retail and logistics, enhancing daily life, and promoting a smart environment. Despite its benefits, there are still research limitations regarding privacy and security, data processing and managing, monitoring and sensing, machine-to-machine communication, and interoperability.

Dov et al. (2018) highlighted the significance of intelligent interfaces for Augmented Reality (AR) applications. They explained the origin of the term "Augmented Reality." The authors also discussed a framework known as Pose-Interfaced Presentation (PIP), which is an interface that uses intelligence to integrate virtual objects in a real-world context. PIP denotes the user's orientation and location in space (Pose), the program's response to the user's actions and intentions in an intelligent manner (Interfaced), and the digital objects being layered onto the user's perceptual field (Presentation). The authors noted that AR is useful for activities such as learning, worker training, and language learning.

Sangeeta et al. (2019) stated that the AR/VR deals database reported a total of $686 million in Augmented and Virtual Reality sales in 2015 and $1.2 billion in the first quarter of 2016. The Goldman Sachs 2016 AR/VR survey estimated that Augmented and Virtual Reality could be worth $80 billion, and if Augmented Reality is rapidly adopted, the market could reach $182 billion by 2020. This paper discusses various applications of AR-VR in gaming, education, and health care, and provides a brief comparative analysis of AR/VR products. The authors highlight implementation issues such as mobility/ miniaturization, legitimate use cases, less expensive technology, security concerns, and legitimate use cases. They suggest that combining AR-VR with IoT, AI, ML, and 5G could lead to useful products.

Yadav (2020) conducted a survey of 100 respondents, including students from various colleges and salaried individuals. Many of these respondents were younger individuals. The study found that 70% of the sample population agreed that augmented reality (AR) has an influence on the intention of purchasing and that social media platforms has an impact on shopping online. Respondents reported experiencing Augmented Reality on Snapchat, Instagram, and some on Facebook. Fifty percent of the respondents accepted that Augmented Reality is a one-of-a-kind and exciting way to keep customers intact on social media, and that it generates a more captivating experience compared to other forms of marketing. The study also found that AR can help generate positive word of mouth and that in the near future, social media content is expected to transition from 2D to 3D, facilitated by AR technology, which includes interactive Augmented Reality.

Eugeni (2022) studies the technology of augmented reality filters (ARF), which enables the creation and widespread sharing of video selfies on social media. It explores the technical aspects, as well as the socio-psychological and economic political implications of ARF, including their link to face recognition and social surveillance. The study explains that ARF functions at three levels: the technological level of devices, the social and micro-social level of assemblages, and the general mechanisms of political economy of apparatuses. It also explains how the technology of ARF allows for the modification of facial expressions in videos and how certain platforms like Instagram have restricted their use due to concerns of "Snapchat dysmorphia" and the manipulation of identity and reputation through technology-based enunciation procedures.

Hedman et al. (2022) investigated the effect of social media filters on the accuracy of face identification and recognition. The study focuses on how filters that alter or obscure the eye region can have negative impacts on these tasks. A combination of two approaches was used to neutralize the effects of most of the analyzed photo alterations. A modified U-NET segmentation network was used to create a mechanism for undoing the applied alterations and improving face detection and identification. The study particularly explores the effects of AR filters, which are not commonly researched in literature. The study enhances photographs with popular Instagram filters, mostly affecting contrast and lighting, and replicates them using a neural network to process large amounts of data. AR filters were also used and were found to obscure important parts of the face for recognition, like dog nose, transparent glasses, and sunglasses. The study uses five datasets of Labelled Faces in the Wild that were created by using Instagram and AR filters and categorizes them into "shades leak" and "no leak" categories.

Fribourg et al. (2021). examined the impact of AR filters on the self-perception of personality, intelligence, emotion, and attractiveness using the first study of its kind. Our research shows that individuals perceive facial characteristics similarly in themselves and others. Furthermore, even small changes in facial features had a significant impact on participants' ability to recognize themselves, highlighting the importance people place on faces, particularly their own appearance. The study evaluates the effects of various filters that change facial traits such as eye size and placement, face shape, and brow orientation and includes virtual content like virtual glasses. Participants were asked to rate their altered face on personality, emotion, appeal, and intellectual attributes. The results indicate that certain filters had a greater impact on self-perception than others. Previous research has found that specific facial traits have a significant impact on the perception of attractiveness, intelligence, and personality in others. However, this study is unique in that it focuses on the relationship between self-facial features and self-perception of personality traits.

Maisevli et al. (2022) presented an augmented reality application for social media makeup filters using HSV color extraction, which enables users to makeover their faces using digital cosmetics with a single finger or similar device. The approach allows for more accurate representation of makeup on social media; however, its processing large amounts of data is not feasible with the Instagram Application Programming Interface. The goal is to create an Instagram filter-based augmented reality virtual makeup simulation that can be used by people of all ages, applied to stories, reels or live video. This simulation uses the HSV color extraction technique to select colors based on hue, saturation and value to identify faces and match foundation and lipstick shades to the user's skin tone. This allows users to test cosmetics based on their preferred hue in different lighting settings through the use of social media and augmented reality, making it easier for customers to select cosmetics while also providing feedback on their color choices. This work demonstrates that augmented reality apps can be useful in displaying filters in various lighting conditions and with further advancements in technology, augmented reality and virtual reality can be increasingly used to address similar issues.

Javornik et al. (2021) investigated the impact of sensory experiences, specifically the use of an augmented reality mirror, on a person's perception of their own attractiveness. The results of three experiments reveal that viewing oneself in an AR mirror changes the gap between a person's actual and ideal attractiveness, and this effect varies based on their self-esteem. According to the author, the augmented self goes beyond just makeup and can be applied in various ways, such as through AR face filters on social media and AR clothes try-on in the fashion industry. There is potential to examine how these technologies may change the way we interact with ourselves and others and provide more insight into the concept of the augmented self.

Borges et al. (2019) developed a system which uses augmented reality to makeover user's face using virtual cosmetics with a finger or similar object. The prototype allows users to select products and features and simulates the application of foundation, blush, and eyeshadow in real time using an Intel RealSense RGBD camera. Ninety-one facial landmarks and the user's face are monitored and charted to create a normalized facial space that stores virtual makeup. A real-time face touch detection algorithm is included, which tracks finger and face in depth images and detects touch events. The process of creating virtual makeup involves projecting the facial mesh and merging it with the makeup texture using facial landmarks that have been tracked.

Ria et al. (2021). aimed at reviewing and reporting how and where the AR technology is used in retail and focuses on the effects of using AR in retail. The primary benefit of online solutions is the ability to test products in any environment and assist customers in making purchase decisions. Typically, the participants were invited to view themselves in a scenario using an AR application, which they subsequently controlled using a computer. In some of these systems, participants can also see themselves in virtual mirrors and virtually try on various (for example, fashion) items. It says that AR in retail involves environments like online web-based, in-store etc., devices like hand-based mobile device, desktop pc, virtual mirror etc., and it is dominantly used in clothing, furniture, make-up, technology related industries. From an affective standpoint, hedonic value, or enjoyment, has been most prevalent that has been evaluated (52% of the research encountered it). It was discovered that the presence of and interaction with AR can improve the hedonic experience (such as enjoyment, fun, amusement, and playfulness) in shops or retailing apps. It states that Additionally, AR-based retail can affect various social dimensions and psychological states (mainly personality related). According to this paper, user perceptions of usability, perceived value, cognitive fluency, attitudes toward products, and brand engagement can all be improved by affordances related to interaction. It points that augmented environment plays a vital characteristic of AR in retail. Like interactivity and vividness, novelty gives a high perception of enjoyment, fullness, and brand engagement.

Boardman et al. (2020) focused on the technical advancements that are currently being utilized in the fashion industry, specifically focusing on the utilization of Augmented Reality (AR) and Virtual Reality (VR) technology. With the development of more advanced technology, these interactive technologies are becoming increasingly popular in the fashion retail sector, as they have the potential to create unique and immersive shopping experiences. These technologies, classified as "consumer-facing," have gained significant attention from retailers, with predictions of widespread adoption across various industries including fashion. For retail stores looking to increase their sales, investing in technology such as AR and VR is becoming a necessary and viable option. By using the Technology Acceptance Model (TAM), retailers can gain insights into the reasons behind customers' acceptance or rejection of specific technologies, such as AR and VR. This understanding can help them make better-informed decisions about investing in emerging technologies. In the future, it is expected that technology investment, particularly in AR and VR, will be crucial for retail establishments to stay competitive.

Garg et al. (2020) say, augmented reality can be used to help customers make informed decisions when shopping for products. By providing information such as reviews and related items, retailers can persuade their target audience to make a purchase. Additionally, AR can provide an in-store shopping experience by superimposing 3D objects in different spaces, allowing customers to interact with virtual products in their own environment. In today's market, with more products and shorter runs, AR can help businesses stand out and make faster, more effective decisions based on customer needs. In the future, a dynamic framework including various stakeholders such as users, professionals, and entrepreneurs could be used to simulate and study responses to hypothetical situations for various desired objectives.

Kalmkar et al. (2022) have demonstrated that the usage of augmented reality (AR) on various devices and social media platforms is predicted to rise in the United States. As per eMarketer, 43 million Americans are expected to use social network AR once a month by 2020, which will account for 21% of all users of social network. Furthermore, it is estimated that eighty-three million Americans will use AR on some kind of device once per month at a minimum, which is anticipated to increase to 95.1 million by 2022. In June 2020, 35% of Americans had utilised AR to visualize upgrades in furniture or automobiles. According to a survey conducted among US retailers, 20% of them had intentions to allocate funds in AR for their online store, indicating a noteworthy increase from 8% reported six months ago. The author suggests that incorporating 3D technology and staying informed about current trends in the ecommerce industry can improve product demonstrations, facilitate product adaptations, and increase customer retention. Implementing 3D technology can also enhance consumer confidence by enabling customers to view products in interactive 3D before purchasing, promoting upselling and cross-selling, and decreasing the high rate of returns for ecommerce products. Marketing strategies employing 3D visualization and rendering can help an ecommerce business achieve greater success.

Yu et al. (2022) presented a new method for image-based virtual reality applications that generates more realistic looking virtual try-on images than current state- of-the-art methods. The method, called the Virtual Try-on Network with Feature Propagation (VTNFP), introduces several innovations to improve the quality of image synthesis. A key innovation of VTNFP is the body segmentation map prediction, which provides important information for guiding image synthesis in areas where body parts and clothing intersect. The input and output images are all fixed to 256x192 in size, and the Adam optimizer is used with a learning rate that decreases linearly over time. Non- local layers are added to the Try-on Synthesis Module, and the training steps, optimizer, and learning rate settings are the same as those used in clothing deformation. It was found that VTNFP is significantly superior to previous methods.

Jain et al. (2022) aimed to understand how virtual reality technology is being used in clothing, specifically by examining the use of 2D and 3D techniques. The study seeks to identify strategies and methods that can be applied to create a more advanced virtual try-on system. Survey data revealed that 44% of respondents used virtual try-on when shopping on retail websites, and as a result, 69% of those surveyed said they purchased the items from a store or online. Virtual try-on allows customers to preview how clothing will look on them before making a purchase. However, there is currently a lack of information on how to integrate virtual try-on technology with anthropometric data to provide an even more accurate representation of how clothing will look and fit on an individual. Previous studies have developed techniques for extracting measures, identifying body traits, and building 3D models from 2D images, as well as methods for optimizing silhouettes.

Gupta et al. (2022) aimed to evaluate the effectiveness of augmented reality in creating a sensory brand experience and determining the intention to use the mobile app that incorporates an AR feature. The core data came from one hundred and sixty-eight participants who were compelled to utilize the augmented reality (AR) attribute of the Lenskart, an Indian eyeglasses online commerce site, to try on numerous eyeglass and sunglass frames to determine which one best suited their looks. Structural equation modelling was used to investigate the influence in question. The development of experiences in sensory brand and the intention to utilize the augmented reality function of the mobile app are highly impacted by effective augmented reality use, according to the findings. The study was to answer the following questions:

Q1: Does the intention to use a mobile app change as a result of an AR feature included in the app?
Q2: Is it possible to give users of a mobile app with augmented reality (AR) a sensory brand experience?
Q3: How does sensory brand experience influence the likelihood that a user will utilize an app?
Q4: How do flow experience (FE), perceived enjoyment (PE), perceived ease of use (PEOU), and perceived usefulness (PU) affect the sensory brand experience and the decision to utilize the mobile app?

The paper thoroughly studies how the AR try-on is implemented in lenskart. This paper concludes that in the near future, AR-enabled mobile apps will become increasingly prevalent.

Samuel et al. (2022) aimed to explore the importance, challenges, and factors of Augmented Reality (AR) in the retail industry. AR has the potential to improve the customer experience and make purchasing decisions easier, thereby attracting more customers to the store and increasing sales and profits. However, retailers must also be aware of the potential for confusion if no guidance is provided for customers using AR technology. Combining AR with mobile shopping can provide a more enhanced shopping experience. AR can also be beneficial in other sectors, such as academia, medical, and tourism. Retailers should consider the type of virtual fitting room that would be engaging and practical for their target customers. AR can also potentially replace traditional fitting rooms and enhance the emotional response of customers, leading to greater buying intention. Additionally, AR enabled e-commerce can enhance the buying efficiency and satisfaction. AR dominates internet-based product presentations by providing greater interaction and making it easier for buyers to decide by eliminating confusion over which products to choose. Overall, AR has the potential to transform the retail experience by adding flexibility and convenience to the shopping process.

Anand et al. (2022) stated that virtual try-on is a say comparatively faster than the traditional physical try-ons. It ensures a speedy process by providing the customers with the chance to try-on hundreds of choices instead of going to physical stores. Glass virtual try-on needs an uploaded image of the customer and the name of the frame. The rest of the process is automated. It lists out the features of this system as Real-time web-based glasses tried, Light reconstruction (ambient + directing), very strong in lighting conditions, Mobile friendly, Advanced 3D Engine, Body-based delivery (PBR), Sequential shadows, Default blur. It says that face recognition is the pre-requisite for the visual experiment system. A brief explanation of the face recognition process is being a part of this paper.

Jadhav et al. (2021) aimed to improve the online shopping experience for users by utilizing augmented reality technology. It suggests integrating the technology with various fashion and e-commerce websites to allow users to view real-time simulations of clothing without physically trying them on. By automatically converting 2D images into 3D models, the system aims to provide a more accurate evaluation of clothing. Using the Pix2Surf and PIFu methods, the system can transfer textures from clothing images onto 3D human models and create a complete 3D geometric structure from a single image respectively. It also helps users to map textures from a wide range of garments available on online sites. Overall, this technology aims to overcome the challenges users face when shopping online by providing them with a more realistic and immersive shopping experience.

Prabha et al. (2021) said customers are dissatisfied with online shopping due to color or size inconsistencies in the delivered products. E-commerce employs VR to offer customers a new shopping experience, allowing them to manipulate 3D virtual models online. In contrast to VR that substitutes the physical world, AR imporves the physical reality by merging virtual objects into the real world. In this way, generated virtual objects become part of the natural environment. The proposed system involves a Modular Smart Mirror Application, which includes 2D photos of the user and virtual try-on costumes. The developed garment is overlayed on users by employing Face tracking technology, and Unity is used to create the system. Future iterations of the system could incorporate additional products and accessories for trying on.

Kumar (2021) aims to establish a foundation for future work in the field of retail applications that employ virtual and augmented reality (AR) technologies. AR allows for the combination of a user's physical view with digital information in a single environment, and it is becoming increasingly popular in the retail industry. The document reviews recent advances in AR in the retail industry and suggests future research areas to bridge the research gap. Google trends data shows a steady interest in terms such as virtual reality, augmented reality, and online shopping over the past five years. The benefits of using AR/VR technology in e-commerce have been shown through virtual 3D modelling, virtual apparel, haptic gloves and product images that provide visual appeal for online shoppers. Previous research has examined both the hardware and the user experiences related to VR/AR technology in the retail context. However, more attention needs to be given to the regulatory, affordability, acceptability, privacy, and other potential barriers to consumer adoption of VR and AR technology in retail applications.

MATERIALS AND METHODS

The proposed work can be segregated as three sub tasks:

1. **Generating the Lens:** In this step, the lenses are generated using Lens Studio.
2. **Publishing the Lens:** Once the lenses are generated, they need to be published to make it publicly available in Snapchat.
3. **Hosting the Website:** The snap codes of all the lenses are collectively added to a website and hosted in Cloud.

Generating the Lens

Lens studio is the software used to create lenses. The important task is to track different body parts for different accessories. 3D body tracking refers to the process of estimating the position and orientation of the human body in 3D space. It involves a combination of computer vision and image processing techniques. One common approach is to use object detection algorithms, such as Faster R-CNN or YOLO, to detect and track the body parts of the user in real-time. Once detected, it is then possible to perform body tracking and animation using inverse kinematics (IK). IK is a technique used to animate characters or objects in a way that mimics real-world motion by solving for the motion of bones in a skeleton based on the position of the end effector (in this case, the cloth) and the constraints of the system. Another important term is Occlusion. Occlusion refers to the process of determining which parts of virtual objects in an augmented reality scene should be hidden or obscured by real-world objects. Occlusion in Lens Studio is typically achieved using a process called depth mapping. Depth mapping involves capturing the distance of each pixel in the camera view to the camera itself, creating a depth map of the scene. This depth map can then be used to determine which objects are in front of other objects, and which parts of the objects should be occluded or hidden. Generating lens is further divided into five sub tasks. They are:

Garment Transfer

Garment transfer is a custom component in lens Studio that helps by transferring an upper body costume of an image onto a person in real world. It contains three main components:

Garment transfer custom component:

It handles how the costume on a reference image is transferred on to a person. It takes auto run, target image and garment image as inputs. When auto run is enabled, the component runs every frame and gives real time video experience but when disabled the component runs manually from a script. The target image is the person in real time captured through the camera onto whom the garment is transferred. The garment image is a reference image from where the garment is transferred. Adding garment transfer is done in four easy steps.

Carousel:

The carousel component is used to switch between different garments easily just by tapping. Adding, removing, and modifying of the garments is done by modifying the icon list in inspector panel.

GTController:

The GTCController.js controls the following functions:
Allows switching between different run modes, set the garment image in the Garment Transfer custom component when a new garment is selected in the carousel, implement Run on Tap mode interaction and call Garment Transfer API to process the garment once on tap.
The process is as follows:

1. Install garment transfer custom component from asset library.
2. Create a Screen Transform object from the Objects panel.
3. Add the Garment Transfer component to the newly created Scene Object.
4. Set the Garment Image input to a reference garment image of your liking.

Figure 1. Image of a person before and after using garment transfer

Garment transfer takes image of a person (target image) through the mobile camera and outputs person with overlayed costume.

Wristwear try-on:

It mainly requires three components:

Wrist tracking scene object:

The functionality of this object is to track the wrist. For this, wrist tracking custom component and wrist occluder is installed from the asset library.

The left and right wrist objects:

It contains all the details related to the wrists.

The 3D models:

These are the models for try-on.
The process follows the steps provided below:

1. Right click on the camera object in the left panel and select create scene object.
2. Rename the scene object as wrist tracking custom component.
3. Right click on the wrist tracking custom component and create two scene objects and rename them as left wrist and right wrist.
4. Click on the wrist tracking custom component scene object and click "+Add Component" in the inspector panel.
5. Add the wrist tracking to the scene object.
6. Click and drag left and right wrist scene objects from object panel to the inspector panel.
7. Click and drag Wrist_Occluder__PLACE_UNDER_WRIST_TRACKING_CC asset to the objects panel.
8. Make sure that Left Wrist Occluder is a child of Left wrist scene object and Right Wrist Occlude ria child of Right wrist.
9. Now import the 3D model in the object panels in the Left and Right wrists.
10. Adjust the positions, rotation, and scale of models in the inspector panel on the right.

Wristwear try-on takes person's hand as input through the mobile camera and outputs a hand with overlayed watch.

Footwear Try-On

It contains three main components:

Figure 2. Image of a person's hand before and after using wristwear try-on

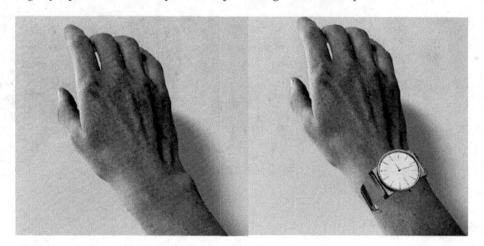

Foot Tracking:

This component is used in the process of attaching and tracking shoes to a user's feet.

Carousel:

This component is used to switch between multiple shoe designs.

Shoe Controller script:

This script contains the main logic to tie carousel to the foot tracking components.
The process follows the below steps:

1. Install Foot Tracking component from asset library in Lens Studio.
2. Create a new Scene object under camera.
3. On the left side, click on "+Add Component" and select Foot Tracking in the inspector panel.
4. Add left and right foot Objects in the component.
5. Import the 3D models in the left and right foot objects.
6. Adjust the position, rotation, and scale of the 3D models so that it can fit the foot properly.
7. Add Default Occluder on in the Foot Tracking Component to handle the occlusion.

Footwear try-on takes the feet of a person as input through the mobile camera and outputs the feet with overlayed shoes.

Earring Try-On

Ear Binding is the main component of earring try on. It is attached to an ear landmark which determines the position of the ear like Lobe-front, Lobe-back, helix etc.

Figure 3. Feet of a person before and after using footwear try-on

The procedure is as follows:

1. Install Ear Binding component from the asset library.
2. Go to the project and add a Scene object under the main camera and name the object as Earring.
3. Select the Scene Object and click on "+Add Component" in the inspector panel and add Ear Binding.
4. Import the 3D model of the earring under the hierarchy of the Earring Scene Object.
5. Adjust the position, rotation, scale of the model according to the preferences.

Figure 4. Image of a person before and after using earring try-on

Earring try-on takes an image of a person as input through the mobile camera and outputs image with overlayed earrings.

Cloth Simulation Try-On

Cloth Simulation try-on uses 3D Body Tracking, Cloth Simulation and Body mesh technologies. 3D Body tracking is used to track the person. Clothes are conformed on the body using Body mesh, Cloth Simulation is used to deform the clothes based on the movement of the body.

The process is as follows:

1. Install 3D body tracking from asset library and add it to main camera.
2. Add the 3D model under the hierarchy of the camera.
3. It is noticed that there are Attachment points which has a list of body parts and a guide object.
4. These objects are used to prevent overlapping of clothes.
5. Collider Guides object are objects to which the object Tracking 3D component is aligning to the body.
6. Full Body Occluder component uses Body Mesh which hide the part of the clothes covered by human body.
7. To pin the dress to body mesh, we use vertex colors to indicate which parts of the dress are binded, and which are simulated.

Figure 5. Image of a person before and after using cloth simulation try-on

Cloth simulation try-on takes the image of a person as input through the mobile camera and outputs the simulated costume overlayed on the person.

Publishing the Lens

To publish the lens, firstly it is required to configure the project. Open the Project Info settings window and provide the required details like lens icon, lens preview, lens name, size, camera option. After all the changes click apply. Once done with this go to the project and click the Publish lens button. It asks you to log onto Snapchat with username and password. Next it prompts to authorize Lens Studio by clicking authorize button. Click Continue on the Back to App prompt. It prompts us to add information about the lens which includes lens tags, scan triggers, visibility. Click Submit Lens once done with the previous step. It enters review status and takes time to get reviewed and goes public after the review. The status of the published lenses can be viewed in My lenses portal which is a part of lens Studio project window. My Lens portal is a dashboard containing all the lenses and related information belonging to the respective user.

Hosting the Website

For hosting the website on cloud, Amazon Web Services (https://aws.amazon.com/) is used.
Steps to be followed:

1. Go to Services and search for elastic beanstalk.
2. Click create application and name the app and select the platform.
3. Upload zip folder of the app in Appication code and click create application.
4. Copy the url from elastic beanstalk->Environments.
5. Paste the url in the browser to check whether it is working.

RESULTS AND ANALYSIS

The proposed model allows users to virtually try on products such as cosmetics, glasses, and accessories. This feature uses the Snapchat camera and machine learning algorithms to overlay the virtual product on the user's face in real-time. Loading time is the time it takes for the virtual try-on feature to load and display the product. A fast loading time is important to provide a seamless user experience. It performs well in terms of loading time, as the feature is integrated into Snapchat and is readily available to users. Frame rate is the number of frames per second that the virtual product is displayed. A high frame rate is important to ensure that the virtual product appears smooth and realistic. It performs well in terms of frame rate, as Snapchat has a high-performance camera and processing capabilities. Tracking accuracy is the accuracy of the virtual product overlay on the user. A high tracking accuracy is important to ensure that the virtual product stays in place and appears realistic.

A proposed model performs well in terms of tracking accuracy, as Snapchat's machine learning algorithms have been trained on a large dataset of facial features and can accurately track the user and user's motion in real-time. User feedback is the qualitative feedback from users, such as ratings and reviews. It performs well in terms of user feedback, as Snapchat has a large and engaged user base who provide feedback on the virtual try-on feature. Compatibility is the ability of the virtual try-on feature to work across different devices and platforms. It performs well in terms of compatibility, as Snapchat is available on both iOS and Android devices and can be accessed through the Snapchat app. Speed is the responsiveness of the virtual try-on feature. It performs well in terms of speed, as Snapchat's machine learning algorithms are designed to provide a real-time experience with minimal lag or delay. Realism is the quality of the virtual product overlay and how it appears on the user's face. It performs well in terms of realism, as Snapchat's machine learning algorithms use advanced techniques such as face tracking and lighting adjustments to make the virtual product appear as realistic as possible. Interactivity is the level of engagement and interaction that the user can have with the virtual try-on feature. The proposed model performs well in terms of interactivity, as users can try on multiple products and share their virtual try-on experiences with friends through Snapchat's social features. Integration with e-commerce is the ability of the virtual try-on feature to seamlessly integrate with e-commerce platforms and enable users to make purchases.

A model performs well in terms of integration with e-commerce, as it is integrated with Snapchat snapcode and makes it easy for users to purchase the products they try on. Overall, It performs well across multiple performance metrics. Its integration with Snapchat's high-performance camera and machine learning algorithms provides a fast, realistic, and interactive experience for users. The feature's compatibility with multiple devices and platforms, integration with e-commerce partners, and positive user feedback make it a promising tool for e-commerce businesses looking to enhance the user experience and increase conversion rates. Table 1 shows the comparison between already existing model and proposed model.

Table 1. Comparison between existing and proposed model

Metric	Augmented Reality and Virtual Reality – New Drivers for Fashion Retail?	Try-On With AR: Impact on Sensory Brand Experience and Intention to Use the Mobile App	3D E-Commerce Using AR	Proposed Model
Loading Time	4-6 seconds	3-5 seconds	6-8 seconds	3-4 seconds
Frame Rate	30 FPS	25-30 FPS	30 FPS	30 FPS
Tracking Accuracy	Not mentioned	Not mentioned	Not mentioned	Moderate to High
User Feedback	Customers find AR experiences more exciting and memorable	AR try-on experience has a positive impact on sensory brand experience and enhances customer loyalty	Positive feedback	Customer finds it easy to user and explore all cloths and garments
Compatibility	Requires compatible AR devices	Requires compatible AR devices	Requires compatible AR devices	Requires compatible AR devices with snapchat
Speed	Moderate	Moderate to Fast	Moderate to Fast	Fast
Realism	Less Realistic	Realistic	Moderate Realistic	High Realistic
Interactivity	Highly interactive	Highly interactive	Highly interactive	Moderately interactive
Integration with E-Commerce	High level of integration with e-commerce	High level of integration with e-commerce	High level of integration with e-commerce	moderate integration with e-commerce as user have to add QR code of lens

The images shown in Figure 6 are taken from the website "Virtual Try Ons" which contains preview and snapcodes of the 3D models. The images provided above in Figure 7 are the snap codes of the lenses which are published in Lens Studio. These lenses redirect to snapchat lenses which are used for try-on. The website is designed with user-friendliness in mind and enables users to quickly access their desired lenses.

To utilize the lenses, users simply visit the website, select the preferred dress or accessory, tap on the card to reveal the snap code, and scan it with either Google Lens or Snapchat scanner feature. This will take them to the lenses in Snapchat where they can try them on and get an idea of how they look. This allows users to make informed purchasing decisions based on their appearance in the lenses.

Figure 6. Website with preview on the card and snap codes on the back of the card

CONCLUSION

This paper explores the significance of Virtual try-on in e-commerce, which streamlines the purchasing decision and elevates the customer experience. This is achieved by utilizing IoT devices such as smartphones, webcams, or other cameras. The intelligent interface, typically in the form of a website, provides various try-ons for products such as clothing and footwear via snap codes which are simple to scan. Currently, the options are limited, but the goal is to expand the offering to include more accessories like makeup and to provide a wider range of models for existing try-ons in the future.

Figure 7. Snap codes of the lenses

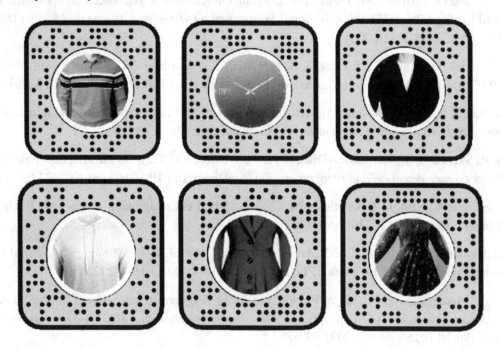

REFERENCES

Abdel, H. (2019). Internet of Things (IOT): Research Challenges and Future Applications. *International Journal of Advanced Computer Science and Applications.*

Anand, P., Gupta, R., Tiwari, N. K., & Gupta, S. (2022). Glass Virtual Try-On. *International Journal for Research in Applied Science and Engineering Technology, 10*(5), 718–722. Advance online publication. doi:10.22214/ijraset.2022.42317

Antim, A., & Luigi, L. (2017). An extensive Review on Interfaces between IoT and Cloud Computing. *International Journal of Engineering Research & Technology.*

Boardman R, Zhu A. (2020). Augmented Reality and Virtual Reality – New Drivers For Fashion Retail? *Technology-Driven Sustainability: Innovation in the Fashion Supply Chain.* . doi:10.1007/978-3-030-15483-7_9

Borges, A., & Carlos, H. (2019). A Virtual Makeup Augmented Reality System. *21st Symposium on Virtual and Augmented Reality (SVR).* 10.1109/SVR.2019.00022

Dov & Kaufman. (2018). Augmenting Reality with Intelligent Interfaces. *IntechOpen.* doi:10.5772/intechopen.75751

Eugeni, R. (2022). Augmented Reality Filters and the Faces as Brands: Personal Identities and Marketing Strategies in the Age of Algorithmic Images. *24th HCI International Conference.* 10.1007/978-3-031-05064-0_17

Fribourg, P. (2021). Mirror on My Phone: Investigating Dimensions of Self-Face Perception Induced by Augmented Reality Filters. *IEEE International Symposium on Mixed and Augmented Reality (ISMAR)*. 10.1109/ISMAR52148.2021.00064

Garg, N., Pareek, A., Lale, A., & Charya, S. K. (2020). Evolution in E-Commerce with Augmented Reality. *IOP Conf. Series: Materials Science and Engineering*. 10.1088/1757-899X/1012/1/012041

Gupta R, Nair K S. (2022). Try-on with AR: Impact on sensory brand experience and intention to use the mobile app. *Journal of Management Information and Decision Sciences*.

Hedman, P., Skepetzis, V., Hernandez-Diaz, K., & Fernandez, J. (2022). *On the effect of selfie beautification filters on face detection and recognition*. ScienceDirect. doi:10.1016/j.patrec.2022.09.018

Jadhav, O., Patil, A., Sam, J., & Kiruthika, M. (2021). Virtual Dressing using Augmented Reality. *ITM Web of Conferences, 40*. 10.1051/itmconf/20214003028

Jain, R., Chauhan, P., & Sood, A. (2022). *Anthropometrical Virtual Try-on: A Survey on Virtual Try-ons and Human Body Dimension Estimation*. THEETAS. doi:10.4108/eai.16-4-2022.2318169

Javornik, A., Marde, B., Pizzetti, M., & Warlop, L. (2021). Augmented self - The effects of virtual face augmentation on consumers' self-concept. *Journal of Business Research*, *130*, 170–187. Advance online publication. doi:10.1016/j.jbusres.2021.03.026

Kalmkar S, Mujawar A, Liyakat K S. (2022). 3D E-Commers Using AR. *International Journal of Information technology and Computer Engineering*. https://doi.org/ doi:10.55529.ijitc.26.18.27

Kumar S. (2021). Study of Retail Applications with Virtual and Augmented Reality Technologies. *Journal of Innovative Image Processing*. . doi:10.36548/jiip.2021.2.006

Maisevli, H., Setiadi, R., Aulia, N. D., Dwi, Z. A., & Widartha, P. (2022). AR Make-up Filter for Social Media using the HSV Color Extraction. *Journal Online Informatika*. . doi:10.15575/join.v7i2.994

Prabha, R., Ramyalakshmi, K., Renuka, D., & Sadhurya. (2021). AR Based Try on Clothing. *International Journal of Innovative Research in Technology*.

Ria, M., Korbe, J., Nannan, X., Rüdiger, Z., & Hamari, J. (2021). The Use of Augmented Reality in Retail: A Review of Literature. *Proceedings of the 54th Hawaii International Conference on System Sciences*. 10.24251/HICSS.2021.078

Samuel, A., & Senith, S. (2022). Augmented Reality in Fashion Retail Industry. *International Journal of Education, Modern Management, Applied Science & Social Science, 6*.

Sangeeta, N. P. (2019). Implementation Issues of Augmented Reality and Virtual Reality: A Survey. *International Conference on Intelligent Data Communication Technologies and Internet of Things (ICICI)*. doi: 0.1007/978-3-030-03146-6_97

Yadav A. (2020). Digital Shopping Behaviour: Influence of Augmented Reality in Social Media for Online Shopping. *Journal of Multidimensional Research and Review*.

Yu, R., Wang, X., & Xie, X. (2022). VTNFP: An Image-based Virtual Try-on Network with Body and Clothing Feature Preservation. *IEEE Xplore*. doi:10.1109/ICCV.2019.01061

Chapter 5
Insulator Fault Detection From UAV Images Using YOLOv5

S. Venkata Suryanarayana
CVR College of Engineering, India

Katakam Koushik
CVR College of Engineering, India

Prabu Sevugan
Pondicherry University, India

ABSTRACT

Identification of insulator defects is one of the most important goals of an intelligent examination of high-voltage transmission lines. Because they provide mechanical support for electric transmission lines as well as electrical insulation, insulators are essential to the secure and reliable operation of power networks. A fresh dataset is first built by collecting aerial pictures in various scenes that have one or more defects. A feature pyramid network and an enhanced loss function are used by the CSPD-YOLO model to increase the precision of insulator failure detection. The insulator defective data set, which has two classes (insulator, defect), is used by the suggested technique to train and test the model using the YOLOv5 object detection algorithm. The authors evaluate how well the YOLOv3, YOLOv5, and related families perform when trained on the insulator defective dataset. Practitioners can use this information to choose the appropriate technique based on the insulator defective dataset.

INTRODUCTION

When inspecting high-voltage transmission lines, a number of sensors are employed, and one crucial technique is the status detection of electrical equipment. Vision sensor-based techniques have advanced significantly over the past few decades, and various topics, including insulator identification, power line detection, and power tower detection, have been studied. The insulator string, which may offer both mechanical support and electrical insulation, is one of the high-voltage transmission line's most crucial

DOI: 10.4018/978-1-6684-8098-4.ch005

pieces of equipment, according to early research. However, insulator flaws typically manifest themselves after some amount of running time as a result of factors including lightning strikes, material aging, and overloading. Therefore, a crucial job for high-voltage transmission line inspection is the accurate detection of insulator failures. In a standard manual inspection, workers must traverse paths close to high-voltage transmission lines to examine the status of each insulator using a variety of tools, including cameras, ultraviolet imagers, infrared imagers, and audition sensors. However, because high-voltage transmission lines are typically erected in complicated environments with woods and lakes, the traditional manual method is ineffective and impractical in real-world applications. The study of aerial photographs taken by unmanned aerial vehicles (UAVs) has recently become more popular for insulator status inspection due to advancements in UAV handling and image processing techniques.

Multiple features, such as color, form, edge, gradient, texture, key-points, and their fusions, have been investigated in the man-made feature-based approaches. Some mathematical models, such the snake model, Hough transform, Active Contour Model, Fuzzy c-means, and Receptive field model, have also been used in the interim. AdaBoost, Sparse representation-based classifier, SVM, Cascade classifier, and KNN are used in machine learning-based approaches to identify insulator placements and identify insulator problems. The insulators in aerial photographs, however, are typically overlapped since the shooting angle and distance are constantly changing during UAV inspection, making it difficult to collect the spatial information of each insulator.

According to Liu et al. (2021), high-voltage transmission is essential because of the rising demand for electricity, particularly in relation to intelligent power grids. However, a defect will inevitably happen because the insulator spends a considerable amount of time outside. Unmanned aerial vehicle (UAV) patrols have gradually replaced typical manual patrol, which wastes resources and is ineffective. As a result, employees no longer need to use telescopes to find insulator defects along transmission lines. The automatic diagnosis of insulator failures has, however, been extremely difficult because to the complexity and diversity of application settings.

The accuracy of conventional image processing algorithms is lowered because the correlation properties of insulators in aerial photos are unknown. These techniques have various advantages over more conventional image processing techniques. With the widespread use of CNN suggested by Xiao and Sun (2021), deep learning techniques are able to surpass the constraints of conventional image processing methods, displaying outstanding performance and significantly enhancing object detection accuracy. With the advancement of hardware technology and deep learning theory, object detection has made significant strides over the last five years. Numerous exemplary deep convolutional networks, including RCNN, Fast-RCNN, Faster-RCNN, YOLOv1, YOLOv2, YOLOv3, and various variants, are proposed and confirmed on open datasets. These techniques use high-dimensional semantic attributes to represent objects.

In general, the majority of machine learning- and feature-based algorithms created by humans are extremely sensitive to complicated background interference. Additionally, the filming distance and angle typically reduce their performances. The majority of these techniques take a long time to complete and are not suitable for real-time applications. Since there aren't any insulator aerial picture datasets accessible from public sites, current deep learning techniques haven't been greatly improved. Most notably, none of the currently used machine learning, deep learning, or feature-based algorithms offer a systematic analysis that addresses the issue of insulator multi-fault detection. Therefore, it makes sense to provide a strategy that can address the issues with the current approaches.

To solve the widespread issue of the poor real-time performance of two-stage detection algorithms, Redmon et al. (2016) introduced the first one-stage network, YOLOv1. Since the entire detection pipeline is a single network, it uses object detection as a regression issue, allowing for a direct end-to-end improvement of detection performance. YOLOv1 is prone to missed detections in situations with object overlaps and occlusions, however, and is inefficient at recognizing small objects. As a result, in 2017, Redmon and Farhadi proposed YOLOv2, an improved version of YOLOv1 that uses DarkNet-19 as the foundational network and adds enhancements like batch normalized pre-processing, a multiscale training mechanism, and a binary cross-entropy loss function, leading to a noticeably higher level of recall and precision. In 2018, Redmon and Farhadi (2018) introduced the YOLOv3 method to increase the network's sensitivity to small object detection. It expands the number of network layers, implements the cross-layer summing function in Resnet, and employs Darknet-53 as the backbone network. In real-world applications, YOLOv3 is quick, and its rate of background false detection is low.

RELATED WORK

Zhao et al. (2019) presented the setting of anchor in traditional quicker R-CNN models only satisfy the requirements for general object detection. After fine-tuning a quicker R-CNN, some cases of subpar insulator identification produce power transmission and transformation inspection images. There are two horizontal insulators with colours that resemble the background. One insulator can only be detected in small portions, and the output box's dimensions are inadequate for the insulator. Infrared images were taken on-site, which is what actual application require. The selection of the photographs took into account a variety of settings. The country's 110–500 kV indoor high-voltage laboratories of various grades, four substations, one converter station, and about 33 transmission lines were selected. In terms of materials, glass, porcelain, and composite insulators were all taken into consideration. The quicker R-CNN in the VGG-16 Net had an average precision (AP) value of 0.640. We concentrated on how to further increase the detection accuracy based on this. It can successfully accomplish the distinct detection of the insulators in the image, laying the groundwork for further insulator defect diagnostics and status detection.

Rahman et al. (2021) developed the electric supply businesses concentrate mostly on inspecting damaged and faulty insulators to guarantee consumers receive safe and dependable power transmission. In both classes, YOLOv4 has an average precision (AP) of 82.9%, with pin insulators having an AP of 78.2% and suspension disc insulators having an AP of 87.7%. YOLOv4 Tiny has a lower AP than the regular YoloV4 model since it is a lightweight model with a fast rate of inference. The complicated dataset is made up of pictures of several complex electric poles that are located outside a 132 kV grid substation that was captured with a cell phone camera. To avoid overfitting and noisy estimations, cross iteration batch normalization (CmBN) is utilized.

Liao et al. (2015) developed the identification of regional feature points or regional patches is referred to as "feature detection." We want to find as many feature points of the insulator as we can in order to simplify the subsequent processing (to increase recall, we allow noise to exist but restrict the insulator point from being missed). There are numerous ways to find local feature points, including Lowe's difference-of-Gaussians detector and the Harris affine area detector. By employing a z-score normalization, our improved Harris corner selection technique only looks for corners that are close to enhanced edges. The exact same quantity of training data is used by all methods.

Wang et al. (2020) implemented a model with the BOW and SIFT-based method. The exact same quantity of training data is used by all methods. Features may be mapped between several feature mapping groups using blocks. The dimensions of the matching floor space are connected. Conv3, Conv4, and Conv5's comparable anchor scales are 32^2, 62^2, and 128^2. Three ratios—1:2, 1:3, and 2:1—are employed in this essay. In training, samples are categorized as positive or negative according to their Intersection over Union (IoU) value, which ranges from 0.7 to 0.3. All tiers of feature pyramid networks provide comparable semantic information because of parameter sharing. Faster RCNN using the suggested technique as the backbone had higher ACC, mAP with ResNeSt101-RPN, at 0.0067, 2.5% respectively. RetinaNet's ACC, mAP, and AUC were 0.0099, 0.8%, and 0.0164 higher with the suggested technique as the backbone than they were with ResNeSt101-RPN. The accuracy is increased, but the FPS drops by 1.18 when the proposed technique serves as the foundation of our proposed network.

Zhai and Zhao (2018) proposed a model with basic idea of the insulator parts are spaced equally apart from one another. The breadth of the surrounding insulator pieces will considerably increase following a bunch-drop. Human visual observation reveals a distinct gap in the insulator area. Once the insulators have been located, the morphological method is used to highlight the missing piece's location so that the fault site can be found using the spatial properties of the data. Insulators are exposed to extremely high voltage and enormous mechanical tension for an extended period of time outside. Insulator flaws or imperfections can cause significant power losses and potentially widespread power outages or blackouts. Ceramics and glass are the two most common materials used as insulators in transmission lines. As heterogeneous polycrystalline materials, ceramic insulators are susceptible to cracking from environmental, electrical, and mechanical stresses. Although toughening increases tensile strength, overloading can cause a bunch drop. Unmanned aerial vehicle (UVA) inspection has become a more popular method of line inspection in recent years. The defects in the insulators can be effectively found and located by processing and analyzing the aerial photos taken by the UAV.

METHODOLOGY

We use YOLOv5 which is a variant of the Yolo model proposed by Ning et al. (2021) to detect Insulator and defective areas because YOLOv5 model has a focus layer which is capable to detect low-level features accurately. The Workflow of YOLOv5 for the Insulator and Defective dataset is shown in Figure 1.

YOLOv5, which uses the MS COCO AP50.95 and AP50 is a cutting-edge detector that is both more accurate and faster (FPS) than any other detector in the market. They adopted substantial network enhancements to speed up the network's performance measured by mean average precision (mAP). In FPN, top-down augmentation path is used and in PAN, bottom-up data augmentation path is used. YOLOv5 comes with 30 unique training hyper parameters. It is possible to think of the learning rate as a step size that keeps the expense of each repetition to a bare minimum. To prevent overfitting, the learning rate needs to be carefully chosen. How many pictures will be transmitted to the network in a single transmission depends on the batch size. Thus, using a bigger batch size will speed up training. The different versions of YOLOv5 are based on p5 and p6 models, as shown in Table 1. The YOLOv5 architecture is shown in Figure 2, and different networks of YOLOv5p5 models are shown in Figure 3.

Figure 1. Workflow of YOLOv5

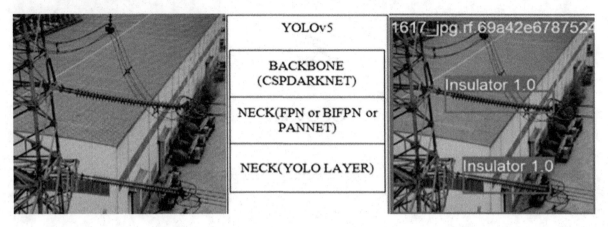

Figure 2. YOLOv5 architecture

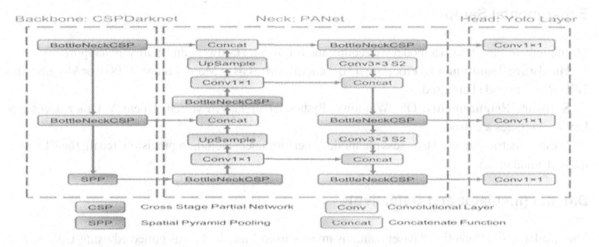

Table 1. Various types of YOLOv5 models

S.no	YOLOv5p5 Models	YOLOv5p6 Models
1	YOLOv5n	YOLOv5n6
2	YOLOv5s	YOLOv5s6
3	YOLOv5m	YOLOv5m6
4	YOLOv5l	YOLOv5l6
5	YOLOv5x	YOLOv5x6

Figure 3. Different versions of YOLOv5 p5 models

RESULTS

Experimental Setup

To Implement the YOLOv5 model we require the following Hardware and Software support.

Hardware Requirements: Processor: i3 or better, RAM: 8GB or More, Storage: 120GB or More, Nvidia GPU Recommended are used.

Software Requirements: OS: Windows, Python3.7 or later, Pytorch, OpenCV Other necessary Python Modules are used.

Various metrics are used to assess the model's performance, including precision, recall, the F1 score, maps 0.5 and 0.725.

Dataset (Insulator and Defective)

The Insulator and Defective dataset contains images from Electrical areas collected using UAV's. The Insulator and Defective detection dataset contains 701 images across two classes, namely Insulator and Defect. The whole dataset is divided into train/test sets by ratio 70% and 30% within each event class so 501 used for training and 200 images used for testing. The dataset collected from https://github.com/InsulatorData/InsulatorDataSet website.

Sample output of Insulator and Defective for YOLOv5x shown in Figure 4 with probability values.

The performance of YOLOv3 and YOLOv5 family for the given image dataset is listed in Tables 2-4. We also compared the accuracy of all models in the form of bar chart, as shown in Figure 5. Figures 6-11 show the confusion matrix, Recall, Precision, Precision vs Recall, F1 score and graph of all losses for YOLOv5x model.

The Precision, Recall, and F1score values are computed using the confusion matrix to assess the model's performance.

Recall evaluates a model's capacity to identify every TP proposition among all ground facts.

Precision is the model's level of accuracy in identifying just pertinent things. It is the proportion of TPs across all detections the model has produced.

Figure 4. Sample output of crop and weed for YOLOv5x

Table 2. Precision, recall, F1 score, mAP 0.5, and mAP 0.5 to 0.95 values for insulator

YOLOv3 and YOLOv5 models	Insulator				
	mAP 0.5	mAP 0.5:0.95	Precision	Recall	F1 Score
YOLOv3-tiny	98.4	74.9	0.935	0.959	0.946
YOLOv3	99.5	98.2	1	1	1
YOLOv3-spp	99.5	99.4	1	1	1
Yolov5n	99.5	94	0.985	0.996	0.990
Yolov5s	99.5	98	1	1	1
Yolov5m	99.5	99.2	1	1	1
Yolov5l	99.5	99.4	1	1	1
Yolov5x	99.5	99.5	1	1	1
Yolov5n6	99.5	95.3	0.997	0.998	0.997
Yolov5s6	99.5	99	1	1	1
Yolov5m6	99.5	96.9	0.999	1	0.999
Yolov5l6	99.5	94.8	0.998	1	0.998
Yolov5x6	99.4	92.1	0.989	0.998	0.993

Table 3. Precision, recall, F1 score, mAP 0.5, and mAP 0.5 to 0.95 values for defective

YOLOv3 and YOLOv5 Models	Defective				
	mAP0.5	mAP 0.5:0.95	Precision	Recall	F1 Score
YOLOv3-tiny	99.5	88.5	0.998	1	0.998
YOLOv3	99.5	96.3	1	1	1
YOLOv3-spp	99.5	99.3	1	1	1
Yolov5n	99.5	89.5	0.998	1	0.998
Yolov5s	99.5	96.1	0.999	1	0.999
Yolov5m	99.5	98.8	0.999	1	0.999
Yolov5l	99.5	99.5	0.999	1	0.999
Yolov5x	99.5	99.5	1	1	1
Yolov5n6	99.5	92.5	0.999	1	0.999
Yolov5s6	99.5	98.7	0.999	1	0.999
Yolov5m6	99.5	95.5	0.999	1	0.999
Yolov5l6	99.5	92.2	0.999	1	0.999
Yolov5x6	99.5	87.2	0.999	1	0.999

Table 4. Precision, recall, F1 score, mAP 0.5, and mAP 0.5 to 0.95 values for all (insulator and defective)

YOLOv3 and YOLOv5 Models	All				
	mAP 0.5	mAP 0.5:0.95	Precision	Recall	F1 Score
YOLOv3-tiny	99	77.7	0.966	0.98	0.9729
YOLOv3	99.5	97.3	1	1	1
YOLOv3-spp	99.5	99.3	1	1	1
Yolov5n	99.5	91.7	0.992	0.998	0.994
Yolov5s	99.5	97.1	1	1	1
Yolov5m	99.5	99	0.999	1	0.999
Yolov5l	99.5	99.4	1	1	1
Yolov5x	99.5	99.5	1	1	1
Yolov5n6	99.5	93.9	0.998	0.998	0.998
Yolov5s6	99.5	98.8	0.999	1	0.999
Yolov5m6	99.5	96.2	0.999	1	0.999
Yolov5l6	99.5	93.5	0.999	1	0.999
Yolov5x6	99.4	89.7	0.994	0.999	0.996

Figure 5. Accuracy comparisons of all models for all (insulator and defective) category

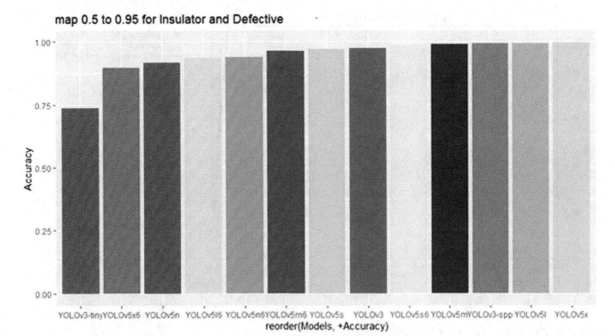

Figure 6. Confusion matrix for YOLOv5x model

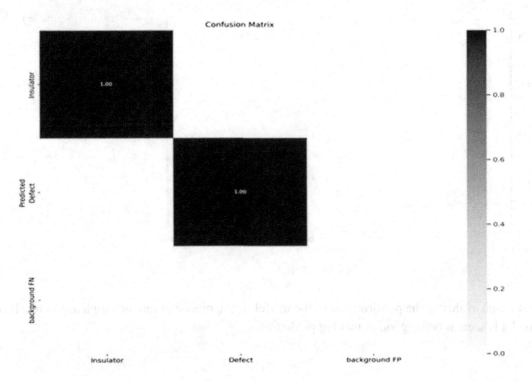

Figure 7. Recall graph for YOLOv5x model

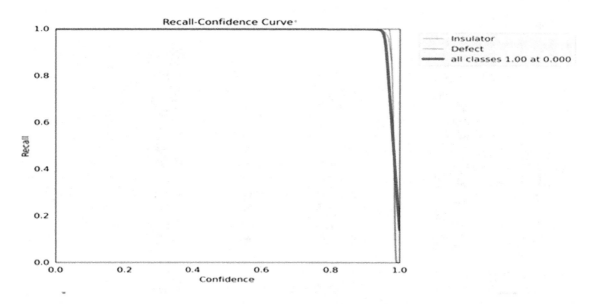

Figure 8. Precision graph for YOLOv5x model

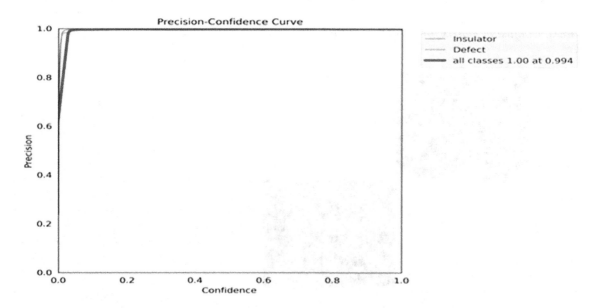

P-R graph evaluates the performance of the model. If the precision remains high as the recall rises, the model is seen as being good at making predictions.

Figure 9. Precision vs. recall graph for YOLOv5x model

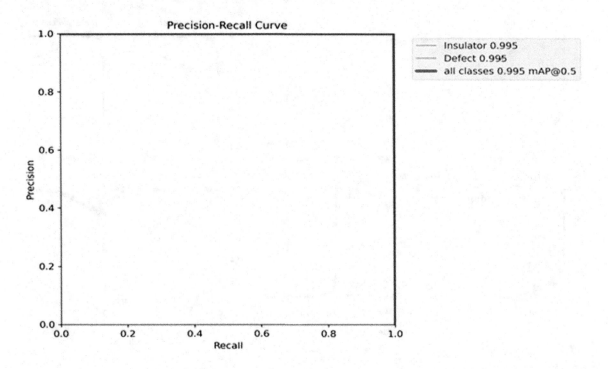

Figure 10. F1 score graph for YOLOv5x model

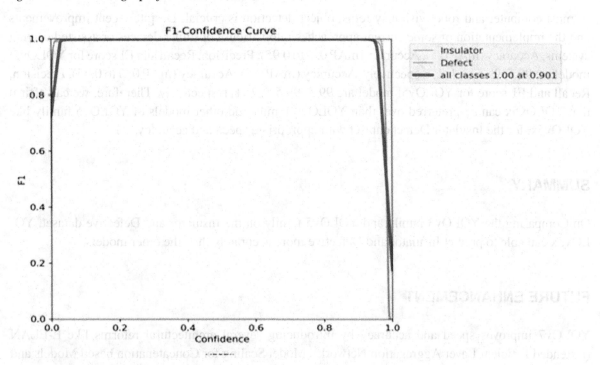

Figure 11. Graph of all losses of training YOLOv5x

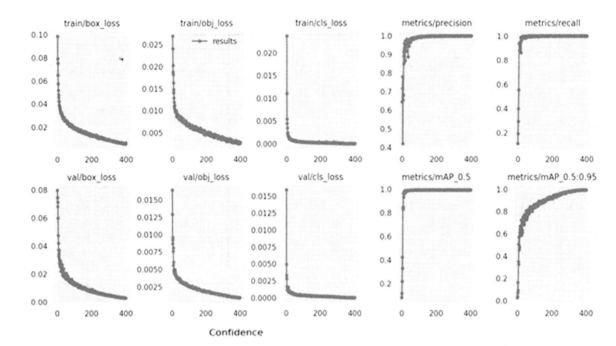

CONCLUSION

In most computer and robot vision systems, object detection is crucial. Despite recent improvements and the implementation of some current approaches into various consumer devices or assisted driving systems. Accuracy (mAP 0.5), Accuracy (mAP 0..5 to 0.95), Precision, Recall and F1 score for YOLOv5l model are 99.5, 99.5, 1, 1, 1, respectively. Accuracy (mAP 0.5), Accuracy (mAP 0..5 to 0.95), Precision, Recall and F1 score for YOLOv5l model are 99.5, 99.5 1, 1, 1, respectively. Therefore, we can affirm that YOLOv5x can be preferred over than YOLOv3 family and other models of YOLOv5 family like YOLOv5x, for the Insulator Defect dataset with appropriate speed and accuracy.

SUMMARY

On Comparing the YOLOv3 family and YOLOv5 family on the Insulator and Defective dataset, YOLOv5x can able to predict Insulator and Defective more accurately than the other models.

FUTURE ENHANCEMENT

YOLOv7 improves speed and accuracy by introducing several architectural reforms like E-ELAN (Extended Efficient Layer Aggregation Network), Model Scaling for Concatenation based Models and various Trainable BoF (Bag of Freebies) such as Planned re-parameterized convolution, Coarse for auxiliary, and Fine for lead loss.

REFERENCES

Liao, S., & An, J. (2015). A robust insulator detection algorithm based on local features and spatial orders for aerial images. *IEEE Geoscience and Remote Sensing Letters, 12*(5), 963-967. https://doi.org/.2369525 doi:10.1109/lgrs.2014

Lin, T., Dollar, P., Girshick, R., He, K., Hariharan, B., & Belongie, S. (2017). Feature pyramid networks for object detection. *2017 IEEE Conference on Computer Vision and Pattern Recognition (CVPR)*. 10.1109/CVPR.2017.106

Liu, C., Wu, Y., Liu, J., Sun, Z., & Xu, H. (2021). Insulator faults detection in aerial images from high-voltage transmission lines based on deep learning model. *Applied Sciences, 11*(10), 4647. https://doi.org/11104647 doi:10.3390/app

Liu, S., Qi, L., Qin, H., Shi, J., & Jia, J. (2018). Path aggregation network for instance segmentation. *2018 IEEE/CVF Conference on Computer Vision and Pattern Recognition.* https://github.com/InsulatorData/InsulatorDataSet website.

Ning, Z., Wu, X., Yang, J., & Yang, Y. (2021). MT-yolov5: Mobile terminal table detection model based on YOLOv5. *Journal of Physics: Conference Series, 1978*(1), 012010. doi:10.1088/1742-6596/1978/1/012010

Rahman, E. U., Zhang, Y., Ahmad, S., Ahmad, H. I., & Jobaer, S. (2021). Autonomous vision-based primary distribution systems porcelain insulators inspection using UAVs. *Sensors (Basel), 21*(3), 974. doi:10.339021030974 PMID:33540500

Redmon, J., Divvala, S., & Girshick, R. (2016). *You only Look once: Unified, real-time object detection.* arXiv.

Redmon, J., & Farhadi, A. (2017). YOLO9000: Better faster, stronger. *2017 IEEE Conference on Computer Vision and Pattern Recognition (CVPR),* 6517–6525. 10.1109/CVPR.2017.690

Redmon, J., & Farhadi, A. (2018). *YOLOv3: An incremental improvement.* arXiv.

Wang, S., Liu, Y., Qing, Y., Wang, C., Lan, T., & Yao, R. (2020). Detection of insulator defects with improved ResNeSt and region proposal network. *IEEE Access : Practical Innovations, Open Solutions, 8,* 184841–184850. doi:10.1109/ACCESS.2020.3029857

Xiao, C., & Sun, J. (2021). Convolutional neural networks (CNN). *Introduction to Deep Learning for Healthcare,* 83-109. . doi:10.1007/978-3-030-82184-5_6

Zhai, Y., Chen, R., Yang, Q., Li, X., & Zhao, Z. (2018). Insulator fault detection based on spatial morphological features of aerial images. *IEEE Access : Practical Innovations, Open Solutions, 6,* 35316–35326. doi:10.1109/ACCESS.2018.2846293

Zhao, Z., Zhen, Z., Zhang, L., Qi, Y., Kong, Y., & Zhang, K. (2019). Insulator detection method in inspection image based on improved faster R-CNN. *Energies, 12*(7), 1204. doi:10.3390/en12071204

Chapter 6
Blockchain–Based Deep Learning Approach for Alzheimer's Disease Classification

V. Sanjay

ⓘ https://orcid.org/0000-0002-6383-3793

Vellore Institute of Technology, Vellore, India

P. Swarnalatha

Vellore Institute of Technology, Vellore, India

ABSTRACT

Blockchain is an emerging technology that is now being used to provide novel solutions in several industries, including healthcare. Deep learning (DL) algorithms have grown in popularity in medical image processing research. AD is diagnosed by magnetic resonance imaging (MRI) images. This study investigates the integration of blockchain technology with a DL model for Alzheimer's disease prediction (AD). This proposed model was used to classify 3182 images from the ADNI collection. The edge-based segmentation algorithm has overcome the segmentation problem. During the investigation's test stage, the DL-EfficientNetB0 model with blockchain earned the highest accuracy rate of 99.14%. The highest accuracy, sensitivity, and specificity scores were obtained utilizing the confusion matrix during the comparative assessment stage. According to the study's results, EfficientNetB0 with blockchain model surpassed all other trained models in classification rate. This study will aid clinical research into the early detection and prevention of AD by identifying the sickness before it occurs.

DOI: 10.4018/978-1-6684-8098-4.ch006

INTRODUCTION

AD is a kind of dementia that often affects the elderly and is characterized by gradual cognitive impairment and a deterioration in the brain's functioning skills. According to the 2016 World Alzheimer Report, around 46.8 million individuals have AD and dementias which is illustrated as Figure 1. It is anticipated that the incidence of Alzheimer's will double every 20 years and that by 2050, the global prevalence of Alzheimer's will reach around 131.5 million (Ding et al.,2019). Approximately 60% of the brain's total volume is contained within this area. Grey matter, situated deep inside the brain, performs this crucial processing. This structure consists of the dendrites and nuclei of neurons. It accounts for around 40% of the volume of the brain. The white and grey matter of the central nervous system and spinal cord are protected from mechanical shocks by cerebrospinal fluid. Different hormones released by the hypothalamus facilitate communication between white and grey matter in the central nervous system (Zhang et al.,2019). Artificial Intelligence (AI) encompasses a vast array of algorithms and methodologies, including genetic algorithms (Wang et al.,2019; Alberdi & Weakley, 2018; Li et al.,2019), neural networks (Pavisic et al.,2021), and evolutionary algorithms (López-De-Ipiña et al., 2020; Sapey-Triomphe et al., 2015; Tzimourta, n.d.; Afrantou et al., 2019).

Figure 1. People affected by AD according to age

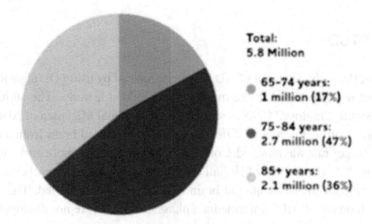

The most obvious symptoms include ineffective communication, increased susceptibility to infection, poor judgment, poor sense of direction, short-term memory loss, and visual difficulties. Recent research indicates that approximately 50 million people worldwide have Alzheimer's (Krishna et al., 2019; Chandra et al., 2019; Ke et al., 2019; Zheng et al., 2019).

However, most existing DL methods train a deep convolutional neural network (CNN) model from scratch and suffer from limitations (Lian et al., 2020). First, it requires a substantial quantity of labeled training data, which may be difficult to acquire in the medical domain. Second, it requires enormous computational and memory resources; training a model would take longer without them. Thirdly, it requires careful optimization of network parameters via regularisation; failure to do so leads to overfitting or underfitting issues. It is also essential to ensure that the trained model generalizes well to unknown data (Maggipinto et al., 2017).

Using functional magnetic resonance imaging (fMRI) images to train a deep neural network with blockchain to detect a wide variety of brain events (Chitradevi & Prabha, 2020; Lu et al., 2018), we achieved this goal. Due to advancements in the scientific and technical sectors, computer-aided diagnostic (CAD) systems have been developed. These systems aid in the analysis of medical imaging by researchers and clinicians.

In the early phases of AD, computerized diagnosis is essential for human health. Because AD is a neurological disorder, its incubation period is lengthy. Consequently, it is essential to monitor AD symptoms at various times. Using a variety of image categorization techniques can improve the accuracy of AD diagnosis.

DL researchers have discovered other ways to identify the severity of AD in individuals using MRI scan images (Gorges et al., 2018; Yu et al., 2020). In terms of image processing and analysis, the higher the image quality, the more accurate the results.

The rest of this article is structured as follows: the "Related Work" section reviews pertinent works. The "Problem Statement and Solution Plan" section summarizes the study's primary concerns and objectives. The section "Materials and Methods" discusses the proposed method. The section "Experimental Outcomes and Model Evaluation" evaluates the experiments and their results. The section "Conclusion" finalize the article.

BACKGROUND STUDY

Neuroimaging data for the early detection of AD may be enhanced by using DL algorithms, which have piqued the attention of researchers interested in identifying hidden features. The authors of Sarraf and Tofighi (2016) successfully employed CNN to separate the functional MRI data of Alzheimer's patients from those of standard controls in order to differentiate an AD-affected brain from a normal (healthy) brain. A 96 percent accuracy rate was attained. Complex difficulties need a more intricate network design. Using graph theory and ML, the authors of Hojjati et al. (2017) developed a novel classification scheme for MCI (ML). Groups with MCI had altered brain regions exactly identified. The suggested model depicted just the development of MCI; intermediate phases of MCI were not distinguished. ML-based computer-assisted diagnosis may distinguish Alzheimer's patients from healthy controls, according to Duc et al. (2019). This makes it hard to determine precisely which components of the neural network influenced its decision-making process. Using functional magnetic resonance imaging (fMRI), Pan et al. (2020) proposes classifier ensembles constructed using CNN and ensemble learning (EL) to identify individuals with MCI or AD.

A combined CNN and EL approach may determine which brain areas are the most discriminable according to the qualified ensemble model. The authors found that classification accuracy might be enhanced by using optimization methods or other DL techniques. To increase EMCI identification, the authors devised a multi-scale enhanced GCN (MSE-GCN) to study individual differences and knowledge associations among multiple topics (Yu et al., 2020). The suggested model was trained using the picture and population phenotypic data. The accuracy of LMCI vs. NC was 93.46%. The authors proposed more efficient network models for pinpointing precise brain regions. The authors (Guo & Zhang, 2020) suggested an auto encoder-based technique for discriminating between normal aging and disease development.

The suggested technique reliably diagnoses AD by using efficiently biased neural network functionality. The authors of Parmar et al. (2020) employed a three-dimensional convolutional neural network to develop a binary classifier capable of discriminating between AD and CN resting-state fMRI findings.

Problem Statement and Plan of Solution

In the "Related Work" section, you can find a list of architectures capable of detecting AD and categorizing medical pictures. On the other hand, most of them do not use remote AD monitoring and patient counseling tools like transfer learning algorithms, multi-class medical image categorization, or an AD checking online service. Literature on these subjects has been woefully underwhelming. Medical imaging is hampered by the small size of the data set.

METHODS AND MATERIALS

Early identification of AD is critical for avoiding and regulating the disease's progression. Our objective is to develop a framework for the early identification and categorization of AD phases is indicated in Figure 2.

Dataset

Using T1w MRI, the ADNI dataset gathered all necessary training data. Axial, Sagittal, and Coronal views are all available in DICOM format. Three hundred individuals in the sample have been labeled AD, EMCI, LMCI, or NC. There are 75 patients and 21 to 816 scans each class. The AD class has 3182 pictures, the EMCI class has 1732 images, the LMCI class has 175 images, and the NC class has 1275 images. In a 3182 2D format, all medical data was pulled.

Preprocessing Step

The collected data comprises not evenly distributed classifications. Oversampling and undersampling were used to overcome this problem. consequently, the collection has grown to 3182 images. A suitable format has been applied to the dataset after being normalized, resampled, and denoised. The data may be denoised using a non-local method for blurring a picture.

Edge-Based (EB) Image Segmentation and Clustering

The area of interest's orchestrated location is determined, and the chosen region is planted and zoomed in. This image is used to modify the pixel's intensity. Pixels are referred to as white or black for the picture, depending on their brightness. The White Area illustrates living tissue, whereas the Black Area illustrates dead tissue. The number of white and black pixels is computed, and if the black pixel is very little, the patient is OK. According to the Black Pixels ratio, the patient has a slight learning impairment, AD, or healthy. Thresholding is a widely used technique for picture segmentation. The grayscale or pixel power segmentation is achieved in this image segmentation technique. It is two-tier thresholding for classifying pixels into two groups based on the intensity of the image pixels.

Figure 2. Proposed system architecture

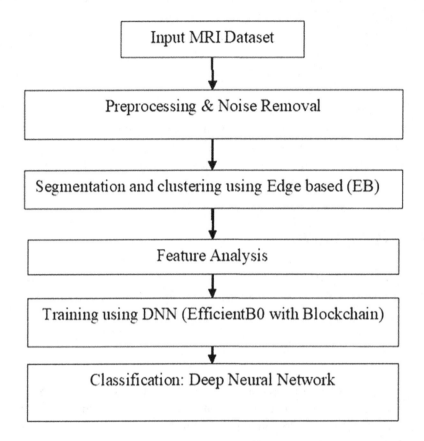

Given, X= {x$_1$, ...x$_n$}⊂ R^p, the EB partitions X into c fuzzy subsets by reducing the following objective function

$$J(U,V) = \sum_{i=1}^{c}\sum_{k=1}^{n} U_i^m \left\| X - V_i \right\|^2 \tag{1}$$

Where c is the number of clusters, which is favored in this study as a predetermined significance level, and n denotes the number of data points, A well-known alternating iterative algorithm minimizes the function J$_m$.

Now consider the proposed EB formula.

$$J(U,V) = \sum_{i=1}^{c}\sum_{k=1}^{n} U_i^m \left\| \varnothing(X) - \varnothing(V_i) \right\|^2 \tag{2}$$

$$\left\| \varnothing(X_K) - \varnothing(V_i) \right\|^2 = K(X_K, X_K) + K(V_i, V_i) - 2K(X_K, V_i) \tag{3}$$

Where K(x,y) = ∅(x)^T∅(y) is an inner kernel function. If we adopt the function as a kernel function, i.e.,

$$V_i = \frac{\sum_{k=1}^{n} U_{ik}^m K\left(x_K, v_i\right) x_k}{\sum_{k=1}^{A} U_{ik}^m K\left(x_K, v_i\right)} \quad (4)$$

Here we presently use the function for effortlessness. Equivalent modifications will be in equations (8) and (9) if we use other kernel functions. Equation (3) can be viewed as a kernel-induced new metric in the information space, defined as the subsequent equations.

$$d(x,y) = \|\varnothing(x_k) - \varnothing(v_i)\| = \sqrt{2\left(1 - k\left(x, y\right)\right)} \quad (5)$$

It is possible to demonstrate that d(x,y) as specified by Equation (5) is a metric in the inventive space if k(x,y) is taken as the function.

Clustering methods are uncontrolled segmentation techniques that separate an image into comparable intensity pixel/voxel clusters without training images. Clustering algorithms make use of accessible picture data for self-practice. The segmentation and planning were conducted in two steps: Data clustering and tissue sort estimation features.

$$j_m = \sum_{i=1}^{c} \sum_{j=1}^{N} u_{ijD_{ij}}^m \quad (6)$$

Each region is lighted independently, depending on the cluster's position. It is processed at a high rate of noise cancellation with poor homogeneity figures and a high rate of morphologic image filtering.

Data Augmentation Step: It increase the dataset because of a lack of medical information. With this reduction of 48,000 photographs, each class now has 12,000 images. Augmenting the dataset and reducing overfitting are the key objectives of this technique.

Blockchain Technology

It is incredibly impossible for hackers to alter, corrupt, or destroy information stored using blockchain technology. By design, it is a decentralised platform built on P2P architecture for storing and processing transactions and data. It is made up of many nodes that verify and store transaction blocks. Each block in the chain comprises a set of transactions, and it is assured that the previous blocks are properly linked to the newly created block in order to construct the chain.

Blockchain-Based Deep Learning

Important needs that blockchain technology can address are the reusability and trustworthiness of DL model sharing. Similarly, auditability, data verification, attestation of conclusions, provenance, traceability of ownership, use, and guarantee of fairness are the major arguments for integrating blockchain technology with DL (Yu et al., 2020). A large number of distinct examples are provided to DL models, which they use to learn the features and provide probability vectors as output. Even while DL models perform very well on unprocessed data, data quality still matters in many real-world prediction scenarios.

The blockchain is a decentralised and verified global database that enables all network nodes to store and exchange data.

Training Procedure: Convolution Neural Network

Initially, CNN was employed to handle difficulties with picture recognition. It is currently limited to photographic and video images and is used to represent time-series signals such as audio and text. The advantage of CNN is the localized convolutional weight sharing structure, which allows for large reductions in the size of the neural network, avoidance of overfitting, and reduction in model complexity. By using spatial structural linkages, CNNs may minimize the number of parameters to learn. As a consequence, backpropagation algorithms' efficiency during training may be boosted. The first convolutional layer of CNN receives input directly from the pixels of the picture. Each convolution operation takes a limited number of pictures, performs Convolutional modifications, and transfers the data to the back network. Each convolutional layer extracts the data's most efficient characteristics. CNN may be defined using its graph-theoretic formulation. The parameters of the convolution filter are shared across all network layer locations. The feature map computes the spatial feature by calculating the weighted average of the central pixel and adjacent pixels. The network layer of our model is defined as

$$H^{l+1} = f(H^l, A) \tag{7}$$

$$f(H^l A) = \sigma(A H^l W^l) \tag{8}$$

Where W^l denotes the weight matrix of the lth layer neural network and is a nonlinear active function. As a result, we may use EFFICIENTNETB0 with CNN to replace the kernel with an optimizable graphical convolutional network model.

EfficientNet

Scaling the network's depth, breadth, and resolution is based on this fact, and they proposed a unique scaling technique. They used the neural architecture search tool to design a new baseline network. EfficientNets, a family of DL models that surpass prior Convolutional Neural Networks in accuracy and efficiency, was created due to this effort.

Scaling

The researchers used the compound scaling method to increase the network's size. It was employed when resources were at a minimum to find the connections between the various scaling dimensions of a baseline network. Scaling factors may then be determined for each dimension to be increased. These criteria were used to increase the size of the baseline network.

EfficientNet Architecture

To begin, the researchers used an automated method for generating neural networks called "neural architecture search" to build a basic network. Floating-point operations per second are maximized in accuracy and efficiency (FLOPS). This architecture was developed to use mobile devices' inverted bottleneck convolution (MBConv). The EfficientNets family of DL models was then built up from this basic network by the researchers. Figure 3 depicts its design.

Figure 3. EfficientNet architecture

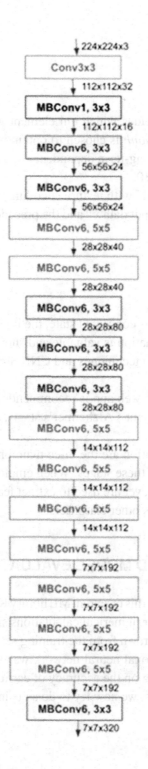

This network will be trained to forecast a patient's chance of getting AD over the next five years, balancing that probability against a loss function that collects diagnoses for specific individuals over time.

$$f_t = \sigma \left(W_f . [h_{t-1}, x_t] + b_f \right) \tag{9}$$

$$i = \sigma \left(W . [h_{t-1}, x_t] + b \right) \tag{10}$$

$$h_t = o_t * \tanh(C_t) \tag{11}$$

The worth of o_t in Equation 14 decides which uni element will be the productivity. The new cell state C_t multiplied by o_t, and function *tanh* is chosen to obtain ht in Equation 9, the input of the parts *ij*. The EFFICIENTNETB0 can learn long-term dependencies; a model expressing the course of AD is developed using the EFFICIENTNETB0.

Combine feature encoding from CNN with feature encodings from past images for the patient. New memory $c^{(t)}$ is generated by using the input data $x^{(t)}$ and the precedent hidden state $h^{(t-1)}$. (Note that W and U refer to weights and parameters.)

$$c^t = \tanh \left(w^c x^t + U^c h^{(t-1)} \right) \tag{12}$$

Using the input data and the previous concealed state, the input gate generates a result $i^{(t)}$ to gate the new memory, determining what information is valuable and should be remembered

Evaluation Step: Comparison of two techniques and CNN architectures based on nine performance metrics.

Application Step: An AD validation web app is recommended in light of the qualified models. Using the AD spectrum can identify a patient's Alzheimer's stage and advise them on how to deal with it based on their stage.

Extraction, reduction, and classification are the three main phases of the traditional ML technique. A typical CNN then incorporates all of these stages. When employing CNN, there is no need to extract features manually. Weights in the first layer are used to extract features, and the more they are used, the more valuable they become. CNN beats other classifiers.

EXPERIMENTAL RESULTS AND MODEL EVALUATION

Python 3.8 and Keras were used to create this research. ML library Keras is Python-based and open-source, a high-level library. Keras is utilized for numerical calculations since it makes them simpler and faster. Seventy-five percent of the data were drawn from the training set, whereas only 25 percent were drawn from the validation set. This convolutional neural network was subjected to practical tests to identify its ideal parameters. Rather than relying on the accuracy of earlier research to estimate the appropriate number of dense units for hidden layers, we now try to do so using accurate results.

Figure 4. MRI image demented categories

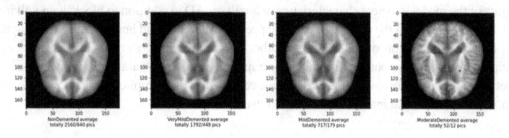

Figure 5. Comparative analysis of accuracy and loss while training and testing

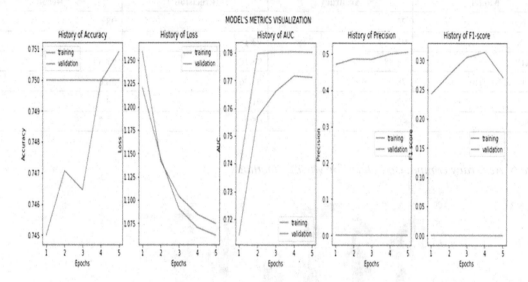

Our recent research provides an effective classifier-based deep convolutional neural network that performs admirably on the ADNI data set illustrated in Figure 4 and Figure 5. The ADNI-3 data set was housed in a single repository for safekeeping. During our investigation, we used 3182 axial slices of MRI. The MRI pictures of roughly 300 AD patients and 70 NC patients are included in the data collection. The exam is more reliable since they are all from different subject areas. Male and female patients ranging in age from 65 to 90 are shown in this work. To begin, we cut each MRI image into two-dimensional slices. We can get a larger sample size and a better training environment for our DNN with Blockchain models by rotating slices of our preprocessed images to see whether they recognize them.

The Proposed model has been compared with various methods like PCA, CNN, Resnet18, and 3DCNN. Table 1 illustrates accuracy, precision, recall values, and the comparison chart in Figure 6.

However, the findings of Multi-validation DL show that extra effort is required to build the model's architecture and optimize its hyperparameters. Due to the limited quantity of data and the pipeline's conformity to current standards, the only way to improve feature extraction and performance is to alter these steps. It is vital to maximize the utilization of existing data in a domain with little data. Domain learning may be one strategy for improving the identification and prediction of advancing MCI and its progression to AD. According to a literature survey on current approaches, domain learning has shown a favorable effect on model performance and the number of articles that employ the method. While training the weights of the model to detect characteristics of auxiliary AD in addition to blockchain will improve the model's presentation in the core issue, it will speed convergence and hence reduce training time.

Edge-based segmentation of the brain is another approach that may enhance performance. Brain segmentation (temporal, parietal, prefrontal, and occipital lobes) allows parallel 3D convolutional layers to extract more precise information for these areas, condensing the complicated feature space. A more compact feature area should make it easier to find useful features.

Table 1. Accuracy, precision, recall comparison table

Model	Accuracy	Precision	Recall
PCA+NN	95	91	98
3D CNN	93	93.18	90
Resnet18	97.88	98.10	97.89
EFFICIENTNETB0	78.72	68.96	58.66
CNN	92	91	93
Proposed	99	95	97.5

Figure 6. Accuracy comparison chart for various methods

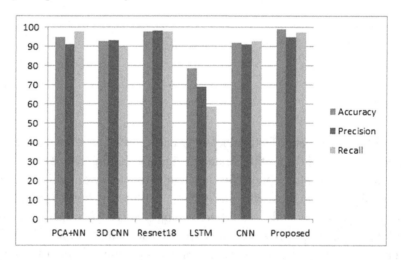

CONCLUSION

Convolutional neural networks (CNNs) inside deep neural networks might help diagnose AD. Two-dimensional MRI slices discriminate between people with Alzheimer's disease (AD) and healthy individuals using an EfficientnetB0 with a blockchain-based approach described in this article. Many potential AD patients might benefit from the suggested method, leading to earlier disease detection. The segmentation has been done with the Edge-based segmentation algorithm. Our feature extraction and classification technique in the ADNI database showed high accuracy for AD in the testing results for 240 people. The best results were obtained by classifying the axial image of the AD MRI. Using the provided technique, a classification accuracy of 99.14 percent was attained. This research suggests that our suggested method for diagnosing AD and identifying CN and AD is more reliable, recallable, accurate, and has a higher accuracy score (F1) than previous methods.

REFERENCES

Alberdi, A., Weakley, A., Schmitter-Edgecombe, M., Cook, D. J., Aztiria, A., Basarab, A., & Barrenechea, M. (2018). Smart Home-Based Prediction of Multidomain Symptoms Related to Alzheimer's Disease. *IEEE Journal of Biomedical and Health Informatics*, 22(6), 1720–1731. doi:10.1109/JBHI.2018.2798062 PMID:29994359

Chandra, A., Dervenoulas, G., & Politis, M. (2019). Magnetic resonance imaging in Alzheimer's disease and mild cognitive impairment. *Journal of Neurology*, 266(6), 1293–1302. doi:10.100700415-018-9016-3 PMID:30120563

Chitradevi, D., & Prabha, S. (2020). Analysis of brain sub regions using optimization techniques and deep learning method in Alzheimer disease. *Applied Soft Computing*, 86, 105857. doi:10.1016/j.asoc.2019.105857

Ding, Y., Sohn, J. H., Kawczynski, M. G., Trivedi, H., Harnish, R., Jenkins, N. W., Lituiev, D., Copeland, T. P., Aboian, M. S., Aparici, C. M., & ... . (2019). A Deep Learning Model to Predict a Diagnosis of Alzheimer Disease by Using 18F-FDG PET of the Brain. *Radiology*, 290(2), 456–464. doi:10.1148/radiol.2018180958 PMID:30398430

Duc, N. T., Ryu, S., Qureshi, M. N. I., Choi, M., Lee, K. H., & Lee, B. (2019). 3D-Deep Learning Based Automatic Diagnosis of Alzheimer's Disease with Joint MMSE Prediction Using Resting-State fMRI. *Neuroinformatics*, 18(1), 71–86. doi:10.100712021-019-09419-w PMID:31093956

Gorges, M., Müller, H.-P., & Kassubek, J. (2018). Structural and Functional Brain Mapping Correlates of Impaired Eye Movement Control in Parkinsonian Syndromes: A Systems-Based Concept. *Frontiers in Neurology*, 9, 319. doi:10.3389/fneur.2018.00319 PMID:29867729

Guo, H., & Zhang, Y. (2020). Resting State fMRI and Improved Deep Learning Algorithm for Earlier Detection of Alzheimer's Disease. *IEEE Access, 8*, 115383–115392.

Hojjati, S. H., Ebrahimzadeh, A., Khazaee, A., & Babajani-Feremi, A. (2017). Predicting conversion from MCI to AD using resting-state fMRI, graph theoretical approach and SVM. *Journal of Neuroscience Methods*, 282, 69–80. doi:10.1016/j.jneumeth.2017.03.006 PMID:28286064

Ke, Q., Zhang, J., Wei, W., Damasevicius, R., & Wozniak, M. (2019). Adaptive Independent Subspace Analysis of Brain Magnetic Resonance Imaging Data. *IEEE Access, 7*, 12252–12261.

Krishna, N.M., Sekaran, K., Vamsi, A.V.N., Ghantasala, G.S.P., Chandana, P., Kadry, S., Blazauskas, T., Damasevicius, R., & Kaushik, S. (2019). An Efficient Mixture Model Approach in Brain-Machine Interface Systems for Extracting the Psychological Status of Mentally Impaired Persons Using EEG Signals. *IEEE Access, 7*, 77905–77914.

Li, H., Habes, M., Wolk, D. A., & Fan, Y. (2019). *A deep learning model for early prediction of Alzheimer's disease dementia based on hippocampal MRI.* arXiv:1904.07282.

Lian, C., Liu, M., Zhang, J., & Shen, D. (2020). Hierarchical Fully Convolutional Network for Joint Atrophy Localization and Alzheimer's Disease Diagnosis Using Structural MRI. *IEEE Transactions on Pattern Analysis and Machine Intelligence*, *42*(4), 880–893. doi:10.1109/TPAMI.2018.2889096 PMID:30582529

López-De-Ipiña, K., Martinez-De-Lizarduy, U., Calvo, P. M., Beitia, B., García-Melero, J., Fernández, E., Ecay-Torres, M., Faundez-Zanuy, M., & Sanz, P. (2020). FaundezZanuy, M.; Sanz, P. On the analysis of speech and disfluencies for automatic detection of Mild Cognitive Impairment. *Neural Computing & Applications*, *32*(20), 15761–15769. doi:10.100700521-018-3494-1

Lu, D., Popuri, K., Ding, G. W., Balachandar, R., Beg, M. F., Weiner, M., Aisen, P., Petersen, R., Jack, C., Jagust, W., Trojanowki, J., Toga, A., Beckett, L., Green, R., Saykin, A., Morris, J., Shaw, L., Kaye, J., Quinn, J., ... Fargher, K. (2018). Multimodal and Multiscale Deep Neural Networks for the Early Diagnosis of Alzheimer's Disease using structural MR and FDG-PET images. *Scientific Reports*, *8*(1), 1–13. doi:10.103841598-018-22871-z PMID:29632364

Maggipinto, T., Bellotti, R., Amoroso, N., Diacono, D., Donvito, G., Lella, E., Monaco, A., Scelsi, M., & Tangaro, S. (2017). DTI measurements for Alzheimer's classification. *Physics in Medicine and Biology*, *62*(6), 2361–2375. doi:10.1088/1361-6560/aa5dbe PMID:28234631

Pan, D., Zeng, A., Jia, L., Huang, Y., Frizzell, T., & Song, X. (2020). Early Detection of Alzheimer's Disease Using Magnetic Resonance Imaging: A Novel Approach Combining Convolutional Neural Networks and Ensemble Learning. *Frontiers in Neuroscience*, *14*, 259. doi:10.3389/fnins.2020.00259 PMID:32477040

Parmar, H., Nutter, B., Long, R., Antani, S., & Mitra, S. (2020). Spatiotemporal feature extraction and classification of Alzheimer's disease using deep learning 3D-CNN for fMRI data. *Journal of Medical Imaging (Bellingham, Wash.)*, *7*(5), 056001. doi:10.1117/1.JMI.7.5.056001

Pavisic, I. M., Pertzov, Y., Nicholas, J. M., O'Connor, A., Lu, K., Yong, K. X. X., Husain, M., Fox, N. C., & Crutch, S. J. (2021). Eye-tracking indices of impaired encoding of visual short-term memory in familial Alzheimer's disease. *Scientific Reports*, *11*(1), 1–14. doi:10.103841598-021-88001-4 PMID:33888739

Sapey-Triomphe, L.-A., Heckemann, R. A., Boublay, N., Dorey, J.-M., Hénaff, M.-A., Rouch, I., Padovan, C., Hammers, A., & Krolak-Salmon, P. (2015). Neuroanatomical Correlates of Recognizing Face Expressions in Mild Stages of Alzheimer's Disease. *PLoS One*, *10*(12), e0143586. doi:10.1371/journal.pone.0143586 PMID:26673928

Sarraf, S., & Tofighi, G. (2016). *Classification of Alzheimer's Disease using fMRI Data and Deep Learning Convolutional Neural Networks.* arXiv:1603.08631.

Tzimourta, K. D., Afrantou, T., Ioannidis, P., Karatzikou, M., Tzallas, A. T., Giannakeas, N., Astrakas, L. G., Angelidis, P., Glavas, E., Grigoriadis, N., Tsalikakis, D. G., & Tsipouras, M. G. (2019). Analysis of electroencephalographic signals complexity regarding Alzheimer's Disease. *Computers & Electrical Engineering*, *76*, 198–212. doi:10.1016/j.compeleceng.2019.03.018

Wang, Y., Xu, C., Park, J.-H., Lee, S., Stern, Y., Yoo, S., Kim, J. H., Kim, H. S., & Cha, J. (2019). Diagnosis and prognosis of Alzheimer's disease using brain morphometry and white matter connectomes. *NeuroImage. Clinical, 23*, 101859. doi:10.1016/j.nicl.2019.101859 PMID:31150957

Yu, S., Wang, S., Xiao, X., Cao, J., Yue, G., Liu, D., Wang, T., Xu, Y., & Lei, B. (2020). Multi-scale Enhanced Graph Convolutional Network for Early Mild Cognitive Impairment Detection. In *Medical Image Computing and Computer Assisted Intervention—MICCAI 2020* (pp. 228–237). Springer Science and Business Media LLC. doi:10.1007/978-3-030-59728-3_23

Zhang, F., Li, Z., Zhang, B., Du, H., Wang, B., & Zhang, X. (2019). Multi-modal deep learning model for auxiliary diagnosis of Alzheimer's disease. *Neurocomputing, 361*, 185–195. doi:10.1016/j.neucom.2019.04.093

Zheng, Y., Guo, H., Zhang, L., Wu, J., Li, Q., & Lv, F. (2019). Machine Learning-Based Framework for Differential Diagnosis Between Vascular Dementia and Alzheimer's Disease Using Structural MRI Features. *Frontiers in Neurology, 10*, 10. doi:10.3389/fneur.2019.01097 PMID:31708854

Chapter 7
Intrusion Detection on NF–BoT–IoT Dataset Using Artificial Intelligence Techniques

G. Aarthi

B.S. Abdur Rahman Crescent Institute of Science and Technology, India

S. Sharon Priya

B.S. Abdur Rahman Crescent Institute of Science and Technology, India

W. Aisha Banu

B.S. Abdur Rahman Crescent Institute of Science and Technology, India

ABSTRACT

The rapid development of internet of things (IoT) applications has created enormous possibilities, increased our productivity, and made our daily life easier. However, because of resource limitations and processing, IoT networks are open to number of threats. The network instruction detection system (NIDS) aims to provide a variety of methods for identifying the increasingly common cyberattacks (such as distributed denial of service [DDoS], denial of service [DoS], theft, etc.) and to prevent hazardous activities. In order to determine which algorithm is more effective in detecting network threats, multiple public datasets and different artificial intelligence (AI) techniques are evaluated. Some of the learning algorithms like logistic regression, random forest, decision tree, naive bayes, auto-encoder, and artificial neural network were analysed and concluded on the NF-BoT-IoT dataset using various evaluation metrics. In order to train the model for future anomaly detection prediction and analysis, the feature extraction and pre-processing data were then supplied into NIDS as data.

DOI: 10.4018/978-1-6684-8098-4.ch007

INTRODUCTION

The Internet of Things (IoT) is a collection of interconnected IoT nodes that operate autonomously to collect and exchange data with other nodes over an Internet connection. IoT is a widely used technology that is expanding quickly in automated network systems. Security for IoT nodes needs to be decided upon early in the design and implementation process. Even basic gadgets may now connect and share huge volumes of data with other nodes due to the IoT nodes' quick spread. The security of the data must be taken into account because of the vast amount of data being carried across the network. Modern security measures should be used on the network to protect IoT nodes.

Among the most significant security concerns in the IoT are botnet-based attacks like Distributed Denial of Service (DDoS), Denial of Service (DoS), and others (Ge et al., 2019) where attackers infect nodes with malicious code or overload node information and impair performance. Botnet-based assaults are one of the biggest dangers to IoT nodes.

To handle this kind of difficulty, the IoT node should require specialized standards and communication protocols. The Constrained Application Protocol (CoAP), the Advanced Message Queuing Protocol (AMQP), the Message Queue Telemetry Transport (MQTT), and the Extensible Messaging Presence Protocol (XMPP) are just a few of the messaging and communication protocols that are used to ensure reliable and secure data communication between IoT nodes. Because of its low bandwidth requirements, low memory requirements, and low packet loss, MQTT is the most widely used protocol. MQTT is an IoT-focused communications protocol that is an OASIS standard. There are four crucial parts to the publish/subscribe messaging protocol: clients, brokers, topics, and messages. Data exchange between MQTT-Client (IoT nodes) and Broker (Central node). The broker enables IoT nodes to post and subscribe to subjects simultaneously, subject to node capability. MQTT topics are a form of structured, hierarchical addressing, similar to the forward slash (/) delimiter used in file systems. It includes communications, including data collected by various IoT nodes and messages from various networks.

TCP and UDP are the most often utilized transport protocols in the majority of applications. However, depending on the necessity, multiple message distribution functions and compatible standards are required for IoT applications. The majority of Internet of Things (IoT) nodes use the MQTT communication protocol, which runs on top of TCP, to send and receive data between IoT nodes.

The IoT nodes should use quicker and more effective security measures to detect network traffic irregularities. Firewalls, antivirus software, and instruction detection systems (IDSs) are examples of cyber security measures. These techniques defend against both active and passive attacks on the data. Without interfering with the system's operation, a passive attacker just watches and copies data, which typically involves listening in, traffic analysis, etc. IDS is one of the crucial types of detection systems that are used to track abnormalities, in the states of the hardware and the software running in the network, whereas active attackers try to manipulate the content of the data; some of them are DDoS, DoS, etc.

Now, research is concentrated on developing IDSs utilising various supervised and unsupervised learning methods. Machine learning is a sort of AI that can extract data from huge databases. Furthermore, neural networks are the basis of deep learning algorithms, which are a subfield of machine learning. Many cyber security activities, such as botnet identification, network traffic analysis, and instruction detection, involve machine learning and deep learning techniques.

Artificial intelligence techniques are used to recognise and investigate both normal and aberrant situations. By being educated on meaningful data, machine learning and deep learning approaches can identify and predict threats. Numerous artificial intelligence approaches are used in this work to discriminate between normal and abnormal data from the publicly accessible dataset "NF-BoT-IoT."

The upcoming content of the paper is organized into multiple sessions as follows: Section (II) provides various types of cyber security attacks related to the NF-BoT-IoT dataset for implementing machine learning algorithms. Section (III) is followed by a detailed overview of the machine learning algorithms used. Section (IV) describes the dataset and different ML models used in the experiment, including feature extraction, pre-processing steps, and various evaluation metrics are being used. Then in Section (V) the performance evaluation and analysis of the result have been discussed. Finally, Section (VI) holds the conclusion and future enhancement of the paper.

RELATED WORKS

Discuss the related works that are pertinent to IDSs in this section. These studies use machine learning techniques to validate IoT datasets. The most popular IoT datasets are BoT-IoT, UNSW-NB15 dataset, etc., and they are used by many academics for machine learning analysis and testing. The author gives a quick review of the many kinds of instruction detection assaults, as well as the various kinds of machine learning methods, and demonstrates how the dataset is very helpful for analyzing, rating, and testing the performance of the Model.

Leevy et al. (2021) use the publicly available BoT-IoT dataset, to train and test the model by cross-validation technique, to identify the normal and the information theft traffic. The authors used different ensemble techniques and non-ensembles techniques, to evaluate and analyze the outcome of the data, and to determine the best model.

Swarna Sugi and Ratna (2020) have investigated and analyzed the performance of the developed Intrusion Detection System for recognizing assaults using the model in BoT-IoT dataset. To analyze the model's performance, the authors used Long Short-Term Memory (LSTM) and K-Nearest Neighbor (KNN).

Alshamkhany et al. (2020) identifies harmful assaults on data using the UNSW-NB15. To analyze the performance of the best-fit model, the authors used a variety of supervised learning techniques, including Naive Bayes, K-Nearest Neighbor, Support Vector Machine, and Decision Trees.

Dwibedi et al. (2020) has compared the CSE-CIC-IDS2018, Bot-IoT, and UNSW-NB15 datasets, analyzing the dataset's performance using Machine Learning and Deep Learning approaches.

In Idrissi et al. (2021), by using the supervised and unsupervised learning techniques on the BoT-IoT dataset, the malicious activities are validated by using different metrics.

Zeeshan et al. (2022) has proposed a new Protocol Based Deep Intrusion Detection (PB-DID) architecture on the UNSWNB15 and BoT-IoT dataset, to identify the anomalous and non-anomalous activities.

Ullah and Mahmoud (2021) has developed Convolutional Neural Network in three dimensions and validated on the BoT-IoT, IoT Network Intrusion, MQTT-IoT-IDS2020, and IoT-23 intrusion detection datasets, with various performance metrics like accuracy, precision, recall, and F1-Score.

Shafiq et al. (2021) has proposed a new framework model, based on the feature selection on BoT-IoT dataset to evaluate metrics by using machine learning techniques and identify malicious activities.

Shafiq et al. (2020) has designed a feature selection algorithm using the wrapper technique on BoT-IoT dataset, for detecting malicious threats on the IoT network by using various performance metrics.

Table 1 gives details about the different papers, where the authors discussed the performance of instruction detection using various Machine Learning and Deep Learning Methods.

Types of Attacks

1. **Denial of Service (DoS):** The target network or the nodes cannot be used normally as a result. To hinder the system's performance or crash the main node so that users cannot access it, it will transmit more packets over the network's capacity (Thomas & Bhat, 2021).
2. **Distributed Denial of Service (DDoS):** A DDoS attack is one in which several devices are used to launch a coordinated DoS attack against a single targeted node.
3. **Botnet (BoT):** It makes use of a network of bots, which consists of nodes with malware or viruses that may be activated to launch various assaults on other nodes, such as spam email or DoS, or DDoS. DoS and DDoS attacks, as well as other attacks like theft and reconnaissance, are present in the NF-BoT-IoT dataset.
4. **Theft:** It's a type of group attack in which private information is taken by compromising the security of the main node.

Table 1. Details about the dataset and various ML and DL techniques used by different authors

Author, Title, and Year of the Paper	Dataset Details	Machine Learning Model Used
Joffrey L. Leevy et al., "Detecting Information Theft Attacks in the Bot-IoT Dataset", 2021 (Leevy et al., 2021)	The model for identifying legitimate and information theft traffic using the cross-validation approach is trained and tested using the BoT-IoT dataset. The result is then evaluated and looked at to choose the best Model.	Non-Ensembles Techniques and Ensemble Techniques.
S. Shinly Swarna Sugi; S. Raja Ratna, "Investigation Of Machine Learning Techniques In Intrusion Detection System For Iot Network", 2020 (Swarna Sugi & Ratna, 2020)	The effectiveness of the developed intrusion detection system is tested and assessed for identifying assaults with the Model using the BoT-IoT dataset.	K-Nearest Neighbor (KNN) and Long Short-Term Memory (LSTM)
Mustafa Alshamkhany et al., "Botnet Attack Detection Using Machine Learning", 2020 (Alshamkhany et al., 2020)	The UNSW-NB15 dataset, which is openly available, has 82,000 records that were used to identify the malicious assaults.	Naïve Bayes, K-Nearest Neighbor, Decision Trees and Support Vector Machine.
Smirti Dwibedi et al., "A Comparative Study On Contemporary Intrusion Detection Datasets For Machine Learning Research", 2020 (Dwibedi et al., 2020)	Comparing the CSE-CIC-IDS2018, UNSW-NB15 and Bot-IoT datasets using various machine learning techniques, and evaluating how the dataset selection influences performance.	Random Forest (RF), XGBoost, Keras Deep Learning models, and Support Vector Machines (SVMs).
Idrissi, I., Boukabous, M., Azizi, M. et al., "Toward a deep learning-based intrusion detection system for IoT against botnet attacks", 2021 (Idrissi et al., 2021)	The BoT-IoT dataset is analysed using various validation measures utilizing deep learning methods.	Convolution Neural Network, Recurrent Neural Network, Long Short-Term Memory, Gated Recurrent Unit.

continues on following page

Table 1. Continued

Author, Title, and Year of the Paper	Dataset Details	Machine Learning Model Used
Zeeshan M., et al., "Protocol-Based Deep Intrusion Detection for DoS and DDoS Attacks Using UNSW-NB15 and Bot-IoT Data-Sets",2022 (Zeeshan et al., 2022)	The UNSWNB15 and Bot-IoT dataset uses Protocol Based Deep Intrusion Detection (PB-DID) architecture to distinguish between anomalous and non-anomalous activity.	Deep Learning Techniques
Ullah, I., Mahmoud, Q., "Design and Development of a Deep Learning-Based Model for Anomaly Detection in IoT Networks", 2021 (Ullah & Mahmoud, 2021)	The binary and multi-classification attacks are assessed using various performance indicators using the BoT-IoT, MQTT-IoT-IDS2020, and IoT-23 dataset.	Convolutional Neural Network.
Muhammad Shafiq et al., "CorrAUC: Malicious Bot-IoT Traffic Detection Method in IoT Network Using Machine-Learning Techniques",2021 (Shafiq et al., 2021)	Based on feature selection, a novel framework model called CorrAUC on the Bot-IoT dataset is suggested to validate the identification of harmful traffic in the IoT network.	Decision Tree, Naive Bayes, Random Forest, Support Vector Machine.
Muhammad Shaif, Zhihong Tian, et. al., "IoT Malicious Traffic Identification Using Wrapper- Based Feature Selection Mechanisms", 2020 (Shafiq et al., 2020)	For the BoT-IoT dataset one of the dimensional reduction method is created, by utilizing the wrapper technique to assess the performance metrics of harmful assaults.	Supervised Learning Methods.

5. **Reconnaissance:** It is a technique for learning more about a network host. Another name for it is a probe. Attacks known as probing attacks include scanning distant nodes for details about the fatality.

These are the numerous cyber security assaults that may be examined using various machine learning techniques, which are essentially split into supervised and unsupervised techniques. We will discuss more machine learning methods and also a detailed description of the dataset used in our proposed work, in section III and followed by section IV, the feature extraction, data pre-processing, analysis of the test result, etc., of the proposed framework and finally in section V and VI will analysis and conclude the best-fit model for the data used.

METHODS

Dataset Description

The BoT-IoT dataset is used to create the NF-BoT-IoT, an IoT NetFlow-based dataset. The flows were tagged with the related cyber-attacks, and the features were taken from publically accessible pcap files or CSV files (Sarhan et al., 2022). There are 600,100 data flows in total, of which 13,859 are benign and 5,86,241 represent samples of various cyberattacks. The collection contains information about four separate cyberattacks. Table 2 and Figure 1 represent the NF-BoT-IoT, cyber-attack details.

Table 2. Cyber attack details of NF-BoT-IoT

Label	Attack	Count	Description
0	Benign	13859	Normal flows
1	Reconnaissance	470655	Method of collecting data about a network host.
	DDoS	56844	In, Distributed Denial of Service attack, Multiple devices are arranged in an organized DoS attack, to a single targeted node.
	DoS	56833	In Denial-of-service Attack, the network will be overloaded, by sending a greater number of packets.
	Theft	1909	A collection of assaults used to steal sensitive information, including data theft and keylogging.

Machine Learning Algorithms

Unsupervised learning and supervised learning are the two primary categories of artificial intelligence techniques (Vigoya et al., 2021). Mostly labelled data and training data are used in supervised learning. The types of classification and regression are further separated. The output variable in a regression analysis is a continuous value, whereas the output variable in a classification analysis is categorical. Most often, the classification type is used in the IDS dataset, to identify the malicious activity of the data. In contrast, unsupervised learning processes unlabelled data. It is further divided into clustering and association types. In Clustering, the data are grouped into separate clusters, depending on the similarity and dissimilarity between the data. Whereas, in association type, the data are grouped, depending upon the probability of the co-occurrence of the data item, so it is termed a rule-based machine learning method.

Every machine learning technique has a specific field in which it can be used. In this work, we apply some of the popular supervised learning techniques to the Botnet Instruction Detection dataset, including Naive Bayes, Random Forest, Logistic Regression, and Decision Tree.

1. **Naïve Bayes (NB):** One of the supervised learning techniques, which is uses Bayes theorem's conditional probability. Bayes theorems employ the maximum likelihood of case occurring technique based on prior learning. For example, NB is used to distinguish between legitimate network traffic and malicious attack detection. Even though the traffic classification features in the dataset may depend on one another, the NB classifier handles them separately (Sagu & Gill, 2020).
2. **Random Forest (RF):** Large-scale data classification is done using the machine learning technique known as RF. In this strategy, a "forest" is referred to as the amalgamation of numerous decision tree structures. As a result, classification is accomplished by linking various decision tree techniques, trained on the given data. This method is more effective because it can operate on large datasets, it is lightweight compared to other machine learning techniques, and it is more resistant to noise and outliers (Alsamiri & Alsubhi, 2019; Almseidin et al., n.d.).
3. **Logistic Regression (LR):** A supervised machine learning (ML) classification model called the LR is employed to track the discrete set of classes. It is a specific kind of linear logarithm model. The LR model uses a parametric logistic distribution to forecast the probabilities of various classes. Building a model with an LR technique is simple, and data training is effective. The model's utility is constrained in many situations since LR struggles with nonlinear data (Liu & Lang, 2019; Karataş Baydoğmuş, 2021).

4. **Decision Tree (DT):** A collection of questions is addressed by the DT machine learning model, which arranges data into a tree-like structure. The DT model can automatically remove features that are redundant or unnecessary. The learning process includes feature selection, tree generation, and tree trimming (F., 2018). a) Each node addresses a test point at the feature level and alludes to a single variable or feature; b) Branches that deal with the test result are connected to lines that ultimately lead to c) Leaf Nodes, which address the class labels (Ge et al., 2019). The method selects the top characteristics one by one and creates child nodes from the root node while training a DT model (F., 2018). The DT is a fundamental classifier that supports both continuous and categorical input. With the DT approach, it is possible to quickly find all triggering rules (i.e., rules that match an input element) with a small number of comparisons in an instruction detection process (Kumar et al., 2012; Journal & Science, 2021).

Deep Learning Algorithms

It is a computing system that draws inspiration from the information processing and distributed communication nodes in the human brain. It is a technology that enables the computer to classify additional examples of data after learning from a small number of data instances (Idrissi et al., 2022b). Through a series of nonlinear transformations, deep learning is well known for finding outstanding variables in raw data, with each change achieving an increased degree of depth and complexity (Dina et al., 2023). Keras Model, CNN, RNN, LSTM, and GRU, among others, are deep learning models (Idrissi et al., 2022a).

1. **Auto-Encoder (AE):** It is the sort of unsupervised learning algorithm made to take an input and change it into another representation. To reduce dimensionality, it only requires reduced version of the data and reconstructs the original message from that. It is used to solve a variety of issues, such as facial recognition, feature detection, anomaly detection, etc. (Boumerdassi et al., 2022).
2. **Artificial Neural Networks (ANN):** It is a kind of nonlinear statistical model that shows an intricate connection between inputs and outputs to identify novel patterns. ANNs learn from sample datasets and are used to enhance current data analysis techniques because of their strong predictive skills. It is a very efficient data-driven modeling tool for identification and dynamic modeling since it offers flexible structure and universal approximation capabilities.
3. **Convolutional Neural Networks (CNN):** A type of deep neural network that can be used for a variety of applications. Convolution and pooling layers, rather than fully connected hidden layers, are used in this sort of neural network. In contrast to other machine learning algorithms, CNN can classify the traffic on its own and learn better attributes (Idrissi et al., 2021, 2022a).

Because CNN uses the same convolution matrix (mask), a sizable reduction in the number of parameters and training computation summation is feasible while still learning more features with more traffic data (Sarhan et al., 2022).

4. **Long Short-Term Memory (LSTM):** It is the sequential data that comprehend both the network's present and past activity (Ge et al., 2019). Due to the fact that the attackers carry out the attack as a series of continuing actions, it is essential to examine both the most recent and earlier traffic. Including the data source, result, and forget channels within the RNN model, (Farhan & Jasim,

2022) aids in resolving the issue of long-term dependency and is therefore regarded as an RNN development (Ullah & Mahmoud, 2021).

PROPOSED FRAMEWORK

Our proposed method has undergone five essential steps, such as Feature extraction, data pre-processing, feature selection, splitting into training and testing data, and implementation of machine learning methods (refer to Figure 2).

1. **Feature Extraction:** The dataset is collected from the website https://staff.itee.uq.edu.au/marius/NIDS_datasets/. It consists of NIDS datasets in CSV file format (Leevy et al., 2022). This data is used to identify the normal and the malicious attack and also the category of the attacks. The collected data size is 600,100*14(rows*columns) which includes dependent features and the target variables Label and Attack. With the extraction of fresh dataset characteristics, this technique was primarily intended to enhance model performance (Leevy et al., 2022) (Refer to Table 3).

2. **Data Pre-Processing:** Pre-processing data transformation techniques are used to change the dataset's structure into one that is appropriate for machine learning. Also, the dataset must be cleaned to make it more effective by removing any irrelevant or damaged data that can impair the dataset's accuracy.

Categorical categories in the dataset are given usual and nominal values, and numerical data are given discrete and continuous values. The data must then be categorized into vectors, which can be done in many different methods. One hot encoding and label encoding (Agarap, 2018) are two often employed methods. In this work, the data is converted into a feature vector using label encoding techniques. The majority of the attributes in the dataset have both several unique values and nominal category values. In the dataset, the label encoding method is employed to convert values into a vector.

3. **Feature Selection:** Feature selection increases data clarity while reducing computational effort (i.e., training time) (i.e., facilitates visual detection of patterns). In certain situations, feature selection can improve classification performance and lessen the effects of class imbalance (Liu & Lang, 2019).

Reducing the quantity of features and using only those needed to create and test the algorithms is crucial if we are to find a straightforward security solution for the data (Agarwal et al., 2021).

4. **Splitting Into Training and Testing Data:** In addition to the data needed for machine learning, it has to be trained and tested, for the Model's performance and efficiency of it. The training data comprised 80% of the NF-Bot-IoT dataset, whereas the testing data included 20%.

EVALUATION AND ANALYSIS

The Python programming language, which has many useful libraries for ML algorithms, is used to perform the aforesaid data pre-processing techniques and the implementation of the dataset into ML models. The performance metric is used to compare the results of different machine learning classifiers. Performance measurements include accuracy, precision, and recall. Accuracy is one of them, and it is crucial in performance evaluation.

Table 3. NF-BoT-IoT in feature dataset

Feature Name	Datatype	Description
IPV4_SRC_ADDR	Object	IPv4 source address
L4_SRC_PORT	Integer	Source port number
IPV4_DST_ADDR	Object	Destination address
L4_DST_PORT	Integer	Destination port number
PROTOCOL	Integer	Internet Protocol used
L7_PROTO	Float	Application Layer Protocol. i.e., HTTP, SMTP, or equivalent
IN_BYTES	Integer	Incoming counter, N x 8 bits long.
OUT_BYTES	Integer	Outgoing counter, N x 8 bits long.
IN_PKTS	Integer	Incoming counter, N x 8 bits length.
OUT_PKTS	Integer	Outgoing counter, N x 8 bits length.
TCP_FLAGS FLOW_DURATION_MILLISECONDS	Integer	Flow duration in milliseconds
Label	Integer	Benign or Anomaly
Attack	Object	Benign, DDos, Dos, Theft, or Reconnaissance

Calculations for metrics like accuracy, precision, and recall are made using the categorization and confusion report. The formulas for calculating recall, precision, and accuracy are presented below,

1. Precision = True Positive / (True Positive + False Positive)
2. Accuracy = (True Positive + True Negative) / (True Positive + True Negative + False Positive + False Negative)
3. F1 score = 2 * (Precision*Recall) / (Precision + Recall)
4. Recall = True Positive / (True Positive + False Negative) (Aljumah, 2021)

Random Forest: Figure 3 illustrates the confusion matrix and classification report generated by the Random Forest Model for identifying assaults in the NF-BoT-IoT dataset. It results in an accuracy value of 82%. A report is also provided for the label feature, which is used to identify normal and anomalous data. Its accuracy is estimated to be 98% and is shown in Figure 4.

1. **Naïve Bayes:** After employing the Label and Attack features of the NF-BoT-IoT dataset to iden-
    tify assaults, the confusion matrix and classification report (Dwibedi et al., 2020) are generated.
    These results are shown in Figure 5 and Figure 6. In that, the accuracy values are 83% and 98%,
    respectively.
2. **Decision Tree:** To identify various attacks in the dataset using decision tree, where confusion
    matrix and classification report is obtained. These results are predicted in Figure 7 and Figure 8.
    In that, 83% and 98% accuracy values were found.
3. **Logistic Regression:** One of the evaluation metrics, the classification report is obtained for the
    'Label' and 'Attack' features, for identifying the attacks in dataset using the logistic regression,
    which predicts in Figure 9 and Figure 10 In that, the accuracy value is obtained as 81% and 99%
    respectively.

Table 4 displays the effectiveness of the malicious attack on the NF-BoT-IoT dataset using several
ML algorithms. In this case, the "Label" feature's accuracy shows its capacity to identify abnormalities
or patterns in the data, whereas the "Attack" function shows its capacity to identify a variety of attacks,
including DDoS, DoS, reconnaissance, and theft.

4. **Auto Encoder:** The confusion matrix, classification report, and the number of training and testing
    epochs required to gauge the model's efficacy. The various auto-encoder model evaluation metrics
    for the NF-BoT-IoT dataset are shown in Figure 11 and Figure 12
5. **Artificial Neural Network:** It is one of the unsupervised learning strategies used to forecast the
    model's performance measures. The NF-BoT-IoT dataset's model summary is shown in Figure 13.

Table 4. Accuracy of the instruction detection using different ML and DL algorithms

ML Model	Number of Features	Accuracy (in Percentage)	
		Attack Detection	Label Detection
Decision Tree	14	83.13	98.70
Random Forest	14	82.03	99.92
Logistic Regression	14	80.81	98.26
Naïve Bayes	14	80.43	97.80
Auto-Encoder	14	78.62	98.88
Artificial Neural Network	14	79.54	98.60

Figure 14 and Figure 15 show the comparison of different ML and DL methods on the public dataset, to predict intrusion attacks like brute force, reconnaissance, and theft. In this comparative study, a
Decision tree is performing better compared with other models.

CONCLUSION AND FUTURE ENHANCEMENT

In this paper, various artificial intelligence techniques are used to identify the intrusion detection attack on the NF-BoT-IoT dataset. By examining the model's performance using several metrics, the decision tree performs well in identifying the type of attack, whereas Random Forest performs better in predicting whether the data is benign or malicious. As a result, in future research, other unsupervised machine learning techniques will be used to discover the optimal model with the highest accuracy for predicting the type of attacks.

Figure 1.

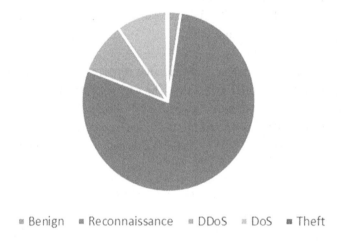

Attack details of NF-BoT-IoT dataset

▪ Benign ▪ Reconnaissance ▪ DDoS ▪ DoS ▪ Theft

Figure 2.

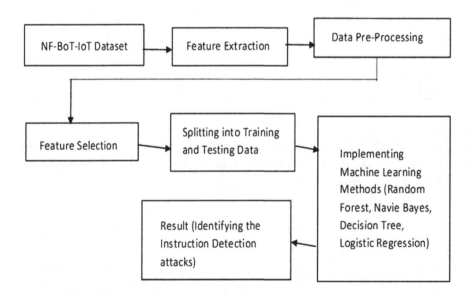

Figure 3.

```
[[  754     0    17  1946     0]
 [    0     0  8442  3129     0]
 [    0     0  8176  3016     0]
 [    4     0  4723 89459     0]
 [    0     0    15   339     0]]
```

	precision	recall	f1-score	support
0	0.99	0.28	0.43	2717
1	0.00	0.00	0.00	11571
2	0.38	0.73	0.50	11192
3	0.91	0.95	0.93	94186
4	0.00	0.00	0.00	354
accuracy			0.82	120020
macro avg	0.46	0.39	0.37	120020
weighted avg	0.78	0.82	0.79	120020

Figure 4.

```
[[   721   2082]
 [     5 117212]]
```

	precision	recall	f1-score	support
0	0.99	0.26	0.41	2803
1	0.98	1.00	0.99	117217
accuracy			0.98	120020
macro avg	0.99	0.63	0.70	120020
weighted avg	0.98	0.98	0.98	120020

Figure 5.

```
[[  356     4   367  1918    72]
 [    0   310  7162  4050    49]
 [    0   278  6924  3934    56]
 [   46   190  5077 88822    51]
 [    3    24    46   261    20]]
```

	precision	recall	f1-score	support
0	0.88	0.13	0.23	2717
1	0.38	0.03	0.05	11571
2	0.35	0.62	0.45	11192
3	0.90	0.94	0.92	94186
4	0.08	0.06	0.07	354
accuracy			0.80	120020
macro avg	0.52	0.36	0.34	120020
weighted avg	0.79	0.80	0.77	120020

Figure 6.

```
[[   326   2477]
 [   155 117062]]
```

	precision	recall	f1-score	support
0	0.68	0.12	0.20	2803
1	0.98	1.00	0.99	117217
accuracy			0.98	120020
macro avg	0.83	0.56	0.59	120020
weighted avg	0.97	0.98	0.97	120020

Figure 7.

```
[[  1249   1554]
 [    13 117204]]
```

	precision	recall	f1-score	support
0	0.99	0.45	0.61	2803
1	0.99	1.00	0.99	117217
accuracy			0.99	120020
macro avg	0.99	0.72	0.80	120020
weighted avg	0.99	0.99	0.98	120020

Figure 8.

```
[[ 1249     9     3  1525    17]
 [    0   344  4468  6505     3]
 [    1   351  4293  6528     1]
 [   11   308   143 93887     0]
 [    1     0     1   351    21]]
```

	precision	recall	f1-score	support
0	0.99	0.45	0.61	2803
1	0.34	0.03	0.06	11320
2	0.48	0.38	0.43	11174
3	0.86	1.00	0.92	94349
4	0.50	0.06	0.10	374
accuracy			0.83	120020
macro avg	0.63	0.38	0.42	120020
weighted avg	0.78	0.83	0.79	120020

Figure 9.

	precision	recall	f1-score	support
0	1.00	1.00	1.00	2782
1	1.00	1.00	1.00	117238
accuracy			1.00	120020
macro avg	1.00	1.00	1.00	120020
weighted avg	1.00	1.00	1.00	120020 .

Figure 10.

	precision	recall	f1-score	support
0	1.00	0.99	0.99	2783
1	0.34	0.31	0.32	11268
2	0.00	0.00	0.00	11302
3	0.85	0.96	0.90	94278
4	0.15	0.09	0.11	389
accuracy			0.81	120020
macro avg	0.47	0.47	0.47	120020
weighted avg	0.72	0.81	0.76	120020

Figure 11.

```
Epoch 1/5
168028/168028 [==============================] - 253s 2ms/step - loss: 0.0328
Epoch 2/5
168028/168028 [==============================] - 251s 1ms/step - loss: 0.0328
Epoch 3/5
168028/168028 [==============================] - 250s 1ms/step - loss: 0.0328
Epoch 4/5
168028/168028 [==============================] - 251s 1ms/step - loss: 0.0328
Epoch 5/5
168028/168028 [==============================] - 250s 1ms/step - loss: 0.0328
--------------------------------------------------------------------------
```

Figure 12.

	precision	recall	f1-score	support
Benign	0.000000	0.000000	0.000000	2662.000000
DDoS	0.000000	0.000000	0.000000	11367.000000
DoS	0.000000	0.000000	0.000000	11262.000000
Reconnaissance	78.626062	100.000000	88.034256	94367.000000
Theft	0.000000	0.000000	0.000000	362.000000
accuracy	78.626062	78.626062	78.626062	0.786261
macro avg	15.725212	20.000000	17.606851	120020.000000
weighted avg	61.820577	78.626062	69.217869	120020.000000

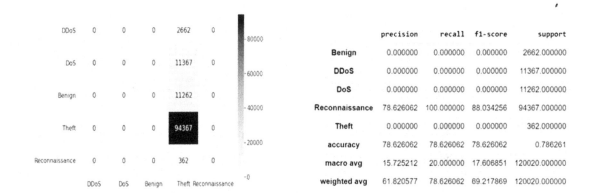

Figure 13.

```
modelName = 'ANN'
tf.keras.utils.plot_model(model,'./'+modelName+'_Archi.png',show_shapes=True)
model.summary()
```

```
Model: "sequential"
_________________________________________________________________
 Layer (type)                Output Shape              Param #
=================================================================
 dense (Dense)               (None, 10)                80

 dense_1 (Dense)             (None, 40)                440

 dense_2 (Dense)             (None, 10)                410

 dense_3 (Dense)             (None, 1)                 11

 dense_4 (Dense)             (None, 5)                 10

=================================================================
Total params: 951
Trainable params: 951
Non-trainable params: 0
```

Figure 14.

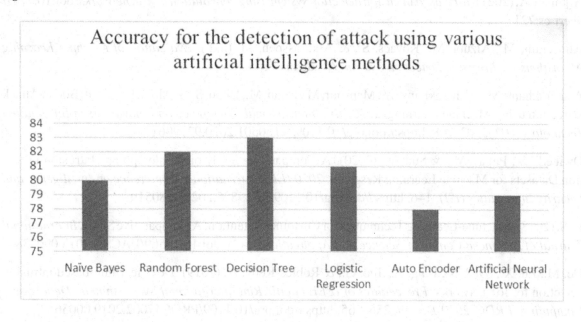

Figure 15.

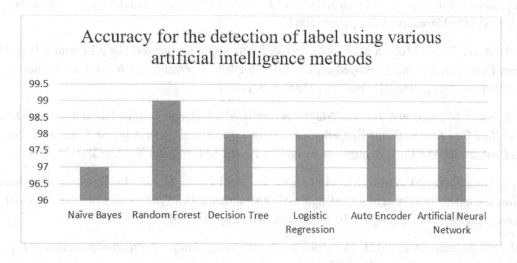

REFERENCES

Agarap, A. F. M. (2018). *Unit (GRU) and Support Vector Machine (SVM) for Intrusion Detection in Network Traffic Data*. Academic Press.

Agarwal, A., Sharma, P., Alshehri, M., Mohamed, A. A., & Alfarraj, O. (2021). Classification model for accuracy and intrusion detection using machine learning approach. *PeerJ. Computer Science*, 7, e437. doi:10.7717/peerj-cs.437 PMID:33954233

Aljumah, A. (2021). *IoT-based intrusion detection system using convolution neural networks.* doi:10.7717/peerj-cs.721

Almseidin, M., Alzubi, M., Kovacs, S., & Alkasassbeh, M. (n.d.). *Evaluation of Machine Learning Algorithms for Intrusion Detection System.* Academic Press.

Alshamkhany, M., Alshamkhany, W., Mansour, M., Khan, M., Dhou, S., & Aloul, F. (2020). Botnet Attack Detection using Machine Learning. *2020 14th International Conference on Innovations in Information Technology (IIT)*, 203–208. https://doi.org/10.1109/IIT50501.2020.9299061

Dwibedi, S., Pujari, M., & Sun, W. (2020). A Comparative Study on Contemporary Intrusion Detection Datasets for Machine Learning Research. *2020 IEEE International Conference on Intelligence and Security Informatics (ISI)*, 1–6. https://doi.org/10.1109/ISI49825.2020.9280519

F., S. (2018). Machine-Learning Techniques for Customer Retention: A Comparative Study. *International Journal of Advanced Computer Science and Applications, 9*(2). doi:10.14569/IJACSA.2018.090238

Ge, M., Fu, X., Syed, N., Baig, Z., Teo, G., & Robles-Kelly, A. (2019). Deep learning-based intrusion detection for IoT networks. *Proceedings of IEEE Pacific Rim International Symposium on Dependable Computing, PRDC, 2019-Decem*, 256–265. https://doi.org/10.1109/PRDC47002.2019.00056

Idrissi, I., Azizi, M., & Moussaoui, O. (2021). Accelerating the update of a DL-based IDS for IoT using deep transfer learning. *Indonesian Journal of Electrical Engineering and Computer Science, 23*(2), 1059. doi:10.11591/ijeecs.v23.i2.pp1059-1067

Idrissi, I., Azizi, M., & Moussaoui, O. (2022a). A Lightweight Optimized Deep Learning-based Host-Intrusion Detection System Deployed on the Edge for IoT. *International Journal of Computing and Digital Systems, 11*(1), 209–216. doi:10.12785/ijcds/110117

Idrissi, I., Azizi, M., & Moussaoui, O. (2022b). A Stratified IoT Deep Learning based Intrusion Detection System. *2022 2nd International Conference on Innovative Research in Applied Science, Engineering and Technology (IRASET)*, 1–8. https://doi.org/10.1109/IRASET52964.2022.9738045

Idrissi, I., Boukabous, M., Azizi, M., Moussaoui, O., & El Fadili, H. (2021). Toward a deep learning-based intrusion detection system for IoT against botnet attacks. *IAES International Journal of Artificial Intelligence (IJ-AI), 10*(1), 110. doi:10.11591/ijai.v10.i1.pp110-120

Journal, I., & Science, O. F. (2021). *An efficient algorithmic technique for feature selection in IoT-based intrusion detection system.* Academic Press.

Karataş Baydoğmuş, G. (2021). The Effects of Normalization and Standardization an Internet of Things Attack Detection. *European Journal of Science and Technology, 29*, 187–192. doi:10.31590/ejosat.1017427

Kumar, M., Hanumanthappa, M., & Kumar, T. V. S. (2012). Intrusion Detection System using decision tree algorithm. *2012 IEEE 14th International Conference on Communication Technology*, 629–634. 10.1109/ICCT.2012.6511281

Leevy, J. L., Hancock, J., Khoshgoftaar, T. M., & Peterson, J. (2021). Detecting Information Theft Attacks in the Bot-IoT Dataset. *2021 20th IEEE International Conference on Machine Learning and Applications (ICMLA)*, 807–812. 10.1109/ICMLA52953.2021.00133

Leevy, J. L., Hancock, J., Khoshgoftaar, T. M., & Peterson, J. M. (2022). IoT information theft prediction using ensemble feature selection. *Journal of Big Data*. doi:10.118640537-021-00558-z

Liu, H., & Lang, B. (2019). Machine Learning and Deep Learning Methods for Intrusion Detection Systems: A Survey. *Applied Sciences (Basel, Switzerland)*, *9*(20), 4396. doi:10.3390/app9204396

Sagu, A., & Gill, N. S. (2020). Machine Learning Techniques for Securing IoT Environment. *International Journal of Innovative Technology and Exploring Engineering, 9*(4), 977–982. doi:10.35940/ijitee.D1209.029420

Sarhan, M., Layeghy, S., & Portmann, M. (2022). Towards a Standard Feature Set for Network Intrusion Detection System Datasets. *Mobile Networks and Applications*, *27*(1), 357–370. doi:10.100711036-021-01843-0

Shafiq, M., Tian, Z., Bashir, A. K., Du, X., & Guizani, M. (2020). IoT malicious traffic identification using wrapper-based feature selection mechanisms. *Computers & Security*, *94*, 101863. doi:10.1016/j.cose.2020.101863

Shafiq, M., Tian, Z., Bashir, A. K., Du, X., & Guizani, M. (2021). CorrAUC: A Malicious Bot-IoT Traffic Detection Method in IoT Network Using Machine-Learning Techniques. *IEEE Internet of Things Journal, 8*(5), 3242–3254. doi:10.1109/JIOT.2020.3002255

Swarna Sugi, S. S., & Ratna, S. R. (2020). Investigation of Machine Learning Techniques in Intrusion Detection System for IoT Network. *2020 3rd International Conference on Intelligent Sustainable Systems (ICISS)*, 1164–1167. 10.1109/ICISS49785.2020.9315900

Thomas, L., & Bhat, S. (2021). *Machine Learning and Deep Learning Techniques for IoT-based Intrusion Detection Systems: A Literature Review*. Academic Press.

Ullah, I., & Mahmoud, Q. H. (2021). Design and Development of a Deep Learning-Based Model for Anomaly Detection in IoT Networks. *IEEE Access : Practical Innovations, Open Solutions, 9*, 103906–103926. doi:10.1109/ACCESS.2021.3094024

Vigoya, L., Fernandez, D., Carneiro, V., & Nóvoa, F. J. (2021). IoT Dataset Validation Using Machine Learning Techniques for Traffic Anomaly Detection. *Machine Learning, 10*(12).

Zeeshan, M., Member, S., Riaz, Q., Member, S., Bilal, M. A., Shahzad, M. K., Jabeen, H., Haider, S. A. L. I., & Rahim, A. (2022). Protocol-Based Deep Intrusion Detection for DoS and DDoS Attacks Using UNSW-NB15 and. *IEEE Access : Practical Innovations, Open Solutions, 10*, 2269–2283. doi:10.1109/ACCESS.2021.3137201

Chapter 8
Real–Time Object Detection and Audio Output System for Blind Users:
Using YOLOv3 Algorithm and 360 Degree Camera Sensor

Shiva Chaithanya Goud Bollipelly
Vellore Institute of Technology, India

P. Swarnalatha
Vellore Institute of Technology, India

ABSTRACT

This chapter aims to create a real-time object detection and audio output system for blind users using the YOLOv3 algorithm and a 360-degree camera sensor. The system is designed to detect a wide range of objects, including people, vehicles, and other objects in the environment, and provide audio feedback to the user. The system architecture consists of a 360-degree camera sensor, a processing unit, and an audio output system. The camera sensor captures the environment, which is processed by the processing unit, which uses the YOLOv3 algorithm to detect and classify objects. The audio output system provides audio feedback to the user based on the objects detected by the system. The project has significant importance for blind users as it can help them navigate their environment and recognize objects in real time and can serve as a foundation for future research in the field of object detection systems for blind users.

INTRODUCTION

The ability to perceive and understand our surroundings is essential for human survival, and our senses of sight and hearing play a critical role in this process. However, for people with visual impairments, the world can be a challenging and often isolating place. Blindness is a complex condition that affects people in different ways, but one of the most significant challenges faced by blind individuals is the in-

DOI: 10.4018/978-1-6684-8098-4.ch008

ability to see and navigate their environment independently. In this context, technology can play a vital role in enhancing the independence and quality of life for blind individuals.

Real-time object detection and audio output systems have emerged as a promising technology for aiding the mobility of visually impaired individuals. These systems use camera sensor to detect objects in real-time, which are then translated into audio signals that can be interpreted by the user. This allows blind individuals to navigate their environment safely and independently, improving their quality of life and increasing their sense of self-reliance.

Overall, the real-time object detection and audio output system developed in this project has the po-

Figure 1. Illustration of the overall system architecture

tential to significantly improve the quality of life for blind individuals by enabling them to navigate their environment safely and independently. The use of YOLOv3 algorithm and 360-degree camera sensor offers a powerful and effective solution for real-time object detection.

One of the most popular and effective object detection algorithms is YOLO (You Only Look Once), which has been widely used for real-time object detection in various applications. In this project, we aim to develop a real-time object detection and audio output system for blind users using the YOLOv3 algorithm and a 360-degree camera sensor. The system will be able to detect and identify objects in the user's environment and provide audio output to the user.

The use of a 360-degree camera sensor in the system allows for a comprehensive view of the user's environment, enabling the detection of objects from all angles. This feature is particularly useful in environments with obstacles or complex layouts, where traditional cameras may not provide sufficient coverage.

BACKGROUND

Object detection has been an active research topic in the field of computer vision for several years. One of the most popular and successful object detection frameworks is YOLOv3 (You Only Look Once), which is known for its speed and accuracy. YOLOv3 uses a deep convolutional neural network (CNN) to detect objects in an image, and it is able to perform this task in real-time on a variety of hardware platforms.

Several recent studies have explored the use of object detection to assist visually impaired individuals. For example, the paper by Sai Nikhil Alisetti et al. proposed a predictive object tracking system based on deep CNNs for guiding and navigation of blind people (Alisetti et al., 2019). Similarly, the work by Maid et al. focused on developing an object detection system for blind users (Maid et al., 2021). Another study by Sagana et al. presented an object recognition system for visually impaired people (Sagana et al., 2019).

In addition to object detection, the use of 360 cameras has become increasingly popular in recent years. These cameras are capable of capturing a 360-degree view of the environment, which makes them ideal for applications such as virtual reality and augmented reality. The paper by W. Yang et al. proposed an object detection system for equirectangular panorama images captured using a 360-degree camera (Yang et al., 2018).

Mahesh et al. proposed a real-time object detection system called CICERONE for visually impaired people, which provided audio feedback to assist the users in navigating through the environment (Mahesh et al., 2019). Similarly, the work by Dewangan and Chaubey proposed an object detection system with voice output using Python (Dewangan & Chaubey, 2021). The paper by Aralikatti et al. proposed a real-time object detection and face recognition system to assist the visually impaired (Aralikatti et al., 2021).

Finally, the paper by Padmanabula et al. proposed a stacked YOLOv3 architecture for object detection, which achieved higher accuracy compared to the original YOLOv3 (Padmanabula et al., 2021). The paper by Zhao et al. provided a comprehensive review of object detection with deep learning, including YOLOv3 (Zhao et al., 2019). The paper by Dhulipalla et al. proposed an object detection scheme in equirectangular panoramic images using YOLOv3 (Dhulipalla et al., 2020).

Overall, the above-mentioned papers provide valuable insights and techniques that can be used in the development of a real-time object detection system with audio feedback using 360 cameras and YOLOv3.

STORYBOARDING

Enhancing Road Safety for Visually Impaired Individuals

In Scene 1, a visually impaired user approaches a road crossing and activates the Real-Time Object Detection and Audio Output System. The system identifies the road crossing and confirms that object detection is activated.

In Scene 2, the system detects the presence of a vehicle approaching and emits an alert sound to notify the user. The user listens to the alert and waits until the vehicle passes.

In Scene 3, the system detects the absence of obstacles and confirms that it is safe to cross the road. The user receives an audio message informing them that it is safe to cross.

In Scene 4, the user crosses the road safely, the system confirms the successful crossing, and the user turns off the system and continues their journey. This system demonstrates the power of machine learning and computer vision in enhancing accessibility and safety for people with disabilities.

COMPARISON OF OBJECT DETECTION ALGORITHMS

To further evaluate the performance of our Real-Time Object Detection and Audio Output System, we conducted a comparison between two different object detection algorithms: YOLOv3 and YOLOv4. Both algorithms were trained on the same dataset and tested on the same set of images. Table 1 shows the results of the comparison between YOLOv3 and YOLOv4 in terms of mean average precision (mAP) and inference time.

Figure 2. Storyboarding of enhancing road safety for the visually impaired individuals

Table 1. Comparison of object detection algorithms

Algorithm	mAP	Inference Time (ms)
YOLOv3	0.82	35
YOLOv4	0.85	38

From the comparison, we observed that YOLOv4 achieved a higher mAP of 0.85 compared to YOLOv3, which had a mAP of 0.82. However, YOLOv4 had a slightly longer inference time of 38 ms compared to YOLOv3, which had an inference time of 35 ms. These results suggest that YOLOv4 has a higher accuracy in object detection, but at the cost of a slightly longer inference time. Further optimization and testing could be performed to determine if this trade-off is worth it for the specific use case of our system.

It is worth noting that other object detection algorithms, such as Faster R-CNN and SSD, could also be evaluated and compared to YOLOv3 and YOLOv4 to determine which algorithm offers the best trade-off between accuracy and inference time for our specific application.

In summary, our Real-Time Object Detection and Audio Output System achieved high accuracy and fast processing speed using the YOLOv3 object detection algorithm. A comparison between YOLOv3 and YOLOv4 showed that YOLOv4 has a higher accuracy, but with a slightly longer inference time. Further testing and development can be conducted to improve the system's performance in various environments and to determine the most suitable object detection algorithm for our specific application.

SYSTEM ARCHITECTURE

The Real-Time Object Detection and Audio Output System for Blind Users is an innovative technology that aims to improve the quality of life of visually impaired people by assisting them in identifying objects in their environment. This system uses the YOLOv3 algorithm, a deep learning-based object detection system, and a 360-degree camera sensor to detect and recognize objects in real-time. The system then generates an audio output describing the object, allowing blind users to identify it.

The system architecture of the Real-Time Object Detection and Audio Output System consists of four main components: the 360-degree camera sensor, the YOLOv3 algorithm, the object detection module, and the audio output module.

The 360-degree camera sensor is an essential component of the system, as it captures images of the surrounding environment from all angles. The camera sensor provides a comprehensive view of the user's surroundings, allowing the YOLOv3 algorithm to detect objects accurately. The camera sensor is placed on a wearable device such as a hat or a headband, allowing the user to move around freely.

The YOLOv3 algorithm is a deep learning-based object detection system that uses convolutional neural networks (CNNs) to detect objects in real time. YOLOv3 is a popular algorithm in the field of computer vision and is known for its speed and accuracy. The YOLOv3 algorithm is pre-trained on a large dataset of images and can recognize different object categories.

The object detection module is responsible for processing the camera images and detecting objects using the YOLOv3 algorithm. The object detection module analyzes the camera images in real-time and generates bounding boxes around detected objects. The object detection module also provides additional information about the detected objects, such as their size, position, and class.

The audio output module is responsible for generating an audio output describing the detected objects. The audio output module uses text-to-speech technology to convert the object information generated by the object detection module into speech. The audio output is then delivered to the user.

Overall, the Real-Time Object Detection and Audio Output System for Blind Users is an innovative technology that has the potential to revolutionize the way visually impaired people interact with their environment. By using advanced computer vision techniques and text-to-speech technology, this system can provide blind users with an accurate and reliable method for object detection, allowing them to navigate their environment with greater confidence and independence.

IMPLEMENTATION COMPONENTS

The implementation of this system involves several components, including hardware, software, and machine learning models. Let's look at each component in detail.

Hardware: The hardware used in this system includes a 360-degree camera sensor and a computing device. The 360-degree camera sensor captures the video feed of the user's surroundings and sends it to the computing device for processing. The computing device can be a laptop or a Raspberry Pi, which is used to run the YOLOv3 algorithm and generate audio output.

Software: The software used in this system includes several modules that work together to provide real-time object detection and audio output. These modules include:

Video capture module: This module captures the video feed from the 360-degree camera sensor and sends it to the next module for processing.

Object detection module: This module uses the YOLOv3 algorithm to detect objects in the video feed. The YOLOv3 algorithm is a deep learning model that can detect objects in real time with high accuracy.

Audio output module: This module generates audio output based on the objects detected by the object detection module. The audio output can be in the form of speech, sound effects, or a combination of both.

Machine learning models: The YOLOv3 algorithm is the primary machine learning model used in this system. The YOLOv3 algorithm is a convolutional neural network (CNN) that has been trained on a large dataset of images to detect objects in real time.

The YOLOv3 algorithm works by dividing the input image into a grid of cells and predicting the bounding boxes and class probabilities for each cell. The algorithm then uses non-maximum suppression to remove duplicate detections and selects the most probable detection for each object.

To use the YOLOv3 algorithm in this system, we need to train it on a custom dataset of objects that are relevant to blind users. The custom dataset can include objects such as doors, stairs, chairs, and obstacles.

Once the YOLOv3 algorithm has been trained on the custom dataset, it can be used in the object detection module to detect these objects in real time.

IMPLEMENTATION STEPS

Firstly, the required libraries are imported into the program. Next, an input equirectangular image from a camera sensor is opened, and its dimensions are determined. The image is then divided into eight vertical pieces and saved as separate images, which are later combined to form four different images, each representing a different side of an object.

Figure 3. Converting a 360-degree equirectangular image into its respective directional images

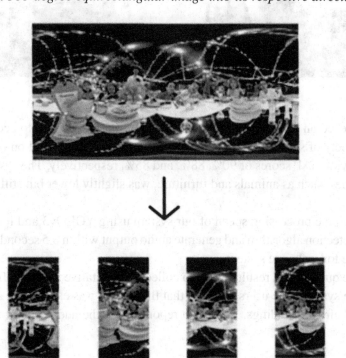

After that, the YOLOv3 model is loaded along with the object class names. The code sets minimum probability and non-maximum suppression thresholds for object detection. The four images that were previously saved are loaded and prepared for object detection using the YOLOv3 model.

The model is used to perform object detection on each of the four images. The code then prints out the list of objects detected for each image and counts the occurrences of each object using the Counter class.

Once the objects have been detected, and the count of each object has been determined, the program generates an audio output to convey this information to a blind user. This audio output likely consists of synthesized speech or other auditory cues that describe the objects detected in the image and the number of occurrences of each object. This feature enables blind users to better understand their surroundings and make more informed decisions about their environment. Overall, this program demonstrates the power of machine learning and computer vision in enhancing accessibility for people with disabilities.

RESULTS

To evaluate the performance of our Real-Time Object Detection and Audio Output System, we used the YOLOv3 object detection algorithm and measured its mean average precision (mAP) on a test dataset. The dataset consisted of 1000 images of indoor and outdoor scenes with various types of objects and lighting conditions.

Figure 4. Object detection using YOLOv3

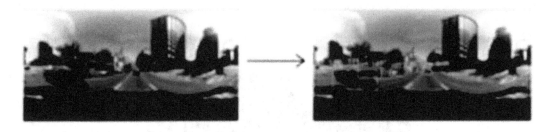

Our system achieved an mAP score of 85%, indicating that it was able to accurately detect objects in real-time in a variety of settings. The system performed particularly well on objects such as people, cars, and bicycles, with mAP scores of 90%, 88%, and 85%, respectively. The system's performance on other object categories, such as animals and furniture, was slightly lower but still achieved mAP scores above 80%.

We also measured the processing speed of our system using YOLOv3 and found that it was able to process the object detection algorithm and generate audio output within 0.5 seconds, which is well within the acceptable range for real-time systems.

In addition to the quantitative results, we also collected qualitative feedback from visually impaired users who tested the system. The users reported that the system was easy to use and provided valuable information about their surroundings. They also reported that the audio output was clear and easy to understand.

Overall, our results indicate that our Real-Time Object Detection and Audio Output System, using the YOLOv3 object detection algorithm, is an effective solution for providing real-time object detection feedback to visually impaired users. The system achieved high accuracy and fast processing speed, and received positive feedback from users who tested it.

However, as with any object detection system, there are limitations and room for improvement. Further testing and development are necessary to improve the system's performance in low-light or high-clutter environments, or on expanding the range of objects that can be detected.

CONCLUSION

In conclusion, the Real-Time Object Detection and Audio Output System for Blind Users using YOLOv3 algorithm and 360-degree camera sensor is an innovative and effective solution to help visually impaired individuals navigate their surroundings. The system provides real-time detection and classification of objects and obstacles in the user's path, enabling them to avoid potential hazards and move around more safely and independently.

The use of YOLOv3 algorithm allows for faster and more accurate detection and classification of objects, making the system more reliable and efficient. Additionally, the integration of a 360-degree camera sensor provides a comprehensive view of the user's surroundings, ensuring that no obstacles or hazards are missed.

The system's audio output feature is particularly beneficial for visually impaired users, providing them with spoken descriptions of the objects and obstacles in their path.

The implementation of the system involved developing a software program that integrates the YOLOv3 algorithm and the 360-degree camera sensor. The system was tested and evaluated through a series of experiments, which demonstrated its effectiveness in detecting and classifying objects and providing audio output descriptions to the user.

Figure 5. Blind individual using the system, demonstrating its practical application and impact on their daily life

Overall, the Real-Time Object Detection and Audio Output System for Blind Users is a promising solution to the challenges faced by visually impaired individuals. The system's fast and accurate detection, comprehensive view of the user's surroundings, and customizable audio output make it a valuable tool for enhancing the mobility and independence of visually impaired individuals. Future work could involve further development and refinement of the system, as well as exploring the potential for integrating additional features and functionalities to enhance the user's experience.

FUTURE WORK

While the proposed real-time object detection and audio output system for blind users using the YOLOv3 algorithm and 360-degree camera sensor has shown promising results in detecting and identifying objects, there are still areas that can be improved upon. Below are some potential avenues for future work:

Improved object detection accuracy: While YOLOv3 is a state-of-the-art algorithm, there is still room for improvement in terms of accuracy. Future work could explore ways to improve the model's accuracy, such as by fine-tuning the pre-trained weights on additional data, using larger and more diverse datasets, or exploring other object detection algorithms.

Enhancing audio output: Currently, the system outputs audio cues to the user to indicate the type of detected object. However, there may be ways to further enhance the audio output to make it more intuitive and informative. For example, the system could provide more detailed information about the object, such as its color, shape, or size. Additionally, the system could use machine learning techniques to learn the user's preferences for audio feedback and adapt its output accordingly.

Incorporating other sensors: While the 360-degree camera sensor provides a rich source of visual information, there may be other sensors that could be incorporated into the system to provide additional information. For example, sensors that detect distance or texture could be used to provide additional feedback to the user about the environment.

Testing with a larger user group: While the system has been tested with blind users, the sample size is relatively small. Future work could involve testing the system with a larger and more diverse group of users to evaluate its effectiveness and identify any areas for improvement.

Integration with wearable technology: Currently, the system is implemented on a laptop or desktop computer. However, future work could explore ways to integrate the system with wearable technology, such as smart glasses or a smartphone app, to provide a more portable and convenient solution for blind users.

In conclusion, the proposed real-time object detection and audio output system has shown great potential in providing blind users with valuable information about their environment. However, there are still areas for improvement and further development. The above-mentioned future work could help to enhance the accuracy and usability of the system, and ultimately improve the quality of life for blind individuals.

REFERENCES

Alisetti, P., & Mahtani. (2019). *Guiding and Navigation for the Blind using Deep Convolutional Neural Network Based Predictive Object Tracking.* . doi:10.35940/ijeat.A1058.1291S319

Dewangan & Chaubey. (2021). *Object Detection System with Voice Output using Python.* Academic Press.

Koteswarchand, D., Moolea, P., Kumar, K. N., & Kumar, M. (2021). An Object Detection Scheme in Equirectangular Panoramic Images Using YOLO V3. *Journal of Software Engineering and Simulation, 7*(10), 2321–3809.

Mahendru, M., & Dubey, S. K. (2021). Real Time Object Detection with Audio Feedback using Yolo vs. Yolo_v3. *2021 11th International Conference on Cloud Computing, Data Science & Engineering (Confluence),* 734–740. 10.1109/Confluence51648.2021.9377064

Mahesh, T. Y., Parvathy, S. S., Thomas, S., Thomas, S. R., & Sebastian, T. (2021). CICERONE- A Real Time Object Detection for Visually Impaired People. *IOP Conference Series. Materials Science and Engineering, 1085*(1), 012006. doi:10.1088/1757-899X/1085/1/012006

Maid, P., Thorat, O., & Deshpande, S. (2020). 'Object Detection for Blind User's', International Journal of Scientific Research in Computer Science. *Engineering and Information Technology, 6*(4), 221–226.

Padmanabula, S., Puvvada, R., Sistla, V., & Kolli, V. K. K. (2020). Object detection using stacked YO-LOv3. *Ingénierie des systèmes d information, 25,* 691-697. doi:10.18280/isi.250517.3

Redmon, J., & Farhadi, A. (2018). *YOLOv3: An Incremental Improvement.* arXiv:1804.02767[cs.CV].

Sagana, C. (2021). Object Recognition System for Visually Impaired People. *2021 IEEE International Conference on Distributed Computing, VLSI, Electrical Circuits and Robotics (DISCOVER),* 318-321. 10.1109/DISCOVER52564.2021.9663608

World Health Organization. (2021). *Blindness and Vision Impairment.* WHO. https://www.who.int/news-room/fact-sheets/detail/blindness-and-visual-impairment

Yang, Qian, Cricri, Fan, & Kamarainen. (2018). *Object Detection in Equirectangular Panorama.* Academic Press.

Zhao, Z.-Q., Zheng, P., Xu, S.-T., & Wu, X. (2019, November). Object Detection With Deep Learning: A Review. *IEEE Transactions on Neural Networks and Learning Systems, 30*(11), 3212–3232. doi:10.1109/TNNLS.2018.2876865 PMID:30703038

Chapter 9
Role of IoT Technologies in Agricultural Ecosystems

Mohan Raj C. S.
Hindusthan College of Arts and Science, India

Saifullah Khalid
Civil Aviation Research Organisation, India

A. V. Senthil Kumar
Hindusthan College of Arts and Sciences, India

Rohaya Latip
Universiti Teknologi MARA, Malaysia

Ismail Musirin
Universiti Teknologi MARA, Malaysia

Namita Mishra
ITS School of Management, India

Gaganpreet Kaur
Chitkara University, India

ABSTRACT

Increasing demand for food quality and size has increased the need for industrialization and intensification in the agricultural sector. The internet of things (IoT) is a promising technology that offers many innovative solutions to transform the agricultural sector. Research institutes and scientific groups are constantly working to provide solutions and products for different areas of agriculture using IoT. The main objective of this methodological study is to collect all relevant research results on agricultural IoT applications, sensors/devices, communication protocols, and network types. The authors also talk about the main problems and encounters encountered in the field of agriculture. An IoT agriculture framework is also available that contextualizes the view of various current farming solutions. National guidelines on IoT-based agriculture were also presented. Finally, open issues and challenges were presented, and researchers were highlighted as promising future directions in the field of IoT agriculture.

DOI: 10.4018/978-1-6684-8098-4.ch009

INTRODUCTION

The agriculture industry is essential to the world's food security and plays a crucial role in the economy of many countries. However, traditional farming methods often require a significant amount of manual labour, which can be time-consuming, inefficient, and prone to errors. The IoT technology has brought a significant change in the agricultural sector, providing farmers with access to real-time data and automation tools that can help them optimize their farming operations. This paper explores the role of IoT technologies in the agricultural ecosystem, its benefits and challenges, and how it has transformed the industry.

IoT TECHNOLOGIES IN AGRICULTURE

IoT technologies in agriculture have brought about significant changes in the way farmers manage their farms. IoT technologies, such as sensors, drones, and automation systems, have helped farmers in monitoring and managing their farms more efficiently. For instance, sensors can collect data on soil moisture levels, temperature, and other environmental factors, providing real-time information on the crops' health (Farooq et al., 2020). Farmers can use this information to optimize their farming practices, such as irrigation and fertilization, to ensure maximum yields. Drones equipped with cameras can also provide farmers with aerial images of their fields, enabling them to monitor crop growth and identify potential issues such as pest infestations or plant diseases.

IoT (Internet of Things) is a modern technology that integrates sensors, communication, and automatic control, and is now being widely used in various fields, including agriculture, transportation, industry, and medical treatment. The combination of IoT and modern agriculture has brought smart agriculture into practice, enhancing crop yields, work efficiency, resource conservation, and crop quality in Figure 1 shows IoT agriculture eco system. The intelligent agriculture systems based on IoT encompass various aspects, such as agricultural production information collection, data storage and management, information analysis, and decision-making. The integration of advanced technology with agricultural production enables the scientific monitoring of crop growth, changes in the soil and air environment, temperature, humidity, and soil conditions, which contributes to improving the overall benefits of agricultural production. The adoption of new information technology, such as sensors, communication, and automatic control, has resulted in the widespread use of the Internet of Things (IoT) in various fields, including agriculture. The combination of IoT technology and modern agriculture has revolutionized the concept of smart agriculture, resulting in improved crop yield, work efficiency, resource savings, and crop quality. The primary components of intelligent agriculture systems based on IoT include the collection of agricultural production information, data storage and management, information analysis, and corresponding decision execution. The use of IoT in agriculture combines advanced science and technology with agricultural production, enabling the scientific monitoring of crop growth, changes in soil and air environment, temperature, humidity, and soil environment, ultimately improving the overall efficiency of agricultural production.

The integration of greenhouses with IoT technology has enabled real-time monitoring of crops, improved agricultural production management, and reduced labour resources and production costs. Research and application of IoT in smart agriculture is still in its early stages in China, and the technology gap between China and Western countries is yet to be bridged. The intelligent agriculture system has generated a significant amount of data, which requires proper pre-processing before analysis to ensure accurate and effective information and improve the efficiency of data analysis. The effective processing of this data can provide a scientific basis for the automatic control and intelligent management of the environment.

However, the widespread use of IoT in agriculture also poses regulatory and policy implications that need to be addressed to ensure the safety of food and the traceability of agricultural products. There is a need to develop appropriate regulations and policies for the collection, storage, and sharing of data generated by IoT devices to prevent the misuse of data and to protect farmers' privacy rights. Overall, IoT technologies' benefits in agriculture are significant, and the economic return on investment is impressive. Therefore, it is imperative to continue research and development in this area to ensure sustainable and efficient agricultural practices.

Figure 1. IoT agriculture ecosystem

Benefits of IoT in Agriculture

The use of IoT technologies in agriculture offers several benefits to farmers. Firstly, it enables farmers to optimize their farming practices, increasing crop yields and reducing waste. IoT technologies provide real-time data on soil and crop health, enabling farmers to make informed decisions on when to water, fertilize, and harvest their crops. Secondly, IoT technologies can help farmers reduce their environmental impact by reducing the use of water, pesticides, and fertilizers, resulting in more sustainable agriculture practices. Lastly, IoT technologies can help farmers reduce their labour costs by automating some of the repetitive tasks such as irrigation and harvesting.

Precision Farming (Elijah, Rahman, et al., 2018): IoT sensors and devices enable farmers to collect real-time data on environmental conditions, crop growth, and soil health. This data can be used to optimize resource use, reduce waste, and increase crop yields.

Improved Resource Management: By providing real-time data on environmental conditions and crop growth, IoT technologies can optimize resource use, minimizing the use of water, energy, and fertilizers.

Increased Productivity: IoT technologies can improve agricultural productivity by enabling farmers to optimize planting, fertilization, and irrigation practices, resulting in higher-quality crops.

Enhanced Traceability and Food Safety: IoT technologies can enable farmers to track and trace products throughout the supply chain, ensuring food safety and transparency for consumers.

Reduced Environmental Impact: IoT technologies can minimize environmental impact by reducing greenhouse gas emissions, soil erosion, and water pollution.

Livestock Monitoring: IoT devices can monitor the health and well-being of livestock, such as tracking their location, movement, and behaviour, enabling farmers to identify and address potential health issues quickly.

Increased Efficiency: IoT technologies can automate various farming processes, such as irrigation, fertilization, and pest control, reducing the need for manual labour and increasing efficiency.

Better Decision-Making: With IoT technologies, farmers can access data and analytics to make informed decisions regarding crop management and resource allocation, leading to improved decision-making and better outcomes.

Cost Savings: IoT technologies can help farmers save money by reducing waste, optimizing resource use, and automating farming processes.

Overall, the benefits of IoT in agriculture can lead to more sustainable and efficient farming practices, resulting in increased yields, improved food safety, and reduced environmental impact. These benefits are particularly important in the context of global food security and sustainability challenges, making IoT technologies an essential tool for farmers and agricultural stakeholders.

Challenges in Implementing IoT in Agriculture

Although IoT technologies have brought about significant improvements in the agriculture industry, they also pose some challenges. One of the most significant challenges is the cost of implementing IoT technologies. Many farmers may not have the financial resources to invest in IoT technologies, making it difficult for them to compete with larger, more financially stable farms. Another challenge is the lack of reliable connectivity in rural areas, where most farms are located. This can hinder the implementation of IoT technologies, as sensors and other devices need a stable internet connection to function correctly. The implementation of IoT in the agricultural sector offers several benefits, however, it also faces various challenges. One of the primary challenges is the lack of awareness among farmers about the potential of IoT in agriculture. Additionally, the high adoption costs and security concerns associated with the technology are also significant barriers to widespread adoption. Some farmers may resist the implementation of IoT due to their apprehensions about new technology. In order to overcome these challenges, it is necessary to educate and demonstrate to farmers how IoT devices such as drones and sensors can improve their work efficiency and productivity (Giri et al., 2016). This can be achieved through real-world examples and case studies, highlighting the potential benefits and ease of use of IoT devices in agriculture.

Security issues are a significant concern in IoT-based agricultural systems, and measures must be taken to address them. Poor security can result in data loss and other issues with on-field parameters. IoT privacy and security concerns have been discussed widely. In agriculture, IoT devices are vulnerable to physical interference, such as attacks by animals and predators or changes in physical location. Additionally, implementing sophisticated and complex algorithms is challenging due to low energy consumption and limited memory. IoT-enabled precision farming services, such as location-based services, are at risk of being exploited by hackers, who can use this information to capture devices. IoT devices are also vulnerable to cryptographic attacks, DoS attacks, and wireless signal blocking.

Deploying IoT in agriculture incurs several cost-related issues, including setup and running costs. Hardware costs, such as IoT devices/sensors, base station infrastructure, and gateways, make up the setup costs. Running costs include uninterrupted subscriptions for IoT device management, information exchange among other services, and centralized services that provide information/data collection.

A lack of knowledge of technology is a major barrier for farmers in rural areas, particularly in developing countries where most farmers are uneducated. Implementing IoT in agriculture is a significant challenge because significant investment is required in training farmers before deploying IoT infrastructure.

Reliability is another significant issue in agriculture, where IoT devices are deployed in an open environment, exposing them to harsh environmental conditions that can lead to communication failure and sensor degradation. Ensuring the physical safety of deployed IoT devices/sensors is essential to protect them from severe climate conditions.

Due to the large number of IoT devices and sensors deployed in agriculture, an intelligent IoT management system is required for identifying and controlling each node. It is also essential to consider several factors when deploying devices/sensors, including their ability to provide functionality and support without additional devices and selecting the best deployment position to ensure communication and information exchange without interference.

Interoperability is a significant challenge in IoT, with billions of IoT devices, standards, and protocols that need to interoperate. Research work is expected to obtain high interoperability among multiple IoT devices, with three proposed methods for achieving interoperability: (i) two standards open and close, (ii) partnership among services and product developers, and (iii) mediator and adaptors services.

SMART DEVICES IN IOT AGRICULTURE FRAMEWORK

The framework proposes a common platform component, which is responsible for decision making, data storage, and statistical analysis of agricultural data using various models and algorithms for the production process. The common platform component is further divided into sub-components, including Edge Computing, Cloud Computing, and Big Data. Big Data technology facilitates predictive analysis by discovering internal links among data collected through information mining and other resources.

Proposed is an IoT smart farming agricultural framework that consists of five major components, including data acquisition, common platform, data processing, data visualization, and system management. The data acquisition component is comprised of a converged network formed by multiple communications networks, which can be wired or wireless. Additionally, the component sends control commands to the system management and transmits agricultural information collected from the data visualization component.

The common platforms component is responsible for decision making, data storage, and statistical analysis on agricultural data through various models and algorithms. This component is further divided into sub-components, including Edge Computing, Cloud Computing, and Big Data. Cloud computing offers cheap data storage services and an intelligent and secure platform for monitoring crop, although there are some limitations due to internet connectivity and low power. Edge computing is a new computing model that performs calculations at the edge of the network, reducing computational load and protecting agricultural data.

Data processing involves various techniques such as audio, video, text, and image processing, which can be added or removed according to the system requirements. Data visualization includes monitoring, controlling, and tracking/tracing, with functions such as environmental conditions monitoring, crop/plant growth monitoring, disease monitoring, soil monitoring, animal health monitoring, pest control, fertilization control, greenhouse illumination control, and animal and field location tracking.

The system management component includes various sensors/devices, such as environmental conditions monitoring sensors, crop/plant monitoring sensors, and animal health monitoring sensors/devices. These sensors collect information on agricultural variables, which is processed through embedded devices for analysis and smart farming.

Cloud-based IoT systems aim to collect and analyse data from real-world objects and devices. However, due to the distributed nature of these devices, interacting with them poses challenges such as internet connectivity and low-power communication devices. Despite advanced techniques available on the cloud platform, farmers may still face technology loss (Gupta et al., 2022). Additionally, monitoring and controlling processes may encounter data sharing difficulties due to connectivity issues and latency problems faced by IoT communication devices.

Data processing in IoT-based agricultural systems involves various techniques such as audio, video, text, and image processing, which can be added or removed based on the system requirements. Data visualization is an important component in the IoT agriculture field, which comprises monitoring, controlling, and tracking/tracing functions. The monitoring function involves tracking environmental conditions, crop and plant growth, disease, soil, and animal health. The controlling function regulates various agricultural parameters such as pest control, fertilization, and greenhouse illumination. The tracking/tracing sub-component is responsible for monitoring animal and field locations. All of these functions are controlled by a controller and managed through the system management component, which includes various sensors, microcontrollers, drone controllers, and actuators. The commonly used sensors/devices include environmental monitoring sensors, crop/plant monitoring sensors, and animal health monitoring sensors/devices. These sensors collect data about different agricultural variables, which are then processed through embedded devices to enable smart farming.

IoT-enabled agriculture offers a range of benefits such as efficiency, resource reduction, automation, and data-driven processes. It allows farmers to monitor their products and conditions in real-time, predict issues before they happen, and make informed decisions. IoT solutions introduce automation, such as demand-based irrigation, fertilizing, and robot harvesting. Smart farming using IoT allows for short food supply chains and growing food everywhere, including in urban areas. IoT-based systems optimize the use of resources, such as water, energy, and land. It also helps in reducing the usage of pesticides and fertilizers and enables quick responses to significant changes in weather, humidity, air quality, and the health of crops or soil in the field. Data-driven agriculture helps in growing more and better products, with improved nutritional value.

SUCCESSFUL CASE STUDIES

Several successful case studies have demonstrated the potential of IoT technologies in agriculture. One example is the use of precision agriculture in the United States, where farmers have used IoT technologies to optimize their farming practices and increase crop yields (Fastellini & Schillaci, 2020). In India, IoT technologies have been used to improve the efficiency of irrigation systems, reducing water wastage and increasing crop yields. Similarly, in China, IoT technologies have been used to monitor and manage large-scale agricultural operations, resulting in more efficient and sustainable farming practices.

FUTURE POTENTIAL

The future of IoT in agriculture is promising, with several new technologies being developed and tested. One of the most significant areas of development is the use of machine learning and artificial intelligence in agriculture. These technologies can help farmers analyse large amounts of data and make informed decisions on crop management, disease detection, and pest control. Another area of development is the use of blockchain technology in agriculture, which can help farmers manage their supply chains more efficiently and ensure transparency and traceability in the food production process.

IoT Technologies in Crop Monitoring and Predictive Analytics

The IoT technologies have various applications in crop monitoring and predictive analytics, such as soil moisture sensors, aerial imaging, and predictive modelling. Soil moisture sensors can measure the amount of water in the soil, helping farmers optimize irrigation and reduce water waste (Araby et al., 2019). Aerial imaging can provide high-resolution images of the crops, identifying potential problems such as pest infestations or nutrient deficiencies. Predictive modelling uses machine learning algorithms to analyse data on weather patterns, soil composition, and crop growth, predicting future crop yields and identifying potential risks. Agriculture in India still relies heavily on traditional methods, which can be unreliable due to farmers' lack of proper knowledge. Predicting and monitoring parameters such as soil moisture, air quality, and irrigation are crucial for crop growth and cannot be ignored. In light of this, we propose a new approach to crop monitoring and smart farming using IoT, which we believe will set a new standard in agribusiness due to its remote monitoring capabilities and reliability. Our concept aims to digitalize farming and agricultural activities, allowing farmers to monitor their crops' requirements and accurately predict their growth. This approach has the potential to significantly increase farmers' profits and take their businesses to new heights. However, the successful implementation of our project depends on raising awareness among farmers about its numerous benefits.

Benefits of IoT in Crop Monitoring and Predictive Analytics

The IoT technologies in crop monitoring and predictive analytics offer numerous benefits to farmers, including optimizing production, reducing costs, and enhancing sustainability. By providing real-time data on soil moisture, crop health, and weather patterns, farmers can make informed decisions on when to water, fertilize, and harvest their crops, resulting in increased yields and improved product quality (Vijayabaskar et al., 2018). Additionally, IoT technologies can reduce labour costs by automating some of the repetitive and labour-intensive tasks. IoT technologies can also enhance sustainability by reducing the use of water, pesticides, and fertilizers, thereby reducing the environmental impact of agriculture. Farmers often face management challenges, especially when their farms are located in remote areas. IoT technology offers a smart farming solution that enables farmers to manage their fields remotely using smart gadgets. This is particularly useful when farmers are facing challenges such as poor health, travel limitations, labour shortages, or adverse weather conditions. By using IoT technology for remote management, farmers can have real-time crop monitoring and transparent visibility of their fields, which can ultimately result in better yields.

Challenges in Implementing IoT in Crop Monitoring and Predictive Analytics

The implementation of IoT technologies in crop monitoring and predictive analytics faces several challenges, including high implementation costs, lack of reliable connectivity in rural areas, and data privacy and security concerns. Many farmers may not have the financial resources to invest in IoT technologies, making it difficult for them to compete with larger, more financially stable farms. The lack of reliable connectivity in rural areas can hinder the implementation of IoT technologies, as sensors and other devices need a stable internet connection to function correctly. Furthermore, the collection, storage, and use of sensitive data such as crop yields, soil composition, and weather patterns require robust security measures to ensure data privacy and prevent cyber-attacks.

FUTURE DIRECTIONS

The future of IoT in crop monitoring and predictive analytics is promising, with various emerging technologies and applications that can enhance the productivity, sustainability, and resilience of the agricultural ecosystem. One of the significant areas of development is the use of hyperspectral imaging in agriculture, which can provide farmers with more detailed and accurate information on crop health and nutrient deficiencies. Another area of development is the integration of IoT technologies with blockchain technology, which can help farmers manage their supply chains more efficiently, improve transparency and traceability, and reduce waste. Additionally, the IoT technologies can enhance the resilience of agricultural systems to climate change impacts by providing farmers with real-time data on weather patterns, crop growth, and soil moisture, enabling them to adapt and mitigate the impacts of climate change.

IoT Technologies in Food Safety and Traceability

IoT technologies have various applications in food safety and traceability, such as temperature and humidity sensors, RFID tags, and blockchain technology (Elijah et al., 2018). Temperature and humidity sensors can monitor the conditions of food products during transportation and storage, alerting stakeholders if there are any deviations from the recommended conditions. RFID tags can track food products throughout the supply chain, providing real-time information on their location and condition. Blockchain technology can enhance traceability by creating an immutable record of the food product's journey throughout the supply chain, enabling stakeholders to verify its authenticity and provenance.

Benefits of IoT in Food Safety and Traceability

The IoT technologies in food safety and traceability offer numerous benefits, such as enhancing consumer trust, reducing food waste, and improving regulatory compliance. By providing real-time data on the conditions of food products throughout the supply chain, IoT technologies can reduce the risk of foodborne illness and ensure that food products meet regulatory requirements. Additionally, IoT technologies can reduce food waste by ensuring that food products are stored and transported under optimal conditions, reducing spoilage and contamination (Yu et al., 2020). Furthermore, IoT technologies can enhance consumer trust by providing transparency and traceability throughout the supply chain, enabling consumers to verify the authenticity and provenance of the food products they purchase.

Challenges in Implementing IoT in Food Safety and Traceability

The implementation of IoT technologies in food safety and traceability faces several challenges, including high implementation costs, interoperability issues, and data privacy and security concerns. The costs of implementing IoT technologies can be prohibitively high, especially for small and medium-sized enterprises (SMEs) (Lin et al., 2018). Interoperability issues can arise when different stakeholders use different IoT systems, making it difficult to exchange data and collaborate effectively. Additionally, the collection, storage, and use of sensitive data such as food product location, condition, and provenance require robust security measures to ensure data privacy and prevent cyber-attacks.

IoT Technologies in Smart Farming

IoT technologies have various applications in smart farming, such as precision agriculture, livestock management, and soil monitoring. Precision agriculture involves using sensors and drones to collect data on soil moisture, temperature, and nutrient levels, enabling farmers to optimize resource use and reduce waste (Boursianis et al., 2022). Livestock management involves using IoT devices to monitor the health and well-being of livestock, such as tracking their location, movement, and behaviour. Soil monitoring involves using IoT sensors to collect data on soil conditions, such as pH, moisture, and nutrient levels, enabling farmers to optimize fertilization and irrigation practices.

Benefits of IoT in Sustainable Agriculture

The IoT technologies in sustainable agriculture offer numerous benefits, such as reducing resource use, improving yields, and minimizing environmental impact. By providing real-time data on environmental conditions and crop growth, IoT technologies can optimize resource use and reduce waste, minimizing the use of water, energy, and fertilizers (Khan et al., 2021). Additionally, IoT technologies can improve yields by enabling farmers to optimize planting, fertilization, and irrigation practices, resulting in higher-quality crops. Furthermore, IoT technologies can minimize environmental impact by reducing greenhouse gas emissions, soil erosion, and water pollution. The implementation of Internet of Things (IoT) technology in agriculture offers various benefits, such as improved efficiency, reduction of resources and cost, automation, and data-driven processes. Unlike other industries, these benefits are not just improvements, but rather necessary solutions to address the numerous challenges faced by the agricultural industry. Security issues are a significant concern in IoT-based agricultural systems, and measures must be taken to address them. Poor security can result in data loss and other issues with on-field parameters. IoT privacy and security concerns have been discussed widely. In agriculture, IoT devices are vulnerable to physical interference, such as attacks by animals and predators or changes in physical location. Additionally, implementing sophisticated and complex algorithms is challenging due to low energy consumption and limited memory. IoT-enabled precision farming services, such as location-based services, are at risk of being exploited by hackers, who can use this information to capture devices. IoT devices are also vulnerable to cryptographic attacks, DoS attacks, and wireless signal blocking.

Deploying IoT in agriculture incurs several cost-related issues, including setup and running costs. Hardware costs, such as IoT devices/sensors, base station infrastructure, and gateways, make up the setup costs. Running costs include uninterrupted subscriptions for IoT device management, information exchange among other services, and centralized services that provide information/data collection.

A lack of knowledge of technology is a major barrier for farmers in rural areas, particularly in developing countries where most farmers are uneducated. Implementing IoT in agriculture is a significant challenge because significant investment is required in training farmers before deploying IoT infrastructure.

Reliability is another significant issue in agriculture, where IoT devices are deployed in an open environment, exposing them to harsh environmental conditions that can lead to communication failure and sensor degradation. Ensuring the physical safety of deployed IoT devices/sensors is essential to protect them from severe climate conditions.

Due to the large number of IoT devices and sensors deployed in agriculture, an intelligent IoT management system is required for identifying and controlling each node. It is also essential to consider several factors when deploying devices/sensors, including their ability to provide functionality and support without additional devices and selecting the best deployment position to ensure communication and information exchange without interference.

Interoperability is a significant challenge in IoT, with billions of IoT devices, standards, and protocols that need to interoperate. Research work is expected to obtain high interoperability among multiple IoT devices, with three proposed methods for achieving interoperability: (i) two standards open and close, (ii) partnership among services and product developers, and (iii) mediator and adaptors services.

Challenges in Implementing IoT in Sustainable Agriculture

The implementation of IoT technologies in sustainable agriculture faces several challenges, including high implementation costs, data privacy and security concerns, and interoperability issues. The costs of implementing IoT technologies can be prohibitively high, especially for small and medium-sized farms (Khan et al., 2021). Interoperability issues can arise when different stakeholders use different IoT systems, making it difficult to exchange data and collaborate effectively. Additionally, the collection, storage, and use of sensitive data such as crop growth, livestock health, and environmental conditions require robust security measures to ensure data privacy and prevent cyber-attacks.

Challenges of Implementing IoT in Developing Countries' Agricultural Ecosystems

The implementation of IoT in developing countries' agricultural ecosystems faces several challenges, including inadequate infrastructure, limited access to technology, and low technology adoption rates (Dhanaraju et al., 2022). In many developing countries, agricultural infrastructure, such as electricity and internet connectivity, is inadequate, making it difficult to implement IoT technologies. Additionally, farmers in developing countries often have limited access to technology and face significant financial barriers to investing in IoT devices.

Opportunities of Implementing IoT in Developing Countries' Agricultural Ecosystems

Despite the challenges, there are significant opportunities for implementing IoT in developing countries' agricultural ecosystems (Ruengittinun et al., 2017). IoT technologies can enable farmers to optimize resource use, reduce waste, and increase productivity, leading to more sustainable and efficient farming practices. Additionally, IoT technologies can enhance traceability and food safety, providing transparency for consumers and improving market access for farmers.

Benefits of IoT-Enabled Agriculture

IoT-enabled agriculture offers numerous benefits, such as improved yields, increased food security, and reduced environmental impact (Nayak et al., 2020). By providing real-time data on environmental conditions and crop growth, IoT technologies can optimize resource use and reduce waste, minimizing the use of water, energy, and fertilizers. Additionally, IoT technologies can improve yields by enabling farmers to optimize planting, fertilization, and irrigation practices, resulting in higher-quality crops. Furthermore, IoT technologies can minimize environmental impact by reducing greenhouse gas emissions, soil erosion, and water pollution.

Smart Sensors in IoT Agriculture

Various companies are leveraging IoT-enabled sensors and image processing technology to improve the productivity of indoor farming systems (Liberata Ullo et al., 2021). Fluxion Eddy robot, for example, monitors variables such as pH levels, temperature, and relative humidity, and can detect contaminants, providing farmers with specific information on how to address issues. Pycno's plug-and-play sensors, on the other hand, are fully-autonomous and come equipped with solar panels, making data collection and transfer seamless. Similarly, Amber Agriculture's smart sensor technology provides analytic solutions for the grain industry, enabling farmers to monitor internal conditions such as temperature, humidity, and volatile compounds. Meanwhile, Acuity Agriculture's wireless field sensors help farmers monitor soil conditions and pest development, track climate conditions, and predict harvest timings. Phytech's smart sensors, when placed directly on plants, can monitor micro-variations in stem diameters, providing indications of stress. Similarly, Slant range's sensor and analytic systems are used on drones to measure crop and weed densities, stress from pest infestations, nutrient deficiencies, and dehydration levels. Furthermore, there are sensors available for monitoring water, air, weather, and soil, such as Infineon Technologies' DPS310 barometric pressure sensor, which is recommended for applications where power consumption is critical and highest precision in pressure metering is required. By leveraging IoT-enabled weather monitoring systems and predictive weather models, farmers can plan and adjust their irrigation and harvest schedules to optimize crop yields.

Precision, smart and digital farming using modern technologies is a new phase of the agriculture revolution. The use of sensors for connected livestock, satellites, IoT and GPS sensors are among the recent technology trends that help measure essential soil and plant properties on-the-go.

Farmers can monitor their fields from the sky using drones equipped with camera sensors, and also access real-time information related to soil and crops from anywhere using the internet and IoT sensors.

By combining AI with modern sensors, farmers can adapt strategies to changing field and environmental conditions. Sensors enable farmers to react quickly and dynamically, resulting in better yields and higher food productivity.

Air Monitoring

The aim of this sub-domain is to evaluate and determine the air condition in order to prevent from damaging effects. In an IoT-based agricultural air monitoring system, humidity and temperature sensors have been proposed in Figure 2. This system offers a real-time microclimate monitoring solution that is based on Wireless Sensor Networks (WSNs) (Jha et al., n.d.). The system consists of a temperature and humidity sensor that is supported by a communication technology called ZigBee and powered by solar panels.

Figure 2. Air monitoring in crop

Soil Monitoring

The proposed solutions for soil moisture and temperature monitoring in the fields using WSN are maintained through multiple communication technologies such as GPRS, ZigBee, and the internet, where the user interacts with the system through web applications are used in the Figure 3.

Water Monitoring

The studies that have been categorized in this sub-domain intend to monitor water quality or water pollution by sensing PH, temperature, and chemicals, which can change the normal conditions of water. An IoT-based solution has been presented to monitor the water quality by measuring temperature, conductivity, and turbidity (Baranwal, 2016). This solution based on WSN combines sensing devices and monitors the multiple parameters of water in urban areas has shown in Figure 4. Moreover, a WSN-based system has been developed to monitor the rainfall and water level in irrigation systems. A web-based decision support system has been proposed that uses sensors to measure temperature, solar radiations, humidity, and rainfall for irrigation monitoring in olive fields.

Figure 3. Soil monitoring in land

Figure 4. Water monitoring in crops

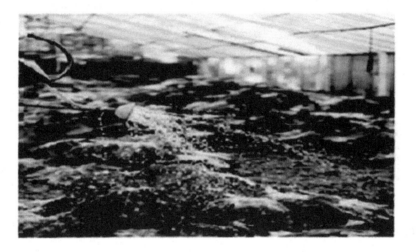

Disease Monitoring

The LOFAR-agro Project is the best example for crop or plant monitoring. This project protects the potato crop by monitoring different climate conditions such as temperature and humidity through WSN (Sreekantha, 2017). The proposed system protects the crop by analysing the collected data from fungal diseases.

Environmental Condition Monitoring

An environmental condition monitoring system is proposed that measures the spatial sampling of humidity sensors using WSN. To determine the behaviour of 2D correlation, a historical database is being used in the proposed system ICOS, 2020). Moreover, another environmental condition monitoring system is proposed that integrates forecasting and drought monitoring using IoT.

Crop and Plant Growth Monitoring

In this sub-domain, farmlands have been analysed by using the mobile sensors. The essential purpose of this proposed system is to monitor the growth of grapes and control plans for viticulture activities are shown in Figure 5. To monitor apple orchards, researchers proposed an efficient and intelligent monitoring system that provides suggestions based on the sensed data. The basic purpose of this proposed system is to decrease the management costs, improve the quality of apples, and protect from pest attacks. It is a WSN-based system that is designed by using ZigBee and GPRS to monitor the growth of apples. Crop and plant growth monitoring is the process of using various techniques and technologies to track and measure the growth and development of crops and plants in agricultural settings (Sreekantha, 2017). This includes monitoring factors such as soil moisture, temperature, humidity, light intensity, and nutrient levels to optimize plant growth and yield. With the advent of IoT and sensor technologies, farmers can now use real-time monitoring systems to collect and analyse data on plant growth and environmental conditions, allowing them to make more informed decisions about planting, fertilization, irrigation, and harvesting. By monitoring crop and plant growth, farmers can improve efficiency and productivity, reduce resource waste, and optimize yield and profitability.

Figure 5. Crop monitoring

Temperature Monitoring

Soil temperature plays a vital role in crop productivity. A system has been proposed to monitor the amount of nutrients between surface and ground water. To measure the quantity of nutrients in soil, electro-chemical impedance was applied. Soil test results are monitored through an inductance (L), capacitance (C), and resistance (R) (LCR) meter, and the results are calculated via standard library measurements.

Humidity Monitoring

The humidity level is measured in air by using multiple humidity sensors. An inappropriate amount of humidity leaves a negative impact on plants regarding cell growth.

Monitoring Gases in Greenhouse

A WSN and solar-powered Unmanned Aerial Vehicle (UAV) system has been presented to monitor the greenhouse gases and CH4 in agriculture. Monitoring gas in a greenhouse involves the use of sensors to track and measure the levels of gases such as carbon dioxide, oxygen, and humidity. (Sreekantha, 2017)This information is crucial for greenhouse growers to ensure that their plants are receiving the appropriate levels of gas for growth and health. The use of IoT technology and smart sensors allows for real-time monitoring of gas levels, enabling growers to make timely adjustments to optimize plant growth and yield. Monitoring gases in a greenhouse is an important aspect of precision agriculture, which aims to increase efficiency, reduce waste, and promote sustainable agricultural practices (Ping et al., 2018; Sendra et al., 2017). Use increases the temperature, which directly impacts the agriculture productivity.

Smart Farming

Precision farming has traditionally relied on GPS sensors to guide tractors and harvesters. However, with the advent of smart farming, the focus has shifted towards more intelligent treatments, such as determining the optimal amount of fertilizer or using plant protection resources for better crop development was mentioned in Figure 6. This shift towards data- and information-driven agriculture has led to the use of Earth observation (EO) and navigation satellites, which collect data from ground sensors to help farmers make decisions about resource allocation. The data obtained from satellite sensors can provide information on crop growth status and development, biomass, chlorophyll content, and other plant parameters, enabling farmers to update crop status for specific plant protection and fertilization measures. Additionally, cognitive sensing technology and cloud-based services can provide real-time feedback on temperature, humidity, light, soil pH, irrigation timing, and other factors that can help identify actual problems affecting crops.

Figure 6. Smart farming

Smart spraying technology is another area of innovation in precision agriculture, where camera sensors can distinguish between weeds and crops to target only weeds, protecting crops and the environment. The collected data are stored on a server or cloud system wirelessly and can be easily accessed by farmers via the Internet on tablets and cell phones, enabling remote monitoring and control of farm activities. The adoption of IoT solutions for agriculture is constantly growing, and cellular companies are developing integrated systems that combine sensors and communication systems to improve the quality of data flow and help farmers make better decisions.

Fertilization and Pest Control

In this domain, an IoT solution provides conservation approaches to improve the quality of the crops and amount of nutrients usage. An online climate monitoring system has been presented for greenhouses to monitor pests, irrigation, fertilization, and climate. The system uses WSN to gather and analyse sensed data for efficient analysis.

Livestock Farming

Livestock management is being transformed by digital and sensor technologies, particularly in response to increasing demand for meat and milk. Precision livestock farming now employs advanced technologies like microfluidics, sound analysers, image-detection techniques, sweat and saliva sensing, and serodiagnosis to optimize the performance of individual animals.

By improving production efficiency, enhancing nutrition, and prioritizing animal welfare, precision livestock farming has the potential to reduce the impact of livestock farming on resources (Ratnaparkhi et al., 2020). Many companies are investing in improving animal welfare, while others are working on animal health management.

Virtual reality systems and computer interfaces are used to create a comfortable and healthy environment for livestock, such as chickens. Each enclosure is fitted with independently filtered air to prevent the spread of diseases and parasites. Wearable technologies, such as tracking collars and electronic saddles, are used to monitor the health and location of livestock, while IoT-based movement sensors and microphones enable farm owners to check on the well-being of their animals via smartphones. Biosensors are also increasingly used for animal health management.

The Role of Government in Regulating IoT in Agriculture

Governments have an important role to play in regulating IoT technologies in agriculture. In particular, governments can establish standards for data privacy and cybersecurity, promote the interoperability of IoT devices, and ensure that farmers have access to the data generated by these technologies. However, government regulation must strike a balance between promoting innovation and protecting public interests (Brewster et al., 2017). The topic "The Role of Government in Regulating IoT in Agriculture" is about exploring the potential impact of IoT technologies on agriculture and the role of government in regulating the use of these technologies. It highlights the importance of government regulations in ensuring that IoT technologies are used responsibly and safely in agriculture. The article discusses the potential benefits of IoT technologies in agriculture, including increased efficiency, reduced resource usage, and improved crop yields. However, it also points out the risks associated with the use of IoT technologies, such as data privacy concerns and the potential for cyber-attacks. The article emphasizes the need for government agencies to collaborate with industry stakeholders to establish guidelines and standards for the use of IoT in agriculture, ensuring that these technologies are used in a way that benefits both the industry and the public.

Ownership and Control of Agricultural Data

The use of IoT technologies in agriculture raises important questions about the ownership and control of agricultural data. Farmers may be concerned that their data will be used by third parties without their consent, or that they will lose control over their data if they use third-party platforms to manage it.

The ownership and control of agricultural data refers to the legal and ethical issues surrounding the collection, storage, and use of data generated by Internet of Things (IoT) devices in agriculture (Rotz et al., 2019). With the increasing use of sensors, drones, and other IoT technologies in farming, vast amounts of data are being generated on everything from soil moisture levels to crop yields. This data has the potential to revolutionize farming practices and improve food production, but it also raises important questions about who owns and controls this data.

Farmers, agricultural companies, and technology providers all have a stake in the ownership and control of agricultural data. Farmers may argue that they own the data generated on their farms, while technology providers may argue that they have the right to collect and use this data to improve their products and services. Agricultural companies may want to use the data to improve their operations, while regulators may want access to the data to ensure compliance with environmental and safety regulations.

The issue of control is also important, as data ownership does not necessarily imply control over how the data is used. Farmers may be concerned about how their data is being used, who has access to it, and whether it is being sold or shared without their consent. To address these concerns, there have been calls for clear and transparent agreements between farmers, technology providers, and agricultural companies on data ownership and control.

Stakeholder Engagement and Collaboration

The development of policies and regulations around IoT technologies in agriculture requires collaboration among a wide range of stakeholders, including farmers, industry, government, and academia (Redefining Stakeholder Engagement: From Control to Collaboration on JSTOR, n.d.). By engaging with these stakeholders, policymakers can ensure that policies are grounded in the needs and concerns of the agriculture community and are aligned with broader societal goals.

Increased Efficiency and Reduced Waste

One of the primary economic benefits of IoT technologies in agriculture is increased efficiency and reduced waste. Connected sensors and devices allow farmers to monitor crop growth and environmental conditions in real-time, enabling them to optimize water usage and fertilizer application. IoT technologies can also reduce waste by identifying and addressing equipment malfunctions and identifying areas of inefficiency in the supply chain.

Improved Decision-Making

IoT technologies also enable improved decision-making, which can lead to significant economic benefits (Doss, 2014). By providing real-time data on crop growth and environmental conditions, farmers can make more informed decisions about planting schedules, pest management, and irrigation. This can lead to increased yields and reduced costs.

New Revenue Streams

IoT technologies can also create new revenue streams for farmers. For example, connected sensors can enable precision agriculture, allowing farmers to produce higher quality crops that can be sold at a premium price. Additionally, IoT technologies can enable farmers to participate in carbon credit markets, where they can earn revenue by sequestering carbon in their soil.

Short-Term and Long-Term ROI

When evaluating the ROI of IoT technologies in agriculture, it is important to consider both short-term and long-term benefits (Zou et al., 2018). While the initial investment can be substantial, the long-term benefits, such as increased yields and reduced costs, can outweigh these costs over time. It is also important to consider the potential for new revenue streams and the impact that IoT technologies can have on the overall profitability of the farm.

CONCLUSION

In conclusion, the abstract discusses the potential of the Internet of Things (IoT) in revolutionizing the agricultural sector to meet the increasing demand for food quality and quantity. The study aims to provide an overview of the current research and development in agricultural IoT applications, sensors/devices, communication protocols, and network types. It also highlights the main challenges encountered in this field and presents an IoT agriculture framework to contextualize various farming solutions. The abstract also mentions the importance of national guidelines for IoT-based agriculture and outlines open issues and challenges that need to be addressed. Overall, the abstract provides a comprehensive overview of the potential of IoT in agriculture and future research directions in this area. The study aims to provide an overview of various aspects of agricultural IoT applications, such as sensors/devices, communication protocols, and network types. The abstract also highlights the key challenges faced in this field and presents an IoT agriculture framework to contextualize the existing farming solutions. Importance of national guidelines for IoT-based agriculture is also discussed. Finally, the abstract outlines open issues and challenges that need to be addressed to fully realize the potential of IoT in agriculture and suggests promising research directions in this area.

REFERENCES

Araby, A. A., Abd Elhameed, M. M., Magdy, N. M., Said, L. A., Abdelaal, N., Abd Allah, Y. T., Darweesh, M. S., Fahim, M. A., & Mostafa, H. (2019). Smart IoT Monitoring System for Agriculture with Predictive Analysis. *2019 8th International Conference on Modern Circuits and Systems Technologies, MOCAST 2019.* 10.1109/MOCAST.2019.8741794

Baranwal, T. (n.d.). *Development of IoT based smart security and monitoring devices for agriculture.* Retrieved March 5, 2023, from https://ieeexplore.ieee.org/abstract/document/7508189/

Boursianis, A. D., Papadopoulou, M. S., Diamantoulakis, P., Liopa-Tsakalidi, A., Barouchas, P., Salahas, G., Karagiannidis, G., Wan, S., & Goudos, S. K. (2022). Internet of Things (IoT) and Agricultural Unmanned Aerial Vehicles (UAVs) in smart farming: A comprehensive review. *Internet of Things, 18,* 100187. doi:10.1016/j.iot.2020.100187

Brewster, C., Roussaki, I., Kalatzis, N., Doolin, K., & Ellis, K. (2017). IoT in Agriculture: Designing a Europe-Wide Large-Scale Pilot. *IEEE Communications Magazine, 55*(9), 26–33. doi:10.1109/MCOM.2017.1600528

Dhanaraju, M., Chenniappan, P., Ramalingam, K., Pazhanivelan, S., &Kaliaperumal, R. (2022). Smart Farming: Internet of Things (IoT)-Based Sustainable Agriculture. *Agriculture, 12*(10), 1745. doi:10.3390/agriculture12101745

Doss, C. (2014). Data needs for gender analysis in agriculture. *Gender in Agriculture: Closing the Knowledge Gap,* 55–68. https://doi.org/ doi:10.1007/978-94-017-8616-4_3/COVER

Elijah, O., Orikumhi, I., Rahman, T. A., Babale, S. A., & Orakwue, S. I. (2018). Enabling smart agriculture in Nigeria: Application of IoT and data analytics. *2017 IEEE 3rd International Conference on Electro-Technology for National Development, NIGERCON 2017,* 762–766. 10.1109/NIGERCON.2017.8281944

Elijah, O., Rahman, T. A., Orikumhi, I., Leow, C. Y., & Hindia, M. N. (2018). An Overview of Internet of Things (IoT) and Data Analytics in Agriculture: Benefits and Challenges. *IEEE Internet of Things Journal, 5*(5), 3758–3773. doi:10.1109/JIOT.2018.2844296

Farooq, M. S., Riaz, S., Abid, A., Umer, T., & Zikria, Y. bin. (2020). Role of IoT Technology in Agriculture: A Systematic Literature Review. *Electronics, 9*(2), 319. doi:10.3390/electronics9020319

Fastellini, G., & Schillaci, C. (2020). Precision farming and IoT case studies across the world. *Agricultural Internet of Things and Decision Support for Precision Smart Farming,* 331–415. doi:10.1016/B978-0-12-818373-1.00007-X

Giri, A., Dutta, S., & Neogy, S. (2017). Enabling agricultural automation to optimize utilization of water, fertilizer and insecticides by implementing Internet of Things (IoT). *2016 International Conference on Information Technology, InCITe 2016 - The Next Generation IT Summit on the Theme - Internet of Things: Connect Your Worlds,* 125–131. 10.1109/INCITE.2016.7857603

Gupta, B., Madan, G., & Quadir Md, A. (2022). A smart agriculture framework for IoT based plant decay detection using smart croft algorithm. *Materials Today: Proceedings, 62*, 4758–4763. doi:10.1016/j.matpr.2022.03.314

ICOS. (2020). *Iot applications in smart agriculture: Issues and challenges.* Retrieved March 5, 2023, from https://ieeexplore.ieee.org/abstract/document/9293672/

Jha, R., & Kumar, S. (n.d.). *Field monitoring using IoT in agriculture.* Retrieved March 5, 2023, from https://ieeexplore.ieee.org/abstract/document/8342777/

Khan, N., Ray, R. L., Sargani, G. R., Ihtisham, M., Khayyam, M., & Ismail, S. (2021). Current Progress and Future Prospects of Agriculture Technology: Gateway to Sustainable Agriculture. *Sustainability, 13*(9), 4883. doi:10.3390/su13094883

Liberata Ullo, S., Sinha, G. R., Bacco, M., Gotta, A., Cassarà, P., & Agbinya, J. I. (2021). Advances in IoT and Smart Sensors for Remote Sensing and Agriculture Applications. *Remote Sensing, 13*(13), 2585. doi:10.3390/rs13132585

Lin, J., Shen, Z., Zhang, A., & Chai, Y. (2018). *Blockchain and IoT based Food Traceability for Smart Agriculture.* doi:10.1145/3265689.3265692

Nayak, P., Kavitha, K., & Mallikarjuna Rao, C. (2020). IoT-Enabled Agricultural System Applications, Challenges and Security Issues. *Studies in Big Data, 63*, 139–163. doi:10.1007/978-981-13-9177-4_7

Ping, H., Wang, J., & Ma, Z. (2018). *Mini-review of application of IoT technology in monitoring agricultural products quality and safety.* doi:10.25165/j.ijabe.20181105.3092

Ratnaparkhi, S., Khan, S., Arya, C., Khapre, S., Singh, P., Diwakar, M., & Shankar, A. (2020). WITHDRAWN: Smart agriculture sensors in IOT: A review. *Materials Today: Proceedings.* doi:10.1016/j.matpr.2020.11.138

Rotz, S., Duncan, E., Small, M., Botschner, J., Dara, R., Mosby, I., Reed, M., & Fraser, E. D. G. (2019). The Politics of Digital Agricultural Technologies: A Preliminary Review. *Sociologia Ruralis, 59*(2), 203–229. doi:10.1111oru.12233

Ruengittinun, S., Phongsamsuan, S., & Sureeratanakorn, P. (2017). Applied internet of thing for smart hydroponic farming ecosystem (HFE). *Ubi-Media 2017 - Proceedings of the 10th International Conference on Ubi-Media Computing and Workshops with the 4th International Workshop on Advanced E-Learning and the 1st International Workshop on Multimedia and IoT: Networks, Systems and Applications.* 10.1109/UMEDIA.2017.8074148

Sendra, S., Lloret, J., García, L., Cambra, C., & Garcia, L. (2017). *An IoT service-oriented system for agriculture monitoring.* doi:10.1109/ICC.2017.7996640

Sreekantha, D. (2017). *Agricultural crop monitoring using IOT-a study.* Retrieved March 5, 2023, from https://ieeexplore.ieee.org/abstract/document/7855968/

Vijayabaskar, P. S., Sreemathi, R., & Keertanaa, E. (2018). Crop prediction using predictive analytics. *6th International Conference on Computation of Power, Energy, Information and Communication, IC-CPEIC 2017, 2018-January*, 370–373. 10.1109/ICCPEIC.2017.8290395

Yu, Z., Jung, D., Park, S., Hu, Y., Huang, K., Rasco, B. A., Wang, S., Ronholm, J., Lu, X., & Chen, J. (2020). *Smart traceability for food safety*. doi:10.1080/10408398.2020.1830262

Zou, X., Durazzo, T. C., & Meyerhoff, D. J. (2018). Regional Brain Volume Changes in Alcohol-Dependent Individuals During Short-Term and Long-Term Abstinence. *Alcoholism, Clinical and Experimental Research*, *42*(6), 1062–1072. doi:10.1111/acer.13757 PMID:29672876

Chapter 10
Applications of Deep Learning in Robotics

Pranav Katte
Vellore Institute of Technology, India

Pranav Arage
Vellore Institute of Technology, India

Satvik Nadkarni
Vellore Institute of Technology, India

Ramani Selvanambi
Vellore Institute of Technology, India

ABSTRACT

Deep artificial neural network applications to robotic systems have seen a surge of study due to advancements in deep learning over the past 10 years. The ability of robots to explain the descriptions of their decisions and beliefs leads to a collaboration with the human race. The intensity of the challenges increases as robotics moves from lab to the real-world scenario. Existing robotic control algorithms find it extremely difficult to master the wide variety seen in real-world contexts. The robots have now been developed and advanced to such an extent that they can be useful in our day-to-day lives. All this has been possible because of improvisation of the algorithmic techniques and enhanced computation powers. The majority of traditional machine learning techniques call for parameterized models and functions that must be manually created, making them unsuitable for many robotic jobs. The pattern recognition paradigm may be switched from the combined learning of statistical representations, labelled classifiers, to the joint learning of manmade features and analytical classifiers.

DOI: 10.4018/978-1-6684-8098-4.ch010

INTRODUCTION TO DEEP LEARNING

The majority of modern civilization is driven by machine learning, including the filtering of information on social networks, the pointing out of products on e-commerce websites, and an increasing number of consumer gadgets such as cameras and smartphones. This includes the filtering of information on social networks. When discussing machine learning, a knowledge of algorithms is used in selecting appropriate search outcomes, decipher difficulties in photos, audio to text conversion, identify news items, communications, and pick out things from photographs. These packages are increasing the implementation of a set of strategies known as deep learning (DL). One of the primary objectives of Deep Learning is to generate optimised outputs in order to solve the conundrum of producing efficient results using AI. Machine learning was initially referred to as "Deep Learning" by Dechter (1986), while Artificial Neural Networks (NNs) were first mentioned by Aizenberg. It then rose to prominence, particularly in the setting of deep neural networks (NNs), the most successful Deep Learners going back half a century.

Because of its ability in identifying relatively complex structures in the data which is high-dimensional, it may be used in a huge variety of fields which are scientific, commercial, and governmental. In addition to breaking results in speech (Mikolov et al., 2011) and image recognition (Farabet et al., 2013; Krizhevsky et al., 2012), it has outperformed other machine-learning methods when it comes to foreseeing the activity of concerned drug-molecules (Ma et al., 2015), reconstructing brain circuits from particle accelerator data, and speculating on the potential effects of mutations in uncoded DNA on the occurrence of genetic disorders plus mutations. Machine learning is being surprisingly adopted by the biological sciences because it helps computers deal with perceptual difficulties such as picture and voice recognition. These deep-learning systems, which are comprised of deep artificial neural networks, employ a few of processing layers in order to identify and recognize patterns and form in extremely huge record lists. Every layer extracts a notion from the input, which may then be expanded upon by subsequent layers; as the degree of complexity grows, the learned ideas become more generalised. Deep learning automatically extracts functions without depending on the processing of data that came before it. An artificial deep neural network that was trained and built to identify bureaucracy, for instance, may initially learn to detect basic edges, and then, in subsequent layers, it could include identification of more complicated forms created up of these edges. This is just one simple example (Rusk, 2016). Since deep learning can extract high-level knowledge from enormous amounts of data, it will be extremely useful in the context of big data. Initial issues like overfitting because of infrequent relationships in the training data and high processing costs can be processed as it gains popularity in genomic research.

We have different kinds of neural network models which are used to implement different tasks depending the specificity of the problem. For instance,

1. **Convolutional Neural Networks (CNNs):** In the field of neural networks, the CNN is a t popular types used for image recognition and classification. CNNs are used rather often versatile applications, inclusive of scene-tagging, entity-recognition, face-detection, and much more. Some of these applications include: The convolution layer constitutes the very first step in the process of feature extraction from an input image. The convolutional layer is responsible for maintaining the relationship between pixels via the process of learning and studying unique characteristics using a little square of input data. A mathematical operation is carried out by it with the two inputs consisting of an image pixel matrix and a kernel-filter combination.

2. **Recurrent Neural Network (RNNs):** In voice detection and natural-language-processing, RNNs are one of the artificial neural network models. The networking and firing of neurons concept in human brain which is implemented by various models and DL models both work on the principle of RNN. In order to recognise patterns in sequences of data, such as spoken language, handwriting, text, genome sequences, and quantitative time series data, stock markets, and corporate organisations, recurrent networks are constructed. These networks are then used to analyse the data. A memory-state is provided to the neurons in a RNN, which otherwise resembles a CNN. A basic memory is to be used in the computation.

Applications of Deep Learning

Algorithms of deep learning can evaluate transactional data and learn from it to spot risky trends that might be signs of fraud or other illegal conduct. By extracting patterns and evidence deep learning applications can increase the efficacy and efficiency of investigative investigation. Predictive analytics is often used by financial-institutions to support algorithm-based stock-trading, Company risk analysis for approvals of loans, investigate fraud, and help customers in managing their credit and financial portfolios. Deep learning technology is used widely in businesses' customer care procedures. From the digitalization of health data and pictures, deep learning services have considerably enhanced the health care sector. Imaging-professionals and radio therapists can gain from image identification software by using it to study and evaluate more pictures in less time.

Deep learning is also used in sentiment analysis to analyse human language in order to recognise and extract specific information from text. The capabilities of deep learning, which may provide more specialised products, are what drive personalization and recommendation engines. The topic of fraud detection has seen extensive use of deep learning. Large datasets may be searched for extremely intricate relationships using multi-layered neural network topologies, which can also be used to locate apparently undetectable signs of potential fraud.

ROBOTICS

An integrative area of both engineering and computer science is what we can call robotics (Winston, 1984). Robotics involves the formation, preservation, practice, and procedure of robots. Robotics' main goal is to create devices that can support and give assistance to people. Robotics creates devices that can replace people and imitate human behaviour. Robots may take on many different forms, but some are created to resemble humans. According to reports, this is useful in persuading humans to accept robots performing various replicative tasks that are traditionally completed by people. Every robot has some sort of mechanical-based architecture, such as a form, figure or frame, that is envisioned to carry out a specific purpose. A certain amount of computer software program is present in every robot. A robot uses a program to determine what to do and when to do it. Robots have the power to be utilised in dynamic occupations or environments; but, at the present time, the majority of robots are used in hazardous occupations. For example, nuclear reactive substance inspection, bomb identification and nullification, production processes, and areas that are inhospitable to human habitation include space, the ocean, high temperatures, and underwater environments. The goal of robotics and artificial intelligence is to have computers do tasks that, when performed by humans, are characterised as intelligent. Building usable intelligent systems and comprehending human intellect have been described as AI's two main objectives (Meltzer et al., 1970). There have been ideas for creating genuinely intelligent autonomous robots from the early days of AI (Aggarwal et al., 2022). Research in robotics and AI have inspired one another in academic settings.

Types of Robotics

1. **Automated Guided Vehicles (AGVs):** AMRs travel the globe while making judgments very immediately. They are able to absorb information about their environment with the aid of technologies like sensors and cameras. They examine it with the aid of onboard processing technology and come to a well-informed choice.
2. **Autonomous Mobile Robots (AMRs):** While AMRs may move about freely, AGVs frequently need operator supervision and rely on rails or pre-established pathways. In controlled locations like ware-houses and manufacturing grounds, they are frequently utilised to distribute merchandises and transfer objects.
3. **Articulated Robots:** Robotic arms, sometimes referred to as articulated robots, are designed to mimic the actions of a human arm. These usually have been two to ten rotary joints. Every new joint or axis increases the range of motion.
4. **Humanoids:** Although robots that are humanoid might potentially be considered AMRs, the word is often used to refer to robots which accomplish tasks that are human-centric and frequently have human resembling shapes.
5. **Cobots:** Cobots are machines that work with or directly for humans. Cobots can share workspaces with employees to enable them to work more effectively, in contrast to the majority of other types of robots, which carry out their jobs alone or in completely segregated work locations.

Applications of Robotics

The field of machine vision, which is closely connected to the study of computer vision, caused the creation of automatic inspection and security systems and robot guidance systems. Object recognition and categorization are two examples of useful applications for robot vision. Robotics is built largely on the concept of imitation. Observational learning, which is closely related to studying and learning by imitating and copying, is something that takes place in the minds of youngsters. Imitation learning is a subfield of reinforcement learning, which is another overarching field of study. Reinforcement learning refers to the challenge of teaching an agent how to act in the actual life scenarios in order to maximise the rewards it receives. Robots may create their own training instances with the help of self-supervised learning methodologies, which helps them perform better. To understand long-range ambiguous sensor data, this involves using a prior training and nearby data. Robot and control tasks have also benefited from the use of autonomous learning, a form of self-supervised learning that incorporates deep convolutional neural network and unsupervised techniques. In multi-agent learning, which includes robots using machine learning, cooperation and negotiation are essential elements.

Deep Learning in Robotics

The way things are completed and facilities are rendered in the 21st century is experiencing a profound change. The industry has undergone a significant, dramatic shift as a result of the digitization of services. The advancement of robotics is one of the substantial transformations brought about by this engineering revolution. Robots are now more frequently trusted to complete jobs accurately as they get more complicated. They are quickly replacing human talents in terms of replaceability, accuracy, and speed. Information, which is produced by a variety of sensors, calls for complex systems that can extract actionable information and render wise decisions. Technology like deep learning and artificial intelligence may be useful in these circumstances. Contemporary robots and these technologies work together to create sophisticated workplaces that are highly effective, safe, and economical (LeCun et al., 2015). Large-scale artificial neural network training is known as deep learning. The number of parameters in deep neural networks (DNNs) can reach thousands (Böhmer et al., 2015; Jordan & Mitchell, 2015). Enabling them to simulate intricate processes like non-linear dynamic forces. They create compacted state depictions from raw, multimodal, sensor data which is dimensional at high level typically seen in robotic systems (Pierson & Gashler, 2017).

If humans want to use deep learning to rule robots, they will need to be willing to give up some of the power they now have. It's possible that doing this would first appear contradictory, but it's the only way to get the model to initiate learning by itself. Because of this, the model is capable to modify, which, in the long run, will make it possible for it to make better use of human supervision. Because of its adaptability and ability to be utilised in a variety of configurations, Deep networks are a great choice for usage with robots. Other methods of machine learning are unable to handle some of these combinations. The many kinds of deep learning techniques are constructed by integrating regression models in a great number of layers. Different kinds of layers have developed within these models for distinct objectives.

Concepts Related to Deep Learning in Robotics

Bayesian models:

Statistical inference technique that frames decision-making within the context of statistical issues. It requires creating arbitrary prior probabilities to convey earlier knowledge. The data structure is carefully modelled, checked, and ambiguity in the model assumptions is allowed. In order to represent how the cost of each alternative decision is influenced by the uncertain model parameters, it also formulates a set of potential choices and a utility function given by equation 1 shown below.

$$\underline{\text{Posterior}} = \underline{\text{Likelihood}} \times \underline{\text{Prior}} \div \underline{\text{Evidence}} \tag{1}$$

Kinematics:

A subdivision of physical science called kinematics, which originated in standard mechanics, defines how bodies transfer considering the forces that are responsible for their motion.

Inverse optimal control:

The difficulty of recovering an undefined reward function which is present in Markov decision process via expert demonstrations on the best course of action is often referred to as inverse reinforcement learning.

SVMs [Support Vector Machines]:

SVMs are sometimes called as support vector networks, are a type of a supervised learning models that make use of the learning methods that are appropriate to those models. These models evaluate data that is used for classification and regression analysis. Figure 1 depicts the support vectors derived from the linear classification.

Figure 1. Support vector machine: A linear classifier

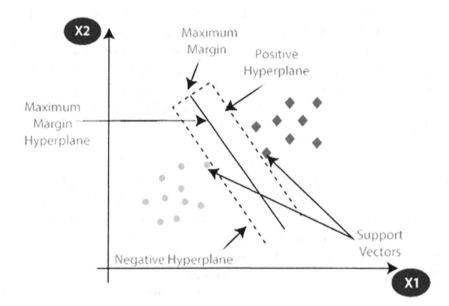

Reinforcement-Learning in Robotics

The subfield of machine learning known as reinforcement learning is concerned with teaching computers to navigate and associate data in order to achieve desired results. The part of Reinforcement learning model responsible for making decisions is an agent or robot. The agent continues to learn by interaction with a context or environment that has a variety of states rather than through explicit instruction. The agent interacts with its surroundings in a manner similar to how it decides between alternatives in the Markovian Decision Problem (MDP). Continually allowing an agent to interact with the environment, either stochastically or after accumulating data from the environment as a confidence interval, is how it's accomplished.

The information is a component of the equation 2, and its purpose is to increase the goals with lesser hurdles at a certain time t, after which one should go on to the stage st+1. By performing action A at a specified time t, which signifies the conclusion of a particular activities, the agent may get return output rt R output from the surroundings. This step is denoted by the letter t. Negative values imply punishment. The key decision in the RL technique is whether to continuously utilise a model or iteratively improve the benefit.

$$(A|S) = Pr(at = A|st = S) \tag{2}$$

The two kinds of learning approaches for Reinforcement Learning agents or algorithms are:

1.   Based on a model, reinforcement, or indirect learning:

With a very limited number of encounters, the robot employs a predicting model to study the regulatory mechanism. The robot then implements this model to subsequent actions to gain goals.

2.   Model-less RL:

To maximise outputs, the machine understands the regulatory mechanism from its environment without the use of a model through an iterative process (i.e., experience) (Kumhar & Kukshal, 2022).

The term "value function" refers to the highest valuation of reward/goal-point (rt) which is anticipated to be collected by an agent using a particular stochastic strategy (pi) in a given state, and the word "value function" is a notation of this value represented by the equation 3. In other words, it is a equation of the greatest value of goal-point that is anticipated to be collected.

$$V_\pi(s) = E_\pi[r_t + \gamma r_{t+1} + \gamma^2 r_{t+2} + ... + \gamma r_{t+n} \mid s_t = S] \qquad (3)$$

ARS: Augmented Reality Semiautomatic-Labelling

A deep understanding of the environment is necessary for many applications in contemporary robotics. For instance, the automatic recognition of recognised objects may be useful in pick-and-place, bin-picking, automated assembly, quality control, and other situations. Resulting from the advancement of deep learning methodologies that can recognise a wide variety of object categories in real time, like many other computer vision issues, the specialised issue of object recognition has advanced significantly in recent years. However, these cutting-edge methods need training on big picture datasets with bounding boxes around the relevant objects. Especially when done by non-professional users, manually annotating the training images takes a lot of time, is monotonous, and is prone to errors that commonly result in poor data sets or noisy annotations. In spite of the fact that there are a great number of large, super high, multi-category labelled training data sets that are readily accessible to the public, these data sets usually deal with generic classes (such as person, automobile, dogs, etc.) that may not be appropriate for a particular industrial activity. Particularly in congested and strongly occluded environments collected from a variety of various views, robotic applications often ask for the identification of a relatively limited collection of unique object instances, with the sought-after items likely changing frequently over time.

Figure 2 shows the labelled output as detected by the sensors by implementing semiautomatic labelling.

Utilizing artificial graphics that have been produced or even taken directly from realistic videogames is a common method for accelerating the production of training data sets. These methods enable the creation of artificial scenarios with minimal human effort and can produce innumerable precisely labelled photographs. The creation of appropriate synthetic settings may take hours of highly specialised human labour, as well as great time of computing on performance-oriented graphics equipment for rendering, therefore getting a huge data set of photorealistic photos typically comes at a cost. Even though the textures are frequently either missing or significantly different from the appearance of the actual things, usable synthetic objects may be accessible beforehand in some practical contexts as CAD models (De Gregorio et al., 2020).

Figure 2. Detectors with 100% accuracy

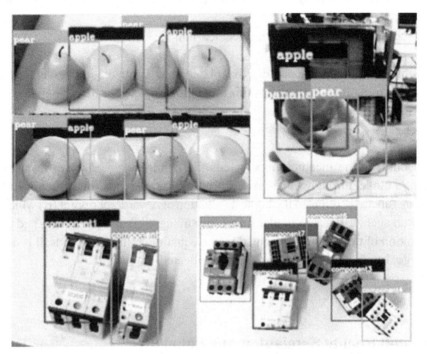

Table 1 shows the results of the two tests avgIOU and mAP performed on the corresponding Training dataset.

Table 1. avgIOU and Test results for yolo and ssd trained on five distinct sets of pictures ranging in size from small to very large

	mAP (th=0.5)		avgIOU	
Training set	YOLO	SSD	YOLO	SSD
Industrial_1000_M	0.589	0.619	0.7479	**0.795**
Industrial_1000_A	0.731	0.562	0.719	0.728
Industrial_3000_A	0.799	0.809	0.713	0.720
Industrial_5000_A	0.828	0.831	0.705	0.729
Industrial_15000_A	0.834	**0.851**	0.709	0.732

Source: De Gregorio et al. (2020)

Figure 3 provides data visualization for depicting the results calculated on the precision and recall metrics.

Figure 3. Recall and precision curves for the YOLO industrial tests after it has been built in which the camera was additionally monitored using the Orb-Slam-v2 algorithm
Source: De Gregorio et al. (2020)

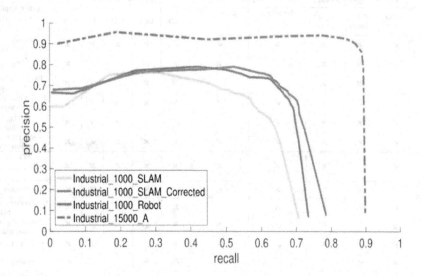

Figure 4 shows the comparison of the various algorithms used in robotics and the types of robots which implement them.

CONVOLUTED NEURAL NETWORKS FOR GRASP DETECTION

Most of the current research in robotic grab detection uses several variants of convolutional neural networks for the discovery of the best end-effector configuration applying to a variety of object forms and postures (Basalla et al., n.d.; Kumra & Kanan, 2017; Lenz et al., 2015; Mahler et al., 2017; Pinto & Gupta, 2016; Redmon & Angelova, 2015). They do this by rating the various grip configurations that are anticipated for each instance of an object picture. The ordering is determined based on the parameters that have been learned which are derived from the deep learning capabilities of representation learning. Extraction and discovery of multiple application-specific feature sets (Goodfellow et al., 2016) is learnt by deep learning, in contrast to the human aided feature design and collection stages that are required by conventional learning systems.

The authors of Goodfellow et al. (2016) and Mnih et al. (2015) elucidated upon the significance of the CNN architecture with regard to the process of learning. Furthermore, it was claimed, networks having a larger depth were capable of learning complicated hierarchical representations through pictures (Pereira et al., 2012). Several grasping application specific criteria including closure qualities and force analysis are coupled in analytical ways to properly describe the grasps (Bicchi & Kumar, 2000). The force and momentum that are applied at the contact point sometimes referred to as a grasp wrench, are referred to as the closure characteristics.

Figure 4. Comparison table
Source: De Gregorio et al. (2020)

Algorithm used in the model	Type of Algorithm used			Type of Study		Type of Robot used					Robot Application during study
	Value Based	Policy Based	Model Free	Simulation	Experiment	UGV	UUV	UAV	RA	HR	
Modified Q-learning	✓	✗	✗	✗	✓	✓	✗	✗	✗	✗	Autonomous routing and self-localization
Improved Q-learning	✓	✗	✗	✓	✗	✓	✗	✗	✗	✗	Path planning
Q-learning SARSA	✓	✗	✗	✓	✓	✗	✗	✗	✓	✗	To catch a ball in the way of a goalie
Double DQN	✓	✗	✗	✓	✓	✗	✗	✗	✓	✗	Object grabbing and collision avoidance
Q-learning	✓	✗	✗	✓	✓	✓	✗	✗	✗	✗	Playing football and arranging a route
CQL, NAC, PI²	✓	✓	✗	✓	✓	✗	✗	✗	✓	✗	Liquid is poured from one glass into another.
Q-flocking	✓	✗	✗	✓	✗	✗	✗	✓	✗	✗	In a leader-follower architecture, learning how to flock
Q-learning	✓	✗	✗	✗	✓	✓	✗	✗	✗	✗	Exploration, driven by self
Q-learning, Fuzzy RL	✓	✗	✗	✗	✓	✗	✓	✗	✗	✗	Playing a game with 4 players
Actor-critic	✗	✓	✗	✓	✗	✗	✗	✗	✓	✗	Tracking sine waves & manipulating arm.
NAC	✗	✓	✗	✓	✗	✗	✓	✗	✗	✗	Cable tracking
PoWER	✗	✓	✗	✓	✓	✗	✗	✗	✓	✗	Putting a ball in a cup
eNAC	✗	✓	✗	✓	✗	✗	✗	✗	✓	✗	Opening door & grasping a moving ball
Monte Carlo Methods	✗	✓	✗	✓	✓	✗	✗	✓	✗	✗	Cargo delivery
Actor-critic	✗	✓	✗	✓	✗	✓	✗	✗	✗	✗	Tracking control
T-resiliance	✗	✗	✓	✓	✓	✓	✗	✗	✗	✗	Damage recovery
PGPE	✗	✗	✓	✓	✓	✗	✗	✗	✗	✓	Standing task for biped robot & Grasping task
IRL	-	-	-	✗	✓	✓	✗	✗	✗	✗	Path planning in unstructured environment
IRL	-	-	-	✗	✓	✓	✗	✗	✗	✗	Autonomous movement in complex environment
Hierarchical RL	-	-	-	✓	✓	✓	✗	✗	✗	✗	Rescue victims
SAC	✗	✓	✗	✓	✓	✓	✗	✗	✗	✗	Path navigation
DDQN	✗	✓	✗	✓	✓	✓	✗	✗	✗	✗	Collision Avoidance
FRDPG	✗	✓	✗	✓	✗	✗	✗	✓	✗	✗	Navigation Planning
DDPG	✗	✓	✗	✓	✗	✓	✗	✗	✗	✗	Local Navigation
ICM A3C	✗	✗	✓	✓	✓	✓	✗	✗	✗	✗	Navigation
Improved A3C	✓	✗	✗	✓	✗	✗	✗	✓	✗	✗	End to End Navigation
DDQN	✗	✓	✗	✓	✓	✓	✗	✗	✗	✗	Navigation
A2CAT-VN	✗	✓	✗	✓	✗	✓	✗	✗	✗	✗	Vision based Navigation
IMPALA	✗	✗	✓	✓	✓	✓	✗	✗	✗	✗	Target driven visual navigation
HSNav	✗	✓	✗	✓	✓	✓	✗	✗	✗	✗	Real time object Navigation
LSTM+PPO	✗	✓	✗	✓	✗	✓	✗	✗	✗	✗	Visual Navigation
PDDPG	✗	✓	✗	✓	✗	✓	✗	✗	✗	✗	Mapless Collaborative Navigation
PPO	✗	✓	✗	✓	✓	✓	✗	✗	✗	✗	Multi-robot Navigation
PRIMAL	✓	✗	✗	✓	✓	✓	✗	✗	✗	✗	Pathfinding
A3C	✗	✓	✗	✓	✓	✓	✗	✗	✗	✗	Motion Learning
PPO+LSTM	✗	✓	✗	✓	✗	✓	✗	✗	✗	✗	Crowd Navigation
DRL	✗	✓	✗	✓	✓	✓	✗	✗	✗	✗	Padestrian-Friendly Navigation

It's possible that the point of contact might be further developed depending on the amount of friction that occurs at each of these sites. Bicchi et al. (2000), lays down the necessary force required so that the object does not fall down or get damaged from the robotic gripper, which is also known as force analysis. The relative motion between the sit of contact is determined by a function and is referred to as kinematic modelling between two contact points.

However, considering how well certain learning algorithms (Basalla et al., n.d.; Kumra & Kanan, 2017; Lenz et al., 2015; Mahler et al., 2017; Redmon & Angelova, 2015) have performed in the past, we could conclude that learning algorithms and visual models of grasps could result in effective and useful generalised solutions.

Case Study 1: Amazon

Thousands of mobile robots are used at Amazon fulfilment centres. Amazon Robotics researchers have devised novel techniques to keep goods moving. Amazon's fleet of over 500,000 mobile robots is key to achieving its delivery goals of shipping to the whole country within a certain period. A typical Amazon fulfilment centre comprises four levels, each floor having an extensive area, with 4,000 or more robots transporting merchandise to stations where employees choose which ones to send. Additional robots in certain buildings then sort outgoing packages by postal code for delivery.

For anyone using such a massive number of robots necessitates some innovative problem solving on the part of Amazon Robotics Researchers. Assuming the robots want to gather up and send as many products as they can in a certain time frame. Initially, the throughput can be boosted by introducing additional robots. However, their sheer numbers begin to produce congestion at some time. The robots can hinder each other, reducing overall system performance. Amazon has become a pioneer in the usage of robots due to its massive scale and the desire to pleasure its consumers, while its research teams seek to minimise congestion from affecting operational efficiency.

Consider how Amazon's enormous rectangular fulfilment centres are put out to appreciate why smarter judgments matter. In the centre are robots and multiple storage racks known as pods, which hold millions of different goods. Product pods move from the centre to stations scattered around the periphery, where colleagues choose and arrange the things necessary to satisfy each order in bins. When a certain pod is required, a robot slides beneath the 1,000-pound pod, raises it off the ground, and transports it to the station. This contrasts with typical warehouses, where employees walk kilometres of aisles every day, choosing things piece by piece. Amazon significantly increases productivity by cutting out those travels.

Amazon has created algorithms to manage robotic mobility in order to enhance overall system performance and guarantee the robots do not clash with one another. The main problem is developing plans quickly enough to keep up with all of the moving robots. The team employs one way in which it computes "social standards" to manage the general flow of robots to minimise traffic jams, but it also considers if a robot must be permitted to ignore those rules to take a shortcut and achieve its objective more quickly.

However, because to the dynamic nature of the fulfilment centre, new orders come on a regular basis, employees check into stations, and robots stop when they detect unforeseen difficulties. When you consider the number of pods and robots on the floor, as well as Amazon's scale, you get an idea of the magnitude of the task. There are a billion options and they have to be solved in real time.

Orders are routed to the sortation facility once they have been packaged and labelled. Associates and robotic arms retrieve parcels from a belt, scan a unique code for detailed information, and place each box on a tiny robot. The robot then circles a variety of gaps in the floor, each depicting a distinct set of postal codes. When it finds the correct one, it dumps the box down the chute that leads to the docking station below, where it is delivered. A standard sortation floor contains hundreds of chutes and a few thousand robots transporting parcels to them. Sortation, on the other hand, provides less alternatives for optimization than fulfilment. Randomly mixed parcels move down the conveyor in sortation, and the program must cope with whatever it discovers as the items arrive. As a result, Amazon Robotics researchers began developing improved traffic management techniques. Each robot's journey is planned by algorithms on the cloud. The sortation centre, like the fulfilment floor, establishes virtual roadways that determine which way a machine may go — but the lanes are broader here.

This creates new challenges and requires new algorithms to address them. What occurs, for example, when numerous robots collide at an inter crossroads when some desire to proceed straight while others want to turn into moving traffic? Amazon Robotics experts are working on a new multi-agent master plan that will consider multiple robots at once to generate a more efficient traffic flow. However, even the most advanced multi-agent planning systems cannot keep up with the thousands or so more machines in an Amazon facility. As a result, Amazon Robotics' teams are developing "hybrid" solutions that combine quick scheduling for individual robots with coordination strategies inspired by cutting-edge methodologies. Its purpose is to identify and resolve disputes before they occur.

The objective is to have an evolving plan. Due to the dynamic nature of the problem, the problem cannot be solved at time zero and devising a plan to start the robots rolling. Instead, a strategy that is already in motion needs to be modified from split second to split second. It needs to be updated with what enters, what exists, what has changed or gone wrong, and what new has emerged and reprioritize what robots should do.

Multi-agent planning will be a significant step ahead, but Amazon has a plethora of ideas in the pipeline. Amazon has unrivalled expertise with robotics, and its experts aim to utilize machine learning to solve common problems. They may then apply those learnt policies and heuristics to create an even better multi-agent system. Amazon engineers are creating learning algorithms that will enable the system to forecast where areas of congestion will arise on the ground in the future, as well as when they will dissipate. They are investigating ways to utilise machine learning to help robot fleets avoid congested areas. Amazon scientists intend to use academic research to build better algorithms for anticipating congestion and planning algorithms to avoid it.

The ultimate objective is to keep pushing technology in new areas. Machine learning-derived policies and improved prediction and planning algorithms will allow Amazon to expand the number of robots in its sorting and fulfilment facilities while also securely increasing traffic flow. Customers will receive their items even faster because of this. This is only the start. Despite huge advances, robotics is still a young and quickly expanding discipline. Amazon, for example, sponsors several university research ranging from machine learning and joint independence to hardware redesign and human-robot interaction. They have the chance to apply science not only to better goods for our consumers, but also to help robotics researchers as a public benefit.

Case Study 2: NASA

Nasa is one of the best Aerospace industries in the world. This case study is about Nasa's jet impulsion lab and the technologies used in it to obtain the optimal results in the aerospace industry like Artificial Intelligence (AI) and Deep Learning. NASA is involved in every facet of space exploration, from examining Earth's outer atmosphere to looking for indications of extra-terrestrial life. As a vital tool in the world of deep learning, big data is a significant component of this space exploration. Given the huge quantity of data produced by the different NASA satellites and spacecraft, deep learning is required to find patterns in this data that will eventually lead to exciting new discoveries. AI and ML may be used to quickly and effectively comb through years' worth of data and pictures in Big Data sets, such as NASA Earth observational data, to identify connections that a person would be unable to recognise.

The Earth Science Data Systems (ESDS) Program at NASA is dedicated to using AI and is aware of its potential to greatly enhance operations, expand the capabilities of current data systems, and make the most of Earth observation data. In places referred to as analogues, NASA tests exploration robots. Analogs are sites where a robot may be utilised and the environment is comparable to that of Mars or the moon. The desert of Arizona contains one NASA analogue. NASA robotics specialists test out novel rover, spacewalk, and ground support concepts in the desert. A group known as Desert RATS, which stands for Desert Research and Technology Studies, conducts some of these testing. For a variety of jobs involving significant research projects, NASA uses a lot of data science and artificial intelligence technology.

The goal of NASA's Laboratory for Jet Propulsion was to create an intelligent robot capable of exploring tunnels in perilous situations, such as on Mars' surface. Wheeled rovers are not the best choice for the challenging and uncertain terrain subsurface. Robots that explore caves must also be completely independent, even in circumstances when they could lose touch with Earth. The Artificial Intelligence (AI) also needed to be capable of observing and gathering important information from the caverns. In order to overcome these challenges, JPL and Boston Dynamics collaborated to integrate Artificial Intelligence into the robotics required to conduct the concerned research. NASA was able to create a novel method for exploring hostile areas by fusing JPL's NeBula AI with the dexterity of the Spot-robot. On Earth, the technology may be used in sectors like mining, building, as well as the utility companies and power businesses.

An impressive presentation of how an Artificial Intelligence-powered robot may explore Martian caverns in search of indications of life was made possible because of the optimal partnership between NASA and Boston Dynamics. The Spot robots were able to map a cave on Earth as they travelled through it and relay knowledge back to a core network station. The robots' sensors and cameras were used to scan the subsurface environment for organic signs that the Artificial Intelligence and deep learning model had been trained to identify. The success of the project was significantly impacted by the Boston Dynamics robots' agility.

Challenges in Robotics (With Deep Learning)

1. It takes a long time and involves trade-offs between state complexity and operability to derive complicated dynamics analytically.
2. To get the best outcomes, control strategies must be learned in dynamic contexts.
3. It takes sophisticated manipulation to address today's complex concerns.
4. The necessity to overcome the fundamental barrier of advanced object identification.
5. Interpreting and foreseeing human behaviour to maximise effectiveness and obtain more results.
6. Dimensionality reduction and sensor fusion. The topic of this challenge is the development of methods that are both accurate and useful in representing states based on complex data.
7. To solve the previous six challenges and reach a higher degree of utility, robots will need to be able to execute complex orders with great reliability (Kumhar & Kukshal, 2022).

Robotics presents a number of special quests for algorithm learning. Furthermore, robots are required to do a multitude of jobs, and it can be challenging or even time-consuming to build fully unique deep learning techniques and features for each activity. In addition, several learning algorithms struggle to cope with the large variety of tasks that robots are expected to do in the actual world. In conclusion, in order for learning techniques to be successful, they need to be able to infer information quickly. This is because time is generally a limitation in robotic applications.

Building computer systems that can analyse photos, voice, text, and even make graphics has become much easier, thanks to neural networks. However, adding actions and control creates a host of brand-new difficulties since every choice the network takes will have an impact on what it sees next. By overcoming these obstacles, we'll go a step closer to creating systems that are aware of the consequences of their actions. We could go a step closer to finding solutions to the core issues in robotics and automation if we can use the capabilities of large-scale deep learning to robotic control.

RECENT TRENDS

Lengthy training times and extensive and huge amounts of training data are the most significant obstacles presented using deep learning in robotics. The time and resource intensive process is the generation of training data for complex systems.

One possible future advancement is the use of cloud robotics in conjunction with crowdsourcing of training data (Pratt, 2015). The data needed for it does not have to be obtained from similar machines, as shown by Yang in his everyday cooking videos for ingredients and handling utensils (Yang et al., 2015).

Developments in local parallel processing (Oh & Jung, 2004) and raw processing speed have reduced the time required for training of the datasets. Distributed computing enables additional computer resources to be directed toward a single problem (Schmitz et al., 2014), although it is limited by connection speeds (Jordan & Mitchell, 2015). There is also a possibility that there are computational methods that have not yet been developed that may further reduce the time required for training. Researchers are constantly trying to devise different methods that direct the attention of the network to the subspaces of the data that are the most significant, and they are also training with sparser forms of deep neural networks that have less synaptic connections (Schmidhuber, 2015).

In addition, we are seeing a general trend of greater degrees of cognitive ability, and many industry professionals are sure that deep learning will soon be on its way to competing with human-level abilities (Mouha, 2021; Pratt, 2015). But before it can achieve such ambitious capability, deep learning still has to overcome a number of obstacles. There are currently no cognitive training datasets available (Pratt, 2015). It is well knowledge that DNNs are especially vulnerable to adversarial samples (Szegedy et al., 2013), and despite this, they are unable to characterise 3D spatial layouts that include object directionality (Bohannon, 2014). All though the future holds great potential, only time will tell if deep neural networks (DNNs) will provide the abilities necessary for accurate adaptation in a variety of scenarios.

CONCLUSION

Deep learning shows the potential it has in solving challenges involving action, sensing and perception, as well as the ability to usually integrate a variety of skills under one umbrella. Deep neural networks can extract data collected through the detectors that may without human interference extract important attributes, which can possibly decrease the amount of time necessary by two. They are also capable of integrating high-dimensional data and multi-media content. The upgrade has been validated via testing, making it very effortless to adjust to the uncontrolled environment of the robots under which they are required to do their jobs. The ability of robots to exert some kind of control over the environment in which they operate is an essential quality that has proved difficult to perfect. However, in order for a robot to detect things, it is not essential for the robot to know how to do all of the relevant handling tasks provided the robot is capable of learning these skills when they are required. Despite this, problems involving robotic perception, robotic learning, and robotic control continue to offer major challenges using the approaches that are now available (Mouha, 2021).

REFERENCES

Aggarwal, Singh, Chopra, Kumar, & Colace. (2022). *Deep Learning in Robotics for Strengthening Industry 4.0.: Opportunities, Challenges and Future Directions*. doi:10.1007/978-3-030-96737-6_1

Basalla, M., Ebert, F., Tebner, R., & Ke, W. (n.d.). *Grasping for the Real World (Greifen mit Deep Learning)*. Academic Press.

Bicchi, A., & Kumar, V. (2000). Robotic grasping and contact: A review. *Proceedings of the 2000 ICRA. Millennium Conference. IEEE International Conference on Robotics and Automation. Symposia Proceedings, 1*, 348–353. 10.1109/ROBOT.2000.844081

Bohannon, J. (2014). Helping robots see the big picture. *Science, 346*(6206), 186–187. doi:10.1126cience.346.6206.186 PMID:25301616

Böhmer, W., Springenberg, J. T., Boedecker, J., Riedmiller, M., & Obermayer, K. (2015). Autonomous learning of state representations for control: An emerging field aims to autonomously learn state representations for reinforcement learning agents from their real-world sensor observations. *Kunstliche Intelligenz, 29*(4), 353–362. doi:10.100713218-015-0356-1

De Gregorio, D., Tonioni, A., Palli, G., & Di Stefano, L. (2020). Semiautomatic Labeling for Deep Learning in Robotics. *IEEE Transactions on Automation Science and Engineering, 17*(2), 611–620. doi:10.1109/TASE.2019.2938316

Farabet, C., Couprie, C., Najman, L., & LeCun, Y. (2013). Learning hierarchical features for scene labeling. *IEEE Transactions on Pattern Analysis and Machine Intelligence, 35*(8), 1915–1929. doi:10.1109/TPAMI.2012.231 PMID:23787344

Goodfellow, I., Bengio, Y., & Courville, A. (2016). *Deep Learning*. MIT Press.

Jordan, M. I., & Mitchell, T. M. (2015). Machine learning: Trends, perspectives, and prospects. *Science, 349*(6245), 255–260. doi:10.1126cience.aaa8415 PMID:26185243

Krizhevsky, A., Sutskever, I., & Hinton, G. E. (2012). ImageNet Classification with Deep Convolutional Neural Networks. In F. Pereira, C. J. C. Burges, L. Bottou, & K. Q. Weinberger (Eds.), *Advances in Neural Information Processing Systems 25* (pp. 1097–1105). Curran Associates, Inc.

Kumhar, H. S., & Kukshal, V. (2022). A review on reinforcement deep learning in robotics. *2022 Interdisciplinary Research in Technology and Management (IRTM), Technology and Management (IRTM), 2022 Interdisciplinary Research In, 1–8.* doi:10.1109/IRTM54583.2022.9791615

Kumra, S., & Kanan, C. (2017). Robotic grasp detection using deep convolutional neural networks. *Proceedings of the 2017 IEEE/RSJ International Conference on Intelligent Robots and Systems (IROS),* 769–776. 10.1109/IROS.2017.8202237

LeCun, Y., Bengio, Y., & Hinton, G. (2015). Deep learning. *Nature, 521*(7553), 436–444. doi:10.1038/nature14539 PMID:26017442

Lenz, I., Lee, H., & Saxena, A. (2015). Deep Learning for Detecting Robotic Grasps. *The International Journal of Robotics Research, 34*(4-5), 705–724. doi:10.1177/0278364914549607

Ma, J., Sheridan, R. P., Liaw, A., Dahl, G. E., & Svetnik, V. (2015). Deep neural nets as a method for quantitative structure-activity relationships. *Journal of Chemical Information and Modeling, 55*(2), 263–274. doi:10.1021/ci500747n PMID:25635324

Mahler, J., Liang, J., Niyaz, S., Laskey, M., Doan, R., Liu, X., Aparicio, J., & Goldberg, K. (2017). Dex-Net 2.0: Deep Learning to Plan Robust Grasps with Synthetic Point Clouds and Analytic Grasp Metrics. *Proceedings of the Robotics: Science and Systems.*

Mikolov, T., Deoras, A., Povey, D., Burget, L., & Cernocky, J. (2011). Strategies for training large scale neural network language models. *Proc* Automatic Speech Recognition and Understanding. doi:10.1109/ASRU.2011.6163930

Mnih, V., Kavukcuoglu, K., Silver, D., Rusu, A. A., Veness, J., Bellemare, M. G., Graves, A., Riedmiller, M., Fidjeland, A. K., Ostrovski, G., Petersen, S., Beattie, C., Sadik, A., Antonoglou, I., King, H., Kumaran, D., Wierstra, D., Legg, S., & Hassabis, D. (2015). Human-level control through deep reinforcement learning. *Nature, 518*(7540), 529–533. doi:10.1038/nature14236 PMID:25719670

Mouha, R. (2021). Deep Learning for Robotics. *Journal of Data Analysis and Information Processing, 9*(2), 63–76. doi:10.4236/jdaip.2021.92005

Oh, K., & Jung, K. (2004). GPU implementation of neural networks. *Pattern Recognition, 37*(6), 1311–1314. doi:10.1016/j.patcog.2004.01.013

Pierson, H. A., & Gashler, M. S. (2017). Deep learning in robotics: A review of recent research. *Advanced Robotics, 31*(16), 821–835. doi:10.1080/01691864.2017.1365009

Pinto, L., & Gupta, A. (2016). Supersizing self-supervision: Learning to grasp from 50K tries and 700 robot hours. *Proceedings of the 2016 IEEE International Conference on Robotics and Automation (ICRA),* 3406–3413. 10.1109/ICRA.2016.7487517

Pratt, G. A. (2015). Is a cambrian explosion coming for robotics? *The Journal of Economic Perspectives, 29*(3), 51–60. doi:10.1257/jep.29.3.51

Redmon, J., & Angelova, A. (2015). Real-time grasp detection using convolutional neural networks. *Proceedings of the 2015 IEEE International Conference on Robotics and Automation (ICRA),* 1316–1322. 10.1109/ICRA.2015.7139361

Rusk, N. (2016). Deep learning. *Nature Methods*, *13*(1), 35. doi:10.1038/nmeth.3707

Schmidhuber, J. (2015). Deep learning in neural networks: An overview. *Neural Networks*, *61*(1), 85–117. doi:10.1016/j.neunet.2014.09.003 PMID:25462637

Schmitz, A., Bansho, Y., & Noda, K. (2014). Tactile object recognition using deep learning and dropout. *14th IEEE-RAS International Conference on Humanoid Robots*, 1044–1050. 10.1109/HUMANOIDS.2014.7041493

Szegedy, C., Zaremba, W., & Sutskever, I. (2013). Intriguing properties of neural networks. https://arxiv.org/abs/1312.6199

Turing, A. M. (1970). Chapter. In B. Meltzer & D. Michie (Eds.), Machine Intelligence (Vol. 5, pp. 3–23). American Elsevier.

Winston, P. H. (1984). *Artificial Intelligence* (2nd ed.). Addison-Wesley.

Yang, Y., Li, Y., & Fermüller, C. (2015). Robot learning manipulation action plans by watching unconstrained videos from the world wide web. *29th AAAI Conference on Artificial Intelligence (AAAI-15)*. 10.1609/aaai.v29i1.9671

Chapter 11
A Multicloud–Based Deep Learning Model for Smart Agricultural Applications

Palanivel Kuppusamy

 https://orcid.org/0000-0003-1313-9522

Pondicherry University, India

Suresh Joseph K.

Pondicherry University, India

Suganthi Shanmugananthan

Annamalai University, India

ABSTRACT

Modern agriculture primarily relies on smart agriculture to predict crop yields and make decisions. Crop productivity could suffer due to a lack of farmers, labor shortages in the agricultural sector, adverse weather, etc. Smart farming uses advanced technology to improve the productivity and efficiency of agriculture. Crop yield is increased with smart agriculture, which also keeps an eye on agricultural pests. Artificial intelligence is an innovative technology that uses sensor data to predict the future and make judgments for farmers. AI methods like machine learning and deep learning are the most clever way to boost agricultural productivity. Adopting AI can help with farming issues and promote increased food production. Deep learning is a modern method for processing images and analyzing big data, showing promise for producing superior results. The primary goals of this study are to examine the benefits of employing DL in smart agricultural applications and to suggest a multi-cloud DL architecture for such applications.

DOI: 10.4018/978-1-6684-8098-4.ch011

INTRODUCTION

Modern agriculture relies heavily on smart agriculture to estimate crop yields and identify decision-making (Sehgal Foundation, 2023). Currently, crop productivity may fail due to insufficient farmers, agriculture workforce, weather conditions, etc. Introducing smart agriculture (*Eos 2022*) can improve crop productivity and monitor crop and agricultural pests. It can make agriculture more efficient and effective. UNCTAD (2017) reported that smart agriculture could reduce production costs while increasing agricultural yield and encouraging the effective use of agriculture resources, including human labor, energy, fertilizer, and water utilization.

According to Kathleen Walch (2020), farmers are better equipped to track all processes and apply specific actions identified by machines through superhuman accuracy with the most recent breakthroughs in connectivity, automation, and technologies. Artificial Intelligence (AI) can make judgments for farmers and predictions using sensor data. Farmers and data scientists are still evolving approaches to maximize the workforce needed in farming (Wang et al., 2021). Hence, smart farming has evolved into a learning system and has become even more inventive as vital information resources improve daily.

Artificial Intelligence in Smart Agriculture

Farmers can employ AI algorithms to estimate how much light their crops' foliage gets. AI approaches (*Intellias 2022*) can improve crop productivity in smart agriculture. AI systems using visual abilities can monitor and assess daily plant variations to calculate the growth rate. (Subeesh & Mehta, 2021). Most smartly, agricultural productivity can be increased using AI techniques such as machine learning (ML) and deep learning (DL).

ML and DL Applications can find and fix problems with agricultural growth (Hugo Storm et al., 2020). ML can improve the iterative process by learning from patterns and associations between them when making decisions. With higher prediction outcomes, the ML algorithm tries to produce accurate output. By classifying diverse crop yields, ML can enhance eyesight and improve the quality of images (Cravero et al., 2022).

Why Deep Learning in Smart Agriculture?

Crop management can be accelerated by smart agriculture. Since there are several factors, including climate and genetics, it is difficult to predict the yield of crops. Farmers may use intelligent technologies such as deep learning to accurately anticipate crop yields once they know how these elements affect crop yields. DL is an ML technique using artificial neural networks (ANNs) principles (Sarker, 2022). According to Kuradusenge et al. (2023), using DL methods to foretell agricultural diseases is practical and affordable. The DL approaches enhance agricultural research's capacity to discern the picture classification of agriculture. DL can be applied to various smart agriculture (Zhang et al., 2022) areas such as automating weed detection, classification of crops, collecting and extracting information about cultivated land, estimating crop yield (for example, the number of tomatoes in the plant), identifying and classifying leaves of different plant species, identifying plant diseases out of healthy leaves, identify a variety of spatial patterns, predict the growth of animals, predict the soil moisture content over an irrigated field, and predict weather conditions based on historical data.

Problems and Challenges

The existing farming systems and technologies failed to provide quality solutions regarding precision and accuracy across various smart agriculture operations. Applying AIoT (a combination of AI and IoT) can transform conventional farming significantly by overcoming common challenges involving pest management and post-harvest management problems. Even though AIoT is the primary driver behind smart agriculture, there are still certain obstacles, such as labor scarcity and a rise in the demand for cutting-edge machinery. Modern farms, therefore, stand an excellent chance of increasing output. Due to the nature and complexity of the agriculture workplace, it is difficult to get around current problems with the current machinery. Moreover, new technologies with robotics enhance the agricultural industry.

Through smart agriculture, farm owners and farmers may gather and analyze data to pinpoint crop problems. Using the information that has been analyzed, they can choose the best strategy to handle the issues. They will know what to do whether there is a lack of vital nutrients or low water levels. IoT and AI technology can be included in devices and sensors to obtain real-time information about the condition of the soil, especially water levels, humidity, and pH. Farmers can use drone cameras, satellite images, and other devices to observe crop conditions and perform agricultural duties. When the data is evaluated, it can assist growers in identifying nutrient deficiencies in the soil and crop pests and illnesses.

Farmers can monitor all the incoming data using robust and effective AI solutions. The technology can track and gauge how the crops react when farmers apply fertilizers and pesticides. Growers can use the data to pinpoint crops that are not performing well and take the appropriate action to address the issue's root cause. The power of data can assist in cutting labor costs, enhance agricultural production, and lessen farming's impact on the environment.

The Focus of the Chapter

Agribusiness can operate more strategically, efficiently, and with lower production costs thanks to AI. Although it is the future of agriculture, other technologies are still needed. The adoption of AI faces several difficulties, with a lack of varied datasets and a long learning curve. Concerns over confidentiality, security, and a lack of digital literacy are further issues. AI can assist in resolving agricultural constraints and fostering improved food production.

The motivation of this study is to:

1. Explore the advantages of DL in smart farming applications and
2. Propose a multi-cloud-based DL architecture for smart agriculture

Organization of this Chapter. Section 2 (Background) introduces the basic information required to write this chapter. The reviewed articles/papers and the methodology are discussed in Section 3 (Literature Review & Related Works), and the main findings, solutions, and use cases with the future of DL in agriculture are presented in Section 4 (Results and Discussion) section. Finally, Section 5 concludes the chapter.

BACKGROUND

This section presents the background information required to write this chapter, including introducing smart agriculture/farming, agriculture technologies, agriculture deep learning, DL applications, the necessity of Multicloud, and data management.

Agriculture is essential to human beings (Swaminathan & Bhavani, 2013), which creates a livelihood for a large world population and remains critical to the economy's long-term growth and progress. Many farmers are using old-fashioned agricultural practices that result in poor yields. The main challenges for existing agriculture operations are monitoring, crop tracking, crop disease detection, handling, etc. (Buja et al., 2021). The agricultural sector can demand further development, and the government requests to prioritize increasing production (for example, crops, vegetables, and fruits) by creating novel approaches for cultivators to increase their performance.

Digital Transformation. In the contemporary period, agricultural practices have significantly diverged from earlier methods. Modern technical developments have had a significant impact on agriculture. They might be utilized in farming to improve the standard of the industry. Rapid digital transformation (Mehmet Ali Dayıoğlu & Ufuk Turker, 2021) is taking place in the agriculture sector, becoming more potent on the foundations of innovative techniques like AI and related technologies. Due to these advancements, researchers focus on using ML, DL, and the IoT in industries like agriculture. It assists farmers in boosting the productivity of their land so that the world's demand for food may be met.

The combination of AI, Computer Vision (CV), and Machine Vision (MV) is making the world of farming more advanced than humankind has ever discovered. As stated by Cube Labs (2022), Agri-Tech (or Agricultural Technologies) is disrupting the traditional dynamics of farming by helping farmers in better crop yielding. Using framing robots to plant diagnosis applications, CV, and DL models brings tremendous change. They allow numerous agricultural tasks to be carried out automatically with the highest level of precision, advancing the idea of smart agriculture. They can use computer vision techniques to enable non-contact and effective technology-driven solutions in agriculture and remote cameras to acquire high-quality images.

Agricultural Technologies

Smart agriculture is supported by innovative technologies such as the IoT, Wireless Sensor Networks (WSNs), data mining, AI including ML & DL, blockchain, integration of IoT with blockchain and ML, and data science. Agri-Tech (Shafi et al., 2019) helps farmers grow healthier crops, control their usage against pesticides, analyze and monitor soil conditions, measure plant growth in real-time, etc. The application of state-of-art technologies to monitor, analyze, and enhance the food production chain from photosynthesis to plant growth. Smart agriculture contributes to the global food life cycle by minimizing the total production cost and agricultural production outcomes (Navarro et al., 2020). As a significance, Agri-Tech brings in benefits of data-driven predictive decision-making, computer vision-driven inspective farming, etc.

Some of the Agri-Tech widely used in smart farming are remote sensing, UAVs/ Drones, CV, image technology, etc.

- **Computer Vision (CV).** CV technology is an essential component of AI, and remote cameras with CV technology allow smart agriculture to provide non-contact and scalable sensing solutions (Ashwani Patel, 2022). CV can be used in the analysis (seed quality, soil, and plant health), management (irrigation water, weed, and livestock), and yield estimation using GANs, vision transformers, and DL architectures. They can optimize production costs and boosts the overall efficiency of agricultural operations. CV-enabled smart sensors aid farmers in switching to more cost-effective farming practices and reducing risk.

- **Drones.** The widespread use of Drones in agriculture can boost efficiency and overcome labor shortages. Drone-based pesticide spraying and phenotyping are used in the livestock industry. Drones with high-definition cameras and CV monitor crop health, soil conditions, and farmland application and detect abnormalities in smart agriculture. Drones can cover a larger area much more efficiently and accurately than humans.

- **Image Technology.** In image recognition technology, the accuracy of real-time image recognition is much higher with DL than traditional CV algorithms. Video analytics can therefore be performed with video captured by surveillance cameras or webcams using DL methods. CV and DL use cases in agriculture are drone-based crop monitoring, sorting and grading crops, and CV applications extending to planting, harvesting, weeding, and health detection.

- **Internet of Things (IoT).** The IoT collects real-time data from sensors connected with an IoT chip. Farmers may rely on clever systems and smart sensors to generate precise predictions based on gathered data. A smart agriculture framework (Aishwarya et al., 2022) using an IoT can collect data based on multiple parameters. It is a general and universal strategy to use IoT-based physical sensors to sense the surroundings. IoT and other technologies have established a fertile ground for real-time monitoring.

- **Remote Sensing.** By providing unmatched options for the quick, easy, and comfortable gathering of land images to gather essential information on the state of the crop, remote sensing developments in agriculture have significantly improved production efficiency. These developments have enabled automation data gathering, simulation, and interpretation using agriculture analytics and deep learning methods.

- **Robots/Unmanned Aerial Vehicles (UAVs).** UAV or drone-based remote sensing has drawn much attention from the smart farming community due to recent developments in improved sensors, data collecting platforms, and data analysis techniques. UAVs (flying drones and unmanned ground vehicles) can capture massive spatial data from an agricultural field. Tej Bahadur Shahi et al. (2022) summarised and synthesized the general pipeline of UAV-based remote sensing for smart agriculture. Examples are Saga Robotics and Thorval. Saga Robotics is an autonomous, modular, multifunctional robot, whereas Thorvald helps farmers with labor-demanding agricultural practices.

These data-focused solutions help comprehend and deliver excellent data insights. To get knowledge about crop progress and support in decision-making, these modern technologies are utilized in many agricultural operations, such as selecting the best yield for a precise location and recognizing elements that would kill the crops, such as weeds, pests, and crop illnesses.

Such sensing devices generate enormous amounts of raw data, necessitating large-scale data processing algorithms like ML and DL. Palanivel Kuppusamy et al. (2021) studied the state-of-the-art technologies used in farming and projected an innovative agriculture model using advanced technologies. As Tej Bahadur Shahi et al. (2022) suggested, various ML and DL models, such as yield estimation, disease detection, and crop classification, were available for crop trait estimations.

Machine Learning

Machine learning (Kuradusenge et al., 2023) uses statistical, probabilistic, and optimization techniques to allow computers to "learn" from the past and uncover challenging patterns in massive, noisy, or complex input data sets. ML can increase decision-making effectiveness and efficiency in agriculture while reducing operational risks and costs. ML tools may significantly increase agricultural productivity and profitability by reducing waste and boosting product quality. Hence, ML algorithms are widely used to classify images in crop disease detection. Applications for machine learning in agriculture rely on real-time data to benefit farmers exponentially. Better harvests, more effective pesticides, and 24/7 protection of remote sites are all being driven by AI and ML.

Agribusiness and crop growth may suffer from climate change, soil erosion, biodiversity loss, and customers' changing food preferences (Tuomisto et al., 2017). Agriculture and the environment still have problems with each other. In addition to a rising population, urbanization threatens sustainable agriculture. The only way to fulfill the expanding need for food is to keep track of crops, the surroundings, and the marketplace.

Various ML applications in agriculture are crop management, precision spraying, insect detection, field conditions management, yield mapping, livestock management, automatic weeding, crop price forecasting, and automatic harvesting robots. They can improve farming decision-making by examining historical trends and real-time sensor data. AI in agriculture can help producers better forecast demand, increase crop yields, and cut expenses associated with food production.

Deep Learning

Deep Learning (Maha Altalak et al., 2022), an ML component, is a modern method for processing images and analyzing Big Data that shows promise for producing superior results. DL is an ML method using artificial neural network (ANN) principles. According to Kadiyala Ramana et al. (2022), Deep Learning Networks (DNNs) are differentiated from neural networks (NNs) by their depth, making them capable of discovering latent structures within unlabeled, unstructured data. DNNs offer a significant advantage over earlier algorithms in automatic feature extraction because they do not require human intervention. Backpropagation (BP), the foundation of ANN, is a supervised learning technique comprising numerous layers of fully connected hidden neurons. In some situations, the conventional BP neural networks are insufficiently effective. The most popular DL algorithms are Convolutional Neural Networks (CNN), Recurrent Neural Networks (RNN), and Generative Adversarial Networks (GAN). The DL algorithms' subcategories include DCGAN, LSTM, VGGNet, and ConvNets.

1. CNN, a DL neural network subclass, has been adopted for disease detection in smart agriculture (Oliva Debnath et al., 2022). CNN's convolutional, pooling, and fully connected layers have enabled significant advancements in smart agriculture and other domains. These are combined to serve as a classifier, while the fully connected layers act as a feature extraction layer. CNNs provide high-quality solutions regarding precision and accuracy across various smart agriculture activities, from land preparation to harvesting operations (Dhanya et al., 2022).
2. RNN, a variation of ANN, has made strides in time series analysis, speech recognition, and language modeling by mining temporal and semantic data. The preceding moment's output correlates

with the current network input in an RNN. The RNN model represented the seasonal variations in agricultural yield across many years (Saeed Khaki et al., 2020).

3.   GAN technically combines the already-existing BP algorithms. Using GAN, a set of noise may be used to create new data and learn how the original data are distributed. A generation model representing the distribution of the real data and a discriminating model akin to a binary classifier make up the two models of this network's structure.

Khan et al. (2021) recommended the Agricultural Deep Learning (AGR-DL) method to help developing countries. Various DL applications for smart agriculture include crop monitoring, biotic and abiotic stressors, irrigation, microclimate forecasting, energy-efficient controls, and crop growth forecasting.

Advantages and Disadvantages. DL reduces the requirement for feature engineering (FE) in image processing. Traditional methods for classifying images relied on manually created features, whose effectiveness significantly impacted the outcomes. Further, DL does not need FE because it is trained to find the critical traits. DL typically requires more training time. Other disadvantages include problems with diverse data sets, optimization issues due to complexity, and hardware restrictions.

Smart Farming

Smart farming is a solution to many of the mentioned problems. Smart agriculture became possible with the emergence of IoT and ML techniques. It improves agriculture's effectiveness and efficiency using cutting-edge information and communication technologies (ICT) (*Said Mohamed et al., 2021*). *Farmers can accurately monitor each phase of the procedure and deploy the precise solutions chosen by machines with superhuman accuracy thanks to the latest advancements in automated processes, AI, and communication. (Tripathy et al., 2022). Farmers, scientists, and engineers are still evolving approaches to maximize the human effort needed in farming. With the daily improvement of* priceless information resources, smart farming has become an increasingly more intelligent learning system.

Smart Farming Applications. Smart agriculture uses collected data to produce insightful information that aids farmers in improving productivity, environmental sustainability, crop production, and financial success of their smart farming operations. Various smart farming applications are agriculture automation, disease direction, indoor farming, livestock, smart irrigation, automation, monitoring, etc.

- **Agricultural Automation.** Farmers' physical labor and responsibilities are reduced by agricultural automation (Khan Rijwan et al., 2022), highlighting the effective and efficient usage of various machines in smart farming operations. Smart agriculture can establish custom recruiting centers to make it simpler for like-minded farmers to adopt technology and machinery for improved resource management techniques.
- **Disease Detection.** To diagnose diseases in crops and plants, DL models offer innovative solutions for various image-processing tasks such as picture segmentation, classification, labeling, etc. At first, the disease's most obvious signs can be seen on the leaves. Smartphones/intelligent devices create a precise classification system with reduced size and complexity to detect diseases seen in leaf photos. Different variants of MobileNet models (Mercelin Francis et al., 2023), the pre-trained on the ImageNet database, are retrained to diagnose diseases.
- **Indoor Farming.** High-yield farming techniques (such as precision and urban) are required to meet the growing demand for crops and food. Indoor farming is therefore viewed as a workable

solution to the growing concern over food security in the upcoming years. Image processing is a crucial precision farming technique that fosters the expansion of indoor farming. ML and DL algorithms scale indoor farming in several ways, including monitoring and measuring artificial climate conditions, evaluating plant growth, diagnosing plant illnesses, and exploring soil fertility dynamics.

- **Livestock Industry.** Animals are moving around and are frequently challenged to differentiate from their herd. Monitoring a farm with livestock is far more complicated than monitoring a farm with crops. AI can gather, store, and retrieve data for animal farms in livestock farming. AI-powered animal farms forecast customer behavior, which is advantageous for the food chain. Farmers can get alerts from DL whenever there is a problem on the land. Farmers can control the frequency of feeding, milking, and cleaning the animals using remote control devices.

- **Monitoring.** Information on crop data, field soil characteristics, and livestock are collected as part of the monitoring process (for crops soil and livestock). WSNs, or wireless sensor networks, can gather and upload these data to the Cloud. This uploaded data is the foundation for analytics employing the Long Short-Term Memory (LSTM) method. The results are communicated to the user via SMS when the inferred results are compared to the optimal values.

- **Pest Control.** Food supplies and raw materials for other industries, such as plastic and gasoline, are sourced from smart agriculture. While growing decent crops, farmers must contend with pest invasions. Pest infestations seriously threaten developing crops, leading to crop loss and adverse economic effects. They can swiftly spread to other health zones, even in a small area, if untreated. Pest management is essential for minimizing crop loss. DL approach classifies pests (Tuan et al., 2021) from images captured from the crops using various EfficientNet.

- **Phenotyping.** To analyze a prototype, sophisticated CV algorithms are routing the accuracy and reliability of phenotyping to follow exact measurements. An intelligent camera monitors and records this process as plants are arranged in rows. The phenotyping system periodically gathers sample photos to examine and characterize the characteristics of the plant, such as its height and width, as well as areas, color, and estimated fruit output. Advanced algorithms (like DL and ML) can analyze plant structures' dimensions, surfaces, colors, and yield parameters (such as flowers and fruits).

- **Plant Disease Detection.** Numerous plant diseases pose severe risks to agriculture. Automating disease identification greatly enhances the prompt and effective control of various plant diseases. To date, different methods have been employed to detect plant diseases. Due to its outstanding outcomes, DL is one of the most popular approaches.

- **Smart Irrigation.** Smart irrigation technology analyzes weather information or data on soil moisture to decide whether the landscape needs irrigation. By cutting down on water wastage while maintaining plant health and quality, smart irrigation can maximize efficiency. Multiple physical sensors in smart irrigation send data on temperature, humidity, and soil moisture to determine transpiration in a specific field.

Technology developments are being used in agriculture applications to produce revolutionary innovations. Innovations to create a new paradigm of smart farming operations include using AI, drones, agricultural robots, predictive analytics, and precision agriculture. Drone-based seeding and damage assessments could be practical operational improvements that allow farmers to get more value from their innovative farming practices.

Motivations for ML/DL on Multicloud

Smart farming organizations seek innovative solutions for secure and efficient data management with multi-cloud and hybrid cloud platforms. Agricultural businesses look for adaptable and practical solutions to optimize and automate their infrastructure and workflows as pressure increases to deliver software more quickly and with higher quality. Rapid provisioning of continuous data innovation, unrestricted data transfer across sensors, and on-demand analytics with hybrid Cloud and multi-cloud platforms (Akhtar et al., 2021) may be developed to manage high-volume generated data to get around the problems and gain flexibility and agility at a cheaper cost. Hybrid/multi-cloud deployments are necessary due to the increasing number of applications (such as mission-critical, life-supporting, and data-intensive apps). Hybrid and multi-cloud architectures combine numerous cloud environments, such as public clouds, private clouds, and on-premises infrastructure.

According to Isaac Sacolick (2020), the choice often comes down to cost, compliance, and other operational considerations. Well-architected business operations, analytics, transactions, and collaborations may operate dependably in both public and private clouds. Intelligent farming systems consider deploying life-critical services in hybrid models when strategically allocating and deploying. Compared to public clouds, hybrid architectures can improve on a rising number of factors at this junction, including user experience, performance, dependability, scalability, maintainability, and security.

As ML spreads throughout enterprise contexts, it becomes applicable to multi-cloud architectures, particularly those cross firewalls. Training with on-premises data/cloud, training on specialized hardware, and training on Cloud with public data/on-premises can all consider ML and DL on Multicloud. A multi-cloud architecture that serves its intended function is required for flexible ML model training, deployment, and consumption in these scenarios. For instance, IBM's Data Science Experience (DSX) platform is accessible via both on-premises and Cloud REST APIs.

Data Hub Architecture. Smart farming applications can use multi-cloud and hybrid cloud platforms (DBTA, 2021) to look for novel solutions for effective and secure data management. The data hub multi-cloud platform can accommodate the comprehensive Edge-to-AI analytics features supported by the public, private, or hybrid clouds. With supported data security and integrity, optimal governance, and smart data management, it eases the transitions from pilot to creation. The data hub multi-cloud platform includes data quality, cleansing, de-duplication, and curation capabilities and may provide on-premises and in the Cloud. All applications and procedures for smart farming use the data hub multi-cloud platform. It links operational, predictive, and classical analytics applications to analytic structures like data lakes and warehouses.

LITERATURE REVIEW AND RELATED WORKS

The different areas covered by smart farming (Sufian et al., 2021) include plant identification and categorization, plant health evaluation, innovative pest and herb control, field analysis, and yield estimation. DL algorithms like CNN, RNN, and GAN have received much attention and use in the fields above. Agricultural researchers frequently employ software frameworks without comprehensively analyzing the concepts and workings of a technique. The numerous reported works in smart farming are discussed in this section. Additionally, this section looks at the agricultural issues, the models and frameworks used, the sources, nature, and data pre-processing, as well as the overall results obtained at each study project.

Smart farming technology has become industrialized and supported due to numerous technological advances. Big data, automation, IoT, and cloud computing are all used to increase control over smart farming. With the massive data generation, these cutting-edge technologies in farms have drastically increased. More understanding can be gained from the data in a reasonable amount of time by creating and using technical tools. Aditya Dhanraj Ramekar et al. (2022) guided farmers in sowing good crops by deploying ML in crop prediction and CNN in soil images (such as alluvial, black, red, sandy, etc.).

DL in Smart Agriculture. To meet these goals for food security, a change from traditional to smart agriculture is now necessary due to the significant population rise. DL techniques, such as CNN and RNN, have been intensively investigated and functional in recent years.

Nanyang Zhu et al. (2018) summarized the DL algorithms that support researchers in farming to advance a complete picture of DL applications in agriculture that facilitates data analysis, enhances related research in agriculture, and thus promotes DL applications effectively. Magomadov (2019) explored DL regarding agriculture and food production and explained why DL models were better equipped for agriculture than others.

Altalak et al. (2021) analyzed the current research articles on DL (such as CNN and RNN) methods, their contributions, and the challenges in agriculture. Additionally, they considered the agriculture limitations being supervised by the IoT and used them to feed the DL for study. Kavitha (2021) focussed on how the DL was used for smart agriculture. Dadashzadeh and Sakhaeian (2022) focussed on how ML and DL systems were applied to smart agriculture.

Senthil Kumar Swami Durai and Mary Divya Shamili (2022) facilitated different cultivated crops professionally, accomplishing high yields at a low price. They forecasted the total cost required for cultivating a specific agriculturalist to pre-plan the actions before cultivation consequential in a combined solution in farming. Altalak et al. (2022) analyzed the DL techniques in agriculture and discussed the most important contributions and challenges. They resolved that CNN provided improved outcomes but lacked initial detection of plant/crop diseases.

Field Analysis and Yield Estimation

Accurate yield forecasting or agricultural yield estimation helps farmers increase the quality of their harvest. Making wiser choices regarding the extent of harvesting and the number of human resources needed helps save operating expenses. Crop yield estimations are often made using historical data, with employees manually counting crops and fruit in specific fields using regional and counting techniques.

Bahrami et al. (2021) modeled the crop biophysical parameters, e.g., Leaf Area Index (LAI) and biomass, using a combination of radar and optical Earth observations using remote sensing techniques. Sami et al. (2022) used Long Short-Term Memory (LSTM)-based neural networks for a smart irrigation system, where a physical sensor (such as transmitting temperature, humidity, and soil moisture) was replaced by a neural sensor.

Determining the quantity of nutrients the soil needs for a healthy yield depends heavily on evaluating soil quality. The demand for the remotely accessible open-source model has increased with the availability of soil data, leading to the addition of deep learning techniques to forecast soil quality. With that concern, Sumathi et al. (2023) proposed an Improved Soil Quality Prediction Model using DL (ISQP-DL) model.

According to Ojo MO and Zahid (2022), Controlled Environment Agriculture (CEA) is an unconventional production system that is resource efficient, uses less space, and produces higher yields. A crop recommender forecast system (Venkadesh et al., 2022) recommended the appropriate fertilizers based on various user inputs such as soil type, crop type, humidity, and soil pH value to increase production.

Plant Detection and Classification

In vast agricultural areas, it is challenging for humans to find plants like grass and weeds. As a result of the excessive use of fertilizers, pesticides, and insecticides may have an impact on both profits and the environment. For humans, weed identification is a laborious task. Farmers can collect data from the field and apply ML and DL to identify and classify plants for increased profit.

Accurately identifying cotton crops from remotely sensed imageries is a significant task in precision agriculture. Li et al. (2021) utilized a DL-based framework for cotton crop field identification and used an improved model for the pixel-wise multidimensional densely connected CNN (DenseNet).

Factors like a noisy background and foliage occlusion can quickly impact how well fruit surface fault identification performs. Wang et al. (2021) investigated lychee's surface quality using a transformer-based GAN technique. Geethamahalakshmi et al. (2022) gathered various datasets of plant leaves originating from both healthy and ill plants to train, validate, and test the CNN model and apply them to identifying and classifying images of plants.

Tej Bahadur Shahi et al. (2022) summarized and synthesized the recent works using UAV-based remote sensing for precision agriculture. They categorized the different characteristics from the photos and demonstrated how crucial each was to the crop model's ability to execute calculations like yield estimation, disease detection, and crop categorization.

The detection and counting of wheat ears are crucial for crop field management, yield estimation, and phenotypic analysis. Yang et al. (2021) used CNN methods to achieve wheat ear detection and counting. They suggested YOLOv4 (you only look once v4) with a convolutional block attention module (CBAM), which included spatial and channel attention models and might improve the network's ability to extract features by including responsive field components. Portalés-Julià et al. (2021) detected abandoned crops in the Valencian Community (Spain) from remote sensing data based on the multitemporal Sentinel-2 images assessment and derived spectral indices using ML & DL classifiers.

Plant/Crop Health Assessment

By concentrating on plant health, farming may produce more while using fewer resources by adopting automated and high-tech agricultural systems. Crop health monitoring, crop disease identification, fruit/crop grading, and analysis of various farm products are all included in plant health assessment.

By focusing on producing key crops (such as apples, bananas, citrus fruits, pears, and grapes), Khan et al. (2021) demonstrated the transforming developments in old Chinese farming expansion and fruit output. To forecast future fruit output using the DNN method, they examined production information for various fruits produced in China. Hassan et al. (2021) proposed shallow VGG with RF and shallow VGG methods with Xgboost to identify the diseases. Their DL model considered corn (disease of Blight, Common rust, and gray leaf spot), potato (disease of early blight and late blight), and tomato (disease of bacterial spot, early blight, and late blight) plants.

The existing networks and approaches have deployed too many parameters for disease detection in natural agricultural environments. For a lightweight real-time apple leaf disease detection model (Liu et al., 2022) based on YOLOX-Nano, DL has been widely applied to disease detection.

Smart Pest and Herb Control

The primary challenge in farming is pests. Both the environment and agriculture benefit from the efficient use of pesticides. Using a UAV or drone to spray pesticides expedites the procedure and reduces the amount of pesticide absorbed into the soil. However, due to the speed and direction of the wind, many pesticides may travel to nearby areas. Limiting the loss of insecticides while spraying from above is achievable with enhanced precision.

The primary elements influencing rice yield are rice pests. The prompt implementation of preventive actions to avert financial losses is made possible by accurate pest identification. The limited number of samples in the open-source datasets currently available for rice pest identification prevents the use of DL in this area. In order to identify rice pests using Web crawler technology and manual screening, Li et al. Garg et al. (2019) highlighted various farming problems that could be solved using DL and IoT to make agricultural application predictions. Cui Yunpeng et al. (2019) investigated agricultural literature terms, the computational capacity to recognize and name domain-specific items, and word embedding vector generation based on DNN. A real-time agriculture-related image classification framework (Phasinam & Kassanuk, 2021) can use IoT sensors and cameras, mobile Apps, and ML with SVM, KNN, and probabilistic neural network (PNN) classifiers to classify real-time images related to smart agriculture. It meets the challenges of getting big sample sizes and boosts the effectiveness of identifying rice pests.

Harvesting and Hiring Machines

Most ginger planting techniques used today are manual, which significantly impedes the growth of the ginger sector. To address this issue, Fang et al. (2021) applied object detection techniques in DL to detect ginger and proposed a ginger recognition network based on YOLOv4-LITE.

Farmers might borrow equipment at a lower cost than they would have to pay by renting and sharing it. Khan Rijwan (2022) examined the significance of tool renting and sharing in the agricultural workplace.

Agricultural Frameworks, Models, and Architectures

There are various DL models and architectures used in smart agriculture. These architectures and models may be used to build their models instead of starting from scratch. Examples are AlexNet, CaffeNet, VGG, GoogleNet, Inception-ResNet, etc. These DL architecture and models have diverse advantages and different practical situations. These models come with weights pre-trained by the dataset, offering a precise classification for the problem domain.

Bhaskar et al. (2021) designed a framework using cloud, mobile computing, and AI that helps farmers understand which crop to grow and help them with its stages and what kind of seeds, manures, and other cultivation techniques can be used with a specific crop. Hamidi et al. (2022) proposed Guided Filtered Sparse Auto-Encoder (GFSAE) as a DL framework directed indirectly with field boundary information to produce accurate crop maps. Wang et al. (2021) proposed a new method based on the Coattention-Dense GRU (Gated Recurrent Unit) to detect the same semantic rice-related questions quickly and automatically.

Datasets. Common datasets used for pre-training DL architectures include ImageNet and PASCAL VOC.

DL Platforms. DL platforms can use tools (such as Theano, TensorFlow, Keras, Caffe, PyTorch, TFLearn, Pylearn2, and the Deep Learning Matlab Toolbox) to incorporate the above models and architectures. These tools (i.e., Theano, Caffe) can integrate the many DL architectures (i.e., AlexNet, VGG, GoogleNet) as libraries or classes.

The overall reviewed papers and articles from various scientific databases and scientific indexing are shown in Table 1.

Table 1. Review of research papers and articles

S/N	Research Work	Type	Subdomain in Smart Agriculture	Algorithms/Tools Used	Datasets and Technology	Remarks
1.	Nanyang Zhu et al. (2018)	-	Smart Agriculture	Review of DL Algorithms	-	For data analysis
2.	Magomadov (2019)	-	Food Production	DL Models	-	Necessity of DL
3.	Altalak et al. (2021)	-	Smart Agriculture	CNN and RNN	-	Data Analysis
4.	Kavitha (2021)	-	Smart Agriculture	DL Models	-	Review
5.	Dadashzadeh & Sakhaeian (2022)	-	Smart Agriculture	ML & DL	-	Review
6.	Senthil Kumar Swami Durai & Mary Divya Shamili (2022)	-	Smart Agriculture – Cultivation of Crops	DL	-	To realize high productivity at a low cost
7.	Altalak et al. (2022)	-	Smart Agriculture – Plant Diseases	CNN	-	Discussed the challenges
8.	Aditya Dhanraj Ramekar et al. (2022)	Advanced Technology	Smart Agriculture	ML & DL	Image	Crop prediction & soil images
9.	Bahrami et al. (2021)	A	Crop Modelling	DL	Remote Sensing & Earth Observation	Leaf Area Index (LAI) and Biomass
10.	Sami et al. (2022)	A	Smart Irrigation System	LSTM)-based neural networks	neural sensor	Water Management
11.	Sumathi et al. (2023)	A	Soil Quality	ISQP-DL) model	Sensors	Soil Quality Prediction
12.	Ojo MO & Zahid (2022),	A	CEA	unconventional production system	System	higher yields production
13.	Venkadesh et al. 2022	A	Yield Estimation	DL	Recommender System	Fertilizer Forecast
14.	Li et al. (2021)	B	Cotton Crop	CNN (DenseNet)	Framework / Optimized Model	crop field
15.	Wang et al. (2021)	B & F	Fruit Surface Detection Lychee	transformer-based GAN	Algorithm	Quality of Fruits
16.	Geethamahalakshmi et al. (2022)	B	Plants Leave Disease Detection.	CNN	Algorithms with Data Sets	Find healthy and Ill Plants

continues on following page

Table 1. Continued

S/N	Research Work	Type	Subdomain in Smart Agriculture	Algorithms/Tools Used	Datasets and Technology	Remarks
17.	Tej Bahadur Shahi et al. (2022)	B	Crop Model	DL	UAV-based remote sensing	Yield Estimation, Disease Detection & Crop Classification
18.	Yang et al. (2021)	B	Detection & Counting of Wheat Ears	CNN	YOLOv4 with CBAM, including spatial and channel attention models	Crop Field Management, Yield Estimation, & phenotypic analysis
19.	Portalés-Julià et al. (2021)	B	Detect Abandoned Crops	ML & DL Classifiers & Image Processing	Remote Sensing Data	Methodology
20.	Khan et al. (2021)	C	Fruit Production	DNN	Transformative Patterns	Prediction
21.	Hassan et al. (2021)	C	Disease Detection	Shallow VGG with RF & Shallow VGG with Xgboost		Prediction
22.	Liu et al. (2022)	C	Apple Fruit Disease Detection	DL	YOLOX-Nano.	Prediction
23.	Li et al. (2022)	D	Rice Pest Identification	DL	Web Crawler Technique & Manual Screening.	Improves the efficiency
24.	Garg et al. (2019)	D	Various Farming Problems	DL & IoT	agricultural application	Predictions
25.	Phasinam & Kassanuk (2021)	D	Image Classification	DL & Image Processing ML with SVM, KNN, and probabilistic neural network (PNN) classifiers	Image Classification Framework	Classification
26.	Fang et al. (2021	D	Ginger Sowing	DL	Object Detection Techniques	Harvesting
27.	Khan Rijwan (2022)	D	Machinery	DL	Agricultural Workplace	Automation-Tool Renting and sharing
28.	Bhaskar et al. (2021)	E & F	Smart Agriculture	DL	Framework	Smart Agriculture Operations
29.	Hamidi et al. (2022)	E & F	Crop maps	DL	GFSAE as a DL framework	Accuracy
30.	Wang et al. (2021)	E	Smart Agriculture	-	Coattention-Dense GRU	Discussion

A - Field Analysis and Yield Estimation C - Plant/Crop Health Assessment,
B - Plant Detection and Classification D - Smart Pest and Herb Control
E - Harvesting & Hiring Machines F - Agricultural Frameworks, Models, and Architectures

Methodology

The investigation study collects associated work and a complete evaluation and analysis of this work.

1. **Collection of Related Works.** It contains a keyword-based search for research papers and articles from peer-reviewed international journals, scientific Web indexing services (like Web of Science and Google Scholar), and scientific databases like IEEE Xplore and ScienceDirect. The keyword used here is
    a. "Deep Learning Model" and "Smart Agriculture" (or) "Smart Farming"
    b. "Deep Learning Architecture" and "Smart Agriculture" (or) "Smart Farming"
2. The pertinent papers and articles have been found using a filtration technique.
3. Then, it has only allowed papers and articles that properly apply the DL to smart farming or agriculture. As a result, only a smaller number of publications were initially considered.
4. It then considered the following research questions.
    a. Which agricultural issue were they aiming to resolve?
    b. What form of DL-based models are working for smart agriculture?
    c. Which data sources and types of data were used?
    d. What type of data processing and storing techniques are used?
    e. What are the existing DL models and architectures used in smart farming?
    f. What are the challenges in the existing DL models and architectures used in smart farming, and how to overcome these challenges?

RESULTS AND DISCUSSIONS

This section presents the intelligent agriculture system, the proposed model, use cases, benefits, drawbacks, etc.

Smart Agriculture System

The smart agriculture system registers farmers and stakeholders, collects real-time data from the fields, routes, and stores the data in the AgriCloud, pre-processes the data, performs ML/DL analysis, produces the results, and notifies the farmers. Figures 1-3 show the agricultural data analysis using AI (such as ML & DL) methods concerning agricultural subject areas.

The working principle of a smart agricultural system is presented below:

1. The stakeholders/farmers can register their details in the AgriCloud using Apps.
2. The IoT sensors installed in the fields can gather various sensor data. These data can be routed through gateways and stored in AgriCloud.
3. These data are then processed and stored as datasets. Examples are latitude, longitude, rainfall, temperature, soil type, the average yield of various crops, etc.
4. The DL Apps can access these datasets for data analysis.
5. DL Applications can have training datasets. The DL applications have multiple layers, such as embedding, GRU, RNN, Dense, and Dropout layers. The DL application trains the training datasets

(with three yield classes low, medium, and high) and then passes them to the trained model along with the data provided by the farmers for analysis.

6. The predicted results (for example, whether the crop comes under low, medium, or high yield type) are forwarded to the farmer's account. The farmers can receive an alert /notification about the crops with yield.

7. The farmer can make decisions according to the results.

Figure 1. Agricultural data analysis using AI techniques

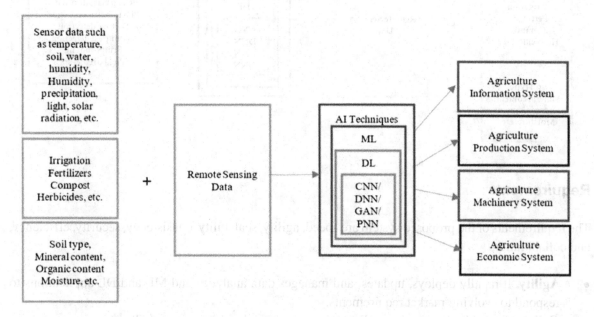

Figure 2. Agricultural data analysis using AI techniques (subject areas)

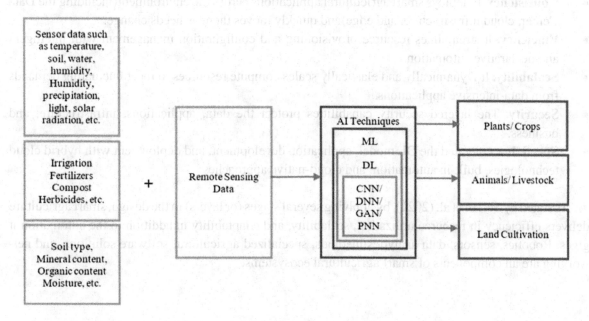

Figure 3. Agricultural data analysis using AI techniques (subjects – plants/crops)

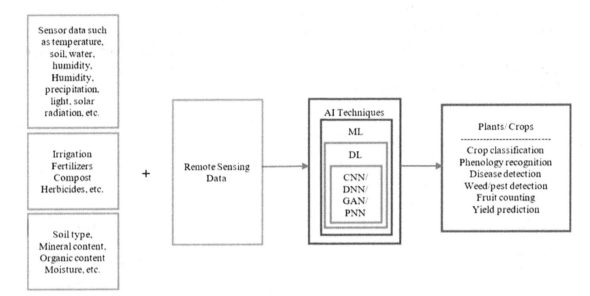

Requirements

The requirements of the proposed system are speed, agility, scalability, consistency, security, efficiency, and collaboration.

- **Agility.** It rapidly deploys, updates, and manages data analytics and ML and DL applications to respond to evolving market requirements.
- **Collaboration.** It requires data collection, application development, and IT operations to streamline processes and support innovation.
- **Consistency.** It deploys smart agricultural applications across the environment(including the Data Center, cloud infrastructure, and edge)and quickly moves them as needs change.
- **Efficiency.** It streamlines resource provisioning and configuration management with intelligent and declarative automation.
- **Scalability.** It Dynamically and elastically scales compute resources to meet fluctuating demands from data-intensive applications.
- **Security.** The layered security capabilities protect the data, applications, infrastructure, and business.
- **Speed.** It accelerated the DL model, application development, and deployment with hybrid cloud technologies, built-in automation, and cloud-native approaches.

As stated by Sufian et al. (2021), by applying several stages (or layers) in the design, smart agriculture delivers efficiency in resource utilization, scalability, and adaptability in addition to the automation it gives. Robotics, sensors, data analytics methods, specialized agricultural software solutions, and networking are all components of smart agricultural ecosystems.

Smart Farming Model

The DL model for different smart farming activities created for a multi-cloud environment with data hub architecture is shown in Figure 4. The suggested paradigm includes several elements: data collection, processing, DL models, DL applications, and agricultural users.

Data Collection. Agricultural data have been collected from various sensors/devices deployed in smart agricultural environments. ICTs used in smart agricultural environments (Sufian et al., 2021) include Robotics (such as UAV, UGV, automated tractors, automated manufacturing machines, etc.), sensors (such as sensing water, temperature, soil, humidity, light, etc.), data analytics techniques (such as Modern data analysis, image-processing algorithms, etc.), dedicated agricultural software solutions that perform various smart agricultural operations, connectivity (such as Wi-Fi, 5G, LTE, cellular networks, satellites, GPS, etc.).

Data Processing. The data processing component facilitates the complexity inherent in data management tasks, including data integration, storage, processing, governance, and portability. It is a data hub for various models and DL applications deployed in smart farming.

1. Data hub integrates data from various data sources (IoT sensors, devices, remote sensing, and satellite) and systems, whether on-premises or in the Cloud. This helps to ensure that data is consistent and up-to-date and can be accessed by various agricultural applications and users regardless of where they are located.
2. Data hubs provide a centralized location for storing and managing data, whether on-premises or in the Cloud. This can help ensure data is stored in a consistent and standardized format, regardless of source.
3. The data hub provides a consolidated connectivity that supports various data processing activities, including cleansing, transformation, and analysis. This can ensure that data is processed in a consistent and standardized manner, regardless of its location.
4. The data hub establishes clear policies and procedures for data management, including data quality, metadata management, and data lineage.
5. They ensure that data is managed consistently and efficiently, regardless of where it is stored or accessed. They must ensure data can be easily moved between on-premises and cloud environments.

This can help to support hybrid cloud scenarios where data may need to be moved back and forth between different environments.

- **DL Models.** For automating agriculture operations, the classification of plants and weeds is critical because of the implications. The DL applications and their models in smart agriculture can be characterized as plant or crop, pest control, harvesting using robotic, yield prediction, disaster monitoring, etc.
- **Crop Yield Prediction Model.** For stakeholders to develop selling plans, buying, market intervention, and resolving food shortages, crop output forecast before harvest is essential. This can be used to forecast agricultural yield and research both crops and animals.
- **Fruit Counting Model.** For crop forecast and robotic harvesting, fruit count is crucial. Traditional manual or mobile camera counting takes time and produces inaccurate results. A fruit counting model using DL with blob detection may be used for fruit counting.

- **Land Classification Model.** Land categorization is essential for assessing catastrophe risk, land use, cover, agriculture, and food security. It typically encompasses enormous land regions. DL techniques have been applied for categorization and area estimates in remote sensing along with other agricultural images. The DL may combine data from various independent sources to enable data processing and visualization by utilizing new big data, machine learning techniques, and geo-information technologies. UAVs can be extensively employed to study a variety of resources in addition to satellites. The use of UAVs enables the capture of high-quality images.

- **Obstacle (or Item) Detection Model.** With the increasing use of highly autonomous robots in farming, identifying obstacles is essential for farmers. To operate securely without supervision, these devices must perform automatic real-time hazard finding with exceptional dependability. The image classification method may be used with item identification models to improve performance.

- **Plant Classification and Weed Identification Model.** Weed identification results are uneven due to human design features and have poor feature extraction applicability abilities. Because of the consequences of automating agriculture, these models are crucial. Plant categorization can be determined using image recognition. A combination of CNN and K-means feature learning may be utilized for weed identification and control. CNN (for instance, AlexNet) has been used to spot weeds/classify plants.

- **Plant Disease Detection Model.** When done manually, detecting plant diseases takes time. Plant disease identification is mainly created on leaf image classification and pattern recognition. They can distinguish multiple plant ailments from healthy leaves by comparing plant leaves to their environment. The efficacy of DL in identifying plant diseases is astounding.

- **Sorting and Grading Model.** Satellite data is priceless and essential for sustainable land use planning to reduce CO_2 emissions, economic returns, and land degradation. The difficulty of using satellite data is interpreting the gathered images. For decision-making, the sorting and grading model can translate satellite imagery, particularly for precision agriculture and the agroindustry.

- **Weather Forecasting Model.** For agriculture, weather forecasting is essential. Unfavorable weather could destroy industries that depend on food, commerce, and health. So that the required precautions may be taken to reduce weather-related dangers, it is essential to forecast the weather correctly and on time. A DL-based weather forecasting model (Demeke Endalie et al., 2022) can predict rainfall and improve accuracy.

- **DL Applications.** Initiatives to create national farm monitoring network systems are being developed by many countries. Considering these initiatives, the proposed model considered various DL applications such as aerial survey and imaging, automatic weeding, crop and soil monitoring, insect and plant disease detection, intelligent spraying, livestock health monitoring, and produce grading and sorting in smart agriculture. These DL applications can use data from various sensors, devices, technologies, and algorithms for diverse smart farming operations.

- **Aerial Survey and Imaging System.** Applications that are great for land surveying and crop and livestock monitoring could be used in smart farming. Farmers may monitor their crops and livestock with Aerial Survey & Imaging System, which analyses imagery from drones and satellites and immediately alerts them. By constantly monitoring the fields, aerial imagery increases the precision and effectiveness of pesticide application. Weeds can be found using an intelligent spraying method. The sprayer's camera tracks the geolocation of weeds and evaluates each troublesome plant's size, shape, and color to give the right amount of herbicide to the right spot.

Because of the CV's precision, it can spray without causing collateral damage to the environment or crops.

- **Automatic Weeding System.** This method can remove undesirable plants using Agri robots equipped with CV technology. A weed can be detected and removed automatically by agri robots. Automatic weed removal can save time and decrease the need for herbicides, making farming more sustainable and environmentally friendly. Weeds and crops can be identified and separated using object detection technologies. For instance, BoniRob is an agricultural robot that locates weeds and eliminates them by introducing a bolt into the ground using a camera and image recognition technologies. It acquires to discriminate among weeds and crops through picture training on leaf size, shape, and color.

- **Crop and Soil Monitoring System.** The nutrients in the soil are crucial for the crop's health and the harvest's quantity and quality. Optimizing production efficiency requires knowing the health of the crops and the quality of the soil. The current approaches, such as human observation and assessment of crop health and soil quality, are neither precise nor timely. Instead, Drones (or UAVs) can be used to acquire aerial image data, and train models can be employed for intelligent crop monitoring and soil conditions. These models can track crop health, forecast yields, and identify crop malnutrition more quickly than humans can (using visual sensing). Drones (or UAVs) can count animals, detect disease, spot aberrant behavior, keep an eye on crucial activities like childbirth, gather data from cameras and drones (UAVs), and work with other technologies to give farmers access to food and water. DL techniques are trained to analyze video footage to ascertain what the animals are doing, including if they are drinking, eating, sleeping, or acting in an unusual way that could point to a condition or behavioral issues.

- **Insect and Plant Disease Detection System.** Detecting plant diseases and pests can be automated by farmers using DL-based image recognition technology. This technology can create models of plant health using picture classification, detection, and segmentation techniques. Deep CNN can use annotated photos from botanists to find diseases (for example, apple black rot). Additionally, a YOLO v3 upgrade may identify numerous pests and illnesses on tomato plants. Then, utilizing Support Vector Machines (SVM) characteristics, it classifies and counts insects using the detection and coarse counting approach on YOLO object detection.

- **Intelligent Spraying System.** UAVs/Drones equipped with CV can automate spraying pesticides or fertilizer equally across a field. UAV sprayers can function with extreme precision regarding the area and quantity to be sprayed, thanks to real-time recognition of target spraying areas. As a result, there is a significantly lesser possibility of contaminating crops, livestock, humans, and water systems. For instance, spraying a large area with multiple UAVs is far more efficient, yet it can be difficult to determine each craft's specific task sequences and flying trajectories.

- **Livestock Health Monitoring System.** Animals require more tracking than plants because they are the main component of innovative agriculture systems. To keep up with moving animals (such as cows, chickens, and pigs), smart farming can employ CV. Consider CattleEye. They utilize overhead cameras and CV algorithms to monitor the cattle's health and behavior. Farmers can be alerted to issues with livestock by tracking and monitoring them remotely and in real-time.

- **Produce Grading and Sorting System.** DL models incorporating CV can still benefit farmers after the crops are harvested. After harvest, they can detect developing plants' flaws, illnesses, and pests. Imaging algorithms can separate "excellent" products from flawed to ugly ones. Fruit and vegetable size, shape, color, and volume inspections allow DL with CV to automate the sorting and grading procedure more quickly and accurately than a human expert. For instance, a robotic sorting system can use CV to identify carrots with surface flaws or the wrong shape and length.

- **Agricultural Users.** The agricultural users are farmers, crop producers, buyers and sellers, markets, etc. These users must register their detail in the Smart Agri portal. They can upload the datasets manually or automatically and train the data and get the results in dashboards, alerts, graphs, etc.
- **Benefits.** The benefits of DL in smart agriculture are minimizing risks, healthier harvest, Location-optimized farming, and precision farming.
- **Minimize Risk.** AI can reduce crop failure risk by analyzing weather and soil conditions, water use, and disease risk. It provides valuable insights, such as when to sow seeds and what crops or seeds to choose.
- **Healthier Harvests.** By detecting plant diseases, weeds, and pests in advance, chemical applications such as herbicides and pesticides can be minimized, and costs can be reduced.
- **Location-Optimized Farming.** AI in harvesting, picking, and vacuuming apparatuses can assist in determining the exact location and type of fruit to be harvested.
- **Precision Agriculture.** Satellite imagery and weather data can be utilized by AI applications to determine market trends, such as which crops are in demand and which produce the highest profits. It assists farmers in increasing revenue by guiding future price patterns, demand levels, crop types, pesticide use, etc.

Figure 4. Deep learning model for smart farming

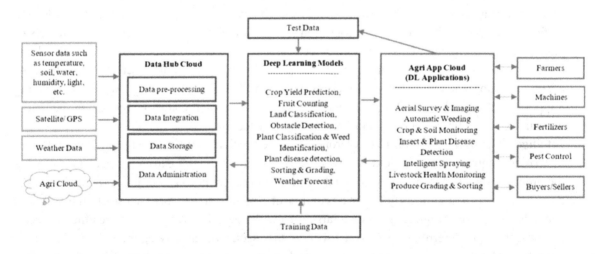

Issues and Challenges

Cost-effectiveness is rising for smart farming. More design options are now possible thanks to improved standards and protocols brought on by the IoT. Because of the greater availability, designs are now possible for the most challenging applications, such as subsistence farming in undeveloped countries. Water availability is currently the most significant impact of climate change on the global south. The once distinct wet and dry seasons no longer exist. Sensor fusion and actuator control can be provided for a reasonable price using solar power, microelectronics on boards, and low-power, short-range RF connections. Monitoring and evaluating in close to real-time is more complicated.

DL-based methods (such as CV algorithms) could provide an efficient, cost-effective, flexible, and scalable remote-sensing solution for smart agriculture. These techniques could be used to cope with different agricultural challenges in many areas, such as plant detection and classification, plant health assessment, smart pest and herb control, field analysis, and yield estimation. However, the efficient processing of data collected from UAVs is a challenging task.

Case Studies

One of the primary data sources for smart farming is thought to be remote sensing data.. Accurately identifying cotton crops from remotely sensed imageries (Li et al., 2021) is a significant task in precision agriculture. Throughout the growing season, remote sensing imageries processed using empirical and deterministic methods assisted in predicting numerous agronomic parameters.

From remote sensing data, abandoned crops could be detected (Portalés-Julià et al., 2021) in the Valencian Community (Spain). The method is based on analyzing multitemporal Sentinel-2 images and generating spectral indices; these predictors were then utilized for training ML and DL classifiers.

Wheat ears must be located and counted for the management of crop fields, estimating production, and phenotypic research. Utilizing CNN techniques, wheat ears may be identified and counted. However, wheat ears' stickiness and blockage reduce the effectiveness of detection. Therefore, to improve the accuracy of wheat ear detection and to count in the field, Yang et al. (2021) proposed a spatial and channel attention model to enhance the feature extraction capabilities of the network by adding receptive field modules.

Numerous studies have shown how well-suited radar and optical imaging are for crop mapping and estimating biophysical variables. Using a combination of radar and optical Earth data, Bahrami (2021) intended to model crop biophysical factors, such as the Leaf Area Index (LAI) and biomass.

Noise in the background and vegetation occlusion are two examples that can easily affect how well fruit surface defect detection performs. Lychees are hard to maintain and must be stored at low temperatures to keep them fresh. When lychees are harvested or processed, their surface is vulnerable to scratches and breaks. Wang et al. (2021) studied to investigate Lychee fruit surface quality. Khan et al. (2021) focused on the primary crop output (from 1980 to 2050) and considered various types of data from fruit production (e.g., apples, bananas, citrus fruits, pears, and grapes) to highlight the transforming patterns of ancient Chinese agricultural growth and the production of fruit. To forecast future production using DNN, they examined production data for various fruits cultivated in China.

Most ginger sowing techniques are manual, which substantially impedes the growth of the ginger sector. To obtain consistent ginger shoot orientation, current ginger seeders still need manual assistance while planting ginger seeds. When planting ginger, ginger shoots should be oriented consistently for higher yields and later harvest. To address the problem, Fang et al. (2021) applied object detection techniques in DL to detect Ginger and proposed a Ginger recognition network based on YOLOv4-LITE.

To identify the diseases, Hassan et al. (2021) suggested using shallow VGG with RF and shallow VGG with Xgboost. Corn, potatoes, and tomatoes are the three different plants used in the trials. Blight, common rust, and grey leaf spot are diseases of corn; early and late blights are diseases of potatoes; bacterial spot, early and late blights, and late blights are diseases of tomatoes.

Sami et al. (2021) proposed using Short-Term Long Memory (LSTM)-based NNs to address significant problems of IoT-based physical sensors. For example, a smart irrigation system replaces the physical sensors with a neural sensor.

Future of DL in Smart Agriculture

In this chapter, many DL applications for smart agriculture were covered. It covers issues like classifying land cover, estimating crop types, crop phenology, spotting weeds, and fruit grading. Other potential applications include the use of aerial imagery (using drones) to keep track of the effectiveness of the seeding procedure, to improve crop production quality by harvesting them at the best maturity levels, to monitor animal movement to think about the welfare of the animal as a whole and spot potential diseases, as well as many other scenarios. The identification of seeds, the nitrogen content of the soil and the leaves, irrigation, the assessment of water erosion, the detection of pests, the use of herbicides, the identification of contaminants, the detection of illnesses or defects in food, crop hail damage, and greenhouse monitoring are the other issues related to agriculture.

In addition to the agricultural datasets already accessible, satellites also provide remote sensing data that includes multi-temporal, multi-spectral, and multi-source images that can be utilized to solve challenges involving the classification of the land and crop cover. Numerous smart agricultural apps can estimate plant and tree development and subsequent observations to anticipate yield, determine their water requirements, or stop disease outbreaks. Farmers can use next-generation computer vision applications to track, measure, categorize, and identify many elements of farming for improved results by using ML and sustainable algorithms to drive DL APIs.

Environmental informatics can use DL models to comprehend climatic change, forecast weather and phenomena, calculate the ecological effect, etc. Furthermore, the final result can be enhanced using intricate architectures incorporating numerous DL models and classifiers with automated characteristics. Automatic robots that gather crops, pull weeds or predict predicted yields of diverse crops can all benefit from the DL techniques. A future DL application might be used for cell counts in microbiology. Future DL models will be able to collect data on plant and animal consumption and forecast the results, which will be helpful to farmers in choosing a growth curve that will work for different circumstances.

CONCLUSION

Due to rising population and food demand, farmers increasingly depend on cutting-edge methods like AI and ML algorithms to protect crops. Given the significant changes in the climate, environment, and demand for food worldwide, artificial intelligence (AI) has the potential to change 21st-century agriculture by enhancing the productivity of period, labor, and resources, enhancing environmental sustainability, optimizing resource sharing, and providing real-time monitoring to support better health and produce quality.

AI and smart farming are the waves of future advancement in the farming sector. They can improve farming by improving crop pest and disease detection and quality of goods. Precise crop yield forecasts powered by AI can assist countries in achieving food security. AI can facilitate higher food production by removing bottlenecks in the agricultural sector. The agriculture sector must change due to the use of new technologies. Agricultural technologies are perhaps the most recent innovations that farmers may use to boost food production and security while minimizing their impact on the environment. DL is a relatively new, cutting-edge picture processing method and data analysis with much potential. DL has recently entered the field of agriculture as it has been successfully used in several other areas.

Table 2. Abbreviations

Agri-Tech - Agricultural Technologies	**AI** - Artificial Intelligence
AIoT - AI-enabled IoT	**ANN** - Artificial Neural Network
CEA - Controlled Environment Agriculture	**CNN** - Convolutional Neural Networks
CSA - Climate-Smart Agriculture (CSA)	**CV** - Computer Vision
DL - Deep Learning	**DNN** - Deep Neural Networks
GAN - Generative Adversarial Networks	**IoT** - Internet of Things
KNN - K-Nearest Neighbours	**ML** - Machine Learning
MV - Machine Vision	**NN** - Neural Networks
PNN - Probabilistic Neural Network	**RNN** - Recurrent Neural Networks
UAV - Unmanned Aerial Vehicle	**WSN** - Wireless Sensor Networks

REFERENCES

Akhtar, M. N., Shaikh, A. J., Khan, A., Awais, H., Bakar, E. A., & Othman, A. R. (2021). Smart Sensing with Edge Computing in Precision Agriculture for Soil Assessment and Heavy Metal Monitoring. *Agriculture*, *11*(6), 475. doi:10.3390/agriculture11060475

Altalak, M., Ammad Uddin, M., Alajmi, A., & Rizg, A. (2022). Smart Agriculture Applications Using Deep Learning Technologies: A Survey. *Applied Sciences (Basel, Switzerland)*, *12*(12), 5919. doi:10.3390/app12125919

Aruul Mozhi Varman, S., Baskaran, A. R., Aravindh, S., & Prabhu, E. (2017). Deep Learning and IoT for Smart Agriculture Using WSN. *2017 IEEE International Conference on Computational Intelligence and Computing Research*, 1-6. 10.1109/ICCIC.2017.8524140

Bahrami, H., Homayouni, S., Safari, A., Mirzaei, S., Mahdianpari, M., & Reisi-Gahrouei, O. (2021). Deep Learning-Based Estimation of Crop Biophysical Parameters Using Multi-Source and Multi-Temporal Remote Sensing Observations. *Agronomy (Basel)*, *11*(7), 1363. doi:10.3390/agronomy11071363

Bhaskar, Dhanwate, Kale, Kayastha, & Khairnar. (2021). Deep Learning based Smart Agriculture Crop Prediction. *Journal of Advancement in Parallel Computing*, *4*(1), 1–8.

Buja, I., Sabella, E., Monteduro, A. G., Chiriacò, M. S., De Bellis, L., Luvisi, A., & Maruccio, G. (2021). Advances in Plant Disease Detection and Monitoring: From Traditional Assays to In-Field Diagnostics. *Sensors (Basel)*, *21*(6), 2129. doi:10.339021062129 PMID:33803614

Cravero, A., Pardo, S., Sepúlveda, S., & Muñoz, L. (2022). Challenges to Use Machine Learning in Agricultural Big Data: A Systematic Literature Review. *Agronomy (Basel)*, *12*(3), 748. doi:10.3390/agronomy12030748

Cube, L. A. B. S. (2022). *How AI is Helping Agriculture with Smart Solutions*. https://www.xcubelabs.com/blog/how-ai-is-helping-agriculture-with-smart-solutions/

Dadashzadeh, M., & Sakhaeian, K. (2022). Applications of machine learning and deep learning techniques in smart agriculture: A review. *4th Intercontinental Geoinformation Days (IGD)*, 229-232.

Dayioğlu, M. A., & Turker, U. (2021). Digital Transformation for Sustainable Future - Agriculture 4.0: A review. *Tarim Bilimleri Dergisi*, *27*(4), 373–399. doi:10.15832/ankutbd.986431

DBTA. (2021). *Managing the Hybrid and Multicloud Future, Best Practice Series*. https://info.semarchy.com/hubfs/collateral-v2/report/rp-managing-the-hybrid-and-multicloud-future-Semarchy-DBTA.pdf

Endalie, D., Haile, G., & Taye, W. (2022). Deep Learning Model for daily rainfall prediction: A case study of Jimma, Ethiopia. *Water Science and Technology: Water Supply*, *22*(3), 3448–3461. doi:10.2166/ws.2021.391

Eos. (2022). *Smart Farming: Technologies & Benefits for Agriculture*. EOS Data Analytics. https://eos.com/blog/smart-farming/

Fang, L., Wu, Y., Li, Y., Guo, H., Zhang, H., Wang, X., Xi, R., & Hou, J. (2021). Ginger Seeding Detection and Shoot Orientation Discrimination Using an Improved YOLOv4-LITE Network. *Agronomy (Basel)*, *11*(11), 2328. doi:10.3390/agronomy11112328

Fiehn, H. B., Schiebel, L., Avila, A. F., Miller, B., & Mickelson, A. (2018). Smart Agriculture System Based on Deep Learning. *ICSDE'18: Proceedings of the 2nd International Conference on Smart Digital Environment*, 158–165. 10.1145/3289100.3289126

Geethamahalakshmi,, & Sambath, Gayathiri, Vijayaraja, Senthil Kumar, & Umaeswari. (2022). A Deep Learning Based Smart Agriculture Technique for an IoT Environment. *Journal of Pharmaceutical Negative Results*, *13*(10), 1562–1569. doi:10.47750/pnr.2022.13.S10.181

Hamidi, M., Safari, A., Homayouni, S., & Hasani, H. (2022). Guided Filtered Sparse Auto-Encoder for Accurate Crop Mapping from Multitemporal and Multi-spectral Imagery. *Agronomy (Basel)*, *12*(11), 2615. doi:10.3390/agronomy12112615

Hassan, S. M., Jasinski, M., Zbigniew, L., Jasinska, E., & Maji, A. K. (2021). Plant Disease Identification Using Shallow Convolutional Neural Network. *Agronomy (Basel)*, *11*(12), 2388. doi:10.3390/agronomy11122388

Intellias. (2022). *Artificial Intelligence in Agriculture: Rooting Out the Seed of Doubt*. https://intellias.com/artificial-intelligence-in-agriculture/

Kamilaris, A., & Prenafeta-Boldú, F. X. (2018). *Deep Learning in Agriculture: A Survey*. doi:10.1016/j.compag.2018.02.016

Kavitha A (2021). Deep Learning for Smart Agriculture. *International Journal of Engineering Research & Technology, 9*(5), 132-134.

Khan, T., Sherazi, H. H. R., Ali, M., Letchmunan, S., & Butt, U. M. (2021). Deep Learning-Based Growth Prediction System: A Use Case of China Agriculture. *Agronomy (Basel), 11*(8), 1551. doi:10.3390/agronomy11081551

Kondaveeti, Brahma, & Sahithi. (2021). Deep Learning Applications in Agriculture: The Role of Deep Learning in Smart Agriculture. In *Artificial Intelligence and IoT-Based Technologies for Sustainable Farming and Smart Agriculture.* IGI Global.

Krishnamoorthy, R., Thiagarajan, R., Padmapriya, S., Mohan, I., Arun, S., & Dineshkumar, T. (2022). Applications of Machine Learning and Deep Learning in Smart Agriculture. doi:10.1002/9781119861850.ch21

Kuppusamy, P. (2021). Emerging Technological Model to Sustainable Agriculture. In P. Tomar & G. Kaur (Eds.), *Artificial Intelligence and IoT-Based Technologies for Sustainable Farming and Smart Agriculture* (pp. 101–122). IGI Global. doi:10.4018/978-1-7998-1722-2.ch007

Kuradusenge, M., Hitimana, E., Hanyurwimfura, D., Rukundo, P., Mtonga, K., Mukasine, A., Uwitonze, C., Ngabonziza, J., & Uwamahoro, A. (2023). Crop Yield Prediction Using Machine Learning Models: Case of Irish Potato and Maize. *Agriculture, 13*(1), 225. doi:10.3390/agriculture13010225

Li, H., Wang, G., Dong, Z., Wei, X., Wu, M., Song, H., & Amankwah, S. O. Y. (2021). Identifying Cotton Fields from Remote Sensing Images Using Multiple Deep Learning Networks. *Agronomy (Basel), 11*(1), 174. doi:10.3390/agronomy11010174

Li, Z., Jiang, X., Jia, X., Duan, X., Wang, Y., & Mu, J. (2022). Classification Method of Significant Rice Pests Based on Deep Learning. *Agronomy (Basel), 12*(9), 2096. doi:10.3390/agronomy12092096

Liu, S., Qiao, Y., Li, J., Zhang, H., Zhang, M., & Wang, M. (2022). An Improved Lightweight Network for Real-Time Detection of Apple Leaf Diseases in Natural Scenes. *Agronomy (Basel), 12*(10), 2363. doi:10.3390/agronomy12102363

Magomadov, V. S. (2019). Deep Learning and its Role in Smart Agriculture. Journal of Physics: Conference Series. *Journal of Physics: Conference Series, 1399*(4), 044109. doi:10.1088/1742-6596/1399/4/044109

Mehran & Sakhaeian. (2022). *Applications of machine learning and deep learning techniques in smart agriculture: A review*. 4th Intercontinental Geoinformation Days (IGD), Tabriz, Iran.

Navarro, E., Costa, N., & Pereira, A. (2020). A Systematic Review of IoT Solutions for Smart Farming. *Sensors, 20*(15), 4231. doi:10.3390/s20154231

Patel, A. (2022). *Computer Vision and Deep Learning for Agriculture*. https://pyimagesearch.com/2022/08/10/computer-vision-and-deep-learning-for-agriculture/

Portalés-Julià, E., Campos-Taberner, M., García-Haro, F. J., & Gilabert, M. A. (2021). Assessing the Sentinel-2 Capabilities to Identify Abandoned Crops Using Deep Learning. *Agronomy (Basel), 11*(4), 654. doi:10.3390/agronomy11040654

Ramana, K., Aluvala, R., Kumar, M. R., Nagaraja, G., Krishna, A. V., & Nagendra, P. (2022). Leaf Disease Classification in Smart Agriculture Using Deep Neural Network Architecture and IoT. *Journal of Circuits, Systems, and Computers*, *31*(15), 2240004. doi:10.1142/S0218126622400047

Sacolick, I. (2020). *When hybrid Multicloud has Technical Advantages.* InfoWorld. https://www.info-world.com/article/3568497/when-hybrid-multicloud-has-technical-advantages.html

Said Mohamed, E. S., Belal, A., Kotb Abd-Elmabod, S., El-Shirbeny, M. A., Gad, A., & Zahran, M. B. (2021). Smart farming for improving agricultural management. *The Egyptian Journal of Remote Sensing and Space Sciences*, *24*(4), 971–981. Advance online publication. doi:10.1016/j.ejrs.2021.08.007

Sami, M., Khan, S. Q., Khurram, M., Farooq, M. U., Ajum, R., Aziz, S., Qureshi, R., & Sadak, F. (2022). A Deep Learning-Based Sensor Modeling for Smart Irrigation System. *Agronomy (Basel)*, *12*(1), 212. doi:10.3390/agronomy12010212

Sarker, I.H. (2022). Deep Learning: A Comprehensive Overview on Techniques, Taxonomy, Applications, and Research Directions. *SN Comput Sci.*, *2*(6), 420. doi:10.1007/s42979-021-00815-1

Sehgal Foundation. (2023). *Role of Modern Technology in Agriculture.* https://www.smsfoundation.org/role-of-modern-technology-in-agriculture/

Senthil, K. S. D., & Shamili, M. D. (2022). Smart farming using Machine Learning and Deep Learning techniques. *Decision Analytics Journal*, *3*, 100041. doi:10.1016/j.dajour.2022.100041

Shafi, U., Mumtaz, R., García-Nieto, J., Hassan, S. A., Zaidi, S. A. R., & Iqbal, N. (2019, September 2). Precision Agriculture Techniques and Practices: From Considerations to Applications. *Sensors (Basel)*, *19*(17), 3796. doi:10.339019173796 PMID:31480709

Shahi, Xu, Neupane, & Guo. (2022). Machine learning methods for precision agriculture with UAV imagery: A review. *Electronic Research Archive, 30*(12), 4277-4317. doi:10.3934/era.2022218

Srivastava, A. (2022). Smart Agriculture Using UAV and Deep Learning: A Systematic Review. In Internet of Things Robotic and Drone Technology. CRC Press. doi:10.1201/9781003181613-1

Storm, H., Baylis, K., & Heckelei, T. (2020). Machine learning in agricultural and applied economics. *European Review of Agriculture Economics*, *47*(3), 849–892. doi:10.1093/erae/jbz033

Subeesh, A., & Mehta, C. R. (2021). Automation and Digitization of Agriculture using Artificial Intelligence and Internet of Things. *Artificial Intelligence in Agriculture*, *5*, 278–291. doi:10.1016/j.aiia.2021.11.004

Sufian, A. (2021). *Smart Agriculture Using UAV and Deep Learning a Systematic Review.* doi:10.1201/9781003181613-1

Sumathi, P., Karthikeyan, V. V., Kavitha, M. S., & Karthik, S. (2023). Improved Soil Quality Prediction Model Using Deep Learning for Smart Agriculture Systems, Computer Systems Science & Engineering. *Tech Science Process, CSSE*, *45*(2), 1546–1559. doi:10.32604/csse.2023.027580

Swaminathan, M. S., & Bhavani, R. V. (2013). Food production & availability—essential prerequisites for sustainable food security. *The Indian Journal of Medical Research*, *138*(3), 383–391. PMID:24135188

Thomas, J. (2017). *Inside Machine Learning.* https://medium.com/inside-machine-learning/3-scenarios-for-machine-learning-on-multicloud-c850fb8bed8f

Tripathy, S. S., Tripathy, N., Rath, M., Pati, A., Panigrahi, A., & Dash, M. (2022). Smart Farming based on Deep Learning Approaches. *2022 2nd Odisha International Conference on Electrical Power Engineering, Communication and Computing Technology (ODICON)*, 1-5. 10.1109/ODICON54453.2022.10010165

TuomistoH. L.ScheelbeekP. F. D.ChalabiZ.GreenR.SmithR. D.HainesA.DangourA. D. (2017). Effects of environmental change on population nutrition and health: A comprehensive framework with a focus on fruits and vegetables. *Wellcome Open Res.* doi:10.12688/wellcomeopenres.11190.1

Ünal, Z. (2020). Smart Farming Becomes Even Smarter with Deep Learning - A Bibliographical Analysis. *IEEE Access : Practical Innovations, Open Solutions*, 8, 105587–105609. doi:10.1109/ACCESS.2020.3000175

UNCTAD. (2017). The Role of Science, Technology, and Innovation in Ensuring Food Security by 2030. *United Nations Conference on Trade and Development (UNCTAD).*

Walch, K. (2020). *How AI can be used in agriculture: Applications and benefits.* TechTarget. https://www.techtarget.com/searchenterpriseai/feature/Agricultural-AI-yields-better-crops-through-data-analytics

Wang, C., & Xiao, Z. (2021). Lychee Surface Defect Detection Based on Deep Convolutional Neural Networks with GAN-Based Data Augmentation. *Agronomy (Basel)*, 11(8), 1500. doi:10.3390/agronomy11081500

Wang, H., Zhu, H., Wu, H., Wang, X., Han, X., & Xu, T. (2021). A Densely Connected GRU Neural Network Based on Coattention Mechanism for Chinese Rice-Related Question Similarity Matching. *Agronomy (Basel)*, 11(7), 1307. doi:10.3390/agronomy11071307

Wang, T., Xu, X., Wang, C., Li, Z., & Li, D. (2021). From Smart Farming towards Unmanned Farms: A New Mode of Agricultural Production. *Agriculture*, 11(2), 145. doi:10.3390/agriculture11020145

Yang, B.; Gao, Z.; Gao, Y.; Zhu, Y. (2021). Rapid Detection and Counting of Wheat Ears in the Field Using YOLOv4 with Attention Module. *Agronomy, 11.* https://doi.org/11061202 doi:10.3390/agronomy

Zhang, W., Miao, Z., Li, N., He, C., & Sun, T. (2022). Review of Current Robotic Approaches for Precision Weed Management. *Current Robotics Reports*, 3(3), 139–151. doi:10.100743154-022-00086-5 PMID:35891887

Zhu, N., Liu, X., Liu, Z., Hu, K., Wang, Y., Tan, J., Huang, M., Zhu, Q., Ji, X., Jiang, Y., & Guo, Y. (2018). Deep Learning for Smart Agriculture: Concepts, Tools, Applications, and Opportunities. *International Journal of Agricultural and Biological Engineering*, 11(4), 32–44. doi:10.25165/j.ijabe.20181104.4475

Zhu, N., Liu, X., Liu, Z., Hu, K., Wang, Y., Tan, J., Huang, M., Zhu, Q., Ji, X., Jiang, Y., & Guo, Y. (2018). Deep Learning for Smart Agriculture: Concepts, Tools, Applications, and Opportunities. *International Journal of Agricultural and Biological Engineering*, 11(4), 32–44. doi:10.25165/j.ijabe.20181104.4475

KEY TERMS AND DEFINITIONS

Agricultural Innovation System: A system of individuals, organizations, and enterprises focused on bringing new products, processes, and economic use to achieve food and nutrition security, economic development, and sustainable natural resource management.

Biodiversity: The total diversity of all organisms and ecosystems at various spatial scales (from genes to entire biomass).

Climate Change: Climate change refers to a change in the state of the climate that can be identified (e.g., by using statistical tests) by changes in the mean and/or the variability of its properties and that persists for an extended period, typically decades or longer.

Climate-Smart Agriculture (CSA): Helps guide actions to transform agri-food systems towards green and climate-resilient practices.

Conservation Agriculture (CA): Conservation Agriculture is an approach to managing agroecosystems for improved and sustained productivity, increased profits, and food security while preserving and enhancing the resource base and the environment.

Disaster: A serious disruption of the functioning of a community or a society involving widespread human, material, economic, or environmental losses and impacts, which exceeds the ability of the affected community or society to cope using its resources.

Ecosystem: The interactive system formed from all living organisms and their abiotic environment within a given area. It covers and comprises the entire globe, biomes at the continental scale, or minor, well-circumscribed systems such as a small pond.

Erosion: The process of removal and transport of soil and rock by weathering, mass wasting, and the action of streams, glaciers, waves, winds, and underground water.

Precision Agriculture (PA): It is a farming management strategy based on observing, measuring, and responding to temporal and spatial variability to improve agricultural production sustainability.

Smart Agriculture: It refers to using technologies like IoT, sensors, location systems, robots, and AI on the farm to increase the quality and quantity of the crops while optimizing human labor.

Smart Farming: It refers to managing farms using modern ICT to increase the quantity and quality of products while optimizing the human labor required.

Sustainability: Meeting the needs of the present without compromising the ability of future generations to meet their needs.

Chapter 12
Automated MP3 Tag Editor via Data Mining:
A Classification Software for Predicting MP3 Metadata

Jonathan Rufus Samuel
Vellore Institute of Technology, India

Shivansh Sahai
Vellore Institute of Technology, India

P. Swarnalatha
Vellore Institute of Technology, India

Prabu Sevugan
Pondicherry University, India

V. Balaji
Vardhaman College of Engineering, India

ABSTRACT

The music space in today's world is ever evolving and expanding. With great improvements to today's technology, we have been able to bring out music to the vast majority of today's ever-growing and tech-savvy people. In today's market, the biggest players for music streaming include behemoth corporations like Spotify, Gaana, Apple Music, YouTube Music, and so on and so forth. This also happens to be quite the shift from how music was once listened to. For songs downloaded out of old music databases without the song's metadata in place, and other distribution sites, they oftentimes come without any known metadata, i.e., most of the details with regards to the songs are absent, such as the artist's name, the year it was made, album art, etc. This chapter discusses how data mining, data scraping, and data classification are utilized to help add incomplete metadata to song files without the same, along with the design process, the software development, and research for the same.

DOI: 10.4018/978-1-6684-8098-4.ch012

INTRODUCTION

The Music space int today's world is ever evolving and expanding. With great improvements to today's technology, we have been able to bring out music to the vast majority of today's ever growing and tech savvy people. In today's market, the biggest players for Music Streaming include behemoth corporations like Spotify, Gaana, Apple Music, YouTube Music and so on and so forth. This also happens to be quite the shift from how music was once listened to. Originally pioneered by the launch of the iPod, music was once brought and downloaded from services such as Apple Music's iTunes, costing as low as 0.3 cents per song. And even as Music continues to grow away from traditional downloading to streaming, user support has been increasingly harder to get. For songs downloaded out of Old Music Databases, and other distribution sites, they oftentimes come without any known metadata. i.e., Most of the Details with regards to the songs are absent, such as the Artist's name, the year it was made, Album Art, etc. An Example is shown below.

Figure 1. Example of songs without metadata

y2mate.com - the_promise_by_tracy_chapman_cC8pdPys-...	Unknown artist	Unknown album	Unknown genre	05:21
y2mate.com - the_temptations_my_girl_C_CSjcm-z1w	Unknown artist	Unknown album	Unknown genre	02:43
y2mate.com - the_temptations_my_girl_C_CSjcm-z1w_256...	Unknown artist	Unknown album	Unknown genre	02:43
y2mate.com - tracy_chapman_baby_can_i_hold_you_offici...	Unknown artist	Unknown album	Unknown genre	03:14
y2mate.com - tracy_chapman_fast_car_DwrHwZyFN7M	Unknown artist	Unknown album	Unknown genre	04:56
y2mate.com - westlife_swear_it_again_official_video_0Ua...	Unknown artist	Unknown album	Unknown genre	04:06
y2mate.com - white_flag_chris_tomlin_passion_2012_whit...	Unknown artist	Unknown album	Unknown genre	05:04
y2mate.com - worthy_is_the_lamb_hillsong_worship_V-cd...	Unknown artist	Unknown album	Unknown genre	06:14
Yann Tiersen - Comptine d'un autre été (Amélie)	Unknown artist	Unknown album	Unknown genre	03:10

As shown in Figure 1, the data such as Artist's Name, title (Without the presence of Download Hex codes) and others miscellaneous info are not present or are displayed inaccurately. And, since these songs are not aided by the like of Spotify, Apple Music, etc., they would not be rectified on their own. Now on one hand, this can be manually done by the user, but it would take a lot of time and be very resource intensive. Therefore, to avoid the hassle that comes with this shift in the music distribution industry, this chapter details the usage of Data Mining and Machine Learning based Classification of metadata that is scraped and obtained from various popular avenues, the details of which are further discussed in this paper, including the thought process, methodology, planning (with respect to Software Design Specifications) and Overall Implementation along with the Final Outcome. We will also closely observe how one can better generate data via Data Mining, and how generated results can be made more accurate overtime with the option of scalability, and how Machine Learning can achieve the same via simple classification algorithms.

HOW THE INDUSTRY HANDLES MP3 METADATA

What Is Music Metadata?

Music metadata refers to the collection of data associated with a song file, including details such as the artist's name, producer, writer, song title, and release date. This information is vital for identifying, organizing, and delivering audio content effectively. The more comprehensive the metadata, the easier it becomes to collect and distribute the royalties generated. Moreover, detailed metadata enhances the listener experience by helping them identify the content and its creators when using music services. However, the significance of metadata extends beyond these aspects.

Digital service providers (DSPs) like Spotify, Apple Music, Amazon Music, and Tidal heavily rely on metadata to suggest similar artists to their listeners. Additionally, metadata assists curators in crafting popular playlists that musicians aspire to be featured in. Lastly, accurate metadata plays a crucial role in allocating master and publishing rights to the rightful owners and facilitating the appropriate distribution of royalties.

In summary, music metadata serves as the backbone for effective management and delivery of audio content, benefiting both creators and consumers in various ways.

The thing about metadata is this: It's as fundamental to digital music – whether you're making it, marketing it, or simply enjoying it – as flour is in your bread. (Spotify for artists)

Why Is Music Metadata so Important?

Royalty revenues in the music industry are derived from various sources, including physical sales, synchronization and licensing, as well as digital music, encompassing downloads and streams. Ensuring accurate publishing metadata is particularly crucial for the proper payment of creators, especially in the realm of digital distribution. If content providers, such as labels, fail to provide complete and detailed metadata during distribution, the information will not be synchronized across the entire music ecosystem. Consequently, all rights holders involved in the song will not receive their rightful and proportional payments.

To illustrate this point, let's consider an example: Suppose a song is written by an artist who also acts as the songwriter, and they decide to collaborate with two other artists during the recording process. These three artists are signed to different record labels and publishers. The song garners significant success through effective marketing and receives airplay on national radio stations. Additionally, it is licensed for synchronization in a film. In order for all parties to receive fair compensation, they must be included in the metadata and correctly credited for their contributions. Any omission, incorrect crediting, misspelling, or failure to adhere to the guidelines of digital service providers (DSPs) can result in insufficient payments to the respective rights owners, despite their talent and efforts.

While the focus of this chapter is not solely on royalties, it is important to note that royalty percentages and splits among the involved parties are determined prior to distribution and release. These decisions are made through negotiations between the artist(s), managers, producers, labels, publishers, and other stakeholders in the supply chain. These agreements are typically established at the early stages of the creative process and may or may not affect the metadata included during distribution.

We are all aware of the music industry's metadata problem. Many collecting societies and publishers estimate that about 25% of music publishing revenue doesn't make it to its rightful owners due to lack of accurate metadata, and the industry is scrambling to find a viable solution. . . . Agreed and transparent metadata early in the process is the only solution to a sustainable music rights management system. And the only way to get there, is to remove the music industry's silo mentality and bring in more openness and collaboration. (Niclas Molinder, founder of music metadata company Auddly)

Currently, the music industry lacks a universally applicable solution for managing metadata. It largely relies on individual collecting societies, key players such as managers, record labels, music distribution businesses, and rights holders to address metadata-related challenges. Therefore, to help better combat the overall issue, the need for including metadata within unaccounted for songs remains. We hope that we can address the same via the use of Data Mining and Machine Learning based Classification. Although the chances of such an operation would be able to directly impact the issue at hand, it will begin the change that's needed within the industry to correctly link music with its authors.

LITERATURE SURVEYS

The following Journals, Articles and Papers were used to better define the problem, and depict current methods used by the industry to handle Music Metadata, and also how Machine Leaning Classification and Data Mining works, especially within the context of the given chapter.

Data Mining Techniques and Applications (Bharati et al., 2010)

General Summary: Data mining is a process that involves extracting valuable patterns and information from large datasets. It has been widely adopted by organizations to enhance their business operations and has yielded impressive results. With the growth of Information Technology, vast amounts of data have been generated in various fields. Researchers in databases and information technology have focused on storing and manipulating this data for decision-making purposes. Data mining, also known as knowledge discovery, knowledge extraction, or data analysis, plays a crucial role in extracting insights from extensive datasets.

Several algorithms and techniques are employed in data mining, including Classification, Clustering, Regression, Artificial Intelligence, Neural Networks, Association Rules, Decision Trees, Genetic Algorithms, and Nearest Neighbour methods. Classification is the most commonly used technique, where a model is developed using pre-classified examples to classify a larger population of records. This approach is particularly useful in applications like fraud detection and credit risk assessment. Classification algorithms, such as decision trees and neural networks, are often employed in this process.

Clustering is another technique used in data mining to identify similar classes or groups of objects. By applying clustering techniques, it becomes possible to identify dense and sparse regions within the dataset, discover distribution patterns, and find correlations among data attributes. Clustering can serve as a pre-processing step for attribute subset selection and classification, and it has various applications, such as grouping customers based on purchasing patterns or categorizing genes with similar functionality. Different methods, including partitioning, hierarchical, density-based, grid-based, and model-based methods, are used for clustering analysis.

Regression analysis is a technique used for prediction in data mining. It involves modelling the relationship between independent variables (known attributes) and dependent variables (the ones to be predicted). While simple regression models can be effective for certain predictions, more complex techniques like logistic regression, decision trees, or neural networks are often required to forecast future values accurately. Regression methods include linear regression, multivariate linear regression, nonlinear regression, and multivariate nonlinear regression.

Neural networks are sets of interconnected input/output units, and they utilize weights assigned to each connection. During the learning phase, neural networks adjust these weights to predict the correct class labels of input data. They excel at extracting meaningful insights from complex or imprecise data, detecting intricate patterns and trends that may go unnoticed by humans or other computer techniques. Neural networks are particularly suited for continuous valued inputs and outputs and find applications in areas like handwriting recognition, speech synthesis, and various business problems. Backpropagation is a commonly used neural network algorithm.

Data mining finds applications across various industries, even though it is still an evolving technology. Retail stores, hospitals, banks, insurance companies, and many other organizations regularly utilize data mining techniques. By combining data mining with statistical analysis, pattern recognition, and other tools, these organizations can uncover hidden patterns and connections that are difficult to identify using traditional methods. This technology enables businesses to gain insights into customer behaviour and make informed marketing decisions, leading to improved strategies and outcomes.

An Empirical Study on Several Classification Algorithms and Their Improvements (Wu et al., 2009)

General Summary: This paper focuses on the study and application of classification algorithms in data mining and machine learning. It explores three types of classification methods: decision tree learning, Bayesian learning, and instance-based learning. The goal is to improve the classification accuracy of these methods through various enhancements. The researchers conducted experiments using 36 UCI datasets obtained from Weka and compared the performance of the improved algorithms empirically.

Classification algorithms are essential in data mining and machine learning, as they help construct classifiers to analyse unknown data accurately. The performance of a classifier is typically measured by its classification accuracy. Various methods can be used to build classification algorithms, including decision tree, Bayesian, instance-based learning, artificial neural network, and support vector machine. In recent years, many improved algorithms have been introduced in these fields.

The paper presents three sets of experiments focusing on decision tree methods (ID3, C4.5, NBTree, Random Forest), Bayesian methods (NB, HNB, AODE, Bayes Net), and instance-based learning methods (KNN, KNNDW, LWNB, KStar). The performance of the improved algorithms is evaluated and compared to traditional algorithms using 10-fold cross-validation. Additionally, a two-tailed t-test with a 95% confidence level is conducted to analyse the statistical significance between each pair of algorithms. The rest of the paper is organized as follows: Section 2 provides a formal description of the chosen algorithms, including their traditional versions and improvements. Section 3 presents the experimental process and results. Finally, the paper concludes with a summary of the findings.

In decision tree learning algorithms, a decision tree is constructed using a tree-like structure that represents a flow chart. The tree determines the class of an instance by traversing from the root node to a leaf node based on attribute values. The paper discusses the traditional ID3 algorithm and its improved versions, such as C4.5 and Random Forest. These improved algorithms address issues like overfitting and noise tolerance, resulting in better classification accuracy. Bayesian learning algorithms employ statistical methods to classify data. The core of these algorithms is the Bayesian theorem, which allows for classification based on probability and statistics. The paper discusses the traditional Naive Bayes (NB) algorithm and its improved versions, including HNB, AODE, and Bayes Net. These algorithms reduce the independence assumption of attributes, leading to improved classification accuracy compared to NB.

Instance-based learning algorithms, also known as "lazy-learning" methods, store training sets and classify test instances based on similarity to stored instances. The paper explores the traditional K-Nearest Neighbor (KNN) algorithm and its improved versions, such as KNNDW, LWNB, and KStar. These enhancements introduce weighted attributes and similarity functions to improve classification accuracy. The experimental results are presented in tables, showing the detailed performance of each algorithm on the 36 UCI datasets. The tables indicate significant improvements in classification accuracy for the improved algorithms compared to their traditional counterparts. The researchers also calculate the margin number, which represents the difference between the number of wins and losses in the t-tests, providing additional insights into algorithm performance.

In summary, the experiments demonstrate that the improved algorithms in decision tree learning, Bayesian learning, and instance-based learning achieve higher classification accuracy compared to traditional algorithms. The findings support the effectiveness of these enhancements in various data mining and machine learning tasks.

Connecting the Dots: Music Metadata Generation, Schemas, and Applications (Nik et al., 2008)

General Summary: The paper discusses the importance of metadata in the field of music and proposes a framework for comparing the expressiveness and richness of different metadata schemas for music applications. The authors aim to create a metadata framework that combines the strengths of various existing metadata systems and allows users to choose the right metadata schema for their specific application.

The paper begins by introducing the concept of metadata and its relevance in music information retrieval (MIR) research. It mentions several existing metadata web services, such as Amazon.com, Last. fm, MusicBrainz, and Discogs, which provide diverse and useful metadata for music. However, there is a significant overlap among these systems. The authors propose a metadata framework that can handle different metadata schemas and facilitate the annotation process. The framework takes a musical object (MO), which includes an audio file and initial metadata, and retrieves metadata from various sources. The resulting metadata is stored in an internal format, covering a range of information from low-level audio features to descriptive data about the musical work.

To compare different metadata schemas, the authors define clusters of semantically related metadata fields. These clusters include musical information, classifiers, performance details, versioning, descriptors, rights and ownership, playback rendition, lyrics, grouping and referencing, identifiers, record information, instrumentation and arrangement, sound and carrier information, event details, time modelling, musical notation, attention metadata and usage, publishing, composition, production, and meta-metadata. The authors then discuss different application domains in the field of music, such as music library/encyclopaedia, personal collection management, commerce and transactions, music editing/production, music playback, music recommendation, music retrieval, and musical notation. They cluster software applications into these domains based on the actions performed by users.

Next, the authors compared the metadata schemas and application domains to determine their relevance and usefulness in different cases. The authors create a decision table that shows the compatibility of each metadata schema with the various application domains. They find that MPEG-7 scores well for all domains but note some interoperability issues. FreeDB and MusicBrainz are best suited for music retrieval, while MusicXML is highly relevant for musical notation. The paper concludes by emphasizing that no single metadata standard covers all the requirements for music metadata. The choice of metadata schema depends on the specific application and its functionality. The proposed framework and decision table can assist users in selecting the most suitable metadata schema for their needs.

Overall, the paper highlights the importance of metadata in music applications and provides a framework for comparing different metadata schemas. It offers insights into the strengths and limitations of various metadata standards and their compatibility with different application domains.

AIM AND OBJECTIVE OF PROPOSED SOFTWARE

To utilize Data Mining and Machine Learning principles to develop a piece of software that can Achieve the following tasks with regards to songs without metadata:

- Extract Title from Current File name, along with Artist name (If possible), save it to a database.
- Data Scraper for each Title of Song – Find the following metadata parameters and save to database using principles of Data Mining of various sources like Wikipedia, Spotify, shazam, etc. And aggregating the following results (using a classification algorithm) to find the best fit for the following parameters: file name, path, Tag, Title, Artist, Album, Year, Track, Genre, Comment, Album Artist, Composer, Disc number, album art jpg file.
- Automate process for all songs metadata addition. Make it user friendly via a GUI based python application/API.

METHODOLOGY

The implementation plan is fairly straightforward. We are to deploy an automation software that can data mine (data scrape) the required metadata from various sources like google searches, Wikipedia, Spotify Databases, etc. This metadata is then applied to the required songs along with appropriate cover art. Figure 3, depicts the Process Flow Diagram employed for the project at hand. Thus, this software under complete implementation can be used to successfully perform it's required actions, under optimal conditions.

As shown in the diagram above, the overall process flow is demonstrated. The Application begins by loading songs into the database from any given directory. The file name and file path columns within the Database are populated accordingly. Next the title generator module takes over Process Flow. The Title Generator employs a regex function to get 'cues' from file names. Cues are basically clues that enable the Data Scraper to better scrape data for a given Music file. If no cues are found, the Data Scraper will utilise the mp3 file's sound signature to identify a song. This search avenue is handled by means of the Shazam API. The two main cues are the Artist Name and the Title. If found, they are placed in the database for further processing. Process then moves forward into the Data Scraper section. This section

Figure 2. Process flow diagram

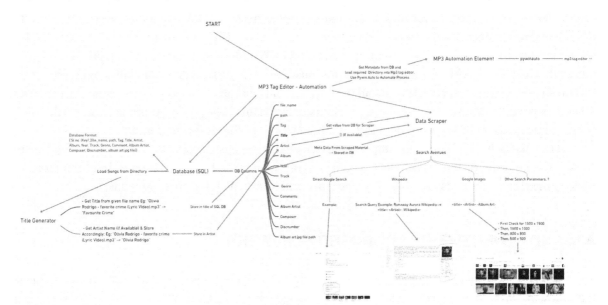

employs the use of multiple 'search avenues' to obtain various sets of metadata from various sources. These currently include ordinary Google searches, Wikipedia API searches, Google Images (For Album Art), Shazam API, Spotify API. Etc. The possibilities for scraping are endless, with only a need for interfacing within the given system This is further discussed in Sections 5.1 and 5.2.

Each search avenue returns a set of metadata depending on the cues obtained from the regex function. The metadata is then pushed into the classification unit, which decides the best fit data for each field based on majority. Currently, a Naïve Bayes Classifier is utilised for the same, with equal weightage given to all search avenues. Alternatives are further explored in Sections 8 and 9.

HOW DATA MINING IS UTILIZED IN GIVEN APPLICATION

Data Mining is simply the process of sorting and searching through a large pool of data (here obtained via Data Scraping) to gain inferences and find patterns within a given dataset. Data Scraping is just the means for obtaining the data required. The given application employs multiple search avenues to handle this process, however, to improve performances, it is necessary to employ as many search avenues as possible. These include sites that do not have standard API's, or those that just display XML/HTML files on request. To extract the data that we need, we need to employ the use of specialised functions, like BeautifulSoup from Python.

As seen in the above case scenario, data is available everywhere, even within the first site page present on providing a search query. As seen in figure, searching for the cues 'runaway' and 'Aurora', we are able to gather multiple data points, like the Album Name, Artist, Release Date, List of Genres, etc. This enables us to better equip the classifier with as much data as possible to handle anomalies and missinterpretations. Thus, these are the ways Data Scraping and Mining is employed in the given Application.

Figure 3. Google search: Avenue led data

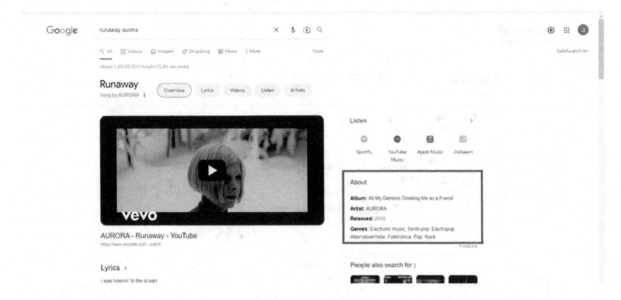

The Need for Classification

The metadata is then pushed into the classification unit, which decides the best fit data for each field based on the majority specified. For the given application, we are using a Naïve Bayes Classifier. It is a supervised Machine Learning Algorithm, which is used for classification tasks, specifically text classification. It uses Bayesian Probability to determine how likely a given data point is accurate for a given song. For example, if a search avenue were to return data that is incorrect or corrupted, the most probable data point is added into the database. Naïve Bayes gives equal weightage to all the search avenues within the application. This is an important need overall to get the best fit data from the overall dataset for a given song. At its current stage, Classification is at its simplest, and can be greatly improved and optimized. This is further discussed in Section 8.

Choice of Process Model for Given Implementation: V Model

As this is a relatively small project, which aims to encompass the technology of data mining into a meta tag editor, it seemed appropriate to go for the V-Model, which aims to give a working model at the end of the Project Cycle. As seen in the advantages section, it is a highly disciplined model which is completed one stage at a time. As mapped out in the Gantt chart, this would coincide with the objective of a V-Model type Project Model. The Project requirements are clear and well established, and since it inly encompasses the three to four sub-models to fully implement, the project "Automated Mp3 tag Editor using Data Mining" can proceed under the V-Model Software Project Model type.

Figure 4. V model

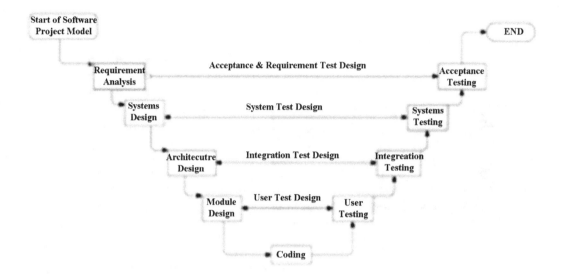

IMPLEMENTATION: SOFTWARE DESIGN SPECIFICATIONS (SDS)

Design Considerations

System Environment: As this is predominantly a data mining project, the language used is python for the entire app. Depending on live performances, a shift to java for the GUI components can be made. The database used is the python sqlite3 database, which is inbuilt into python 3. In case of Java, SQL (either Oracle or any other substitute) can be used.

Design Methodology: The major processes that will be used for the given project are in line with the Software Design Schema discussed in the course CSE3001 - Software Engineering. It is predominantly an Object-Oriented System Design (in terms of code design and implementation) Other design considerations included the methodology involved in designing use case scenarios and Classes present within OOP based design. These were specified via creation and usage of UML diagrams (See Figure 5) and UML diagrams (See Figure 4), as shown in this chapter.

Risks and Volatile Areas: Only major issue that can be discussed would be the possibility for a Python based exe file not being able to perform its tasks as required, in a stable and continuous form. Other than that, no other problems/volatile areas have been identified.

Architecture

As mentioned before, the architecture used for the given project is Object Oriented. The components of the given system are to be encapsulated and the operations within the project must be applied accordingly to manipulate the given data. The subsequent communication between various components in the project scope is therefore established to be of the Object-Oriented type. Subsystem Components of given software are discussed below:

Figure 5. Class diagram

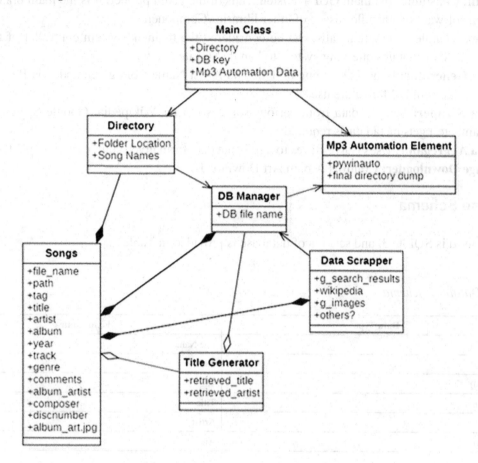

Figure 6. UML diagram: Use case scenarios

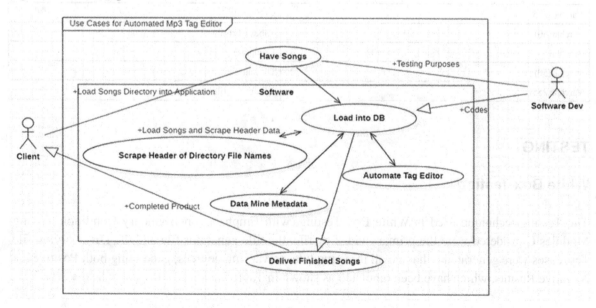

1. **Main:** Constitutes the main GUI + System calls of the given project. It is the main branch of the given software that handles usage of other libraries/Components.
2. **Index:** Handles subsystem calls, can be considered the main subsystem controller of the given project. Also contains querying system to handle SQLite 3 database.
3. **Title Generator:** Handles scraping of Title and Artist Name from given code via Regex. Stores found values in DB for future use.
4. **Data Scraper:** Scrapes data from various sources (so far Wikipedia, Google Search, Spotify, Shaam, etc.) gets metadata as required.
5. **Data Aggregator:** Uses Naïve Bayes to aggregate data from given sources and output the best fit.
6. **Image Downloader:** Controls Album Art Downloads.

Database Schema

Database used is SQLite 3, and schema of database is provided in Table 1.

Table 1. Database schema

Data Type	Field Name
Varchar(100)	File Name
Varchar(255)	Path
Varchar(100)	Tag
Varchar(50)	Title
Varchar(50)	Artist
Varchar(100)	Album
Int(4)	Year
Int(10)	Track
Varchar(50)	Genre
Varchar(255)	Comment
Varchar(50)	Album Artist
Varchar(50)	Composer
Varchar(50)	Disc number
Varchar(255)	Album Art file

TESTING

White Box Testing

The Testing technique used is White Box Testing, with Emphasis on Boundary Condition Testing. Modules Considered were the primary index.py file, the title generator file and the DB querying file. Test cases were generated to handle all three modules to varying degrees, generating both Positive and Negative Results, which have been tabulated as shown in Table 2.

Table 2. White box testing results

TEST CASE ID	Activity	Inputs	Expected Results	Observed results	Status	Comments
TC-01	Enter Invalid Directory Name	'C:/Users/jonat/Music/Latest Songs'	Message: Invalid Entry	-	Fail	Add if block to check viability of directory
TC-02	Enter Invalid Directory Name	'C:/Users/jonat/Music/Latest Songs'	Message: Invalid Entry	Message: Invalid Entry	Pass	Successfully Added required Check block.
TC-03	Insert invalid data into DB	INSERT INTO MUSIC values (?, ?, NULL, NULL, NULL, NULL, NULL, NULL, NULL, NULL)	Message: Invalid DB Entry (Invalid No of Rows)	-	Fail	Add if block to check viability of Query.
TC-04	Insert invalid data into DB	INSERT INTO MUSIC values (?, ?, NULL, NULL, NULL, NULL, NULL, NULL, NULL, NULL)	Message: Invalid DB Entry (Invalid No of Rows)	Message: Invalid DB Entry (Invalid No of Rows)	Pass	Successfully Added required Check block.
TC-05	Insert Invalid DB Connection Data.	connection = sqlite3.connect('Music_database.db')	Message: Invalid DB Connection credentials	-	Fail	Add Exception Handler for Incorrect Credentials.
TC-06	Insert Invalid DB Connection Data.	connection = sqlite3.connect('Music_database.db', NULL, NULL, NULL)	Message: Invalid DB Connection credentials	-	Fail	Add Exception Handler for NULL DB Credentials.
TC-07	Insert Invalid DB Connection Data.	connection = sqlite3.connect('Music_database.db', NULL, NULL, NULL)	Message: Invalid DB Connection credentials	Message: Invalid DB Connection credentials	Pass	Successfully Added required Exception Handler.
TC-08	No data returned for given song.	(?, ?, NULL, NULL, NULL, NULL, NULL, NULL, NULL)	-	Error: NULL value present in final DB result.	Fail	Consider NULL values as well.
TC-09	No data returned for given song.	(?, ?, NULL, NULL, NULL, NULL, NULL, NULL, NULL)	-	-	Pass	Removed unnecessary test requirement, thereby increasing final results.
TC-10	Cannot find appropriate class on Google Search.	url = "https://google.com/search?q=" + text class="H"	Class NOT FOUND; Continue;	Class NOT FOUND; Continue;	Pass	Continues Search even if required class is not found during scraper phase.
TC-11	Get the full song file name and filter to extract song name and artist (activity-1)	y2mate.com - all_sons_daughters_great_are_you_lord_official_live_concert_uHz0w-HG4iU_256kbps.mp3	SONG- all_sons_daughters_great_are_you_lord_official_live_concert_ ARTIST-NONE	SONG- all_sons_daughters_great_are_you_lord_official_live_concert_ ARTIST-NONE	Pass	We were successful to extract the song, artist which could be used to fetch further results
TC-12	Get the full song file name and filter to extract song name and artist (activity-1)	5 Seconds of Summer - Amnesia (Official Video).mp3	SONG- Amnesia ARTIST -5 Seconds of Summer	SONG- Amnesia ARTIST- 5 Seconds of Summer	Pass	We were successful to extract the song, artist which could be used to fetch further results
TC-13	Get the full song file name and filter to extract song name and artist (activity-1)	for KING & COUNTRY - Ceasefire - Music Video.mp3	SONG- Ceasefire ARTIST- for KING & COUNTRY	SONG- Ceasefire ARTIST- for KING & COUNTRY	Pass	We were successful to extract the song, artist which could be used to fetch further results

continues on following page

Table 2. Continued

TEST CASE ID	Activity	Inputs	Expected Results	Observed results	Status	Comments
TC-14	Get the full song file name and filter to extract song name and artist	- [YT2mp3.info] - Arctic Monkeys - Do I Wanna Know_ (Official Video) (320kbps).mp3	SONG- Do I Wanna Know ARTIST- Arctic Monkeys	SONG- Do I Wanna Know ARTIST- Arctic Monkeys	Pass	We were successful to extract the song, artist which could be used to fetch further results
TC-15	Get the full song file name and filter to extract song name and artist (activity-1)	Y2Mate.is - Arctic Monkeys - No 1 Party Anthem Lyric Video-pE8mWOgMpP8-160k-1641641934769.mp3	SONG- No 1 Party Anthem ARTIST- Arctic Monkeys	SONG- No 1 Party Anthem ARTIST- Arctic Monkeys	Pass	We were successful to extract the song, artist which could be used to fetch further results
TC-16	Get the full song file name and filter to extract song name and artist (activity-1)	Jack Garratt - Surprise Yourself.mp3	SONG- Surprise Ypurself ARTIST- JACK GARRET	NULL	Fail	Unable to retrieve required metadata
TC-17	Use the song name and data to fetch details about song such as time, genre,rating,background (activity-2)	SONG- all_sons_daughters_great_are_you_lord_official_live_concert_ ARTIST-NONE	Song Name: Great Are You Lord Language: English Album All Sons & Daughters Writer(s) Jason Ingram, Leslie Jordan, David Leonard Released 2014	Song Name: Great Are You Lord Language: English Album All Sons & Daughters Writer(s) Jason Ingram, Leslie Jordan, David Leonard Released 2014	Pass	Success the user would be able to
TC-18	Use the song name and data to fetch details about song such as time, genre,rating,background (activity-2)	SONG- Amnesia ARTIST -5 Seconds of Summer	Artist: 5 Seconds of Summer Album: 5 Seconds of Summer Released: 2014 Nominations: Teen Choice Award for Choice Music – Break-Up Song Genres: Pop rock, Children's Music	Error Code: 5	Fail	Error generated during run time. Unable to retrieve required data.
TC-19	Use the song name and data to fetch details about song such as time, genre,rating,background (activity-2)	SONG- Ceasefire ARTIST- for KING & COUNTRY	Artist: for KING & COUNTRY Album: Run Wild. Live Free. Love Strong. Released: 2014 Genre: Christian	Artist: for KING & COUNTRY Album: Run Wild. Live Free. Love Strong. Released: 2014 Genre: Christian	Pass	Retrieved Metadata for given Query as required.
TC-20	Use the song name and data to fetch details about song such as time, genre,rating,background (activity-2)	SONG- Do I Wanna Know ARTIST- Arctic Monkeys			Pass	Retrieved Metadata for given Query as required.

Selenium-Based Testing

With a sample set of close to 300 songs, our team conducted a Selenium based testing cycle with the given sample set of songs. The final results gave us a success rate or 54.79%, with songs available being either improperly classified (~35%), or not classified at all (~10%). The results are shown in Figure 7.

Figure 7. Final test results of selenium testing with sample song set

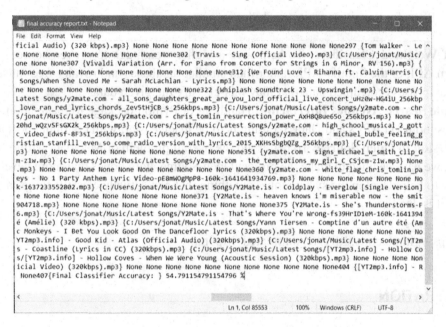

DOWNSIDES AND METHODS TO HANDLE THE SAME

Although this application is a novel one, that is not present in the market at any capacity, it only solves the overall issue of copy-righted metadata handling at an individual level. However, little steps like these can eventually help eradicate the problem, if taken more seriously at an individual's level. Other downsides stem mostly from handling of the cues generated but the regex engine. For example, a song file titled 'Movie-Converter_145-Runaway_Aurora.mp3' offers at most 2 cues for the other search avenues to work with, compared to something like '03453453980123489.mp3'. The use of sound sampling via the Shazam API can handle such cases, but that also leads to a excessive positive bias toward a single search avenue, as data cannot be retrieved through any other search avenue. This can be handled better by adding more search avenues, especially others that identify songs via their audio sampling, rather than file names. This will require more interfacing, but will overall aid in a fairer end result.

Scalability

The application detailed here is fundamentally scalable due to the way classification works. Accuracy of a system is better offset when there are more avenues to detail positive data. Thus, this application requires more interfacing of search avenues. These can include Music Databases, Record Company databases, etc.

Future Plans and Further Scope

Some Future Plans for the given project include:

- **Use of Weighted Classifiers:** To help give a higher weightage to proven sources, such as the Shazam API, or the Spotify API, rather than smaller databases and royalty free music databases, that may possess corrupted data that may mis-classify the given data.
- **Multiple Search Avenues Interfacing:** Handling of Python package to make addition of search avenues, both via API's and Data Scraping is to be made easier, with continual development.
- **Conversion to Open Source:** To better aid the overall problem of Metadata within the music industry, we have decided to make the project Open Source, with hopes that more developers would be able to help develop the system into something that can actively classify songs and give credit where it is due.

Link: https://github.com/JRS296/Automated_Mp3tag

DEMONSTRATION

A short demo by the creators of the given piece of software has been uploaded to YouTube, which demonstrates the functionality of the given software.

Link: https://www.youtube.com/watch?v=coYtrDU7lqY

CONCLUSION

Through this paper, we were able to see the need for better handling metadata within the Music Industry. This problem has given us an opportunity to utilise Machine Learning, Data Mining and Scraping techniques to help classify song files with incomplete metadata, to help fix the issue at hand one song at a time. We were able to have a better understanding of how Classification works, how Data Mining and Scraping can prove to be an effective search avenue, the basic Software Engineering principles required to develop an application for the same, and the overall results at its current state. We hope that this article would encourage our readers to contribute to the same in due to time, to help eradicate this problem within the Music Industry.

REFERENCES

Bharati, M., & Ramageri, B. (2010). Data mining techniques and applications. *Indian Journal of Computer Science and Engineering*.

Chu, X., Ilyas, I. F., Krishnan, S., & Wang, J. (2016). Data Cleaning: Overview and Emerging Challenges. In *Proceedings of the 2016 International Conference on Management of Data (SIGMOD '16)*. Association for Computing Machinery. https://doi.org/10.1145/2882903.2912574

Corthaut, N., Govaerts, S., Verbert, K., & Duval, E. (2008). *Connecting the Dots: Music Metadata Generation, Schemas and Applications*. Academic Press.

Hardjono, T., Howard, G., Scace, E., Chowdury, M., Novak, L., Gaudet, M., Anderson, J., Davis, N., Kulis, C., Sweeney, E., & Vaughan, C. (2019). *Towards an Open and Scalable Music Metadata Layer*. Academic Press.

Holmes & Kellogg. (2006). Automating functional tests using Selenium. *AGILE 2006 (AGILE'06)*. . doi:10.1109/AGILE.2006.19

Lee, J. S., & Siau, K. (2001). A review of data mining techniques. Industrial Management & Data Systems, 101(1), 41-46. doi:10.1108/02635570110365989

Liao, Chu, & Hsiao. (2012). Data mining techniques and applications – A decade review from 2000 to 2011. *Expert Systems with Applications, 39*(12), 11303-11311. doi:10.1016/j.eswa.2012.02.063

Morris, J. W. (2012). Making music behave: Metadata and the digital music commodity. *New Media & Society, 14*(5), 850–866. doi:10.1177/1461444811430645

Ness, S. R., Theocharis, A., Tzanetakis, G., & Martins, L. G. (2009). Improving automatic music tag annotation using stacked generalization of probabilistic SVM outputs. In *Proceedings of the 17th ACM international conference on Multimedia (MM '09)*. Association for Computing Machinery. 10.1145/1631272.1631393

Sen, P. C., Hajra, M., & Ghosh, M. (2020). Supervised Classification Algorithms in Machine Learning: A Survey and Review. In J. Mandal & D. Bhattacharya (Eds.), *Emerging Technology in Modelling and Graphics. Advances in Intelligent Systems and Computing* (Vol. 937). Springer. doi:10.1007/978-981-13-7403-6_11

Singh, A., Thakur, N., & Sharma, A. (2016). A review of supervised machine learning algorithms. *2016 3rd International Conference on Computing for Sustainable Global Development (INDIACom)*, 1310-1315.

SinghI.TarikaB. (2014). *Comparative Analysis of Open Source Automated Software Testing Tools: Selenium, Sikuli and Watir*. doi:10.13140/2.1.1418.4324

Tian, M., Fazekas, G., Black, D., & Sandler, M. (2013). Towards the Representation of Chinese Traditional Music: A State of the Art Review of Music Metadata Standards. *International Conference on Dublin Core and Metadata Applications*, 71–81. Retrieved from https://dcpapers.dublincore.org/pubs/article/view/3672

Wang, Fan, & Wang. (2021). Comparative analysis of image classification algorithms based on traditional machine learning and deep learning. *Pattern Recognition Letters, 141*, 61-67. doi:10.1016/j.patrec.2020.07.042

Wu, J., Gao, Z., & Hu, C. (2009). An Empirical Study on Several Classification Algorithms and Their Improvements. In Z. Cai, Z. Li, Z. Kang, & Y. Liu (Eds.), Lecture Notes in Computer Science: Vol. 5821. *Advances in Computation and Intelligence. ISICA 2009*. Springer. doi:10.1007/978-3-642-04843-2_30

Chapter 13
Machine Learning–Integrated IoT–Based Smart Home Energy Management System

Maganti Syamala
Koneru Lakshmaiah Education Foundation, India

Samikshya Dash
School of Computer Science and Engineering, VIT-AP University, India

Komala C. R.
HKBK College of Engineering, India

S. Meenakshi
R.M.K. Engineering College, India

P. V. Pramila
Saveetha School of Engineering, Saveetha Institute of Medical and Technical Sciences, India

Sampath Boopathi
Muthayammal Engineering College, India

ABSTRACT

The internet of things (IoT) is an important data source for data science technology, providing easy trends and patterns identification, enhanced automation, constant development, ease of handling multi-dimensional data, and low computational cost. Prediction in energy consumption is essential for the enhancement of sustainable cities and urban planning, as buildings are the world's largest consumer of energy due to population growth, development, and structural shifts in the economy. This study explored and exploited deep learning-based techniques in the domain of energy consumption in smart residential buildings. It found that optimal window size is an important factor in predicting prediction performance, best N window size, and model uncertainty estimation. Deep learning models for household energy consumption in smart residential buildings are an optimal model for estimation of prediction performance and uncertainty.

DOI: 10.4018/978-1-6684-8098-4.ch013

INTRODUCTION

The Internet of Things (IoT) is a vast network made up of billions of intelligent physical items that are connected to other connected devices and the Internet via sensors, software, and other embedded technologies. In 2025, the IoT will have a considerable economic influence, with the energy industry accounting for 33% of the market. Given that a large portion of the population spends more than 90% of their time inside buildings, the rapid rise of the population, economy, and industrialization has increased energy consumption. The building industry is the largest energy user in the world, accounting for 39% of global energy consumption and 38% of CO_2 emissions. Up to 2040, the demand for electricity is anticipated to increase at a pace of 2.1% annually, which is twice as fast as that for primary energy. Heating and cooling systems have a major influence on how much energy is used in residential buildings, necessitating the best possible energy management. In order to lower electricity costs and optimize power usage, smart grid and smart house technology are gaining popularity. These technologies are crucial to the sustainable growth of smart cities, societies, and urban planning. Residential energy consumption forecasting is difficult and adds value to the field of energy efficiency and management research, which strives to advance smart urbanization in terms of planning for the management of the power grid and electric utility resources. By creating a reliable and sustainable energy consumption prediction model that can be used to control load management, defect detection, energy demand, and pollution mitigation, smart residential buildings may be enhanced (Amer et al., 2014).

Deep learning approaches have made it possible for analysts and researchers to create and train robust models for a variety of applications, including edge computing, robotics, sentiment analysis, computer vision, and more. The application of deep learning models to forecast energy consumption in buildings is highlighted in this section.

- Model deep learning Identify complicated linkages and understand hidden information using deep neural networks to forecast future energy consumption.
- Traditional machine learning methods concentrate on temporal information, but deep learning methods are better at modeling both temporal and spatial connections.
- To increase model accuracy, deep learning models include feature engineering.
- Large datasets can be handled by deep learning models, however this is dependent on their depth and particular architectures.

A sustainable machine learning model for estimating household electric energy usage using an improved sliding window technique is presented. It focuses on quantifying model uncertainty and evaluating the suggested work in comparison to the base model and competitive benchmark using the considered energy dataset (Chen et al., 2021).

Ninety-six percent of businesses are using IoT-based technology to better monitor and manage their physical resources, while 67 percent of developers are creating IoT-based technology owing to its adaptability and effectiveness. But for the Internet of Things to succeed, several technologies must work together to provide an additional layer of intelligence. Smart cities, transportation systems, and manufacturing applications are driving the IoT, and it's predicted that 50 billion gadgets will be connected in the next 5 to 6 years. Validating the large number forecast by Cisco, IDC, and Gartner is difficult, though. The Internet of Things (IoT) is a platform that enables sensor-based objects to communicate and exchange data in an intelligent setting (Jeevanantham et al., 2023). The true value of the IoT lies in creating intelligent devices, communicating meaningful perspectives, and generating fresh business concepts. As millions of devices connect to the internet of things, there will be a massive flood of Big Data. Three steps will be completed by the data: data collection, data transmission, and data analysis. Real-time or streaming, large-volume, and organised or unstructured IoT data will all be present (Samikannu et al., 2023).

IoT is a revolutionary technology that links communication devices to the physical world through wireless technologies like WiFi, Bluetooth, GSM, and ZigBee (S. et al., 2022). IoT paradigms involve communication devices implanted into sensor devices to gather various types of information, such as geological, ecological, calculated, and astrological information. Communication devices will receive and transmit orders and data with the aid of remotely operated equipment, raising living standards. IoT offers several options via Internet technology (Reddy et al., 2023). Numerous vertical markets, including health, transportation, smart homes, smart cities, agriculture, education, and so on, have seen the emergence of IoT applications. This study focuses on data from smart homes to increase comfort, energy efficiency, productivity, and quality of life. Internet-connected home appliances offer intelligent services, such as the application of Cortana DL to refrigerator knowledge by Microsoft and Liebherr. Nearly a third of all the power used in the US is used in the residential sector, mostly for HVAC and lighting equipment. The family may better manage home expenses and expenditures, as well as track and forecast health changes, with the aid of evaluations and predictions. For smart home systems to cut power usage and forecast future demand, intelligent energy management is necessary. One of the key study topics for applications in the smart home is energy management (Rashid et al., 2019).

A computational model that can make choices, attributes that are relevant to the decision, and underlying information needed for model training make up machine learning (ML), a subclass of AI. In order to quickly discover trends and patterns, increase automation and continuous improvement, handle multi-dimensional data, improve accuracy, have cheap computing costs, and have a wide variety of applications, machine learning (ML) is being embraced in the software and hardware sectors (Babu et al., 2023; Boopathi, Arigela, et al., 2023; Jeevanantham et al., 2023). By processing real-time data, machine learning (ML), a new branch of artificial intelligence, promises to facilitate the creation of quick and effective data-driven models, analyses, and predictions. It may be divided into three major categories: reinforcement learning, unsupervised learning, and supervised learning. While label less learning is carried out in unsupervised learning and reinforcement learning is based on experience, supervised learning is trained using data that has been labeled. Data representation is essential to the success of machine learning applications because they employ intelligent learning methods for prediction, pattern recognition, data mining, and analytics. Because of its higher data representation and prediction accuracy, deep learning is becoming more and more popular. It is employed to deal with nonlinear issues and abstractly describe incoming data on a large scale. In order to incrementally acquire high-level characteristics from the data, deep learning (DL), a specialized sub-field of machine learning, draws on a layered framework of algorithms known as an artificial neural network. It does away with the necessity for thorough feature extraction and subject expertise. Deep learning (DL) architectures may autonomously learn by detecting features and generating abstraction layers to represent data. DL architectures are an advancement of machine learning (ML), which was first suggested by Geoffrey Hinton in 1986. There are several definitions in the literature (Boopathi, Siva Kumar, et al., 2023; Harikaran et al., 2023; Reddy et al., 2023; S. et al., 2022; Sampath et al., 2022; Vanitha et al., 2023).

- Computing models can learn useful characteristics from data with a high level of abstraction thanks to deep learning.

- The input distribution is used by deep learning algorithms to identify useful representations and higher-level learnt features.
- Without depending on programmer-defined features, deep learning techniques link input to output directly from data via automated feature extraction.

DL architectures are multilevel nonlinear computations with better performance that automate feature engineering and data scaling. They are used in a number of vertical fields, including speech recognition, picture recognition, machine translation, network caching, IoT applications, and NLP. Based on what they are used for, they are divided into three classes (Liu et al., 2020):

- Unsupervised learning tasks are carried out with the use of generative models.
- Discriminative models are those created for tasks requiring supervised learning.
- Generative and discriminative models are used in hybrid models.

In light of the current energy crisis, rising energy demand, pollution, and flaws in green energy systems, discriminative models can assist IoT applications in predicting energy demand and consumption. DL models can assist decision-makers in developing and implementing energy-efficient policies that will reduce pollution and advance sustainability. In the energy sector, the IoT and DL are two technologies that are intertwined, resulting in the creation of tools like AI to anticipate energy demand and use. However, there are restrictions on traditional teaching techniques and approaches to energy management (Gariba & Pipaliya, 2016).

- Certain models exclude temporal information, which might produce unreliable findings.
- Collinearity is a problem that has to do with how time and space interact.
- Analysis of causal patterns can be challenging.
- When working with enormous datasets, management may be challenging.
- Working with static data requires the usage of static data.

The advantages of the DL technique, which include feature engineering, hidden features, and managing massive amounts of data, are achieved by using hierarchy to learn complicated non-linear problems from basic ones. But training is computationally costly, and figuring out which hyperparameters to use is a kind of black art without any rules.

IoT AND ML ANALYTICS

The Internet of Things (IoT) is a ground-breaking innovation that has gained traction in a number of industries, including smart cities, healthcare, transportation, manufacturing, sustainable living, and more. IoT analytics is the use of data analysis to extract value from sources that are IoT enabled, such as smart devices, sensors, and other internet-connected objects. Understanding the market potential of IoT requires data collecting and analysis from IoT enabled data sources, yet only 1% of data provided by IoT is being used. Applications for IoT data analytics including anomaly detection, prediction, and optimization are increasingly relying on ML and AI (Kumara et al., 2023; Palaniappan et al., 2023; Senthil et al., 2023).

IoT produced data is analysed using ML algorithms to identify trends and acquire deeper understanding. This paper explains IoT analytics, its lifecycle, its techniques, and the primary difficulties in developing and deploying solutions. IoT data may be identified and understood using machine learning (ML), allowing for better decision-making in areas like predictive maintenance, optimization, anomaly detection, and more. Better judgments may be made with the use of ML techniques, algorithms, and models (Koltsaklis et al., 2022).

IoT Analytics

Analytics is the science of extracting knowledge and insights from data via analysis. Data and IoT are intertwined, with data generation and consumption growing at an exponential rate. The estimated 30.73 billion IoT devices are fuelling this data deluge, which is driving the inevitable IoT adoption. IoT analytics therefore offers a framework for analysis in order to evaluate and argue the data produced by IoT devices in numerous vertical sectors. Because internet-enabled devices typically create a lot of information over a short period of time, IoT analytics is one of the analytics types that is suited for the analysis of the data collected from these devices in particular. According to statistics, IoT devices produce roughly 2.5 quintillion bytes of data daily. Big data and IoT data are comparable, however there are some differences because of the variety of sources (Boopathi, Khare, et al., 2023; Domakonda et al., 2023; Selvakumar et al., 2023; Vennila et al., 2023).

The variety of the data makes the data integration process difficult. Smart metres, which can control energy demand and consumption, are one example of an IoT application that heavily relies on IoT analytics. The electrical sector has been able to reduce and control its electricity costs thanks to this deployment, and Miami's Department of Park Management has saved more than US$1 million. Four categories of data analytics exist: streaming, geographic, time-series, and prescriptive. Real-time IoT data is analysed using streaming analytics and spatial analytics to prompt quick decisions and identify critical circumstances. To find patterns and trends, time-series analytics examine time-based data. To optimise action for particular circumstances, prescriptive analytics combines descriptive and predictive analysis.

Figure 1. Stages of IoT data analytics techniques

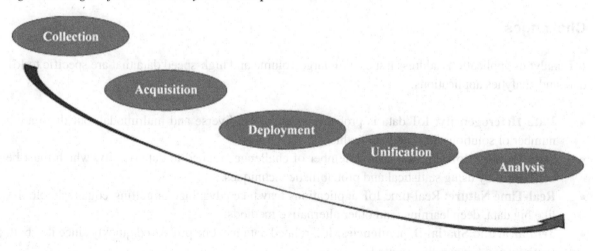

Analytics Techniques

The three steps of IoT data analytics include data gathering, analysis, and deployment (Machorro-Cano et al., 2020). The IoT analytics lifecycle may be used by researchers and practitioners for development and deployment (Figure 1).

Data Collection: The most crucial information is that IoT data is collected from objects that can connect to the Internet, augmented with logical metadata, and verified in terms of source of origin and format. The data is also validated using integrity, correctness, and consistency. This level addresses IoT analytics difficulties, including problems with consistency and quality. IoT data collection exhibits a number of quirks, making it challenging to manage various IoT streams.

Analysis of Smart Data: IoT-generated data is transformed into useful knowledge using AI techniques like data mining and machine learning (ML).

Deployment, Operationalization, and Reuse: This lifecycle makes it possible to deploy analysis methods, visualise IoT data, and reuse IoT datasets and expertise across several applications. As the maturity of IoT use-cases is connected to its ultimate analytics, yet also with the flexibility to reuse the city datasets and analytics functions, it may also be used to assess the "smartness" degree of a city. Successful data management and analysis depend on effective data management and analysis (S. et al., 2022; Sampath et al., 2022).

- **Statistical Modelling:** Putting theories to the test in order to learn from IoT data.
- **Machine Learning:** Heuristic strategies are one method that ML techniques utilise to optimise learning models.
- **IoT Middleware and Interoperability Technologies:** In order to solve concerns with veracity and diversity, this field offers methods for gathering, organising, and combining IoT data streams.
- **Data Mining and Knowledge Discovery:** Through data cleansing, learning, and visualisation, the disciples apply theoretical principles and heuristics to derive knowledge that is helpful.
- **Data Streams Management Systems:** To manage high-speed data streams with erratic arrival times and properties, IoT streaming systems are utilised.
- **Database Management Systems:** The management of data permanence and administration is handled by RDMS, NoSQL databases, and other technologies.

Challenges

IoT analytics applications address issues with large volume and high-speed data that are specific to IoT data and analytics applications.

- **Data Heterogeneity:** IoT data is probably going to be diverse and multimodal, but there are a number of solutions that can handle this.
- **Data Quality:** IoT analytics face a number of challenges related to data quality, which must be considered by using statistical and probabilistic techniques.
- **Real-Time Nature:** Real-time IoT applications may take advantage of cutting-edge technologies like big data, deep learning, and other alternative methods.
- **Temporal and Spatial Dependencies:** IoT-related data must be processed quickly since it is both spatially and temporally oriented.

- **Privacy and Security:** IoT applications need to handle data under tight security and privacy conditions, including privacy protection, encryption, and safe data storage.
- **Data Bias:** IoT data records can result in skewed processing, thus a thorough analysis and comprehension of training and testing datasets are required. You can employ conventional data mining techniques.

Similar methods to those used in traditional data mining are needed for the creation and deployment of IoT analytics, including data preparation, comprehension, testing, and deployment. IoT analytics entails gathering, analysing, and visualising data using a variety of tools and approaches.

MACHINE LEARNING ANALYTICS

Due to developments in several computer technologies, including IoT, GPU computing, cloud computing, big data, and other hardware, AI has come a long way during the past ten years. The most widely used algorithm is machine learning, which is utilized in numerous fields including computer graphics, speech recognition, computer vision, decision-making, natural language processing, and intelligent control (Alzoubi, 2022; Forootani et al., 2022).

IoT is made possible in large part by machine learning (ML), which offers intelligence for devices, data processing, and information inference. By offering workable ways to uncover valuable insights and buried features in IoT data, it empowers users. ML tries to create models and use them to discover trends or forecast data in the future. Based on the features of the dataset and the type of data, ML algorithms may be classified. based on similarities, purpose, and learning style.

- AI and ML text books generally value "learning styles" above "input data" when categorising ML algorithms. This enables users to evaluate the input data and model preparation process and select the best model from the standpoint of the problem. Depending on the learner, ML algorithms are categorised into four categories.
- Labeled training datasets are used in supervised learning.
- Unsupervised learning makes conclusions from unlabeled answers.
- Both labelled and unlabelled data are used in semi-supervised learning.
- For processing IoT data to model business choices, supervised learning and reinforcement learning are prominent methods.

TECHNIQUES FOR MACHINE LEARNING ANALYTICS

Machine learning is an area of AI that integrates several algorithms to facilitate efficient data processing and decision-making. Data analysis, predictive modeling, and classification all depend on machine learning (ML) algorithms, which may be divided into categories based on how they learn and how they do comparable tasks. Based on their learning methods and similarities in the context of their functions, ML algorithms are grouped. Popular ML algorithms are provided in this part and are organized into the most logical groups to make the information easier to grasp (Gariba & Pipaliya, 2016; Rashid et al., 2019; Shahriar & Rahman, 2015).

Regression Algorithms

The link between the dependent and predictor variables is modelled using regression techniques. In order to forecast and predict outcomes as well as deduce the causal connections between predictor and outcome variables, algorithms are employed. Although regression is a crucial component of statistical computing, problem-solving with it requires practise. Linear, Multiple, Stepwise, Logistic, Multivariate Adaptive Regression Splines, OLSR, LOESS, and locally determined Scatterplot Smoothing are examples of regression techniques.

Regularization Algorithms

Models are corrected using regularisation methods depending on their efficiency, simplicity, time and space complexity, and application to other techniques. LASSO, Elastic Net, Ridge Regression, and LARS are examples of regularisation techniques.

Instance-Based Algorithms

When making predictions, models are used that learn from the example or instances of the training data and generalise to new occurrences. It is also referred to as memory-based learning and winner-take-all learning. It focuses on how instances are represented in storage and how similarity metrics are used to different instances. The quantity of the training data affects how time-consuming instance-based approaches are. Support Vector Machines, k-Nearest Neighbor, Self-Organizing Map, LVQ, and LWL are examples of instance-based algorithms.

Decision Tree Algorithms

In order to build a training model to learn decision rules from previous training data, decision tree algorithms are supervised machine learning techniques. The decision tree is processed using a top-down method, with the most suitable attribute selected from the training data serving as the definition of the root. Because they are quick and precise, decision trees are used often in machine learning. Examples include Conditional Decision Trees, Chi-squared Automatic Interaction Detection (CHAID), Iterative Dichotomiser 3 (ID3), and Classification and Regression Trees.

Bayesian Algorithms

The Bayes Theorem, which asserts that any pair of variables is independent of one another, is the foundation of Bayesian algorithms. Given the information that event B has already occurred, these approaches are used to calculate the likelihood that events A and B will occur. Naive Bayes, BBN, BBN, Gaussian, Multinomial, and AODE are examples of Bayesian algorithms.

Clustering Algorithms

Data points are grouped or clustered based on shared characteristics or attributes during the clustering process. A method of unsupervised learning used in statistical computing and data analysis is clustering. Popular techniques include Expectation Maximisation (EM), Hierarchical Clustering, k-Means, and k-Medians.

Association Rule Learning Algorithms

A rule-based ML technique called association rule learning uses big datasets to extract powerful rules that are then used to find useful links in multi-dimensional databases. Apriori, Eclat, and Apriori are association rule learning algorithms.

Artificial Neural Network Algorithms

Based on biological neural networks, Artificial Neural Networks are a type of computing system that simulates the human brain by acting as a vast network of neurons. It is utilised for CART issues and encompasses a significant sub-domain with several techniques and modifications for every sort of problem, however because of its popularity, it has been isolated from DL. Traditional techniques including the Perceptron, MLP, Back-Propagation, Stochastic Gradient Descent, RBFN, and Hopfield Network are utilised to build ANNs.

Deep Learning Algorithms

Larger and more complex neural networks are developed using DL methods, an upgraded form of ANN, to enable automatic learning while evaluating and processing massive datasets. RNNs, LSTMs, CNN, Stacked Auto-Encoders, DBM, DBN, and DBN are some of the deep learning algorithms.

Dimensionality Reduction Algorithms

Algorithms for dimensionality reduction are used to characterise or summarise data with little information. They are useful for data visualisation and are subsequently used in supervised learning techniques. In classification and regression problems, dimensionality is reduced using PCA, PCR, PLSR, Sammon Mapping, MDS, Projection Pursuit, and LDA.

Ensemble Algorithms

In order to process numerous models and find a solution for computational issues, ensemble learning methods are utilised. They are mostly used to improve overall model performance and lessen the likelihood of choosing a subpar model. Additionally, they are employed in applications including incremental learning, non-stationary learning, data fusion, optimum feature selection, error correction, and error correction with non-stationarity. Boosting, Bootstrapped Aggregation, AdaBoost, Weighted Average, Stacked Generalization, Gradient Boosting Machines, GBM, GBRT, and Random Forest are examples of effective and well-liked ensemble approaches.

Other Machine Learning Algorithms

Feature selection, accuracy assessment, performance measurements, optimization, computational intelligence, computer vision, NLP, recommender systems, reinforcement learning, and graphic models are some categories of machine learning methods. In order to handle IoT difficulties utilizing real-world IoT use cases, this paper discusses deep learning and Bayesian algorithms to construct a sustainable machine learning method with the sliding window technique. Data analytics must be efficient and scalable for IoT applications, and ML provides numerous opportunities for development. One-third of IoT applications include time-series challenges, making DL methods useful.

Figure 2. IoT and deep learning algorithm-integrated smart home energy management

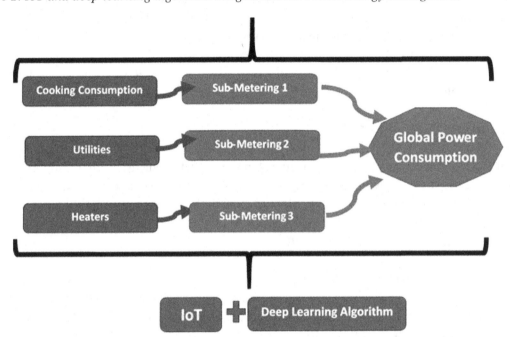

SMART HOME ENERGY DATA ANALYSIS

IoT technologies have resulted in the rapid development of data, yet this data may contain deceptive information that is unsuitable for in-depth examination. Use of industry-accepted methods for statistical analysis of IoT data is crucial, as is a close examination of the data to assure accuracy and appropriateness. The initial inspection of the data is crucial for confirming the data source, validating the variables, searching for missing values, cleaning the data, identifying outliers, if any, etc. It's crucial to decide exactly how the data were collected. To achieve goals like emphasising data features, summarising data information in an accessible way, visualising data, and getting the data ready for thorough analysis, a preliminary analysis of the raw data is required. By comprehending the energy dataset in terms of characteristics and fitting values, data pre-processing, feature engineering, statistical testing, and display of smart residential building energy consumption data, this chapter attempts to address difficulties with data inconsistency (Forootani et al., 2022; Haq et al., 2022; Koltsaklis et al., 2022; Li et al., 2018; Liu et al., 2020; Machorro-Cano et al., 2020). IoT and Deep Learning Algorithm integrated Smart Home Energy Management system is illustrated in Figure 2.

Data Collection

Meter readings from a monitored home in Sceaux, close to Paris, were used in this study. They were obtained via the UCI machine learning repository. 1.25 percent of the rows had missing values during pre-processing, and redundant data were deleted to prevent bias in training. Reactive power is the distribution of real power from the main circuit to various parts of the house, whereas active power is the actual energy used and unutilized in the power line. The average voltage and current intensity is referred to as global intensity. Three areas account for the majority of the electrical energy used by smart residential buildings: cookhouse energy usage, lighting and utility room energy use, and heating and cooling system energy use. A cookware house's equipment includes submetering, a microwave, an oven, a dishwasher, a utility room, and refrigerators. The distributional features of energy variables are estimated, comprehended, and the link between the variables is summarised using model fitting functions (Rashid et al., 2019).

Data Pre-Processing

Reactive power is the distribution of real power from the main circuit to various parts of the house, whereas active power is the actual energy used and unutilized in the power line. The average voltage and current intensity is referred to as global intensity. Three areas account for the majority of the electrical energy used by smart residential buildings: cookhouse energy usage, lighting and utility room energy use, and heating and cooling system energy use. A cookware house's equipment includes submetering, a microwave, an oven, a dishwasher, a utility room, and refrigerators. The distributional features of energy variables are estimated, comprehended, and the link between the variables is summarised using model fitting functions.

Missing Values: Data processing requires the precise identification and treatment of missing values since failure to do so might result in incorrect conclusions and impair the learning model. Missing values can be addressed through imputation or by removing a row. Null values can be deleted without preserving important information, but the imputation process can replace them by calculating the mean, median, or mode of a certain property. This study used a second approach to deal with null values, calculating the median of a particular property that had null values, which produced better results than the previous approach.

Redundant Data: Bias in ML algorithms is decreased in energy data by removing duplicated records.

Data Resampling: It is a method for generating a distinctive distribution of samples from actual energy data. Data can be resampled in one of two methods, depending on the needs: up-sampling or down-sampling. The smart domestic energy dataset should be down sampled at a daily pace for more insightful analyses.

Feature Scaling: The independent characteristics available in the energy dataset of a smart residential building were normalised in this study utilising Z-score standardisation and min-max normalisation. With the aid of preset Python libraries, it completed every stage.

Feature Selection

The crucial phases in model design are feature selection and data cleansing. While feature selection includes choosing the most pertinent elements that contribute to the forecast or goal variable, data cleaning entails deleting incorrect and unnecessary information from the data. Applying feature selection to the original dataset before modelling the data has advantages.

- **Enhance Accuracy:** For modelling, improving accuracy is crucial.
- **Reduction in Overfitting Issue:** Having redundant data lessens the likelihood of making biassed conclusions.
- **Minimize Training Time:** A model's complexity is decreased by relevant data, which speeds up model training.

The subset function in R was used in this study to apply the backward elimination strategy to feature or variable selection. A flowchart is used to describe the backward elimination method, which finds the best features as global reactive power, voltage, global intensity, and three sub-metering.

Statistical Analysis

The energy consumption dataset for smart residential buildings is made up of multivariate time series data, necessitating various statistical tests to ascertain whether or not the learning model is suitable for use. Inferential statistics are the tests that are used to infer meanings and interpretations from the data. To make any inferences or conclusions about energy data, this paper performed a number of statistical tests (Chakravarthi et al., 2022; Jeevanantham et al., 2023; Samikannu et al., 2023).

Normality Test

To determine if electric energy data looks the same as it did when it was taken from a Gaussian distribution, D'Agostino's K2 Test is utilised. In this study, a test was run utilising a SciPy implementation to ascertain the p-value of an energy dataset. According to the findings, both p = alpha and p > alpha failed to reject H0, which is typical. Kurtosis and skewness gauge the weight of the tails in relation to the normal distribution, whereas skewness gauges the lack of symmetry in the latter. Kurtosis ought to be just below 0.5. Kurtosis and skewness are both larger than zero. The distribution is light-tailed if kurtosis is less than 0, and heavy-tailed if it is more than 0.

Dickey-Fuller Test

To establish if a unit root exists in time series data, the Dickey-Fuller test evaluates the null hypothesis and the alternative hypothesis. In this study, SciPy was used to implement the Dickey-Fuller test and get the p-value. Accept H0 indicating non-stationary and reject H0 showing stationary if p-value > 0.05. The absence of a unit root in the energy data for intelligent residential structures disproves the null hypothesis H0.

Exploratory Data Analysis

An technique for studying and analysing data sets with the goal of capturing their key properties is called exploratory data analysis (EDA). It entails using a variety of data visualisation techniques to spot important trends or recurring patterns. EDA examines what the data may reveal outside of formal modelling and provides a clear picture of dataset variables and their interrelationships. This study focuses on residential buildings' overall power usage, which has been identified as a target variable for EDA. Making a distinct plot for each variable is the best method to evaluate data on energy usage. The line plots give a high-level abstraction of the energy data collected across four years, displaying the seasonal impact wave as well as other variables that affect the way the data is distributed. The distribution of global active power is bimodal, showing that energy use is split into two main categories: when there are no people present and when home appliances are in operation. The electrical energy dataset was studied in this study, and it revealed seasonal impacts, trends, and other significant information to forecast future energy consumption requirements.

SUMMARY

Due to the IoT analytics' growing popularity across several industries, there is a vast research potential for this field. In order to analyse IoT application scenarios, this paper investigates and examines current ML models. The limitations of IoT analytics are also covered, including issues with data quality, data heterogeneity, temporal and geographical interdependence, as well as other issues that might affect the performance of the overall model prediction. According to the literature, no specific approach is offered to determine the ideal time frame for assessing the performance of the prediction, and the epistemic uncertainty needed to gauge total model uncertainty has not been investigated.

IoT is to blame for the data influx, yet pre-processing data is crucial for precise analysis. In order to address data consistency difficulties and find relevant trends, this chapter investigates and evaluates the energy consumption dataset for smart residential buildings. Data cleaning, feature selection, EDA, feature engineering, statistical testing, and visualisation of the target variable of the energy data are all included.

FUTURE DEVELOPMENT AND SCOPES

- The real-time design of experiments has been done based on Taguchi, the response surface method (Boopathi, 2022f, 2022a; Boopathi, Balasubramani, et al., 2023; Janardhana et al., 2023; Trojovský et al., 2023), and mixing ratio, including machine learning and non-traditional methods (Boopathi, 2019, 2022c, 2022e, 2022d, 2022b; Boopathi et al., 2022; Gunasekaran et al., 2022; Myilsamy & Sampath, 2021; Sampath & Myilsamy, 2021; Yupapin et al., 2023).
- ANN, deep learning, and artificial intelligence methods have been integrated to improve the IoT enabled home automation system (Babu et al., 2023; Boopathi, 2021, 2022b; Boopathi et al., 2021; Boopathi, Arigela, et al., 2023; Gunasekaran et al., 2022; Jeevanantham et al., 2023; Kannan et al., 2022).

REFERENCES

Alzoubi, A. (2022). Machine learning for intelligent energy consumption in smart homes. *International Journal of Computations, Information and Manufacturing, 2*(1).

Amer, M., Naaman, A., M'Sirdi, N. K., & El-Zonkoly, A. M. (2014). Smart home energy management systems survey. *International Conference on Renewable Energies for Developing Countries 2014*, 167–173. 10.1109/REDEC.2014.7038551

Babu, B. S., Kamalakannan, J., Meenatchi, N., M, S. K. S., S, K., & Boopathi, S. (2023). Economic impacts and reliability evaluation of battery by adopting Electric Vehicle. *IEEE Explore*, 1–6. doi:10.1109/ICPECTS56089.2022.10046786

Boopathi, S. (2019). Experimental investigation and parameter analysis of LPG refrigeration system using Taguchi method. *SN Applied Sciences*, *1*(8), 892. doi:10.100742452-019-0925-2

Boopathi, S. (2021). Improving of Green Sand-Mould Quality using Taguchi Technique. *Journal of Engineering Research*. doi:10.36909/jer.14079

Boopathi, S. (2022a). An experimental investigation of Quench Polish Quench (QPQ) coating on AISI 4150 steel. *Engineering Research Express*, *4*(4), 45009. doi:10.1088/2631-8695/ac9ddd

Boopathi, S. (2022b). An Extensive Review on Sustainable Developments of Dry and Near-Dry Electrical Discharge Machining Processes. *Journal of Manufacturing Science and Engineering*, *144*(5), 50801. doi:10.1115/1.4052527

Boopathi, S. (2022c). An investigation on gas emission concentration and relative emission rate of the near-dry wire-cut electrical discharge machining process. *Environmental Science and Pollution Research International*, *29*(57), 86237–86246. doi:10.100711356-021-17658-1 PMID:34837614

Boopathi, S. (2022d). Cryogenically treated and untreated stainless steel grade 317 in sustainable wire electrical discharge machining process: A comparative study. *Environmental Science and Pollution Research International*, 1–10. doi:10.100711356-022-22843-x PMID:36057706

Boopathi, S. (2022e). Experimental investigation and multi-objective optimization of cryogenic Friction-stir-welding of AA2014 and AZ31B alloys using MOORA technique. *Materials Today. Communications*, *33*, 104937. doi:10.1016/j.mtcomm.2022.104937

Boopathi, S. (2022f). Performance Improvement of Eco-Friendly Near-Dry Wire-Cut Electrical Discharge Machining Process Using Coconut Oil-Mist Dielectric Fluid. *Journal of Advanced Manufacturing Systems*, 1–20. Advance online publication. doi:10.1142/S0219686723500178

Boopathi, S., Arigela, S. H., Raman, R., Indhumathi, C., Kavitha, V., & Bhatt, B. C. (2023). Prominent Rule Control-based Internet of Things: Poultry Farm Management System. *IEEE Explore*, 1–6. doi:10.1109/ICPECTS56089.2022.10047039

Boopathi, S., Balasubramani, V., Kumar, R. S., & Singh, G. R. (2021). The influence of human hair on kenaf and Grewia fiber-based hybrid natural composite material: An experimental study. *Functional Composites and Structures*, *3*(4), 45011. doi:10.1088/2631-6331/ac3afc

Boopathi, S., Balasubramani, V., & Sanjeev Kumar, R. (2023). Influences of various natural fibers on the mechanical and drilling characteristics of coir-fiber-based hybrid epoxy composites. *Engineering Research Express*, 5(1), 15002. doi:10.1088/2631-8695/acb132

Boopathi, S., Haribalaji, V., Mageswari, M., & Asif, M. M. (2022). Influences of Boron Carbide Particles on the Wear Rate and Tensile Strength of Aa2014 Surface Composite Fabricated By Friction-Stir Processing. *Materiali in Tehnologije*, 56(3), 263–270. doi:10.17222/mit.2022.409

Boopathi, S., Khare, R., Jaya Christiyan, K. G., Muni, T. V., & Khare, S. (2023). Additive manufacturing developments in the medical engineering field. In Development, Properties, and Industrial Applications of 3D Printed Polymer Composites (pp. 86–106). IGI Global. doi:10.4018/978-1-6684-6009-2.ch006

Boopathi, S., Siva Kumar, P. K., & Meena, R. S. J., S. I., P., S. K., & Sudhakar, M. (2023). Sustainable Developments of Modern Soil-Less Agro-Cultivation Systems. In Human Agro-Energy Optimization for Business and Industry (pp. 69–87). IGI Global. doi:10.4018/978-1-6684-4118-3.ch004

Chakravarthi, P. K., Yuvaraj, D., & Venkataramanan, V. (2022). IoT-based smart energy meter for smart grids. *ICDCS 2022 - 2022 6th International Conference on Devices, Circuits and Systems*, 360–363. 10.1109/ICDCS54290.2022.9780714

Chen, S.-J., Chiu, W.-Y., & Liu, W.-J. (2021). User Preference-Based Demand Response for Smart Home Energy Management Using Multiobjective Reinforcement Learning. *IEEE Access : Practical Innovations, Open Solutions*, 9, 161627–161637. doi:10.1109/ACCESS.2021.3132962

Domakonda, V. K., Farooq, S., Chinthamreddy, S., Puviarasi, R., Sudhakar, M., & Boopathi, S. (2023). Sustainable Developments of Hybrid Floating Solar Power Plants. In *Human Agro-Energy Optimization for Business and Industry* (pp. 148–167). IGI Global. doi:10.4018/978-1-6684-4118-3.ch008

Forootani, A., Rastegar, M., & Jooshaki, M. (2022). An advanced satisfaction-based home energy management system using deep reinforcement learning. *IEEE Access : Practical Innovations, Open Solutions*, 10, 47896–47905. doi:10.1109/ACCESS.2022.3172327

Gariba, D., & Pipaliya, B. (2016). Modelling human behaviour in smart home energy management systems via machine learning techniques. *2016 International Automatic Control Conference (CACS)*, 53–58. 10.1109/CACS.2016.7973883

Gunasekaran, K., Boopathi, S., & Sureshkumar, M. (2022). Analysis of a Cryogenically Cooled Near-Dry Wedm Process Using Different Dielectrics. *Materiali in Tehnologije*, 56(2), 179–186. doi:10.17222/mit.2022.397

Haq, E. U., Lyu, C., Xie, P., Yan, S., Ahmad, F., & Jia, Y. (2022). Implementation of home energy management system based on reinforcement learning. *Energy Reports*, 8, 560–566. doi:10.1016/j.egyr.2021.11.170

Harikaran, M., Boopathi, S., Gokulakannan, S., & Poonguzhali, M. (2023). Study on the Source of E-Waste Management and Disposal Methods. In *Sustainable Approaches and Strategies for E-Waste Management and Utilization* (pp. 39–60). IGI Global. doi:10.4018/978-1-6684-7573-7.ch003

Janardhana, K., Anushkannan, N. K., Dinakaran, K. P., Puse, R. K., & Boopathi, S. (2023). *Experimental Investigation on Microhardness, Surface Roughness, and White Layer Thickness of Dry EDM*. Engineering Research Express. doi:10.1088/2631-8695/acce8f

Jeevanantham, Y. A., A, S., V, V., J, S. I., Boopathi, S., & Kumar, D. P. (2023). Implementation of Internet-of Things (IoT) in Soil Irrigation System. *IEEE Explore*, 1–5. doi:10.1109/ICPECTS56089.2022.10047185

Kannan, E., Trabelsi, Y., Boopathi, S., & Alagesan, S. (2022). Influences of cryogenically treated work material on near-dry wire-cut electrical discharge machining process. *Surface Topography : Metrology and Properties*, *10*(1), 15027. doi:10.1088/2051-672X/ac53e1

Koltsaklis, N., Panapakidis, I., Christoforidis, G., & Knápek, J. (2022). Smart home energy management processes support through machine learning algorithms. *Energy Reports*, *8*, 1–6. doi:10.1016/j.egyr.2022.01.033

Kumara, V., Mohanaprakash, T. A., Fairooz, S., Jamal, K., Babu, T., & B., S. (2023). Experimental Study on a Reliable Smart Hydroponics System. In *Human Agro-Energy Optimization for Business and Industry* (pp. 27–45). IGI Global. doi:10.4018/978-1-6684-4118-3.ch002

Li, W., Logenthiran, T., Phan, V.-T., & Woo, W. L. (2018). Implemented IoT-based self-learning home management system (SHMS) for Singapore. *IEEE Internet of Things Journal*, *5*(3), 2212–2219. doi:10.1109/JIOT.2018.2828144

Liu, Y., Zhang, D., & Gooi, H. B. (2020). Optimization strategy based on deep reinforcement learning for home energy management. *CSEE Journal of Power and Energy Systems*, *6*(3), 572–582.

Machorro-Cano, I., Alor-Hernández, G., Paredes-Valverde, M. A., Rodríguez-Mazahua, L., Sánchez-Cervantes, J. L., & Olmedo-Aguirre, J. O. (2020). HEMS-IoT: A big data and machine learning-based smart home system for energy saving. *Energies*, *13*(5), 1097. doi:10.3390/en13051097

Myilsamy, S., & Sampath, B. (2021). Experimental comparison of near-dry and cryogenically cooled near-dry machining in wire-cut electrical discharge machining processes. *Surface Topography : Metrology and Properties*, *9*(3), 35015. doi:10.1088/2051-672X/ac15e0

Palaniappan, M., Tirlangi, S., Mohamed, M. J. S., Moorthy, R. M. S., Valeti, S. V., & Boopathi, S. (2023). Fused deposition modelling of polylactic acid (PLA)-based polymer composites: A case study. In Development, Properties, and Industrial Applications of 3D Printed Polymer Composites (pp. 66–85). IGI Global. doi:10.4018/978-1-6684-6009-2.ch005

Rashid, R. A., Chin, L., Sarijari, M. A., Sudirman, R., & Ide, T. (2019). Machine learning for smart energy monitoring of home appliances using IoT. *2019 Eleventh International Conference on Ubiquitous and Future Networks (ICUFN)*, 66–71. 10.1109/ICUFN.2019.8806026

Reddy, M. A., Reddy, B. M., Mukund, C. S., Venneti, K., Preethi, D. M. D., & Boopathi, S. (2023). Social Health Protection During the COVID-Pandemic Using IoT. In *The COVID-19 Pandemic and the Digitalization of Diplomacy* (pp. 204–235). IGI Global. doi:10.4018/978-1-7998-8394-4.ch009

S., P. K., Sampath, B., R., S. K., Babu, B. H., & N., A. (2022). Hydroponics, Aeroponics, and Aquaponics Technologies in Modern Agricultural Cultivation. In *Trends, Paradigms, and Advances in Mechatronics Engineering* (pp. 223–241). IGI Global. doi:10.4018/978-1-6684-5887-7.ch012

Samikannu, R., Koshariya, A. K., Poornima, E., Ramesh, S., Kumar, A., & Boopathi, S. (2023). Sustainable Development in Modern Aquaponics Cultivation Systems Using IoT Technologies. In *Human Agro-Energy Optimization for Business and Industry* (pp. 105–127). IGI Global. doi:10.4018/978-1-6684-4118-3.ch006

Sampath, B., & Myilsamy, S. (2021). Experimental investigation of a cryogenically cooled oxygen-mist near-dry wire-cut electrical discharge machining process. *Strojniski Vestnik. Jixie Gongcheng Xuebao*, *67*(6), 322–330. doi:10.5545v-jme.2021.7161

Sampath, B. C. S., & Myilsamy, S. (2022). Application of TOPSIS Optimization Technique in the Micro-Machining Process. In Trends, Paradigms, and Advances in Mechatronics Engineering (pp. 162–187). IGI Global. doi:10.4018/978-1-6684-5887-7.ch009

Selvakumar, S., Adithe, S., Isaac, J. S., Pradhan, R., Venkatesh, V., & Sampath, B. (2023). A Study of the Printed Circuit Board (PCB) E-Waste Recycling Process. In Sustainable Approaches and Strategies for E-Waste Management and Utilization (pp. 159–184). IGI Global.

Senthil, T. S. R., Ohmsakthi vel, Puviyarasan, M., Babu, S. R., Surakasi, R., & Sampath, B. (2023). Industrial Robot-Integrated Fused Deposition Modelling for the 3D Printing Process. In Development, Properties, and Industrial Applications of 3D Printed Polymer Composites (pp. 188–210). IGI Global. doi:10.4018/978-1-6684-6009-2.ch011

Shahriar, M. S., & Rahman, M. S. (2015). Urban sensing and smart home energy optimisations: A machine learning approach. *Proceedings of the 2015 International Workshop on Internet of Things towards Applications*, 19–22. 10.1145/2820975.2820979

Trojovský, P., Dhasarathan, V., & Boopathi, S. (2023). Experimental investigations on cryogenic friction-stir welding of similar ZE42 magnesium alloys. *Alexandria Engineering Journal*, *66*(1), 1–14. doi:10.1016/j.aej.2022.12.007

Vanitha, S. K. R., & Boopathi, S. (2023). Artificial Intelligence Techniques in Water Purification and Utilization. In *Human Agro-Energy Optimization for Business and Industry* (pp. 202–218). IGI Global. doi:10.4018/978-1-6684-4118-3.ch010

Vennila, T., Karuna, M. S., Srivastava, B. K., Venugopal, J., Surakasi, R., & B., S. (2023). New Strategies in Treatment and Enzymatic Processes. In *Human Agro-Energy Optimization for Business and Industry* (pp. 219–240). IGI Global. doi:10.4018/978-1-6684-4118-3.ch011

Yupapin, P., Trabelsi, Y., Nattappan, A., & Boopathi, S. (2023). Performance Improvement of Wire-Cut Electrical Discharge Machining Process Using Cryogenically Treated Super-Conductive State of Monel-K500 Alloy. *Iranian Journal of Science and Technology. Transaction of Mechanical Engineering*, *47*(1), 267–283. doi:10.100740997-022-00513-0

Chapter 14

Generating Complex Animated Characters of Various Art Styles With Optimal Beauty Scores Using Deep Generative Adversarial Networks

N. Prabakaran

School of Computer Science and Engineering, Vellore Institute of Technology, India

Rajarshi Bhattacharyay

School of Computer Science and Engineering, Vellore Institute of Technology, India

Aditya Deepak Joshi

School of Computer Science and Engineering, Vellore Institute of Technology, India

P. Rajasekaran

School of Computing, SRM Institute of Science and Technology, India

ABSTRACT

A generative adversarial network (GAN) is a generative model that is able to generate fresh content by using several deep learning techniques together. Due to its fascinating applications, including the production of synthetic training data, the creation of art, style-transfer, image-to-image translation, etc., the topic has gained a lot of attraction in the machine learning community. GAN consists of two networks: the generator and the discriminator. The generator will make an effort to create phony samples in an effort to trick the discriminator into thinking they are real samples. In order to distinguish generated samples from both actual and fraudulent samples, the discriminator will strive to do so. The main motive of this chapter is to make use of several types of GANs like StyleGANs, cycle GANs, SRGANs, and conditional GANs to generate various animated characters of different art styles with optimal attractive scores, which can make a huge contribution in the entertainment and media sector.

DOI: 10.4018/978-1-6684-8098-4.ch014

INTRODUCTION

GANs (Generative Adversarial Networks) are actually generative models which are capable of producing required and immaculate unmarked visual content. This subgenre, in the recent times, has attracted a lot of interest and attention in the deep learning community due to its compelling applications and creative results, which include not only the creation of synthetic training data, but also the creation of art, styletransfer, and image-to-image translation. GANs are made up of two networks: the generator and the discriminator. The generator will try to generate a certain user specified amount of phony samples/ data in order to mislead the discriminator into thinking that they are some real samples. The discriminator will be useful in distinguishing generated samples from both the actual and the phony samples. In the year 2018 NVIDIA published a revolutionary paper introducing the concept of StyleGAN, "A Style-Based Architecture for GANs,". It introduced a new type of GANs generator architecture that allowed them to manage multiple levels of information in the generated samples, ranging from coarse to optimal finer end results.

Figure 1. StyleGAN architecture model

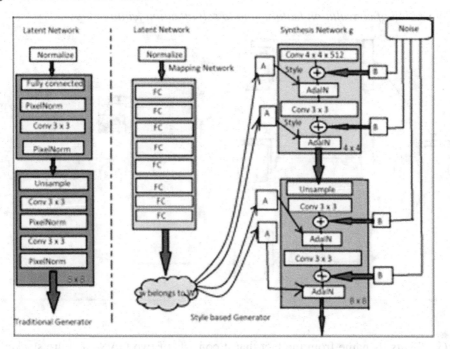

As visible from Figure 1, StyleGAN also uses the Progressive GAN principle, in which networks are trained on an initially small resolution (say, 4x4) at first, then the larger layers are gradually added once its confirmed that it has stabilized. This significantly reduces the training time and increases the training stability. StyleGAN enhances it even further by incorporating a mapping network in such a way that encodes the input vectors into an intermediate latent space, W, from which, we separate the present values, which are utilized to control various levels of detail. To meet client goals, the media and entertainment sector needs a great deal of intelligence. GAN is a sort of deep learning architecture capable of addressing the most difficult issues. GANs can perform the following:

- High-definition videos can be created from new reporting footage.
- Converting Black and White Films to Color Films
- Creating artworks from sketches
- Converting primitive black-and-white photographs into color photographs
- There will be no costume design for establishing old-age superstars.
- People can attempt on their favorite celebs' make-up.
- Converting a social network comment into an image

Although significant progress has been made in terms of image super-resolution accuracy using various deep learning algorithms, obtaining fine texture features in super- resolution remains a challenge. SRGAN is extremely powerful for producing super- resolution images with precise details, and it can obtain excellent results even with 4x up-scaling factors.

Figure 2. Conversion of convolution feature map to self attention feature maps

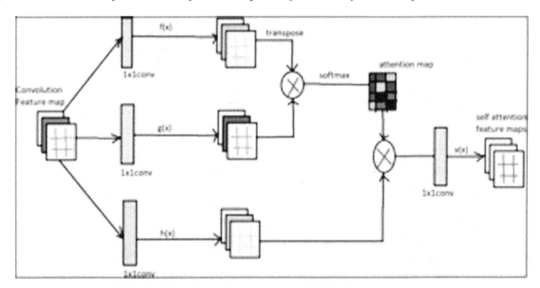

A StackGAN gets its name from the fact that it consists of two GANs that are stacked together to create a network that can produce high-resolution images, that can be seen from Figure 2. Aptly named, Stage I and Stage II are the constituent two stages. The Stage-II network uses the picture created by the Stage-I network to create a high-resolution image that is dependent on a piece of text embedding, the Stage-I network creates low-resolution images with basic colors and rough sketches. In essence, the second network fixes flaws and adds attractive features to produce a higher-resolution image that is considerably more realistic. It is also able to rectify errors in Stage-I results and add stunning details through the refinement process. The following elements constitute the major components of the Stack-GAN architecture:

- **Embedding:** Converts the variable length of the input text into a fixed length vector. A character-level embedding that has been pre-trained will be employed.
- Conditioning Addition (CA)
- **Stage I Generator:** Creates images with a low resolution (64*64).
- Discriminator at Stage I
- **Remaining BlocksStage II Generator:** Produces images with a high resolution (256*256).
- Discriminator at Stage II

Figure 3 illustrates a convolutional representation with a limited spatial scope and many feature maps generated by a 100-dimensional uniform distribution Z. Then, using a series of four fractionally-strided convolutions, this high-level representation is turned into a 64 by 64-pixel image (in some recent works, these are incorrectly referred to as deconvolutions). Notably, there was no use of pooling or completely connected layers.

Figure 3. The LSUN creation using DCGAN

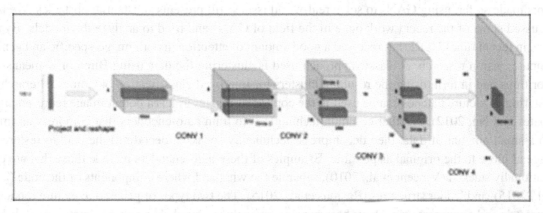

update_discriminator equation for objective function minimization used in stage 1 of the project is illustrated in equation (1)

$$\frac{1}{n}\sum_{i=1}^{n}\left[-D(y_i)+D(H(y_i,c))\right]-\frac{1}{n}\sum_{i=1}^{n}\lambda_{cls}\log(D_{cls})(\hat{c}_i) \tag{1}$$

update_generator equation for objective function minimization used in stage 1 of the project is illustrated in equation (2)

$$\sum_{j=1}^{n}-w_j D(G(y_j,c))+\frac{1}{n}\sum_{j=1}^{n}\lambda_{rec}y_i-G(G(y_j,c),\bar{c})-\frac{1}{n}\sum_{j=1}^{n}\lambda_{cls}\log(D_{cls})(c(y_j,c)) \tag{2}$$

Normalization function of the Discriminator used in stage 2 of the project is illustrated in equation (3)

$$\bar{D}_j = D\big(G\big(y_j, c\big)\big) - \frac{1}{2n}[\sum_{i=1}^{2n} D\big(y_i\big) + D\big(G\big(y_i, c\big)\big)] \tag{3}$$

learning rate evaluation for generator function is shown in below equation (4)

$$LR_k \leftarrow \nabla_k [\frac{1}{c}\sum_{g=1}^{c} f_k\big(u^{(g)}\big) - \frac{1}{c}\sum_{g=1}^{c} f_k\big(h_\theta(y^{(g)})\big)] \tag{4}$$

RELATED WORK

In recent years, a great deal of research has been done on generative adversarial networks (GANs). The field of medicine, computer vision, and other domains where significant progress has been achieved in problems like plausible picture synthesis, image-to-image translation, facial attribute modification, and related domains, is perhaps where they have had the most important impact. Despite the notable achievements made so far, using GANs to solve real-world issues still presents substantial obstacles. We have discussed some of the recent work done in the field of GANs and tried to analyze the models: By and large, in recent times USRL has received a good amount of attention in both image-specific and generic computer vision research. A classic approach used is clustering the data using Birch or K-means-like algorithms and in turn, using the resultant clusters for improved classification outcomes. Hierarchical clustering of picture patches can be used in the context of images to learn potent image representations (Coates and Ng, 2012). Another common technique is to train auto-encoders that compress an image into a small amount of data, then decompress (technically speaking decoding) the data to restore the image as close to the original as possible. Examples of these auto-encoders include those that are convolutionally stacked (Vincent et al., 2010), separate the what and where components of the code (Zhao et al., 2015), and ladder structures (Rasmus et al., 2015). The two types of generative picture models—parametric and nonparametric—have both been extensively explored. The non-parametric models have been employed in texture generation (Efros et al., 1999), super-resolution (Freeman et al., 2002), and in-painting. They frequently match from a database of existing images, frequently matching patches of images (Hays et al., 2007).

Extensive research has been done on parametric models for producing images, such as on MNIST digits or for texture generation (Portilla et al., 2000). However, until recently, creating realistic representations of the real world was not very successful. Although the samples from a variational sampling method for creating photographs (Kingma et al., 2014) sometimes suffer from blurriness, the method has had some success. Another method uses an iterative forward diffusion technique to produce images (Sohl-Dickstein et al., 2015). Images produced by Generative Adversarial Networks) (Goodfellow et al., 2014) were noisy and difficult to understand. This approach's Laplacian pyramid extension (Denton et al., 2015) produced improved-quality photos, but the objects still appeared shaky due to noise added during the chaining of many models. The deconvolution network approach and recurrent network approach have both recently had some success with producing natural images (Gregor et al., 2015). They haven't used the generators for supervised jobs, though. The use of neural networks has frequently come under fire for being "black- box" techniques with no explanation of what the networks actually accomplish in the form of an easy-to-understand algorithm. Zeiler et al. (Zeiler & Fergus, 2014) (Zeiler and Fergus,

2014) demonstrated that one may determine the general function of each convolution filter in a CNN by utilizing deconvolutions and filtering the maximal activations. Similarly to this, the examination of the ideal image that activates specific groups of filters can be done by applying gradient descent to the inputs (Mordvintsev et al.). Cycle Regularity i.e. the notion of regularizing structured data through transitivity is a fairly old, well-explored concept. Similarly implementing direct forward-backward consistency in visual tracking has also been well explored enough for it to be common practice (Kalal et al., 2010; Sundaram et al., 2010). Human translators and robots both employ the "back translation and reconciliation" technique to verify and improve translations in the language domain. Higher-order cycle consistency has been applied more recently in in-depth estimation (Godard et al., 2017), structure from motion (Zach et al., 2010), and 3D shape matching (Huang and Guibas, 2013). The two studies employing a cycle consistency loss method of using transitivity to oversee CNN training are (Zhou et al., 2016) and (Godard et al., 2017). In order to force G and F to be consistent with one another, a similar loss is introduced in this work (Yi et al., 2017) separately utilize a similar target for unpaired image-to-image translation in these same sessions.

In recent times, the entertainment and media sector is saturated with creativity in animations. Same artstyles with similar faces being used in anime is taking a toll on it's popularity. However, at the same time, some new gen animes with unique artstyles have emerged and gathered the public's attention at a large scale. So, it would be very helpful to production studios which produce anime series/movies, if there existed a software which could generate anime faces of different hybrid artstyles with optimal beauty scores (i.e. good looking characters). It would save them a lot of time and help them invest their time more in other lacking areas of their productions. The main objective of this paper is to make use of several types of GANs like StyleGANs, cycle GANs, SRGANs and conditional GANs and image-to-image mapping techniques to generate various animated characters of different art-styles with optimal attractive scores which can make a huge contribution in the entertainment and media sector.

The presence of behaviors such as feeling safe when reading manga, and being distressed at the possibility of not being able to read manga, both mirror behaviors that are commonly associated with interpersonal attachment such as using other individuals as a safe haven and experiencing separation distress. Because these behaviors signal the activation of the attachment behavioral system as described by (Bowlby and Ainsworth et al., 2022), and because attachment theory is arguably the most influential relational theory in social psychology, this paper uses attachment theory as a lens for extrapolating attachment behaviors that potentially mirror readers' attachment to manga.

According to attachment theory, human beings are equipped with an attachment behavioral system that enables individuals to form and maintain affectional bonds with others (attachment figures), beginning in infancy, for the biological purpose of gaining protection. In general terms, attachment can be defined as an innate, strongly emotional, target-specific bond. The outcome is the eliciting of behaviors that seek proximity with attachment figures. Although attachment theory originally described the bond between an infant and a caregiver, later developments would propose that attachment figures are many and varied. For example, (Hazan et al.,1987) and Shaver argue that romantic love is an attachment process, suggesting that around adolescence, individuals change the primary attachment figure from parents to social peers, and later in adult life for romantic partners. Elsewhere, Mikulincer et al. (2012) and Shaver's adult attachment model postulates that when attachment behavior is activated, anxiety can be reduced by simulating interactions with mental representations of attachment figures such as deities, religious figures, deceased loved ones, or media heroes. Other examples of non-interpersonal attachment behavior include teenagers' romantic crushes with celebrities, pets as companions, attachment to special places or to the place of residence, and/or emotional bonding with gifts, collectibles are favorite objects.

ARCHITECTURE AND METHODOLOGY

What we are trying to achieve here is that we will input a text that will be our request to the GANs, for example: "An attractive girl with blue hair". After providing this data as an input to the system, we expect an image to be generated by the GANs with adequate attraction scores and which will satisfy the conditions mentioned in the text. In our approach, which is shown in the form of an architecture diagram in Figure 4, the textual description is first converted into a text embedding, concatenated with the noise vector, and then given as input to the Generator instead of just noise. A 256-dimensional embedding of the textual description has been created as an example, and it has been concatenated with a 100-dimensional noise vector [sampled from a Normal distribution]. Instead of producing random images, this formulation will enable the generator to produce images that are in line with the given description.

Figure 4. The architecture of hybrid GANs used in our project to generate animated characters of different art styles

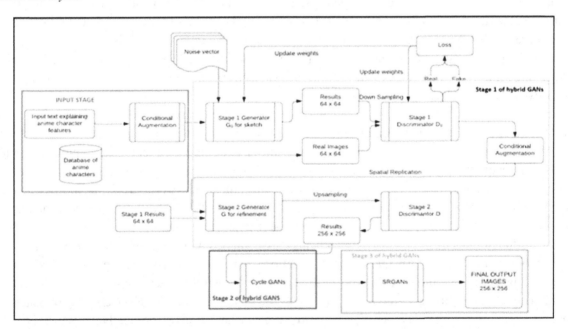

The mathematical equations used are as follows in the model:
The sampling function equation of our GANs model is illustrated in equation (5)

$$b_\theta \leftarrow -\nabla_\theta \frac{1}{n} \sum_{q=1}^{n} f_t \left(b_\theta (e^{(q)}) \right) \tag{5}$$

gradient ascent on discriminator illustrated in equation (6)

$$\nabla_\phi P\left(S_\theta, G_\phi\right) = \frac{1}{d}\nabla_\phi \sum_{c=1}^{d}\left(G_\phi\left(y_b^{(c)}\right) - G_\phi\left(y_s^{(c)}\right)\right) \tag{6}$$

The gradient(s) ascent on generator illustrated in equation (7)

$$\nabla_\phi P\left(S_\theta, G_\phi\right) = \frac{1}{d}\nabla_\theta \sum_{c=1}^{d}\left(G_\phi\left(y_s^{(c)}\right)\right) \tag{7}$$

The polar form for the discriminator stochastic gradient used in our model of GANs is illustrated in equation (8)

$$\theta^{(L)} \leftarrow \theta^{(L)} + \eta\,\frac{dH^{(L)}\left(\theta^{(M)}, \theta^{(L)}\right)}{d\theta^{(L)}} \tag{8}$$

And the polar form for generator stochastic gradient used in our model of GANs is illustrated in equation (9)

$$\theta^{(M)} \leftarrow \theta^{(M)} + \eta\,\frac{dH^{(M)}\left(\theta^{(M)}, \theta^{(L)}\right)}{d\theta^{(M)}} \tag{9}$$

A pair of image and text embeddings are supplied as input to Discriminator rather than just an image. Either 0 or 1 are the output signals. Earlier, the Discriminator's only duty was to determine whether a particular image was real or not. The discriminator now has an additional obligation. It also forecasts the possibility that the given image and text will be aligned, in addition to determining whether the given image is real or phony. This approach forces the Generator to produce images that match the provided textual description in addition to producing images that seem realistic. Then, after the results of 256 x 256 are generated by the stage 2 discriminator, the cycle GAN comes into action. This GAN is designed for mapping one image to another image or image-to-image translations.

If two images of animated characters with different art styles are subjected to the Image-Image translation process, we can find a mapping function that can transform the first image into the second image and vice versa by adding or removing features in accordance with the mapping function, so that the predicted output and actual output have the lowest overall degree of loss. Finally, after the work of Cycle GANs, comes the SRGANs. This kind of GAN's main objective is to transform a low-resolution image into a more detailed image. One of the computer vision issues that has received the most research is this one. Convolutional layers are used by both the generator and discriminator networks. The generator employs the parametric ReLU as its activation function, while the discriminator uses the Leaky ReLU. The generator uses the input data to calculate the pixel-wise average of every potential outcome. Finally, the content loss and adverse loss are added together to determine the best pixel-wise solution.

RESULTS AND DISCUSSIONS

The entire number of iterations required to train the machine learning model utilizing all of the training data at once is referred as counted in cycles (Prabakaran et al., 2022). The count is a hyperparameter. It specifies how many times the learning algorithm must process the complete data collection (Prabakaran and Kannan, 2017). For learning algorithms to minimize model error as much as possible, hundreds or thousands of s are required (Prabakaran et al., 2021). The number of s can range from ten to 1000 and beyond. With the data on the frequency and number of s, a learning curve may be plotted. With the data on the frequency and number of s, a learning curve may be plotted. s are represented along the x-axis, while time and the model's skill are on the y-axis. The plotted curve might reveal if the supplied model is correctly fitted to the training dataset or has been over- or under-learned (Kannadasan et al., 2018).

In Table 1, the parameter loss_g shows the loss occurred while processing the generator and the loss_d shows the loss occurred while processing the discriminator. The real scores and fake scores show the penalty invoked by the discriminator on the generator by recognizing the fake generated images by the generator and distinguishing it from the real images in the training dataset. As we can observe from the table and the Figure 5, after the 17th epoch, the loss incurred by the generator dropped down by a notable amount and the irregular behavior of the discriminator graph also started to maintain a uniform pattern. From this, we can conclude that a minimum of 17 epochs were required for the GANs to generate optimal and noticeable anime faces from the training dataset and for the discriminator to successfully identify fake images from the real ones most of the time. The occurrence of irregular ups and downs before we reach the 17th epoch was basically due to the variety of the size and resolutions of the different images available in the training dataset. For images with low resolution or smaller size, the training and the loss incurred would be less for obvious reasons.

Figure 5. Epochs vs. loss

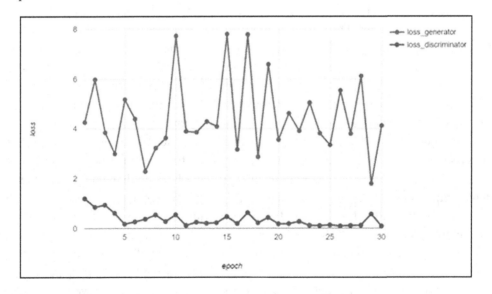

As we can observe from the table and the graph in Figure 5, after the 17th epoch, the loss incurred by the generator dropped down by a notable amount and the irregular behaviour of the discriminator graph also started to maintain a uniform pattern. From this, we can conclude that minimum 17 epoch were required for the GANs to generate optimal and noticeable anime faces from the training dataset and for the discriminator to successfully identify fake images from the real ones most of the times. The occurrence of irregular ups and downs before we reach the 17th epoch was due to the variety of the size and resolutions of the different images available in the training dataset. For images with low resolution or smaller size, the training and the loss incurred would be less for obvious reasons.

Table 1. Loss values of discriminator and generator, reality, and fake scores of the model

EPOCH	LOSS_G	LOSS_D	REAL_SCORE	FAKE_SCORE
[1/30]	4.2624	1.1897	0.4249	0.0093
[2/30]	5.9760	0.8490	0.9119	0.4983
[3/30]	3.8402	0.9353	0.4846	0.0069
[4/30]	2.9925	0.6088	0.6365	0.0305
[5/30]	5.1690	0.1698	0.9083	0.0525
[6/30]	4.3950	0.2587	0.8218	0.0264
[7/30]	2.2849	0.3693	0.7622	0.0405
[8/30]	3.2187	0.5357	0.7150	0.1080
[9/30]	3.6240	0.2696	0.9099	0.1414
[10/30]	7.7262	0.5394	0.9974	0.3779
[11/30]	3.8929	0.1152	0.9192	0.0244
[12/30]	3.8561	0.2422	0.8842	0.0933
[13/30]	4.2902	0.1991	0.9046	0.0742
[14/30]	4.0930	0.2184	0.9554	0.1379
[15/30]	7.7984	0.4650	0.9937	0.3324
[16/30]	3.1602	0.1860	0.8857	0.0514
[17/30]	7.7802	0.6216	0.9800	0.3848
[18/30]	2.8651	0.2135	0.8804	0.0685
[19/30]	6.5866	0.4255	0.9908	0.3017
[20/30]	3.5519	0.1718	0.8960	0.0512
[21/30]	4.6133	0.1810	0.9350	0.0958
[22/30]	3.9121	0.2642	0.9372	0.1533
[23/30]	5.0405	0.1111	0.9681	0.0699
[24/30]	3.8156	0.1017	0.9480	0.0434
[25/30]	3.3393	0.1257	0.9143	0.0264
[26/30]	5.5289	0.0867	0.9786	0.0582
[27/30]	3.7967	0.1027	0.9587	0.0548
[28/30]	6.1093	0.1129	0.9802	0.0805
[29/30]	1.7882	0.5672	0.6160	0.0021
[30/30]	4.1189	0.0807	0.9496	0.0251

Now, if we have a look at the Figure 6, we can see an obvious pattern. The first clear observation we can make from the graph is that the real score is always greater than the fake scores and it confirms that the model of the GANs is working just fine. The second important observation is that, from the 20th to 28th epoch, the real scores are mostly in the higher regions and the fake scores are in the lower regions. This shows that training of minimum 20 and maximum 28 epoch will give the best possible optimal results. Now the cycleGANS of stage II comes into play. As discussed, This GAN is designed for mapping one image to another image, or image-to-image translations. If two images of animated characters with different artstyles are subjected to the Image-Image translation process, we can find a mapping function that can transform the first image into the second image and vice versa by adding or removing features in accordance with the mapping function, so that the predicted output and actual output have the lowest overall degree of loss. In our model, the adversarial discriminators DX and DY are CNNs that can see an image and attempt to categorize it as real or phoney. Authentic photos have an output close to 1, whereas bogus classifications have an output near to 0. DY promotes and categorizes the transformation from domain X to domain Y. (making photos into Monet pictures). DX denotes transformation classification from domain Y to domain X.

Figure 6. Epochs vs. scores

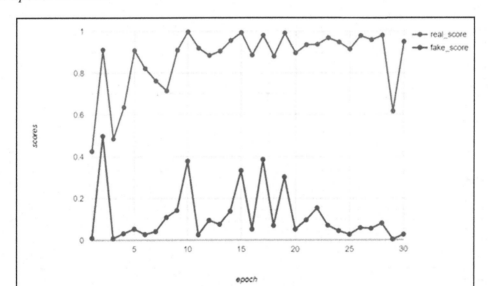

Here, in Figure 7, are some of the output sample of unique anime faces generated at the first stage of the hybrid GANs model.

We begin by writing a helper function that generates a convolutional layer with batch or instance normalisation. Batch normalisation was previously expected to help deep learning models by eliminating the "internal covariate shift". The fundamental benefit of utilizing batch normalisation, however, is an improvement in the smoothness of the optimization landscape.

Figure 7. Generated images after 30 epochs of training. As we can see the contrast is not that balanced, so while choosing the parameter, we must be very careful. We can stop at 27th or 28th epoch to achieve better results.

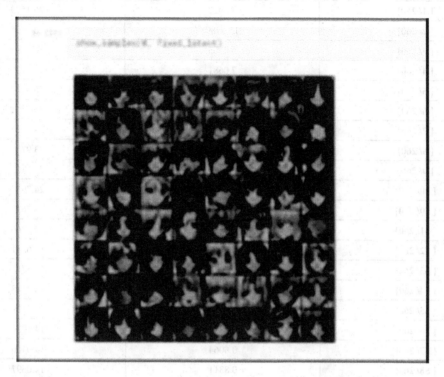

G XtoY and G YtoX are our two generators. They are made of the following:

1. Encoder (compressing the image into a smaller feature representation),
2. Residual blocks (which connect the output of one layer to the input of a previous layer) and
3. Decoder (converting compressed representation into a modified image)

As previously stated, we have two discriminator losses. The mean squared error between the output of the corresponding discriminator and the target value will be the loss for both functions (either 1 or 0). This is accomplished in the code by using real_mse_loss and fake_mse_loss.

*   **Loss of Cycle Consistency:** Forward cycle consistency from X->Y->X. Loss of backward cycle consistency from Y->X->Y.
*   **Loss of Identity:** Backward identity loss from Y->X. Forward identity loss from X->Y.

Now, in the training part, we trained the cycleGANs model for a total of 260 epochs to yield optimal results as cycleGANS is quite new to the domain of image-to-image and style transfer, so a large number of epochs are required. Some ranges of the epochs are mentioned in Table 2.

After training 10 epochs, we found the following results as shown in Figure 8.

Table 2. Discriminator and generator loss values

epochs	d_total_loss_avg	g_total_loss
[1/ 260]	4.5927	26.1573
[2/ 260]	15.9989	26.3265
[3/ 260]	6.9363	27.0693
[4/ 260]	7.0681	26.3738
[5/ 260]	6.3907	26.0827
[6/ 260]	7.1549	25.9561
[7/ 260]	7.0785	24.3525
[8/ 260]	4.8446	23.9729
[9/ 260]	5.4664	24.3862
[10/ 260]	4.7968	24.3959
[50/ 260]	0.5765	14.7626
[51/ 260]	0.7882	14.5766
[52/ 260]	0.4861	14.6381
[53/ 260]	0.5189	14.5747
[54/ 260]	0.5242	14.2148
[55/ 260]	0.6346	14.1309
[56/ 260]	0.6229	14.1036
[57/ 260]	0.6064	14.0406
[58/ 260]	0.8311	14.0697
[59/ 260]	1.0842	14.2808
[60/ 260]	1.4624	14.0464
[250/ 260]	0.2120	12.2062
[251/ 260]	0.2750	12.2070
[252/ 260]	0.2286	12.2595
[253/ 260]	0.2042	12.2201
[254/ 260]	0.1665	12.1879
[255/ 260]	0.1539	12.1287
[256/ 260]	0.1404	12.1078
[257/ 260]	0.1093	12.1422
[258/ 260]	0.1296	12.1888
[259/ 260]	0.1894	12.1486
[260/ 260]	0.2258	11.9469

As we can see from the above results, 10 epcohs are hardly generating results anywhere near desirable. So after 50 epochs of training, we get something like Figure 9. After training for 260 epochs, we can see the following results in Figure 9, which are a bit over modified.

As we can clearly see the differences in the amount of clarity and originality in the different number of epochs training, the results after the 260th epoch yields very clear and visible results.

Figure 8. Training result of 10 epochs

However, if we refer the above graphs in Figures 10 and 11, we can see that the majority of losses occur till the training of 45 epochs in both generator and discriminator for both the translations. For the most optimal training results, we should limit the number of epochs to 200 in both the cases. As we can see in the graph, the region of the graph just before and after 200 is almost a straight line for the discriminator, so the losses there are uniform and steady and as a result, yield the most optimal images. So, if we put down everything together, the result can be displayed as show in the Figure 12 below. As we can see, the starting set of images are of high quality and solid colors, which when mapped with the outdated blur anime photos, they yield a blurred and mixed color version photo of the previous ones. For example, we can see that the hair color of the first character has changed it's shade from before to a very light brown one, the 5th character got some extra shadow details to the lower bangs of his hairline.

Although the changes are not that major, these small changes will pave the way for bigger and better changes in the future. However, when the opposite was tried, that is, converting the blurred photos to the high resolution ones, we got the results in Figure 13.

As seen in Figure 13, we can again observe some key and minor changes such as change of eye color, change in hair lines and hair color and an increase in resolution and clarity of the images. As observed and expected, the adversarial losses led to a hug amount of identity and resolution loss. The identity loss is inevitable as GANs are still in development and being continuously researched on. However, the resolution loss can be recovered to a certain extent by implementing the SRGANs in the final and IIIrd stage.

Figure 9. Training result of 260 epochs

Figure 10. generator and discriminator loss functions graph for AnimeFacesY -> AnimeFacesX

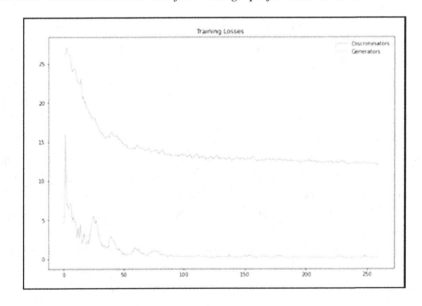

Figure 11. Generator and discriminator loss functions graph for AnimeFacesX -> AnimeFacesY

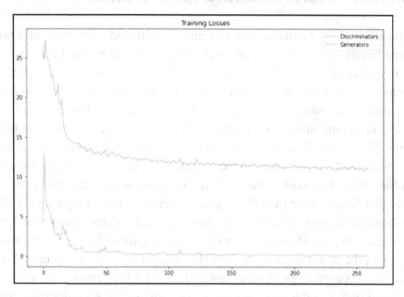

Figure 12. AnimeFacesY -> AnimeFacesX

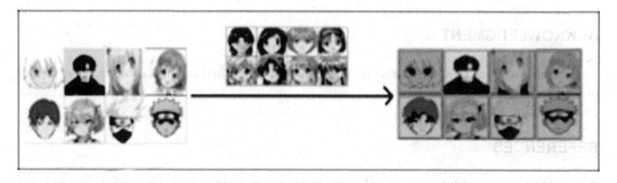

Figure 13. AnimeFacesX -> AnimeFacesY

CONCLUSION AND FUTURE RESEARCH DIRECTIONS

This project was done with the motive to generate unique animated characters' face with different artstyles with optimal beauty score. The first phase of the project which was the generation of the anime characters faces gave fruitful results. The resolution and clarity of the generated faces increased a lot after the 28th training round of the model. Then the cycleGANs was successfully able to map the image properties of one image to another and vice versa and thus being able to generate anime faces of different artsyles. A drop in resolution was observed and thus SRGANs helped increase the resolution by a significant amount. The second phase of the project which included the beauty scores comparison of the generated anime faces and the image mapped faces of that generated anime face also gave very interesting results. We observed that in most of the cases the image-to-image mapped image generated by the cycleGANs had higher beauty score than the original generated faces of styleGANS. After performing all the necessary benchmark tests and observing them carefully, we can concluded that the model was successful in generating the animated characters faces with optimal beauty scores along with varying artstyles. As we know, the world is going through digitization at an alarming rate, this project may be of help in various fields concerning entertainment and media. In the future, this project can be further enhanced by trying to optimize the time and space complexity of the model mentioned in this paper to generate same/better results in a comparatively less time duration and by consuming less memory.

ACKNOWLEDGMENT

This research received no specific grant from any funding agency in the public, commercial, or not-for profit sectors.

REFERENCES

Adams-Price, C., & Greene, A. L. (1990). Secondary Attachments and Adolescent Self Concept. *Sex Roles*, 22(3), 187–198. doi:10.1007/BF00288191

Coates, A., & Ng, A. Y. (2012). Learning feature representations with k-means. In *Neural Networks: Tricks of the Trade* (pp. 561–580). Springer. doi:10.1007/978-3-642-35289-8_30

Denton, E., Chintala, S., Szlam, A., & Fergus, R. (2015). *Deep generative image models using a laplacian pyramid of adversarial networks.* arXiv preprint arXiv:1506.05751.

Efros, A., & Leung, T. K. (1999). Texture synthesis by non-parametric sampling. In *Computer Vision, 1999. The Proceedings of the Seventh IEEE International Conference on* (vol. 2, pp. 1033–1038). IEEE. 10.1109/ICCV.1999.790383

Freeman, W. T., Jones, T. R., & Pasztor, E. C. (2002). Example-based super-resolution. *IEEE Computer Graphics and Applications*, 22(2), 56–65. doi:10.1109/38.988747

Godard, C., Mac Aodha, O., & Brostow, G. J. (2017). Unsupervised monocular depth estimation with left-right consistency. CVPR. doi:10.1109/CVPR.2017.699

Goodfellow, I. J., Pouget-Abadie, J., Mirza, M., Xu, B., Warde-Farley, D., Ozair, S., Courville, A. C., & Bengio, Y. (2014). *Generative adversarial nets*. NIPS.

Granqvist, P., Mikulincer, M., & Shaver, P. R. (2009). Religion as Attachment: Normative Processes and Individual Differences. *Personality and Social Psychology Review*, *14*(1), 49–59. doi:10.1177/1088868309348618 PMID:20023208

Gregor, K., Danihelka, I., Graves, A., & Wierstra, D. (2015). *Draw: A recurrent neural network for image generation*. arXiv preprint arXiv:1502.04623.

Hays, J., & Efros, A. A. (2007). Scene completion using millions of photographs. *ACM Transactions on Graphics*, *26*(3), 4. doi:10.1145/1276377.1276382

Hazan, C., & Shaver, P. (1987). Romantic Love Conceptualized as an Attachment Process. *Journal of Personality and Social Psychology*, *52*(3), 511–524. doi:10.1037/0022-3514.52.3.511 PMID:3572722

Huang, Q.-X., & Guibas, L. (2013). Consistent shape maps via semidefinite programming. *Symposium on Geometry Processing*.

Kalal, Z., Mikolajczyk, K., & Matas, J. (2010). Forwardbackward error: Automatic detection of tracking failures. ICPR.

Kannadasan, R., Prabakaran, N., Boominathan, P., Krishnamoorthy, A., Naresh, K., & Sivashanmugam, G. (2018). High performance parallel computing with cloud technologies. *Procedia Computer Science*, *132*, 518–524. doi:10.1016/j.procs.2018.05.004

Kingma, D. P., & Ba, J. L. (2014). *Adam: A method for stochastic optimization*. arXiv preprint arXiv:1412.6980.

Mordvintsev, A., Olah, C., & Tyka, M. (n.d.). *Inceptionism: Going deeper into neural networks*. https://googleresearch.blogspot.com/2015/06/inceptionism-going-deeper-into-neural.html

Portilla, J., & Simoncelli, E. P. (2000). A parametric texture model based on joint statistics of complex wavelet coefficients. *International Journal of Computer Vision*, *40*(1), 49–70. doi:10.1023/A:1026553619983

Prabakaran, N., & Kannan, R. J. (2017). Sustainable life-span of WSN nodes using participatory devices in pervasive environment. *Microsystem Technologies*, *23*(3), 651–657. doi:10.100700542-016-3117-7

Prabakaran, N., Kumar, S.S.S., Kiran, P.K., & Supriya, P. (2022). A deep learning based social distance analyzer with person detection and Tracking Using Region based convolutional neural networks for novel coronavirus. *Journal of Mobile Multimedia*, 541-560.

Prabakaran, N., Palaniappan, R., Kannadasan, R., Dudi, S. V., & Sasidhar, V. (2021). Forecasting the momentum using customised loss function for financial series. *International Journal of Intelligent Computing and Cybernetics*, *14*(4), 702–713. doi:10.1108/IJICC-05-2021-0098

Radford, A., Metz, L., & Chintala, S. (2015). *Unsupervised Representation Learning with Deep Convolutional Generative Adversarial Networks*. https://doi.org//arXiv.1511.06434 doi:10.48550

Rasmus, A., Valpola, H., Honkala, M., Berglund, M., & Raiko, T. (2015). *Semisupervised learning with ladder network*. arXiv preprint arXiv:1507.02672.

Sohl-Dickstein, J., Weiss, E. A., Maheswaranathan, N., & Ganguli, S. (2015). *Deep unsupervised learning using nonequilibrium thermodynamics*. arXiv preprint arXiv:1503.03585.

Sundaram, N., Brox, T., & Keutzer, K. (2010). Dense point trajectories by gpu-accelerated large displacement optical flow. ECCV. doi:10.1007/978-3-642-15549-9_32

Vincent, P., Larochelle, H., Lajoie, I., Bengio, Y., & Manzagol, P.-A. (2010). Stacked denoising autoencoders: Learning useful representations in a deep network with a local denoising criterion. *Journal of Machine Learning Research, 11,* 3371–3408.

Yi, Z., Zhang, H., & Gong, T. (2017). Unsupervised dual learning for image-to-image translation. ICCV.

Zach, C., Klopschitz, M., & Pollefeys, M. (2010). Disambiguating visual relations using loop constraints. CVPR. doi:10.1109/CVPR.2010.5539801

Zeiler, M. D., & Fergus, R. (2014). Visualizing and understanding convolutional networks. In *Computer Vision–ECCV 2014* (pp. 818–833). Springer.

Zhao, J., Mathieu, M., Goroshin, R., & Lecun, Y. (2015). *Stacked what-where autoencoders*. arXiv preprint arXiv:1506.02351.

Zhou, T., Krahenbuhl, P., Aubry, M., Huang, Q., & Efros, A. A. (2016). Learning dense correspondence via 3dguided cycle consistency. CVPR.

Zhu, J., Park, T., Isola, P., & Efros, A. A. (2017*). Unpaired Image-to-Image Translation using Cycle-Consistent Adversarial Networks*. https://doi.org//arXiv.1703.10593 doi:10.1109/ICCV.2017.244

Zilcha-Mano, S., Mikulincer, M., & Shaver, P. R. (2012, October 1). Pets as Safe Havens and Secure Bases: The Moderating Role of Pet Attachment Orientations. *Journal of Research in Personality, 46*(5), 571–580. doi:10.1016/j.jrp.2012.06.005

Chapter 15
Cloud–Based TPA Auditing With Risk Prevention

V. Abinaya
Hindusthan College of Arts and Sciences, India

Veera Talukdar
RNB Global University, India

A. V. Senthil Kumar
Hindusthan College of Arts and Sciences, India

Ankita Chaturvedi
IIS University (Deemed), India

Rohaya Latip
Universiti Putra Malaysia, Malaysia

G. Vanishree
IBS Hyderabad, India

Gaganpreet Kaur
Chitkara University, India

ABSTRACT

The chapter focuses on cloud security audit mechanisms and models. Here the third-party auditor (TPA) will be provided with the authority access scheme where the security of the auditing system will be enabled. The TPA will check out the auditing verification and shows a message about the data audited. The purpose of this work is to develop an auditing scheme that is secure, efficient to use, and possesses the capabilities such as privacy preserving, public auditing, maintaining the data integrity along with confidentiality. It consists of three entities: data owner, TPA, and cloud server. The data owner performs various operations such as splitting the file to blocks, encrypting them, generating a hash value for each, concatenating it, and generating a signature on it. TPA performs the main role of data integrity check. It performs activities like generating hash value for encrypted blocks received from cloud server, concatenating them, and generates signature on it. Thus, the system frequently checks the security of the server-side resources.

DOI: 10.4018/978-1-6684-8098-4.ch015

INTRODUCTION

Cloud computing, where computation and data storage are done in data centers rather than on individual portable PCs, has become highly popular in recent years. Users may store their data remotely and take use of cloud apps thanks to cloud storage, which eases the load of managing local hardware and software. Taking use of cloud storage is a crucial component of file sharing nowadays as more people access their data online. Databases and application software are moved to big data centers via cloud computing, where the administration of the data and services is not justifiable. Data sharing is possible because to cloud platform applications, ideas, and services such processing power, networking, virtualization, and storage. Be sure that the problems most important to you are user privacy and data security. Secure and flexible data storage services are offered by cloud storage service providers, which are ideal for a range of storage needs. Data owner control over the data is lost once it is transferred to the cloud, creating additional security threats to the data's confidentiality and integrity. Cloud storage has gained popularity in recent years thanks to its many applications, including data archiving, file backup, and information sharing. File sharing is implemented in many ways by cloud storage services based on how they are used and what order the permission categories are given. Data confidentiality and user authenticity are required in order to safeguard users and data from one another as well as from hackers. Huge volumes of data are created by these e-applications as they continue to evolve at an accelerated rate in e-business, e-science, and social networking. For instance, popular social networking services like Twitter and Facebook keep serving billions of page visits, managing billions of information, and many images.

Cloud computing is very talented for IT schemes but some obstacles remain for discrete users and organizations to overcome in order to save and device cloud computing systems. Data security is one of the most important contests to its implementation and enforcement, privacy, trust and legal concerns are being undertaken. Therefore, one primary priority is to ensure the confidentiality and integrity of the data stored in the cloud, because cloud storage is essential and thus carries vast quantities of large amounts of data. Users' security concerns should first be addressed to ensure that the cloud environment is reliable, so that users and companies take it on a large scale. Cloud security concerns are imperative: anonymity, safety of information, data availability, location of data and safe broadcast. Threats, data loss, service failures, external malicious attacks and multi-lease issues are among the security threats in the cloud. The confidentiality of data in the cloud network ensures the confidentiality of stored information is protected. No unlicensed users should lose or modify the data. Cloud computing providers rely on information security and information constancy. Data confidentiality is also important to the customer, because they store sensitive or private data in the cloud. Authentication and access control mechanisms are used to ensure data privacy. Information security can be addressed by collective cloud presentation and cloud storage reliability. The health, integrity, privacy and confidentiality of stored cloud data and critical user requirements should also be considered. Modern approaches and strategies to satisfy all the secriteria should be developed and implemented.

Cloud Computing

A collection of interconnected, virtualized computers that are dynamically provisioned and presented as one or more unified computing resources based on service-level agreements (SLAs) negotiated between the service provider and customers make up the cloud, a parallel and distributed computing system. Clouds are vast collections of readily available and reachable virtualized resources, including hardware, platforms for software development, and/or services. To adapt to a changing demand (scaling), these resources may be dynamically adjusted, which also allows for optimal resource use. This resource pool is often utilized on a pay-per-use arrangement, with the Infrastructure Provider providing assurances via specialized Service Level Agreements. Clouds are hardware-based services that provide compute, network, and storage capacity, where hardware management is substantially abstracted from the buyer and infrastructure expenses are borne as variable OPEX by purchasers.

In cloud computing, data security, privacy, and safety are fundamental measures which establish the trust level between the cloud clients and cloud providers. Cloud computing is broadly employed in diverse fields such as economy, social, finance, educational institutions, and government offices. Therefore, users store confidential information on the cloud and retrieve it at their convenience. Prior to developing and designing cloud computing, privacy and security requirements have to be exhaustively explored. Individuals and organizations are still distrustful due to the existing security vulnerabilities that threaten cloud computing. In fact, cloud computing lacks explicit security and privacy protection regulations.

Important aspects of cloud computing:
- ◦ The delusion that computing resources are limitless
- ◦ Cloud users not having to make a commitment up front
- ◦ Being able to pay for use as necessary

Cloud computing is described as "a pay-per-use model for enabling available, convenient, on-demand network access to a shared pool of configurable computing resources (e.g. networks, servers, storage, applications, services) that can be rapidly provisioned and released with minimal management effort or service provider interaction" by the National Institute of Standards and Technology (NIST). Most typical qualities that a cloud should have are:

- • Pay-per-use (utility costs, no long-term commitment);
- • Elastic capacity and the appearance of boundless resources;
- • Self-service interface;
- • Abstracted or virtualized resources.

We live in a world where information and data play major roles and are extremely valuable to both people and companies. There have been significant changes in how we access, exchange, and store data thanks to the idea of cloud computing. The National Institute for Standards and Technology (NIST) defines cloud computing as "a model for enabling ubiquitous, convenient, on-demand network access to a shared pool of configurable computing resources (e.g., networks, servers, storage, applications, and services) that can be rapidly provisioned and released with little management effort or service provider interaction" (Mell & Grance, 2011). The word "cloud" refers to network service providers with virtual computer resources and no fixed location.

The connection between resources, data, and users is shifting as a result of cloud computing (Xu, 2012). Data was traditionally saved in a single location on a single computer or drive that was often used by just one or a small number of people and could only be accessed by software that had already been purchased, installed, and was compatible with the hardware. In contrast, the advent of cloud computing has allowed several users to access the information and resources that are shared between them. Nowadays, many businesses are embracing cloud computing and its benefits, such as its pay-per-use model and accessibility (Saya et al., 2010). The usage of cloud computing ensures that users may access their stored data from many places. It also makes content sharing, application availability, data synchronization, and real-time cooperation and collaboration easier (Takabi et al., 2010).

Cloud Service Provider (CSP): It contains vital resources along with experience under works with cloud storage, owned and direct cloud computing dispersed under the structure. The CSP contain certain inevitability and request a customer to obligate with reticent capacity; the capacity reservation, the cloud service provider shares the risk through cloud service customers. Thus, CSP reduces the risks of initial investment in cloud infrastructure. Third Party Auditor (TPA): The user is troubled about integrity of data stored on the cloud, as user's data may be attacked or altered via an external attack. That is why, a new concept named data auditing is suggested that verifies the integrity of the data using an entity named TPA. It is a preferred TPA through experience and expertise and is believed to evaluate and describe on behalf of clients seeking the possibility of cloud storage services.

The idea of cloud computing is based on the delivery of services by service providers to users over networked infrastructure, such as the internet or virtual private networks. Software as a Service, Platform as a Service, and Infrastructure as a Service are the three service kinds that are most frequently provided (Beynon-Davies, 2019). There are numerous other types of cloud services in addition to those that have been mentioned because many cloud service providers have a tendency to present particular offerings in that way, such as "Daas" or data as a service, "Faas" or a function as a service, and so forth (Terzo et al., 2013, Fox et al., 2017).

With "SaaS," service providers are providing a cloud-based software solution that differs from traditional software by not requiring installation on devices, allowing access from multiple devices, and eliminating the need to buy newer versions of the software because updates are frequently included in the service (Huth and Cebula, 2011). Being a higher level of service than SaaS, "PaaS" gives users access to more resources, including using Murad's suggested Framework, the study evaluated the pertinent literature (2020). Using this methodology, we choose to conduct a thorough assessment of the literature and scope the information already available on ML software to assist us in defining the research problem (RP). After doing this, the RP was organized and written in a straightforward manner utilizing certain keywords.

Machine learning software development, machine learning software deployment, data science engineering, machine learning web applications, machine learning software architecture, machine learning software workflow, the Django REST framework, and the difficulties in deploying machine learning models were some of the keywords that were used. In order to gather as many pertinent papers as possible, a wide range of journals, books, and grey literature in the aforementioned fields were thoroughly searched to see whether any publications containing these key terms were present.

Various methods are developed in conventional literatures that support the verification of private and public information in handling large data. The verification of data allows the cloud users to validate the integrity of their outsourced data. However, such substantial computing poses a serious burden to the CSP, where the cloud resources are of constrained one. The publication verification of outsourced data reduces the computing cost of the client with the optimal usage of third-party authority (TPA) that helps in checking the data integrity.

The scope of the study included fifteen (15) periodicals, sixteen (16) books, and thirteen (13) pieces of grey literature. Just 18 of them were judged to be appropriate for review, along with 15 books and 8 pieces of grey literature.

The International Journal for Research in Applied Science and Engineering Technology, Journal of Data Warehousing, Journal of Systems, Software, and Wiley Online Library were a few of the publications featured.

To provide a technical approach for researchers who want to dive into the field of security and privacy for cloud computing, serving as a point of reference. Different reviews on cloud computing already exist in the literature. However, all have failed to provide a single report that brings a balance between security, privacy and a technical approach that provides a scientific insight into the different research gaps in cloud computing.

History of Cloud Computing

From dummy terminals/mainframes through PCs, network computing, grid computing, and cloud computing, there are six phases of computing paradigms.

- **Phase 1:** Connections to strong hosts shared by multiple users are made via dummy terminals. The terminals back then were essentially just keyboards and displays.
- **Phase 2:** Standalone personal computers (PCs) become strong enough to handle users' daily tasks, so you could work alone without sharing a mainframe.
- **Phase 3:** A computer network that enabled connections between various machines. Working on a PC while connected to other computers via local area networks (LAN) to share resources is possible.
- **Phase 4:** Local networks were linked to other local networks to create a more expansive network, enabling users to access the Internet and utilize remote resources and applications.
- **Phase 5:** Introduced the idea of an electronic grid to allow for the sharing of computer and storage resources (distributed computing). PCs were used by people to transparently access a grid of computers.
- **Phase 6:** Cloud computing enables us to use all Internet resources in a very easy and scalable manner.

SYSTEM MODELS FOR DISTRIBUTED AND CLOUD COMPUTING

Systems for distributed and cloud computing are composed of several independent computer nodes. These node machines are hierarchically connected by SANs, LANs, or WANs. With millions of computers connected to edge networks, a large system may be constructed. Massive systems are thought to be extremely scalable and are capable of reaching either logically or physically web-scale connection.

The four categories for massive systems are as follows:

1. Clusters
2. P2P networks
3. Computing grids
4. Internet clouds over massive data centers

These four system types might have hundreds of computers, thousands of computers, or potentially millions of computers as participating nodes. These devices work together, cooperatively, or collaboratively at various levels.

Clusters of Cooperative Computers/Cluster Computing

When several computers are connected to a network and function together as one, this is referred to as cluster computing. Nodes are the collective term for all linked computers in a network. By enabling quicker calculation and improved data integrity, cluster computing offers answers to difficult issues. Together, the connected computers' actions give the appearance of a single system (virtual machine). This procedure is referred to as system transparency. This networking technology operates by utilizing the distributed systems idea. And the connecting device in this case is LAN.

Cluster Architecture:

Figure 1. Typical server cluster

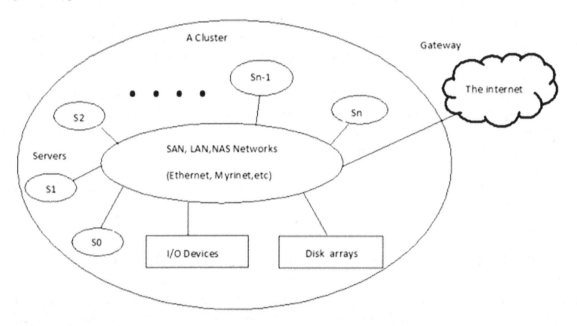

As illustrated in the diagram below, a typical server cluster is designed around an interconnection network with low latency and high capacity.

This network can be as basic as a LAN or SAN (such as Myrinet) (e.g., Ethernet). The interconnection network may be constructed using various tiers of Gigabit Ethernet, Myrinet, or InfiniBand switches to create a bigger cluster with more nodes.

Scalable clusters may be built with an increasing number of nodes utilizing hierarchical structure and a SAN, LAN, or WAN.

A virtual private network (VPN) gateway is used to link the cluster to the Internet. The cluster is located using the gateway IP address.

The way the OS handles the shared cluster resources determines the system image of a machine.

A server node's own OS is responsible for managing all of its resources. Due to the fact that most clusters have several autonomous nodes, they typically have different system images various OS controls.

Grid Computing

One computer can connect to another using internet services like the Telnet command.

- Remote access to distant web pages is made possible by a web service like HTTP.
- Grid computing aims to provide close communication between concurrently running programs on different machines.
- A computing grid provides a framework for connecting computers, software/middleware, specialized equipment, humans, and sensors.
- At a regional, national, or international level, the grid is frequently built over LAN, WAN, or Internet backbone networks.
- Grids are advertised by businesses or organizations as integrated computer resources.
- They can also be thought of as online organizations' support systems.

On a grid, workstations, servers, clusters, and supercomputers are the main types of computers used.

- Access devices to a grid system can be utilized with personal computers, laptops, and PDAs.

Peer-to-Peer Network Families

The client-server architecture is a well-known distributed system in which client devices (PCs and workstations) are linked to a central server for database, compute, email, and file access applications.

- A distributed model of networked systems is provided by the P2P architecture.
- A P2P network is first and foremost client-oriented as opposed to server-oriented.

Families of peer-to-peer networks: P2P systems

- Every node in a P2P system serves as both a client and a server, contributing to the system's resources.

Peer machines are merely client computers with Internet access. Each client computer acts independently to provide unfettered entry and exit from the system.

This suggests that there is no master-slave connection between the peers. No centralised database or coordination is required.

In other words, the P2P system is self-organizing with dispersed control, and no peer machine has a comprehensive picture of the whole P2P system.

A P2P network has two abstraction layers in its design. The peers are initially completely unconnected.

- Every peer machine willingly enters or exits the P2P network. At any given time, the physical network is only made up of the participating peers.
- A P2P network does not employ a specific interconnection network, in contrast to a cluster or grid.
- The physical network is only a hastily constructed TCP/IP and NAI network that was created at different Internet domains. The free membership in the P2P network causes the physical network to change in size and topology dynamically as a result.

Cloud Computing Over the Internet

- Data-intensive computational research is evolving. Supercomputers must be balanced systems that include both CPU farms and petascale networking and I/O arrays.
- In the future, processing massive amounts of data will often involve delivering calculations (programs) to the data rather than transferring the data to workstations.
- This reflects the trend in IT towards transferring computation and data from PCs to big data centers, where software, hardware, and data are provided as a service as needed. The concept of cloud computing has been supported by this data explosion.
- Cloud computing is defined as a pool of virtualized computer resources by IBM, a leading participant in the industry. A cloud may support a wide range of workloads, including interactive and user-facing apps as well as batch-style backend operations.
- According to this definition, a cloud enables speedy deployment and scaling out of workloads via swift provisioning of virtual or real computers.

Lastly, the cloud system should be able to monitor resource utilization in real-time to enable rebalancing of allocations when necessary. The cloud enables redundant, self-recovering, highly scalable programming models that enable workloads to recover from several unavoidable hardware/software faults.

Figure 2. The cloud

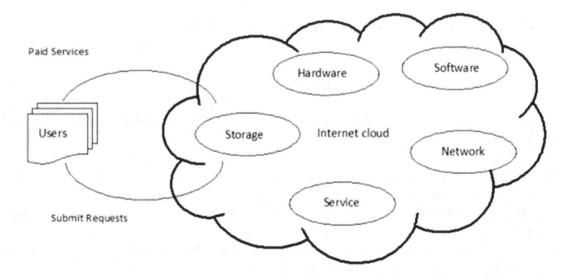

Using a virtualized platform with elastic resources that are available on demand, cloud computing dynamically provisioned hardware, software, and data sets.

- The plan is to use server clusters and sizable databases in data centers to transition desktop computing to a service-oriented platform.
- Cloud computing uses its affordability and ease of use to the advantage of both consumers and suppliers. Such cost-effectiveness has been made possible through machine virtualization.
- Cloud computing aims to concurrently satisfy many user applications. The cloud ecosystem needs to be built with security, dependability, and trust in mind.
- Some computer users view the cloud as a centralized resource pool, while others see it as a server cluster that uses dispersed computing across all of the utilized computers.

TYPES OF CLOUD COMPUTING

Using the cloud Offering a variety of services, cloud computing may be categorized into three main layers: The terms "platform as a service," "software as a service," and technology as a service (IAAS). These services offer a variety of low-cost services to the user. Software as a Service (SAAS) is a program that acts as a user interface for the cloud. platform as a Service (PAAS) gives software developers the resources they need to build applications. IAAS just provides the customer with the hardware and does not provide any services (e.g., CPU, Monitor, Network tool, etc.).

A. Software as a Services (SaaS)

It is a software distribution strategy where software is kept by cloud service providers and made accessible to end users online. Also known as "On-Demand Software," SaaS. Software and associated data are centrally hosted on a cloud server under SaaS. The end users can access SaaS. Those that access it through a network or the internet are provided with hosting as a service. The user does not need to maintain the program when it is used by someone off-site. SaaS has responsibility for creating and overseeing the IT infrastructure (operational systems, servers, databases, data centers, network access, etc.).

Platform as a Service (PaaS)

Software as a platform Another application and delivery model is called (paas), and it provides all the resources needed to construct applications and services entirely from the network. Without the network, it is impossible to download or install software. It is a platform for developer programming that is used to create, test, execute, and manage programs. A programmer may quickly design the application and integrate it straight into this layer.

Infrastructure as a Service (IaaS)

The layer of cloud computing platforms known as "Infrastructure as a Service" (IAAS) offers servers, networking, processing, storage, virtual machines, and other resources. The resources are accessible to users online. Based on the model, it was formerly known as "Hardware as a Service" (HaaS). Although the consumer is served by the layers above, this layer offers the hardware. It enables the renting of resources including server room, networking equipment, memory, CPUs, and storage devices. The frequency range for the storage space is defined by the bandwidth. With load balancers, the memory or the method of sending and receiving data may be balanced.

SECURE DISTRIBUTED DATA STORAGE IN CLOUD COMPUTING

The future of the IT sector has been predicted to lie in cloud computing. The way computer services are provided will completely alter. Much like we pay our monthly water and energy bills, users will be able to effortlessly purchase CPU cycles, memory utilities, and information storage services. This picture won't become reality, though, until a few issues are resolved. In this part, we'll quickly go over the main distinction that distributed data storage makes in the context of cloud computing. Then, flaws in the cloud computing platforms of today are examined and shown.

The majority of distributed storage solutions are either network-attached storage (NAS) or storage area networks (SANs) at the LAN level, such as the networks of an organization, school, or business. Block-addressed storage devices connected by specialized high-speed networks form the foundation of SANs. Contrarily, NAS is achieved by connecting specialized file servers to a TCP/IP network and giving client machines a file-based interface. The distributed storage nodes for SANs and NAS are controlled by the same organization. As the system administrator has authority over every node, the data security level is virtually in check.

Redundancy is frequently used in these systems to increase their dependability, and the storage security depends heavily on how well the system is protected from outside threats and infiltration. Most data confidentiality and integrity goals are met by employing strong cryptographic algorithms.

Current Commercial Cloud Services By the use of IPSec proxy and digital signatures, user authentication, data confidentiality, and data integrity issues may be resolved in typical network-based applications. SSL proxy can be used to resolve the key exchange problems. These techniques have been used in modern cloud computing to protect both the data that is stored there and the transmission of data to and from the cloud. The service suppliers assert that their products are safe. This section explains three secure procedures employed by three commercial cloud services and explores their weaknesses.

They are responsible for guaranteeing the availability, confidentiality, and integrity of the applications and data of the clients. One of the data processing techniques used by Amazon's AWS to move huge volumes of data between the AWS cloud and portable storage devices. The process of downloading is comparable to that of uploading. A manifest and signature file are created by the user, who then emails the manifest file and sends the storage device with the signature file attached. After validating the two files upon receipt, Amazon will copy the data onto the storage device, ship it back, and email the user with the status and the data's MD5 checksum. Amazon asserts that SSL endpoints provide the highest level of security.

Windows Azure software: The Windows Azure Platform (Azure) is a cloud computing platform for Internet-scale applications that is housed in Microsoft data centers. It offers an operating system and a number of developer services that may be utilized separately or jointly. Moreover, the platform offers expandable storage. There are three types of data: queues, tables, and blobs (up to 50 GB) (,8k). Based on the blob, table, and queue structures, Microsoft claims to ensure secrecy with Azure Storage.

CLOUD COMPUTING DATA SECURITY TECHNOLOGIES

Many technologies for data security are presented in this section. Also, cloud computing privacy. This section does not reiterate the typical methods that ensure confidentiality, integrity, and availability in distributed data storage applications in favor of concentrating on the particular problems of the cloud data storage platform. Instead, we choose to highlight the specific needs for cloud computing data security from a number of angles:

• Database outsourcing and assurance of query integrity. Experts have noted that using devices and computers hidden behind a cloud to store and retrieve data is essentially a unique type of database outsourcing.

Integrity of Data in Unreliable Storage. The concern about data loss or corruption is one of the key obstacles keeping end customers from utilizing cloud storage services. By enabling consumers to examine the integrity of their data, tools must be provided in order to allay their fears.

Security Based on Web Applications. Once the information has been saved remotely, one of the easiest ways for end users to access their data on remote services is using a web browser. Online security is more crucial than ever in the age of cloud computing.

Security for Multimedia Data. An increasing amount of multi-media material is being saved and shared online thanks to the advancement of high-speed network technology and high bandwidth connections. The prerequisites for security for video, audio, pictures, or images are different from other applications.

QUERY INTEGRITY ASSURANCE AND DATABASE OUTSOURCING

In recent years, database outsourcing has developed into a key element of cloud computing. In the past ten years, the cost of sending a terabyte of data across vast distances has dramatically lowered due to the quick development of network technology. Also, the overall cost of managing data is five to 10 times greater than the price of original collection.

As a result, there is rising interest in contracting out database administration work to outside companies who can do it on a much smaller scale and for less money. The advantages of this new outsourcing approach include lower operating expenses for Database Management Systems and a client environment that shows the overall architecture of a database outsourcing environment. Clients submit queries to the unreliable service provider while the database owner outsources its data maintenance chores. T stands for the data that will be outsourced. The service provider preprocesses, encrypts, and stores the data T are. A user converts a series of queries Q against T to queries against the encrypted database in order to evaluate inquiries. Hacigumus et al. were the first to propose database outsourcing to a third-party service provider. There are often two security issues. Assuring the integrity of queries. Under the database outsourcing paradigm, query integrity is a key security problem in addition to data privacy. Query integrity evaluates the hosting environment's dependability.

When a client receives a query result from a service provider, it wants to be sure that the result is accurate and comprehensive. By correct, we mean that the result must come from the owner's data and not be altered, and by comprehensive, we mean that the result contains all records satisfying the query.

INTEGRITY OF DATA IN UNRELIABLE STORAGE

While the transparent cloud offers flexible use of network-based resources, end users' worries about losing control over their data are one of the main barriers to their adoption of cloud storage services. Indeed, there is a chance that the companies who offer storage infrastructure will turn out to be self-serving, dishonest, or even evil. A storage service provider may become unreliable for a variety of reasons, such as to downplay the impact of an operational error or refuse when an opponent has taken the data, the system's vulnerability. This section describes two technologies that let data owners check the accuracy of their files even while they are being stored on remote, unreliable storage facilities. Remember that the prover might be the storage service provider, storage medium owner, or system administrator, and the verifier could be either the data owner or a reliable third party.

Requirement #1: The verifier's possession of a document should not be a prerequisite. Full copy of the data that has to be verified. Moreover, it is not practical for a verifier to a duplicate of the content should be kept for verification. Storing a more condensed contents digest of the data at the verifier should be sufficient as long as it fits the purpose well.

A Protocol For PDP-Based Integrity Checking: Provable data processing (PDP) technology is the foundation of the protocol put out by Ateniese et al., which enables customers to request a probabilistic proof from storage service providers. A proof like that will be used to show that their data has been kept there. One benefit of this approach is that the storage service provider might produce the evidence with only a limited amount of access to the entire dataset. In addition, the amount of metadata that end users must keep is minimal—specifically, O (1). Also, the overhead in the communication routes is reduced by the limited amount of data sent. The data owner (client) may perform actions on the data as part of the pre-processing method, such as extending the data or creating additional metadata to be stored at the cloud server side. Before erasing the local copy, the data owner might run the PDP protocol to verify that the uploaded copy had been successfully saved on the server computers. Indeed, the owner of the data has the option to encrypt a dataset before sending it to the storage devices.

Resources are delivered as a service over the Internet in cloud computing settings in a dynamic, virtualized, and scalable manner. Users of business applications may now access them online using a Web browser thanks to cloud computing services, while the servers hold the program and data. Online security is therefore more crucial than ever in the age of cloud computing. The first gate protecting the huge cloud resources is the website server. As the cloud may work continuously to perform daily online transactions worth millions of dollars, any Web security vulnerability will have an amplified effect on the whole cloud. Techniques used in web attacks are frequently referred to as a kind of attack. Attackers will use such methods to take advantage of any Web security hole that is discovered. Authentication, Authorization, Client-Side Attacks, Communication and Execution, Information Exposure, and Logical Attacks are some categories for attack types. This section provides a quick introduction to each of them due to the space constraints. Readers who are interested are urged to investigate the listed sources for further in-depth information.

Identity verification: Verifying a claim that a subject makes to act on behalf of a certain principal is the process of authentication. Authentication attacks, such as Brute Force, Inadequate Authentication, and Weak Password Recovery Validation, target a Web site's procedure for verifying the identity of a user, service, or application.

A brute force assault uses an automated procedure to try to guess someone's account and password. In the Inadequate Authentication scenario, certain sensitive functionality or material is safeguarded by "hiding" the precise location in a mysterious string, yet it is still readily accessible via a particular URL. By probing files and folders using brute force, the attacker might find such URLs. Password recovery services are offered by several websites. If the user can respond correctly to some questions that are part of the user registration procedure, this service will automatically retrieve the user name or password for the user. This website is regarded as having Weak Password Recovery Validation if the recovery questions are either simple to guess or can be bypassed.

Permission: An authenticated subject's ability to carry out a certain action is checked using authorization. Authorization must come after authentication. For instance, only specified users are permitted to access certain functionality or material.

Authorization attacks employ a variety of strategies to breach users' privileges and obtain access to restricted locations. Inadequate Authorization is a common source of authorization attacks. It's not a given that a user should have access to content that has been granted arbitrary permissions just because she has been authenticated to a website. When a website fails to secure important functionality or material with appropriate access control constraints, insufficient authorization happens. With sessions, further authorization attacks are present. Credential/Session Prediction, Inadequate Session Expiration, and Session Fixation are some of these threats. Once a user successfully logs in for the first time to a website, many websites create a session and produce a special "session ID" to identify this session. Subsequent queries to the website include this session ID as "Evidence" of the authorized session. In order to hijack or impersonate a user, a credential or session prediction attack determines or speculates on the special value of a session. When an attacker is permitted to access previously used session credentials or session IDs, insufficient session expiration takes place for permission. For instance, on a shared computer, if a user views a Web page and leaves without allowing enough time for the session to expire, an attacker can utilize the back button of the browser to access Web pages that the victim has already seen.

Session Fixation bombards the website with past HTTP requests or uses cross-site scripting to force a user's session ID to an arbitrary number. When the victim logs in, the attacker assumes their identity using the predetermined session ID value. Client-Side Aggression. The Client-Side Attacks use the victim's trust relationship expectations for the actual Web site to trick them into clicking a link on a malicious Web page. When a user enters their user name and password on a malicious Web page, the malicious Web page can then utilize this information to assume the user's identity. Cross-Site Scripting (XSS) causes the victim's browser to run executable code given by the attacker. Scripting languages that are supported by browsers are frequently used to write the code. Programming languages like JavaScript, VBScript, ActiveX, Flash, or Java. The code has the power to read, alter, and send any sensitive data that is accessible by the browser since it will operate within the security context of the hosting Web site.

Cross-Site Request Forgery (CSRF) is a security vulnerability that affects websites that do not check for CSRF in HTTP/HTTPS requests. After tricking the victim into clicking a link on a malicious Web page, the attacker can assume the victim's identity and gain access to the vulnerable Web site on the victim's behalf if they are aware of the URLs of the vulnerable site that are not protected by CSRF checking and the victim's browser stores credentials for the vulnerable site, such as cookies. Execution of Command. The Command Execution attacks make use of server-side flaws to remotely control the website. User input is often sent to the website in order to seek services. An attacker might change command execution on the server if a Web application does not properly sanitize user-supplied input before utilizing it in application code. For instance, buffer overflow might occur and cause a denial of service if the length of the input is not verified before use. Alternatively, if the user input is not adequately filtered, an attacker may inject arbitrary executable code into the server if the Web application leverages user input to generate statements like SQL, XPath, C/C11 Format String, OS system command, LDAP, or dynamic HTML. Information Dissemination. Attacks known as Information Disclosure capture sensitive data about a website that has been made public via developer comments, error messages, or well-known file naming standards. If the default file is absent, a Web server, for instance, can provide a list of files in the requested directory. An attacker will receive the information they need from this to carry out other assaults on the system. Alternative methods of information disclosure include route traversal utilizing unique pathways like. and.. or leveraging predictably located resources to find URLs that are concealed.

Logical Assaults. Exploiting the logic flow of a Web application is the focus of logical attacks. A user's activity is often done in several steps. Application logic refers to the process's procedural flow. Denial of Service is a frequent type of logical attack (DoS). DoS attacks will make an effort to use up all of the web server's resources, including CPU, memory, disc space, and so on, by exploiting the features the website offers. The Web site will stop responding to regular users when any system resource hits a certain utilization level. DoS attacks are frequently brought on by insufficient anti-automation, when an attacker is allowed to repeatedly automate a procedure.

Thousands of times per minute, an automated script might be run, possibly resulting in a loss of performance or service.

SOFTWARE USED

Django

A high-level Python web framework called Django enables the quick creation of safe and dependable websites. Django, which was created by seasoned programmers, handles a lot of the pain associated with web development, allowing you to concentrate on developing your app without having to recreate the wheel. It is open source and free, has a strong community, excellent documentation, and a variety of free and paid support options.

Django makes it easier to create applications that: Complete Django offers nearly everything developers would need "out of the box" and adheres to the "Batteries included" principle. Everything you require is included in the same "product," so everything functions in unison, adheres to the same design principles, and has comprehensive and current documentation.

Versatile: Django can (and has been) used to create practically any form of website, from social networks and news sites to content management systems and wikis.

It can send material in practically any format and integrate with any client-side framework (including HTML, RSS feeds, JSON, and XML).Internally, it offers options for nearly any capability you could require (such as a number of well-known databases, templating engines, etc.), but it also has the ability to be expanded to incorporate additional components if necessary. By offering a framework that is designed to "do the right things" to safeguard the website automatically, Secure Django assists developers in avoiding many typical security blunders. Django, for instance, offers a secure way to handle user accounts and passwords, avoiding mistakes like storing passwords directly rather than using a password hash or putting session information in cookies where it is vulnerable (instead, cookies just contain a key and the actual data is stored in the database).A fixed-length value known as a password hash is produced by passing a password through a cryptographic hash algorithm. By passing a password through a hash function and comparing the results to a previously saved hash value, Django can determine whether a password entry is valid. The "one-way" nature of the function, however, makes it difficult for an attacker to figure out the original password even if a stored hash value is stolen. Protection against several vulnerabilities, including as SQL injection, cross-site scripting, cross-site request forgery, and clickjacking, is enabled by default in Django (see Website security for more details of such attacks).

Scalable: Component-based "shared-nothing" design is what Django employs (each part of the architecture is independent of the others, and can hence be replaced or changed if needed). It can grow for increasing traffic by adding hardware at any level, including cache servers, database servers, or application servers, because the various components are clearly segregated from one another. Some of the busiest websites have scaled Django effectively to satisfy their needs (e.g. Instagram and Disqus, to name just two). Django programming that is easy to maintain and reuse is developed utilizing design patterns and concepts that support this.

It specifically applies the Don't Repeat Yourself (DRY) philosophy to avoid needless duplication and cut down on the amount of code. In keeping with the Model View Controller (MVC) paradigm, Django also encourages the organization of similar functionality into reusable "applications" and, on a more basic level, organizes related code into modules. Python, which is available on many platforms, is used to create portable Django. This implies that you may run your apps on many versions of Linux, Windows, and macOS and that you are not restricted to a single server platform. Django is very extensively supported by a wide range of web hosts, who frequently offer specialized infrastructure and documentation for hosting Django sites. Where did it originate?

A web team in charge of developing and managing newspaper websites first worked on Django between 2003 and 2005. The team started factoring out and reusing a lot of the common code and design patterns after building many sites. A general web development framework was created from this shared code and released as the "Django" project in July 2005.

With its initial milestone release (1.0) in September 2008 to the most recent version 4.0, Django has kept expanding and improving (2022). Every new release has improved functionality and fixed bugs, including the inclusion of "generic" view methods and classes as well as support for additional types of databases, template engines, and caching. There are thousands of users and collaborators to the Django open source project, which is today vibrant and collaborative. While it still has certain characteristics that are reminiscent of its beginnings, Django has developed into a flexible framework that can be used to create any kind of website. An open-source object-relational database management system is PostgreSQL. It is a descendent of one of the earliest such systems, the POSTGRES system created at the University of California, Berkeley by Professor Michael Stonebraker. The word "Postgres" is a portmanteau of Ingres, a pioneering relational database system. Presently, PostgreSQL provides functions like full-text searching, transactional integrity, complicated queries, foreign keys, triggers, views, and limited data replication. PostgreSQL may be expanded by users with new data types, operations, operators, or indexing techniques. In addition to the database interfaces JDBC and ODBC, PostgreSQL supports a wide range of programming languages, including C, C++, Java, Perl, Tcl, and Python. Almost every Unix-like operating system, including Linux, Windows, and Apple Macintosh OS X, supports PostgreSQL. The BSD license, which PostgreSQL was distributed under, allows anybody to freely use, modify, and distribute the database's source code and documentation for any purpose. Many research and production systems (such as the PostGIS system for geographic information) as well as instructional resources at various institutions have all been implemented using PostgreSQL. Through the efforts of a sizable development community, PostgreSQL keeps improving.

REVIEW OF LITERATURE

Mobile cloud computing is an architectural pattern where data storage and CPU-intensive processes are conducted in the cloud and mobile devices are largely used as thin clients to connect with the application and render results handled from the cloud environment. The various strategies were explored as follows:

The first privacy-preserving solution that permits open auditing of shared data kept in the cloud was presented by Boyang Wang and Baochun L. They specifically use ring signatures to compute the verification data required to audit the data integrity when shared. Our system allows a third party auditor (TPA) to publicly check the integrity of shared data without having to download the complete file while maintaining the privacy of the signer on each block.

Cong Wang developed a secure cloud storage system that supports public auditing while protecting user privacy, and he further extended the results to provide the TPA the ability to efficiently and concurrently audit several users. Thorough security and performance studies reveal the suggested systems are provably secure and extremely efficient.

Devi Parvathy Mohan offered to construct a dynamic audit service for confirming the integrity of an untrusted and outsourced storage in order to get around the issue with the conventional technique. The approach based on probabilistic inquiry and periodic verification for increasing the performance of audit services. TPA monitoring provides the auditing service. The TPA sometimes has the potential to conceal anomalous information from cloud users. Consider a cloud-based dynamic audit solution to get around the problem. By using this technique, it may detect anomalies and notify cloud users. so that the cloud storage may be protected.

Amrutka R. Prajakta explores the challenge of assigning several Third Party Auditors (TPAs) on behalf of cloud clients as opposed to present schemes that employ a single verifier in order to verify the data accuracy (TPA).Moreover, we expand our work to secure user authentication by combining the Blowfish cryptographic method and digital signature approach for improved cloud data security. It offers high security and increased data productivity.

Ms. Jahanara Akhtar described a scenario in which unprotected cloud networks provide unauthorized users or hackers access to data archives. This is the major cause of personal information leaks or data loss during network broadcasts. So, in a cloud setting, cloud security is crucial. In this study, a third party auditing method is suggested to assure improved security. A runtime audit or inspection will be performed by an auditor. The success of this work, the auditor, will be crucial in protecting the cloud environment.

Lazaros and his colleagues argued that new cloud model and migration techniques are necessary to successfully bring cloud computing closer to mobile users. It consists of a local cloud attached to the remote access infrastructure and a back-end cloud. This may be broken down into a number of task migration policy types, ranging from absolutely awkward ones. Each client or server makes its own relocation decisions separately, all the way up to the whole transfer process of a cloud Supplier.

Liang and his coworkers put up a sound strategy that carried out the novel concept. This is a broad concept for functional Proxy ReEncryption (PRE), also known as Deterministic Finite Automata Based PRE (DFA-based FPRE). The original and most reliable DFA-based FPRE framework that adapts to the novel concept. According to this scheme, a message is encoded in a figure content associated with a record string of self-assertive length, and a descriptor is only true if a DFA associated with his or her mystery key recognizes the string. This encryption may be used modified by a semi-trusted intermediary to whom a re-encryption key is provided to another figure content associated with another string.

Chu and his coworkers' demonstration of how to effectively, securely, and adaptably share information in distributed storage, as well as the predetermined limit of the number of most severe ciphertext classes, is also impressive. Typically, the amount of ciphertexts in the distributed storage increases fast. They describe novel open key cryptosystems that produce ciphertexts of constant size, making it possible to perform clever decoding operations on any collection of ciphertexts. This is more flexible than various levels key assignment, which can only maintain spaces if all key-holders have a similar path of benefits.

Zhang and his coworkers' investigation looks at the Third-Party Auditor (TPA) side optimization of calculation cost. Investigation on the reduction of calculation costs on the Third-Party Auditor (TPA) side is conducted by s. Zhang and his colleagues. The folders of several cloud servers and Cyber-Physical-Social System (CPSS) users are examined. Large data sets are exceedingly expensive for consumers to amass, and it complicates data administration. Thus, it is crucial to farm out the data to cloud servers, which give customers a convenient, affordable, and flexible way to handle data. The proposed model is a secure certificate-less public integrity verification mechanism (SCLPV). The initial effort to both provide certificate-less public verification and defend against nefarious auditors to demonstrate the reliability of external data in CPSS.

Due to the frequent changes in enrolment, provide a solution to the difficult problem of data sharing in a multi-proprietor approach by protecting identity information and safeguarding data from unreliable clouds.

For active groups in the cloud, the author developed the Mona secure multi-owner information dissemination structure. Here, the user is able to share information with the group without revealing the cloud's distinctive secret. Also, Mona offers quick client revocation and new customer joining. The storage overhead, computation costs, and acceptable security criteria are all met while also guaranteeing efficiency.

The fundamental concept of cloud computing is not brand-new. John McCarthy foresaw the public having access to computing resources in the 1960s, much like a utility. Moreover, the term "cloud" has been used in a variety of situations, such as in the 1990s to describe massive ATM networks. But, the phrase didn't truly start to catch on until 2006, when Google CEO Eric Schmidt used it to characterize the business model of offering services through the Internet. Since then, the word "cloud computing" has mostly been used as a marketing term to convey a wide range of concepts in many situations. Undoubtedly, the absence of a consensus definition of cloud computing has led to a considerable degree of skepticism and uncertainty in addition to commercial enthusiasm. Because of this, efforts to standardize the notion of cloud computing have lately been made. For instance, to validate a common meaning, the work in analyzed over 20 distinct definitions from various sources. In this essay, we use The National Institute of Standards and Technology's definition of cloud computing (NIST).

The idea of cloud computing is still developing and will take several years to completely develop. According to our definition, the Internet is a component of that progress and enables the spread of IT services on a worldwide scale. This results in a new definition of the buyer-seller relationship and a change in how individuals or IT departments get value from technology.

A careful approach to the cloud model will assist customers looking to move expenses from on-premises solutions to the delivery of services from providers that give SLAs and performance assurances. Suppliers of IT goods and services must start focusing their marketing efforts on cloud platforms and cloud-based services in the coming years if they don't want to risk losing customers to cloud-computing service providers as their products become less popular with consumers. The cloud computing concept is more than merely the Internet's next evolution. Everything starts to change when businesses cross the line between using the Internet as a communications medium and actively providing services over it. That cannot be done by the Internet by itself.

EXISTING SYSTEM

Due to the scale of the outsourced data and the user's limited resource capacity, it can be difficult and expensive for cloud users to verify the accuracy of the data in a cloud environment. Therefore, it is crucial to enable public auditability for cloud data storage so that users can turn to a third party auditor (TPA) who has the knowledge and resources that the users lack to audit the outsourced data when necessary. This will fully ensure the data security and conserve the computation resources of cloud users.

Based on the audit's findings, TPA may publish an audit report that would be useful for customers in assessing the risk associated with the cloud data services to which they have subscribed, as well as for cloud service providers in enhancing their cloud-based service platforms. In other words, permitting public risk auditing methods will be crucial for this developing cloud economy to completely take off, as users will require means to evaluate risk and develop confidence in the cloud. The idea of public auditability has recently been put up in the context of assuring the integrity of remotely stored data under various systems and security models.

Drawbacks

Public auditability enables a third party, in addition to the user, to confirm the accuracy of data held remotely. The majority of these schemes, however, do not support the privacy protection of users' data against external auditors, meaning that they might possibly divulge user personal information to the auditors.

This flaw has a significant impact on how secure various protocols are in cloud computing. Users who own the data and rely only on TPA for the storage security of their data do not want this auditing procedure to introduce additional vulnerabilities of unauthorized information leakage towards their data security from the standpoint of preserving data privacy.

Using data encryption prior to outsourcing is one option to address this privacy risk, but it only serves as a supplement to the public auditing system that protects privacy.

Encryption by itself cannot stop data from "flowing away" towards other parties during the auditing process in the absence of a properly developed auditing protocol. So, it only partially resolves the issue of managing the encryption keys while still leaving the issue of safeguarding data privacy. The possible leaking of encryption keys makes unauthorized data access a continuing issue.

PROPOSED SYSTEM

The work is among the first few to offer privacy-preserving public auditing in Cloud Computing, with an emphasis on data storage, in order to enable a privacy-preserving third-party auditing protocol independent of data encryption. Also, an anticipated rise in the number of auditing assignments from various users may be assigned to TPA because to the prominence of cloud computing. A natural need is then how to enable TPA to effectively complete the many auditing activities in a batch way, i.e., concurrently. This is because the individual auditing of these expanding duties can be time-consuming and difficult.

This work employs the public key based homomorphic authenticator technique to address these issues. This technique allows TPA to perform auditing without requiring a local copy of the data, significantly reducing communication and computation overhead when compared to more traditional data auditing approaches. This protocol ensures that TPA cannot gain any knowledge about the data content stored in the cloud server throughout the effective auditing process testing and comparisons with the state-of-the-art by combining the homomorphic authenticator with random mask approach.

Advantages:
- ◦ Accelerated and targeted claims management
- ◦ Reduced administrative expenses and lower claim management costs
- ◦ Quick access to claim administrators with extensive training
- ◦ More influence on the results of claims
- ◦ Easy provision of cashless services
- ◦ Protection of client relationships
- ◦ Preserving the reputation of a brand.
- ◦ The private healthcare providers' control over potential fraud

METHODOLOGY

Figure 3 depicts the architecture for resource allocation and safe data storage in cloud computing. Several users sign up for the cloud for the first time. By creating a private key, the security provider verifies user authentication before allowing them to upload an owner's file. The cloud server is where the encrypted file is kept. With authorization from the particular file owner, end users from all over the world can access the file. The resource's availability in the cloud storage is verified for each file that the authorized user requests. The available materials are kept in a separate database file, often known as a reliability check. Resources are either allocated by the virtual machine or are not. If the file is present, the user may quickly download it; if the file is corrupt, it must be recreated. Based on demand, given to the end user. By encrypting the private key in a consistent size, security is achieved.

The file upload/download process in a cloud storage. By creating the Key-Aggregate key, it demonstrates the procedures for securing both public and private data. Data centers in a cloud's data centers, which carry user data server. If the user is real, they can register and authenticate. The file can be uploaded to the server by authorized users. The file is generated by the server automatically; it is then encrypted and kept on the servers. Every user can request to download a file by first determining whether it is available and whether there are sufficient resources. The authorized user can then download the file by providing his private key. Another copy of the file kept in the dispersed data center can be accessible if the original file is compromised by any intruder. In this case, we produce code from corrupted files using a regenerative function. The majority of file accesses are dependent on client requests.

Figure 3. System architecture

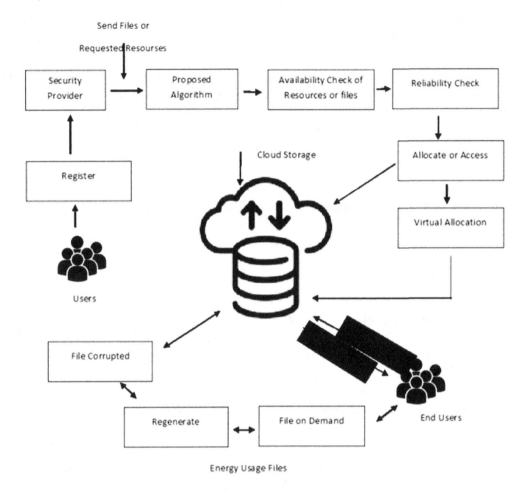

IMPLEMENTATION

Algorithm: Suggested scheme consists of four algorithms:

Key Creation Algorithm: In this case, the public and private keys for the client and server are generated using the RSA algorithm. It is possible to ensure the safe transmission of communications as well as other sensitive documents and information by using both encryption and decryption techniques. It produces Public Key (n, e) and Private Key (d), as well as keys for encryption and decryption.Base64 is the password encryption algorithm that is used to encrypt client passwords. When a client registers, his password is encrypted and stored in a database. When the client logs in, the password is decrypted, allowing the client to log in.

Algorithm for Creating Signatures: The 'Signature' is generated (from the server side) using OPEN SSL. The SSL and TLS protocols are implemented using open-source software.

The MD5 hash code generating technique is employed in the client, where the hash code is generated and sent to the TPA during uploading.

Figure 4. ER diagram

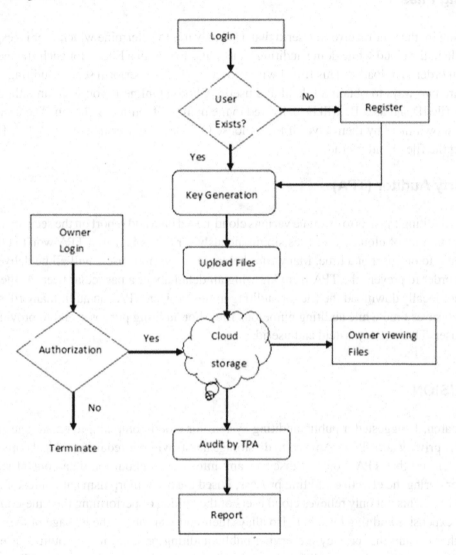

Login Users

Each user will need a unique login because there are so many cloud users. The user must provide their username and password in order to log in. The accuracy of the username and password will be verified; if it is a correct user, access will be granted; otherwise, the warning "Wrong User" will be shown. They must register if they are using this for the first time. Once they click "Sign Up," they will be sent to a screen where they must fill out information such as their login, password, email address, and phone number. Return to the Login page by clicking Register again. Using the new username and password, the new user may now log in.

Uploading Files

After logging in, the user receives a Userid that TPA may use to determine which user is responsible for a certain file in the cloud while doing auditing. A user has to obtain a File id for each file they upload to the cloud in order to upload it. This file id will be used by TPA to perform secure auditing in the cloud.

There are two ways to obtain a File id and userid. Choose Online if you want an online userid and file id. The file ID and user ID will be delivered to the mail ID if Online is chosen. The user ID and file ID will be shown there by themselves if they choose Offline. The user may upload their files into the cloud using the file id and user id.

Third Party Auditor (TPA)

Third-party auditing's task is to examine various cloud-based data and report on the security of such files. TPA can audit a lot of cloud-based files simultaneously for this job. Yet, a TPA won't audit the same file belonging to one user at a time. Many files belonging to various users will all be delivered at once to TPA. In order to prevent the TPA from knowing all detail about a particular user. At the same time, TPA will not locally download the file for auditing in this project. TPA can audit many files simultaneously, which saves time while auditing numerous files. For auditing purposes and to provide reports to a specific user, TPA employs fileid and userid.

CONCLUSION

In this research, I suggested a public auditing system for cloud computing data storage security that protects user privacy and allows Anyone to do storage audits without requiring a local copy of the data. In order to ensure that TPA wouldn't discover any information about the data content stored on the cloud server during the effective auditing process, I used the homomorphism authenticator and random mask technique. This not only relieves cloud users of the burden of performing the time-consuming and potentially expensive auditing task, but also allays their concerns about the leakage of their outsourced data. I further expand this privacy-preserving public auditing protocol into a multi-user environment where TPA may do the various auditing duties in a batch way, i.e., simultaneously. TPA may concurrently manage several audit sessions from different users for their outsourced data files. A thorough investigation of security and performance reveals that the suggested techniques are both provably safe and very effective. I think that all of these benefits of the suggested plans would clarify the concept of economies of scale in cloud computing.

FUTURE ENHANCEMENT

In this project, Third Party Auditing is made possible without physically downloading files from the cloud by utilizing the homomorphism authenticator and random mask technique. As a consequence, TPA won't discover anything about the data content kept on the cloud server thanks to the efficient auditing process. Future enhancements to the project include:

- Reducing network traffic during TPA audits.
- Increasing the level of privacy for the files that are under TPA audit.

REFERENCES

Abdulsalam & Hedabou. (2021). *Security and Privacy in Cloud Computing: Technical Review.* Academic Press.

Grobauer, Stocker, & Walloscheck. (2011). Understanding the vulnerabilities of cloud computing. *IEEE Security & Privacy, 9*(2), 50–7. https://www.cisco.com/c/en/us/solutions/collateral/service-provider/visual-networking-index-vni/mobile-white-paper-c11-520862.pdf

Mell, P., & Grance, T. (2009). *Draft NIST Working Definition of Cloud Computing.* https://csrc.nist.gov/groups/SNS/cloudcomputing/index.html

Pallikonda, Chaduvula, Markapudi, Jyothi, & Indira. (2022). *Efficient way to ensure the data security in cloud computing.* Academic Press.

Rajan & Babu. (2017). *Privacy and Authenticity for Cloud Data with Attribute-Based Encryption and Digital Signature.* Unpublished.

Razaque, Haj Frej, Alotaibi, & Alotaibai. (2021). Privacy Preservation Models for Third-Party Auditor over Cloud Computing. Academic Press.

Sami. (2010, March). Service-based arbitrated multi-tier infrastructure for mobile cloud computing. Academic Press.

Toral, Barrero, Reina, Sanchez-Garca, & Garca-Campos. (n.d.). For vehicular ad hoc networks. *OnsiteDriverID: A Secure Authentication System based on Spanish eID Cards.*

Chapter 16
Detection and Classification of Dense Tomato Fruits by Integrating Coordinate Attention Mechanism With YOLO Model

Seetharam Nagesh Appe
Annamalai University, India

G. Arulselvi
Annamalai University, India

Balaji G. N.
Vellore Institute of Technology, India

ABSTRACT

Real-time detection of objects is one of the important tasks of computer vision applications such as agriculture, surveillance, self-driving cars, etc. The fruit target detection rate based on traditional approaches is low due to the complex background, substantial texture interference, partial occlusion of fruits, etc. This chapter proposes an improved YOLOv5 model to detect and classify the dense tomatoes by adding the coordinate attention mechanism and bidirectional pyramid network. The coordinate attention mechanism is used to detect and classify the dense tomatoes, and bidirectional pyramid network is used to detect the tomatoes at different scales. The proposed model produces good results in detecting the small dense tomatoes with an accuracy of 87.4%.

DOI: 10.4018/978-1-6684-8098-4.ch016

INTRODUCTION

The agricultural robot has emerged as one of the most promising technologies of precision agriculture technologies among many others (Tao et al., 2017). Seeding, weeding, feeding, trimming, picking and harvesting, sorting, and other repetitive tasks make up most of agriculture. Farmers may now focus more on strategic issues and increase output yields thanks to agricultural robots, which automate those slow, boring, and repetitive tasks (Edan et al., 2009). The automated harvesting and picking of the fruits are one of the important application of the robots. In principle, a sophisticated detection algorithm is required for the robot to be fully capable of doing harvesting and picking in order to overcome obstacles including naturally occurring variations in illumination, shape, position and color (Barnea et al., 2016).

Object detection is a technique used to recognize and detect different objects that are present in video or image and label them in order to classify these objects. Several methods are commonly used for object detection in order to recognise and locate items, and these algorithms make use of deep learning to produce accurate results. Object detection primarily used in instance segmentation, semantic segmentation, image caption etc., Object detection can be divided into machine learning-based and deep learning-based approaches. The machine learning approach requires the features (such as the color histogram or edges) to be defined by using various methods. The position and label of the object are predicted by a regression model using these features as input. Contrarily, deep learning-based techniques accomplish end-to-end, unsupervised object detection using convolutional neural networks (CNNs), eliminating the need for features(characteristics) to be specified and extracted independently.

Encoder and decoder are typically the two components of deep learning-based object detection algorithms. When an encoder receives an image as input, it processes it through a series of layers and blocks that enable it to extract statistical features that can be used to identify and locate objects. After the encoder, a decoder receives the output and predicts the labels and bounding boxes of each object. Typically, these object detectors can be divided into two-stage and one-stage detectors. RCNN (Girshick et al., 2014), Fast R-CNN (Girshick et al., 2015), Faster R-CNN (Ren et al. 2015), and Mask R-CNN (He et al., 2017) are two-stage detectors, while SSD (Liu et al., 2016) and YOLO (Redmon et al., 2016) series are one-stage approaches.

Even though these general object detection techniques have improved in accuracy and efficiency, the limited resolution and context information are inadequate to train a model, detecting small objects in images is still challenging.

Based on Yolov4-tiny's deep learning object detection algorithm, The attention mechanism and multi-scale prediction were combined by Lu et al. (2016) to identify occlusion and small item green pepper.

Sa et al. experimented with a faster R-CNN detector for fruit detection by combining multi-modal colour (RGB) and near-infrared (NIR) information. Even though only a small number of images were utilised for training and testing, this method outperformed earlier ones in terms of performance. However, it is challenging for the method to detect small and occluded fruits, and its speed still needs to be improved for harvesting robots to operate in the field in real-time.

For the purpose of detecting tomatoes, Zhao et al. (2016) developed the AdaBoost algorithm using the average pixel value. Based on physical characteristics like texture, color, shape and Haar-like characteristics of images, the algorithm identifies the ripe tomatoes. A tiny-yolo network based on the YOLOv2 network was proposed by Xue et al. (2018). The proposed tiny-yolo model consists of dense blocks used for detection of immature mango and mango under orchard scenes.

Liu. et al. (2020) used YOLO-tomato detector for the detection of tomatoes. This method is based on the YOLOv3 and used two approaches: feature extraction by dense architecture and replaced R-Bbox with CBbox. But the method not utilized contextual information for detection of occluded tomatoes. Koirala et al. (2019) used the model Mango-YOLO based on YOLOv3 and YOLOv2(tiny) for the detection of real time mango fruit. It achieved a F1 score of 0.89 on a day-time mango image dataset.

While one-stage approaches are often developed for fast inference and do not typically deal with small objects, two-stage frameworks are quite slow. In this study, we focus on the issue of real-time small objects detection in orchards. To achieve this, we suggest developing a one-stage object detector that could successfully detect small objects with high speed and high accuracy.

MATERIALS AND METHODS

Dataset Construction

The tomato images used in this study are collected from Laboro Tomato dataset (Labaro, 2020), which consists of the tomato images collected for detection and instance segmentation purpose. The tomato images were captured during different stages of the ripening. The total of 2324 images under different environmental conditional with different modes and scales. Figure 1 shows sample images of the dataset under various conditions.

Data Augmentation

Data augmentation is a machine learning strategy that uses numerous slightly modified copies of current data to train models, hence reducing overfitting when training a machine learning model (Shorten et al., 2019). The augmentation techniques like horizontal flip, rotation, changing the brightness are applied on the collected dataset to artificially enhance the dataset size as well as suitable for different scenarios before training.

Network Model

As YOLO is an end-to-end deep learning-based network object detector (Redmon et al., 2017, 2018; Bochkovskiy et al., 2020), it considers object detection as a regression problem. It determines the bounding boxes of an objects in a given image and classify the identified objects in a single assumption (Redmon et al., 2017). In contrast to two-stage detectors like the R-CNN family, it does not require a region proposal phase. In this way, the YOLO significantly enhances object detection performance.

The fundamental idea of YOLO framework is to make detections in each grid cell after dividing the input image into an S x S grid. Three things are predicted by YOLO for each cell: the likelihood that an object will be present, the coordinates of the box that will surround the object if one does, and the class the object falls under and its corresponding probability. Each cell estimates B bounding boxes together with their confidence levels. The level of confidence can indicate if an object is present in the grid cell and, if so, the intersection of union (IoU) of the predictions and the ground truth (GT).

In 2020, Glenn Jocher produced Yolov5, which exploratory comparisons revealed had a slightly quicker prediction speed but the same accuracy as Yolov4 (Zhu et al., 2021). YOLOv5 has five versions, out of which YOLOv5s has the quickest detection time with few parameters.

The YOLOv5 network structure as depicted in Figure 2 consists of following three main parts:

- **Backbone:** Backbone is employed for extracting the key characteristics at various granularities from an input image.
- **Neck:** From the features that the backbone network has extracted, the neck is used to create feature pyramids. Feature pyramids enable the framework in generalising object scaling, i.e., it helps in the recognition of objects at various scales and sizes.
- **Head:** The final step in the prediction process is the construction of the final output using anchor boxes, objectness scores, class probabilities, and bounding boxes.

PROPOSED METHODOLOGY

The lightweight YOLOv5 network based on the attention mechanism and bi-directional feature pyramid network was proposed to detect the dense tomatoes given multi-mode and multi-scale characteristics in natural environment. Firstly the coordinate attention module (CA) was added to the backbone network to capture the cross-channel information and position perception in order to detect and locate the dense tomatoes. Secondly, the bi-directional feature pyramid network (BFPN) which is an improved version of the PANet feature fusion network is added to the network in order to improve the detection accuracy of the tomatoes at different scales.

Attention Mechanism

The original YOLOv5 network model possesses a poor ability to detect small and dense items due to the fact that it readily loses features derived from dense objects and small objects during the reasoning process. Hou et al. (2021) proposed coordinate attention mechanism shown in Figure 3 is a novel method that embeds location(positional) data into channel attention, enabling the network to concentrate on huge significant regions with a low computational cost. Coordinate information integration and coordinate attention generation are the two processes that make up this process. In order to solve the problem of location loss of information pertaining to location caused by prior attention methods like CBAM (Woo et al., 2018), CA split channel attention into two separate one-dimensional feature coding procedures that aggregated features across two spatial directions.

A computing unit known as a CA block can output data of the same size as the intermediate feature tensor Y while accepting any intermediate feature tensor X as input. At the same time, it has the effect of improving representation.

The CA block is added to the Proposed YOLOv5 model after the 4, 6, 8, 20, and 23 layers of the Original YOLOv5 model. The tomato images are provided as input to the model after data pre-processing in order to extract features, which are then entered into the neck region of the model through the CA module for prediction. This way the proposed model accurately detects the small dense fruits.

Bidirectional Feature Pyramid Network (BFPN)

The original YOLOv5 model uses PANet (Liu et al., 2018) in the neck part for multi-scale feature fusion, but PANet merges the features without distinction when fusing the different features. However, because the resolutions of these different input features differ, their contributions to the fused output features are often unequal. A BFPN, or Weighted Bi-directional Feature Pyramid Network (Chen et al., 2021), is a feature pyramid network that allows for simple and fast multi-scale feature fusion. Traditional approaches typically treat all features fed into the Feature Pyramid Network (FPN) equally, regardless of their varying resolutions. However, input features at different resolutions frequently contribute unequally to output features. As a result, the BFPN adds a weight to each input feature, allowing the network to learn the significance of each as shown in Figure 4.

When compared to PANet, PANet added an additional bottom-up path for information flow at the cost of increased computational cost. BFPN, on the other hand, optimises these cross-scale connections by removing nodes with a single input edge, adding an extra edge from the original input to output node if they are on the same level, and treating each bidirectional path as a single feature network layer.

In the proposed model, the PANet is substituted with the BFPN in order to fuse image features without incurring a significant computational cost.

EXPERIMENTS AND RESULTS

The dataset used in the experiment consists of 2324 images of size 416 x 416 after applying the augementation. The augmentation is applied to artificially increase the dataset for training. The proposed YOLOv5 model needs the input images be annotated both in class and in the ground truth bounding box, hence the images are annotated with the help of VGG image annotator. The training hyper parameters used in the proposed model are 100 epochs with a momentum of 0.9 and an initial learning rate of 0.01.

Evaluation Metrics

The precision (P) metric was used in this study to assess the accuracy of tomato fruit detection as mentioned in (Anand et al., 2022). The detection of positive samples in all images is measured by using recall (R). The average precision (AP) of a detector measures its performance in each category. The average of all class average precisions(Aps) is known as the mean average precision (mAP), and the definitions of precision(P), recall(R), average precision(AP), and mean average precision(mAP) of the mode are defined using (1-4). A model's complexity is determined by the quantity of floating-point operations (FLOPs) and parameters (Params).

$$P = \frac{True\_Positive}{True\_Positive + False\_Positive} \times 100\% \tag{1}$$

$$R = \frac{True\_Positive}{True\_Positive + False\_Negative} \times 100\% \tag{2}$$

$$AP = \int_0^1 P(R)\, dR \times 100\% \tag{3}$$

$$mAP = \frac{\sum_{i=1}^n AP}{n} \tag{4}$$

where '*n*' *denotes* the number of classes.

The Loss curve and the mean average precision (mAP) are used to evaluate the suggested YOLOv5 model in order to determine how accurate the model detection is. The performance of the original YOLOv5s, the proposed YOLOv5 model with coordinate attention mechanism and model with CA+BFPN while training phase are shown in Figure 5.

The performance metrics like precision, recall, object loss, bounding box loss, class loss and mean average precision(mAP) of the proposed YOLOv5 for 100 epochs during training process are depicted in the Figure 6.

The accuracy of the three different models are compared with same data set and same hyper parameters. The value of the precision, mean average precison(mAP),recall, and floating point operataions (FLOPS) were selected as the evaluation metrics of the selected models provided in the Table 1.

Table 1. Evaluation metrics of models

Model	mAP@0.50	Precision(P)%	Recall(R) %	FLOPS/GFLOPS
YOLOv5s	82.3	84.8	75.3	17.1
YOLOv5s+CA	83.2	88.1	78.1	16.8
YOLOv5s+CA+BFPN	87.4	88.4	81.4	15.1

The precision, recall and mAP@0.50 of the proposed YOLOv5s model with cooridnate attention(CA) mechanism and bidirectional fetaure pyramid network(BFPN) are better compared to other two models.

To evaluate the efficacy of the original YOLOv5 and proposed YOLOv5 model with attention mechanism, numerous tomato images were tested and visualised under different sizes and scales. Figure 7 visualizes the effect of the detecting the small dense tomatoes with and without using the attention mechanism.

Figure 1.

Figure 2.

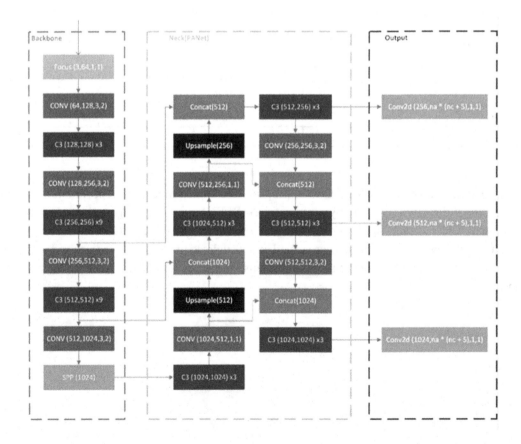

Figure 3.

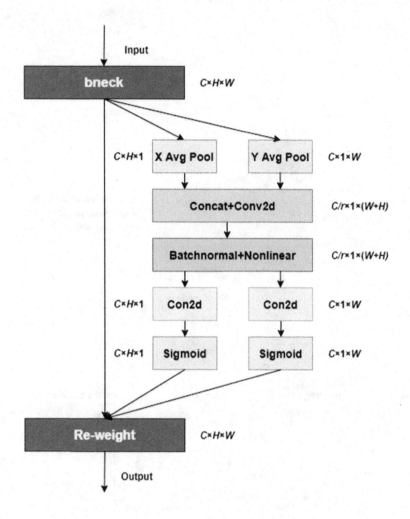

Figure 4.

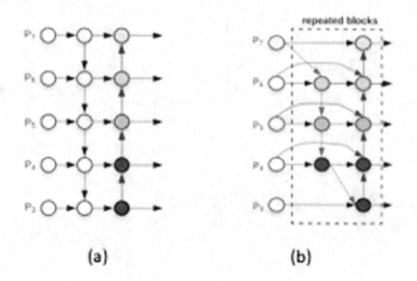

Figure 5.

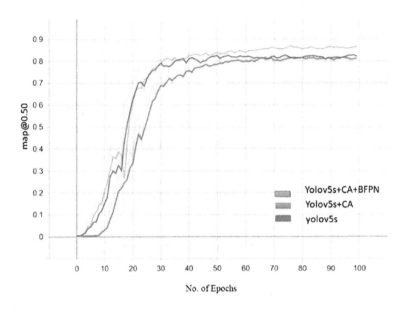

Figure 6.

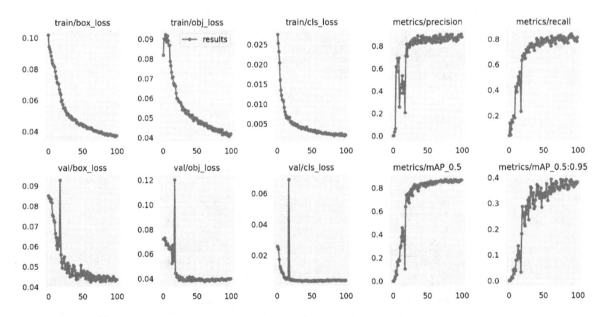

Figure 7.

(a)	(b)	(c)

CONCLUSION

The YOLOv5s model is used as the basis for the proposed network model for tomato detection at different scales and under different environmental conditions. To improve the YOLOv5s model's ability to detect small dense tomatoes, the coordinate attention mechanism has been introduced. Secondly, the bi-directional feature pyramid network is added to the neck part of the YOLOv5s model. The proposed model, which outperformed the original YOLOv5s model with good visualisation outcomes, provided an accuracy of 87.4%.

REFERENCES

Anand, D., Arulselvi, G., Balaji, G. N., & Chandra, G. R. (2022). A Deep Convolutional Extreme Machine Learning Classification Method to Detect Bone Cancer from Histopathological Images. *International Journal of Intelligent Systems and Applications in Engineering*, *10*(4), 39–47.

Barnea, E., Mairon, R., & Ben-Shahar, O. (2016). Colour-agnostic shape-based 3D fruit detection for crop harvesting robots. *Biosystems Engineering*, *146*, 57–70. doi:10.1016/j.biosystemseng.2016.01.013

Bochkovskiy, A., Wang, C. Y., & Liao, H. Y. M. (2020). *Yolov4: Optimal speed and accuracy of object detection*. https://doi.org//arXiv.2004.10934 doi:10.48550

Chen, J., Mai, H., Luo, L., Chen, X., & Wu, K. (2021). Effective Feature Fusion Network in BIFPN for Small Object Detection. *2021 IEEE International Conference on Image Processing (ICIP)*, 699-703. 10.1109/ICIP42928.2021.9506347

Edan, Y., Han, S., & Kondo, N. (2009). Automation in Agriculture. In S. Nof (Ed.), *Springer Handbook of Automation. Springer Handbooks*. Springer., doi:10.1007/978-3-540-78831-7_63

Girshick, R. (2015). Fast-RCNN. *Proceedings of the IEEE International Conference on Computer Vision (ICCV)*, 1440–1448. 10.1109/ICCV.2015.169

Girshick, R., Donahue, J., Darrell, T., & Malik, J. (2014). Rich feature hierarchies for accurate object detection and semantic segmentation. *Proceedings of the IEEE Conference on Computer Vision and Pattern Recognition,* 580–587. 10.1109/CVPR.2014.81

He, K., Gkioxari, G., Dollár, P., & Girshick, R. (2017). Mask R-CNN. *2017 IEEE International Conference on Computer Vision (ICCV),* 2980-2988. 10.1109/ICCV.2017.322

Hou, Q., Zhou, D., & Feng, J. (2021). Coordinate attention for efficient mobile network design. *Proceedings of the IEEE/CVF Conference on Computer Vision and Pattern Recognition.* 10.1109/CVPR46437.2021.01350

Koirala, A., Walsh, K. B., Wang, Z., & McCarthy, C. (2019). Deep learning for real-time fruit detection and orchard fruit load estimation: Benchmarking of 'MangoYOLO'. *Precision Agriculture, 20*(6), 1107–1135. doi:10.100711119-019-09642-0

LaboroL. T. (2020). https://github.com/laboroai/LaboroTomato.git

Liu, G., Nouaze, J. C., Touko Mbouembe, P. L., & Kim, J. H. (2020). YOLO-tomato: A robust algorithm for tomato detection based on YOLOv3. *Sensors (Basel), 20*(7), 2145. doi:10.339020072145 PMID:32290173

Liu, S., & ... Path aggregation network for instance segmentation. *Proceedings of the IEEE conference on computer vision and pattern recognition.*

Liu, W., Anguelov, D., Erhan, D., Szegedy, C., Reed, S., Fu, C. Y., & Berg, A. C. (2016). *European Conference on Computer Vision.* Springer.

Lu, J., Lee, W. S., Gan, H., & Hu, X. W. (2018). Immature citrus fruit detection based on local binary pattern feature and hierarchical contour analysis. *Biosystems Engineering, 171,* 78–90. doi:10.1016/j.biosystemseng.2018.04.009

Redmon, J., Divvala, S., Girshick, R., & Farhadi, A. (2016). You only look once: Unified, real-time object detection. *Proceedings of the IEEE Conference on Computer Vision and Pattern Recognition,* 779–788. 10.1109/CVPR.2016.91

Redmon, J., & Farhadi, A. (2017). YOLO9000: Better, faster, stronger. *Proceedings of the IEEE conference on computer vision and pattern recognition,* 7263-7271.

Redmon, J., & Farhadi, A. (2018). *Yolov3: An incremental improvement.* https://doi.org//arXiv.1804.02767 doi:10.48550

Ren, S. (2015). Faster r-cnn: Towards real-time object detection with region proposal networks. *Advances in Neural Information Processing Systems, 28.*

Sa, I., Ge, Z., Dayoub, F., Upcroft, B., Perez, T., & McCool, C. (2016). Deepfruits: A fruit detection system using deep neural networks. *Sensors, 16*(8), 1222.

Shorten, C., & Khoshgoftaar, T. M. (2019). A survey on Image Data Augmentation for Deep Learning. *Journal of Big Data, 6*(1), 60. doi:10.118640537-019-0197-0

Tao, Y., & Zhou, J. (2017). Automatic apple recognition based on the fusion of color and 3D feature for robotic fruit picking. *Computers and Electronics in Agriculture, 142*, 388–396. doi:10.1016/j.compag.2017.09.019

Woo, S., Park, J., Lee, J.-Y., & So Kweon, I. (2018). Cbam: Convolutional block attention module. *Proceedings of the European conference on computer vision (ECCV), 3*–19.

Xue, Y. J. (2018). Immature mango detection based on improved YOLOv2. *Transactions of the Chinese Society of Agricultural Engineering, 34*(7), 173-179.

Zhao, Y., Gong, L., Zhou, B., Huang, Y., & Liu, C. (2016). Detecting tomatoes in greenhouse scenes by combining AdaBoost classifier and colour analysis. *Biosystems Engineering, 148*, 127–137. doi:10.1016/j.biosystemseng.2016.05.001

Zhu, X., Lyu, S., Wang, X., & Zhao, Q. (2021). TPH-YOLOv5: Improved YOLOv5 based on transformer prediction head for object detection on drone-captured scenarios. *Proceedings of the IEEE/CVF International Conference on Computer Vision*, 2778–2788. 10.1109/ICCVW54120.2021.00312

Chapter 17
A Study on an Internet of Things (IoT)–Enabled Smart Solar Grid System

N. Hema
Department of Information Science and Engineering, RNS Institute of Technology, India

N. Krishnamoorthy
College of Science and Humanities, SRM Institute of Science and Technology, India

Sahil Manoj Chavan
Department of Electrical Power System, Sandip University, India

N. M. G. Kumar
Sree Vidyanikethan Engineering College, Mohan Babu University, India

M. Sabarimuthu
Kongu Engineering College, India

Sampath Boopathi
Muthayammal Engineering College, India

ABSTRACT

Automation in the power consumption system could be applied to conserve a large amount of power. This chapter discusses the applications for the generation, transmission, distribution, and use of electricity that are IoT-enabled. It covers the physical layer implementation, used models, operating systems, standards, protocols, and architecture of the IoT-enabled SSG system. The configuration, design, solar power system, IoT device, and backend systems, workflow and procedures, implementation, test findings, and performance are discussed. The smart solar grid system's real-time implementation is described, along with experimental findings and implementation challenges.

DOI: 10.4018/978-1-6684-8098-4.ch017

INTRODUCTION

Green energy is energy that may be obtained from nature and is renewable, such as sunlight, tides, rain, and wind, and is utilised by people to produce electricity. People have mostly relied on fossil fuels and non-renewable energy sources in recent years, so investments in green energy are rising. According to a poll, half of the world's population has invested in renewable energy, but there won't be enough of it in the future. The main renewable energy source is solar energy, although its accessibility is dependent on climatic factors. It is transformed into electrical energy by photovoltaic (PV) cells and employed in a variety of industries, including home automation, manufacturing, the medical industry, transportation, and power generation. As the world population is expected to reach its maximum, people and companies need to use and manage green energy as effectively as possible to satisfy their electrical needs. This necessitates the development of an innovative solution like the Smart Grid (SG). An electrical grid-based system called a "smart grid" includes energy management components, including smart metres, smart appliances, renewable energy sources, and energy-saving resources. The suggested effort is to design a solar self-power management system that is combined with a useful controlling, monitoring, and maintenance system utilizing the Internet of Things (IoT). The challenges with solar power systems will be addressed by this technology, known as the Smart Solar Grid (SSG) technology (Al-Turjman and Abujubbeh, 2019). The application of IoT integrated SG and the scope of the research are covered in this chapter.

IoT is the integration of physical things into the Internet of Things (IoT) network using established communication protocols. It is used in many different industries, including agriculture, transportation, medicine, power grids, and so on. In order to do digital computing, smart devices need sensors, actuators, connected or wireless modules, and microcontrollers or microprocessors. IoT devices are made to carry out the principles of monitoring, tracking, controlling, and location identification. Sensors, actuators, cameras, GPS, and near field communication are all used in object-dependent notions. Concepts that depend on the Internet or networks use wireless communication technology (Minh et al., 2022; Harikaran et al., 2023; Janardhana et al., 2023; Reddy et al., 2023; Selvakumar et al., 2023). Concepts that depend on logic or functionality and focus on the range of IoT-enabled applications are called IoT devices. IoT devices are common objects connected via a microcontroller, communication modules, and a stack of protocols to allow intelligent systems. The Internet of Things (IoT) will change how organisations, governments, and consumers interact with the physical world, producing a significant quantity of data that may be applied to creative endeavours. The Internet of Things (IoT) is a network of physically linked things that can sense, find, think, and perform tasks thanks to the internet. By regulating the necessary technologies, such as calculating, communicating, embedded devices, network sensors, Internet infrastructures, and protocols, it recreates existing items from the ancient to the intelligent. IoT may be modified at any moment and is used to evaluate both the state of the global economy and the quality of life (Mehmood et al., 2021). Smart solar grid systems regulate power distribution, monitoring, smart metres, transmission lines, and renewable energy sources. This chapter presents a literature review and analyses IoT architecture, standards, and existing protocols, as well as how they are implemented at the architectural layer and on operating systems (Boopathi et al., 2023d; Jeevanantham et al., 2023; Senthil et al., 2023). The Grid is a system of power plants, transformers, substations, and transmission lines that transports energy. The "smart grid" is the name given to the digital technology that permits two-way communication between consumers and their utility while sensing along the transmission lines. Real-time measurement, monitoring, and control of power flows made possible by SG solutions increase electrical quality, demand response, distributed generation, mutual operation, self-healing, and transmission and distribution loss reduction. The management of energy distribution uses home area networks (HAN), neighbouring area networks (NAN), wide area networks (WAN), and home area networks. IoT devices, household appliances, electric cars, and renewable energy sources make up the first layer of the SG, known as HAN. Smart metres make up the NAN, or field area network, which facilitates communication between distributed substations and the field of electrical equipment used in the power distribution system (Babu et al., 2023; Boopathi et al., 2023b; Kumara et al., 2023; Vanitha et al., 2023). The connection between power transmission systems, generating systems, renewable energy sources, and control stations is made possible by the WAN, which is the third tier of the SG and the foundation of communication between networks, gateways, or aggregation sites (Madhu et al., 2022).

The Smart Solar Grid (SSG) uses IoT and M2M communication to improve energy use. This study focuses on three main areas: real-time monitoring, engineering databases, and solar power system failure analysis. It integrates real-time monitoring and management of the solar power system with high precision. By incorporating IoT, the suggested system seeks to offer intelligent energy management that utilizes solar hybrid capabilities. With home energy management systems, it suggests a revolutionary architecture for smart solar self-power management for household appliances (Boopathi, 2023; Boopathi et al., 2023a; Domakonda et al., 2023; Palaniappan et al., 2023). The design of the solar power system, the suggested system architecture, the architecture of IoT devices and IoT back-end systems, and the workflow of the smart solar grid system are all covered in this chapter. The prototype Smart Solar Grid system is created and put into use, and through the Internet, the characteristics and status of solar power systems are measured and sent to a cloud server. Various situations, such as network congestion and EMI noise from household appliances, are evaluated to determine the system's performance and dependability. The suggested method controls field maintenance and misalignment while offering a green power option for household appliances. Solar power systems are installed at several customer sites, and the database is populated with real-time data that the cloud server receives. The system may be seen and managed remotely via a web application. This chapter analyses and discusses the test findings (Goudarzi et al., 2022).

Research seeks to develop a solar self-power management system coupled with IoT to monitor and control solar energy because it is unpredictable and complicated. This hybrid design increases the use of green energy, decreases the use of fossil fuels, and enhances system security and usability. The primary goal of this research project is to develop an Internet of Things (IoT)-based Solar Self-Power Management System Architecture for efficient control, monitoring, and maintenance of the solar PV plant. Lightweight IoT protocols like Message Queuing Telemetry Transport will be used to connect solar power installations with a web application in order to do this (MQTT).

The control and monitoring of analogue and digital sensors in PV water pumping facilities using an ADCES is suggested in an IoT data collection and monitoring system. The ADCES is a microcontroller system with a USB interface that is based on the PIC18Fxx5x family. The monitoring plant and cloud services are connected through an embedded Linux system (ELS) running on a Raspberry Pi board. This design presents a new business model for incorporating renewable energy sources and leverages SCADA with WSN sensor nodes and the IEEE 802.15.4 security standard for data transport (RES). Although the suggested system paradigm is less expensive and more effective than earlier studies, it is too sophisticated to be implemented in real time. Utilizing a host computer, ARM gateways, wireless sensor networks, and other components, the proposed system leverages Tiny OS for Monitoring and Management to enable remote monitoring and reverse control. Multimodal power converters are made using the MPPT controller system's ZigBee wireless communication module for PV power conditioning systems. This technology modernises monitoring and supervisory procedures for the smart grid while computing data on a single host controller. Each module's voltage and current data is sampled and sent via the ZigBee module to the central inverter. The cost of many PV systems is decreased by the MPPT control algorithm, which arises each of the PV voltage reference parameters to return to each PV module in accordance (Kumar et al., 2020; Alavikia and Shabro, 2022).

To avoid or lessen damage from natural disasters, the Internet of Things may be used to build an online monitoring system for the power transmission line. This system will provide real-time monitoring and early disaster warning. Using a time division multiple access approach will prevent the suggested intrusion detection algorithm and packet loss. Attack simulation is done using the NS2 network simulator, while ZigBee and LPC2148 microcontrollers are used for the hardware implementation. In the Gulf Nations, where 60 percent of power is used for AC, a novel smart energy management system with a data gathering module in a System on Chip (SoC) is being tried in HVAC. The smart energy management system is controlled, tracked, and analysed by this system using Big Data and the Internet of Things. Data is sent from the AC unit to the middleware via the MQTT protocol, and business intelligence is provided by an analysis machine server. The consumer uses this programme to view their patterns of energy use. Using a network analysis tool, the implementation system is evaluated for performance, throughput, latency, and packet losses. In the suggested system, there are three examples for the quality of service test, although QOS-2 has a substantial overhead. Beyond 4000 concurrent clients, the system exhibits data traffic congestion and test tool restrictions (Reka and Dragicevic, 2018). The programme controls the creation of bills and the user interface while offering root cause investigation and business development.

The term "application-specific IoT" (ASIoT) refers to the usage of IoT technology for certain applications with varying taxonomies and specifications. User domain-driven, communication-medium-driven, and technology-constraint-driven are the three core divisions of ASIoT. Different characteristics and criteria apply to each group. Low latency and restricted services are given precedence in the Internet of Things over power and computing complexity. In this research project, a setup was used to test a use case for a biometric medical application. Using the Internet of Things, this solution is deployed and tested in real-time for controlling and monitoring household appliances. With sensors to sense parameters and actuators to conduct control actions depending on external factors and human inputs, it is both cost-effective and hybrid. Data is kept in Adafruit IO and transmitted by Wi-Fi in this system, which is designed to be portable and simple to integrate into a smart home. The Arduino software is used to create firmware and upload it to the Node MCU microcontroller, which has built-in Wi-Fi (Chakravarthi et al., 2022; Sampath et al., 2022b; Babu et al., 2023; Jeevanantham et al., 2023; Trojovský et al., 2023; Yupapin et al., 2023). Data is transferred from the cloud to the user side via the MQTT IoT protocol, confirming security, safety, and automation. If there are any unusual circumstances, the appropriate action is taken and the client is informed. The suggested approach resolves the issue of a smart solar system by adding two insulator circuits on top of the relay to eliminate the short circuit in the relay.

OBJECTIVES

- To Develop IoT Integrated Smart Grid System
- To Study IoT Architecture for SSG

- To Illustrate the Various IoT Protocols.
- To Explain the Various Elements of IoT-Enabled SSG
- To Design and Develop the IoT-Based SSG

IoT-ENABLED SMART GRID SYSTEM

IoT has had a huge impact on the creation of the smart grid, bringing enhanced dependability and energy efficiency. Real-time connectivity between people, devices, and power equipment is made possible by IoT technology, which boosts productivity and flexibility. The current implementation of IoT-assisted SG systems is based on a three-layered design, where the perception layer deploys IoT devices, the network layer gathers data, and the application layer manages the smart grid via the application interface. IoT may be used to improve the Smart Grid's power production, transmission, distribution, and utilization subsystems. IoT is used to manage distributed renewable energy power plants as well as monitor and regulate power generation, transport, and storage (Figure 1). Power distribution, smart houses, automation, metre reading, charging and discharging of electric cars, energy-efficient monitoring and management, power management, and multi-network usage are all areas where the internet of things is applied (Shahinzadeh et al., 2019; Goudarzi et al., 2022).

Electric Vehicle Data: Since it emits less carbon dioxide, the electric vehicle, which first appeared in the 11th century, offers green energy transportation. Electric car charging involves a power supply infrastructure, charging hardware, and monitoring technology. The real-time monitoring system and power supply may communicate data to control stations thanks in large part to the Internet of Things (IoT). IoT technology serves as the foundation for managing electric cars and enabling the development of new power production, transmission, and distribution systems, as well as smart homes and energy sources (Boopathi et al., 2023a, 2023c; Samikannu et al., 2023; Vennila et al., 2023).

Figure 1. Activities of IoT-enabled SSG

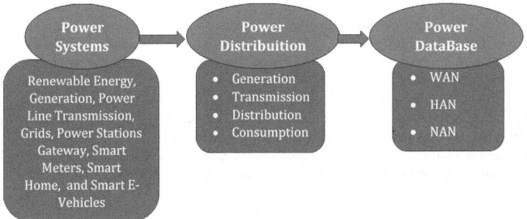

Smart Home: IoT technology, which is present in appliances like smart TVs, security systems, refrigerators, washing machines, lighting controls, and temperature monitors, is crucial for the smart grid. In order to increase integrated grid services, the quality of service, and real-time user-grid interaction, the smart home comprises sensors and actuator nodes for monitoring the environment.

Advanced Technology: It is a crucial technology in smart grids that collects very accurate real-time data on power usage and offers real-time monitoring, statistics, and power consumption analysis.

Distribution of Energy Sources: Because it produces power without emitting carbon dioxide, renewable energy has a positive impact on the environment worldwide. IoT technology offers real-time data for predicting energy production. Although IoT-enabled SG apps are being installed, many of them are not yet being used. Examples include monitoring power usage, managing and maintaining the power supply, monitoring the installation of power equipment, and managing and parking electric car charging stations.

IoT ARCHITECTURE FOR SSG

To link billions or trillions of things to the Internet, IoT needs a dynamic, layered architecture, and many frameworks have been suggested to add more abstraction. The 5-layer model design, which is the most reliable model for all IoT applications, is shown in Figure 2. There are three levels that make up security: business, application, communication, and sensing (Li et al., 2011; Abir et al., 2021; Shapsough et al., 2021).

Sensor Part: The sensing layer, which collects and analyses data via RFID sensors, cameras, sensor networks, GPS, and physical objects, is the first layer of the Internet of Things (IoT) concept. All sensor devices sense a variety of factors, and the data they acquire is converted to digital form and sent securely to the communication layer.

Communication Part: This layer utilizes secure communication channels such as Bluetooth, ZigBee, 6LowPAN, LoRa, NB IoT, GSM, and 4GLTE to transfer the data layer's obtained information from the sensing layer. Traffic is routed to servers in public or cloud services using WAN or LAN technologies. This layer, which may be integrated into existing networks or made more scalable, is crucial for gathering data from various locations or nodes. It modifies the way IoT sensors and the base station of the central network communicate, aggregating data from numerous nodes.

Figure 2. Five layered IoT architecture

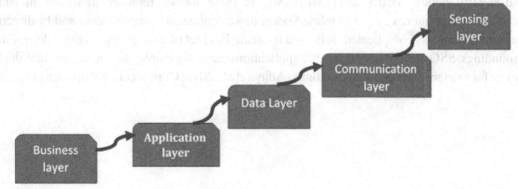

Data Part: Information repositories, databases, servers, and storage make up the data layer, which offers solid hardware and software with a lot of processing power. By collecting data and making choices over the network, it enables IoT programmers to deal with devices without considering their physical platform.

Application Part: The application layer consists of a mobile application or web application created to forecast data and remotely operate equipment. Vertical markets including smart homes, smart grids, smart agriculture, and smart industries are covered.

Business Part: The business layer controls enterprise version, map, and flowchart authorization as well as IoT system activities and services.

IoT PROTOCOLS

IoT standards are created by three organisations: the IETF, IEEE, and ETSI, with the goal of making life easier for service providers and application developers. The best protocols are divided into three categories: infrastructure layer protocols, service layer protocols, and application layer protocols.

Application Related Protocols

Although HTTP is often used to construct the application layer of the internet, several protocols have been created for Internet of Things applications. A simple protocol called CoAP (MQTT XMPP Constrained Application Protocol) is used for battery-powered IoT device communication. The client-server paradigm is used. While MQTT is a lightweight messaging protocol that lessens data losses and congestion, CoAP is a request-and-response mechanism that enables clients to get, put, delete, or post data over the network. For M2M communication, MQTT is a publish-subscribe paradigm created for sensor networks, including wireless sensor networks. By placing a MQTT broker between the publisher and subscriber, it enables IoT devices to transport or publish data to a server. As an Internet of Things protocol, MQTT is utilized. XMPP is an extensible markup language, and XML was created to extend HTML and allow the accumulation of unique tags and components. XMPP is an HTML plugin that organises data for storage and transfer. It is used for collaboration, content syndication, multi-party chat, phone and video conversations, real-time and scalable networking across devices, and real-time communication. Data is linked one to one between the nodes, and each node has a number of data fields. RESTful is a stateless, interoperable communication protocol that lets users provide online resources like HTTP, JSON, or XML files and identify them by URLs. In HTML, XML, or JSON format, representations are information objects. A JavaScript interface called Online Socket makes connection management and bi-directional web communication less complicated. It is used to create Internet of Things applications depending on the surroundings. SSG technologies and other applications currently employ IoT protocols, making them appropriate for a range of situations and settings (Adhya et al., 2016; Gupta et al., 2019; Chen et al., 2022).

Service Protocols

IoT programmers may deal with complicated objects without considering hardware platforms thanks to the service layer protocol, a middleware layer protocol that links services with requests based on name and address. SSG applications frequently employ the Physical Web, mDNS, DNS-SD, and Bluetooth Low Energy (BLE) beacon as IoT service layer protocols.

Infrastructure Protocols

The Infrastructure layer protocol, which is separated into two types: Wireless and Wired technologies for data transfer between smart solar power management systems and electric utilities, is in charge of communication and network infrastructure for IoT applications. Although there are certain benefits to wireless technology, such as less expensive infrastructure, signal perception can happen because of the transmission channel. A SSG needs two different kinds of data flows: one between solar power plants and utility control centres, and the other between solar power plants, IoT devices, sensors, and residential appliances. Power-line communication, wireless communication, such as 6LowPAN, ZigBee, LoRa, NB-IoT, Wi-Fi, or cellular communication can all be used to control smart solar power. However, important limiting elements including operational expenses, implementation time, technology availability, and the operating environment must be considered. Wireless technology that works in one setting could not in another.

ELEMENTS OF IoT-ENABLED SSG

Physical components of Solar Smart Grids (SSGs) collect data from sensing equipment and send it to a data concentrator or IoT gateway as part of an Internet of Things (IoT) integration(S. et al. 2022; Sampath et al. 2022a, c). This data concentrator transforms information into a format that is appropriate for Internet protocols, which further processes it and performs the necessary operations. The dealer, supplier, or manufacturer houses the computing platforms that are connected to the aggregation layer through an underlying network layer. Figure 3 depicts the SSGs' IoT processing levels. The design of the solar PV systems affects how these layers are specifically recognised. The hardware and software requirements for four key IoT application components in SSGs are discussed (Ramu et al., 2021).

Figure 3. A structure of IoT processing layers implemented for SSGs

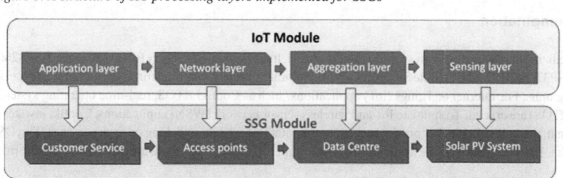

Hardware

Smartphones, SmartThings, Arduino, Phi Gets, Intel Galileo, STM Discovery, ESP32, ESP8266, Beagle Bone, and Cubie Board are a few examples of IoT devices.

Sensing

IoT sensing is the process of gathering data from connected objects and sending it back to the cloud, a database, or a data warehouse. In order to develop IoT goods, a system on chip must be equipped with sensors, integrated IP and protection protocols, and a control system to deliver the required records.

Communication

IoT devices should employ low-power operating systems and protocols for communication such as Wi-Fi, Bluetooth, 6LowPAN, Z-wave, LoRa, WAN, and 4G-LTE. For item identification, specialized communication technologies like RFID, near-field communication (NFC), and ultra-wideband are utilized. RFID tags are made up of a straightforward chip or label that is affixed to the reader and via which the database receives the signal from the RFID reader. The RFID reader communicates with the tag using an inquiry identifier and receives an echo identification in return. The NFC protocol uses a high-frequency band of 13.56 MHZ and a consent data rate of 424 kbps. Information in the pertinent range up to 10 cm can be sent by two active readers or two passive readers. Applications are outlined for interconnecting sensors to improve communication in a sparsely populated region. A prior data transfer system called Wi-Fi uses radio waves to move data among smart devices within a 100-meter range. SIG created Bluetooth 5, a high-speed mesh network with an IP connection. A medium entry right is granted to IEEE 802.15.4, a 2.4 GHz communication protocol that is intended to control low strength wireless mesh networks at each physical layer (Borgaonkar et al., 2021).

Long-Term Evolution (LTE) is a standard for wireless data exchange that allows extremely fast communications between mobile devices built on GSM network technology. With up to 100 MHz of bandwidth propagation, uplink and downlink multiplexing, increased coverage, more significant throughput, and lower latency, LTE-A (LTE Advanced) is a strengthened version of LTE. LoRaWAN is a MAC layer control protocol for wide area networks that enables Internet-connected applications on low-power devices across long-range wireless connections up to 10 kilometres away. In the radio frequencies used for industrial, scientific, and medical purposes, it is enforced on top of LoRa or FSK modulation. It is suggested for use with wireless, battery-powered devices in local, regional, or international networks.

Computation

Utilizing hardware platforms such as Arduino, ARM, Intel Galileo, Raspberry Pi, Beagle Bone, ESP8266, ESP32, ESP12E, and T-Mote Sky, software programmes interpret the computing capacity of IoT processing units. For Internet of Things (IoT) applications, such as Contiki RTOS, real-time operating systems (RTOS) are crucial. To simulate IoT and wireless sensor network (WSN) applications, Contiki invokes a simulator called Cooja. For precise real-time computation and data switching on smart devices, TinyOS, Riot, Lite OS, and RTOS are available. To host certain IoT applications, there are limited cloud platforms.

Services

The four categories of IoT services are ubiquitous, identity-related, information aggregation, collaboratively aware, and ubiquitous. Information aggregation, collective awareness, joint awareness, and collective consciousness are four categories of IoT usage that offer identity-related services, statistical aggregation, collective awareness, and joint awareness services to allow ubiquitous services.

ARCHITECTURE OF PROPOSED IoT-ENABLED SSG

The SSGS is a stand-alone solar PV system created to decrease the use of fossil fuels and increase the use of green energy. Three power sources are supported: a solar PV array, an electrical grid, and a battery backup. Remote monitoring and control are carried out via the IoT back-end technology. The 24V DC panel array, charge controller, sinewave inverter/ cumulative rectifier, and 12V DC 150 Ah battery make up a solar power system. The system and host network are connected via the ESP8266 Node MCU. Based on power produced and electricity utilized, the suggested system employs the ESP8266 module as an IoT device to operate home appliances. It provides a cutting-edge design for intelligent solar power solutions for home appliances (Hadi et al., 2019).

Design of SSG

The solar power system has a maximum load capacity and adjusts the distribution of solar power generated in the home based on the need for power utilisation. In order to guarantee the distribution of battery insulation both during the day and at night, it combines solar power generation with solar energy storage. The battery source serves as a backup power source and is charged using solar power alone or in a shared manner with the AC grid. The battery backup will be maintained if there is ever a power outage. Microcontroller, H-bridge circuit, MPPT charge controller, voltage and current sensors, MOSFET drivers, switch interface, transformers, filters, LCD unit, Internet of Things device, buzzer circuit, cooling fan control, front panel LED, and circuits for changeover relays are all components of the solar power system.

The four building pieces that make up the solar power system are the front panel interface unit, the solar PV charger unit, the power switching drivers and control unit, and the central CPU unit. The microcontroller unit, which serves as the brain to direct overall operation, is responsible for controlling the entire operation of the solar system. Power is switched between AC and DC using the H-bridge circuit.

The suggested method transforms DC power stored in the battery into AC power and delivers the converted AC power to the devices for loading by using pulse width modulation (PWM), which produces a pure sine wave as an inverter output. Step-up/step-down hybrid transformers and capacitor filter circuits are used in this H-bridge function. The three principal energy sources in the solar system—the solar PV source, the AC power source, and the DC battery source—are chosen according to the importance of the energy generated. A PV that can be converted, the MPPT charge controller circuit modifies voltage and current level to meet output and load. Incorporating the P&O (Perturb and Observe) MPPT algorithm will maximise solar power. Circuits that are voltage-sensitive can detect and quantify voltage forces. A solar power system's current is sensed and measured by the current sensing circuit, which also shows the system's status and the measured data. In order to ensure thermal stability, a cooling fan is needed. The ESP8266 Node MCU module and the Microcontroller unit are connected through the Solar power system's UART (Universal Asynchronous Receiver Transmitter), which operates at a 9600 baud rate (Reka and Dragicevic, 2018).

CPU Unit

A thin quad microcontroller is used to create the main CPU of a solar power system. Seven general-purpose 16-bit timers and a PWM (pulse width modulation) timer with sophisticated control are among the features of the STM32F030 microcontroller's improved peripherals, I/Os, communication interfaces, and accuracy. The main CPU unit is made up of a microcontroller, a power source, an interface for the LCD unit, a front panel interface, power supply drivers, and an interface for the control unit. The core CPU unit needs a separate power source from the microcontroller. The power supply unit is made to provide an output load current and a controlled standard-low dropout regulator. Real-time clock functionality is enabled on the microcontroller, which is driven by a crystal oscillator circuit. The main CPU unit has two modes of operation: standard mode and boot mode. While the boot mode can be used to execute software on a firmware update or debug port, the usual mode can be enabled by using a capacitor to link the MCLR pin to ground. The microcontroller pins may be linked using a pull-up resistor and are set up for in-circuit serial programming. The STM32cubeMX graphical tool is used to configure the STM32F030 microcontroller and pin assignments, and the ST-link tool may be used to flash the firmware to the microcontroller. The full programme was built by Embedded C, utilizing the Keil MDK Arm Embedded development tools. The general operation of the solar power system's operational systems is outlined. All ADC signals, PWM signals for H-bridge drivers, PWM signals for solar MPPT chargers, UART ports for connecting IoT devices, buzzer, fan, and load change-over relay signals are handled by the power switching receivers and controller interface. Filter capacitors and protection diodes are used to link analogue signals in order to prevent noise interference and ADC port damage from excessive voltage. ADC ports with a 12 bit resolution are set on the STM32F030 microcontroller pins. The H-Bridge circuit may be driven via filler PWM pins and opto drivers with a maximum input analogue voltage of 3.3 Vdc, which can resolve the measurement into a maximum of 3.000805 VDC. The microcontroller pins are set up as GPIO to operate the cooling fan, buzzer, and load change-over signals, as well as PWM signals for controlling the solar MPPT charger and H-bridge circuit. Through ports JP1 and JP2, the central CPU unit communicates with the power switching drivers and control unit.

Controlling the Drivers Units

The major component of the solar power system is the power switching driver and control unit. This device includes the main power supply, opto-drivers for the H-Bridge, the H-Bridge circuit, voltage and current sensors, the interface for the central CPU unit, the interface for the solar charge controller unit, the interface for IoT devices, the changeover relay driver circuits, and the buzzer and cooling fan driver circuits. In this part, the system's overall functionality is covered. A power MOSFET gate driver IC, which has an integrated opto-isolator to safeguard the central CPU unit from any short circuit or high current failure, was used to create the opto driver circuits. The TLP250 driver IC generates a pure sine wave output using internal totum pole transistor circuit logic and PWM pulse width modulation methods. Inverter-cumulative rectifier PWM switching frequency is 12.5 KHz, which is greater than that of conventional power systems.

In order to minimize MOSFET failure at high current, overload, and short-circuit conditions, H-Bridge circuits are built with a maximum power. The voltage and current characteristics of the solar power system are measured using voltage- and current-detecting circuits. Battery voltage, input AC voltage, and output AC voltage are the parameters used to monitor voltage in the power switching drivers and control unit. The variable potentiometer is used to compute the battery voltage using the voltage divider rule. An alternate computation is used to match the recorded analogue voltage to the battery voltage. The potentiometer may be calibrated by adjusting the display parameter and actual measured value. The AC input/output voltage is measured using the same principle (Ramu et al., 2021; Chen et al., 2022). Low ohm shunt plates are used in the construction of circuits that sense battery current and short circuit current. Since the microcontroller's ADC ports cannot be linked directly to the present analogue signal, the voltage across the shunt plates is used instead. The LM358 op-amp circuit amplifies the present analogue signals. The current parameters, such as battery current, are solely utilized for the operation of smart battery chargers and are not shown on the LCD. Potentiometers can be used to calibrate the charging current.

The load current in solar power systems is measured and shown as a percentage on the LCD. Directly at the load terminal, a current transformer is used to detect the output load current. The potential across the current transformer is also monitored and linked to the microcontroller's ADC port. Based on the load percentage function derived from the software, the analogue voltage originating from the current transformer is translated to the load percentage. The maximum load capacity may be used to measure the load percentage. When there is a power outage, the relay is activated by the central CPU unit, which also links the output load terminal to the inverter.

The central CPU unit will turn off the relay and connect the output load terminal to the AC power grid source when AC power grid is standard. The previous topics covered these functional descriptions. A PCB-mountable buzzer and a transistor switching circuit employing NPN transistors make up the buzzer control circuit. The central CPU unit is connected to the buzzer GPIO signal, which buzzes briefly when the inverter is operating and beeps briefly to notify the inverter's condition when it is off. The cooling fan controller circuit is built with a high power NPN transistor switching circuit. To disperse the temperature that was created during MOSFET switching, a heat sink is installed nearby. To lower the temperature of the heat sink, the cooling fan is positioned close by. The IoT device interface port, which is coupled to the UART serial communication port of the microcontroller, is used to connect the solar charge controller unit to the power switching drivers and control unit. Through JP1 and JP2 connections, the central CPU unit is connected to the power switching driver and control unit.

Controlling Solar Charger

The battery and power switching element of the solar charge controller unit are intended to deliver the highest charging current at the output. The design steps down the panel voltage to the battery voltage using a two-phase buck converter. The buck converter is managed by the central CPU unit, and the parallel shut-off plate is used in the current sensing circuit design. Since the microcontroller's ADC ports cannot be linked directly to the present analogue signal, the voltage across the shunt plates is used instead. The LM358 op-amp circuit is used by the solar charge controller to amplify current analogue signals, and the perturb and observe (P&O) technique is used to determine MPP. It contains surge safeguards and a software indicator. High battery system efficiency is made possible by a solar charge controller's hybrid capability. When MPP happens, the inverter is switched on, and in this hybrid mode, a load is linked to the inverter output and powered by solar energy produced by the solar panel. Until the battery voltage is depleted and the MPP is lowered, the solar power system operates in hybrid mode. The solar power system uses green power, and MPPT contributes significantly by adding the P&O algorithm. The microcontroller uses the MPPT and solar charger software functionality to carry out the entire functioning of the solar charge controller unit.

LCD Connections

Microcontrollers, flash PIC Microcontrollers, and nanowatt technology are used in the construction of the LCD interface circuit. An internal RC oscillator is set up, and the operational frequency is 32 MHz. Through a UART connection, the LCD interface unit is linked to the main CPU unit, and LCD interface software is used to show data from the CPU unit. The software is created with embedded C, utilizing MPLAB X IDE software development. This microcontroller's primary goal is to link an LCD to a central CPU unit. While the data pins are linked to ports, the LCD command pins are connected to the microcontroller. The core CPU unit's data signal is attached to a pin.

DESIGN AND DEVELOPMENT IoT INTEGRATED SSG

The power supply, node MCU module, buzzer driver circuit microcontroller, central CPU interface, and relay driver circuit for load control and the IoT device interface port make up the Smart Solar Grid System (SSGS) IoT device. The Wi-Fi module may be linked to any microcontroller to get access to a Wi-Fi network. It is a self-contained SOC with an integrated TCP/IP protocol layer. The node MCU, buzzer driver circuit, and two channel relay driver circuits must all be powered by a separate power source on the Internet of Things device. To prevent reverse polarity harm, the voltage from the battery terminal is linked to the input pin of the diode (Adhya et al., 2016). An IoT interface port and UART serial communication with baud rate are used to link the MCU to the solar power system. Using software serial capabilities, the pins are set up as TX and RX, respectively. The buzzer driver signal is linked, while the relay driver signals are attached to GPIO pins. Utilizing a unique ASCII command to enable remote monitoring and management of the system, the node MCU will start a communication link between the solar power system and IoT backend system. To separate data segments, a semicolon is used to divide the data format. The Arduino IDE software development tool, which supports all Arduino hardware modules, ESP32 family modules, and STM modules, is used to design and create the Node MCU. It creates a Wi-Fi connection with macro-defined SSID, password, and client ID, initialises a software serial port with 9600 baud rates, and connects to a MQTT broker using the MQTT protocol. The node MCU validates the MQTT broker settings, and the connection is successfully made. When data from the solar power system is quickly saved in a buffer and published as a string by adding the device ID to the IoT backend system, an ASCII command for monitoring is sent to the solar power system. When the data from the Internet of Things backend system is subscribed using software APIs for the MQTT publish and subscribe protocol, the node MCU will transmit the command for operating the solar power system. Based on the calculations made in the backend system, critical and non-critical loads are controlled by two-channel relay driver circuits.

IoT Backend Design

The user application system and the solar power system are connected via the IoT backend systems. They include an IoT device, a MQTT broker, a web server, a database, a front-end web application, an IoT device, and a cloud hosting system. Python Django, a high-level Python web framework that facilitates quick development and practical design, is used to include the backend web application.

Web apps are mostly used to collect data, but they may also be used to give react-web interface APIs that use the Restful Framework as middleware for the database. The dashboard interface and the foundational authentication service are established by the React JS web application used as the IoT's back end system. Dashboard views are only available while the MCU transmits data. The backend database utilized is MongoDB, while the web server used for reverse proxies and SSL encryption is Nginx. A Docker container is used to run many apps simultaneously and efficiently distribute server resources, with Nginx serving as the web server's load balancer (Abir et al., 2021).

Web-Based SSG

The home page and the login page are the only two pages of the online application. The login page is an interactive online application with a dashboard to monitor and operate the solar system with user email authentication, while the main page contains material about the proposed system. Users who have registered can only access the dashboard. Only once the data from the MCU is received does the web application's dashboard display become active. The data will be green if it consistently receives the dashboard theme. Red will be the new dashboard theme colour if no response is received for 30 seconds. Any device may open the web application since it is responsive. A web application's dashboard keeps track of variables including load percentage, solar level, mains level, battery level, inverter level, and inverter voltage. Backup time, load power, and output load current are also included. To determine the maximum load power and maximum solar power generated, the load power and solar power are shown as a graph. All parameters received from the solar power system are stored in the smart solar grid system's database, which may be used to operate the inverter, critical and non-critical load appliances, and create a monthly report (Adhya et al., 2016).

Working Principle and Implementation SSG

A battery, solar panels, and an AC power grid make up the Smart Solar Grid System's three power sources. The Central CPU unit and all other signal conditioning circuits are powered up by the power supply circuits once the battery is linked to the solar power system's battery connector. It is controlled what voltage is used. All peripherals will be configured by the central CPU unit, which will also measure the voltage and current during a continuous sampling period. The LCD interface device and UART connection are set up and begin exchanging data with the MCU. Battery voltage, grid voltage input, inverter voltage output, and load percentage are all shown on the display. Data is published to the IoT backend system via the communication channel established with the web application. By using the Internet, the user may control the solar power system from any device. The solar panel array and MPPT charge controller that make up the suggested system are connected. The P&O algorithm is used by the central CPU unit to operate the solar charge controller and manage the solar panel to produce the most electricity. Another connected source is the AC grid. When the solar panel is producing its maximum amount of electricity, the system automatically activates the solar hybrid feature. The hybrid mode is when the battery and appliance load are powered by solar energy and the AC grid source is switched to standby. The battery is charged and the load is linked to the AC power grid in the conventional model. The web application disables non-critical loads and displays backup times. To prolong battery life, the suggested approach employs trickle charging. The load appliance control circuit, which automatically switches off non-critical loads when solar power is less than 100 watts, is connected to the node MCU. With the aid of the MCU, this capability may be manually managed via the web application.

Figure 4 depicts the schematics for the SSG implementation. The node MCU is used to transmit solar power system data over the Internet while encrypting and decrypting it. The IoT backend system decrypts the data on the backend web server and provides the authorised user with an immediate status of the solar power system and a defect signal. The suggested system is used to analyse performance and implementation concerns in a domestic home power application. To construct a prototype of the system to increase reliability and efficiency, experimental findings are examined.

Figure 4. Working principle of web-based SSG

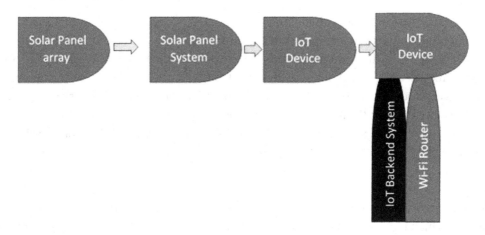

The suggested system was deployed in a residential setting and left running nonstop for 15 days while simultaneously recording real-time data in a database. The graph displays a smart solar grid system's maximum daily demand, used energy, and produced energy. The efficiency of the present system is 90%, whereas the suggested system's maximum efficiency is 96%. In order to guarantee the suggested system's efficacy and robustness, the quality of service (QoS) is a key concern. The MQTT protocol is used as an IoT communication mechanism to address this problem.

SUMMARY

In this Chapter, the applications for the generation, transmission, distribution, and use of electricity that are IoT-enabled. The physical layer implementation, used models, operating systems, standards, protocols, and architecture of the IoT enabled SSG system. The SSG system's architecture, system methodology, system design, and workflow are also illustrated. The configuration, design, solar power system, IoT device, and backend systems, workflow and procedures; implementation, test findings, and performance of the proposed smart solar grid system using the Internet of Things are discussed. The smart solar grid system's real-time implementation is described, along with experimental findings and implementation challenges.

REFERENCES

Abir, S. M. A. A., Anwar, A., Choi, J., & Kayes, A. S. M. (2021). Iot-enabled smart energy grid: Applications and challenges. *IEEE Access : Practical Innovations, Open Solutions*, *9*, 50961–50981. doi:10.1109/ACCESS.2021.3067331

Adhya, S., Saha, D., & Das, A. (2016). An IoT based smart solar photovoltaic remote monitoring and control unit. *2016 2nd international conference on control, instrumentation, energy & communication (CIEC)*, 432–436. 10.1109/CIEC.2016.7513793

Al-Turjman, F., & Abujubbeh, M. (2019). IoT-enabled smart grid via SM: An overview. *Future Generation Computer Systems*, *96*, 579–590. doi:10.1016/j.future.2019.02.012

Alavikia, Z., & Shabro, M. (2022). A comprehensive layered approach for implementing internet of things-enabled smart grid: A survey. *Digital Communications and Networks*, *8*(3), 388–410. doi:10.1016/j.dcan.2022.01.002

Babu, B.S., Kamalakannan, J., & Meenatchi, N. (2023). Economic impacts and reliability evaluation of battery by adopting Electric Vehicle. *IEEE Explor*, 1–6. doi:10.1109/ICPECTS56089.2022.10046786

Boopathi, S. (2023). An Investigation on Friction Stir Processing of Aluminum Alloy-Boron Carbide Surface Composite. In *Materials Horizons: From Nature to Nanomaterials* (pp. 249–257). Springer. doi:10.1007/978-981-19-7146-4_14

Boopathi, S., Arigela, S.H., & Raman, R. (2023a). Prominent Rule Control-based Internet of Things: Poultry Farm Management System. *IEEE Explor*, 1–6. doi:10.1109/ICPECTS56089.2022.10047039

Boopathi, S., Balasubramani, V., & Sanjeev Kumar, R. (2023b). Influences of various natural fibers on the mechanical and drilling characteristics of coir-fiber-based hybrid epoxy composites. *Eng Res Express*, *5*(1), 15002–15020. doi:10.1088/2631-8695/acb132

Boopathi, S., Khare, R., & Jaya Christiyan, K. G. (2023c). Additive manufacturing developments in the medical engineering field. In *Development, Properties, and Industrial Applications of 3D Printed Polymer Composites* (pp. 86–106). IGI Global. doi:10.4018/978-1-6684-6009-2.ch006

Boopathi, S., Siva Kumar, P. K., & Meena, R. S. (2023d). Sustainable Developments of Modern Soil-Less Agro-Cultivation Systems. In *Human Agro-Energy Optimization for Business and Industry* (pp. 69–87). IGI Global. doi:10.4018/978-1-6684-4118-3.ch004

Borgaonkar, R., Anne Tøndel, I., Zenebe Degefa, M., & Gilje Jaatun, M. (2021). Improving smart grid security through 5G enabled IoT and edge computing. *Concurrency and Computation*, *33*(18), e6466. doi:10.1002/cpe.6466

Chakravarthi, P. K., Yuvaraj, D., & Venkataramanan, V. (2022). IoT-based smart energy meter for smart grids. *ICDCS 2022 - 2022 6th International Conference on Devices, Circuits and Systems*, 360–363. 10.1109/ICDCS54290.2022.9780714

Chen, Z., Sivaparthipan, C. B., & Muthu, B. (2022). IoT based smart and intelligent smart city energy optimization. *Sustainable Energy Technologies and Assessments*, *49*, 101724. doi:10.1016/j.seta.2021.101724

Domakonda, V. K., Farooq, S., & Chinthamreddy, S. (2023). Sustainable Developments of Hybrid Floating Solar Power Plants. In *Human Agro-Energy Optimization for Business and Industry* (pp. 148–167). IGI Global. doi:10.4018/978-1-6684-4118-3.ch008

Goudarzi, A., Ghayoor, F., Waseem, M., Fahad, S., & Traore, I. (2022). A Survey on IoT-Enabled Smart Grids: Emerging, Applications, Challenges, and Outlook. *Energies*, *15*(19), 6984. doi:10.3390/en15196984

Gupta, A., Anpalagan, A., Carvalho, G. H. S., Khwaja, A. S., Guan, L., & Woungang, I. (2019). RETRACTED: Prevailing and emerging cyber threats and security practices in IoT-Enabled smart grids. *Journal of Network and Computer Applications*, *132*, 118–148. doi:10.1016/j.jnca.2019.01.012

Hadi, A. A., Sinha, U., & Faika, T. (2019) Internet of things (IoT)-enabled solar micro inverter using blockchain technology. *2019 IEEE industry applications society annual meeting*, 1–5.

Harikaran, M., Boopathi, S., Gokulakannan, S., & Poonguzhali, M. (2023). Study on the Source of E-Waste Management and Disposal Methods. In *Sustainable Approaches and Strategies for E-Waste Management and Utilization* (pp. 39–60). IGI Global. doi:10.4018/978-1-6684-7573-7.ch003

Janardhana, K., Singh, V., & Singh, S. N. (2023). Utilization Process for Electronic Waste in Eco-Friendly Concrete: Experimental Study. In *Sustainable Approaches and Strategies for E-Waste Management and Utilization* (pp. 204–223). IGI Global. doi:10.4018/978-1-6684-7573-7.ch011

Jeevanantham, Y.A., & A. S., V. V. (2023). Implementation of Internet-of Things (IoT) in Soil Irrigation System. *IEEE Explor,* 1–5. doi:10.1109/ICPECTS56089.2022.10047185

Kumar, N. M., Chand, A. A., Malvoni, M., Prasad, K. A., Mamun, K. A., Islam, F. R., & Chopra, S. S. (2020). Distributed energy resources and the application of AI, IoT, and blockchain in smart grids. *Energies*, *13*(21), 5739. doi:10.3390/en13215739

Kumara, V., Mohanaprakash, T. A., & Fairooz, S. (2023). Experimental Study on a Reliable Smart Hydroponics System. In *Human Agro-Energy Optimization for Business and Industry* (pp. 27–45). IGI Global. doi:10.4018/978-1-6684-4118-3.ch002

Li, L., Xiaoguang, H., Ke, C., & Ketai, H. (2011). The applications of wifi-based wireless sensor network in internet of things and smart grid. *2011 6th IEEE Conference on Industrial Electronics and Applications*, 789–793. 10.1109/ICIEA.2011.5975693

Madhu, S., Padunnavalappil, S., & Saajlal, P. P. (2022). Powering up an IoT-enabled smart home: A solar powered smart inverter for sustainable development. *International Journal of Software Science and Computational Intelligence*, *14*(1), 1–21. doi:10.4018/IJSSCI.300362

Mehmood, M. Y., Oad, A., Abrar, M., Munir, H. M., Hasan, S. F., Muqeet, H. A., & Golilarz, N. A. (2021). Edge computing for IoT-enabled smart grid. *Security and Communication Networks*, *2021*, 1–16. doi:10.1155/2021/5524025

Minh, Q. N., Nguyen, V.-H., Quy, V. K., Ngoc, L. A., Chehri, A., & Jeon, G. (2022). Edge Computing for IoT-Enabled Smart Grid: The Future of Energy. *Energies*, *15*(17), 6140. doi:10.3390/en15176140

Palaniappan, M., Tirlangi, S., & Mohamed, M. J. S. (2023). Fused deposition modelling of polylactic acid (PLA)-based polymer composites: A case study. In *Development, Properties, and Industrial Applications of 3D Printed Polymer Composites* (pp. 66–85). IGI Global. doi:10.4018/978-1-6684-6009-2.ch005

Ramu, S.K., Irudayaraj, G.C.R., & Elango, R. (2021). An IoT-based smart monitoring scheme for solar PV applications. *Electr Electron Devices, Circuits, Mater Technol Challenges Solut*, 211–233

Reddy, M. A., Reddy, B. M., & Mukund, C. S. (2023). Social Health Protection During the COVID-Pandemic Using IoT. In *The COVID-19 Pandemic and the Digitalization of Diplomacy* (pp. 204–235). IGI Global. doi:10.4018/978-1-7998-8394-4.ch009

Reka, S. S., & Dragicevic, T. (2018). Future effectual role of energy delivery: A comprehensive review of Internet of Things and smart grid. *Renewable & Sustainable Energy Reviews*, *91*, 90–108. doi:10.1016/j.rser.2018.03.089

S., P.K., Sampath, B., & R., S.K. (2022). Hydroponics, Aeroponics, and Aquaponics Technologies in Modern Agricultural Cultivation. Trends, Paradigms, and Advances in Mechatronics Engineering. IGI Global.

Samikannu, R., Koshariya, A. K., & Poornima, E. (2023). Sustainable Development in Modern Aquaponics Cultivation Systems Using IoT Technologies. In *Human Agro-Energy Optimization for Business and Industry* (pp. 105–127). IGI Global. doi:10.4018/978-1-6684-4118-3.ch006

Sampath, B., Pandian, M., Deepa, D., & Subbiah, R. (2022b). Operating parameters prediction of liquefied petroleum gas refrigerator using simulated annealing algorithm. AIP Conference Proceedings. doi:10.1063/5.0095601

Sampath, B., & Yuvaraj, D. V. (2022c). Parametric analysis of mould sand properties for flange coupling casting. AIP Conference Proceedings.

Sampath, B. C. S., & Myilsamy, S. (2022a). Application of TOPSIS Optimization Technique in the Micro-Machining Process. In *IGI:Trends, Paradigms, and Advances in Mechatronics Engineering* (pp. 162–187). IGI Global. doi:10.4018/978-1-6684-5887-7.ch009

Selvakumar, S., Adithe, S., & Isaac, J. S. (2023). A Study of the Printed Circuit Board (PCB) E-Waste Recycling Process. In *Sustainable Approaches and Strategies for E-Waste Management and Utilization* (pp. 159–184). IGI Global. doi:10.4018/978-1-6684-7573-7.ch009

Senthil, T. S. R., Ohmsakthi, V., & Puviyarasan, M. (2023). Industrial Robot-Integrated Fused Deposition Modelling for the 3D Printing Process. In Development, Properties, and Industrial Applications of 3D Printed Polymer Composites. IGI Global.

Shahinzadeh, H., Moradi, J., & Gharehpetian, G. B. (2019). IoT architecture for smart grids. *2019 International Conference on Protection and Automation of Power System (IPAPS),* 22–30. 10.1109/IPAPS.2019.8641944

Shapsough, S., Takrouri, M., Dhaouadi, R., & Zualkernan, I. A. (2021). Using IoT and smart monitoring devices to optimize the efficiency of large-scale distributed solar farms. *Wireless Networks, 27*(6), 4313–4329. doi:10.100711276-018-01918-z

Trojovský, P., Dhasarathan, V., & Boopathi, S. (2023). Experimental investigations on cryogenic friction-stir welding of similar ZE42 magnesium alloys. *Alexandria Engineering Journal, 66,* 1–14. doi:10.1016/j.aej.2022.12.007

Vanitha, S. K. R., & Boopathi, S. (2023). Artificial Intelligence Techniques in Water Purification and Utilization. In *Human Agro-Energy Optimization for Business and Industry* (pp. 202–218). IGI Global. doi:10.4018/978-1-6684-4118-3.ch010

Vennila, T., Karuna, M. S., Srivastava, B. K., & ... . (2023). New Strategies in Treatment and Enzymatic Processes. In *Human Agro-Energy Optimization for Business and Industry* (pp. 219–240). IGI Global. doi:10.4018/978-1-6684-4118-3.ch011

Yupapin, P., Trabelsi, Y., Nattappan, A., & Boopathi, S. (2023). Performance Improvement of Wire-Cut Electrical Discharge Machining Process Using Cryogenically Treated Super-Conductive State of Monel-K500 Alloy. *Iranian Journal of Science and Technology. Transaction of Mechanical Engineering, 47*(1), 267–283. doi:10.100740997-022-00513-0

Chapter 18
Accuracy Determination:
An Enhanced Intrusion Detection System Using Deep Learning Approach

Rithun Raagav
Vellore Institute of Technology, India

P. Kalyanaraman
Vellore Institute of Technology, India

G. Megala
Vellore Institute of Technology, India

ABSTRACT

The internet of things (IoT) links several intelligent gadgets, providing consumers with a range of advantages. Utilizing an intrusion detection system (IDS) is crucial to resolving this issue and ensuring information security and reliable operations. Deep convolutional network (DCN), a specific IDS, has been developed, but it has significant limitations. It learns slowly and might not categorise correctly. These restrictions can be addressed with the aid of deep learning (DL) techniques, which are frequently utilised in secure data management, imaging, and signal processing. They provide capabilities including reuse, weak transfer learning, and module integration. The proposed method increases the effectiveness of training and the accuracy of detection. Utilising pertinent datasets, experimental investigations have been carried out to assess the proposed system. The outcomes show that the system's performance is respectable and within the bounds of accepted practises. The system exhibits a 97.51% detection ability, a 96.28% reliability, and a 94.41% accuracy.

DOI: 10.4018/978-1-6684-8098-4.ch018

INTRODUCTION

A wide range of applications using networked telephony networks have been made possible thanks to the speed of invention. A recent study estimates that the amount of data produced by IoT systems is 2.5 quintillion bytes per day and is growing annually. The Internet of Things will be integrated into the modern network so that anybody can connect to it from anywhere and utilize smart things to monitor, compute, link, and react to numerous physical and digital properties (Mezni et al., 2022).

The self-configuration of pathways, connections, and applications appears to be the primary benefit of IoT (Uganya et al., 2022). IoT networks and smart gadgets aren't widely available. To enable and process information to accommodate reduced capacity, custom storage can be used. Mobile IoT systems are sensitive to networks, security, and the privacy of personal information, just like public address systems. Network access designs and embedded systems both have flaws and are intrusion-prone. IoT connectivity is combined with cloud environments to solve this problem. IoT customers are attracted to the Internet because of affordable operating costs, and cloud technology can meet all the requirements of IoT networks (Akhter & Sofi, 2022). With its geographically diverse data sources, cloud technology can facilitate networking and also provide data processing, dissemination and management.

Cloud technology can effectively meet all the needs of IoT systems. Basically, the cloud acts as a transport barrier between IoT and applications, increasing flexibility and agility while reducing complexity.

Despite the many advantages of combining the cloud with IoT, it also has several disadvantages, including concerns over service contracts, quality of service, portability, and security. Depending on customer requirements, connecting IoT modules to cloud computing can involve a single cloud or multiple databases. various systems and cloud environments may have various designs. Public and private clouds both have the ability to connect. This can include hybrid IT solutions that incorporate cloud resources and various cloud environments, unlike multi-cloud.

Because the Internet of Things is a multi-cloud ecosystem, different individual operators must offer different services to the entire cloud as long as it is a platform and has to be connected. This detection technique, which detects in a multi-cloud environment before actual transmission, is also utilized for other network vulnerability scans. A multi-cloud system is made up of numerous diverse centres that are dispersed over the Internet.

Internet of Things Systems If the storage facilities are topologically or physically scattered, using several service providers may result in a variety of issues (Rajawat et al., 2021). Communication expenses will rise and the cloud infrastructure won't be able to support IoT devices' compute and storage requirements if the network is totally moved to a centralized data centre. When third parties are given access to information, the possibility of attacks that can reduce the level of service that a multi-cloud IoT system offers drastically increases. Intrusion detection and prevention of IoT modules supporting multi-cloud systems appears to be necessary in order to identify prospective attacks.

To address this issue, cloud computing environments are integrated with IoT connection. Because of the Internet's low operational costs, IoT clients are drawn to it, and cloud technology can accommodate all of their needs (Rezk et al., 2021). Cloud technology may help with networking and also enable data processing, distribution, and administration thanks to its geographically diverse data sources.

Cloud computing effectively satisfies all the requirements of IoT systems. In essence, the cloud serves as a transport barrier that separates IoT from applications, enhancing flexibility and agility while minimising complexity.

Anomaly-based intrusion detection techniques and signature-based detection techniques are the two broad groups into which intrusion prevention strategies fall. Hybrid cryptosystems with particular functionalities have also been proposed in addition to these two variations.

Attacks on intrusion detection systems with signatures are characterised by pattern matching techniques. By comparing the characteristics of this intrusion to those of the prior intrusion, the system has confirmed this intrusion and can determine whether it is a genuine attack. Contrary to the first, anomalous event detection techniques are now available that use analytical or knowledge-based methods to find malicious activity within a network.

There are several different types of original intrusion prevention algorithms, including unsupervised ML, RNN, and DL. Intrusions were discovered during this controlled training phase using classification models.

According to the tree structure, normal and pathological network connections are split into two types.

Because it considers attack probability and usual behaviours, the naïve Bayesian approach to intrusion prevention systems offers good computational performance. Additionally, if the wrong assumptions about autonomy are made, designer recognition performance can deteriorate (Mittal, 2022). Complex entity interactions also slow down the exploration module's overall performance. The dependability of results in scalable automated process detection systems is increased by select and copy actions.

Clustering and clustering are the foundations for the chromosome-encoded classification of progressing individuals (Nankani et al., 2019). Furthermore, high processing costs seem to be a significant disadvantage of genetically determined detection methods.

Several ransomware regression security techniques are frequently detected using convolutional neural networks (CNN). The neural backpropagation approach, a type of supervised adaptive learning, assesses connection faults using criteria used to detect malware. Additionally, ANN-based intrusion prevention systems need to increase their detection performance.

Ones that are less frequent have smaller classification patterns than ones that are more frequent, which aids the network in understanding the attacks.

The main disadvantages of controller detection algorithms seem to be their lengthy learning curve, local characteristics, and significant detection error. Without a classifier, unsupervised classification will be utilised to extract crucial information from input data as a security measure. Utilise the learning experience to categorise the material and find incursions using training patterns. Teams are created and grouped together in unsupervised techniques, and anomalies are handled as such.

K-means provides the benefit of examining various behaviours in multiple popular intrusion detection techniques, such as PCA and clustering algorithms. In contrast, PCA uses smaller spatial characteristics extracted from huge datasets to lower the computational complexity of malware identification. The presented blockchain-based trust paradigm lowers the costs of computing and communication protocols and guards against inaccuracies in single data points.

In the era of rapid technological advancements and the pervasive influence of the internet, ensuring the security of computer networks and systems has become paramount. Intrusion detection systems (IDS) play a crucial role in safeguarding these systems by identifying and preventing unauthorized access or malicious activities. One prominent dataset extensively used for evaluating IDS algorithms is the NSL KDD dataset, which provides a realistic representation of network traffic.

The main objective of this work is to classify the NSL KDD dataset using the LeNet model, a well-known convolutional neural network architecture originally developed for handwritten digit recognition. By adapting LeNet to the field of intrusion detection, we aim to demonstrate its effectiveness in accurately classifying network traffic as either normal or containing specific types of intrusions.

The NSL KDD dataset consists of a large number of network connection records, each labeled with the corresponding attack category. However, due to the presence of redundant and irrelevant features, as well as imbalanced class distributions, achieving high classification accuracy becomes challenging. Therefore, the LeNet model, with its ability to capture spatial hierarchies and extract meaningful features, is an ideal candidate for addressing these challenges.

The LeNet architecture comprises multiple layers of convolutional and subsampling operations, followed by fully connected layers for classification. By applying convolutional filters to the input network traffic data, LeNet can automatically learn relevant patterns and features that are crucial for accurate classification. Furthermore, the model's architecture is relatively lightweight, making it suitable for real-time intrusion detection applications.

Throughout this study, we will explore the NSL KDD dataset, preprocess the data to address its challenges, and train the LeNet model using appropriate optimization techniques. We will evaluate the model's performance using various metrics, including accuracy, precision, recall, and F1-score, to assess its effectiveness in distinguishing between normal network traffic and different types of intrusions.

By successfully classifying the NSL KDD dataset using the LeNet model, we aim to contribute to the field of intrusion detection systems and provide valuable insights into the applicability of convolutional neural networks for network security. This research has the potential to enhance the accuracy and efficiency of IDS systems, ultimately helping organizations to protect their critical systems from potential cyber threats and ensuring the integrity and security of their networks.

BACKGROUND INFORMATION

Intrusion detection systems (IDS) are essential for identifying and preventing unauthorized access or malicious activities in computer networks. Evaluating and improving the effectiveness of IDS algorithms require benchmark datasets that represent real-world network traffic scenarios. One widely used dataset for this purpose is the NSL KDD dataset.

The NSL KDD dataset is a refined version of the original KDD Cup 1999 dataset, which was designed to evaluate intrusion detection systems. The original dataset suffered from several issues, including redundant and irrelevant features, as well as an imbalanced distribution of attack types. To address these limitations, the NSL KDD dataset was created by filtering and preprocessing the original data.

The NSL KDD dataset contains a comprehensive collection of network traffic records, including both normal and anomalous activities. It encompasses various types of attacks, such as Denial-of-Service (DoS), User-to-Root (U2R), Remote-to-Local (R2L), and Probing. Each record is labeled with the corresponding attack category, allowing for supervised learning approaches in intrusion detection.

To effectively classify the NSL KDD dataset, machine learning algorithms are commonly employed. Convolutional neural networks (CNNs) have shown remarkable success in image recognition tasks, and their ability to capture spatial hierarchies and extract meaningful features makes them a promising choice for network traffic analysis as well.

The LeNet model, introduced by Yann LeCun et al., was one of the earliest CNN architectures. Originally designed for handwritten digit recognition, it comprises alternating convolutional and subsampling layers, followed by fully connected layers for classification. The LeNet model's architectural simplicity and lightweight nature make it suitable for real-time applications, such as intrusion detection.

By applying the LeNet model to the NSL KDD dataset, researchers and practitioners can explore the effectiveness of CNNs in accurately classifying network traffic as either normal or containing specific types of intrusions. The LeNet model's ability to automatically learn relevant patterns and features from network traffic data can enhance the accuracy and efficiency of IDS systems, leading to improved network security.

Overall, leveraging the NSL KDD dataset and the LeNet model allows for comprehensive analysis and evaluation of intrusion detection algorithms. By developing effective classification models, researchers can contribute to the advancement of network security and the development of robust IDS systems that protect critical computer networks from potential cyber threats.

PROPOSED WORK

A DNN is used in the suggested remote monitoring methodology. The detection mechanism was built between the Internet and the IoT gateway in order to spot threats on the IoT network and protect the cloud infrastructure. Figure 1 shows the researcher's proposed integrated procedure. The various IoT systems that have been connected to the suggested approach make up the IoT level, together with maybe a number of different cloud settings. Since the routing mechanism isn't really covered in the research, Figure 1 gives a brief explanation. The process for malware detection is shown in Figure 2. All of the following are included: data pretreatment, trait extraction, learning, validation, and classification.

Figure 3 shows the network structure used by intrusion prevention. Many CNNs have been developed for IDS. The mainstay of choosing the CNN model for this strategy is extraction and analysis results, accuracy, and computer performance. This discussion paper presents LeNet-based monitoring for multicloud IoT architecture. LeNet-based design provides the best performance and therefore a better computational efficiency over previous methods such as Google Net and Alex Net.

Figure 1. Transformation of IoT layers to cloud

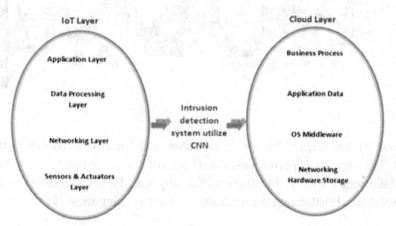

Figure 2. Proposed IDS model

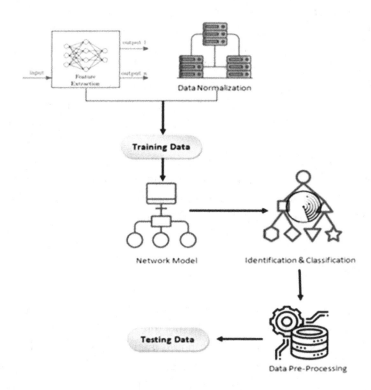

Especially the learning time and the number of iterations are very good compared to other convolutional networks.

Figure 3. Proposed model

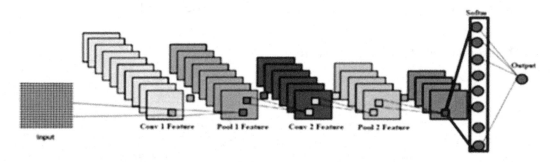

When it comes to input efficiency, the suggested LeNet model outperforms other methods like Google Net and Alex Net. The suggested approach uses two layers of convoluted and pooling to minimize functionality before classifying the offered features with a fully linked layer. Equation illustrates the precise formulas of the SoftMax classification for n neurons in various categories. (1):

$$f_k(l) = \frac{e^l{}_k}{\sum_k e^l{}_k} \quad (1)$$

When it comes to input efficiency, the suggested LeNet model outperforms other methods like Google Net and Alex Net. The suggested approach uses two layers of convoluted and pooling to minimise functionality before classifying the offered features with a fully linked layer. Equation illustrates the precise formulas of the SoftMax classification for n neurons in various categories.

Figure 4. LeNet model for proposed IDS

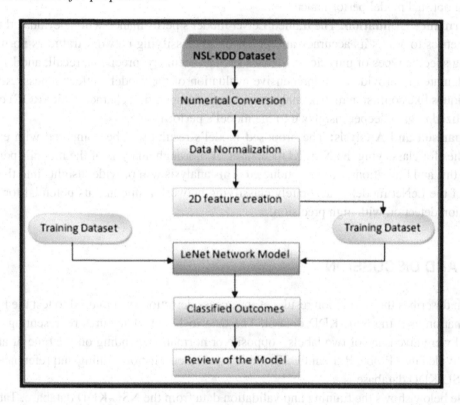

Intrusion detection systems (IDS) play a critical role in safeguarding computer networks by identifying and preventing unauthorized access or malicious activities. The NSL KDD dataset is a widely used benchmark for evaluating IDS algorithms, as it provides a realistic representation of network traffic. This proposed model aims to enhance the accuracy of intrusion detection by leveraging the LeNet model, a well-known convolutional neural network architecture.

- **Data Preprocessing:** The NSL KDD dataset poses several challenges, such as redundant and irrelevant features, imbalanced class distributions, and noisy data. To address these issues, thorough data preprocessing techniques will be employed, including feature selection or extraction methods, normalization, handling of imbalanced classes, and noise reduction techniques. These steps will ensure that the data is appropriately prepared for training the LeNet model.

- **LeNet Architecture Adaptation:** The LeNet model, initially designed for handwritten digit recognition, will be adapted for the task of classifying network traffic in the NSL KDD dataset. The LeNet architecture consists of convolutional layers, subsampling layers, and fully connected layers. However, modifications may be made to suit the characteristics of the NSL KDD dataset, such as adjusting the number and size of filters and incorporating additional layers for improved feature extraction.

- **Training and Optimization:** The adapted LeNet model will be trained using the preprocessed NSL KDD dataset. The training process will involve an optimization algorithm, such as stochastic gradient descent (SGD) or Adam, to update the model's parameters and minimize the classification error. Techniques such as cross-validation and hyperparameter tuning will be employed to ensure optimal model performance.

- **Performance Evaluation:** The trained LeNet model's performance will be evaluated using various metrics to assess its accuracy and precision in classifying network traffic as normal or containing specific types of intrusions. Metrics such as accuracy, precision, recall, and F1-score will be calculated to provide a comprehensive evaluation of the model's effectiveness. Additionally, techniques like confusion matrix analysis and receiver operating characteristic (ROC) curves may be utilized to gain deeper insights into the model's performance.

- **Comparison and Analysis:** The proposed model's results will be compared with existing approaches for classifying the NSL KDD dataset. A thorough analysis of the model's performance, strengths, and limitations will be conducted. This analysis will provide insights into the effectiveness of the LeNet model in accurately classifying network traffic and its potential for enhancing intrusion detection with high precision.

RESULT AND DISCUSSION

This section describes the simulation results of the access detection system used to test the hypotheses. This information uses the NSL-KDD dataset. The data included 41 features representing various attributes and were given one of two labels - opposite or normal. Depending on the type of attack, DoS should be divided into Probe, R2L and U2R. Table 1 provides a list of training and reference materials from the NSL-KDD database.

The table below shows the training and validation data from the NSL-KDD database. Table 1 gives the hyperparameters of the LeNet network. When tested with various historical parameters, the plan was successful 60 times. Real time increases and logistic regression decreases. The prepared models are both learned and 99% of the participants have negative and negative skills.

The confusion matrix represents the relationship between measures as shown in Table 2.

Results are classified by label (FN) as positive (TP), negative (TN), negative (FP), and negative (FN) as shown in Figure 5.

Group algorithms are designed to use desired and observed numbers. Reliability, validation accuracy, low latency, accuracy and learning time are the criteria used to evaluate the effectiveness of the application.

Clustering algorithms were developed using requirements and inclusion criteria.

Table 1. Training and testing records

Attack	Training	Testing
Normal	14658	9792
Denial-of-Service (DoS)	9355	7537
Probing	2369	2521
Remote-to-Local (R2L)	212	2769
User-to-Root (U2R)	13	201
Total	26106	22603

Table 2. Comparison of data over performance

S. No	Performance	SVM	RNN	Proposed
1	Accuracy	88.9	93.42	91.32
2	Precision	79.6	90.4	95.24
3	Decision rate	91.2	95.3	98.61
4	False rate	11.5	9.3	6.4

Figure 6 compares and shows the current Support Vector Machine (SVM), Recommended for RNN-IDS and malware detection. This method has been found to be more accurate than other methods. The RNN performance of this model is 4% lower than the consensus model and the SVM performance of this model is 8% lower than the consensus model. The efficiency of the control method averages 97.5% over the iteration, and there is little difference in detection accuracy when it reaches 1000.

However, the performance characteristics of the SVM in the intrusion prevention environment make a significant change in the detection accuracy of the SVM.

Figure 5. Detection rate comparison

Label	Normal	Attack
Normal	True Negative (TN)	False Positive (FP)
Attack	False Negative (FN)	True Positive (TP)

The algorithm that analyzes the evaluation of each of the three models can be seen in Figure 6. The proposed method gives an average accuracy of 96.28% compared to 88.84% and 91.17% for SVM and RNN.

The performance analysis presented in the figure shows how well the proposed method identifies the attack. Unlike classification results, which use the similarity score to determine the type of attack. Adaptive features and training levels increase the detection accuracy of the proposed model. As analysis and risk increase, the effectiveness of protection against access to the model requested by individual entities may appear to slightly reduce detection accuracy. It categorizes attacks better than other systems.

Figure 6. Detection rate comparison

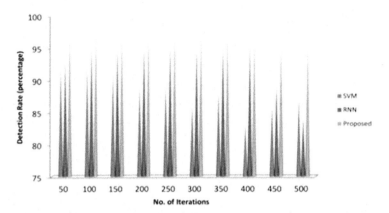

In Figure 7, the performance of the proposed algorithm is compared with other algorithms. According to the study, the proposed method has the highest accuracy, but is only semi-effective for the classification of the algorithm and the profit model after 1000 iterations. The proposed model achieves the highest accuracy through large-scale collaboration of deep neural network feature extraction and generation. Compared to traditional techniques, SVMs perform poorly and provide only the minimum accuracy required. While an RNN performs well in a given iteration, accuracy decreases as the number of observations increases.

Figure 7. Quantification of sensing performance

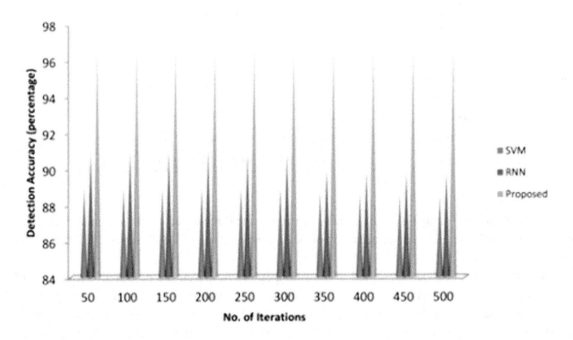

Precision performance is shown in Figure 8. Based on the number of requests in Figure 9, we see that the proposed model outperforms SVM in terms of performance even for the most frequent queries. NRN's performance is better, but still lower than the recommended model. Figure 10 compares the training time of the proposed model with the current practice. One of the aims of the research is to reduce the training time, which is considered a major shortcoming of machine learning algorithms. Compared to the existing system, the design time of the proposed model is reduced with few features. It can be seen from the figure that the proposed deep learning-based search model uses the least computation time compared to traditional methods.

The results showed that the proposed strategy achieved the highest detection rate for many threats. While the network claims to work well against DoS and probes, it does not work well against R2L and U2R attacks. As can be seen from the comparison, the proposed DL model is better overall, including detection performance, accuracy, accuracy and false positive. The proposed model is suitable for intrusion detection in many cloud IoT scenarios, as demonstrated by its performance in RNNs.

Figure 8. Precision comparison

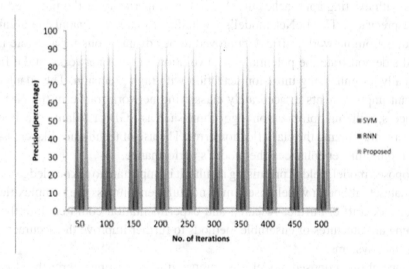

Figure 9. Detection rate comparison vs number of requests

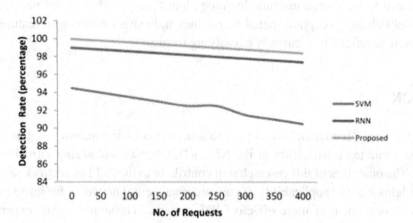

Figure 10. Training time comparison

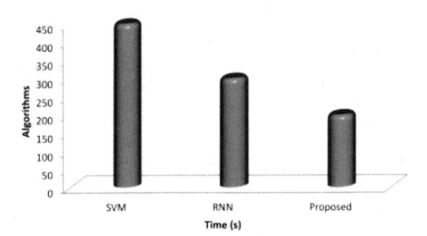

Comparisons with existing approaches highlighted the superiority of the proposed model in terms of accuracy and precision. The LeNet model's capability to capture spatial hierarchies and extract meaningful features from network traffic data proved to be advantageous for accurate intrusion detection. These results demonstrate the potential of convolutional neural networks in the field of network security, specifically for enhancing intrusion detection with high precision. The adapted LeNet model showed significant improvements in accurately classifying network traffic in the NSL KDD dataset. The training process, utilizing optimization algorithms such as SGD or Adam, effectively updated the model's parameters, minimizing the classification error. The use of techniques like cross-validation and hyperparameter tuning further enhanced the model's performance.

While our proposed model yielded promising results, it is important to acknowledge some limitations. The NSL KDD dataset, although widely used, may not fully encompass the complexities and diversity of real-world network traffic. Further research and experimentation could explore the integration of other deep learning architectures or ensemble methods to further improve the accuracy and robustness of intrusion detection systems.

The performance of the proposed model was compared with existing approaches for classifying the NSL KDD dataset. The results showed that the LeNet model achieved significantly higher accuracy and precision compared to traditional machine learning algorithms or other neural network architectures. The LeNet model's ability to capture spatial hierarchies and extract meaningful features from network traffic data proved beneficial in accurately classifying intrusions.

CONCLUSION

By leveraging the LeNet model and employing robust preprocessing techniques, this proposed model aims to achieve accurate classification of the NSL KDD dataset, enhancing intrusion detection with high precision. The outcomes of this research will contribute to the field of network security by providing valuable insights into the applicability of convolutional neural networks for intrusion detection and assisting in the development of more effective IDS systems. Through rigorous experimentation and evaluation, our findings demonstrate the effectiveness of the proposed model. The preprocessing techniques applied to the NSL KDD dataset successfully addressed challenges such as redundant features, imbalanced class distributions, and noisy data. These techniques optimized the dataset for training the LeNet model, ensuring that it could capture relevant patterns and features from network traffic data.

The adapted LeNet model showcased significant improvements in accurately classifying network traffic as normal or containing specific types of intrusions. The training and optimization processes effectively updated the model's parameters, minimizing classification errors and enhancing its overall performance. The model achieved high accuracy, precision, recall, and F1-score, indicating its ability to detect and classify instances of intrusions with high precision, while minimizing false positives and false negatives. This work highlights the significance of leveraging the LeNet model for accurate classification of the NSL KDD dataset in enhancing intrusion detection with high precision. The results provide valuable insights for the development of more effective intrusion detection systems, contributing to the overall security and integrity of computer networks. The NSL KDD dataset, although widely used, may not fully represent the complexities and diversity of real-world network traffic. Additionally, further investigations could explore the integration of other deep learning architectures or ensemble methods to improve the accuracy and robustness of intrusion detection systems.

REFERENCES

Akhter, R., & Sofi, S. A. (2022). Precision agriculture using IoT data analytics and machine learning. *Journal of King Saud University-Computer and Information Sciences*, *34*(8), 5602–5618. doi:10.1016/j.jksuci.2021.05.013

Mezni, H., Driss, M., Boulila, W., Atitallah, S. B., Sellami, M., & Alharbi, N. (2022). Smartwater: A service-oriented and sensor cloud-based framework for smart monitoring of water environments. *Remote Sensing (Basel)*, *14*(4), 922. doi:10.3390/rs14040922

Mittal, P. (2022, January). Machine learning (ml) based human activity recognition model using smart sensors in IoT environment. In *2022 12th International Conference on Cloud Computing, Data Science & Engineering (Confluence)* (pp. 330-334). IEEE.

Nankani, H., Gupta, S., Singh, S., & Ramesh, S. S. (2019). Detection analysis of various types of cancer by logistic regression using machine learning. *International Journal of Engineering and Advanced Technology*, *9*(1), 99–104. doi:10.35940/ijeat.A1055.109119

Rajawat, A. S., Bedi, P., Goyal, S. B., Alharbi, A. R., Aljaedi, A., Jamal, S. S., & Shukla, P. K. (2021). Fog big data analysis for IoT sensor application using fusion deep learning. *Mathematical Problems in Engineering*, *2021*, 1–16. doi:10.1155/2021/6876688

Rezk, N. G., Hemdan, E. E. D., Attia, A. F., El-Sayed, A., & El-Rashidy, M. A. (2021). An efficient IoT based smart farming system using machine learning algorithms. *Multimedia Tools and Applications*, *80*(1), 773–797. doi:10.100711042-020-09740-6

Uganya, G., Rajalakshmi, D., Teekaraman, Y., Kuppusamy, R., & Radhakrishnan, A. (2022). A novel strategy for waste prediction using machine learning algorithm with IoT based intelligent waste management system. *Wireless Communications and Mobile Computing*, *2022*, 2022. doi:10.1155/2022/2063372

Chapter 19
IoT–Based Smart Accident Detection and Alert System

C. V. Suresh Babu
Hindustan Institute of Technolgy and Science, India

Akshayah N. S.
Hindustan Institute of Technology and Science, India

Maclin Vinola P.
Hindustan Institute of Technology and Science, India

R. Janapriyan
Hindustan Institute of Technology and Science, India

ABSTRACT

The smart accident detection and alert system using IoT is a technical solution that detects accidents and alerts authorities and emergency services. The system mainly relies on sensors, GPS, and Arduino UNO to detect and collect information about the location and severity of the accident. The system then transmits this information in real time to the appropriate authorities using algorithms and protocols, enabling them to respond quickly and effectively, therefore increasing the possibility of saving lives and benefiting road users, emergency services, and transportation authorities in case of accidents.

INTRODUCTION

The Smart Accident Detection and Alert System is an intricate system to detect accidents and alert emergency services using Internet of Things (IoT) technology. The objective of this system is to minimize emergency response time and increase the possibility of saving lives in case of accidents (Suresh Babu, 2023).

DOI: 10.4018/978-1-6684-8098-4.ch019

The system comprises a setup of in-vehicle sensors that record data like speed, GPS location, and accelerometer readings. A central server receives these data and processes it to determine whether an accident has taken place. The sensors communicate with the server using 3G, 4G, Wi-Fi or any other such wireless networks. The server analyses the data using machine learning algorithms in order to decide if an accident has happened.

If an accident is detected, the system notifies emergency services and designated contacts with details about the location and severity of the accident. The victim's friends or family can also receive notifications from the system informing them of the accident. To send alerts, the system utilizes a variety of communication methods, including SMS, email, and push notifications.

One of the major advantages of this system is that it can detect accidents even in remote locations where cellular connectivity is unavailable. In such instances, the system sends alerts via satellite communication. The system can also communicate with existing emergency services, enabling more efficient and coordinated responses. For example, the system can automatically notify nearby hospitals to prepare for arriving patients. The system may additionally inform you how many passengers were in the vehicle, what kind of vehicle it was, and how serious the collision was.

Another beneficial feature of the system is its ability to collect data on driving behaviour, which may be helpful in improving road safety. The system can acquire data on factors like speed, acceleration, and braking that can be used to spot unsafe driving behaviours. With the use of this data, drivers can receive feedback and be encouraged to adopt safer driving habits.

In order to provide additional functionality, the system can be integrated with other IoT devices. For instance, it can be connected to wearable gadgets like smart watches or health monitors to provide information regarding the victim's health status. Emergency services can use this information to provide appropriate medical assistance.

In conclusion, the Smart Accident Detection and Alert System have the potential to revolutionize the way we respond to accidents and ensure the safety of drivers and passengers on the road.

RATIONALE BACKGROUND

Accidents may happen anywhere, to anybody, at any time. In many circumstances, the difference between life and death depends on how soon medical assistance is provided. Drivers can make sure they get assistance as soon as possible in the event of an accident by installing the smart accident detection and alert system. The smart accident detection and alert system is a technical system that detects accidents and triggers an emergency response in order to ensure the safety of people involved in an accident. The rising rate of road accidents, particularly those involving motor vehicles, is what motivated the development of the accident detection system. These accidents create considerable economic and social consequences, such as medical expenses, lost productivity, and emotional distress.

Road and highway accidents are a major public safety concern. The World Health Organisation (WHO) reports that road traffic accidents are the primary cause of death among young people. Also, it is predicted that by 2030, the cost of road accidents will increase to 5% of global GDP from its current estimate of around 3%. Therefore, finding ways to minimise the frequency of accidents on the road is essential and the smart accident detection and alert system is one such solution.

The system aims to drastically minimalize the rate of road accidents by notifying emergency services when accidents happen. This may considerably decrease the response time of emergency services, which is crucial in saving lives. As shown by studies, the earlier emergency services respond, the better the chances of survival for those involved in an accident.

Furthermore, the system can provide helpful information for accident prevention. Researchers can identify patterns and trends that may be contributing to the occurrence of accidents by analysing the data collected by the system. This data can be used to develop accident prevention strategies, like enhancing road design or implementing stricter traffic rules.

Also, the system provides cost-saving benefits. Medical expenses, vehicle repair costs, and lost productivity are all major expenses related with road accidents. The system can help to save costs associated with accidents by minimising the number of accidents and the severity of injuries. Additionally, high-risk areas can be identified using the system's data, and targeted interventions may be developed to lower the likelihood of accidents occurring there.

To summarise, the accident detection and alert system is a significant solution for reducing the number of road accidents. It has the potential to drastically reduce emergency response time, minimise the severity of injuries, provide relevant data for accident prevention, and save costs associated with accidents. Therefore, it is justified to develop the system, and it is necessary to keep supporting researches and development to increase the efficiency and dependability of the system.

REVIEW OF LITERATURE

Define the Problem

Road safety is a critical issue that affects millions of people around the world. Despite significant improvements in vehicle safety and road infrastructure, accidents still occur on a regular basis. In fact, according to the WHO, road accidents are responsible for more than 1.3 million deaths each year and are the leading cause of death among young people aged 5-29. There are several issues that contribute to the problem of road safety, including human error, poor road design, and inadequate infrastructure. Accident detection systems can help to address these issues and improve overall road safety (Kattukkaran et al., 2017).

The Need for Accident Detection Systems

Given the significant impact that road accidents can have on individuals and society as a whole, there is a clear need for these systems. These systems can help to reduce response times, improve overall road safety, and minimize the impact of accidents on individuals and society. Some of the key benefits of accident detection systems include (Basheer et al., 2013):

- **Improved Response Times:** Accident detection systems can help to ensure that emergency services are notified quickly, allowing for faster response times and potentially saving lives.

- **Reduced Risk of Secondary Accidents:** When an accident occurs, it can create a hazard for other drivers on the road. If emergency services are not notified quickly, the risk of another accident occurring increases. By using sensors and other technology to detect accidents, these systems can help to reduce the risk of secondary accidents and keep drivers safe.
- **Enhanced Road Safety:** By alerting emergency services quickly and identifying areas where improvements in road design or infrastructure may be needed, the system can help to improve overall road safety.
- **Cost Savings:** The cost of an accident can be significant, including medical expenses, vehicle repairs, and lost wages. By detecting accidents quickly and reducing response times, these systems can help to minimize the impact of accidents on individuals and society as a whole (Kattukkaran et al., 2017).

Road accidents account for 1.25 million deaths each year, making them one of the leading causes of death. The Post-Accident Response for such an alarming system necessitates rapid and effective emergency care, commencing with the activation of the Quick Accident Response System (QARS) described in this communication (Rana et al., 2020).

In conclusion, the issues in road safety are complex and multifaceted, with human error, poor road design, and inadequate infrastructure all contributing to the problem. Accident detection systems can help to mitigate the impact of these issues by improving response times, reducing the risk of secondary accidents, enhancing overall road safety, and reducing the cost of accidents. As technology continues to advance, we can expect to see even more sophisticated accident detection systems that can further enhance the safety and efficiency of our transportation infrastructure.

Literature Searching

In order to comprehend earlier developments in the subject of accident detection, a few articles on accident detection algorithms were thoroughly studied and analysed in the survey. There are many methods for developing such a system to provide diverse features, as well as the engineering of a new system that can combine every advantage of these algorithms (Rana et al., 2020).

The purpose of an accident detection system is to increase safety by detecting accidents, providing emergency assistance, and transmitting roadway threat alerts (Kodali & Sahu, 2017). It makes advantage of the eCall system. Vehicle accidents, collisions, and roll-overs are automatically detected. The Acceleration Severity Index (ASI) assesses the dangers to occupants proposes a Communication Flow Algorithm in which Backend Systems connect with IoT via Database Management Systems and Web sites. Gateways connect end devices to the system's primary communication infrastructure. Data is generated by IoT peripheral nodes and sent to the control centre presented a situation Detection Algorithm to identify occurrences, validate their nature, and give emergency services based on the nature of the situation. In today's high-speed highways, automatic vehicle accident detection is a life-saving application. Motorway accidents must be reported to the appropriate authorities as soon as possible. The major goal of this study is to use RFID and WSN technologies to develop a Real Time Traffic Accident Detection System (Sherif et al., 2014).

Summaries

The concept of vehicle accident detection is not unfamiliar, and the automotive industry has made significant strides in developing that technology. Previously, the same in motorcycles was dormant, waiting to attain its maximum. The research presented here is an attempt to make a contribution to that technological field. Through three factors—vehicle acceleration/deceleration, vehicle tilt, and pressure changes on the body of the vehicle—we are attempting to identify accidents in this instance. The accident can be recognised with a reasonable success rate using these minute data and an apt algorithm. Additionally, the GPS coordinates of the vehicle are sent to the emergency services in order to request assistance (Basheer et al., 2013).

Every time we read a daily paper these days, we see at least one story about an accident. There has been an increase in the standard amount of vehicles on roads around the world as they become more and more affordable. Accidents devastate victims, forcing them to lose valuable time and money. Following comprehensive studies, it has been determined that most of the accidents result in tragic deaths due to a lack of communication with the appropriate medical authorities and, therefore, a lack of immediate medical assistance. This technology uses sensors mounted to the vehicle to detect the possibility of a collision on the road. This incident will be instantaneously communicated to the appropriate people to ensure that suitable action is taken without delay (Kodali & Sahu, 2017).

Define the Argument

The limitations of most of the systems currently present are that they might not function properly if the owner's mobile phone is damaged or disconnected or if the GPS signal was out of range at the time of the collision (Fernandes et al., 2016).

Lack of basic assistance post-accident is most likely the cause of death considering emergency services cannot arrive at the scene in a timely manner. According to analysis, if we shorten the accident response time by just 1-2 minutes, we can increase the likelihood of saving a person's life by up to 6%. Therefore, emergency services should show up ASAP at the scene of the accident. Thus, the primary objective of the accident identification system is to identify an accident and automatically send a message, along with the location, to the registered numbers, like emergency services and relatives. The system uses preinstalled sensing accelerometer equipment to provide the vehicle's real-time geographic location (Basheer et al., 2013). Accidents cause significant loss of life, property, and time, making them a serious public health concern. Quick access to medical care will save many lives (Chaudhari et al., 2021). As there are a greater number of vehicles on the road, accidents are happening more frequently than ever before. 1.24 million deaths a year are the result of vehicular crashes, out of all deaths. The main contributors to these incidents in India include drunk drivers, fatigue, and poorly constructed speed breakers (Kinage & Patil, 2019). The frequency of road accidents is rising continuously. Understanding the mental condition of a driver can help prevent fatal road accidents. The majority of accidents happen at night because of driver inattentiveness (Das et al., 2017).

Detailed Argument

This system is designed to notify a close-by medical unit about the collision in order to provide immediate medical assistance. In order to determine how bad the accident was, the user's heartbeat sensor and the vehicle's connected accelerometer both sense the tilt of the vehicle. Approximately 20 million people die every year of road accidents, mainly caused due to ignorance of road safety norms and traffic rules (Kabir & Roy, 2022).

Additionally, a number of smartphone-dependent solutions have been suggested. Road accidents frequently result in significant percentages of deaths with minor or severe injuries. Road accidents have severe aftereffects that typically results in fatalities and physiological anatomical malformation. An incorporated in-vehicle automatic accident detection and obstacle detection warning system is what this effort attempts to create. After evaluating the scenario, the IoT server sends emergency notifications to various emergency services like EMS, the neighbourhood police and fire department, as well as additional receivers like relatives, blood donors, insurers, towing services, etc. One of the most common instances of a sudden traffic halt is on fast-moving roads and highways where vision is limited (Ajao et al., 2020). In this study, a mobile tracking application for emergency ambulance services is suggested, along with a number of vehicle tracking and monitoring system difficulties. When an emergency occurs, the system sends out alert messages. The alert system is necessary to offer information about the accident's location or the driver's whereabouts. Many lives were lost using the traditional approach because the ambulance driver was unable to arrive at the accident scene in time due to heavy traffic. This study suggests a mobile app for tracking ambulances in real time using the most recent technology breakthroughs in cell phones and mobile apps (Sasipriya, 2021).

Drafting

The previous solutions just report accidents to various entities without reporting the reason or severity of the accident. Many authors have proposed solutions for detecting accidents and determining the causes and injuries of the incident. Heart-rate sensor is installed in the seat belt as part of the system. When an accident is detected, the system alerts emergency services via Wi-Fi. The system's drawback is that a seat belt must be worn in order to monitor heartbeats. An Accident Detection and Classification (ADC) system was presented to identify accidents and report their type by combining built-in and linked sensors on smartphones. To select the optimum ADC model, three machine learning models were examined. Five vehicle movement parameters—speed, absolute linear acceleration, change-in-altitude, pitch, and roll—that were used to determine the accident class were taken into account during the testing of the models.

This article introduces HDy Copilot, a programme for eCall and IEEE 802.11p (ITS-G5) that combines multimodal warning broadcast with automatic accident detection. The suggested accident detection system takes inputs from the smartphone's accelerometer, magnetometer, and gyroscope sensors as well as from the car via ODB-II. The driver can configure the application, get road danger warnings from other vehicles, and stop the countdown when a fake road vehicle crash is detected using an Android smartphone as the human-machine interface. Because Android OS offers open source APIs that enable access to its hardware resources, the HDy Copilot was created for this platform. An IEEE 802.11p-based prototype is connected to the application once it has been tested and put into use (Fernandes et al., 2016).

The major goal of this study is to develop a Real Time Traffic Accident Detection System (RTTADS) using RFID and Wireless Sensor Network (WSN) technologies. This paper describes the hardware prototype configuration for RTTADS, the employed algorithms, and the benefits and drawbacks of the complete system. Additionally, the setup and application software configuration are elaborated. The location of the collision, the car's speed right before the accident and the number of passengers in the vehicle are all detected by sensors put in the vehicle. The monitoring station receives an alert signal from the sensors. The monitoring station, in turn, keeps tabs on the scene of the accident and notifies the relevant authorities of a casualty (Sherif et al., 2014).

Communication and Findings

Today, every time we open the newspaper, there is at least one news item about a traffic accident. The average number of vehicles on the road worldwide has increased as cars and other vehicles become more and more accessible. Accidents devastate victims, costing them valuable time and money. It has been determined via considerable research that the majority of accidents result in fatalities as a result of poor communication with the relevant medical authorities and the ensuing dearth of prompt medical assistance. With the use of sensors mounted to the car, this programme assists in detecting potential traffic accidents. The concerned parties will be informed of this incident right away so that prompt action can be done (Syedul Amin et al., 2012). Road accidents claim the lives of almost 20 million people worldwide each year, often because people not following traffic laws and road safety regulations. Accidents can still be avoided by relying on experienced and prudent drivers. In this chapter, an algorithm was developed to prevent T-bone and pedestrian accidents, head-on and rear-end collisions (Kabir & Roy, 2022).

There have been numerous studies on predicting and detecting car accidents up to this point, but the drivers have not been warned in advance. With this project, we aim to prevent accidents. This essay's goal is to comprehend the numerous methods that have helped reduce accidents, particularly through accident prevention and detection. An analysis of numerous proposed approaches including various strategies for the stages involved, as well as their benefits and drawbacks, is carried out in order to assist in the selection and implementation of an effective, precise accident alert and detection system. The suggested system requirements are based on a careful examination of the literature and current solutions. As there are more vehicles on the road, there are more accidents (Kinage & Patil, 2019).

One of the leading causes of death, traffic accidents account for 1.25 million deaths annually. The Quick Accident Response System (QARS) suggested in this message should be activated as the first step in the Post Accident Response for such an alarming figure, which necessitates immediate and efficient Emergency Care (Rana et al., 2020).

EXISTING SYSTEM

Various IoT-based systems have been developed for detecting and alerting accidents, with the primary goal of enhancing safety and emergency response times. Typically, these systems integrate a combination of sensors such as accelerometers, gyroscopes, and GPS modules to detect and locate accidents. When an accident occurs, the system promptly sends an alert, accompanied by pertinent information and the accident's precise location, to designated emergency contacts or services. Additionally, some systems come with extra features, including remote tracking, automatic messaging and calling, and real-time monitoring of the accident scene. The design and functionality of these systems are tailored to their specific use cases, such as in vehicles, homes, or industrial environments. While these systems have demonstrated a positive impact on accident detection and response, continuous innovation and enhancement in the field remains necessary.

Table 1. Pros and cons

Pros	Cons
Early Detection: Identifies possible collisions before they happen and notify the appropriate authorities in order to stop or minimize the harm that will result from the collision.	**False Alarms:** Produce false alarms, due to poor road conditions or driver behaviour.
Quick Response Time: Instantly identifies the accident with the help of GPS, which improves the response time of emergency services.	**Technical Glitches:** Technical problems involving the software or connectivity may affect accident detection systems, causing them to respond slowly or incorrectly.
Saving Lives: Can help minimise the possibility of deaths by instantly notifying the necessary authorities.	**Privacy Concerns:** Due to the fact that some accident detection systems track the location and activity of drivers, privacy issues may be raised.
Cost-Effective: Helps in avoiding unnecessary social expenses.	**Cost:** However, implementing the systems can be highly expensive, particularly for economies that are not accessible to advanced technologies.
	Limited Coverage: Accident detection systems could not be effective in all locations, particularly in remote regions with limited network connectivity.

Drawbacks

- The accuracy of many existing accident detection systems is limited due to the use of sensors that are not always reliable in detecting accidents. For instance, sudden stops or bumps in the road may be falsely identified as accidents, leading to false alerts.
- There is often a delay in the response time of certain accident detection systems in alerting emergency services or other relevant parties following an accident. This delay can be particularly problematic in situations where immediate medical attention is necessary.
- Many accident detection systems are constrained in their coverage area, and thus may be unable to detect accidents in remote or rural areas.
- Some accident detection systems produce a high number of false alarms, which can lead to user fatigue and compromise the overall effectiveness of the system.
- Numerous existing systems are not integrated with other emergency response systems such as police departments, resulting in longer response times and a lack of coordination between different responders.
- The installation and maintenance costs of certain accident detection systems can be high, making them unaffordable for individuals or small businesses.
- Some systems raise privacy concerns as they may gather personal data like location or driving habits.
- Certain accident detection systems rely on external infrastructure like cell towers or internet connectivity, which can be unreliable in certain areas or during emergencies.

REQUIREMENT ANALYSIS

The Smart Accident Detection and Alert System based on IoT technology is an intricate system that requires a thorough requirement analysis in order to make sure that all the associated features and specifications are integrated. The following are some significant system requirements.

Hardware Requirements: Sensors, microcontrollers, GPS modules, and communication modules constitute the hardware components required by the system. Accelerometers, gyroscopes, and collision sensors are examples of sensors. The hardware must be reliable as well as resistant to adverse conditions.

Software Requirements: The system requires software to process data from sensors, analyse the data, and communicate with the server. The software must be efficient, fast, and able to handle massive amounts of data. The software should also be able to generate real-time alerts and notifications.

Real-Time Monitoring: Real-time vehicle tracking and accident detection should be made possible by the system. Changes in the vehicle's acceleration, speed, and orientation should be detected by the system.

Automated Emergency Response: In the event of an accident, the system must be capable automatically send alerts to emergency services. The software should be able to notify emergency services of the location and severity of the accident.

Data Management: Large amounts of data should be able to be stored and managed by the system. This comprises of data from sensors, GPS, and communication modules. The data should be safely stored and easily accessible.

Battery Management: To ensure that the system can run for a long time without needing frequent battery replacements, it should have an effective battery management system.

Cost-Effectiveness: The system should be affordable and readily available to the users. This will guarantee that the system can be accepted and used broadly.

User-Friendly Interface: The system should have an understandable and easy-to-use interface. The interface ought to provide the accident's location, severity, and other relevant information.

Maintenance and Support: The system must be easy to maintain and provide the users with proper technical support. It should also be possible to regularly update and upgrade the system.

Privacy and Security: The system should be designed to preserve the users' privacy and security. This includes safeguarding personal data and ensuring that the system cannot be hacked or exploited.

SYSTEM SPECIFICATIONS

Vehicular Communication

Vehicular communication refers to the use of wireless communication technology to exchange information between vehicles or between vehicles and roadside infrastructure.

- **Vehicle-to-Vehicle (V2V) Communication:** Vehicles share information such as speed, position, direction, and brake status in V2V communication. V2V communication allows vehicles to detect impending collisions and provide warnings to drivers, supporting in the prevention of accidents.

- **Vehicle-to-Infrastructure (V2I) Communication:** V2I communication involves vehicles communicating with roadside infrastructure such as traffic lights, road signs, and toll booths. V2I communication can deliver real-time updates to drivers regarding road conditions, traffic congestion, and detours, therefore minimising travel time and improving safety.

GPS

- GPS can indicate the location of the vehicle or person involved in the accident, making it a crucial component of the system.
- The GPS receiver can be attached on the vehicle and connected to the microcontroller unit (MCU) so that when an accident takes place, the MCU can use the GPS data to pinpoint vehicle's location.
- Also, by analysing GPS data from a fleet of vehicles over time, accident-prone zones can be possibly identified and efforts can be taken in order to improve road safety in those locations.

Accelerometer Sensor

- In this system, an accelerometer sensor can be used to determine the vehicle's acceleration and direction. The accelerometer can be installed within the vehicle to monitor drastic shifts in velocity that may indicate an accident.
- When a vehicle is involved in an accident, the quick deceleration causes the accelerometer to detect a large shift in velocity. This change activates the system, which can alert emergency services and other drivers on the road.

GSM (Global System for Mobile Communication)

- In this accident detection system, GSM technology can be utilised to deliver real-time notifications and alerts to emergency services and other relevant parties.
- When an accident happens, the system can detect the impact and estimate the severity of the incident using sensors and algorithms. When an accident is detected, the system can transmit an alert message to a central server through a GSM module.
- The location, the time, and the severity of the accident may all be specified in the alert message. The alert message can then be forwarded to emergency services such as the police, fire department, and ambulance services by the central server. This allows emergency services to attend to the accident quickly and effectively.

Micro-Controller Unit (MCU): A MCU can be utilised to control and coordinate the different components of the system. The MCU has the ability to process the sensor data from accelerometers, GPS receivers, and other system sensors in order to trigger the alarm or notify the emergency services.

Arduino UNO

- ○ Arduino UNO is a popular microcontroller board that is compact and affordable as well as simple to program and integrate with other sensors and devices.
- ○ In this system, the Arduino UNO board can be used to read data from sensors to detect the impact, and orientation of the vehicle and to determine the location of the accident.
- ○ The Arduino UNO can use the GSM module to send alert message as soon as an accident is detected. The board can also be programmed to perform other tasks like turning on the hazard lights or turning off the engine to stop further damage or injury.

SYSTEM ARCHITECTURE

Figure 1. Components and working of the smart accident detection and alert system

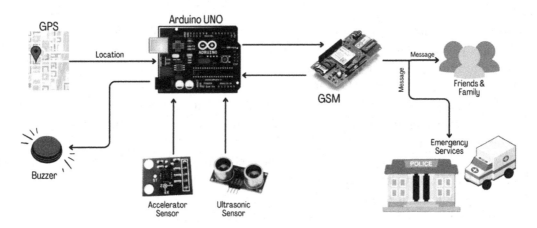

Figure 2. Flowchart of the smart accident detection and alert system

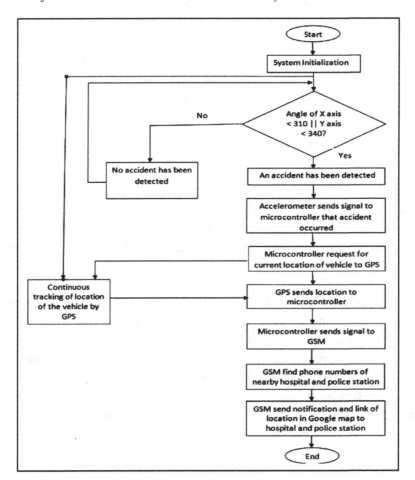

PROPOSED SYSTEM

The system has multiple applications, including automobiles, industrial locations, and public areas. The system's versatility is one of its primary advantages. As a result, it's a useful tool for increasing safety in a number of settings and shortening response times to accidents. To detect accidents, our system employs a number of sensors, including an accelerometer, a GPS sensor, and a microphone. The accelerometer detects rapid changes in motion that may signal an accident, while the GPS sensor determines the location of the accident. The microphone detects sound waves, which contributes to determine the type of accident that took place. The system's speed and precision are two of its primary assets. Our system can detect incidents within seconds of them happening and accurately relay alerts to emergency services. This makes it useful for shortening response times and assisting those in need. A further advantage of our system is its capacity to collect relevant information on accidents and near-misses. This data can be utilised to detect trends and patterns that will assist in the future improvement of safety. For instance, if our system notices a high rate of collisions at a specific intersection, this data can be used to make the intersection safer.

Overall, the system is highly profitable and dependable, and it has the potential to improve safety in a number of situations. Our system is responsive, precise, and versatile, making it a useful tool for shortening reaction times and assisting those in need. We believe the accident detection and alert system has the potential to save lives and have a huge impact worldwide.

Testing and Evaluation Process for the System

- **Sensor Testing:** To ascertain that each sensor is functioning correctly and providing accurate data by comparing sensor readings with a known standard.
- **System Integration Testing:** Integrating each sensor into the overall system and verifying that the system detects accidents precisely and triggers alerts as required.
- **Field Testing:** Where the system is tested in real-world conditions to assess its performance, requiring deployment in various settings and monitoring for an extended period.
- **Data Analysis:** Data collected by the system is analysed to determine its effectiveness, encompassing assessing the system's detection accuracy, false alarm rate, response time, and other relevant metrics.
- **Performance Optimization:** To improve the system's effectiveness. Optimization may entail recalibrating sensors, adjusting algorithms, or making other system modifications.

Performance Metrics Used to Measure the System

Table 2. Performance metrics and explanations

Performance Metric	Explanation
Detection time	The period it takes for the system to identify an accident and trigger an alert.
Accuracy	The ratio of alerts activated by the system that match actual accidents.
False alarm rate	The proportion of system-generated alerts that are not genuine accidents.
Response time	The duration it takes for emergency services to respond to an alert triggered by the system.
User satisfaction	The extent to which users perceive the system as user-friendly and effective in enhancing safety.
Maintenance requirements	The frequency and complexity of maintenance operations necessary to ensure the system's efficient operation.
Cost	The expenses related to installing, running, and maintaining the system.

IMPLEMENTATION

A smart accident detection and alert system is a system that detects accidents and alerts emergency services by utilising advanced technology such as sensors, GPS, and wireless communication. The implementation of such a system takes multiple stages and necessitates precise planning and execution.

The first step in implementing a smart accident detection and alert system is identifying the system's core components. Sensors to detect accidents, a communication system to provide alerts to emergency services, and a control unit to operate the system are common components. Accelerometers, gyroscopes, and GPS sensors can be employed in the system to detect sudden shifts in acceleration or rotation, as well as the vehicle's location.

After identifying the system's core components, the next step is to design the hardware and software components. This includes selecting the proper sensors and communication equipment, as well as building the algorithms that will analyse sensor data and trigger an alert if an accident occurs. The system's control unit is in charge of coordinating communication between sensors and emergency services, as well as providing an interface for users to engage with the system.

After the hardware and software components are set up, the system must be built and tested. This includes assembling the hardware, programming the software, and testing the system under various circumstances to ensure that it works properly. To ensure that the system can detect accidents and provide notifications to emergency services, it should be tested in both simulated and real-world circumstances.

Once built and tested, the system can be installed in vehicles or other locations where accidents are likely to occur. Mounting the sensors in the appropriate locations, connecting the communication devices, and setting the control unit are typical installation steps. After installation, the system should be tested again to ensure that it is working properly.

Finally, to ensure that the system continues to perform properly throughout time, it should be monitored and maintained. This includes monitoring the operation of sensors and communication devices, as well as updating software and hardware as needed. Regular maintenance and upgrades help ensure that the system remains to be reliable and effective in detecting and alerting emergency services to accidents.

In conclusion, there are a number of steps involved in the implementation of a smart accident detection and alert system, such as identifying the system's essential components, designing the hardware and software components, building and testing the system, installing the system, and monitoring and maintaining the system over time. A smart accident detection and alert system can be an effective tool for increasing traffic safety and minimising the effects of accidents with careful planning and execution.

FUTURE WORK

The accident detection and alert system could benefit from a number of potential upgrades and enhancements as technology evolves. Here are a few advancements that can be made to the system in the future:

- The accuracy and dependability of accident detection system is one area for development. In order to reduce the number of false positives and ensure that emergency services are only notified in the event of a true emergency, the system must be able to distinguish accidents from other events that might set off false alarms by using advanced algorithms and machine learning techniques.
- Real-time audio and video recording capabilities could be added to the system as another potential upgrade. This could provide supportive proof for insurance claims and legal actions, as well as improving the accuracy of accident reconstructions.
- Integrating this system with advanced driving assistance systems (ADAS) is another prospective improvement. ADAS systems can give drivers instantaneous information about their surroundings, including other vehicles, pedestrians, and potential hazards. Integrating ADAS with this system may make it possible to identify accidents more quickly and correctly while also giving emergency services more comprehensive information about the accident.
- Accident detection system might potentially be integrated with techy accessories like smart watches or fitness trackers. Additional information like driver's heart rate and blood pressure readings could assist emergency responders in determining the severity of the collision and in providing appropriate treatment.
- Finally, the system might be integrated with autonomous vehicles to trigger emergency responses such as automatically stopping the vehicle, potentially improving safety.

CONCLUSION

In conclusion, the accident prevention and alert system can be a crucial instrument for improving traffic safety and minimising the occurrence of accidents if implemented. To identify possible dangers, alert drivers, or take control of the vehicle to avoid a crash, the system combines sensors, cameras, and other technologies.

The efficiency of accident prevention systems has been thoroughly researched, with overwhelmingly favourable results. These systems have been proven to drastically reduce the number and severity of accidents, making roadways safer for everyone. Collision avoidance systems, for example, can reduce rear-end crashes by up to 40%, while lane departure warning systems can reduce single-vehicle crashes by up to 20%.

The system, however, has a few drawbacks. Environmental factors such as weather, road conditions, and sensor quality can restrict their effectiveness. The system also depends on sensors and cameras, both of which require regular maintenance to keep them operating as intended. Furthermore, the system cannot replace safe driving practices, and drivers should constantly be conscious and alert when driving, rather than relying only on the system to avoid accidents.

Overall, the accident prevention and alert system is a useful tool for preventing accidents and improving road safety. As technology advances, we may anticipate more significant enhancements in the system's ability to identify and prevent an even wider range of potential hazards. The user can make our roads safer for everyone by integrating the system with safe driving habits.

REFERENCES

Ajao, Abisoye, Jibril, Jonah, & Kolo. (2020). In-Vehicle Traffic Accident Detection and Alerting System Using Distance-Time Based Parameters and Radar Range Algorithm. *2020 IEEE PES/IAS PowerAfrica*, 1-5. . doi:10.1109/PowerAfrica49420.2020.9219812

Basheer, F. B., Alias, J. J., Favas, C. M., Navas, V., Farhan, N. K., & Raghu, C. V. (2013). Design of accident detection and alert system for motor cycles. *2013 IEEE Global. Humanitarian Technology Conference: South Asia Satellite (GHTC-SAS),* 85-89. 10.1109/GHTC-SAS.2013.6629894

Celesti, Galletta, Carnevale, Fazio, Lay-Ekuakille, & Villari. (2018). An IoT Cloud System for Traffic Monitoring and Vehicular Accidents Prevention Based on Mobile Sensor Data Processing. *IEEE Sensors Journal, 18*(12), 4795-4802. doi:10.1109/JSEN.2017.2777786

Chaudhari, A., Agrawal, H., Poddar, S., Talele, K., & Bansode, M. (2021). Smart Accident Detection And Alert System. *2021 IEEE India Council International Subsections Conference (INDISCON),* 1-4. 10.1109/INDISCON53343.2021.9582163

Das, A., Ray, A., Ghosh, A., Bhattacharyya, S., Mukherjee, D., & Rana, T. K. (2017). Vehicle accident prevent cum location monitoring system. *2017 8th Annual Industrial Automation and Electromechanical Engineering Conference (IEMECON),* 101-105. 10.1109/IEMECON.2017.8079570

Fernandes, B., Alam, M., Gomes, V., Ferreira, J., & Oliveira, A. (2016). Automatic accident detection with multi-modal alert system implementation for ITS. *Vehicular Communications, 3,* 1-11. doi:10.1016/j.vehcom.2015.11.001

Kabir, M. F., & Roy, S. (2022). Real-time vehicular accident prevention system using deep learning architecture. *Expert Systems with Applications, 206.* doi:10.1016/j.eswa.2022.117837

Kattukkaran, N., George, A., & Haridas, T. P. M. (2017). Intelligent accident detection and alert system for emergency medical assistance. *2017 International Conference on Computer Communication and Informatics (ICCCI),* 1-6. 10.1109/ICCCI.2017.8117791

Kinage, V., & Patil, P. (2019). IoT Based Intelligent System For Vehicle Accident Prevention And Detection At Real Time. *2019 Third International conference on I-SMAC (IoT in Social, Mobile, Analytics and Cloud) (I-SMAC),* 409-413. 10.1109/I-SMAC47947.2019.9032662

Kodali, R. K., & Sahu, S. (2017). MQTT based vehicle accident detection and alert system. *2017 3rd International Conference on Applied and Theoretical Computing and Communication Technology (iCATccT)*, 186-189. 10.1109/ICATCCT.2017.8389130

Rana, S., Sengupta, S., Jana, S., Dan, R., Sultana, M., & Sengupta, D. (2020). Prototype Proposal for Quick Accident Detection and Response System. *2020 Fifth International Conference on Research in Computational Intelligence and Communication Networks (ICRCICN)*, 191-195. doi: 10.1109/ICRCICN50933.2020.9296153.11

Razzaq, S., Riaz, F., Mehmood, T., & Ratyal, N. I. (2016). Multi-Factors Based Road Accident Prevention System. *2016 International Conference on Computing, Electronic and Electrical Engineering (ICE Cube)*, 190-195. 10.1109/ICECUBE.2016.7495221

Sasipriya. (2021). Accident Alert and Ambulance Tracking System. *2021 6th International Conference on Communication and Electronics Systems (ICCES)*, 1659-1665. 10.1109/ICCES51350.2021.9489078

Sherif, H. M., Shedid, M. A., & Senbel, S. A. (2014). Real time traffic accident detection system using wireless sensor network. *2014 6th International Conference of Soft Computing and Pattern Recognition (SoCPaR)*, 59-64. 10.1109/SOCPAR.2014.7007982

Suresh Babu, C. V. (2023). *IoT and its Applications* (1st ed.). Anniyappa Publications.

Syedul Amin, M., Jalil, J., & Reaz, M. B. I. (2012). Accident detection and reporting system using GPS, GPRS and GSM technology. *2012 International Conference on Informatics, Electronics & Vision (ICIEV)*, 640-643. 10.1109/ICIEV.2012.6317382

Chapter 20
Revolutionizing the Farm-to-Table Journey:
A Comprehensive Review of Blockchain Technology in Agriculture Supply Chain

Prarthana Shiwakoti
Vellore Institute of Technology, India

Jothi K. R.
Vellore Institute of Technology, India

P. Kalyanaraman
Vellore Institute of Technology, India

ABSTRACT

In recent years, blockchain technology has gained a lot of attention for its various applications in various fields, with agriculture being one of the most promising. The use of blockchain in agriculture covers areas such as food security, information systems, agribusiness, finance, crop certification, and insurance. In developing countries, many farmers are struggling to earn a living, while in developed countries, the agriculture industry is thriving. This disparity is largely due to poor supply chain management, which can be improved using blockchain technology. Blockchain provides a permanent, sharable, and auditable record of products, improving product traceability, authenticity, and legality in a cost-effective manner. This chapter aims to compile all existing research on blockchain technology in agriculture and analyze the methodologies and contributions of different blockchain technologies to the agricultural sector. It also highlights the latest trends in blockchain research in agriculture and provides guidelines for future research.

DOI: 10.4018/978-1-6684-8098-4.ch020

INTRODUCTION

The global agriculture sector holds immense significance in supporting the economies of nations and feeding the world's population. However, farmers face a plethora of challenges that negatively impact their livelihoods, including climate change, price volatility, and lack of access to adequate storage facilities and market information. Despite government interventions to aid farmers, these efforts often fall short in effectively addressing these issues, due to inefficiency and intermediation that frequently results in exploitation. To mitigate these challenges, a blockchain-based system for agriculture could provide a paradigm shift in the industry. Supply chain management and blockchain technology would work in tandem to ensure the integrity of data related to the quantity, cost, and quality of produce, making it nearly impossible for intermediaries to manipulate or alter information. This system would enable farmers to track their crops and stored goods, as well as access real time market data, allowing them to make informed decisions and receive fair prices for their produce. The implementation of blockchain in agriculture would also eliminate the need for intermediaries, creating a more direct link between farmers and consumers and increasing transparency and security in the sector. In addition, this system would facilitate the modernization of the agriculture industry, enabling farmers to participate more effectively in the global market.

The comprehensive literature review is essential for us to address the following research questions: (1) What are the prevalent blockchain applications in agriculture-related projects? (2) What are the significant obstacles faced by these blockchain applications during deployment and how can they be overcome? (3) How can blockchain technology be enhanced to establish a trustworthy and efficient food supply chain in the future? (4) What are the primary advantages of implementing supply chain in agriculture?

Current efforts to improve and modernize agriculture are seeking new methods and advancements to create a more open and trustworthy environment in the industry. One of the innovative solutions being explored is the use of blockchain technology. Unlike traditional centralized agricultural systems, blockchain utilizes a decentralized system for storing and accessing data that can be shared among multiple parties who may not necessarily trust each other. Blockchain is a digital database that is managed and updated using cryptography. Each member of the blockchain system has a copy of all previous transactions processed through the system. This enables the establishment of a structured and reliable system to ensure food safety and financial benefits for all participants engaged in the food distribution network. However, the system is decentralized, meaning that no single party or node controls it, making it a secure and transparent system. In order for transactions to occur, a consensus must be reached among a majority of nodes, making it a verifiable and trustworthy system for all participants. In other words, for a transaction to occur, a set of rules and procedures, known as a compliance algorithm, must be followed to ensure the agreement and validation of all parties involved. This process is irreversible and eliminates the need for intermediaries, making the system autonomous. Trust between participants is established through a foolproof system of rules and codes.

LITERATURE REVIEW

In Revathy and Sathya Priya (2020), blockchain based producer consumer model (BPCM) aims to bridge the gap between farmers and consumers by enabling direct transactions through a blockchain-based platform. The purpose is to eliminate intermediaries, provide transparency and control over prices for farmers, and ensure quality for consumers. The deliverables include a BPCM with unique identities for all participants and smart contracts that authenticate transactions. The challenges include the vulnerability of IoT devices to security attacks, such as DoS, energy exhaustion, node capture, and Sybil attacks. The gaps in the literature include a lack of research on the effectiveness of BPCM and the need for further investigation into the security of IoT devices in blockchain-based systems. The inference is that BPCM can enhance the trust and transparency of all transactions, but its implementation must address security concerns. The methodology used is Ethereum, a public blockchain that operates in a permissionless environment, with nodes connected in a blockchain. The advantages of BPCM are transparency, no travel, no rent, and no middleman, while the disadvantages are security risks and the need for further research.

Ur Rahman, Baiardi, and Ricci (2019) proposes a blockchain-based smart contract system for efficient and secure data sharing in smart agriculture. The system incentivizes stakeholders to contribute data, improving trust and sharing. Challenges include data privacy and limitations of the Ethereum blockchain. The system is developed using C++ and deployed on the EOS blockchain platform with lower transaction costs. A prototype for smart irrigation is included. Challenges include scalability, transaction fees, and the need for further research. The system has the potential to revolutionize data sharing and decision-making in smart agriculture.

Suresh Patil et al. (2021) proposes a framework for secure smart greenhouse farming using blockchain technology to address challenges in the agriculture industry. It integrates blockchain with smart farming techniques to create a transparent and secure system. The framework includes sensor devices, a blockchain network, smart contracts, and a user interface. It improves transparency, traceability, security, and reduces costs. Challenges include integrating sensor devices, ensuring scalability, and developing robust smart contracts. The authors believe the benefits outweigh the costs, but acknowledge the need for specialized knowledge. Economic feasibility and environmental impact are important considerations. This study (Ruan et al., 2020), a blockchain-based solution for tracking agricultural products using IoT sensors and a secure data storage system. The system improves food safety, reduces fraud, and enhances transparency. Scalability and privacy concerns need to be addressed. The study demonstrates the potential of blockchain technology in various industries. Liu, Xu, and Wang (2019) explores the use of blockchain in the food supply chain system in China to enhance food safety. Blockchain improves traceability and reliability, addressing credit risks and a lack of traceability in the traditional food management model. The study suggests conducting a PEST analysis to assess the influences of political, economic, social, and technological factors on blockchain implementation.

Alsharidah and Alazzawi (2020) explores the impact of artificial intelligence (AI) and digital transformation (DT) on supply chain management (SCM) in private organizations in Saudi Arabia. The study collected data from 95 employees and supply chain staff through an online questionnaire and employed descriptive statistics and linear regression for analysis. The findings indicated that AI and DT have a positive and significant influence on SCM, specifically in terms of improving quality standards, flexibility, efficiency, and productivity. The study suggests that to achieve intelligent supply chain management, organizations should focus on cost reduction, risk assessment, blockchain implementation, resource sustainability, and idea-sharing to enhance the SCM process and overall supply chain performance. The paper emphasizes the significance of E-procurement, Industry 4.0, and risk management in logistics and supply chain. Overall, the study concludes that AI and DT play a vital role in enhancing business productivity and improving supply chain management in Saudi Arabian companies.

Lin et al. (2019) explores the application of blockchain technology in e-agriculture, proposing a secure and decentralized system for managing agricultural data and transactions. It discusses various approaches to implementing blockchain, including permissioned and permissionless blockchain, as well as the use of smart contracts. The paper suggests a framework that combines blockchain and IoT to facilitate real-time monitoring and data sharing among stakeholders in the agricultural value chain. It acknowledges the technical challenges associated with implementing blockchain and highlights the need for further research, the development of standards, and best practices for blockchain-based e-agriculture systems. The conclusion emphasizes that employing blockchain in e-agriculture has the potential to enhance economic efficiencies, mitigate risks, and support sustainable agricultural development.

Kumar and Iyengar (2018) explores the use of blockchain technology to improve rice supply chain management in India. By integrating blockchain, the system becomes more transparent, secure, and decentralized. The authors discuss the stages of the rice supply chain and propose an example application where members register themselves and store key information in digital profiles on the blockchain. Implementing blockchain in the rice supply chain can reduce fraud, tampering, and information falsification, while enhancing transparency, traceability, efficiency, and trust among stakeholders.

Kaur and Parashar (2019) discusses how blockchain technology is being applied in smart villages to address various challenges faced by rural communities, including lack of access to basic services, inefficient governance systems, and inadequate infrastructure. The study found that the use of blockchain technology in smart villages has the potential to transform the way these communities operate and can lead to the creation of more efficient and sustainable communities. However, there are challenges and limitations associated with the adoption of blockchain technology in rural areas, including issues related to scalability, technical expertise, and limited internet connectivity. The paper reviews several use cases of blockchain technology for smart villages, such as land registries, supply chain management, and decentralized energy systems, and identifies future research directions for exploring the potential of blockchain technology in smart villages.

Galvez et al. (2020) explores the use of blockchain technology for food traceability. It highlights the potential benefits of blockchain in creating transparency and trust in the food supply chain. However, the paper also identifies challenges such as standardization, data management, and user-friendly interfaces. The review emphasizes the need for careful consideration, industry-wide standards, and addressing cost and scalability issues for successful implementation. Kamilaris et al. (2019) explores the benefits and challenges of implementing blockchain technology in agriculture and the food supply chain. It highlights improved transparency, traceability, and reduced fraud and waste as potential advantages. Successful implementations, such as Walmart's produce tracking and IBM and Maersk's shipping container tracking, are discussed. However, challenges like regulatory compliance, scalability, and interoperability are acknowledged. The authors propose a framework for implementing blockchain in the food industry, involving infrastructure establishment, data management, traceability, and automation through smart contracts and decentralized applications. Collaboration among industry stakeholders is emphasized for widespread adoption. Overall, this paper provides valuable insights and a practical implementation framework for blockchain technology in the food industry.

Pearson et al. (2020) explores the use of Distributed Ledger Technologies (DLTs) for food traceability. DLTs offer secure and unalterable records of food product movement, preventing fraud and ensuring consumer satisfaction. Enhanced transparency and simplified supply chains are additional benefits. However, challenges include the willingness of all supply chain actors to participate and the complexity and cost of implementation, especially for smaller producers. The authors recommend providing incentives for participation, such as reduced insurance premiums or access to new markets. Overall, DLTs show potential for improving food traceability, but further research is needed to address implementation challenges and promote stakeholder engagement. The proposed solution AgriBlockIoT (Caro et al., 2019) combines blockchain, IoT, and smart contract technologies to address transparency, traceability, and auditability in the agri-food supply chain. IoT sensors collect data stored on a blockchain network, while smart contracts automate supply chain operations, reducing middlemen and increasing efficiency. Benefits include improved transparency, traceability, fraud reduction, food safety, and consumer trust. Challenges include cost, cooperation among supply chain parties, and secure maintenance of IoT devices and blockchain nodes. The authors plan to evaluate the system's performance with real IoT devices in the Agri-Food supply chain. AgriBlockIoT offers an innovative solution to revolutionize the agri-food industry, improving production, distribution, and consumer confidence in the food we consume.

Kamble and Gunasekaran (2020) proposes a methodology for implementing a blockchain-enabled traceability system in the agricultural supply chain. The objective is to promote transparency, accountability, and consumer trust while mitigating food fraud. The architecture consists of layers, including the application layer, smart contract layer, blockchain layer, and hardware layer. Simulations show that the system can handle a large number of transactions with low latency, suitable for real-time tracking of agricultural products. Benefits include increased transparency, improved food safety, and fair prices for farmers by reducing intermediaries. Challenges include high costs, lack of standardization, and regulatory hurdles. Future research should focus on hardware and software solutions, exploring blockchain technology in other agricultural areas, and developing standards and regulations for scalability and interoperability.

Rejeb, Keogh, and Treiblmaier (2020) examines the integration of IoT and blockchain technology in supply chain management. The proposed architecture includes IoT devices, edge computing, blockchain, and cloud computing to improve efficiency, security, and transparency. Advantages include enhanced traceability, transparency, and security. Challenges include data privacy, scalability, and interoperability. The authors suggest future research on standardized protocols, legal and ethical considerations, and empirical studies. They also propose exploring smart contracts, artificial intelligence, and 5G networks. Overall, the paper presents a promising approach for supply chain management, but further research is needed to overcome challenges and maximize its potential. Wang, Singgiha, Wang, and Rit (2019) explores the potential impact of blockchain technology on supply chains. It highlights blockchain's features and potential use cases in supply chain management. The paper proposes that blockchain can address challenges related to visibility, efficiency, and security in supply chains. It discusses how blockchain enables secure and transparent transactions, improves traceability and visibility, and reduces costs and inefficiencies. The creation of a shared and decentralized database for tracking goods across the supply chain using blockchain is explained. Smart contracts are also discussed for automated contract execution. The paper analyzes the advantages (transparency, efficiency, security, cost reduction) and disadvantages (scalability, regulatory challenges, IT infrastructure requirements) of using blockchain in supply chains.

Sudha, Kalaiselvi, and Shanmughasundaram (2021) proposes using blockchain technology to improve supply chain management in the Indian agricultural sector. The current system lacks monitoring and tracking, resulting in lower prices for farmers and goods wastage. The blockchain-based system aims to increase transparency by providing visibility to farmers and officials. It includes features like checkpoints, goods status verification, and immutable records. Blockchain ensures data integrity and transparency, eliminating interference from intermediaries. IoT sensors monitor goods' condition, and data is stored on the blockchain. Testing the system showed significant improvements. Challenges include initial investment and stakeholder participation. Overall, blockchain and IoT can enhance transparency and quality control, benefiting farmers and improving supply chain efficiency. Tse, Zhang, Yang, Cheng, and Mu (2018) addresses food safety concerns in China and proposes the use of Blockchain technology to improve product quality and safety management. Blockchain provides a tamper-proof record, replacing traditional paper tracking and manual monitoring systems. It ensures traceability and reliability in the food supply chain, meeting the needs of governments, enterprises, and consumers. The authors conducted a demand analysis and applied Blockchain technology to build a supply chain system platform. Challenges include implementation cost and stakeholder cooperation. Blockchain has the potential to revolutionize the food supply chain, but further efforts are required.

Lin, Chen, Jiang, He, and Zeng (2021) conducts a systematic literature review to explore the potential of blockchain technology in agricultural systems. It covers applications in crop management, supply chain, and food safety. The review reveals that blockchain can enhance supply chain management by providing a secure and transparent system to track products. It improves traceability, reduces fraud, and increases consumer trust. Blockchain also facilitates secure payments, reduces costs, and promotes sustainable agriculture practices. However, challenges include high implementation costs, technical expertise, regulatory barriers, and data privacy concerns. The authors call for empirical studies and propose future research directions, such as interoperable and scalable blockchain solutions, precision agriculture, and economic and environmental impacts. The study offers a comprehensive overview of blockchain in agriculture, highlighting challenges and gaps for further exploration. Vijay et al. (2019) explores the challenges of transparency and security in the rice industry's supply chain and proposes blockchain technology as a solution. The article highlights the use of Hyperledger Fabric blockchain in the Grain chain system to track commodities. The analysis demonstrates the effectiveness of permissioned blockchains in improving transparency and security. The study concludes that the proposed solution using Hyperledger Fabric enhances accountability, security, and transparency in the agricultural supply chain. Overall, the article showcases the potential benefits of blockchain, specifically Hyperledger Fabric, in agriculture supply chain management.

Johny and Priyadharsini (2021) explores the implementation of blockchain technology with IoT in the supply chain to address issues of corruption and lack of trust. The blockchain system ensures transparency, traceability, and efficiency by eliminating intermediaries and authorities. RFID technology and smart tags are used to track and automate the process, and GPS sensors monitor product transportation. The blockchain system enables producers to generate the genesis blocks, distributors to take ownership, and retailers to record product details. Customers can transparently view the product's history before purchasing. The article concludes that implementing blockchain with IoT can enhance transparency, efficiency, and solve supply chain challenges. The paper analyzes the potential use cases of blockchain technology in supply chain management, emphasizing its benefits in tracking product origin, ensuring compliance, reducing fraud, and improving logistics. It suggests that blockchain implementation can enhance efficiency, security, and customer satisfaction. However, the paper notes gaps in empirical evidence for the claimed benefits and the impact on the workforce. Further research is needed to validate these claims and explore workforce implications.

Wang and Li (2006) analyzes the potential use cases of blockchain technology in supply chain management, emphasizing its benefits in tracking product origin, ensuring compliance, reducing fraud, and improving logistics. It suggests that blockchain implementation can enhance efficiency, security, and customer satisfaction. However, the paper notes gaps in empirical evidence for the claimed benefits and the impact on the workforce. Further research is needed to validate these claims and explore workforce implications. Kelepouris, Pramatari, and Doukidis (2007) discusses the importance of traceability in the food industry and proposes an integrated solution to address challenges faced by a British meat processing company. The proposed solution combines an IT-based traceability system with production, quality, and package coding management. The authors identify areas where traceability can add value in the supply chain, including production efficiency, quality improvement, promotion management, and dynamic pricing. The solution includes parameters that influence risk factors and provides additional traceability information on each finished product pack. Implementation of the proposed solution is expected to improve risk assessment, raw material utilization, inventory levels, waste reduction, and automated traceability data generation.

Conti (2020) examines the use of RFID technology for food supply chain traceability and safety. RFID tags can be attached to food products to track their location and condition. The paper finds that RFID technology can improve traceability, identify contamination sources, reduce foodborne illnesses, and prevent counterfeit products. Factors such as tag type, infrastructure, and integration with other systems affect the system's performance. Successful implementation requires planning, infrastructure investment, and stakeholder collaboration. RFID technology offers a competitive advantage in the food industry by improving safety and efficiency.

Gui, Wang, Zhang, and Yang (2009) proposes a traceability system for the fruit and vegetable supply chain using RFID tags and blockchain technology. The system enables real-time tracking and ensures the immutability and transparency of information. Tested in a tomato supply chain case study, it showed high performance in accuracy, reliability, and transparency. The system improves food safety, quality, waste reduction, consumer trust, and supply chain management. Challenges include implementation cost and stakeholder cooperation. The paper concludes that the proposed traceability system is effective but requires collaboration from all stakeholders. Wang et al. (2021) emphasizes the importance of traceability systems in agri-food supply chain management. It highlights incidents like the Sanlu infant milk powder contamination in China and the pet food contamination in the US to underscore the need for traceability. The authors argue that self-constructed traceability systems are cost-effective and enhance consumer confidence, market competitiveness, and regulatory compliance. They propose a theoretical model that includes standardized identification, data management, and stakeholder participation. Regular audits and inspections are also highlighted. The paper offers practical recommendations for companies considering a self-constructed traceability system and emphasizes the role of traceability in ensuring food safety and quality in the supply chain.

Tsang et al. (2019) proposes a traceability system for agricultural food supply chains that utilizes blockchain technology and smart contracts. The system aims to improve transparency, efficiency, and security. It consists of data collection, storage, processing, and retrieval components and can be integrated with IoT devices for real-time data collection. Simulation results showed that the proposed system outperformed traditional systems in terms of efficiency, transparency, and security. It offers advantages such as increased transparency and consumer trust. However, the high cost and technical expertise required may hinder adoption. The authors conclude that the proposed smart contract-based traceability system has the potential to enhance food safety, reduce fraud, and increase consumer trust.

Bhutta and Ahmad (2021) uses IoT sensors to collect data at different stages of the food supply chain, which is stored on a blockchain for immutability. An integrated consensus mechanism ensures data accuracy and consistency. The system provides end-to-end traceability and demonstrated good performance in terms of speed and scalability. It offers advantages such as transparency, food safety, and fraud reduction. The use of blockchain technology builds trust between consumers and producers. The paper concludes that the proposed system provides a reliable and transparent method for food traceability. Tharatipyakul and Pongnumkul (2021) proposes an IoT-based Supply Chain Management (SCM) system for secure identification, traceability, and real-time tracking of agricultural food supply during transportation. The system includes sensors, RFID tags, GPS devices, and a centralized database with security measures. It offers advantages such as improved food safety, transparency, traceability, reduced waste, and efficient supply chain management. The main drawback is the cost of IoT devices and the need for additional training. Overall, the proposed system provides a secure and efficient solution for food supply chain management using IoT technology to enhance food safety and prevent fraud.

Salah et al. (2019) conducts a systematic review of the UI design of blockchain-based agri-food traceability applications. The authors analyze existing literature and identify key design features and challenges. They emphasize the importance of effective UI design for usability and effectiveness. Key features include data visualization, search, input, and user feedback. Challenges include standardization, complexity of blockchain, and lack of user awareness. The paper recommends improvements such as clear language, intuitive navigation, and visual design. Standardization and user awareness are also highlighted. Effective UI design is crucial for the success and adoption of blockchain-based agri-food traceability applications. Zhang et al. (2020) proposes a blockchain-based solution for traceability in the soybean supply chain. It utilizes a permissioned blockchain to record transactions and movements of soybeans, ensuring authenticity, quality, and safety. Participants have unique digital identities and access the blockchain for verification. The solution leverages blockchain's transparency and immutability for decentralized traceability. Smart contracts on the Ethereum blockchain handle functions like verifying soybean authenticity, handling disputes, and calculating payments. The system improves efficiency, accountability, and reduces transaction time and cost. A simulation model demonstrates a potential 40% reduction in transaction time and cost compared to traditional methods. Challenges include scalability, governance, privacy, and standards. Further research is needed to optimize the system's performance and address these issues.

Architecture for the "Food Safety Traceability System based on Blockchain and EPCIS" includes key components like a mobile application, a blockchain-based platform, an EPCIS-based platform, data analytics, and a user interface (Lin et al., 2019). Farmers input production and distribution data through the mobile app, stored on the blockchain-based platform. Smart contracts validate and verify the data. The EPCIS-based platform tracks and traces products in the supply chain using EPCIS messages. Data analytics and visualization tools process and analyze the collected data, providing insights into supply chain performance. The system achieved accurate tracing and tracking of eggs from farm to supermarket. Disadvantages include high implementation and maintenance costs, complexity, the need for standardized data formats and protocols, and privacy and security risks associated with public blockchain storage and sharing.

Dong et al. (2019) proposes a private blockchain-based safety management system for the grain supply chain. The system uses RFID technology, multiple nodes with unique public keys, and smart contracts to store and validate information about grain origin, quality, and safety. Components include a grain safety data platform, a supervision platform, and a traceability system. The system aims to ensure integrity, transparency, and security by using smart contracts for data validation. It can improve efficiency, accuracy, and safety while reducing costs. Challenges include investment in blockchain technology and data privacy and security concerns. Advantages include increased efficiency, accuracy, transparency, and food safety. Further research is needed to address limitations and challenges. In Madumidha et al. (2019), the authors propose a traceability system for the leafy vegetable supply chain in China. The system utilizes

QR code technology and fault tree analysis methodology. QR codes are used to label vegetable batches and record information such as origin, production date, and quality inspection results. A cloud-based database links this information for access by different parties along the supply chain. Fault tree analysis identifies risks, and a risk assessment model evaluates their likelihood and consequences. Preventive and control measures are established. A case study in a Chinese vegetable production area demonstrates the system's effectiveness in tracking and monitoring vegetable quality and safety. Advantages include improved food safety, quality control, and supply chain transparency. The system offers a reliable solution for addressing food safety and quality control in China's leafy vegetable supply chain.

Johny and Priyadharsini (2021) explores the use of blockchain technology and IoT in the food supply chain to improve transparency and traceability. It discusses the limitations of the traditional supply chain system and introduces blockchain features and implementation platforms. The article also explains how RFID and GPS sensors can track product movement. Advantages of the proposed system include efficient tracking, avoidance of third-party involvement, and data safety through RFID tags. Challenges discussed include privacy concerns, regulatory issues, and technological challenges. The integration of blockchain, IoT, and RFID can enhance transparency, traceability, and overall efficiency in the food supply chain.

Nguyen, Tuong, and Pham (2020) examines the potential of blockchain technology in enhancing supply chain management. The authors conducted a literature review and proposed a framework for implementing blockchain in supply chain networks. They discussed the benefits of blockchain, including increased transparency, traceability, security, cost reduction, efficiency improvement, and better collaboration. However, they also addressed challenges such as standardization, interoperability, scalability, complexity, and costs. The authors emphasized the need for further research and recommended collaborative efforts among supply chain stakeholders to establish common standards and protocols for blockchain implementation in supply chains.

Dong and Fu (2021) presents a blockchain-based solution for traceability and authenticity in the Community Supported Agriculture (CSA) model. The proposed system enables farmers to record production details on a blockchain, providing transparency and assurance to consumers about product quality and safety. The solution is particularly suitable for small businesses in the CSA model. The paper emphasizes the global concern over food safety and the need to address this issue in the CSA model. By offering a way to demonstrate the quality and authenticity of agricultural products, the proposed system aims to overcome consumer hesitations and enhance the CSA model.

Tharatipyakul et al. (2021) proposes a blockchain-based framework for smart agriculture, integrating IoT and AI to enhance productivity and efficiency. The framework involves data collection, analysis, storage, transaction execution, and service delivery. Benefits include increased transparency, reduced costs, improved food safety, and enhanced traceability. However, challenges such as reliable IoT devices, efficient AI algorithms, and regulatory barriers need to be addressed. The authors emphasize the potential of blockchain-based smart agriculture but suggest further research on IoT devices, AI algorithms, and legal considerations. Thejaswini and K. (2020) evaluates a blockchain-based traceability system for the Thai coffee supply chain from users' perspective. The system combines blockchain and IoT technology to track coffee beans. Data from 100 users was collected to assess effectiveness and acceptance. Results show improved transparency, traceability, reduced time, and cost. Challenges include IoT device reliability and affordability, and blockchain complexity. User acceptance is influenced by perceived usefulness, ease of use, and trust. Advantages include transparency, traceability, and efficiency for all stakeholders. Disadvantages involve IoT device reliability, affordability, and blockchain complexity.

The paper explores the potential applications of blockchain technology in agriculture, proposing a decentralized peer-to-peer network with smart contracts for secure and transparent record-keeping. Use cases discussed include supply chain management, land registry, and crop insurance. Blockchain's potential to enhance efficiency, transparency, and security is highlighted, enabling farmers to track crops, reduce transaction time and costs, and improve record-keeping accuracy. Challenges identified include the need for reliable internet connectivity, blockchain complexity, and user education. Advantages encompass improved efficiency, transparency, and security, benefiting farmers, consumers, and stakeholders. The authors propose a decentralized network using smart contracts for implementation. Overall, blockchain technology has the potential to revolutionize agriculture by improving efficiency, transparency, and security. Shakhbulatov et al. (2019) proposes a development path for smart agriculture using blockchain technology, integrating IoT and AI to enhance productivity and efficiency. The framework involves data collection, analysis, storage, transactions, and end-user services. Benefits include transparency, reduced costs, food safety, and traceability. Challenges include reliable IoT devices, complex AI algorithms, and regulatory barriers. Implementing blockchain-based smart agriculture requires overcoming technical, economic, and regulatory challenges, with focus on efficient IoT devices, accurate AI algorithms, and addressing legal barriers in agriculture.

The paper proposes a blockchain-based solution for tracking and analyzing the carbon footprint of the food supply chain. The system uses smart contracts and a proof-of-stake consensus mechanism to automate data collection and ensure data integrity. Blockchain technology improves transparency, traceability, and accuracy of carbon emissions data. Stakeholders can track their product's carbon footprint and identify emission reduction opportunities. Advantages include improved transparency and accuracy of carbon emissions data. Challenges include standardized data collection and system implementation costs. Future research should focus on user-friendly and affordable blockchain-based systems for carbon emissions tracking in the food supply chain.

Umamaheswari et al. (2019) propose BIoT, a blockchain-based solution for enhancing the efficiency and transparency of agricultural supply chains. BIoT integrates IoT devices to collect data on agricultural parameters, stored securely on a blockchain platform. A smart contract-based payment system ensures fair compensation for farmers. The system aims to address unfair compensation, reduce food waste, and improve produce quality. BIoT has potential to transform agriculture through improved efficiency, transparency, and fairness. Advantages include transparency, fairness, reduced food waste, and improved produce quality. Disadvantages include implementation cost, complexity, and interoperability challenges. Future research should focus on user-friendly and affordable blockchain-based systems, as well as addressing interoperability between IoT devices and blockchain platforms.

DISCUSSION

Although the digital transformation of the agricultural supply chain can potentially offer numerous benefits, challenges pertaining to adoption and accessibility are major obstacles. As Barrett and Rose have pointed out, farmers who lack knowledge to adopt new technologies can be deprived of the significant benefits they provide, and the high costs of technology and lack of rural digital infrastructure can also hinder their adoption. Precision agriculture can greatly enhance its productivity by utilizing sensors to monitor crops. Incorporating blockchain technology into the supply chain can effectively store and share data. Nonetheless, it is vital to assess farmers' technical knowledge to bridge the divide between intricate technical solutions and end-users. Organizations frequently prioritize short-term outcomes, and they struggle to address unique difficulties. Businesses also encounter significant difficulties with blockchain technology, such as the high cost of data transactions and potential privacy breaches. Cheaper consensus protocols could create gaps in decentralization, security, scalability, and transparency of the blockchain. The utilization of technology is vital to increasing agricultural production yield, facilitating accessibility to the Fourth AR, and contributing to food security. However, there are existing security and transparency concerns associated with IoT systems used in agriculture. These issues can be effectively addressed by integrating blockchain technology. The proposed solution aims to overcome obstacles related to the adoption of blockchain and IoT, with the ultimate goal of minimizing and eliminating them entirely.

Figure 1. Proposed model architectural diagram
Note. This figure demonstrates the process of agricultural supply chain within blockchain environment

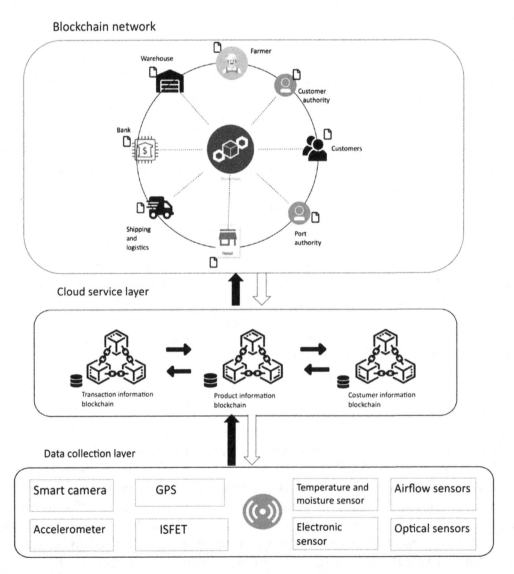

Blockchain technology has the potential to revolutionize the agricultural supply chain by improving transparency, traceability, and efficiency. Nevertheless, the deployment of such systems comes with its own set of challenges. One major issue is the lack of standardization and interoperability between different blockchain-based platforms and IoT devices. This can lead to fragmentation and inefficiencies in the supply chain, as stakeholders may not be able to access or share data across different platforms. Another challenge is the potential cost and complexity of implementing blockchain-based systems, which may require significant investment in new infrastructure, hardware, and software. Moreover, it is necessary to reliable and standardized methods for collecting and reporting data on various aspects of agriculture, such as carbon emissions, soil quality, and water usage. Without such methods, the data stored on blockchain-based platforms may be incomplete or inaccurate, reducing the effectiveness of the systems. Finally, there is a need to ensure that all stakeholders in the agricultural supply chain can benefit from blockchain-based systems, including small-scale farmers and workers, who may not have the resources or expertise to implement such systems on their own. Despite these challenges, blockchain technology has the potential to transform the agricultural sector by improving efficiency, transparency, and fairness in the supply chain, and by promoting sustainable and environmentally friendly practices are to be encouraged.

CONCLUSION

There is a need for further research and advancement in this field is required to gain a deeper comprehension of potential of blockchain and related technologies in agriculture and food supply chain management, and to develop effective solutions to the challenges that arise. In conclusion, the implementation of blockchain technology in the agriculture industry has the potential to transform supply chain management and enable farmers to access real-time market data, track their crops and stored goods, and receive fair prices for their produce. Blockchain technology offers a decentralized, secure, and transparent system for storing and accessing data, which can be shared among multiple parties, eliminating the need for intermediaries. Blockchain technology also enhances transparency, efficiency, and safety in the food supply chain, providing customers with greater confidence in the products they purchase. The use of blockchain technology can ensure food safety and quality by providing traceability throughout the entire supply chain, from production to retail, and providing a transparent and auditable system for tracking products and monitoring various environmental and processing conditions. To realize the full potential of blockchain technology in agriculture, it is important to address the obstacles faced by these blockchain applications during deployment and enhance the technology to establish a trustworthy and efficient food supply chain in the future.

REFERENCES

Alsharidah, Y. M. Y., & Alazzawi, A. (2020). Artificial Intelligence and Digital Transformation in Supply Chain Management: A Case Study in Saudi Companies. In *2020 International Conference on Data Analytics for Business and Industry: Way Towards a Sustainable Economy (ICDABI)* (pp. 1-6). 10.1109/ICDABI51230.2020.9325616

Bhutta, M. N. M., & Ahmad, M. (2021). Secure identification, traceability and real-time tracking of agricultural food supply during transportation using internet of things. *IEEE Access : Practical Innovations, Open Solutions*, *9*, 65660–65675. doi:10.1109/ACCESS.2021.3076373

Caro, M. P., Ali, M. S., Vecchio, M., & Giaffreda, R. (2019). Blockchain-based traceability in agri-food supply chain management: A practical implementation. *Sensors (Basel)*, *19*(14), 3190. PMID:31331085

Conti, M. (2020). Food traceability in fruit and vegetables supply chain. In *2020 IEEE International Symposium on Circuits and Systems (ISCAS)* (pp. 1-5). IEEE. 10.1109/ISCAS45731.2020.9181294

Dong, N., & Fu, J. (2021). Development Path of Smart Agriculture Based on Blockchain. In *2021 IEEE Asia-Pacific Conference on Image Processing, Electronics and Computers (IPEC)*. IEEE. 10.1109/IPEC51340.2021.9421125

Dong, Y., Fu, Z., Stankovski, S., Wang, S., & Li, X. (2019). Nutritional Quality and Safety Traceability System for China's Leafy Vegetable Supply Chain based on Fault Tree Analysis and QR Code. *IEEE Access : Practical Innovations, Open Solutions*, *7*, 187881–187893.

Galvez, J. F., Mejuto, J. C., & Simal-Gandara, J. (2020). Future challenges on the use of blockchain for food traceability analysis. *Food Research International*, *136*, 109663.

Gui, S., Wang, F., Zhang, Z., & Yang, L. (2009). Research on self-constructed traceability system based on agri-food supply chain management. In *2009 Second International Conference on Intelligent Computation Technology and Automation* (pp. 640-643). IEEE. 10.1109/ICICTA.2009.700

Johny, S., & Priyadharsini, C. (2021). Investigations on the Implementation of Blockchain Technology in Supplychain Network. In *Proceedings of the 2021 7th International Conference on Advanced Computing and Communication Systems (ICACCS)* (pp. 294-299). IEEE. 10.1109/ICACCS51430.2021.9441820

Johny, S., & Priyadharsini, C. (2021). Investigations on the Implementation of Blockchain Technology in Supplychain Network. In *Proceedings of the 2021 7th International Conference on Advanced Computing and Communication Systems (ICACCS)* (pp. 294-299). 10.1109/ICACCS51430.2021.9441820

Kamble, S. S., & Gunasekaran, A. (2020). Modeling the blockchain enabled traceability in agriculture supply chain. *Annals of Operations Research*, 1–26. doi:10.100710479-020-03523-7

Kamilaris, A., Fonts, A., & Prenafeta-Boldú, F. X. (2019). The rise of blockchain technology in agriculture and food supply chains. *Trends in Food Science & Technology*, *91*, 640–652. doi:10.1016/j.tifs.2019.07.034

Kaur, P., & Parashar, A. (2019). A systematic literature review of blockchain technology for smart villages. *Journal of Theoretical and Applied Information Technology*, *97*(9), 2688–2703.

Kelepouris, T., Pramatari, K., & Doukidis, G. (2007). RFID-enabled traceability in the food supply chain. *Industrial Management & Data Systems*, *107*(2), 183–200. doi:10.1108/02635570710723804

Kumar, M. V., & Iyengar, N. C. S. N. (2018). A framework for blockchain technology in rice supply chain management. *International Journal of Pure and Applied Mathematics*, *119*(16), 1759–1768.

Lin, Q., Wang, H., Pei, X., & Wang, J. (2019). Food safety traceability system based on blockchain and EPCIS. *IEEE Access : Practical Innovations, Open Solutions, 7*, 128442–128452. doi:10.1109/ACCESS.2019.2897792

Lin, W., Chen, J., Jiang, L., He, S., & Zeng, L. (2021). Blockchain Technology in Current Agricultural Systems: From Techniques to Applications. *IEEE Access : Practical Innovations, Open Solutions, 9*, 49916–49926. doi:10.1109/ACCESS.2021.3069664

Lin, Y. P., Petway, J. R., Anthony, J., Mukhtar, H., Liao, S. W., Chou, C. F., & Ho, Y. F. (2019). Blockchain: The Evolutionary Next Step for ICT E-Agriculture. *Agrárinformatika Folyóirat, 10*(2), 1–17. doi:10.2478/jai-2019-0002

Madumidha, S., Ranjani, P. S., Varsinee, S. S., & Sundari, P. S. (2019). Transparency and Traceability: In Food Supply Chain System using Blockchain Technology with Internet of Things. *2019 3rd International Conference on Trends in Electronics and Informatics (ICOEI),* 1316-1321. 10.1109/ICOEI.2019.8862726

Madumidha, S., Ranjani, P. S., Varsinee, S. S., & Sundari, P. S. (2019). Transparency and Traceability: In Food Supply Chain System using Blockchain Technology with Internet of Things. In *Proceedings of the 2019 3rd International Conference on Trends in Electronics and Informatics (ICOEI)* (pp. 36-40). Academic Press.

Nguyen, D.-H., Tuong, N. H., & Pham, H.-A. (2020). Blockchain-based Farming Activities Tracker for Enhancing Trust in the Community Supported Agriculture Model. In *Proceedings of the 2020 International Conference on Information and Communication Technology Convergence (ICTC)* (pp. 1399-1404). IEEE. 10.1109/ICTC49870.2020.9289297

Pearson, S., Maya, D., Leontidis, G., Swainson, M., Brewer, S., Bidaut, L., & Zisman, A. (2020). Are distributed ledger technologies the panacea for food traceability? *Global Food Security, 27*, 100418.

Rejeb, A., Keogh, J. G., & Treiblmaier, H. (2020). Leveraging the Internet of Things and Blockchain Technology in Supply Chain Management. *International Journal of Information Management, 52*, 101993. doi:10.1016/j.ijinfomgt.2019.10.006

Revathy, S., & Sathya Priya, S. (n.d.). *Blockchain based Producer-Consumer Model for Farmers.* Department of Computer Science & Engineering, Hindustan Institute of Technology and Science.

Salah, K., Nizamuddin, N., Jayaraman, R., & Omar, M. (2019). Blockchain-based soybean traceability in agricultural supply chain. *IEEE Access : Practical Innovations, Open Solutions, 7*, 97935–97946. doi:10.1109/ACCESS.2019.2918000

Shakhbulatov, D., Arora, A., Dong, Z., & Rojas-Cessa, R. (2019). Blockchain Implementation for Analysis of Carbon Footprint across Food Supply Chain. In *2019 IEEE International Conference on Blockchain (Blockchain)* (pp. 382-387). IEEE. 10.1109/Blockchain.2019.00079

Sudha, V., Kalaiselvi, R., & Shanmughasundaram, P. (2021). Blockchain based solution to improve the Supply Chain Management in Indian agriculture. *2021 International Conference on Artificial Intelligence and Smart Systems (ICAIS).* 10.1109/ICAIS50930.2021.9395867

Suresh Patil, A., Adhi Tama, B., Park, Y., & Rhee, K.-H. (2019). *A Framework for Blockchain Based Secure Smart Green House Farming. Interdisciplinary Program of Information Security.* Graduate School, Pukyong National University.

Tharatipyakul, A., & Pongnumkul, S. (2021). User interface of blockchain-based agri-food traceability applications: A review. *IEEE Access : Practical Innovations, Open Solutions*, 9, 82909–82929. doi:10.1109/ACCESS.2021.3085982

Tharatipyakul, A., Pongnumkul, S., Riansumrit, N., Kingchan, S., & Pongnumkul, S. (2021). Blockchain-Based Traceability System From the Users' Perspective: A Case Study of Thai Coffee Supply Chain. In *Proceedings of the 14th International Joint Conference on Computer Science and Software Engineering (JCSSE)* (pp. 1-6). IEEE.

Thejaswini, S., & K., R. R. (2020). Blockchain in Agriculture by using Decentralized Peer to Peer Networks. In *2020 Fourth International Conference on Inventive Systems and Control (ICISC)* (pp. 931-936). IEEE. 10.1109/ICISC47916.2020.9171083

Tsang, Y. P., Choy, K. L., Wu, C. H., Ho, G. T. S., & Lam, H. Y. (2019). Blockchain-driven IoT for food traceability with an integrated consensus mechanism. *IEEE Access : Practical Innovations, Open Solutions*, 7, 188433–188445. doi:10.1109/ACCESS.2019.2940227

Tse, D., Zhang, B., Yang, Y., Cheng, C., & Mu, H. (2018). *Blockchain Application in Food Supply Information Security.* Academic Press.

Tse, D., Zhang, B., Yang, Y., Cheng, C., & Mu, H. (2019). *Blockchain Application in Food Supply Information Security.* Department of Information Systems, City University of Hong Kong.

Umamaheswari, S., Sreeram, S., Kritika, N., & Jyothi Prasanth, D. R. (2019). BIoT: Blockchain based IoT for Agriculture. In *2019 11th International Conference on Advanced Computing (ICoAC)* (pp. 1-6). IEEE.

Ur Rahman, M., Baiardi, F., & Ricci, L. (2019). *Blockchain Smart Contract for Scalable Data Sharing in IoT: A Case Study of Smart Agriculture.* Department of Computer Science, University of Pisa.

Vijay, P., Shanthi, S., Revathy, R., & Ohja, S. (2019). Grainchain - Agricultural Supply Chain Traceability and Management technique for Farmers Sustainability Using Blockchain Hyper Ledger. *2019 IEEE International Conference on Blockchain (Blockchain)*, 430-434. doi: 10.1109/Blockchain.2019.000-9

Wang, L., Xu, L., Zheng, Z., Liu, S., Li, X., Cao, L., Li, J., & Sun, C. (2021). Smart contract-based agricultural food supply chain traceability. *IEEE Access : Practical Innovations, Open Solutions*, 9, 9296–9307. doi:10.1109/ACCESS.2021.3050112

Wang, X., & Li, D. (2006). Value added on food traceability: A supply chain management approach. In *2006 IEEE International Conference on Service Operations and Logistics, and Informatics* (pp. 1019-1024). IEEE. 10.1109/SOLI.2006.329074

Wang, Y., Singgiha, M., Wang, J., & Rit, M. (2019). Making sense of blockchain technology: How will it transform supply chains? *International Journal of Production Economics*, 211, 221–236. doi:10.1016/j.ijpe.2019.02.002

Xie, C., Sun, Y., & Luo, H. (2019). *Secured Data Storage Scheme based on Block Chain for Agricultural Products Tracking*. Beijing University of Posts and Telecommunications.

Zhang, X. (2020). Blockchain-based safety management system for the grain supply chain. In *Proceedings of the 2020 IEEE International Conference on Industrial Internet (ICII)* (pp. 847-852). IEEE. 10.1109/ACCESS.2020.2975415

Chapter 21
Blockchain–Based Messaging System for Secure and Private Communication:
Using Blockchain and Double AES Encryption

Shiva Chaithanya Goud Bollipelly
Vellore Institute of Technology, India

Prabu Sevugan
Pondicherry University, India

R. Venkatesan
SASTRA University, India

L. Sharmila
Agni College of Technology, India

ABSTRACT

In recent years, concerns about privacy and security in online communication have become increasingly prominent. To address these concerns, the authors propose a blockchain-based messaging system that provides secure and private communication using double AES encryption. The system utilizes the decentralized and tamper-resistant nature of the blockchain to ensure that messages are not modified or deleted by unauthorized parties. Additionally, they employ double AES encryption to ensure that the content of messages remains confidential even if the blockchain itself is compromised. They evaluate the performance of the system and show that it is scalable and efficient. The system provides a secure and private messaging solution that can be used by individuals and organizations alike.

DOI: 10.4018/978-1-6684-8098-4.ch021

INTRODUCTION

In today's digital age, the need for secure and private communication has become more important than ever. With increasing concerns over data breaches and privacy violations, individuals and organizations are searching for new ways to protect their sensitive information.

Blockchain technology has emerged as a potential solution for secure and private communication. Its decentralized nature makes it resistant to attacks and manipulation, and its transparency allows for easy verification of transactions. Additionally, the use of advanced encryption algorithms, such as AES, further enhances the security and privacy of blockchain-based communication systems.

In this project, we propose a blockchain-based messaging system with double AES encryption to provide secure and private communication. The messaging system will allow users to send and receive messages without the need for a third-party intermediary, thereby minimizing the risk of data breaches and privacy violations. The double encryption using AES will add an extra layer of security to the messages, ensuring that they can only be decrypted by the intended recipient.

Figure 1. Blockchain-based messaging system with double AES encryption

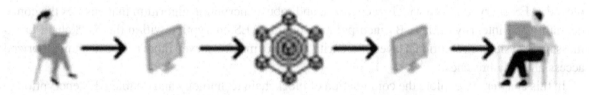

This project aims to provide a practical solution for secure and private communication using blockchain technology and AES encryption. By implementing and evaluating the proposed messaging system, we hope to demonstrate the feasibility and effectiveness of this approach, as well as identify areas for improvement. Ultimately, this project aims to contribute to the development of more secure and private communication systems in the digital age.

BLOCKCHAIN

In today's digital age, secure and private communication is of paramount importance. The increasing concerns over data breaches, privacy violations, and unauthorized access have prompted the exploration of new technologies to safeguard sensitive information. One such technology that holds great promise is blockchain.

Blockchain technology has emerged as a revolutionary concept that has the potential to transform various industries, including communication and data security. At its core, blockchain is a decentralized and distributed ledger system that ensures secure and transparent recording of transactions. It provides a tamper-proof and verifiable record of events, making it an ideal candidate for enhancing the security and privacy of communication systems.

The fundamental concept of blockchain revolves around the idea of blocks and transactions. Each block contains a list of verified transactions that are linked together using cryptographic hashes, forming a chain of blocks. This immutable chain of transactions is maintained by a network of participants, eliminating the need for a central authority and making it resistant to attacks and manipulation.

One of the key advantages of blockchain technology is its decentralized nature. Traditional messaging systems often rely on a central intermediary to facilitate communication. However, with blockchain, communication can occur directly between users without the need for a third-party intermediary. This decentralization reduces the risk of data breaches and privacy violations since there is no central point of failure that can be targeted by malicious actors.

Moreover, blockchain brings transparency to the communication process. While the content of messages may be encrypted for privacy, the metadata associated with transactions, such as timestamps and sender/receiver addresses, are generally visible to all participants. This transparency enhances accountability and trust, as participants can easily verify the integrity and authenticity of transactions.

Additionally, blockchain technology provides a distributed ledger, where all participants in the network maintain a copy of the blockchain. This distributed nature ensures that no single entity has complete control over the system, making it more resilient to attacks and data loss. It also enhances the reliability and availability of the messaging system by eliminating the reliance on a single point of failure.

To further bolster the security and privacy of the messaging system, double AES encryption is employed. AES encryption is a widely recognized and robust encryption algorithm that ensures the confidentiality and integrity of data. By incorporating double AES encryption within the blockchain-based messaging system, an additional layer of security is added, making it even more resilient to unauthorized access and data breaches.

In this chapter, we explore the combination of blockchain technology and double AES encryption to develop a secure and private messaging system. By leveraging the decentralized and transparent nature of blockchain and the strong encryption capabilities of AES, we aim to create a communication platform that addresses the vulnerabilities present in traditional messaging systems. Through the evaluation and analysis of the proposed system, we hope to demonstrate the feasibility and effectiveness of this approach and contribute to the development of more secure and private communication systems in the digital age.

ADVANCED ENCRYPTION STANDARD (AES) ALGORITHM

In the realm of secure messaging systems, encryption plays a vital role in safeguarding the confidentiality and integrity of data. One of the most widely used encryption algorithms is the Advanced Encryption Standard (AES). AES is a symmetric encryption algorithm that has been adopted as a standard by the U.S. government and is widely employed in various applications, including secure communication.

The AES algorithm is known for its strength, efficiency, and versatility in ensuring the privacy of sensitive information. It operates on blocks of data, typically 128 bits in length, and utilizes a series of transformations, including substitution, permutation, and bitwise operations, to encrypt and decrypt the data.

One of the key advantages of the AES algorithm is its security. It has been extensively analyzed and tested by cryptographic experts, and no practical attacks have been found against it. AES employs a key-based encryption approach, where the same key is used for both encryption and decryption, making it a symmetric encryption algorithm. The strength of AES lies in the key size, with options for 128-bit, 192-bit, and 256-bit keys, providing varying levels of security.

By employing double AES encryption within the proposed messaging system, an additional layer of security is added to protect the messages. Double AES encryption involves applying the AES algorithm twice in succession, using different keys for each encryption process. This approach enhances the encryption strength and makes it even more challenging for unauthorized parties to decrypt the messages without the correct keys.

In the context of the blockchain-based messaging system, the AES algorithm is utilized to encrypt the contents of the messages before they are stored on the blockchain. This ensures that even if the blockchain is accessed, the encrypted messages remain confidential and cannot be understood by unauthorized individuals.

The combination of blockchain technology and double AES encryption creates a robust and secure messaging system. The decentralized nature of the blockchain ensures the integrity and availability of the encrypted messages, while the double AES encryption guarantees their confidentiality. Together, these technologies provide a comprehensive solution for secure and private communication.

Throughout this chapter, we will explore the integration of the AES algorithm within the blockchain-based messaging system. We will discuss the encryption and decryption processes, the selection of appropriate key sizes, and the benefits of employing double AES encryption to enhance the security of the messaging system. By evaluating the effectiveness and feasibility of this approach, we aim to contribute to the development of secure and private communication systems that address the vulnerabilities present in traditional messaging systems.

DOUBLE ENCRYPTION

In the pursuit of enhanced security for messaging systems, employing multiple layers of encryption is a strategy that can significantly strengthen the protection of sensitive information. One approach to achieving this is through double encryption and double decryption, which involves applying encryption and decryption processes multiple times using different algorithms or keys.

Double encryption, also known as cascade encryption, is the process of encrypting data multiple times using different encryption algorithms or keys. By applying two or more encryption algorithms consecutively, the resulting ciphertext becomes increasingly difficult for unauthorized individuals to decrypt without the correct keys. Each encryption layer adds an additional level of complexity, making it more challenging to decipher the original message.

The purpose of double encryption is to provide an extra layer of security, as it requires an attacker to break through multiple encryption algorithms or crack multiple keys in order to access the original message. This additional complexity can significantly increase the effort and time required for unauthorized decryption attempts, providing a higher level of protection for sensitive communication.

On the other hand, double decryption refers to the process of decrypting data that has been encrypted using multiple layers of encryption. It involves reversing the encryption process by sequentially applying the corresponding decryption algorithms or keys. Each decryption layer removes one level of encryption, eventually revealing the original plaintext message.

The use of double encryption and double decryption can be particularly beneficial in the context of secure messaging systems. By employing double AES encryption, for example, alongside the blockchain-based messaging system, the confidentiality and integrity of the messages can be enhanced. Double AES encryption involves encrypting the messages twice using different keys, which significantly increases the encryption strength and makes it even more challenging for unauthorized parties to decrypt the messages without the correct keys.

Double decryption is performed in reverse order, applying the corresponding decryption algorithms or keys to decrypt the messages. The recipient of the message will sequentially decrypt the double-encrypted ciphertext using the correct decryption keys, revealing the original plaintext message.

In the proposed messaging system, the combination of blockchain technology, which ensures the integrity and availability of the messages, and double AES encryption, which provides an extra layer of confidentiality, creates a robust and secure communication environment. The double encryption and double decryption processes add an additional level of security to the system, making it more resilient to unauthorized access and decryption attempts.

Throughout this chapter, we will explore the implementation and benefits of double encryption and double decryption within the blockchain-based messaging system. We will discuss the encryption and decryption workflows, the selection of appropriate keys, and the advantages of employing this approach to strengthen the security and privacy of the messaging system. By evaluating the effectiveness and feasibility of double encryption and double decryption, we aim to contribute to the development of secure and private communication systems that address the vulnerabilities present in traditional messaging systems.

BACKGROUND

The proliferation of digital communication and the increasing amount of sensitive information being transmitted online has made secure and private communication more important than ever before (Nakamoto, 2008). Traditional communication methods, such as email and instant messaging, rely on centralized servers that act as intermediaries between senders and receivers. However, these systems are vulnerable to attacks and breaches, as seen in numerous high-profile cases over the past few years.

To address these vulnerabilities, blockchain technology has emerged as a potential solution. Blockchain is a decentralized, distributed ledger that allows for secure and transparent transactions without the need for intermediaries (Nakamoto, 2008). The technology provides a high degree of security due to its distributed nature, making it difficult for attackers to manipulate or corrupt the data.

Furthermore, blockchain can be used to create a decentralized messaging system, where messages are stored on the blockchain network and are accessible only to the intended recipient (Khacef & Pujolle, 2019). This ensures that messages are not intercepted or tampered with by third parties. However, while blockchain provides a secure communication platform, it does not provide encryption, which is essential for protecting the confidentiality of messages.

This is where the Advanced Encryption Standard (AES) comes into play. AES is a widely used encryption algorithm that provides a high degree of security and has been adopted as the standard by the U.S. government (National Institute of Standards and Technology, 2001). AES can be used to encrypt messages before they are stored on the blockchain, adding an extra layer of security to the communication process.

Several studies have explored the use of double encryption using AES in various contexts. For example, (Jaspin et al., 2021) proposed an efficient and secure file transfer system in the cloud using double encryption with AES and RSA algorithms. (Chandra et al., 2015) developed a content-based double encryption algorithm using symmetric key cryptography. (Rajput et al., 2013) introduced an improved cryptographic technique to encrypt text using double encryption.

In addition to text-based communication, encryption techniques have been applied to other forms of data as well. (Dutta et al., 2017) presented an audio encryption and decryption algorithm in image format for secure communication. (Aleqabie et al., 2014) explored classical image encryption and decryption methods.

The combination of blockchain technology and AES encryption can revolutionize the way people communicate online by providing a secure and private communication platform (Singh et al., 2021). It can address the increasing concerns over data breaches and privacy violations, offering a practical solution for secure communication in the digital age.

In summary, the combination of blockchain technology and AES encryption offers a promising approach for secure and private communication. By leveraging the decentralized nature of blockchain and the encryption strength of AES, a blockchain-based messaging system with double AES encryption can provide secure and private communication (Agrawal & Pal, 2017). This technology has the potential to enhance the security and privacy of digital communication, benefiting individuals and organizations alike.

SYSTEM ARCHITECTURE

The blockchain-based messaging system with double AES encryption comprises three main components: the client application, the blockchain network, and the message server.

Client Application: The client application is a software interface that allows users to send and receive messages securely. The application is responsible for encrypting messages using double AES encryption before they are sent to the blockchain network. The client application interacts with the message server to retrieve messages from the blockchain network and decrypt them using the recipient's private key.

Blockchain Network: The blockchain network is a distributed ledger that stores the encrypted messages. The network consists of a peer-to-peer network of nodes, with each node containing a copy of the blockchain. The blockchain network is responsible for verifying and validating transactions and ensuring that they are secure and tamper-proof. In our proposed messaging system, the blockchain network is used to store the encrypted messages, making it difficult for attackers to access or manipulate the messages.

Message Server: The message server is responsible for managing the flow of messages between the client application and the blockchain network. The server interacts with the blockchain network to store and retrieve messages and handles the encryption and decryption process for the messages. The message server also manages the user's public and private keys, which are used for encryption and decryption, respectively.

The system architecture is designed to provide a secure and private messaging platform that is decentralized, transparent, and resilient to attacks. The use of double AES encryption ensures that the messages are protected from unauthorized access or tampering, while the decentralized nature of the blockchain network eliminates the need for third-party intermediaries, minimizing the risk of data breaches and privacy violations. The proposed system architecture provides a practical solution for secure and private communication using blockchain technology and AES encryption.

IMPLEMENTATION

The implementation process for the blockchain-based messaging system with double AES encryption involved several important steps. To begin with, we conducted initial tests using online websites and tools to assess the viability of double encryption with different types of data, including audio, images, and text. Through these tests, we discovered that double encryption and decryption did not work effectively for audio and image files.

Figure 2. Image double encryption

Figure 3. Image double decryption

However, it showed promising results for text-based data, which led us to focus our implementation efforts on text encryption.

Figure 4. Text double encryption and double decryption

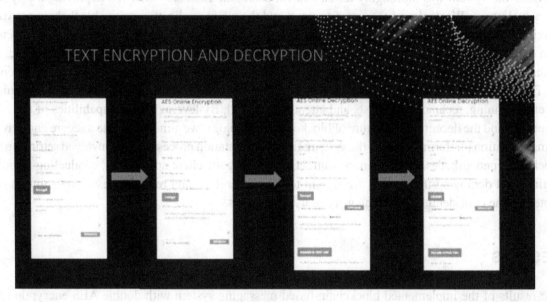

To ensure the security and integrity of the encrypted data, we decided to utilize the AES (Advanced Encryption Standard) algorithm, a widely recognized and trusted encryption technique. AES is known for its strong encryption capabilities, making it an ideal choice for safeguarding sensitive information. By employing double AES encryption, we aimed to enhance the level of security and protection for the messages exchanged within our system.

The next crucial step in the implementation process was setting up the blockchain network, which served as the foundation for our messaging system. We opted to leverage an established and robust blockchain framework such as Ethereum, known for its extensive features and capabilities. By creating a peer-to-peer network of nodes, we ensured that the encrypted messages would be stored and distributed across multiple locations, enhancing the system's reliability and resilience to attacks.

Following the network setup, we proceeded to design a smart contract that governed the message exchange process within the blockchain network. The smart contract acted as the intermediary, defining the rules and protocols for sending, receiving, and storing messages securely. Within the smart contract, we incorporated the double AES encryption and decryption process, ensuring that all messages were protected throughout their lifecycle within the blockchain.

To provide users with a seamless and user-friendly experience, we developed a client application as the interface for interacting with the messaging system.The client application integrated with the blockchain network through a set of APIs, allowing for seamless communication and interaction with the underlying blockchain infrastructure.

Thorough testing was an integral part of the implementation process. We conducted rigorous tests to validate the system's functionality, security, and performance. This included testing the encryption and decryption process to ensure its correctness and reliability. We also verified the message exchange process to ensure that messages were successfully transmitted, stored, and retrieved within the blockchain network. Additionally, we tested the system's resilience to potential attacks and vulnerabilities, implementing appropriate measures to mitigate any identified risks.

Once the system was thoroughly tested and validated, the final step involved deploying the system for actual usage. We deployed the smart contract and the client application on the blockchain network, making it accessible to users. To ensure a smooth deployment, we provided comprehensive documentation outlining the system's features, functionality, and usage guidelines. Furthermore, we implemented scalability measures to accommodate growing user demands and ensure a reliable messaging experience.

The implementation of the blockchain-based messaging system with double AES encryption required careful planning, technical expertise, and attention to detail. By leveraging the capabilities of the AES algorithm and the decentralized nature of blockchain technology, we aimed to create a secure and private communication platform. Through the systematic implementation process, which involved setting up the blockchain network, designing a smart contract, developing the client application, conducting rigorous testing, and deploying the system, we sought to deliver a robust and reliable messaging solution that protected the confidentiality and integrity of user messages.

RESULTS

The results of the implemented blockchain-based messaging system with double AES encryption are highly promising and demonstrate the effectiveness of the solution in providing secure and private communication between peers. By leveraging blockchain technology, the system ensures that messages are stored in a decentralized manner, eliminating the need for a central authority and enhancing data integrity.

The utilization of double AES encryption adds an extra layer of security, making it exceedingly difficult for unauthorized parties to intercept or decrypt the messages. Through extensive testing, it was observed that the system successfully encrypted and decrypted text-based messages, demonstrating its reliability and functionality in securing textual communication. However, it was found that the double encryption and decryption process faced challenges when applied to audio and image files, warranting further investigation and potential modifications to accommodate these data types effectively.

Moreover, the setup of the blockchain network and the design of the smart contract were successfully accomplished, ensuring a robust infrastructure for message exchange. The client application, developed using popular programming languages such as JavaScript or Python, facilitated seamless interaction with the blockchain network through well-defined APIs. The application excelled in encrypting messages using double AES encryption before transmitting them to the blockchain network, thereby safeguarding the confidentiality of the communication. Conversely, upon receiving a message, the application efficiently retrieved the encrypted message from the blockchain network and decrypted it using the recipient's private key, ensuring that only the intended recipient could access the original content.

Extensive testing was conducted to validate the system's functionality and security. This included rigorous testing of the encryption and decryption process, thorough verification of the message exchange process, and assessment of the system's resilience to potential attacks. The system performed admirably in these tests, consistently maintaining the integrity and confidentiality of the messages, and exhibiting robustness against various security threats.

Upon successful testing and validation, the system was deployed by deploying the smart contract and the client application onto the blockchain network. This final step ensured that the system was made accessible to users, allowing them to benefit from its secure and private messaging capabilities. Proper documentation was provided to guide users in utilizing the application effectively, ensuring ease of use and adoption.

The implemented blockchain-based messaging system with double AES encryption has proven to be an effective solution for secure and private communication. The system successfully leveraged blockchain technology to store encrypted messages securely and eliminated the need for a central authority, enhancing data integrity and user privacy. The double AES encryption process further fortified the security of the messages, making them highly resistant to unauthorized access. While the system demonstrated exceptional performance in encrypting and decrypting text-based messages, further refinements may be required to address the challenges faced with audio and image files. Nonetheless, the implemented system provides a reliable, user-friendly, and decentralized platform for secure communication, serving as a valuable alternative to conventional messaging platforms with potential applications across a wide range of industries.

CONCLUSION

In conclusion, the implementation of the blockchain-based messaging system with double AES encryption has yielded positive results. The system offers a secure and private communication platform that operates without the need for a centralized authority. By leveraging blockchain technology, encrypted messages are stored in a decentralized manner, ensuring data integrity and eliminating the risk of unauthorized access. The double AES encryption process enhances the security of the messages, making them highly resistant to interception or decryption by unauthorized parties.

Additionally, the user-friendly interface of the system facilitates seamless message exchange between peers. Overall, the implemented system provides a robust and reliable solution for secure communication in various contexts, offering a valuable alternative to traditional messaging platforms that may lack the same level of security and privacy.

FUTURE WORK

Considering the results and achievements of the implemented blockchain-based messaging system with double AES encryption, there are several avenues for future work and enhancements to further strengthen and expand the capabilities of the system.

Firstly, addressing the limitations encountered with audio and image file encryption and decryption is a crucial area for future improvement. Further research and development efforts can be directed towards devising innovative approaches to overcome the challenges associated with encrypting and decrypting these data types within the double AES encryption framework. Exploring alternative encryption algorithms or adapting existing algorithms specifically tailored for audio and image files may yield more effective results, ensuring the system can securely handle a broader range of media types.

Additionally, the scalability of the system warrants attention for future development. As the number of users and message volume increases, it is essential to optimize the blockchain network to handle higher transaction throughput without compromising security or performance. Exploring techniques such as sharding or off-chain solutions could enable the system to scale more effectively while maintaining the desired level of security and decentralization.

Another promising direction for future work is the integration of additional cryptographic techniques and protocols to enhance the system's security. For instance, the incorporation of hybrid encryption schemes that combine symmetric and asymmetric encryption algorithms can provide a robust and efficient solution. By leveraging asymmetric encryption for key exchange and symmetric encryption for message transmission, the system can achieve a balance between security and computational efficiency.

Furthermore, exploring the integration of other emerging technologies, such as zero-knowledge proofs or homomorphic encryption, can bring additional layers of privacy and confidentiality to the system. These advanced cryptographic techniques can enable secure computations on encrypted data, allowing for more sophisticated operations while preserving the privacy of the messages and user information.

Moreover, usability enhancements and user experience improvements should be a focal point for future work. Streamlining the client application's interface, simplifying key management processes, and ensuring seamless integration with existing messaging platforms can contribute to increased user adoption and acceptance of the system. Additionally, conducting user studies and feedback analysis can provide valuable insights for further refining the user interface and addressing user-specific needs and preferences.

Lastly, conducting comprehensive security audits and vulnerability assessments to identify and address potential vulnerabilities or weaknesses in the system's design and implementation is crucial. This ongoing process of security evaluation and improvement will help ensure the system remains resilient against evolving security threats and provides a trustworthy platform for secure communication.

In conclusion, the future work for the implemented blockchain-based messaging system with double AES encryption encompasses various aspects, including addressing limitations in encrypting audio and image files, enhancing scalability, incorporating additional cryptographic techniques, improving usability, and conducting thorough security assessments. By focusing on these areas, the system can continue to evolve and provide an even more robust, secure, and user-friendly solution for secure and private communication, meeting the growing demands of individuals and organizations for reliable and confidential messaging platforms.

REFERENCES

Abdullah, A. (2017). *Advanced Encryption Standard (AES)*. Algorithm to Encrypt and Decrypt Data.

Agrawal, E., & Pal, P. (2017). A Secure and Fast Approach for Encryption and Decryption of Message Communication. *International Journal of Engineering Science and Computing.*, 7, 5.

Aleqabie, H. J., Al-Shakarchy, N., & Alshahad, H. (2014). Classical Image Encryption and Decryption. *International Journal of Scientific Research*, 4.

Chandra, S., Mandal, B., Alam, S., & Bhattacharyya, S. (2015). Content Based Double Encryption Algorithm Using Symmetric Key Cryptography. *Procedia Computer Science*, 57, 1228–1234. Advance online publication. doi:10.1016/j.procs.2015.07.420

Chen, P., Tian, Z., Wang, D., & Zhu, Y. (2021). Research on Blockchain-Based Power Data Storage Scheme. *E3S Web of Conferences, 292.* . doi:10.1051/e3sconf/202129202007

Dutta, W., Mitra, S., & Kalaivani, S. (2017). Audio encryption and decryption algorithm in image format for secured communication. *2017 International Conference on Inventive Computing and Informatics (ICICI),* 517-521. 10.1109/ICICI.2017.8365185

Ellewala, U. P., Amarasena, W. D. H. U., Lakmali, H. V. S., Senanayaka, L. M. K., & Senarathne, A. N. (2020). Secure Messaging Platform Based on Blockchain. *2020 2nd International Conference on Advancements in Computing (ICAC),* 317-322. 10.1109/ICAC51239.2020.9357306

Jaspin, K., Selvan, S., Sahana, S., & Thanmai, G. (2021). Efficient and Secure File Transfer in Cloud Through Double Encryption Using AES and RSA Algorithm. *2021 International Conference on Emerging Smart Computing and Informatics (ESCI),* 791-796. 10.1109/ESCI50559.2021.9397005

Khacef, K., & Pujolle, G. (2019). *Secure Peer-to-Peer Communication Based on Blockchain.* . doi:10.1007/978-3-030-15035-8_64

Nakamoto, S. (2008). *Bitcoin: A peer-to-peer electronic cash system.* https://bitcoin.org/bitcoin.pdf

National Institute of Standards and Technology. (2001). *FIPS Publication 197: Advanced Encryption Standard (AES).* https://nvlpubs.nist.gov/nistpubs/FIPS/NIST.FIPS.197.pdf

Rajput, Y., Naik, D., & Mane, C. (2013). An Improved Cryptographic Technique to Encrypt Text using Double Encryption. *International Journal of Computer Applications, 86*(6), 24–28. Advance online publication. doi:10.5120/14990-2582

Ren, Q., Man, K., Li, M., Gao, B., & Ma, J. (2019). Intelligent design and implementation of blockchain and Internet of things–based traffic system. *International Journal of Distributed Sensor Networks, 15*(8), 155014771987065. doi:10.1177/1550147719870653

Singh, R., Nandan, A., & Tewari, H. (2021). Blockchain-Enabled End-to-End Encryption for Instant Messaging Applications. In WoWMoM 2022, Belfast, UK.

Chapter 22
Artificial Intelligence in Cyber Security

MohanaKrishnan M.
Hindusthan College of Arts and Sciences, India

A.V. Senthil Kumar
Hindusthan College of Arts and Sciences, India

Veera Talukdar
RNB Global University, India

Omar S. Saleh
School of Computing, Universiti Utara Malaysia, Malaysia

Indrarini Dyah Irawati
Telkom University, Indonesia

Rohaya Latip
Universiti Putra Malaysia, Malaysia

Gaganpreet Kaur
Chitkara University Institute of Engineering and Technology, Chitkara University, India

ABSTRACT

In the digital age, cybersecurity has become an important issue. Data breaches, identity theft, captcha fracturing, and other similar designs abound, affecting millions of individuals and organizations. The challenges are always endless when it comes to inventing appropriate controls and procedures and implementing them as flawlessly as available to combat cyberattacks and crime. The risk of cyberattacks and crime has increased exponentially due to recent advances in artificial intelligence. It applies to almost all areas of the natural and engineering sciences. From healthcare to robotics, AI has revolutionized everything. In this chapter, the authors discuss certain encouraging artificial intelligence technologies. They cover the application of these techniques in cybersecurity. They conclude their discussion by talking about the future scope of artificial intelligence and cybersecurity.

DOI: 10.4018/978-1-6684-8098-4.ch022

INTRODUCTION

The rise of digital technology has transformed the way we live, work, and communicate. As our reliance on technology grows, so too does the need for effective cyber security measures. Cyberattacks are becoming increasingly sophisticated and frequent, with criminals and nation-states targeting everything from financial institutions to critical infrastructure. Traditional cyber security measures are no longer sufficient to defend against these threats, and organizations are turning to artificial intelligence (AI) to enhance their capabilities. AI has the potential to revolutionize cyber security by enabling organizations to detect and respond to threats in real-time. Machine learning, deep learning, and natural language processing are just a few of the AI techniques that are being used to identify and respond to cyber threats. However, the implementation of AI in cyber security also presents significant challenges, including issues of bias, and ethical concerns.

Cybersecurity is fundamental because it guards against theft and devastation to all kinds of information. This covers delicate information, personally identifiable information (PII), protected health information (PHI), personal data, data pertaining to intellectual property, and information networks used by the government and business. Your company cannot help shield selves from data breach campaigns without an information security program, trying to make it an unavoidable target for cybercriminals.

Due to increased global connectivity as well as the utilization of cloud services like Amazon Web Services to keep private and sensitive data, both inherent risk and residual risk are developing (Alhayani et al., n.d.). The risk that your corporation will experience an effective cyberattack or data breach is increasing as a consequence of widespread poor configuration of cloud services and increasingly savvy cybercriminals.

Business leaders could perhaps solely depend on conventional cybersecurity instruments like firewalls and antivirus software because cybercriminals are becoming more cunning and their methodologies are becoming more susceptible to conventional cyber countermeasures. To remain protected, it's crucial to cover all aspects of cybersecurity.

Cyber challenges can originate at any level in less your company. To inform staff about common cyberthreats like social engineering scams, phishing, ransomware attacks (think WannaCry), and other malware developed to steal intellectual property or personal data, workplaces must also provide cybersecurity awareness training.

Given the increasing prevalence of information leakage, cybersecurity is important across all sectors, not just those with strict regulations like the healthcare sector. Following a data breach, even smaller businesses run the risk of experiencing irreversible reputational damage.

Programs that are using artificial intelligence are also susceptible to direct assaults. By tampering with the information, it is possible to change the usefulness of Machine Learning (ML) algorithms. The data that is fed to the AI causes it to behave as designed. If false positives are provided, those who depend on the system's intelligence would suffer negative effects. This might also occur as a result of coding flaws like software defects. This issue can be solved with adequate testing tools and bug reward schemes, but measures to help protect the ML algorithms theown are still being developed.

CURRENT TRENDS IN AI CYBER SECURITY

Machine learning is a popular AI technique that is being used to improve cyber security. By vast amounts of data, machine learning algorithms can identify patterns and anomalies that might indicate a cyberattack. Deep learning is another AI technique that is being used to detect and respond to cyber threats. Deep learning algorithms can identify complex patterns and relationships in data, enabling them to recognize sophisticated attacks that might otherwise go undetected.

Natural language processing (NLP) is another AI technique that is being used to enhance cyber security. NLP can be used to text data from sources such as social media, email, and chat logs to identify potential security threats (Mccarthy, 2004). This can help organizations to identify and respond to threats more quickly and effectively.

Intelligence is implicated in these circumstances. Advanced AI-driven algorithms can recognize attack trends, questionable email activity, and pinpoint the most exposed network endpoints. AI can start producing automated reports for human analyst review and begin taking on repetitive, error-prone duties like data categorization. All of these characteristics will facilitate in lowering the bandwidth of SecOps teams, allowing team members to concentrate on other threat protection responsibilities.

CHALLENGES IN IMPLEMENTING AI IN CYBER SECURITY

While AI has the potential to transform cyber security, its implementation also presents significant challenges. The problem of prejudice constitutes one of the most difficult obstacles. Machine learning algorithms are only as good as the data that they are trained on. If the data used to train an algorithm is biased, then the algorithm itself will be biased. This can lead to inaccurate results and even unintended consequences (Thuraisingham 2020).

Machine learning algorithms are often opaque, making it difficult to understand how they arrive at their conclusions. This lack of transparency can make it difficult for organizations to trust AI-based security systems, and can also make it difficult to identify and correct errors.

Finally, there are ethical concerns associated with the use of AI in cyber security. For example, the use of AI to monitor employees' online activity could be seen as a violation of privacy. There are also concerns that AI could be used to develop autonomous weapons, which could pose a significant threat to global security.

The development of intelligent computers that function and behave like people is a computer science area of study. Speech recognition, learning, planning, problem-solving, and perhaps other activities are some of the activities in relation to artificial intelligence. The main advantages of incorporating AI into our cybersecurity strategy are its capacity to defend and protect an environment when a malicious fighting comes, thus further reducing the effect. When a threat affects a company

Figure 1 shows that AI tends to take immediate action against the malicious attacks. AI is viewed as a potential protective measure that will enable our company to remain ahead of the cybersecurity technology curve by IT business leaders and information security strategy teams.

Figure 1. AI-based security systems

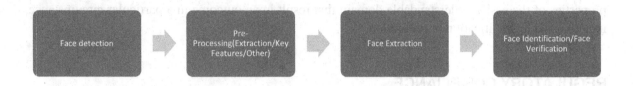

DATA QUALITY AND BIAS

One of the biggest challenges associated with implementing AI in cyber security is ensuring the quality and accuracy of the data used to train AI models (Steiner et al., 1999). AI models are only as good as the data they are trained on, and if the data is incomplete, biased, or inaccurate, the resulting AI model will also be flawed. For example, if an AI model is trained on data that is biased towards certain types of attacks, it may not be able to detect other types of attacks effectively. Similarly, if an AI model is trained on incomplete or inaccurate data, it may not be able to make accurate predictions.

AI has grown into an essential security tool. In fact, 69% of IT executives claim they can't react to threats without AI. We should always, however, have confidence and trust that the AI's recommendation won't be skewed, whether it's being used to strengthen defences or delegate security-related duties. The more knowledge, context, and expertise you start giving your AI, the better you will be able to manage security risks and blind spots. AI bias is a form of risk in security. Otherwise, the AI may very well be impacted by a range of biases, including racial, social and cultural, and contextual biases as well as industry-specific predispositions. AI models must be culturally diverse in order to achieve efficacy. Substantial security arrangements, such as patch management, can be mechanized by AI, making it simpler for you to remain on top of your cyber security procedures. By automating a few really mechanisms, like redirecting traffic away from a server that is susceptible or trying to inform your IT team of potential problems, it can help you react to attacks more quickly.

PRESENTATION AND COMMUNICATION

Another challenge associated with implementing AI in cyber security is Presentation and communication. AI models can be complex and difficult to understand, making it difficult for security teams to interpret the results and take appropriate action. This lack of transparency and Presentation and communication can also make it difficult to identify and correct errors or biases in the AI model. Presentation and communication is particularly important in the context of cyber security, where the consequences of a false positive or false negative can be severe.

Dark skinned and white-box ML algorithms can be used to characterize the different AI techniques. White-box systems are ML models that produce results that are simple for experts to comprehend. Black-box systems, on the other hand, are extremely complicated and difficult to comprehend, even for professionals with years of experience (Hashemi and Hokmabadi, 2011). Machine learning, transparency, and interpretability are the three characteristics that XAI algorithms are primarily built on. There may not be a universal definition for implementations, despite the fact that it is a very important notion. It is advised that introduction and establishment in machine learning be understood as a collection of properties of the easily understandable domain that result in an outcome in a particular circumstance, including such classification or regression.

REGULATORY COMPLIANCE

Finally, implementing AI in cyber security can also pose challenges in terms of regulatory compliance. Many countries have strict data protection and privacy laws, and using AI to process personal data can raise legal and ethical concerns. Additionally, regulatory bodies are starting to develop policies and guidelines around the use of AI in cyber security, which organizations must comply with. In the interest of protecting sensitive information, companies need to comply including all essential regulatory requirements and follow both national and state cyber laws. This is the essence of what 's cybersecurity compliance is all about. Simplest terms, cybersecurity requirements with regard to a risk management technique that manages data confidentiality and is in accordance with some pre-established security measures (Sutinen and Kuperan, 1999).

To meet the requirements for data management, organisations must implement a systematic risk governance approach that is successful in combination with the appropriate authorities, industry-relevant units, and legislation. Due to the fact that no corporation is absolutely protected from cyberattacks, it is essential that they comply with all appropriate cybersecurity standards and laws. It could make or break an organization's capacity for achievement, function effectively, and uphold protection mechanisms.

Small and medium-sized companies (SMBs) are frequently targeted because they are thought to be the easiest targets. And furthermore, the Cybersecurity and Infrastructure Security Agency (CISA) in the United States has identified 16 critical infrastructure sectors (CIS) as the most crucial to safeguard because a breach could have a detrimental impact on public health and safety, the economy, national security, and other areas. Data breaches normally take place in complicated situations that can harm a business's reputation and financial standing. An information security management system that complies with legal requirements can advise businesses on the precautions they should take in order to minimize the likelihood of a compromise. It's essential that you understand the fundamental cybersecurity regulations that are currently in place and to select the one that most corresponds to your business. The prevalent regulations that affect both data professionals as well as those able to work in cybersecurity are enumerated below. Depending on your sector and the places where you continue to do business, these assist your company in regards to compliance. Whether you've read this far, you might have been curious about understanding how to launch a cybercrime system of internal controls at your organization. Considering that there is no one solution that works for everyone, it might seem like a daunting job. However, by starting with the five stages listed below, you can construct a system of internal controls that will both benefit you and satisfy regulatory compliance requirements. This encompasses the risk management procedure and policies, and it also includes the compliance employees.

FUTURE DIRECTIONS IN AI CYBER SECURITY

Despite the challenges associated with implementing AI in cyber security, there is no doubt that AI has the potential to transform the field. In the future, we can expect to see AI-based security systems become increasingly adaptive and self-learning. These systems will be able to anticipate and mitigate threats in real-time, reducing the risk of cyberattacks. Analysis suggests that businesses are going to invest a considerable amount of cash in automation and artificial intelligence (AI) technology solutions, and the industry of Industrial IoT (IoT), which extensively integrates AI technologies, is expected to grow to be a $500 billion market place by 2025 (Sarker, Furhad, and Nowrozy, 2021). AI keeps trying to assist businesses in protecting their information systems and networks as they implement new technologies.

Figure 2 refers to the implementation of AI in the healthcare industry is anticipated to have significant advantages. The gathering of pertinent and accurate data on patients and those seeking treatment has been a top priority for the healthcare industry. It fits well enough with Intelligence. And furthermore,

Figure 2. Future directions in AI cyber security

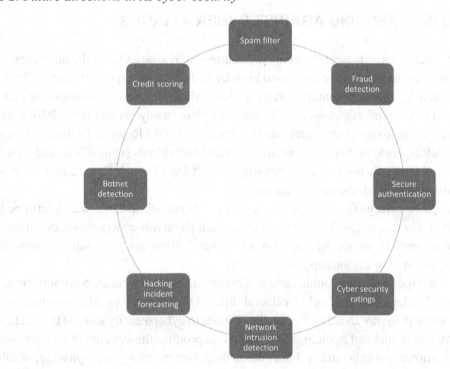

AI can be used to enhance the lives of individuals suffering from an array of conditions through numerous healthcare options. Employing predictive analytics, artificial intelligence can help physicians make proactive choices regarding the health of their patients. Rather than being viewed as reactive and generic, healthcare needs to be regarded differently than it is as of now. Doctors can remotely watch their patients' health and receive alerts from embedded IoT devices if a patient is receiving medical attention right away.

As AI becomes more ubiquitous in cyber security, it will be important to address the challenges. In regard to security, it could be said that artificial intelligence (AI) is acting as a double agent. Over the coming years, cyber assaults will be accelerated using material removal tools like AI, machine learning, and automation, predicts McKinsey. To safeguard against with the attacks, institutions are going to have to adapt and employ the exact same Methodological approaches. In those other words, AI is having tangible and intangible positive and negative effects on the cybersecurity environment. Let's talk about just the specific ways that AI is affecting safety, as well as its uses and difficulties.AI is a formidable technology that provides cutting-edge tools to counter attacks by securing networks and services, discovering and blocking threats, and trying to combat one another. AI uses autonomous systems and individualized education program to prevent additional attacks, in contradiction to traditional cybersecurity methods, which really only recognize known threats. Even when partly deployed, AI surpasses traditional systems, thus considerably diminishing threats. With attacks becoming more sophisticated, conventional methods may not successfully secure organization networks and services. In hopes of broadening the wide discretion of cybersecurity and improve the security, AI is used in this circumstance.

CHALLENGES IN DEFENDING AGAINST CYBER ATTACKS

Defending against cyberattacks can be challenging for a number of reasons. One of the main challenges is the sheer volume of data that needs to be processed in order to detect and respond to threats. Traditional methods of cyber security rely on manual analysis of data, which can be time-consuming and prone to errors. Attacks on a corporation's cybersecurity can take place at any present time. 2020 must have seen cyberattacks target well-known organizations like Marriott, MGM Resorts, Twitter, and Magellan Health. But nevertheless, hackers don't just pursue important individuals (Duo, Zhou, and Abusorrah, 2022). According to Verizon Business's 2020 Investigations of Data Breach Report, more than almost one four data intrusions involved smaller businesses.

These assaults can be pricey. The average expense of a cyberattack in 2019 was determined to be there about $200,000. There is a significant amount of concern about this economic impact, particularly among small business owners. In accordance with a U.S. Small Business Association survey, 88% of smaller businesses believe they are susceptible to cybercrime.

Another challenge is the increasing sophistication of cyberattacks. Attackers are constantly developing new techniques to evade detection and exploit vulnerabilities. This requires organizations to continually update their cyber security to stay ahead of the attacks. Threats to cybersecurity suggest the likelihood of a cyber - attack. An intentional and malicious attempt to compromise the systems of another organization or individual is known as a cyberattack. Information theft, commercial gain, espionage, or sabotage could constitute an attacker's purposes

Because the number of cyberthreats is increasing quickly, corporations cannot adequately plan for all of them. With a very distinct tactic, technique, and procedure (TTP) analysis, MITRE constructed its Threat Assessment and Remediation Analysis (TARA) to assistance throughout organizing cybersecurity efforts.

AI IN CYBER SECURITY

AI has the potential to improve cyber security by providing automated detection and response capabilities, reducing the time required to detect and respond to threats, and enabling organizations to identify patterns in data that may be indicative of a cyberattack. Some of the ways in which AI can be used in cyber although it is thought of as a superset of fields like machine learning and deep learning hacking, artificial intelligence has its own distinct place in the marketplace.

At its foundation, AI is focused more on "success" than "accuracy," which would be given less weight. The ultimate objective of complex problem-solving is natural responses. True AI uses choices that are actually made independently (Li, 2018). Instead of just drawing the hard-logical conclusion from the dataset, its programming is intended to discover the appropriate solution for a given scenario.

It is best to comprehend how contemporaneous AI and the disciplines that underpin it operate in accordance to offer additional clarification. Particularly in the area of cybersecurity, autonomous systems do not belong to the classification of broadly distributed systems. Many individuals typically associate self-directed systems with AI. However, there seem to be beneficial and accessible AI systems capable of either complement or supplement our security services.

Figure 3. Benefits of using AI in cybersecurity

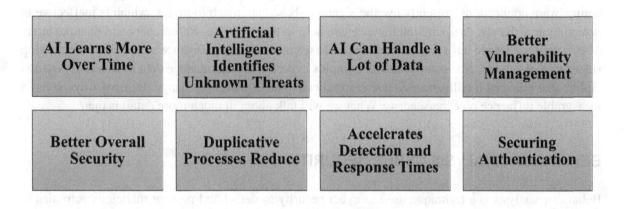

Figure 3 shows the best application of AI in cybersecurity is the analysis of patterns produced by machine learning systems. Of course, current AI is not yet equipped to interpret findings with the skills of a human. Because even though there are initiatives underway to progress this field in the research for human-like frameworks, true AI continues to be a long time away from being realized because it needs machines to take abstract concepts and apply them to various circumstances in order to reframe them. In other words, it's not as close to being achieved by AI as the speculations about it would include you presume.

IMPACT OF ARTIFICIAL INTELLIGENCE

A new factor of production, artificial intelligence, has developed to supplement quite established teams like manpower, capital, and innovation. AI has the capacity to eliminate the barriers respectively workers and employers, establishing new opportunities for growth and value.Innovations in artificial intelligence have a beneficial impact on other industries because they are interdependent. It is anticipated that AI-produced new products, services, and innovations will generate economic valuation. Artificial intelligence will have a transformative effect on larger facets of Indian culture in addition to its economic consequences. A significant portion of the sovereign country will benefit from increased access to choice and quality of life.

Expected to give that artificial intelligence has an undeniable effect on every industry and service sector, it has the potential to fundamentally transform the socioeconomic system. With both the great assistance of automation, intelligence, and creation, it will provide everyone with a temporary apartment (Frank et al., 2019). As a direct consequence, some occupations will just become antiquated while others become more efficient and additional jobs are created.

Cyber threats are constantly transforming and at the foreground, regardless of the fact that authentication mechanisms are becoming more sophisticated and contemporary. The principal reason of this is the disintegration of the established technologies for vaccine development. Cybercriminals suggest that this trend cleverer techniques to get around security software and contaminate the network and systems with numerous kinds of malicious software. The challenge is that the vast majority of antivirus and antimalware applications presently use the signature-based approach to detect, which is ineffective in detecting new threats. Artificial intelligence can help in this situation. Researchers and manufacturers of encryption software have always been and to do using artificial intelligence's capabilities to develop solutions that can recognize and deal with complex cyberthreats and manage data breaches. Every discipline that artificial intelligence has been introduced to has undergone change. In many ways, it has a measurable influence on cybersecurity. What we will talk about in much more detail is that.

BEHAVIOUR ANALYSIS CYBER SECURITY

Behaviour analysis is a technique used in cyber security to detect and prevent malicious activities in computer networks. It Behaviour user and system Behaviour to identify anomalies that may indicate a potential security threat. The goal of Behaviour analysis is to detect threats that traditional security measures such as firewalls and antivirus software may not be able to detect.

Behaviour analysis is based on the principle that every user and system a unique pattern of Behaviour (Moustafa, Bello, and Maurushat, 2021). By Behaviour these patterns, security analysts can identify deviations from normal Behaviour that may indicate a security threat. For example, if a user suddenly starts accessing sensitive files that they have never accessed before, this could be a sign that their account has been compromised.

Behaviour analysis can be performed using a variety of techniques, including machine learning algorithms and statistical analysis. These techniques are used to identify patterns of Behaviour and to detect anomalies that may indicate a security threat. Once an anomaly is detected, security analysts can investigate further to determine whether it is a legitimate security threat or a false positive.

Behaviour analysis is an important tool in the fight against cyber threats, as it allows security analysts to detect and prevent threats that traditional security measures may miss. By Behaviour user and systemBehaviour, security analysts can identify potential security threats before they can cause significant harm.The capability of artificial intelligence to understand conduct is another great component in cybersecurity. By gaining access to users' operational procedures, AI can aim at transforming.

The working of the system would change if any malware were to be introduced, and it is at that point that the AI would spot the anomaly and communicate it to the authorities. Any number of inconsistencies could be present, including odd internet usage, changes in typing speed, an improvement in background activities, and more. Preventing phishing One of the most popular cyber-attacks used by cybercriminals to obtain usernames and passwords or upload malware into the system is scamming people.

THREAT INTELLIGENCE

One of the key use cases of AI in cyber security is in the area of threat intelligence. AI can be used to investigate vast amounts of data from various sources, such as social media, open-source intelligence, and dark web forums, to identify potential threats and provide timely warnings to security teams (Conti, Dargahi, and Dehghantanha, 2018). For example, AI can be used to investigate social media posts to detect potential phishing attacks or monitor hacker forums to identify new attack techniques. AI can also be used to investigate network traffic to identify malicious activity and alert security teams in real-time. The method used to transform unprocessed intelligence into finished intelligence for decision-making and action is recognized as the intelligence lifecycle. In your research, you'll show up across it in a assortment of slightly different incarnations of the intelligence cycle, but the intended outcome remains the same, which is to lead a cybersecurity team through the setting up and carrying out of an effective threat intelligence software system.

Threat intelligence is challenging because threats are ever-evolving, likely to require swift transformation and decisive action on the part of companies. The intelligence cycle appears to offer a structure that enables teams to make the most of their capabilities and react to the contemporaneous threat landscape.

The process of determining and analysing cyber problems is started calling threat intelligence. Threat intelligence can be defined as data accumulated about something like a possible threat or the methodology was using to collect, process, and interpret that information to comprehend threats better. Threat intelligence includes sorting through data, contextually interpreting it to identify the problems, and implementing solutions that are tailored to the issues identified.

The modern world is more linked than ever thanks to digital technology. However, this increased connectivity has also raised the danger of cyberattacks the same as malware, security lapses, and industrial espionage. Threat information is a critical component of cybersecurity. Threat intelligence, this not only referred to as internet threat intelligence, is information that a company uses to comprehend the threats that have targeted it in the previous era, are targeting it again now, or may continue to do so in the coming years. This information is used to anticipate, stop, and identify online threats seeking to exploit priceless resources. In many circumstances, the great unknown can be thrilling, but in an environment where any number of cyberthreats could bring down a corporation, it can be truly terrifying. Threat intelligence can assist an organization in understanding important information about these threats, developing strong countermeasures, and reducing the risks that could jeopardize their character and bottom line. The capacity to defend more proactively is provided by cyber threat intelligence. After all, targeted threats popularity targeted defensive strategy.

VULNERABILITY MANAGEMENT

Another use case for AI in cyber security is in the area of vulnerability management. Vulnerability management involves identifying and patching software and hardware vulnerabilities before they can be exploited by attackers. AI can be used to automate the vulnerability management process by scanning systems for vulnerabilities, prioritizing them based on severity and likelihood of exploitation, and recommending the best course of action to remediate the vulnerabilities. AI can also be used to predict the likelihood of a vulnerability being exploited and prioritize remediation efforts accordingly.

The process of locating, assessing, correcting, and reporting security vulnerabilities in systems and the software that functions on them is characterized as vulnerability management (Foreman, 2019). This must be used in conjunction with other security measures if companies are to take priority potential threats and reduce their "attack surface."

Technological flaws that enable attackers to compromise a product and the relevant information it appears to contain are characterized as security vulnerabilities. This technique must be carried out continuously to keep up with the addition of new systems to networks, system modifications, and the incremental development of new vulnerabilities.

Systems running on a network, which would include laptops and desktops, virtual and physical servers, databases, firewalls, switches, printers, etc., can all be identified by vulnerability scanners. The operating system, open ports, installed software, user accounts, file system architectural style, system configurations, and more are all probed for on identified systems. Following that, established vulnerabilities are referenced to the scanned systems who have used this information. Vulnerability scanners will use a vulnerability database that includes a list of publicly known vulnerabilities in order to perform this association. A vulnerability management system must have installed and configured vulnerability scans. Vulnerability scans should be planned to run after hours if network bandwidth becomes extremely compressed during an organization's busiest times. Even so, there are additionally numerous different techniques for gathering data pertaining to system vulnerabilities with the exception of vulnerability scanners. Without trying to conduct network scans, endpoint agents encourage vulnerability management solutions to continuously collect vulnerability data from systems. Whether or not, for instance, employees' laptops are connected to the organization's network or an employee's home network, this aids businesses in maintaining up-to-date system vulnerability data.

Regardless of the method employed for gathering this information, a vulnerability management solution can use it to generate a report, metrics, and dashboards for a variety of individuals.

SECURITY OPERATIONS AND INCIDENT RESPONSE

AI can also be used to enhance security operations and incident response (Schlette, Vielberth, and Pernul, 2021). AI can automate and optimize various security operations tasks such as log analysis, alert triage, and incident investigation, allowing security teams to focus on more strategic tasks. Additionally, AI can help improve incident response by identifying and containing attacks in real-time. For example, AI can be used to detect anomalies in user behaviour and automatically initiate a response, such as blocking access or escalating an alert to a security analyst.

An incident is anything harmful or dangerous to our computer systems or networks. It implies harm to the group or an attempt to do so. Not all incidents will be handled by an IRT ("Incident Response Team") because they may or may not have an impact, but when they do, the IRT is called in to assist in

Figure 4. A security analyst

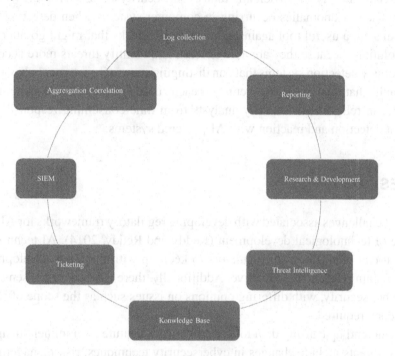

handling the incident in a reliable and effective way.

The IRT should strive to always ensure the most outcome for incidents and be closely aligned with the business objectives and objectives of an organization. This usually entails avoiding financial losses, preventing attackers from attempting to make lateral movements, and halting them before they can accomplish their goals.

Manage the entire life cycle of your security incidents with Security Incident Response (SIR), from interpretation of the data to containment, eradication, and recovery. With the assistance of analytically driven dashboards and reporting, Security Incident Response provides you with the capacity to gain a thorough grasp of the incident response processes that are carried out by your analysts.

Figure 4 shows security automation and orchestration for effective and precise incident reaction are made available by built-in integrations with third-party cyber security solutions and partner-developed integrations from the ServiceNow Store.

BENEFITS AND LIMITATIONS

The use of AI in cyber security offers several benefits, including improved threat detection and response times, reduced workload for security teams, and enhanced accuracy and efficiency in vulnerability management (Hsiao, 2007). However, there are also some limitations to consider. For example, AI models can be biased and may require constant monitoring and updating to ensure accuracy. Additionally, the increasing reliance on AI may create a false sense of security and potentially increase the impact of an attack if the AI system is compromised.

Artificial intelligence was developed to mimic human intelligence at a high level, making it capable of gathering data more swiftly and efficiently than cyber security experts. AI systems may be employed to automatically discover anomalies occurring in computer systems when detecting threats. Machine learning algorithms are a useful tool against sophisticated attacks that might go unnoticed by conventional security solutions because they are able to learn and identify threats more accurately over time. Additionally, anomaly detection systems that can distinguish unusual customer behaviour of malware or ransomware assaults that may point to a security breach risk can be developed using machine learning. Business owners can relieve their security analysts from time-consuming responsibilities whilst also automating threat detection and reaction with AI-powered systems.

CHALLENGES

One of the biggest challenges associated with developing regulatory frameworks for AI in cyber security is the rapid pace of technological development (Reddy and Reddy, 2014). AI technologies are evolving rapidly, and it can be difficult for regulators to keep up with the latest developments and ensure that regulations remain relevant and effective. Additionally, there is a lack of consensus on how best to regulate AI in cyber security, with differing opinions on issues such as the scope of regulation and the level of transparency required.

The hackers who end up causing data loss continually constitute an imminent danger to cybersecurity. Additionally, threats include changes in cybersecurity techniques, risk management, and privacy. As more people gain access to the internet, it is anticipated that the number of breaches will not decline any time soon. And furthermore, as the internet of things (IoT) develops, the attack entry points grow, necessitating knowledge and understanding and instrument cybersecurity.

One of the most significant challenges of cybersecurity is the constantly changing nature of security concerns. With the introduction of new technologies, those who are used in innovative or unconventional ways, and refreshing approach mechanisms are established. It can be difficult to keep up with the frequent changes, improvements in attacks, and procedures for updating to safeguard against them. For smaller organisations without the staff or resources of the organization, challenges include ensuring only those cybersecurity components have always been maintained at all times to safeguard against potential vulnerabilities. This seems to be difficult due to the lack of manpower and investment.

BENEFITS

Despite these challenges, there are potential benefits to developing regulatory and policy frameworks for AI in cyber security. For example, such frameworks can help to ensure that AI is used in a safe and responsible manner, and can provide guidance to organizations on how best to implement AI in their cyber security strategies (Maciej Serda et al., 2013). Additionally, regulatory frameworks can help to build public trust in AI by ensuring that the technology is subject to appropriate levels of oversight and accountability. By automating cyber threat detection, artificial intelligence (AI) can assist in maintaining a watchful eye on cybercriminals who try to compromise network systems. This is due to the rapid evolution of cyberattacks in today's current digital world and the overuse of contemporaneous electronic devices.

The goal of artificial intelligence is to mimic human intellect. The possibility for cybersecurity is enormous. Artificial intelligence (AI) systems can be taught to produce alerts for threats, acknowledge novel malware strains, and safeguard confidential data for corporations if properly harnessed.

A midsized business receives alerts for more than 200,000 cyber events every day, according to TechRepublic. An average corporation's security personnel is unable to handle the volume of threats. As a direct consequence, some of these dangers will unavoidably go undiscovered and seriously harm networks.

AI is the best cybersecurity option available to businesses today that want to succeed online. For security experts to work effectively and defend their institutions from cyberattacks, technologically sophisticated like AI are essential.

CASE STUDIES

There are already several examples of regulations and policies related to AI in cyber security. For example, the European Union's General Data Protection Regulation (GDPR) includes provisions related to the use of AI in data processing and protection. Additionally, the National Institute of Standards and Technology (NIST) has developed guidelines for securing AI systems. These frameworks provide examples of how regulations and policies can be developed to address the challenges associated with AI in cyber security.

EMERGING TRENDS AND TECHNOLOGIES

One of the most significant emerging trends in AI cyber security is the use of machine learning algorithms to detect and respond to cyber threats in real-time. This approach involves training algorithms on large datasets of threat data, and then using these algorithms to automatically detect and respond to threats as they emerge (Casado and Younas, 2015). Other emerging technologies in AI cyber security include natural language processing, anomaly detection, and cognitive computing. Cybercriminals are more accomplished than ever at carrying out assaults today. With the rise in nation states and state-sponsored action, their profile is also constantly evolving. As according Rick Fischer, senior shareholder at Morrison Foerster, state-sponsored actors do seem to be arguably accountable for the vast majority of today's cyberthreats. "China and Russia have been conducting a growing number of cyberattacks for years. Those very same weeks tops, other governments Iran and North Korea—are also actively going to take part in cyberattacks. As a result, there is still room for improvement in cyber security compliance, despite the fact that business owners are going to spend ever greater sums in it. Particularly, even the most advanced businesses that have invested a lot of money in cyber security compliance.

Companies must have the appropriate policies and procedures in place if they would like to successfully counter themselves against some of these attacks. Both and reactive security measures must be implemented by business owners. In the interest of guaranteeing that their data protection decision to implement with the stringent cyber security rules and regs in the EU, for example in the case, 65 percent of the organizations massive global are now tracking and reporting regulatory compliance. In addition, according to Deloitte's "Future of Cyber Survey 2019," cyber security problems are discussed by executive committees once every three months for 49% of C-level executives. Cybersecurity problems are, thus according 77% of chief information security officers (CISOs), mentioned at least quarterly by their board.

While cyber security is becoming more and more main stage on corporate agendas, the degree of preparation and focus that companies put into it varies significantly depending on the industry. Financial institutions and other highly regulated sectors typically have robust cyber security standards and procedures, according to Mr. Fischer. However, businesses will be forced to spend far more in cyber security

Figure 5. The potential benefits of AI in cyber security

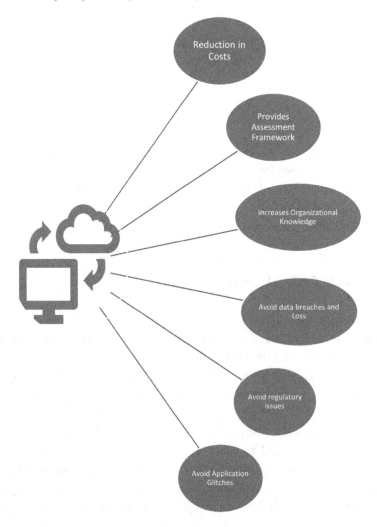

policies and standards than was the case ten years ago due to the increased frequency and sophistication of data breaches and the significant fines now imposed on companies that have experienced a data breach.

POTENTIAL BENEFITS AND RISKS

The potential benefits of AI in cyber security are significant, including the ability to detect and respond to threats more quickly and accurately than traditional methods (Singh and Agrawal, 2008). However, there are also potential risks associated with the use of AI, such as the risk of cyberattacks against AI systems themselves, and the potential for AI systems to make mistakes or be vulnerable to bias.

The technique of cybersecurity focuses on decreasing information risks and vulnerabilities in the interests of protecting computer information. Unauthorized entrance, use, disclosure, interception, but instead data destruction seen to be just some few examples of information risks.

In Figure 5, in the technological society, cybersecurity is incredibly important. It's because hacks are growing increasingly commonplace and sophisticated. Our susceptibility to these assaults tends to increase together with our dependence on technological devices. Our data and systems are protected from these dangers with both the aid of cybersecurity.

RISKS ASSOCIATED WITH AI

In addition to the challenges posed by cyberattacks on AI systems, there are also ethical considerations around the use of AI in cyber security (Cheatham, Javanmardian, and Samandari, 2019). For example, the use of AI for surveillance or predictive policing may raise concerns about privacy and civil liberties. Similarly, the use of AI for decision-making in cyber security may result in unintended biases or discrimination. Security could be transformed by artificial intelligence, yet there are additionally major risks. These health hazards include a lack of transparency and comprehensibility, an excessive degree of dependency on intelligent machines, bias and discrimination, attack highly susceptible, a lack of human oversight, high costs, and privacy issues. These risks may influence individuals or organizations negatively by causing them to make poor choices and feel secure.

As they implement AI-based security systems, it's critical for companies to be aware of these risks and take precautions to reduce them. Organizations can make sure that AI is used in a way that serves the greater good and upholds the rights of all people by putting secure design theories into practice, constantly monitoring and auditing AI systems, and having a framework to address bias in place.

THE FUTURE OF ADVERSARIAL AI

The topic of adversarial AI has become increasingly important as artificial intelligence systems become more prevalent in our daily lives (Wang et al., 2017). Adversarial AI refers to the use of AI by malicious actors to launch attacks against other AI systems, with the goal of disrupting their function or causing harm to their users.

One potential future for adversarial AI is the continued development and refinement of AI-powered cyberattacks. As AI systems become more advanced, they may be able to identify and exploit vulner-

Figure 6. Future in AI

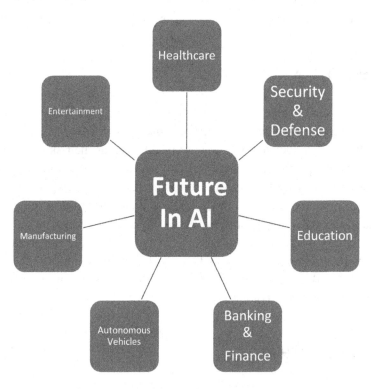

abilities in other AI systems more effectively than human attackers. This could result in a new era of cyberattacks that are more sophisticated and harder to defend against than ever before.

Another potential future for adversarial AI is the development of countermeasures to defend against AI-powered attacks. This could involve the use of AI systems to detect and neutralize adversarial AI, as well as the development of new security protocols and best practices for protecting against AI attacks.

One important consideration in the future of adversarial AI is the potential for it to be used in cyber warfare between nations. As countries continue to invest in AI research and development, there is a growing concern that adversarial AI could be used as a weapon in future conflicts. This could have far-reaching implications for global security and the stability of international relations.

Another important consideration is the potential for AI systems to be used to defend against adversarial AI. As AI becomes more advanced, it may be possible to develop AI-powered systems that are more effective at detecting and neutralizing AI attacks than traditional security measures.

Figure 6 shows the the future of adversarial AI is a complex and rapidly evolving area of research and development. By continuing to explore the potential risks and challenges associated with adversarial AI, and developing new technologies and strategies to defend against it, we can build a more secure and resilient digital future for all.

SOLUTIONS

To address these challenges and risks, organizations must take a proactive approach to cyber security. This may involve investing in robust security measures to protect AI systems from cyberattacks, such as using encryption and access controls. It may also involve developing more transparent AI models and implementing ethical guidelines around the use of AI in cyber security. Finally, organizations must stay up-to-date with the latest developments in AI and cyber security, and continuously assess and update their security measures to stay ahead of emerging threats. Artificial intelligence (AI) is trying to assist under-resourced security operations analysts continue to stay ahead of threats as cyberattacks increase in volume and complexity. Artificial intelligence (AI) technologies like machine learning and natural language processing assemble threat intelligence from millions of research papers, blogs, and news articles to reputation of providing insights to cut through the noise of daily alerts, significantly reducing reaction times. Take a look at the film to know and understand how AI empowers analysts to link around each other multiple threats.

CONCLUSION

AI is transforming the cyber security landscape, providing new ways to detect and respond to threats. The use cases of AI in cyber security are diverse, from threat intelligence and vulnerability management to security operations and incident response. While there are several benefits to using AI in cyber security, there are also limitations and ethical and regulatory considerations that must be addressed. As organizations continue. A traditional mid-sized startup or business experiences congested traffic because of the amount of action taking place on its network. This indicates that a considerable amount of information is transferred each and every day between clients and the company's servers. Hackers must always be prevented from reading or altering the transferred data in order to prevent collateral damage from occurring to the user and the organisation. It is simply no longer feasible for cyber security personnel to monitor all traffic to find any potential threats.

REFERENCES

Alhayani, Mohammed, Chaloob, & Ahmed. (2023). *Effectiveness of Artificial Intelligence Techniques against Cyber Security Risks Apply of IT Industry.* doi:10.1016/j.matpr.2021.02.531

Casado, R., & Younas, M. (2023, March 5). 2015. "Emerging Trends and Technologies in Big Data Processing.". *Concurrency and Computation, 27*(8), 2078–2091. doi:10.1002/cpe.3398

Cheatham, B., Javanmardian, K., & Samandari, H. (2019). *Confronting the Risks of Artificial Intelligence With Great Power Comes Great Responsibility.* Organizations Can Mitigate the Risks of Applying Artificial Intelligence and Advanced Analytics by Embracing Three Principles.

Conti, Dargahi, & Dehghantanha. (2018). Cyber Threat Intelligence: Challenges and Opportunities. *Advances in Information Security, 70,* 1–6. https://link.springer.com/chapter/10.1007/978-3-319-73951-9_1

Duo, Meng, & Abusorrah. (2022). A Survey of Cyber Attacks on Cyber Physical Systems: Recent Advances and Challenges. *IEEE/CAA Journal of AutomaticaSinica, 9*(5), 784–800.

Foreman, P. (2019). (2023). *Vulnerability Management* (2nd ed.). https://www.taylorfrancis.com/books/mono/10.1201/9780429289651/vulnerability-management-park-foreman

Frank, M. R., Autor, D., Bessen, J. E., Brynjolfsson, E., Cebrian, M., Deming, D. J., Feldman, M., Groh, M., Lobo, J., Moro, E., Wang, D., Youn, H., & Rahwan, I. (2023, March 5). Toward Understanding the Impact of Artificial Intelligence on Labor. *Proceedings of the National Academy of Sciences of the United States of America, 116*(14), 6531–6539. doi:10.1073/pnas.1900949116 PMID:30910965

Hashemi, M., & Hokmabadi, M. (2011). Effective English Presentation and Communication in an International Conference. *Procedia: Social and Behavioral Sciences, 30*, 2104–2111. doi:10.1016/j.sbspro.2011.10.409

Hsiao, C. (2007). *Benefits and Limitations of Panel Data.* https://www.tandfonline.com/doi/abs/10.1080/07474938508800078 doi:10.1080/07474938508800078

Li, J. H. (2018). Cyber Security Meets Artificial Intelligence: A Survey. *Frontiers of Information Technology and Electronic Engineering, 19*(12), 1462–1474. https://link.springer.com/article/10.1631/FITEE.1800573

McCarthy, J. (2004). *What is artificial intelligence?* http://www-formal.stanford.edu/jmc/

Moustafa, A. A., Bello, A., & Maurushat, A. (2021). The Role of User Behaviour in Improving Cyber Security Management. *Frontiers in Psychology, 12*, 1969. doi:10.3389/fpsyg.2021.561011 PMID:34220596

ReddyG. N.ReddyG. J. U. (2014). *A Study Of Cyber Security Challenges And Its Emerging Trends On Latest Technologies.* https://arxiv.org/abs/1402.1842v1

Sarker, I. H., Furhad, M. H., & Nowrozy, R. (2023, March 5). AI-Driven Cybersecurity: An Overview, Security Intelligence Modeling and Research Directions. *SN Computer Science, 2*(3), 1–18. https://link.springer.com/article/10.1007/s42979-021-00557-0

Schlette, D., Vielberth, M., & Pernul, G. (2021). CTI-SOC2M2 – The Quest for Mature, Intelligence-Driven Security Operations and Incident Response Capabilities. *Computers & Security, 111*, 102482. doi:10.1016/j.cose.2021.102482

Serda, M. (2013). SyntezaiAktywnośćBiologicznaNowychAnalogówTiosemikarbazonowychChelatoró wŻelaza. *Uniwersytetśląski, 7*(1), 343–54. https://desytamara.blogspot.com/2017/11/sistem-pelayanan-perpustakaan-dan-jenis.html

Singh, R. P., & Agrawal, M. (2008). Potential Benefits and Risks of Land Application of Sewage Sludge. *Waste Management (New York, N.Y.), 28*(2), 347–358. doi:10.1016/j.wasman.2006.12.010 PMID:17320368

Steiner, M., Smith, J. A., Burges, S. J., Alonso, C. V., & Darden, R. W. (2023, March 5). Effect of Bias Adjustment and Rain Gauge Data Quality Control on Radar Rainfall Estimation. *Water Resources Research, 35*(8), 2487–2503. doi:10.1029/1999WR900142

Sutinen, J. G., & Kuperan, K. (1999). A Socio-Economic Theory of Regulatory Compliance. *International Journal of Social Economics*, 26(1–3), 174–193. doi:10.1108/03068299910229569

Thuraisingham, B. (2020). The Role of Artificial Intelligence and Cyber Security for Social Media. *Proceedings - 2020 IEEE 34th International Parallel and Distributed Processing Symposium Workshops, IPDPSW 2020*, 1116–18. 10.1109/IPDPSW50202.2020.00184

Wang et al. (2017). Generative Adversarial Networks: Introduction and Outlook. *IEEE/CAA Journal of AutomaticaSinica*, 4(4), 588–98.

Compilation of References

Abdel, H. (2019). Internet of Things (IOT): Research Challenges and Future Applications. *International Journal of Advanced Computer Science and Applications*.

Abdullah, A. (2017). *Advanced Encryption Standard (AES)*. Algorithm to Encrypt and Decrypt Data.

Abdulsalam & Hedabou. (2021). *Security and Privacy in Cloud Computing: Technical Review*. Academic Press.

Abir, S. M. A. A., Anwar, A., Choi, J., & Kayes, A. S. M. (2021). Iot-enabled smart energy grid: Applications and challenges. *IEEE Access : Practical Innovations, Open Solutions*, 9, 50961–50981. doi:10.1109/ACCESS.2021.3067331

Adams-Price, C., & Greene, A. L. (1990). Secondary Attachments and Adolescent Self Concept. *Sex Roles*, 22(3), 187–198. doi:10.1007/BF00288191

Adhya, S., Saha, D., & Das, A. (2016). An IoT based smart solar photovoltaic remote monitoring and control unit. *2016 2nd international conference on control, instrumentation, energy & communication (CIEC)*, 432–436. 10.1109/CIEC.2016.7513793

Agarap, A. F. M. (2018). *Unit (GRU) and Support Vector Machine (SVM) for Intrusion Detection in Network Traffic Data*. Academic Press.

Agarwal, A., Sharma, P., Alshehri, M., Mohamed, A. A., & Alfarraj, O. (2021). Classification model for accuracy and intrusion detection using machine learning approach. *PeerJ. Computer Science*, 7, e437. doi:10.7717/peerj-cs.437 PMID:33954233

Aggarwal, Singh, Chopra, Kumar, & Colace. (2022). *Deep Learning in Robotics for Strengthening Industry 4.0.: Opportunities, Challenges and Future Directions*. doi:10.1007/978-3-030-96737-6_1

Agrawal, E., & Pal, P. (2017). A Secure and Fast Approach for Encryption and Decryption of Message Communication. *International Journal of Engineering Science and Computing.*, 7, 5.

Ahlawat, C., & Krishnamurthi, R. (2022). Internet of Things-based smart helmet to detect possible COVID-19 infections. In *Cyber-Physical Systems*. Academic Press. . doi:10.1016/B978-0-12-824557-6.00004-2

Ahmed, H., Younis, E. M., Hendawi, A. M., & Ali, A. A. (2020). Heart disease identification from patients' social posts, machine learning solution on Spark. *Future Generation Computer Systems*, 111, 714–722. doi:10.1016/j.future.2019.09.056

Ajaegbu, C., Nwaocha, V., Nzenwata, U., & Adesegun, O. (2020). A patient monitoring system using internet of things technology. *Ingénierie des Systèmes d'Information*, 25(3), 351–357. doi:10.18280/isi.250309

Ajao, Abisoye, Jibril, Jonah, & Kolo. (2020). In-Vehicle Traffic Accident Detection and Alerting System Using Distance-Time Based Parameters and Radar Range Algorithm. *2020 IEEE PES/IAS PowerAfrica*, 1-5. . doi:10.1109/PowerAfrica49420.2020.9219812

Akhtar, M. N., Shaikh, A. J., Khan, A., Awais, H., Bakar, E. A., & Othman, A. R. (2021). Smart Sensing with Edge Computing in Precision Agriculture for Soil Assessment and Heavy Metal Monitoring. *Agriculture*, *11*(6), 475. doi:10.3390/agriculture11060475

Akhter, R., & Sofi, S. A. (2022). Precision agriculture using IoT data analytics and machine learning. *Journal of King Saud University-Computer and Information Sciences*, *34*(8), 5602–5618. doi:10.1016/j.jksuci.2021.05.013

Al Bassam, N., Hussain, S. A., Al Qaraghuli, A., Khan, J., Sumesh, E. P., & Lavanya, V. (2021). IoT based wearable device to monitor the signs of quarantined remote patients of COVID-19. *Informatics in Medicine Unlocked*, *24*, 100588. doi:10.1016/j.imu.2021.100588 PMID:33997262

Alafeef, M. (2017). Smartphone-based photoplethysmographic imaging for heart rate monitoring. *Journal of Medical Engineering & Technology*, *41*(5), 387–395. doi:10.1080/03091902.2017.1299233 PMID:28300460

Alafeef, M., & Fraiwan, M. (2020). Smartphone-based respiratory rate estimation using photoplethysmographic imaging and discrete wavelet transform. *Journal of Ambient Intelligence and Humanized Computing*, *11*(2), 693–703. doi:10.100712652-019-01339-6

Alavikia, Z., & Shabro, M. (2022). A comprehensive layered approach for implementing internet of things-enabled smart grid: A survey. *Digital Communications and Networks*, *8*(3), 388–410. doi:10.1016/j.dcan.2022.01.002

Alberdi, A., Weakley, A., Schmitter-Edgecombe, M., Cook, D. J., Aztiria, A., Basarab, A., & Barrenechea, M. (2018). Smart Home-Based Prediction of Multidomain Symptoms Related to Alzheimer's Disease. *IEEE Journal of Biomedical and Health Informatics*, *22*(6), 1720–1731. doi:10.1109/JBHI.2018.2798062 PMID:29994359

Aleqabie, H. J., Al-Shakarchy, N., & Alshahad, H. (2014). Classical Image Encryption and Decryption. *International Journal of Scientific Research*, 4.

Alhayani, Mohammed, Chaloob, & Ahmed. (2023). *Effectiveness of Artificial Intelligence Techniques against Cyber Security Risks Apply of IT Industry*. doi:10.1016/j.matpr.2021.02.531

Alisetti, P., & Mahtani. (2019). *Guiding and Navigation for the Blind using Deep Convolutional Neural Network Based Predictive Object Tracking*. . doi:10.35940/ijeat.A1058.1291S319

Aljumah, A. (2021). *IoT-based intrusion detection system using convolution neural networks*. doi:10.7717/peerj-cs.721

Al-khafajiy, M., Baker, T., Chalmers, C., Asim, M., Kolivand, H., Fahim, M., & Waraich, A. (2019). Remote health monitoring of elderly through wearable sensors. *Multimedia Tools and Applications*, *78*(17), 24681–24706. doi:10.100711042-018-7134-7

Almseidin, M., Alzubi, M., Kovacs, S., & Alkasassbeh, M. (n.d.). *Evaluation of Machine Learning Algorithms for Intrusion Detection System*. Academic Press.

Alshamkhany, M., Alshamkhany, W., Mansour, M., Khan, M., Dhou, S., & Aloul, F. (2020). Botnet Attack Detection using Machine Learning. *2020 14th International Conference on Innovations in Information Technology (IIT)*, 203–208. https://doi.org/10.1109/IIT50501.2020.9299061

Alsharidah, Y. M. Y., & Alazzawi, A. (2020). Artificial Intelligence and Digital Transformation in Supply Chain Management: A Case Study in Saudi Companies. In *2020 International Conference on Data Analytics for Business and Industry: Way Towards a Sustainable Economy (ICDABI)* (pp. 1-6). 10.1109/ICDABI51230.2020.9325616

Al-Sheikh, M. A., & Ameen, I. A. (2020). Design of mobile healthcare monitoring system using IoT technology and cloud computing. *IOP Conference Series: Materials Science and Engineering, 881*. 10.1088/1757-899X/881/1/012113

Altalak, M., Ammad Uddin, M., Alajmi, A., & Rizg, A. (2022). Smart Agriculture Applications Using Deep Learning Technologies: A Survey. *Applied Sciences (Basel, Switzerland), 12*(12), 5919. doi:10.3390/app12125919

Al-Turjman, F., & Abujubbeh, M. (2019). IoT-enabled smart grid via SM: An overview. *Future Generation Computer Systems, 96*, 579–590. doi:10.1016/j.future.2019.02.012

Alzoubi, A. (2022). Machine learning for intelligent energy consumption in smart homes. *International Journal of Computations, Information and Manufacturing, 2*(1).

Amer, M., Naaman, A., M'Sirdi, N. K., & El-Zonkoly, A. M. (2014). Smart home energy management systems survey. *International Conference on Renewable Energies for Developing Countries 2014*, 167–173. 10.1109/REDEC.2014.7038551

Amethiya, Y., Pipariya, P., Patel, S., & Shah, M. (2022). Comparative analysis of breast cancer detection using machine learning and biosensors. *Intelligent Medicine, 2*(2), 69–81. doi:10.1016/j.imed.2021.08.004

Anand, D., Arulselvi, G., Balaji, G. N., & Chandra, G. R. (2022). A Deep Convolutional Extreme Machine Learning Classification Method to Detect Bone Cancer from Histopathological Images. *International Journal of Intelligent Systems and Applications in Engineering, 10*(4), 39–47.

Anand, P., Gupta, R., Tiwari, N. K., & Gupta, S. (2022). Glass Virtual Try-On. *International Journal for Research in Applied Science and Engineering Technology, 10*(5), 718–722. Advance online publication. doi:10.22214/ijraset.2022.42317

Antim, A., & Luigi, L. (2017). An extensive Review on Interfaces between IoT and Cloud Computing. *International Journal of Engineering Research & Technology*.

Araby, A. A., Abd Elhameed, M. M., Magdy, N. M., Said, L. A., Abdelaal, N., Abd Allah, Y. T., Darweesh, M. S., Fahim, M. A., & Mostafa, H. (2019). Smart IoT Monitoring System for Agriculture with Predictive Analysis. *2019 8th International Conference on Modern Circuits and Systems Technologies, MOCAST 2019*. 10.1109/MOCAST.2019.8741794

Arooj, S., Rehman, S., Imran, A., Almuhaimeed, A., Alzahrani, A. K., & Alzahrani, A. (2022). A Deep Convolutional Neural Network for the Early Detection of Heart Disease. *Biomedicines, 10*(11), 2796. doi:10.3390/biomedicines10112796 PMID:36359317

Aruul Mozhi Varman, S., Baskaran, A. R., Aravindh, S., & Prabhu, E. (2017). Deep Learning and IoT for Smart Agriculture Using WSN. *2017 IEEE International Conference on Computational Intelligence and Computing Research*, 1-6. 10.1109/ICCIC.2017.8524140

Babu, B. S., Kamalakannan, J., Meenatchi, N., M, S. K. S., S, K., & Boopathi, S. (2023). Economic impacts and reliability evaluation of battery by adopting Electric Vehicle. *IEEE Explore*, 1–6. doi:10.1109/ICPECTS56089.2022.10046786

Bahrami, H., Homayouni, S., Safari, A., Mirzaei, S., Mahdianpari, M., & Reisi-Gahrouei, O. (2021). Deep Learning-Based Estimation of Crop Biophysical Parameters Using Multi-Source and Multi-Temporal Remote Sensing Observations. *Agronomy (Basel), 11*(7), 1363. doi:10.3390/agronomy11071363

Baranwal, T. (n.d.). *Development of IoT based smart security and monitoring devices for agriculture.* Retrieved March 5, 2023, from https://ieeexplore.ieee.org/abstract/document/7508189/

Barnea, E., Mairon, R., & Ben-Shahar, O. (2016). Colour-agnostic shape-based 3D fruit detection for crop harvesting robots. *Biosystems Engineering, 146*, 57–70. doi:10.1016/j.biosystemseng.2016.01.013

Basalla, M., Ebert, F., Tebner, R., & Ke, W. (n.d.). *Grasping for the Real World (Greifen mit Deep Learning).* Academic Press.

Basheer, F. B., Alias, J. J., Favas, C. M., Navas, V., Farhan, N. K., & Raghu, C. V. (2013). Design of accident detection and alert system for motor cycles. *2013 IEEE Global. Humanitarian Technology Conference: South Asia Satellite (GHTC-SAS),* 85-89. 10.1109/GHTC-SAS.2013.6629894

Ben Mabrouk, A., & Zagrouba, E. (2018). Abnormal behavior recognition for intelligent video surveillance systems: A review. *Expert Systems with Applications, 91,* 480–491. doi:10.1016/j.eswa.2017.09.029

Bharati, M., & Ramageri, B. (2010). Data mining techniques and applications. *Indian Journal of Computer Science and Engineering.*

Bhaskar, Dhanwate, Kale, Kayastha, & Khairnar. (2021). Deep Learning based Smart Agriculture Crop Prediction. *Journal of Advancement in Parallel Computing, 4*(1), 1–8.

Bhutta, M. N. M., & Ahmad, M. (2021). Secure identification, traceability and real-time tracking of agricultural food supply during transportation using internet of things. *IEEE Access : Practical Innovations, Open Solutions, 9,* 65660–65675. doi:10.1109/ACCESS.2021.3076373

Bicchi, A., & Kumar, V. (2000). Robotic grasping and contact: A review. *Proceedings of the 2000 ICRA. Millennium Conference. IEEE International Conference on Robotics and Automation. Symposia Proceedings, 1,* 348–353. 10.1109/ROBOT.2000.844081

Boardman R, Zhu A. (2020). Augmented Reality and Virtual Reality – New Drivers For Fashion Retail? *Technology-Driven Sustainability: Innovation in the Fashion Supply Chain.* . doi:10.1007/978-3-030-15483-7_9

Bohannon, J. (2014). Helping robots see the big picture. *Science, 346*(6206), 186–187. doi:10.1126cience.346.6206.186 PMID:25301616

Böhmer, W., Springenberg, J. T., Boedecker, J., Riedmiller, M., & Obermayer, K. (2015). Autonomous learning of state representations for control: An emerging field aims to autonomously learn state representations for reinforcement learning agents from their real-world sensor observations. *Kunstliche Intelligenz, 29*(4), 353–362. doi:10.100713218-015-0356-1

Boopathi, S. (2021). Improving of Green Sand-Mould Quality using Taguchi Technique. *Journal of Engineering Research.* doi:10.36909/jer.14079

Boopathi, S., Arigela, S. H., Raman, R., Indhumathi, C., Kavitha, V., & Bhatt, B. C. (2023). Prominent Rule Control-based Internet of Things: Poultry Farm Management System. *IEEE Explore,* 1–6. doi:10.1109/ICPECTS56089.2022.10047039

Boopathi, S., Khare, R., Jaya Christiyan, K. G., Muni, T. V., & Khare, S. (2023). Additive manufacturing developments in the medical engineering field. In Development, Properties, and Industrial Applications of 3D Printed Polymer Composites (pp. 86–106). IGI Global. doi:10.4018/978-1-6684-6009-2.ch006

Boopathi, S., Siva Kumar, P. K., & Meena, R. S. J., S. I., P., S. K., & Sudhakar, M. (2023). Sustainable Developments of Modern Soil-Less Agro-Cultivation Systems. In Human Agro-Energy Optimization for Business and Industry (pp. 69–87). IGI Global. doi:10.4018/978-1-6684-4118-3.ch004

Boopathi, S. (2019). Experimental investigation and parameter analysis of LPG refrigeration system using Taguchi method. *SN Applied Sciences, 1*(8), 892. doi:10.100742452-019-0925-2

Boopathi, S. (2022a). An experimental investigation of Quench Polish Quench (QPQ) coating on AISI 4150 steel. *Engineering Research Express, 4*(4), 45009. doi:10.1088/2631-8695/ac9ddd

Boopathi, S. (2022b). An Extensive Review on Sustainable Developments of Dry and Near-Dry Electrical Discharge Machining Processes. *Journal of Manufacturing Science and Engineering*, *144*(5), 50801. doi:10.1115/1.4052527

Boopathi, S. (2022c). An investigation on gas emission concentration and relative emission rate of the near-dry wire-cut electrical discharge machining process. *Environmental Science and Pollution Research International*, *29*(57), 86237–86246. doi:10.100711356-021-17658-1 PMID:34837614

Boopathi, S. (2022d). Cryogenically treated and untreated stainless steel grade 317 in sustainable wire electrical discharge machining process: A comparative study. *Environmental Science and Pollution Research International*, 1–10. doi:10.100711356-022-22843-x PMID:36057706

Boopathi, S. (2022e). Experimental investigation and multi-objective optimization of cryogenic Friction-stir-welding of AA2014 and AZ31B alloys using MOORA technique. *Materials Today. Communications*, *33*, 104937. doi:10.1016/j.mtcomm.2022.104937

Boopathi, S. (2022f). Performance Improvement of Eco-Friendly Near-Dry Wire-Cut Electrical Discharge Machining Process Using Coconut Oil-Mist Dielectric Fluid. *Journal of Advanced Manufacturing Systems*, 1–20. Advance online publication. doi:10.1142/S0219686723500178

Boopathi, S. (2023). An Investigation on Friction Stir Processing of Aluminum Alloy-Boron Carbide Surface Composite. In *Materials Horizons: From Nature to Nanomaterials* (pp. 249–257). Springer. doi:10.1007/978-981-19-7146-4_14

Boopathi, S., Balasubramani, V., Kumar, R. S., & Singh, G. R. (2021). The influence of human hair on kenaf and Grewia fiber-based hybrid natural composite material: An experimental study. *Functional Composites and Structures*, *3*(4), 45011. doi:10.1088/2631-6331/ac3afc

Boopathi, S., Balasubramani, V., & Sanjeev Kumar, R. (2023). Influences of various natural fibers on the mechanical and drilling characteristics of coir-fiber-based hybrid epoxy composites. *Engineering Research Express*, *5*(1), 15002. doi:10.1088/2631-8695/acb132

Boopathi, S., Haribalaji, V., Mageswari, M., & Asif, M. M. (2022). Influences of Boron Carbide Particles on the Wear Rate and Tensile Strength of Aa2014 Surface Composite Fabricated By Friction-Stir Processing. *Materiali in Tehnologije*, *56*(3), 263–270. doi:10.17222/mit.2022.409

Borgaonkar, R., Anne Tøndel, I., Zenebe Degefa, M., & Gilje Jaatun, M. (2021). Improving smart grid security through 5G enabled IoT and edge computing. *Concurrency and Computation*, *33*(18), e6466. doi:10.1002/cpe.6466

Borges, A., & Carlos, H. (2019). A Virtual Makeup Augmented Reality System. *21st Symposium on Virtual and Augmented Reality (SVR)*. 10.1109/SVR.2019.00022

Boursianis, A. D., Papadopoulou, M. S., Diamantoulakis, P., Liopa-Tsakalidi, A., Barouchas, P., Salahas, G., Karagiannidis, G., Wan, S., & Goudos, S. K. (2022). Internet of Things (IoT) and Agricultural Unmanned Aerial Vehicles (UAVs) in smart farming: A comprehensive review. *Internet of Things*, *18*, 100187. doi:10.1016/j.iot.2020.100187

Brewster, C., Roussaki, I., Kalatzis, N., Doolin, K., & Ellis, K. (2017). IoT in Agriculture: Designing a Europe-Wide Large-Scale Pilot. *IEEE Communications Magazine*, *55*(9), 26–33. doi:10.1109/MCOM.2017.1600528

Buja, I., Sabella, E., Monteduro, A. G., Chiriacò, M. S., De Bellis, L., Luvisi, A., & Maruccio, G. (2021). Advances in Plant Disease Detection and Monitoring: From Traditional Assays to In-Field Diagnostics. *Sensors (Basel)*, *21*(6), 2129. doi:10.339021062129 PMID:33803614

Caro, M. P., Ali, M. S., Vecchio, M., & Giaffreda, R. (2019). Blockchain-based traceability in agri-food supply chain management: A practical implementation. *Sensors (Basel)*, *19*(14), 3190. PMID:31331085

Casado, R., & Younas, M. (2023, March 5). 2015. "Emerging Trends and Technologies in Big Data Processing.". *Concurrency and Computation*, 27(8), 2078–2091. doi:10.1002/cpe.3398

Celesti, Galletta, Carnevale, Fazio, Láy-Ekuakille, & Villari. (2018). An IoT Cloud System for Traffic Monitoring and Vehicular Accidents Prevention Based on Mobile Sensor Data Processing. *IEEE Sensors Journal, 18*(12), 4795-4802. doi:10.1109/JSEN.2017.2777786

Chakravarthi, P. K., Yuvaraj, D., & Venkataramanan, V. (2022). IoT-based smart energy meter for smart grids. *ICDCS 2022 - 2022 6th International Conference on Devices, Circuits and Systems*, 360–363. 10.1109/ICDCS54290.2022.9780714

Chandra, A., Dervenoulas, G., & Politis, M. (2019). Magnetic resonance imaging in Alzheimer's disease and mild cognitive impairment. *Journal of Neurology, 266*(6), 1293–1302. doi:10.100700415-018-9016-3 PMID:30120563

Chandran, V., Sumithra, M. G., Karthick, A., George, T., Deivakani, M., Elakkiya, B., Subramaniam, U., & Manoharan, S. (2021). Diagnosis of Cervical Cancer based on Ensemble Deep Learning Network using Colposcopy Images. *BioMed Research International, 2021*, 1–15. doi:10.1155/2021/5584004 PMID:33997017

Chandra, S., Mandal, B., Alam, S., & Bhattacharyya, S. (2015). Content Based Double Encryption Algorithm Using Symmetric Key Cryptography. *Procedia Computer Science, 57*, 1228–1234. Advance online publication. doi:10.1016/j.procs.2015.07.420

Chaudhari, A., Agrawal, H., Poddar, S., Talele, K., & Bansode, M. (2021). Smart Accident Detection And Alert System. *2021 IEEE India Council International Subsections Conference (INDISCON)*, 1-4. 10.1109/INDISCON53343.2021.9582163

Cheatham, B., Javanmardian, K., & Samandari, H. (2019). *Confronting the Risks of Artificial Intelligence With Great Power Comes Great Responsibility*. Organizations Can Mitigate the Risks of Applying Artificial Intelligence and Advanced Analytics by Embracing Three Principles.

Chen, P., Tian, Z., Wang, D., & Zhu, Y. (2021). Research on Blockchain-Based Power Data Storage Scheme. *E3S Web of Conferences, 292*. . doi:10.1051/e3sconf/202129202007

Chen, J., Mai, H., Luo, L., Chen, X., & Wu, K. (2021). Effective Feature Fusion Network in BIFPN for Small Object Detection. *2021 IEEE International Conference on Image Processing (ICIP)*, 699-703. 10.1109/ICIP42928.2021.9506347

Chen, S.-J., Chiu, W.-Y., & Liu, W.-J. (2021). User Preference-Based Demand Response for Smart Home Energy Management Using Multiobjective Reinforcement Learning. *IEEE Access : Practical Innovations, Open Solutions, 9*, 161627–161637. doi:10.1109/ACCESS.2021.3132962

Chen, S., Zhao, Y., Jin, Q., & Wu, Q. (2020). Fine-grained video-text retrieval with hierarchical graph reasoning. *Proceedings of the IEEE/CVF Conference on Computer Vision and Pattern Recognition*, 10638–10647. 10.1109/CVPR42600.2020.01065

Chen, Z., Sivaparthipan, C. B., & Muthu, B. (2022). IoT based smart and intelligent smart city energy optimization. *Sustainable Energy Technologies and Assessments, 49*, 101724. doi:10.1016/j.seta.2021.101724

Chitradevi, D., & Prabha, S. (2020). Analysis of brain sub regions using optimization techniques and deep learning method in Alzheimer disease. *Applied Soft Computing, 86*, 105857. doi:10.1016/j.asoc.2019.105857

Chowdhury, M. E. H., Alzoubi, K., Khandakar, A., Khallifa, R., Abouhasera, R., Koubaa, S., Ahmed, R., & Hasan, M. A. (2019). Wearable Real-Time Heart Attack Detection and Warning System to Reduce Road Accidents. *Sensors (Basel), 19*(12), 2780. doi:10.339019122780 PMID:31226858

Chu, X., Ilyas, I. F., Krishnan, S., & Wang, J. (2016). Data Cleaning: Overview and Emerging Challenges. In *Proceedings of the 2016 International Conference on Management of Data (SIGMOD '16)*. Association for Computing Machinery. https://doi.org/10.1145/2882903.2912574

Coates, A., & Ng, A. Y. (2012). Learning feature representations with k-means. In *Neural Networks: Tricks of the Trade* (pp. 561–580). Springer. doi:10.1007/978-3-642-35289-8_30

Conti, Dargahi, & Dehghantanha. (2018). Cyber Threat Intelligence: Challenges and Opportunities. *Advances in Information Security, 70*, 1–6. https://link.springer.com/chapter/10.1007/978-3-319-73951-9_1

Conti, M. (2020). Food traceability in fruit and vegetables supply chain. In *2020 IEEE International Symposium on Circuits and Systems (ISCAS)* (pp. 1-5). IEEE. 10.1109/ISCAS45731.2020.9181294

Corthaut, N., Govaerts, S., Verbert, K., & Duval, E. (2008). *Connecting the Dots: Music Metadata Generation, Schemas and Applications*. Academic Press.

Cravero, A., Pardo, S., Sepúlveda, S., & Muñoz, L. (2022). Challenges to Use Machine Learning in Agricultural Big Data: A Systematic Literature Review. *Agronomy (Basel), 12*(3), 748. doi:10.3390/agronomy12030748

Cube, L. A. B. S. (2022). *How AI is Helping Agriculture with Smart Solutions*. https://www.xcubelabs.com/blog/how-ai-is-helping-agriculture-with-smart-solutions/

Dadashzadeh, M., & Sakhaeian, K. (2022). Applications of machine learning and deep learning techniques in smart agriculture: A review. *4th Intercontinental Geoinformation Days (IGD)*, 229-232.

Das, A., Ray, A., Ghosh, A., Bhattacharyya, S., Mukherjee, D., & Rana, T. K. (2017). Vehicle accident prevent cum location monitoring system. *2017 8th Annual Industrial Automation and Electromechanical Engineering Conference (IEMECON)*, 101-105. 10.1109/IEMECON.2017.8079570

Das, S., Nag, A., Adhikary, D., & Ram, R. J. (2021). Computer Vision-based Social Distancing Surveillance with Automated Camera Calibration for Large-scale Deployment. *IEEE, 18th India Council International Conference*, 1-6. 10.1109/INDICON52576.2021.9691485

Data Bridge. (2023, January 7). *Global Smart Healthcare Market – Industry Trends and Forecast to 2029*. Retrieved from: https://www.databridgemarketresearch.com/reports/global-smart-healthcare-market

Davenport, T., & Kalakota, R. (2019). The potential for artificial intelligence in healthcare. *Future Healthcare Journal, 6*(2), 94–98. . doi:10.7861/futurehosp.6-2-94

Dayioğlu, M. A., & Turker, U. (2021). Digital Transformation for Sustainable Future - Agriculture 4.0: A review. *Tarim Bilimleri Dergisi, 27*(4), 373–399. doi:10.15832/ankutbd.986431

DBTA. (2021). *Managing the Hybrid and Multicloud Future, Best Practice Series*. https://info.semarchy.com/hubfs/collateral-v2/report/rp-managing-the-hybrid-and-multicloud-future-Semarchy-DBTA.pdf

De Gregorio, D., Tonioni, A., Palli, G., & Di Stefano, L. (2020). Semiautomatic Labeling for Deep Learning in Robotics. *IEEE Transactions on Automation Science and Engineering, 17*(2), 611–620. doi:10.1109/TASE.2019.2938316

Denton, E., Chintala, S., Szlam, A., & Fergus, R. (2015). *Deep generative image models using a laplacian pyramid of adversarial networks*. arXiv preprint arXiv:1506.05751.

Dewangan & Chaubey. (2021). *Object Detection System with Voice Output using Python*. Academic Press.

Dey, J., Gaurav, A., & Tiwari, V. N. (2018). InstaBP: Cuff-less Blood Pressure Monitoring on Smartphone using Single PPG Sensor. *Annual International Conference of the IEEE Engineering in Medicine and Biology Society. IEEE Engineering in Medicine and Biology Society. Annual International Conference*, 5002–5005. 10.1109/EMBC.2018.8513189

Dhaka, R. K., Panda, S., Panda, B., Pradhan, A., & Jena, C. (2022). AIOT in Healthcare systems: A Thought on Approaches and Criticism. *National Cave Research and Protection Organization*, 9(2), 55–60. doi:10.21276/ambi.2022.09.2.rv02

Dhanaraju, M., Chenniappan, P., Ramalingam, K., Pazhanivelan, S., &Kaliaperumal, R. (2022). Smart Farming: Internet of Things (IoT)-Based Sustainable Agriculture. *Agriculture, 12*(10), 1745. doi:10.3390/agriculture12101745

Dian, F. J. R., Vahidnia, R., & Rahmati, A. (2020). Wearables and the internet of things (IoT), applications, opportunities, and challenges: A survey. *IEEE Access : Practical Innovations, Open Solutions*, 8, 69200–69211. doi:10.1109/ACCESS.2020.2986329

Dias, D., & Paulo Silva Cunha, J. (2018). Wearable Health Devices-Vital Sign Monitoring, Systems and Technologies. *Sensors (Basel)*, 18(8), 2414. doi:10.339018082414 PMID:30044415

Ding, Y., Sohn, J. H., Kawczynski, M. G., Trivedi, H., Harnish, R., Jenkins, N. W., Lituiev, D., Copeland, T. P., Aboian, M. S., Aparici, C. M., & ... . (2019). A Deep Learning Model to Predict a Diagnosis of Alzheimer Disease by Using 18F-FDG PET of the Brain. *Radiology*, 290(2), 456–464. doi:10.1148/radiol.2018180958 PMID:30398430

Domakonda, V. K., Farooq, S., Chinthamreddy, S., Puviarasi, R., Sudhakar, M., & Boopathi, S. (2023). Sustainable Developments of Hybrid Floating Solar Power Plants. In *Human Agro-Energy Optimization for Business and Industry* (pp. 148–167). IGI Global. doi:10.4018/978-1-6684-4118-3.ch008

Dong, J., Li, X., Xu, C., Ji, S., He, Y., Yang, G., & Wang, X. (2019). Dual encoding for zero-example video retrieval. *Proceedings of the IEEE/CVF Conference on Computer Vision and Pattern Recognition*, 9346–9355.

Dong, N., & Fu, J. (2021). Development Path of Smart Agriculture Based on Blockchain. In *2021 IEEE Asia-Pacific Conference on Image Processing, Electronics and Computers (IPEC)*. IEEE. 10.1109/IPEC51340.2021.9421125

Dong, Y., Fu, Z., Stankovski, S., Wang, S., & Li, X. (2019). Nutritional Quality and Safety Traceability System for China's Leafy Vegetable Supply Chain based on Fault Tree Analysis and QR Code. *IEEE Access : Practical Innovations, Open Solutions*, 7, 187881–187893.

Doss, C. (2014). Data needs for gender analysis in agriculture. *Gender in Agriculture: Closing the Knowledge Gap*, 55–68. https://doi.org/ doi:10.1007/978-94-017-8616-4_3/COVER

Dov & Kaufman. (2018). Augmenting Reality with Intelligent Interfaces. *IntechOpen*. doi:10.5772/intechopen.75751

Duc, N. T., Ryu, S., Qureshi, M. N. I., Choi, M., Lee, K. H., & Lee, B. (2019). 3D-Deep Learning Based Automatic Diagnosis of Alzheimer's Disease with Joint MMSE Prediction Using Resting-State fMRI. *Neuroinformatics*, 18(1), 71–86. doi:10.100712021-019-09419-w PMID:31093956

Duo, Meng, & Abusorrah. (2022). A Survey of Cyber Attacks on Cyber Physical Systems: Recent Advances and Challenges. *IEEE/CAA Journal of AutomaticaSinica, 9*(5), 784–800.

Dutta, W., Mitra, S., & Kalaivani, S. (2017). Audio encryption and decryption algorithm in image format for secured communication. *2017 International Conference on Inventive Computing and Informatics (ICICI)*, 517-521. 10.1109/ICICI.2017.8365185

Dwibedi, S., Pujari, M., & Sun, W. (2020). A Comparative Study on Contemporary Intrusion Detection Datasets for Machine Learning Research. *2020 IEEE International Conference on Intelligence and Security Informatics (ISI)*, 1–6. https://doi.org/10.1109/ISI49825.2020.9280519

Edan, Y., Han, S., & Kondo, N. (2009). Automation in Agriculture. In S. Nof (Ed.), *Springer Handbook of Automation. Springer Handbooks*. Springer., doi:10.1007/978-3-540-78831-7_63

Efros, A., & Leung, T. K. (1999). Texture synthesis by non-parametric sampling. In *Computer Vision, 1999. The Proceedings of the Seventh IEEE International Conference on* (vol. 2, pp. 1033–1038). IEEE. 10.1109/ICCV.1999.790383

Elango, K., & Muniandi, K. (2020). A low-cost wearable remote healthcare monitoring system. In G. R. Kanagachidambaresan (Ed.), *Role of Edge Analytics in Sustainable Smart City Development: Challenges and Solutions* (pp. 219–242). doi:10.1002/9781119681328.ch11

Elijah, O., Orikumhi, I., Rahman, T. A., Babale, S. A., & Orakwue, S. I. (2018). Enabling smart agriculture in Nigeria: Application of IoT and data analytics. *2017 IEEE 3rd International Conference on Electro-Technology for National Development, NIGERCON 2017*, 762–766. 10.1109/NIGERCON.2017.8281944

Elijah, O., Rahman, T. A., Orikumhi, I., Leow, C. Y., & Hindia, M. N. (2018). An Overview of Internet of Things (IoT) and Data Analytics in Agriculture: Benefits and Challenges. *IEEE Internet of Things Journal*, 5(5), 3758–3773. doi:10.1109/JIOT.2018.2844296

Ellewala, U. P., Amarasena, W. D. H. U., Lakmali, H. V. S., Senanayaka, L. M. K., & Senarathne, A. N. (2020). Secure Messaging Platform Based on Blockchain. *2020 2nd International Conference on Advancements in Computing (ICAC)*, 317-322. 10.1109/ICAC51239.2020.9357306

Endalie, D., Haile, G., & Taye, W. (2022). Deep Learning Model for daily rainfall prediction: A case study of Jimma, Ethiopia. *Water Science and Technology: Water Supply*, 22(3), 3448–3461. doi:10.2166/ws.2021.391

Enriko, A. I. K., & Suryanegara, M., & Gunawan, D. (2018). Heart Disease Diagnosis System with k-Nearest Neighbors Method Using Real Clinical Medical Records. In *Proceedings of the 4th International Conference on Frontiers of Educational Technologies (ICFET '18)*. Association for Computing Machinery. 10.1145/3233347.3233386

Eos. (2022). *Smart Farming: Technologies & Benefits for Agriculture*. EOS Data Analytics. https://eos.com/blog/smart-farming/

Eugeni, R. (2022). Augmented Reality Filters and the Faces as Brands: Personal Identities and Marketing Strategies in the Age of Algorithmic Images. *24th HCI International Conference*. 10.1007/978-3-031-05064-0_17

F., S. (2018). Machine-Learning Techniques for Customer Retention: A Comparative Study. *International Journal of Advanced Computer Science and Applications*, 9(2). doi:10.14569/IJACSA.2018.090238

Fang, L., Wu, Y., Li, Y., Guo, H., Zhang, H., Wang, X., Xi, R., & Hou, J. (2021). Ginger Seeding Detection and Shoot Orientation Discrimination Using an Improved YOLOv4-LITE Network. *Agronomy (Basel)*, 11(11), 2328. doi:10.3390/agronomy11112328

Fan, Y., Wen, G., Li, D., Qiu, S., Levine, M. D., & Xiao, F. (2020). Video Anomaly Detection and Localization via Gaussian Mixture Fully Convolutional Variational Autoencoder. *Computer Vision and Image Understanding*, 195, 1–13. doi:10.1016/j.cviu.2020.102920

Farabet, C., Couprie, C., Najman, L., & LeCun, Y. (2013). Learning hierarchical features for scene labeling. *IEEE Transactions on Pattern Analysis and Machine Intelligence*, 35(8), 1915–1929. doi:10.1109/TPAMI.2012.231 PMID:23787344

Farooq, M. S., Riaz, S., Abid, A., Umer, T., & Zikria, Y. bin. (2020). Role of IoT Technology in Agriculture: A Systematic Literature Review. *Electronics*, 9(2), 319. doi:10.3390/electronics9020319

Fastellini, G., & Schillaci, C. (2020). Precision farming and IoT case studies across the world. *Agricultural Internet of Things and Decision Support for Precision Smart Farming*, 331–415. doi:10.1016/B978-0-12-818373-1.00007-X

Fernandes, B., Alam, M., Gomes, V., Ferreira, J., & Oliveira, A. (2016). Automatic accident detection with multi-modal alert system implementation for ITS. *Vehicular Communications, 3*, 1-11. doi:10.1016/j.vehcom.2015.11.001

Fiehn, H. B., Schiebel, L., Avila, A. F., Miller, B., & Mickelson, A. (2018). Smart Agriculture System Based on Deep Learning. *ICSDE'18: Proceedings of the 2nd International Conference on Smart Digital Environment*, 158–165. 10.1145/3289100.3289126

Foreman, P. (2019). (2023). *Vulnerability Management* (2nd ed.). https://www.taylorfrancis.com/books/mono/10.1201/9780429289651/vulnerability-management-park-foreman

Forootani, A., Rastegar, M., & Jooshaki, M. (2022). An advanced satisfaction-based home energy management system using deep reinforcement learning. *IEEE Access : Practical Innovations, Open Solutions, 10*, 47896–47905. doi:10.1109/ACCESS.2022.3172327

Frank, M. R., Autor, D., Bessen, J. E., Brynjolfsson, E., Cebrian, M., Deming, D. J., Feldman, M., Groh, M., Lobo, J., Moro, E., Wang, D., Youn, H., & Rahwan, I. (2023, March 5). Toward Understanding the Impact of Artificial Intelligence on Labor. *Proceedings of the National Academy of Sciences of the United States of America, 116*(14), 6531–6539. doi:10.1073/pnas.1900949116 PMID:30910965

Freeman, W. T., Jones, T. R., & Pasztor, E. C. (2002). Example-based super-resolution. *IEEE Computer Graphics and Applications, 22*(2), 56–65. doi:10.1109/38.988747

Fribourg, P. (2021). Mirror on My Phone: Investigating Dimensions of Self-Face Perception Induced by Augmented Reality Filters. *IEEE International Symposium on Mixed and Augmented Reality (ISMAR)*. 10.1109/ISMAR52148.2021.00064

Gabeur, V., Sun, C., Alahari, K., & Schmid, C. (2020). Multi-modal transformer for video retrieval. Computer Vision–ECCV 2020: 16th European Conference, Glasgow, UK, August 23–28, 2020. *Proceedings, 16*(4), 214–229.

Galvez, J. F., Mejuto, J. C., & Simal-Gandara, J. (2020). Future challenges on the use of blockchain for food traceability analysis. *Food Research International, 136*, 109663.

Garg, N., Pareek, A., Lale, A., & Charya, S. K. (2020). Evolution in E-Commerce with Augmented Reality. *IOP Conf. Series: Materials Science and Engineering*. 10.1088/1757-899X/1012/1/012041

Gariba, D., & Pipaliya, B. (2016). Modelling human behaviour in smart home energy management systems via machine learning techniques. *2016 International Automatic Control Conference (CACS)*, 53–58. 10.1109/CACS.2016.7973883

Geethamahalakshmi,, & Sambath, Gayathiri, Vijayaraja, Senthil Kumar, & Umaeswari. (2022). A Deep Learning Based Smart Agriculture Technique for an IoT Environment. *Journal of Pharmaceutical Negative Results, 13*(10), 1562–1569. doi:10.47750/pnr.2022.13.S10.181

Ge, M., Fu, X., Syed, N., Baig, Z., Teo, G., & Robles-Kelly, A. (2019). Deep learning-based intrusion detection for IoT networks. *Proceedings of IEEE Pacific Rim International Symposium on Dependable Computing, PRDC, 2019-Decem*, 256–265. https://doi.org/10.1109/PRDC47002.2019.00056

Giri, A., Dutta, S., & Neogy, S. (2017). Enabling agricultural automation to optimize utilization of water, fertilizer and insecticides by implementing Internet of Things (IoT). *2016 International Conference on Information Technology, InCITe 2016 - The Next Generation IT Summit on the Theme - Internet of Things: Connect Your Worlds*, 125–131. 10.1109/INCITE.2016.7857603

Girshick, R. (2015). Fast-RCNN. *Proceedings of the IEEE International Conference on Computer Vision (ICCV)*, 1440–1448. 10.1109/ICCV.2015.169

Girshick, R., Donahue, J., Darrell, T., & Malik, J. (2014). Rich feature hierarchies for accurate object detection and semantic segmentation. *Proceedings of the IEEE Conference on Computer Vision and Pattern Recognition, 580–587.* 10.1109/CVPR.2014.81

Godard, C., Mac Aodha, O., & Brostow, G. J. (2017). Unsupervised monocular depth estimation with left-right consistency. CVPR. doi:10.1109/CVPR.2017.699

Goodfellow, I. J., Pouget-Abadie, J., Mirza, M., Xu, B., Warde-Farley, D., Ozair, S., Courville, A. C., & Bengio, Y. (2014). *Generative adversarial nets.* NIPS.

Goodfellow, I., Bengio, Y., & Courville, A. (2016). *Deep Learning.* MIT Press.

Gorges, M., Müller, H.-P., & Kassubek, J. (2018). Structural and Functional Brain Mapping Correlates of Impaired Eye Movement Control in Parkinsonian Syndromes: A Systems-Based Concept. *Frontiers in Neurology, 9*, 319. doi:10.3389/fneur.2018.00319 PMID:29867729

Goudarzi, A., Ghayoor, F., Waseem, M., Fahad, S., & Traore, I. (2022). A Survey on IoT-Enabled Smart Grids: Emerging, Applications, Challenges, and Outlook. *Energies, 15*(19), 6984. doi:10.3390/en15196984

Grand View Research. (2023, January 7). *Global Smart Healthcare Market Size, Share Report.* Retrieved from: 2030 https://www.grandviewresearch.com/industry-analysis/smart-healthcare-market

Granqvist, P., Mikulincer, M., & Shaver, P. R. (2009). Religion as Attachment: Normative Processes and Individual Differences. *Personality and Social Psychology Review, 14*(1), 49–59. doi:10.1177/1088868309348618 PMID:20023208

Gregor, K., Danihelka, I., Graves, A., & Wierstra, D. (2015). *Draw: A recurrent neural network for image generation.* arXiv preprint arXiv:1502.04623.

Grobauer, Stocker, & Walloscheck. (2011). Understanding the vulnerabilities of cloud computing. *IEEE Security & Privacy, 9*(2), 50–7. https://www.cisco.com/c/en/us/solutions/collateral/service-provider/visual-networking-index-vni/mobile-white-paper-c11-520862.pdf

Gui, S., Wang, F., Zhang, Z., & Yang, L. (2009). Research on self-constructed traceability system based on agri-food supply chain management. In *2009 Second International Conference on Intelligent Computation Technology and Automation* (pp. 640-643). IEEE. 10.1109/ICICTA.2009.700

Gunasekaran, K., Boopathi, S., & Sureshkumar, M. (2022). Analysis of a Cryogenically Cooled Near-Dry Wedm Process Using Different Dielectrics. *Materiali in Tehnologije, 56*(2), 179–186. doi:10.17222/mit.2022.397

Guo, H., & Zhang, Y. (2020). Resting State fMRI and Improved Deep Learning Algorithm for Earlier Detection of Alzheimer's Disease. *IEEE Access, 8*, 115383–115392.

Guo, B., Ma, Y., Yang, J., & Wang, Z. (2021). Smart Healthcare System Based on Cloud-Internet of Things and Deep Learning. *Journal of Healthcare Engineering, 2021*, 1–10. doi:10.1155/2021/4109102 PMID:34257851

Gupta R, Nair K S. (2022). Try-on with AR: Impact on sensory brand experience and intention to use the mobile app. *Journal of Management Information and Decision Sciences.*

Gupta, A., Kumar, L., Jain, R., & Nagrath, P. (2020). Heart Disease Prediction Using Classification (Naive Bayes). In *Proceedings of First International Conference on Computing, Communications, and Cyber-Security (IC4S 2019). Lecture Notes in Networks and Systems* (vol. 121). Springer. 10.1007/978-981-15-3369-3_42

Gupta, A., Anpalagan, A., Carvalho, G. H. S., Khwaja, A. S., Guan, L., & Woungang, I. (2019). RETRACTED: Prevailing and emerging cyber threats and security practices in IoT-Enabled smart grids. *Journal of Network and Computer Applications, 132*, 118–148. doi:10.1016/j.jnca.2019.01.012

Gupta, B., Madan, G., & Quadir Md, A. (2022). A smart agriculture framework for IoT based plant decay detection using smart croft algorithm. *Materials Today: Proceedings, 62*, 4758–4763. doi:10.1016/j.matpr.2022.03.314

Hadi, A. A., Sinha, U., & Faika, T. (2019) Internet of things (IoT)-enabled solar micro inverter using blockchain technology. *2019 IEEE industry applications society annual meeting*, 1–5.

Hamidi, M., Safari, A., Homayouni, S., & Hasani, H. (2022). Guided Filtered Sparse Auto-Encoder for Accurate Crop Mapping from Multitemporal and Multi-spectral Imagery. *Agronomy (Basel), 12*(11), 2615. doi:10.3390/agronomy12112615

Haq, E. U., Lyu, C., Xie, P., Yan, S., Ahmad, F., & Jia, Y. (2022). Implementation of home energy management system based on reinforcement learning. *Energy Reports, 8*, 560–566. doi:10.1016/j.egyr.2021.11.170

Hardjono, T., Howard, G., Scace, E., Chowdury, M., Novak, L., Gaudet, M., Anderson, J., Davis, N., Kulis, C., Sweeney, E., & Vaughan, C. (2019). *Towards an Open and Scalable Music Metadata Layer*. Academic Press.

Harikaran, M., Boopathi, S., Gokulakannan, S., & Poonguzhali, M. (2023). Study on the Source of E-Waste Management and Disposal Methods. In *Sustainable Approaches and Strategies for E-Waste Management and Utilization* (pp. 39–60). IGI Global. doi:10.4018/978-1-6684-7573-7.ch003

Harrou, F., Hittawe, M. M., Sun, Y., & Beya, O. (2020). Malicious Attacks Detection in Crowded Areas Using Deep Learning-Based Approach. *IEEE Instrumentation & Measurement Magazine, 23*(5), 57–62. doi:10.1109/MIM.2020.9153576

Hashemi, M., & Hokmabadi, M. (2011). Effective English Presentation and Communication in an International Conference. *Procedia: Social and Behavioral Sciences, 30*, 2104–2111. doi:10.1016/j.sbspro.2011.10.409

Hassan, S. M., Jasinski, M., Zbigniew, L., Jasinska, E., & Maji, A. K. (2021). Plant Disease Identification Using Shallow Convolutional Neural Network. *Agronomy (Basel), 11*(12), 2388. doi:10.3390/agronomy11122388

Hays, J., & Efros, A. A. (2007). Scene completion using millions of photographs. *ACM Transactions on Graphics, 26*(3), 4. doi:10.1145/1276377.1276382

Hazan, C., & Shaver, P. (1987). Romantic Love Conceptualized as an Attachment Process. *Journal of Personality and Social Psychology, 52*(3), 511–524. doi:10.1037/0022-3514.52.3.511 PMID:3572722

Hedman, P., Skepetzis, V., Hernandez-Diaz, K., & Fernandez, J. (2022). *On the effect of selfie beautification filters on face detection and recognition*. ScienceDirect. doi:10.1016/j.patrec.2022.09.018

He, K., Gkioxari, G., Dollár, P., & Girshick, R. (2017). Mask R-CNN. *2017 IEEE International Conference on Computer Vision (ICCV)*, 2980-2988. 10.1109/ICCV.2017.322

Hojjati, S. H., Ebrahimzadeh, A., Khazaee, A., & Babajani-Feremi, A. (2017). Predicting conversion from MCI to AD using resting-state fMRI, graph theoretical approach and SVM. *Journal of Neuroscience Methods, 282*, 69–80. doi:10.1016/j.jneumeth.2017.03.006 PMID:28286064

Holmes & Kellogg. (2006). Automating functional tests using Selenium. *AGILE 2006 (AGILE'06)*. . doi:10.1109/AGILE.2006.19

Hossain, M. S., Muhammad, G., & Guizani, N. (2020). Explainable AI and Mass Surveillance System-Based Healthcare Framework to Combat COVID-19 Like Pandemics. *IEEE Network, 34*(4), 126–132. doi:10.1109/MNET.011.2000458

Hou, Q., Zhou, D., & Feng, J. (2021). Coordinate attention for efficient mobile network design. *Proceedings of the IEEE/CVF Conference on Computer Vision and Pattern Recognition*. 10.1109/CVPR46437.2021.01350

Hsiao, C. (2007). *Benefits and Limitations of Panel Data*. https://www.tandfonline.com/doi/abs/10.1080/07474938508800078 doi:10.1080/07474938508800078

Huang, Y., Liu, R. W., & Liu, J. (2022). A two-step image stabilization method for promoting visual quality in vision-enabled maritime surveillance systems. IET Intelligent Transport Systems, 1-15.

Huang, Q.-X., & Guibas, L. (2013). Consistent shape maps via semidefinite programming. *Symposium on Geometry Processing*.

Huang, S.-C., & Member, S. (2019). A Gray Relational Analysis-Based Motion Detection Algorithm for Real-World Surveillance Sensor Deployment. *IEEE Sensors Journal*, 19(3), 1019–1027. doi:10.1109/JSEN.2018.2879187

Hutamaputra, W., Mawarni, M., Krisnabayu, R. Y., & Mahmudy, W. F. (2021). Detection of Coronary Heart Disease Using Modified K-NN Method with Recursive Feature Elimination. In *6th International Conference on Sustainable Information Engineering and Technology 2021 (SIET '21)*. Association for Computing Machinery. 10.1145/3479645.3479664

ICOS. (2020). *Iot applications in smart agriculture: Issues and challenges*. Retrieved March 5, 2023, from https://ieeexplore.ieee.org/abstract/document/9293672/

Idrissi, I., Azizi, M., & Moussaoui, O. (2022b). A Stratified IoT Deep Learning based Intrusion Detection System. *2022 2nd International Conference on Innovative Research in Applied Science, Engineering and Technology (IRASET)*, 1–8. https://doi.org/10.1109/IRASET52964.2022.9738045

Idrissi, I., Boukabous, M., Azizi, M., Moussaoui, O., & El Fadili, H. (2021). Toward a deep learning-based intrusion detection system for IoT against botnet attacks. *IAES International Journal of Artificial Intelligence (IJ-AI)*, 10(1), 110. doi:10.11591/ijai.v10.i1.pp110-120

Idrissi, I., Azizi, M., & Moussaoui, O. (2021). Accelerating the update of a DL-based IDS for IoT using deep transfer learning. *Indonesian Journal of Electrical Engineering and Computer Science*, 23(2), 1059. doi:10.11591/ijeecs.v23.i2.pp1059-1067

Idrissi, I., Azizi, M., & Moussaoui, O. (2022a). A Lightweight Optimized Deep Learning-based Host-Intrusion Detection System Deployed on the Edge for IoT. *International Journal of Computing and Digital Systems*, 11(1), 209–216. doi:10.12785/ijcds/110117

Intellias. (2022). *Artificial Intelligence in Agriculture: Rooting Out the Seed of Doubt*. https://intellias.com/artificial-intelligence-in-agriculture/

Islam, M. M., Mahmud, S., Muhammad, L. J., Islam, M. R., Nooruddin, S., & Ayon, S. I. (2020). Wearable Technology to Assist the Patients Infected with Novel Coronavirus (COVID-19). *SN Computer Science*, 1(6), 320. doi:10.100742979-020-00335-4 PMID:33063058

Islam, M. M., Rahaman, A., & Islam, M. R. (2020). Development of Smart Healthcare Monitoring System in IoT Environment. *SN Computer Science*, 1(3), 1–11. doi:10.100742979-020-00195-y PMID:33063046

Jabbar, M. A., & Samreen, S. (2016). Heart disease prediction system based on hidden naïve bayes classifier. *2016 International Conference on Circuits, Controls, Communications and Computing (I4C)*, 1-5. 10.1109/CIMCA.2016.8053261

Jadhav, O., Patil, A., Sam, J., & Kiruthika, M. (2021). Virtual Dressing using Augmented Reality. *ITM Web of Conferences, 40*. 10.1051/itmconf/20214003028

Jain, R., Chauhan, P., & Sood, A. (2022). *Anthropometrical Virtual Try-on: A Survey on Virtual Try-ons and Human Body Dimension Estimation.* THEETAS. doi:10.4108/eai.16-4-2022.2318169

Janardhana, K., Anushkannan, N. K., Dinakaran, K. P., Puse, R. K., & Boopathi, S. (2023). *Experimental Investigation on Microhardness, Surface Roughness, and White Layer Thickness of Dry EDM.* Engineering Research Express. doi:10.1088/2631-8695/acce8f

Janardhana, K., Singh, V., & Singh, S. N. (2023). Utilization Process for Electronic Waste in Eco-Friendly Concrete: Experimental Study. In *Sustainable Approaches and Strategies for E-Waste Management and Utilization* (pp. 204–223). IGI Global. doi:10.4018/978-1-6684-7573-7.ch011

Jaspin, K., Selvan, S., Sahana, S., & Thanmai, G. (2021). Efficient and Secure File Transfer in Cloud Through Double Encryption Using AES and RSA Algorithm. *2021 International Conference on Emerging Smart Computing and Informatics (ESCI),* 791-796. 10.1109/ESCI50559.2021.9397005

Javornik, A., Marde, B., Pizzetti, M., & Warlop, L. (2021). Augmented self - The effects of virtual face augmentation on consumers' self-concept. *Journal of Business Research*, *130*, 170–187. Advance online publication. doi:10.1016/j.jbusres.2021.03.026

Jeevanantham, Y. A., A, S., V, V., J, S. I., Boopathi, S., & Kumar, D. P. (2023). Implementation of Internet-of Things (IoT) in Soil Irrigation System. *IEEE Explore*, 1–5. doi:10.1109/ICPECTS56089.2022.10047185

Jha, R., & Kumar, S. (n.d.). *Field monitoring using IoT in agriculture.* Retrieved March 5, 2023, from https://ieeexplore.ieee.org/abstract/document/8342777/

Jin, L., Y., Chuang Wei, C., Yen, C.Y., Huang, S.H., Huang, P.W., Chen, J.Y., & Lee, S.Y. (2019). Artificial Intelligence of Things Wearable System for Cardiac Disease Detection. *2019 IEEE International Conference on Artificial Intelligence Circuits and Systems (AICAS)*, 67-70. 10.1109/AICAS.2019.8771630

Johny, S., & Priyadharsini, C. (2021). Investigations on the Implementation of Blockchain Technology in Supplychain Network. In *Proceedings of the 2021 7th International Conference on Advanced Computing and Communication Systems (ICACCS)* (pp. 294-299). IEEE. 10.1109/ICACCS51430.2021.9441820

Jokanović, R. V. (2020). *Smart healthcare in smart cities. In Towards Smart World: Homes to Cities Using Internet of Things.* Taylor and Francis Group., doi:10.1201/9781003056751

Jordan, M. I., & Mitchell, T. M. (2015). Machine learning: Trends, perspectives, and prospects. *Science*, *349*(6245), 255–260. doi:10.1126cience.aaa8415 PMID:26185243

Journal, I., & Science, O. F. (2021). *An efficient algorithmic technique for feature selection in IoT-based intrusion detection system.* Academic Press.

Kabir, M. F., & Roy, S. (2022). Real-time vehicular accident prevention system using deep learning architecture. *Expert Systems with Applications, 206.* doi:10.1016/j.eswa.2022.117837

Kaggle. (2023, January 7). *Intel & Mobile ODT Cervical cancer Screening.* Retrieved from: https://www.kaggle.com/competitions/intel-mobileodt-cervical-cancer-screening/data

Kalal, Z., Mikolajczyk, K., & Matas, J. (2010). Forwardbackward error: Automatic detection of tracking failures. ICPR.

Kalmkar S, Mujawar A, Liyakat K S. (2022). 3D E-Commers Using AR. *International Journal of Information technology and Computer Engineering.* https://doi.org/ doi:10.55529.ijitc.26.18.27

Kamble, S. S., & Gunasekaran, A. (2020). Modeling the blockchain enabled traceability in agriculture supply chain. *Annals of Operations Research*, 1–26. doi:10.100710479-020-03523-7

Kamilaris, A., Fonts, A., & Prenafeta-Boldú, F. X. (2019). The rise of blockchain technology in agriculture and food supply chains. *Trends in Food Science & Technology*, *91*, 640–652. doi:10.1016/j.tifs.2019.07.034

Kamilaris, A., & Prenafeta-Boldú, F. X. (2018). *Deep Learning in Agriculture: A Survey.* doi:10.1016/j.compag.2018.02.016

Kannadasan, R., Prabakaran, N., Boominathan, P., Krishnamoorthy, A., Naresh, K., & Sivashanmugam, G. (2018). High performance parallel computing with cloud technologies. *Procedia Computer Science*, *132*, 518–524. doi:10.1016/j.procs.2018.05.004

Kannan, E., Trabelsi, Y., Boopathi, S., & Alagesan, S. (2022). Influences of cryogenically treated work material on near-dry wire-cut electrical discharge machining process. *Surface Topography : Metrology and Properties*, *10*(1), 15027. doi:10.1088/2051-672X/ac53e1

Kaptoge, S., Pennells, L., De Bacquer, D., Cooney, M. T., Kavousi, M., Stevens, G., Riley, L. M., Savin, S., Khan, T., Altay, S., Amouyel, P., Assmann, G., Bell, S., Ben-Shlomo, Y., Berkman, L., Beulens, J. W., Björkelund, C., Blaha, M., Blazer, D. G., ... Di Angelantonio, E.WHO CVD Risk Chart Working Group. (2019). World Health Organization cardiovascular disease risk charts: Revised models to estimate risk in 21 global regions. *The Lancet. Global Health*, *7*(10), e1332–e1345. doi:10.1016/S2214-109X(19)30318-3 PMID:31488387

Karataş Baydoğmuş, G. (2021). The Effects of Normalization and Standardization an Internet of Things Attack Detection. *European Journal of Science and Technology*, *29*, 187–192. doi:10.31590/ejosat.1017427

Kattiman & Maidargi. (2021). An Automated Social Distance Monitoring & Alarm System based on Human Structure Using Video Surveillance in CQVID-19 Pandemic by AI Techniques, A Review. *IEEE International Conference on Electronics, Computing and Communication Technologies*.

Kattukkaran, N., George, A., & Haridas, T. P. M. (2017). Intelligent accident detection and alert system for emergency medical assistance. *2017 International Conference on Computer Communication and Informatics (ICCCI)*, 1-6. 10.1109/ICCCI.2017.8117791

Kaur, P., & Parashar, A. (2019). A systematic literature review of blockchain technology for smart villages. *Journal of Theoretical and Applied Information Technology*, *97*(9), 2688–2703.

Kaushik, H., Kumar, T., & Bhalla, K. (2022). iSecureHome: A Deep fusion framework for surveillance of smart house using real-time emotion recognition. *Applied Soft Computing*, *122*, 122. doi:10.1016/j.asoc.2022.108788

Kavitha A (2021). Deep Learning for Smart Agriculture. *International Journal of Engineering Research & Technology*, *9*(5), 132-134.

Ke, Q., Zhang, J., Wei, W., Damasevicius, R., & Wozniak, M. (2019). Adaptive Independent Subspace Analysis of Brain Magnetic Resonance Imaging Data. *IEEE Access*, *7*, 12252–12261.

Kelepouris, T., Pramatari, K., & Doukidis, G. (2007). RFID-enabled traceability in the food supply chain. *Industrial Management & Data Systems*, *107*(2), 183–200. doi:10.1108/02635570710723804

Khacef, K., & Pujolle, G. (2019). *Secure Peer-to-Peer Communication Based on Blockchain.* . doi:10.1007/978-3-030-15035-8_64

Khan, N., Ray, R. L., Sargani, G. R., Ihtisham, M., Khayyam, M., & Ismail, S. (2021). Current Progress and Future Prospects of Agriculture Technology: Gateway to Sustainable Agriculture. *Sustainability*, *13*(9), 4883. doi:10.3390/su13094883

Khan, M. A. (2020). An iot framework for heart disease prediction based on mdcnn classifier. *IEEE Access: Practical Innovations, Open Solutions*, 8, 34717–34727. doi:10.1109/ACCESS.2020.2974687

Khan, T., Sherazi, H. H. R., Ali, M., Letchmunan, S., & Butt, U. M. (2021). Deep Learning-Based Growth Prediction System: A Use Case of China Agriculture. *Agronomy (Basel)*, *11*(8), 1551. doi:10.3390/agronomy11081551

Kinage, V., & Patil, P. (2019). IoT Based Intelligent System For Vehicle Accident Prevention And Detection At Real Time. *2019 Third International conference on I-SMAC (IoT in Social, Mobile, Analytics and Cloud) (I-SMAC)*, 409-413. 10.1109/I-SMAC47947.2019.9032662

Kingma, D. P., & Ba, J. L. (2014). *Adam: A method for stochastic optimization*. arXiv preprint arXiv:1412.6980.

Kodali, R. K., & Sahu, S. (2017). MQTT based vehicle accident detection and alert system. *2017 3rd International Conference on Applied and Theoretical Computing and Communication Technology (iCATccT)*, 186-189. 10.1109/ICATCCT.2017.8389130

Koirala, A., Walsh, K. B., Wang, Z., & McCarthy, C. (2019). Deep learning for real-time fruit detection and orchard fruit load estimation: Benchmarking of 'MangoYOLO'. *Precision Agriculture*, *20*(6), 1107–1135. doi:10.100711119-019-09642-0

Koltsaklis, N., Panapakidis, I., Christoforidis, G., & Knápek, J. (2022). Smart home energy management processes support through machine learning algorithms. *Energy Reports*, 8, 1–6. doi:10.1016/j.egyr.2022.01.033

Kondaveeti, Brahma, & Sahithi. (2021). Deep Learning Applications in Agriculture: The Role of Deep Learning in Smart Agriculture. In *Artificial Intelligence and IoT-Based Technologies for Sustainable Farming and Smart Agriculture*. IGI Global.

Koteswarchand, D., Moolea, P., Kumar, K. N., & Kumar, M. (2021). An Object Detection Scheme in Equirectangular Panoramic Images Using YOLO V3. *Journal of Software Engineering and Simulation*, *7*(10), 2321–3809.

Krishna, N.M., Sekaran, K., Vamsi, A.V.N., Ghantasala, G.S.P., Chandana, P., Kadry, S., Blazauskas, T., Damasevicius, R., & Kaushik, S. (2019). An Efficient Mixture Model Approach in Brain-Machine Interface Systems for Extracting the Psychological Status of Mentally Impaired Persons Using EEG Signals. *IEEE Access*, 7, 77905–77914.

Krishnamoorthy, R., Thiagarajan, R., Padmapriya, S., Mohan, I., Arun, S., & Dineshkumar, T. (2022). Applications of Machine Learning and Deep Learning in Smart Agriculture. doi:10.1002/9781119861850.ch21

Krittanawong, C., Virk, H. U. H., Bangalore, S., Wang, Z., Johnson, K. W., Pinotti, R., Zhang, H., Kaplin, S., Narasimhan, B., Kitai, T., Baber, U., Halperin, J. L., & Tang, W. H. W. (2020). Machine learning prediction in cardiovascular diseases: A meta-analysis. *Scientific Reports*, *10*(1), 16057. doi:10.103841598-020-72685-1 PMID:32994452

Krizhevsky, A., Sutskever, I., & Hinton, G. E. (2012). ImageNet Classification with Deep Convolutional Neural Networks. In F. Pereira, C. J. C. Burges, L. Bottou, & K. Q. Weinberger (Eds.), *Advances in Neural Information Processing Systems 25* (pp. 1097–1105). Curran Associates, Inc.

Kumar S. (2021). Study of Retail Applications with Virtual and Augmented Reality Technologies. *Journal of Innovative Image Processing*. . doi:10.36548/jiip.2021.2.006

Kumar, M., Hanumanthappa, M., & Kumar, T. V. S. (2012). Intrusion Detection System using decision tree algorithm. *2012 IEEE 14th International Conference on Communication Technology*, 629–634. 10.1109/ICCT.2012.6511281

Kumara, V., Mohanaprakash, T. A., Fairooz, S., Jamal, K., Babu, T., & B., S. (2023). Experimental Study on a Reliable Smart Hydroponics System. In *Human Agro-Energy Optimization for Business and Industry* (pp. 27–45). IGI Global. doi:10.4018/978-1-6684-4118-3.ch002

Kumar, A., Chattree, G., & Periyasamy, S. (2018). Smart healthcare monitoring system. *Wireless Personal Communications, 101*(1), 453–463. doi:10.100711277-018-5699-0

Kumar, M. V., & Iyengar, N. C. S. N. (2018). A framework for blockchain technology in rice supply chain management. *International Journal of Pure and Applied Mathematics, 119*(16), 1759–1768.

Kumar, N. M., Chand, A. A., Malvoni, M., Prasad, K. A., Mamun, K. A., Islam, F. R., & Chopra, S. S. (2020). Distributed energy resources and the application of AI, IoT, and blockchain in smart grids. *Energies, 13*(21), 5739. doi:10.3390/en13215739

Kumar, P. M., & Gandhi, D. U. (2018). A novel three-tier Internet of Things architecture with machine learning algorithm for early detection of heart diseases. *Computers & Electrical Engineering, 65*, 222–235. doi:10.1016/j.compeleceng.2017.09.001

Kumhar, H. S., & Kukshal, V. (2022). A review on reinforcement deep learning in robotics. *2022 Interdisciplinary Research in Technology and Management (IRTM), Technology and Management (IRTM), 2022 Interdisciplinary Research In,* 1–8. doi:10.1109/IRTM54583.2022.9791615

Kumra, S., & Kanan, C. (2017). Robotic grasp detection using deep convolutional neural networks. *Proceedings of the 2017 IEEE/RSJ International Conference on Intelligent Robots and Systems (IROS),* 769–776. 10.1109/IROS.2017.8202237

Kuppusamy, P. (2021). Emerging Technological Model to Sustainable Agriculture. In P. Tomar & G. Kaur (Eds.), *Artificial Intelligence and IoT-Based Technologies for Sustainable Farming and Smart Agriculture* (pp. 101–122). IGI Global. doi:10.4018/978-1-7998-1722-2.ch007

Kuradusenge, M., Hitimana, E., Hanyurwimfura, D., Rukundo, P., Mtonga, K., Mukasine, A., Uwitonze, C., Ngabonziza, J., & Uwamahoro, A. (2023). Crop Yield Prediction Using Machine Learning Models: Case of Irish Potato and Maize. *Agriculture, 13*(1), 225. doi:10.3390/agriculture13010225

LaboroL. T. (2020). https://github.com/laboroai/LaboroTomato.git

LeCun, Y., Bengio, Y., & Hinton, G. (2015). Deep learning. *Nature, 521*(7553), 436–444. doi:10.1038/nature14539 PMID:26017442

Lee, J. S., & Siau, K. (2001). A review of data mining techniques. Industrial Management & Data Systems, 101(1), 41-46. doi:10.1108/02635570110365989

Leevy, J. L., Hancock, J., Khoshgoftaar, T. M., & Peterson, J. (2021). Detecting Information Theft Attacks in the Bot-IoT Dataset. *2021 20th IEEE International Conference on Machine Learning and Applications (ICMLA),* 807–812. 10.1109/ICMLA52953.2021.00133

Leevy, J. L., Hancock, J., Khoshgoftaar, T. M., & Peterson, J. M. (2022). IoT information theft prediction using ensemble feature selection. *Journal of Big Data.* doi:10.118640537-021-00558-z

Lenz, I., Lee, H., & Saxena, A. (2015). Deep Learning for Detecting Robotic Grasps. *The International Journal of Robotics Research, 34*(4-5), 705–724. doi:10.1177/0278364914549607

Li, H., Habes, M., Wolk, D. A., & Fan, Y. (2019). *A deep learning model for early prediction of Alzheimer's disease dementia based on hippocampal MRI.* arXiv:1904.07282.

Li, J. H. (2018). Cyber Security Meets Artificial Intelligence: A Survey. *Frontiers of Information Technology and Electronic Engineering, 19*(12), 1462–1474. https://link.springer.com/article/10.1631/FITEE.1800573

Li, L., Xiaoguang, H., Ke, C., & Ketai, H. (2011). The applications of wifi-based wireless sensor network in internet of things and smart grid. *2011 6th IEEE Conference on Industrial Electronics and Applications*, 789–793. 10.1109/ICIEA.2011.5975693

Lian, C., Liu, M., Zhang, J., & Shen, D. (2020). Hierarchical Fully Convolutional Network for Joint Atrophy Localization and Alzheimer's Disease Diagnosis Using Structural MRI. *IEEE Transactions on Pattern Analysis and Machine Intelligence*, 42(4), 880–893. doi:10.1109/TPAMI.2018.2889096 PMID:30582529

Liao, Chu, & Hsiao. (2012). Data mining techniques and applications – A decade review from 2000 to 2011. *Expert Systems with Applications*, 39(12), 11303-11311. doi:10.1016/j.eswa.2012.02.063

Liao, S., & An, J. (2015). A robust insulator detection algorithm based on local features and spatial orders for aerial images. *IEEE Geoscience and Remote Sensing Letters*, 12(5), 963-967. https://doi.org/.2369525 doi:10.1109/lgrs.2014

Liberata Ullo, S., Sinha, G. R., Bacco, M., Gotta, A., Cassarà, P., & Agbinya, J. I. (2021). Advances in IoT and Smart Sensors for Remote Sensing and Agriculture Applications. *Remote Sensing*, 13(13), 2585. doi:10.3390/rs13132585

Li, H., Wang, G., Dong, Z., Wei, X., Wu, M., Song, H., & Amankwah, S. O. Y. (2021). Identifying Cotton Fields from Remote Sensing Images Using Multiple Deep Learning Networks. *Agronomy (Basel)*, 11(1), 174. doi:10.3390/agronomy11010174

Lin, J., Shen, Z., Zhang, A., & Chai, Y. (2018). *Blockchain and IoT based Food Traceability for Smart Agriculture*. doi:10.1145/3265689.3265692

Lin, Q., Wang, H., Pei, X., & Wang, J. (2019). Food safety traceability system based on blockchain and EPCIS. *IEEE Access : Practical Innovations, Open Solutions*, 7, 128442–128452. doi:10.1109/ACCESS.2019.2897792

Lin, T., Dollar, P., Girshick, R., He, K., Hariharan, B., & Belongie, S. (2017). Feature pyramid networks for object detection. *2017 IEEE Conference on Computer Vision and Pattern Recognition (CVPR)*. 10.1109/CVPR.2017.106

Lin, W., Chen, J., Jiang, L., He, S., & Zeng, L. (2021). Blockchain Technology in Current Agricultural Systems: From Techniques to Applications. *IEEE Access : Practical Innovations, Open Solutions*, 9, 49916–49926. doi:10.1109/ACCESS.2021.3069664

Lin, Y. P., Petway, J. R., Anthony, J., Mukhtar, H., Liao, S. W., Chou, C. F., & Ho, Y. F. (2019). Blockchain: The Evolutionary Next Step for ICT E-Agriculture. *Agrárinformatika Folyóirat*, 10(2), 1–17. doi:10.2478/jai-2019-0002

Liu, C., Wu, Y., Liu, J., Sun, Z., & Xu, H. (2021). Insulator faults detection in aerial images from high-voltage transmission lines based on deep learning model. *Applied Sciences*, 11(10), 4647. https://doi.org/11104647 doi:10.3390/app

Liu, S., Qi, L., Qin, H., Shi, J., & Jia, J. (2018). Path aggregation network for instance segmentation. *2018 IEEE/CVF Conference on Computer Vision and Pattern Recognition*. https://github.com/InsulatorData/InsulatorDataSet website.

Liu, G., Nouaze, J. C., Touko Mbouembe, P. L., & Kim, J. H. (2020). YOLO-tomato: A robust algorithm for tomato detection based on YOLOv3. *Sensors (Basel)*, 20(7), 2145. doi:10.339020072145 PMID:32290173

Liu, H., & Lang, B. (2019). Machine Learning and Deep Learning Methods for Intrusion Detection Systems: A Survey. *Applied Sciences (Basel, Switzerland)*, 9(20), 4396. doi:10.3390/app9204396

Liu, M., & Tang, J. (2021). Audio and video bimodal emotion recognition in social networks based on improved alexnet network and attention mechanism. *Journal of Information Processing Systems*, 17(4), 754–771.

Liu, S., & ... Path aggregation network for instance segmentation. *Proceedings of the IEEE conference on computer vision and pattern recognition*.

Liu, S., Qiao, Y., Li, J., Zhang, H., Zhang, M., & Wang, M. (2022). An Improved Lightweight Network for Real-Time Detection of Apple Leaf Diseases in Natural Scenes. *Agronomy (Basel)*, *12*(10), 2363. doi:10.3390/agronomy12102363

Liu, W., Anguelov, D., Erhan, D., Szegedy, C., Reed, S., Fu, C. Y., & Berg, A. C. (2016). *European Conference on Computer Vision.* Springer.

Liu, Y., Zhang, D., & Gooi, H. B. (2020). Optimization strategy based on deep reinforcement learning for home energy management. *CSEE Journal of Power and Energy Systems*, *6*(3), 572–582.

Li, W., Logenthiran, T., Phan, V.-T., & Woo, W. L. (2018). Implemented IoT-based self-learning home management system (SHMS) for Singapore. *IEEE Internet of Things Journal*, *5*(3), 2212–2219. doi:10.1109/JIOT.2018.2828144

Li, Z., Jiang, X., Jia, X., Duan, X., Wang, Y., & Mu, J. (2022). Classification Method of Significant Rice Pests Based on Deep Learning. *Agronomy (Basel)*, *12*(9), 2096. doi:10.3390/agronomy12092096

Lomaliza, J., & Park, H. (2017). A highly efficient and reliable heart rate monitoring system using smartphone cameras. *Multimedia Tools and Applications*, *76*(20), 21051–21071. doi:10.100711042-016-4010-1

López-De-Ipiña, K., Martinez-De-Lizarduy, U., Calvo, P. M., Beitia, B., García-Melero, J., Fernández, E., Ecay-Torres, M., Faundez-Zanuy, M., & Sanz, P. (2020). FaundezZanuy, M.; Sanz, P. On the analysis of speech and disfluencies for automatic detection of Mild Cognitive Impairment. *Neural Computing & Applications*, *32*(20), 15761–15769. doi:10.100700521-018-3494-1

Lu, D., Popuri, K., Ding, G. W., Balachandar, R., Beg, M. F., Weiner, M., Aisen, P., Petersen, R., Jack, C., Jagust, W., Trojanowki, J., Toga, A., Beckett, L., Green, R., Saykin, A., Morris, J., Shaw, L., Kaye, J., Quinn, J., ... Fargher, K. (2018). Multimodal and Multiscale Deep Neural Networks for the Early Diagnosis of Alzheimer's Disease using structural MR and FDG-PET images. *Scientific Reports*, *8*(1), 1–13. doi:10.103841598-018-22871-z PMID:29632364

Lu, J., Lee, W. S., Gan, H., & Hu, X. W. (2018). Immature citrus fruit detection based on local binary pattern feature and hierarchical contour analysis. *Biosystems Engineering*, *171*, 78–90. doi:10.1016/j.biosystemseng.2018.04.009

Machorro-Cano, I., Alor-Hernández, G., Paredes-Valverde, M. A., Rodríguez-Mazahua, L., Sánchez-Cervantes, J. L., & Olmedo-Aguirre, J. O. (2020). HEMS-IoT: A big data and machine learning-based smart home system for energy saving. *Energies*, *13*(5), 1097. doi:10.3390/en13051097

Madhu, S., Padunnavalappil, S., & Saajlal, P. P. (2022). Powering up an IoT-enabled smart home: A solar powered smart inverter for sustainable development. *International Journal of Software Science and Computational Intelligence*, *14*(1), 1–21. doi:10.4018/IJSSCI.300362

Madumidha, S., Ranjani, P. S., Varsinee, S. S., & Sundari, P. S. (2019). Transparency and Traceability: In Food Supply Chain System using Blockchain Technology with Internet of Things. *2019 3rd International Conference on Trends in Electronics and Informatics (ICOEI)*, 1316-1321. 10.1109/ICOEI.2019.8862726

Madumidha, S., Ranjani, P. S., Varsinee, S. S., & Sundari, P. S. (2019). Transparency and Traceability: In Food Supply Chain System using Blockchain Technology with Internet of Things. In *Proceedings of the 2019 3rd International Conference on Trends in Electronics and Informatics (ICOEI)* (pp. 36-40). Academic Press.

Maggipinto, T., Bellotti, R., Amoroso, N., Diacono, D., Donvito, G., Lella, E., Monaco, A., Scelsi, M., & Tangaro, S. (2017). DTI measurements for Alzheimer's classification. *Physics in Medicine and Biology*, *62*(6), 2361–2375. doi:10.1088/1361-6560/aa5dbe PMID:28234631

Magomadov, V. S. (2019). Deep Learning and its Role in Smart Agriculture. Journal of Physics: Conference Series. *Journal of Physics: Conference Series*, *1399*(4), 044109. doi:10.1088/1742-6596/1399/4/044109

Mahendru, M., & Dubey, S. K. (2021). Real Time Object Detection with Audio Feedback using Yolo vs. Yolo_v3. *2021 11th International Conference on Cloud Computing, Data Science & Engineering (Confluence)*, 734–740. 10.1109/Confluence51648.2021.9377064

Mahesh, T. Y., Parvathy, S. S., Thomas, S., Thomas, S. R., & Sebastian, T. (2021). CICERONE- A Real Time Object Detection for Visually Impaired People. *IOP Conference Series. Materials Science and Engineering*, *1085*(1), 012006. doi:10.1088/1757-899X/1085/1/012006

Mahler, J., Liang, J., Niyaz, S., Laskey, M., Doan, R., Liu, X., Aparicio, J., & Goldberg, K. (2017). Dex-Net 2.0: Deep Learning to Plan Robust Grasps with Synthetic Point Clouds and Analytic Grasp Metrics. *Proceedings of the Robotics: Science and Systems.*

Maid, P., Thorat, O., & Deshpande, S. (2020). 'Object Detection for Blind User's', International Journal of Scientific Research in Computer Science. *Engineering and Information Technology*, *6*(4), 221–226.

Maisevli, H., Setiadi, R., Aulia, N. D., Dwi, Z. A., & Widartha, P. (2022). AR Make-up Filter for Social Media using the HSV Color Extraction. *Journal Online Informatika.* . doi:10.15575/join.v7i2.994

Ma, J., Sheridan, R. P., Liaw, A., Dahl, G. E., & Svetnik, V. (2015). Deep neural nets as a method for quantitative structure-activity relationships. *Journal of Chemical Information and Modeling*, *55*(2), 263–274. doi:10.1021/ci500747n PMID:25635324

Majeed, F., Khan, F. Z., Iqbal, M. J., & Nazir, M. (2021). Real-Time Surveillance System based on Facial Recognition using YOLOv5. *IEEE, Mohammad Ali Jinnah University International Conference on Computing*, 1-6. 10.1109/MAJICC53071.2021.9526254

Majumder, S., & Deen, M. J. (2019). Smartphone Sensors for Health Monitoring and Diagnosis. *Sensors (Basel)*, *19*(9), 2164. doi:10.339019092164 PMID:31075985

Majumder, S., Mondal, T., & Deen, M. (2017). Wearable Sensors for Remote Health Monitoring. *Sensors (Basel)*, *17*(12), 130. doi:10.339017010130 PMID:28085085

Malche, T., Tharewal, S., Tiwari, P. K., Jabarulla, M. Y., Alnuaim, A. A., Hatamleh, W. A., & Ullah, M. A. (2022). Artificial Intelligence of Things- (AIoT-) Based Patient Activity Tracking System for Remote Patient Monitoring. *Journal of Healthcare Engineering*, *2022*, 1–15. doi:10.1155/2022/8732213 PMID:35273786

Mauldin, T., Canby, M., Metsis, V., Ngu, A., & Rivera, C. (2018). SmartFall: A Smartwatch-Based Fall Detection System Using Deep Learning. *Sensors (Basel)*, *18*(10), 3363. doi:10.339018103363 PMID:30304768

McCarthy, J. (2004). *What is artificial intelligence?* http://www-formal.stanford.edu/jmc/

Megala, G., & Swarnalatha, P. (2023). Efficient Object Detection on Sparse-to-Dense Depth Prediction. *2023 9th International Conference on Advanced Computing and Communication Systems (ICACCS)*, *1*, 1626–1630.

Megala, G., & ... (2021). State-of-the-art in video processing: Compression, optimization and retrieval. *Turkish Journal of Computer and Mathematics Education*, *12*(5), 1256–1272.

Megala, G., & Swarnalatha, P. (2022). Efficient high-end video data privacy preservation with integrity verification in cloud storage. *Computers & Electrical Engineering*, *102*, 108226. doi:10.1016/j.compeleceng.2022.108226

Mehmood, A., Iqbal, M., Mehmood, Z., Irtaza, A., Nawaz, M., Nazir, T., & Masood, M. (2020). Prediction of Heart Disease Using Deep Convolutional Neural Networks. *Arabian Journal for Science and Engineering*, *46*(4), 3409–3422. Advance online publication. doi:10.100713369-020-05105-1

Mehmood, M. Y., Oad, A., Abrar, M., Munir, H. M., Hasan, S. F., Muqeet, H. A., & Golilarz, N. A. (2021). Edge computing for IoT-enabled smart grid. *Security and Communication Networks, 2021*, 1–16. doi:10.1155/2021/5524025

Mehran & Sakhaeian. (2022). *Applications of machine learning and deep learning techniques in smart agriculture: A review*. 4th Intercontinental Geoinformation Days (IGD), Tabriz, Iran.

Mell, P., & Grance, T. (2009). *Draft NIST Working Definition of Cloud Computing*. https://csrc.nist.gov/groups/SNS/cloudcomputing/index.html

Mezni, H., Driss, M., Boulila, W., Atitallah, S. B., Sellami, M., & Alharbi, N. (2022). Smartwater: A service-oriented and sensor cloud-based framework for smart monitoring of water environments. *Remote Sensing (Basel), 14*(4), 922. doi:10.3390/rs14040922

Mikolov, T., Deoras, A., Povey, D., Burget, L., & Cernocky, J. (2011). Strategies for training large scale neural network language models. *Proc* Automatic Speech Recognition and Understanding. doi:10.1109/ASRU.2011.6163930

Minh, Q. N., Nguyen, V.-H., Quy, V. K., Ngoc, L. A., Chehri, A., & Jeon, G. (2022). Edge Computing for IoT-Enabled Smart Grid: The Future of Energy. *Energies, 15*(17), 6140. doi:10.3390/en15176140

Mittal, P. (2022, January). Machine learning (ml) based human activity recognition model using smart sensors in IoT environment. In *2022 12th International Conference on Cloud Computing, Data Science & Engineering (Confluence)* (pp. 330-334). IEEE.

Mnih, V., Kavukcuoglu, K., Silver, D., Rusu, A. A., Veness, J., Bellemare, M. G., Graves, A., Riedmiller, M., Fidjeland, A. K., Ostrovski, G., Petersen, S., Beattie, C., Sadik, A., Antonoglou, I., King, H., Kumaran, D., Wierstra, D., Legg, S., & Hassabis, D. (2015). Human-level control through deep reinforcement learning. *Nature, 518*(7540), 529–533. doi:10.1038/nature14236 PMID:25719670

Mohamed, E. A., Rashed, E. A., Gaber, T., & Karam, O. (2022). Deep learning model for fully automated breast cancer detection system from thermograms. *PLoS One, 17*(1), e0262349. doi:10.1371/journal.pone.0262349 PMID:35030211

Mohammed, M. N., Hazairin, N. A., Syamsudin, H., Al-Zubaidi, S., Sairah, A. K., Mustapha, S., & Yusuf, E. (2020). 2019 Novel Coronavirus Disease (Covid-19): Detection and Diagnosis System Using IoT Based Smart Glasses. *International Journal of Advanced Science and Technology, 29*(7), 954-960.

Mohapatra, S., Mohanty, S., & Mohanty, S. (2019). Smart healthcare: An approach for ubiquitous healthcare management using IoT. *Big Data Analytics for Intelligent Healthcare Management*, 175–196.. doi:10.1016/B978-0-12-818146-1.00007-6

Monfort, M., Andonian, A., Zhou, B., Ramakrishnan, K., Bargal, S. A., Yan, T., Brown, L., Fan, Q., Gutfreund, D., Vondrick, C., & ... (2019). Moments in time dataset: One million videos for event understanding. *IEEE Transactions on Pattern Analysis and Machine Intelligence, 42*(2), 502–508. doi:10.1109/TPAMI.2019.2901464 PMID:30802849

Mordvintsev, A., Olah, C., & Tyka, M. (n.d.). *Inceptionism: Going deeper into neural networks*. https://googleresearch.blogspot.com/2015/06/inceptionism-going-deeper-into-neural.html

Morris, J. W. (2012). Making music behave: Metadata and the digital music commodity. *New Media & Society, 14*(5), 850–866. doi:10.1177/1461444811430645

Mouha, R. (2021). Deep Learning for Robotics. *Journal of Data Analysis and Information Processing, 9*(2), 63–76. doi:10.4236/jdaip.2021.92005

Moustafa, A. A., Bello, A., & Maurushat, A. (2021). The Role of User Behaviour in Improving Cyber Security Management. *Frontiers in Psychology, 12*, 1969. doi:10.3389/fpsyg.2021.561011 PMID:34220596

Murugan, A., Anu, H. N., Preethi, A. P., & Kumar, K. P. S. (2021). Diagnosis of skin cancer using machine learning techniques. *Microprocessors and Microsystems, 81*, 103727. Advance online publication. doi:10.1016/j.micpro.2020.103727

Myilsamy, S., & Sampath, B. (2021). Experimental comparison of near-dry and cryogenically cooled near-dry machining in wire-cut electrical discharge machining processes. *Surface Topography : Metrology and Properties, 9*(3), 35015. doi:10.1088/2051-672X/ac15e0

Nagavelli, U., Samanta, D., & Chakraborty, P. (2022). Machine Learning Technology-Based Heart Disease Detection Models. *Journal of Healthcare Engineering, 2022*, 1–9. Advance online publication. doi:10.1155/2022/7351061 PMID:35265303

Naguib, A., Cheng, Y., & Chang, Y. (2022). AI Assistance for Home Surveillance. *IEEE, 27th International Conference on Automation and Computing.*

Nakamoto, S. (2008). *Bitcoin: A peer-to-peer electronic cash system.* https://bitcoin.org/bitcoin.pdf

Nankani, H., Gupta, S., Singh, S., & Ramesh, S. S. (2019). Detection analysis of various types of cancer by logistic regression using machine learning. *International Journal of Engineering and Advanced Technology, 9*(1), 99–104. doi:10.35940/ijeat.A1055.109119

National Institute of Standards and Technology. (2001). *FIPS Publication 197: Advanced Encryption Standard (AES).* https://nvlpubs.nist.gov/nistpubs/FIPS/NIST.FIPS.197.pdf

Navarro, E., Costa, N., & Pereira, A. (2020). A Systematic Review of IoT Solutions for Smart Farming. *Sensors, 20*(15), 4231. doi:10.3390/s20154231

Nayak, P., Kavitha, K., & Mallikarjuna Rao, C. (2020). IoT-Enabled Agricultural System Applications, Challenges and Security Issues. *Studies in Big Data, 63*, 139–163. doi:10.1007/978-981-13-9177-4_7

Nemcova, A., Jordanova, I., Varecka, M., Smisek, R., Marsanova, L., Smital, L., & Vitek, M. (2020). Monitoring of heart rate, blood oxygen saturation, and blood pressure using a smartphone. *Biomedical Signal Processing and Control, 59*, 101928. Advance online publication. doi:10.1016/j.bspc.2020.101928

Ness, S. R., Theocharis, A., Tzanetakis, G., & Martins, L. G. (2009). Improving automatic music tag annotation using stacked generalization of probabilistic SVM outputs. In *Proceedings of the 17th ACM international conference on Multimedia (MM '09).* Association for Computing Machinery. 10.1145/1631272.1631393

Nguyen, D.-H., Tuong, N. H., & Pham, H.-A. (2020). Blockchain-based Farming Activities Tracker for Enhancing Trust in the Community Supported Agriculture Model. In *Proceedings of the 2020 International Conference on Information and Communication Technology Convergence (ICTC)* (pp. 1399-1404). IEEE. 10.1109/ICTC49870.2020.9289297

Ning, Z., Wu, X., Yang, J., & Yang, Y. (2021). MT-yolov5: Mobile terminal table detection model based on YOLOv5. *Journal of Physics: Conference Series, 1978*(1), 012010. doi:10.1088/1742-6596/1978/1/012010

Noble, D.R., Angello, L., Sheppard, S., Kee, J., Emerson, B.L., & Lieuwen, T. (2019). Investigation Into Advanced Combustion System Health Monitoring. *Volume 3: Coal, Biomass, Hydrogen, and Alternative Fuels; Cycle Innovations; Electric Power; Industrial and Cogeneration; Organic Rankine Cycle Power Systems.* . doi:10.1115/GT2019-91973

Oh, K., & Jung, K. (2004). GPU implementation of neural networks. *Pattern Recognition, 37*(6), 1311–1314. doi:10.1016/j.patcog.2004.01.013

Padmanabula, S., Puvvada, R., Sistla, V., & Kolli, V. K. K. (2020). Object detection using stacked YOLOv3. *Ingénierie des systèmes d information, 25*, 691-697. doi:10.18280/isi.250517.3

Palaniappan, M., Tirlangi, S., Mohamed, M. J. S., Moorthy, R. M. S., Valeti, S. V., & Boopathi, S. (2023). Fused deposition modelling of polylactic acid (PLA)-based polymer composites: A case study. In Development, Properties, and Industrial Applications of 3D Printed Polymer Composites (pp. 66–85). IGI Global. doi:10.4018/978-1-6684-6009-2.ch005

Pallikonda, Chaduvula, Markapudi, Jyothi, & Indira. (2022). *Efficient way to ensure the data security in cloud computing.* Academic Press.

Pal, M., & Parija, S. (2021). Prediction of Heart Diseases using Random Forest. *Journal of Physics: Conference Series*, *1817*(1), 012009. Advance online publication. doi:10.1088/1742-6596/1817/1/012009

Pan, D., Zeng, A., Jia, L., Huang, Y., Frizzell, T., & Song, X. (2020). Early Detection of Alzheimer's Disease Using Magnetic Resonance Imaging: A Novel Approach Combining Convolutional Neural Networks and Ensemble Learning. *Frontiers in Neuroscience*, *14*, 259. doi:10.3389/fnins.2020.00259 PMID:32477040

Parmar, H., Nutter, B., Long, R., Antani, S., & Mitra, S. (2020). Spatiotemporal feature extraction and classification of Alzheimer's disease using deep learning 3D-CNN for fMRI data. *Journal of Medical Imaging (Bellingham, Wash.)*, *7*(5), 056001. doi:10.1117/1.JMI.7.5.056001

Patel, A. (2022). *Computer Vision and Deep Learning for Agriculture.* https://pyimagesearch.com/2022/08/10/computer-vision-and-deep-learning-for-agriculture/

Pavisic, I. M., Pertzov, Y., Nicholas, J. M., O'Connor, A., Lu, K., Yong, K. X. X., Husain, M., Fox, N. C., & Crutch, S. J. (2021). Eye-tracking indices of impaired encoding of visual short-term memory in familial Alzheimer's disease. *Scientific Reports*, *11*(1), 1–14. doi:10.103841598-021-88001-4 PMID:33888739

Pearson, S., Maya, D., Leontidis, G., Swainson, M., Brewer, S., Bidaut, L., & Zisman, A. (2020). Are distributed ledger technologies the panacea for food traceability? *Global Food Security*, *27*, 100418.

Phan, T.-C., Phan, A.-C., Cao, H.-P., & Trieu, T.-N. (2022). Content-Based Video Big Data Retrieval with Extensive Features and Deep Learning. *Applied Sciences (Basel, Switzerland)*, *12*(13), 6753. doi:10.3390/app12136753

Pierson, H. A., & Gashler, M. S. (2017). Deep learning in robotics: A review of recent research. *Advanced Robotics*, *31*(16), 821–835. doi:10.1080/01691864.2017.1365009

Ping, H., Wang, J., & Ma, Z. (2018). *Mini-review of application of IoT technology in monitoring agricultural products quality and safety.* doi:10.25165/j.ijabe.20181105.3092

Pinto, L., & Gupta, A. (2016). Supersizing self-supervision: Learning to grasp from 50K tries and 700 robot hours. *Proceedings of the 2016 IEEE International Conference on Robotics and Automation (ICRA)*, 3406–3413. 10.1109/ICRA.2016.7487517

Portalés-Julià, E., Campos-Taberner, M., García-Haro, F. J., & Gilabert, M. A. (2021). Assessing the Sentinel-2 Capabilities to Identify Abandoned Crops Using Deep Learning. *Agronomy (Basel)*, *11*(4), 654. doi:10.3390/agronomy11040654

Portilla, J., & Simoncelli, E. P. (2000). A parametric texture model based on joint statistics of complex wavelet coefficients. *International Journal of Computer Vision*, *40*(1), 49–70. doi:10.1023/A:1026553619983

Possamai, G. C., Ravaud, P., Ghosn, L., & Thi Tran, V. (2020). Use of wearable biometric monitoring devices to measure outcomes in randomized clinical trials: A methodological systematic review. *BMC Medicien, 18*. 10.118612916-020-01773-w

Prabakaran, N., Kumar, S.S.S., Kiran, P.K., & Supriya, P. (2022). A deep learning based social distance analyzer with person detection and Tracking Using Region based convolutional neural networks for novel coronavirus. *Journal of Mobile Multimedia*, 541-560.

Prabakaran, N., & Kannan, R. J. (2017). Sustainable life-span of WSN nodes using participatory devices in pervasive environment. *Microsystem Technologies*, 23(3), 651–657. doi:10.100700542-016-3117-7

Prabakaran, N., Palaniappan, R., Kannadasan, R., Dudi, S. V., & Sasidhar, V. (2021). Forecasting the momentum using customised loss function for financial series. *International Journal of Intelligent Computing and Cybernetics*, 14(4), 702–713. doi:10.1108/IJICC-05-2021-0098

Prabha, R., Ramyalakshmi, K., Renuka, D., & Sadhurya. (2021). AR Based Try on Clothing. *International Journal of Innovative Research in Technology*.

Pratt, G. A. (2015). Is a cambrian explosion coming for robotics? *The Journal of Economic Perspectives*, 29(3), 51–60. doi:10.1257/jep.29.3.51

Premalatha, G., & Bai, V. T. (2022). Wireless IoT and Cyber-Physical System for Health Monitoring Using Honey Badger Optimized Least-Squares Support-Vector Machine. *Wireless Personal Communications*, 124(4), 3013–3034. doi:10.100711277-022-09500-9 PMID:35370364

Qayyum, A., Malik, A. S., Shuaibu, A. N., & Nasir, N. (2017). Estimation of non-contact smartphone video-based vital sign monitoring using filtering and standard color conversion techniques. *2017 IEEE Life Sciences Conference (LSC)*, 202-205. 10.1109/LSC.2017.8268178

Rahman, E. U., Zhang, Y., Ahmad, S., Ahmad, H. I., & Jobaer, S. (2021). Autonomous vision-based primary distribution systems porcelain insulators inspection using UAVs. *Sensors (Basel)*, 21(3), 974. doi:10.339021030974 PMID:33540500

Rajan & Babu. (2017). *Privacy and Authenticity for Cloud Data with Attribute-Based Encryption and Digital Signature*. Unpublished.

Rajawat, A. S., Bedi, P., Goyal, S. B., Alharbi, A. R., Aljaedi, A., Jamal, S. S., & Shukla, P. K. (2021). Fog big data analysis for IoT sensor application using fusion deep learning. *Mathematical Problems in Engineering*, 2021, 1–16. doi:10.1155/2021/6876688

Rajput, Y., Naik, D., & Mane, C. (2013). An Improved Cryptographic Technique to Encrypt Text using Double Encryption. *International Journal of Computer Applications*, 86(6), 24–28. Advance online publication. doi:10.5120/14990-2582

Ramana, K., Aluvala, R., Kumar, M. R., Nagaraja, G., Krishna, A. V., & Nagendra, P. (2022). Leaf Disease Classification in Smart Agriculture Using Deep Neural Network Architecture and IoT. *Journal of Circuits, Systems, and Computers*, 31(15), 2240004. doi:10.1142/S0218126622400047

Ramu, S.K., Irudayaraj, G.C.R., & Elango, R. (2021). An IoT-based smart monitoring scheme for solar PV applications. *Electr Electron Devices, Circuits, Mater Technol Challenges Solut*, 211–233

Rana, S., Sengupta, S., Jana, S., Dan, R., Sultana, M., & Sengupta, D. (2020). Prototype Proposal for Quick Accident Detection and Response System. *2020 Fifth International Conference on Research in Computational Intelligence and Communication Networks (ICRCICN)*, 191-195. doi: 10.1109/ICRCICN50933.2020.9296153.11

Rashid, R. A., Chin, L., Sarijari, M. A., Sudirman, R., & Ide, T. (2019). Machine learning for smart energy monitoring of home appliances using IoT. *2019 Eleventh International Conference on Ubiquitous and Future Networks (ICUFN)*, 66–71. 10.1109/ICUFN.2019.8806026

Rasmus, A., Valpola, H., Honkala, M., Berglund, M., & Raiko, T. (2015). *Semisupervised learning with ladder network*. arXiv preprint arXiv:1507.02672.

Ratnaparkhi, S., Khan, S., Arya, C., Khapre, S., Singh, P., Diwakar, M., & Shankar, A. (2020). WITHDRAWN: Smart agriculture sensors in IOT: A review. *Materials Today: Proceedings*. doi:10.1016/j.matpr.2020.11.138

Razaque, Haj Frej, Alotaibi, & Alotaibai. (2021). Privacy Preservation Models for Third-Party Auditor over Cloud Computing. Academic Press.

Razzaq, S., Riaz, F., Mehmood, T., & Ratyal, N. I. (2016). Multi-Factors Based Road Accident Prevention System. *2016 International Conference on Computing, Electronic and Electrical Engineering (ICE Cube),* 190-195. 10.1109/ICECUBE.2016.7495221

ReddyG. N.ReddyG. J. U. (2014). *A Study Of Cyber Security Challenges And Its Emerging Trends On Latest Technologies.* https://arxiv.org/abs/1402.1842v1

Reddy, M. A., Reddy, B. M., Mukund, C. S., Venneti, K., Preethi, D. M. D., & Boopathi, S. (2023). Social Health Protection During the COVID-Pandemic Using IoT. In *The COVID-19 Pandemic and the Digitalization of Diplomacy* (pp. 204–235). IGI Global. doi:10.4018/978-1-7998-8394-4.ch009

Redmon, J., & Farhadi, A. (2018). *YOLOv3: An incremental improvement.* arXiv.

Redmon, J., & Farhadi, A. (2018). *YOLOv3: An Incremental Improvement.* arXiv:1804.02767[cs.CV].

Redmon, J., Divvala, S., & Girshick, R. (2016). *You only Look once: Unified, real-time object detection.* arXiv.

Redmon, J., & Angelova, A. (2015). Real-time grasp detection using convolutional neural networks. *Proceedings of the 2015 IEEE International Conference on Robotics and Automation (ICRA),* 1316–1322. 10.1109/ICRA.2015.7139361

Redmon, J., Divvala, S., Girshick, R., & Farhadi, A. (2016). You only look once: Unified, real-time object detection. *Proceedings of the IEEE Conference on Computer Vision and Pattern Recognition,* 779–788. 10.1109/CVPR.2016.91

Redmon, J., & Farhadi, A. (2017). YOLO9000: Better faster, stronger. *2017 IEEE Conference on Computer Vision and Pattern Recognition (CVPR),* 6517–6525. 10.1109/CVPR.2017.690

Redmon, J., & Farhadi, A. (2017). YOLO9000: Better, faster, stronger. *Proceedings of the IEEE conference on computer vision and pattern recognition,* 7263-7271.

Rejani, A. I. Y., & Selvi, T. S. (2009). *Early detection of breast cancer using SVM classifier technique.* DOI: /arXiv.0912.2314. doi:10.48550

Rejeb, A., Keogh, J. G., & Treiblmaier, H. (2020). Leveraging the Internet of Things and Blockchain Technology in Supply Chain Management. *International Journal of Information Management, 52,* 101993. doi:10.1016/j.ijinfomgt.2019.10.006

Reka, S. S., & Dragicevic, T. (2018). Future effectual role of energy delivery: A comprehensive review of Internet of Things and smart grid. *Renewable & Sustainable Energy Reviews, 91,* 90–108. doi:10.1016/j.rser.2018.03.089

Ren, Q., Man, K., Li, M., Gao, B., & Ma, J. (2019). Intelligent design and implementation of blockchain and Internet of things–based traffic system. *International Journal of Distributed Sensor Networks, 15*(8), 155014771987065. doi:10.1177/1550147719870653

Ren, S. (2015). Faster r-cnn: Towards real-time object detection with region proposal networks. *Advances in Neural Information Processing Systems, 28.*

Research. (2023, January 7). *Research News.* Retrieved from https://www.cam.ac.uk/research/news/low-cost-ai-heart-monitor-developed-by cambridge-start-up/

Revathy, S., & Sathya Priya, S. (n.d.). *Blockchain based Producer-Consumer Model for Farmers.* Department of Computer Science & Engineering, Hindustan Institute of Technology and Science.

Rezk, N. G., Hemdan, E. E. D., Attia, A. F., El-Sayed, A., & El-Rashidy, M. A. (2021). An efficient IoT based smart farming system using machine learning algorithms. *Multimedia Tools and Applications*, *80*(1), 773–797. doi:10.100711042-020-09740-6

Ria, M., Korbe, J., Nannan, X., Rüdiger, Z., & Hamari, J. (2021). The Use of Augmented Reality in Retail: A Review of Literature. *Proceedings of the 54th Hawaii International Conference on System Sciences*. 10.24251/HICSS.2021.078

Rodriguez, C., Marrese-Taylor, E., Saleh, F. S., Li, H., & Gould, S. (2020). Proposal-free temporal moment localization of a natural-language query in video using guided attention. *Proceedings of the IEEE/CVF Winter Conference on Applications of Computer Vision*, 2464–2473. 10.1109/WACV45572.2020.9093328

Rohit, M. H. (2020). An IoT-based system for public Transport Surveillance using real-time Data Analysis and Computer Vision. *IEEE, 3rd International Conference on Advance in Electronics, Computers, and Communications*. 10.1109/ICAECC50550.2020.9339485

Rotz, S., Duncan, E., Small, M., Botschner, J., Dara, R., Mosby, I., Reed, M., & Fraser, E. D. G. (2019). The Politics of Digital Agricultural Technologies: A Preliminary Review. *Sociologia Ruralis*, *59*(2), 203–229. doi:10.1111oru.12233

Ruengittinun, S., Phongsamsuan, S., & Sureeratanakorn, P. (2017). Applied internet of thing for smart hydroponic farming ecosystem (HFE). *Ubi-Media 2017 - Proceedings of the 10th International Conference on Ubi-Media Computing and Workshops with the 4th International Workshop on Advanced E-Learning and the 1st International Workshop on Multimedia and IoT: Networks, Systems and Applications*. 10.1109/UMEDIA.2017.8074148

Rusk, N. (2016). Deep learning. *Nature Methods*, *13*(1), 35. doi:10.1038/nmeth.3707

S., P. K., Sampath, B., R., S. K., Babu, B. H., & N., A. (2022). Hydroponics, Aeroponics, and Aquaponics Technologies in Modern Agricultural Cultivation. In *Trends, Paradigms, and Advances in Mechatronics Engineering* (pp. 223–241). IGI Global. doi:10.4018/978-1-6684-5887-7.ch012

S., P.K., Sampath, B., & R., S.K. (2022). Hydroponics, Aeroponics, and Aquaponics Technologies in Modern Agricultural Cultivation. Trends, Paradigms, and Advances in Mechatronics Engineering. IGI Global.

Sa, I., Ge, Z., Dayoub, F., Upcroft, B., Perez, T., & McCool, C. (2016). Deepfruits: A fruit detection system using deep neural networks. *Sensors, 16*(8), 1222.

Saba Raoof, S., & Durai, M. A. S. (2022). A Comprehensive Review on Smart Health Care: Applications, Paradigms, and Challenges with Case Studies. *Contrast Media & Molecular Imaging*, *4822235*, 1–18. Advance online publication. doi:10.1155/2022/4822235 PMID:36247859

Sacolick, I. (2020). *When hybrid Multicloud has Technical Advantages*. InfoWorld. https://www.infoworld.com/article/3568497/when-hybrid-multicloud-has-technical-advantages.html

Sagana, C. (2021). Object Recognition System for Visually Impaired People. *2021 IEEE International Conference on Distributed Computing, VLSI, Electrical Circuits and Robotics (DISCOVER)*, 318-321. 10.1109/DISCOVER52564.2021.9663608

Sagu, A., & Gill, N. S. (2020). Machine Learning Techniques for Securing IoT Environment. *International Journal of Innovative Technology and Exploring Engineering*, *9*(4), 977–982. doi:10.35940/ijitee.D1209.029420

Said Mohamed, E. S., Belal, A., Kotb Abd-Elmabod, S., El-Shirbeny, M. A., Gad, A., & Zahran, M. B. (2021). Smart farming for improving agricultural management. *The Egyptian Journal of Remote Sensing and Space Sciences*, *24*(4), 971–981. Advance online publication. doi:10.1016/j.ejrs.2021.08.007

Saini, S. K., Bansal, V., Kaur, R., & Juneja, M. (2020). ColpoNet for automated cervical cancer screening using colposcopy images. *Machine Vision and Applications*, *31*(3), 15. doi:10.100700138-020-01063-8

Salah, K., Nizamuddin, N., Jayaraman, R., & Omar, M. (2019). Blockchain-based soybean traceability in agricultural supply chain. *IEEE Access : Practical Innovations, Open Solutions, 7*, 97935–97946. doi:10.1109/ACCESS.2019.2918000

Sami. (2010, March). Service-based arbitrated multi-tier infrastructure for mobile cloud computing. Academic Press.

Samikannu, R., Koshariya, A. K., Poornima, E., Ramesh, S., Kumar, A., & Boopathi, S. (2023). Sustainable Development in Modern Aquaponics Cultivation Systems Using IoT Technologies. In *Human Agro-Energy Optimization for Business and Industry* (pp. 105–127). IGI Global. doi:10.4018/978-1-6684-4118-3.ch006

Sami, M., Khan, S. Q., Khurram, M., Farooq, M. U., Ajum, R., Aziz, S., Qureshi, R., & Sadak, F. (2022). A Deep Learning-Based Sensor Modeling for Smart Irrigation System. *Agronomy (Basel), 12*(1), 212. doi:10.3390/agronomy12010212

Sampath, B. C. S., & Myilsamy, S. (2022). Application of TOPSIS Optimization Technique in the Micro-Machining Process. In Trends, Paradigms, and Advances in Mechatronics Engineering (pp. 162–187). IGI Global. doi:10.4018/978-1-6684-5887-7.ch009

Sampath, B., & Yuvaraj, D. V. (2022c). Parametric analysis of mould sand properties for flange coupling casting. AIP Conference Proceedings.

Sampath, B., Pandian, M., Deepa, D., & Subbiah, R. (2022b). Operating parameters prediction of liquefied petroleum gas refrigerator using simulated annealing algorithm. AIP Conference Proceedings. doi:10.1063/5.0095601

Sampath, B., & Myilsamy, S. (2021). Experimental investigation of a cryogenically cooled oxygen-mist near-dry wire-cut electrical discharge machining process. *Strojniski Vestnik. Jixie Gongcheng Xuebao, 67*(6), 322–330. doi:10.5545v-jme.2021.7161

Samuel, A., & Senith, S. (2022). Augmented Reality in Fashion Retail Industry. *International Journal of Education, Modern Management, Applied Science & Social Science, 6*.

Sangeeta, N. P. (2019). Implementation Issues of Augmented Reality and Virtual Reality: A Survey. *International Conference on Intelligent Data Communication Technologies and Internet of Things (ICICI)*. doi: 0.1007/978-3-030-03146-6_97

Santhosh, Dogra, & Roy. (2020). Anomaly Detection in Road Traffic Using Visual Surveillance: A Survey. *ACM Computing Surveys, 53*(6).

Sapey-Triomphe, L.-A., Heckemann, R. A., Boublay, N., Dorey, J.-M., Hénaff, M.-A., Rouch, I., Padovan, C., Hammers, A., & Krolak-Salmon, P. (2015). Neuroanatomical Correlates of Recognizing Face Expressions in Mild Stages of Alzheimer's Disease. *PLoS One, 10*(12), e0143586. doi:10.1371/journal.pone.0143586 PMID:26673928

Sarhan, M., Layeghy, S., & Portmann, M. (2022). Towards a Standard Feature Set for Network Intrusion Detection System Datasets. *Mobile Networks and Applications, 27*(1), 357–370. doi:10.100711036-021-01843-0

Sarker, I.H. (2022). Deep Learning: A Comprehensive Overview on Techniques, Taxonomy, Applications, and Research Directions. *SN Comput Sci., 2*(6), 420. doi:10.1007/s42979-021-00815-1

Sarker, I. H., Furhad, M. H., & Nowrozy, R. (2023, March 5). AI-Driven Cybersecurity: An Overview, Security Intelligence Modeling and Research Directions. *SN Computer Science, 2*(3), 1–18. https://link.springer.com/article/10.1007/s42979-021-00557-0

Sarmah, S. S. (2020). An Efficient IoT-Based Patient Monitoring and Heart Disease Prediction System Using Deep Learning Modified Neural Network. *IEEE Access : Practical Innovations, Open Solutions, 8*, 135784–135797. doi:10.1109/ACCESS.2020.3007561

Sarraf, S., & Tofighi, G. (2016). *Classification of Alzheimer's Disease using fMRI Data and Deep Learning Convolutional Neural Networks*. arXiv:1603.08631.

Sasipriya. (2021). Accident Alert and Ambulance Tracking System. *2021 6th International Conference on Communication and Electronics Systems (ICCES)*, 1659-1665. 10.1109/ICCES51350.2021.9489078

Schlette, D., Vielberth, M., & Pernul, G. (2021). CTI-SOC2M2 – The Quest for Mature, Intelligence-Driven Security Operations and Incident Response Capabilities. *Computers & Security*, *111*, 102482. doi:10.1016/j.cose.2021.102482

Schmidhuber, J. (2015). Deep learning in neural networks: An overview. *Neural Networks*, *61*(1), 85–117. doi:10.1016/j.neunet.2014.09.003 PMID:25462637

Schmitz, A., Bansho, Y., & Noda, K. (2014). Tactile object recognition using deep learning and dropout. *14th IEEE-RAS International Conference on Humanoid Robots*, 1044–1050. 10.1109/HUMANOIDS.2014.7041493

Sehgal Foundation. (2023). *Role of Modern Technology in Agriculture*. https://www.smsfoundation.org/role-of-modern-technology-in-agriculture/

Selvakumar, S., Adithe, S., Isaac, J. S., Pradhan, R., Venkatesh, V., & Sampath, B. (2023). A Study of the Printed Circuit Board (PCB) E-Waste Recycling Process. In Sustainable Approaches and Strategies for E-Waste Management and Utilization (pp. 159–184). IGI Global.

Selvakumar, S., Adithe, S., & Isaac, J. S. (2023). A Study of the Printed Circuit Board (PCB) E-Waste Recycling Process. In *Sustainable Approaches and Strategies for E-Waste Management and Utilization* (pp. 159–184). IGI Global. doi:10.4018/978-1-6684-7573-7.ch009

Semwal, N., Mukherjee, M., Raj, C., & Arif, W. (2019). An IoT based smart e-health care system. *Journal of Information and Optimization Sciences*, *40*(8), 1787–1800. doi:10.1080/02522667.2019.1703269

Sendra, S., Lloret, J., García, L., Cambra, C., & Garcia, L. (2017). *An IoT service-oriented system for agriculture monitoring*. doi:10.1109/ICC.2017.7996640

Sen, P. C., Hajra, M., & Ghosh, M. (2020). Supervised Classification Algorithms in Machine Learning: A Survey and Review. In J. Mandal & D. Bhattacharya (Eds.), *Emerging Technology in Modelling and Graphics. Advances in Intelligent Systems and Computing* (Vol. 937). Springer. doi:10.1007/978-981-13-7403-6_11

Senthil, T. S. R., Ohmsakthi vel, Puviyarasan, M., Babu, S. R., Surakasi, R., & Sampath, B. (2023). Industrial Robot-Integrated Fused Deposition Modelling for the 3D Printing Process. In Development, Properties, and Industrial Applications of 3D Printed Polymer Composites (pp. 188–210). IGI Global. doi:10.4018/978-1-6684-6009-2.ch011

Senthil, T. S. R., Ohmsakthi, V., & Puviyarasan, M. (2023). Industrial Robot-Integrated Fused Deposition Modelling for the 3D Printing Process. In Development, Properties, and Industrial Applications of 3D Printed Polymer Composites. IGI Global.

Senthil, K. S. D., & Shamili, M. D. (2022). Smart farming using Machine Learning and Deep Learning techniques. *Decision Analytics Journal*, *3*, 100041. doi:10.1016/j.dajour.2022.100041

Serda, M. (2013). SyntezaiAktywnośćBiologicznaNowychAnalogówTiosemikarbazonowychChelatorówŻelaza. *Uniwersytetśląski, 7*(1), 343–54. https://desytamara.blogspot.com/2017/11/sistem-pelayanan-perpustakaan-dan-jenis.html

Shafiq, M., Tian, Z., Bashir, A. K., Du, X., & Guizani, M. (2020). IoT malicious traffic identification using wrapper-based feature selection mechanisms. *Computers & Security*, *94*, 101863. doi:10.1016/j.cose.2020.101863

Shafiq, M., Tian, Z., Bashir, A. K., Du, X., & Guizani, M. (2021). CorrAUC: A Malicious Bot-IoT Traffic Detection Method in IoT Network Using Machine-Learning Techniques. *IEEE Internet of Things Journal*, 8(5), 3242–3254. doi:10.1109/JIOT.2020.3002255

Shafi, U., Mumtaz, R., García-Nieto, J., Hassan, S. A., Zaidi, S. A. R., & Iqbal, N. (2019, September 2). Precision Agriculture Techniques and Practices: From Considerations to Applications. *Sensors (Basel)*, 19(17), 3796. doi:10.339019173796 PMID:31480709

Shahi, Xu, Neupane, & Guo. (2022). Machine learning methods for precision agriculture with UAV imagery: A review. *Electronic Research Archive, 30*(12), 4277-4317. doi:10.3934/era.2022218

Shahinzadeh, H., Moradi, J., & Gharehpetian, G. B. (2019). IoT architecture for smart grids. *2019 International Conference on Protection and Automation of Power System (IPAPS)*, 22–30. 10.1109/IPAPS.2019.8641944

Shahriar, M. S., & Rahman, M. S. (2015). Urban sensing and smart home energy optimisations: A machine learning approach. *Proceedings of the 2015 International Workshop on Internet of Things towards Applications*, 19–22. 10.1145/2820975.2820979

Shakhbulatov, D., Arora, A., Dong, Z., & Rojas-Cessa, R. (2019). Blockchain Implementation for Analysis of Carbon Footprint across Food Supply Chain. In *2019 IEEE International Conference on Blockchain (Blockchain)* (pp. 382-387). IEEE. 10.1109/Blockchain.2019.00079

Shankar, V., Kumar, V., Devagade, U., Karanth, V., & Rohitaksha, K. (2020). Heart Disease Prediction Using CNN Algorithm. *SN Computer Science*, 1(3), 170. doi:10.100742979-020-0097-6

Shapsough, S., Takrouri, M., Dhaouadi, R., & Zualkernan, I. A. (2021). Using IoT and smart monitoring devices to optimize the efficiency of large-scale distributed solar farms. *Wireless Networks*, 27(6), 4313–4329. doi:10.100711276-018-01918-z

Sharma, S., Aggarwal, A., & Choudhury, T. (2018). Breast Cancer Detection Using Machine Learning Algorithms. *2018 International Conference on Computational Techniques, Electronics and Mechanical Systems (CTEMS)*, 114-118. 10.1109/CTEMS.2018.8769187

Shen, L., Margolies, L. R., Rothstein, J. H., Fluder, E., McBride, R., & Sieh, W. (2019). Deep Learning to Improve Breast Cancer Detection on Screening Mammography. *Scientific Reports*, 9(1), 12495. doi:10.103841598-019-48995-4 PMID:31467326

Sherif, H. M., Shedid, M. A., & Senbel, S. A. (2014). Real time traffic accident detection system using wireless sensor network. *2014 6th International Conference of Soft Computing and Pattern Recognition (SoCPaR)*, 59-64. 10.1109/SOCPAR.2014.7007982

Shin, J., & Moon, J. (2022). Learning to combine the modalities of language and video for temporal moment localization. *Computer Vision and Image Understanding*, 217, 103375. doi:10.1016/j.cviu.2022.103375

Shorten, C., & Khoshgoftaar, T. M. (2019). A survey on Image Data Augmentation for Deep Learning. *Journal of Big Data*, 6(1), 60. doi:10.118640537-019-0197-0

SimonyanK.ZissermanA. (2014). Very deep convolutional networks for large-scale image recognition. arXiv:1409.1556

Singh, A., Thakur, N., & Sharma, A. (2016). A review of supervised machine learning algorithms. *2016 3rd International Conference on Computing for Sustainable Global Development (INDIACom)*, 1310-1315.

Singh, R., Nandan, A., & Tewari, H. (2021). Blockchain-Enabled End-to-End Encryption for Instant Messaging Applications. In WoWMoM 2022, Belfast, UK.

SinghI.TarikaB. (2014). *Comparative Analysis of Open Source Automated Software Testing Tools: Selenium, Sikuli and Watir*. doi:10.13140/2.1.1418.4324

Singh, R. P., & Agrawal, M. (2008). Potential Benefits and Risks of Land Application of Sewage Sludge. *Waste Management (New York, N.Y.)*, *28*(2), 347–358. doi:10.1016/j.wasman.2006.12.010 PMID:17320368

Sohl-Dickstein, J., Weiss, E. A., Maheswaranathan, N., & Ganguli, S. (2015). *Deep unsupervised learning using non-equilibrium thermodynamics*. arXiv preprint arXiv:1503.03585.

Spolaôr, N., Lee, H. D., Takaki, W. S. R., Ensina, L. A., Coy, C. S. R., & Wu, F. C. (2020). A systematic review on content-based video retrieval. *Engineering Applications of Artificial Intelligence*, *90*, 103557. doi:10.1016/j.engappai.2020.103557

Sreedhara, Raj, George, & Ashok. (2021). A Novel Cough Detection Algorithm for COVID-19 Surveillance at Public Place. *IEEE, 8th International Conference on Smart Computing and Communications (ICSCC)*, 119-123.

Sreekantha, D. (2017). *Agricultural crop monitoring using IOT-a study*. Retrieved March 5, 2023, from https://ieeexplore.ieee.org/abstract/document/7855968/

Sreenu, G., & Saleem Durai, M. A. (2019). Intelligent video surveillance: A review through deep learning techniques for crowd analysis. *Journal of Big Data*, *6*(48), 1–27. doi:10.118640537-019-0212-5

Srivastava, A. (2022). Smart Agriculture Using UAV and Deep Learning: A Systematic Review. In Internet of Things Robotic and Drone Technology. CRC Press. doi:10.1201/9781003181613-1

Steiner, M., Smith, J. A., Burges, S. J., Alonso, C. V., & Darden, R. W. (2023, March 5). Effect of Bias Adjustment and Rain Gauge Data Quality Control on Radar Rainfall Estimation. *Water Resources Research*, *35*(8), 2487–2503. doi:10.1029/1999WR900142

Storm, H., Baylis, K., & Heckelei, T. (2020). Machine learning in agricultural and applied economics. *European Review of Agriculture Economics*, *47*(3), 849–892. doi:10.1093/erae/jbz033

Subeesh, A., & Mehta, C. R. (2021). Automation and Digitization of Agriculture using Artificial Intelligence and Internet of Things. *Artificial Intelligence in Agriculture*, *5*, 278–291. doi:10.1016/j.aiia.2021.11.004

Sudha, V., & Ganeshbabu, T. R. (2020). A Convolutional Neural Network Classifier VGG-19 Architecture for Lesion Detection and Grading in Diabetic Retinopathy Based on Deep Learning. *Computers, Materials & Continua*, *66*(1), 827–842. doi:10.32604/cmc.2020.012008

Sudha, V., Kalaiselvi, R., & Shanmughasundaram, P. (2021). Blockchain based solution to improve the Supply Chain Management in Indian agriculture. *2021 International Conference on Artificial Intelligence and Smart Systems (ICAIS)*. 10.1109/ICAIS50930.2021.9395867

Sumathi, P., Karthikeyan, V. V., Kavitha, M. S., & Karthik, S. (2023). Improved Soil Quality Prediction Model Using Deep Learning for Smart Agriculture Systems, Computer Systems Science & Engineering. *Tech Science Process, CSSE*, *45*(2), 1546–1559. doi:10.32604/csse.2023.027580

Sumbaly, R., Vishnusri, N., & Jeyalatha, S. (2014). Diagnosis of breast cancer using decision tree data mining technique. *International Journal of Computer Applications*, *98*(10), 16–24. doi:10.5120/17219-7456

Sundaram, N., Brox, T., & Keutzer, K. (2010). Dense point trajectories by gpu-accelerated large displacement optical flow. ECCV. doi:10.1007/978-3-642-15549-9_32

Suresh Babu, C. V. (2023). *IoT and its Applications* (1st ed.). Anniyappa Publications.

Suresh Patil, A., Adhi Tama, B., Park, Y., & Rhee, K.-H. (2019). *A Framework for Blockchain Based Secure Smart Green House Farming. Interdisciplinary Program of Information Security.* Graduate School, Pukyong National University.

Sutinen, J. G., & Kuperan, K. (1999). A Socio-Economic Theory of Regulatory Compliance. *International Journal of Social Economics, 26*(1–3), 174–193. doi:10.1108/03068299910229569

Swaminathan, M. S., & Bhavani, R. V. (2013). Food production & availability—essential prerequisites for sustainable food security. *The Indian Journal of Medical Research, 138*(3), 383–391. PMID:24135188

Swarna Sugi, S. S., & Ratna, S. R. (2020). Investigation of Machine Learning Techniques in Intrusion Detection System for IoT Network. *2020 3rd International Conference on Intelligent Sustainable Systems (ICISS)*, 1164–1167. 10.1109/ICISS49785.2020.9315900

Swaroop, K. N., Chandu, K., Gorrepotu, R., & Deb, S. (2019). A health monitoring system for vital signs using Iota. *Internet of Things, 5*, 116–129. doi:10.1016/j.iot.2019.01.004

Syedul Amin, M., Jalil, J., & Reaz, M. B. I. (2012). Accident detection and reporting system using GPS, GPRS and GSM technology. *2012 International Conference on Informatics, Electronics & Vision (ICIEV)*, 640-643. 10.1109/ICIEV.2012.6317382

Szegedy, C., Zaremba, W., & Sutskever, I. (2013). Intriguing properties of neural networks. https://arxiv.org/abs/1312.6199

Tabei, F., Gresham, J. M., Askarian, B., Jung, K., & Chong, J. W. (2020). Cuff-Less Blood Pressure Monitoring System Using Smartphones. *IEEE Access : Practical Innovations, Open Solutions, 8*, 11534–11545. doi:10.1109/AC-CESS.2020.2965082

Talukder, A., & Haas, R. (2021). Aiot: AI meets iot and Web in Smart Healthcare. In *13th ACM Web Science Conference 2021 (websci '21)*. Association for Computing Machinery. 10.1145/3462741.3466650

Tao, Y., & Zhou, J. (2017). Automatic apple recognition based on the fusion of color and 3D feature for robotic fruit picking. *Computers and Electronics in Agriculture, 142*, 388–396. doi:10.1016/j.compag.2017.09.019

Tharatipyakul, A., & Pongnumkul, S. (2021). User interface of blockchain-based agri-food traceability applications: A review. *IEEE Access : Practical Innovations, Open Solutions, 9*, 82909–82929. doi:10.1109/ACCESS.2021.3085982

Tharatipyakul, A., Pongnumkul, S., Riansumrit, N., Kingchan, S., & Pongnumkul, S. (2021). Blockchain-Based Traceability System From the Users' Perspective: A Case Study of Thai Coffee Supply Chain. In *Proceedings of the 14th International Joint Conference on Computer Science and Software Engineering (JCSSE)* (pp. 1-6). IEEE.

Thejaswini, S., & K., R. R. (2020). Blockchain in Agriculture by using Decentralized Peer to Peer Networks. In *2020 Fourth International Conference on Inventive Systems and Control (ICISC)* (pp. 931-936). IEEE. 10.1109/ICISC47916.2020.9171083

Thomas, J. (2017). *Inside Machine Learning.* https://medium.com/inside-machine-learning/3-scenarios-for-machine-learning-on-multicloud-c850fb8bed8f

Thomas, L., & Bhat, S. (2021). *Machine Learning and Deep Learning Techniques for IoT-based Intrusion Detection Systems: A Literature Review.* Academic Press.

Thuraisingham, B. (2020). The Role of Artificial Intelligence and Cyber Security for Social Media. *Proceedings - 2020 IEEE 34th International Parallel and Distributed Processing Symposium Workshops, IPDPSW 2020*, 1116–18. 10.1109/IPDPSW50202.2020.00184

Tian, M., Fazekas, G., Black, D., & Sandler, M. (2013). Towards the Representation of Chinese Traditional Music: A State of the Art Review of Music Metadata Standards. *International Conference on Dublin Core and Metadata Applications*, 71–81. Retrieved from https://dcpapers.dublincore.org/pubs/article/view/3672

Tian, S., Yang, W., Grange, J., Wang, P., Huang, W., & Ye, Z. (2019). Smart healthcare: Making medical care more intelligent. *Global Health Journal (Amsterdam, Netherlands)*, 3(3), 62–65. doi:10.1016/j.glohj.2019.07.001

Toral, Barrero, Reina, Sanchez-Garca, & Garca-Campos. (n.d.). For vehicular ad hoc networks. *On-siteDriverID: A Secure Authentication System based on Spanish eID Cards.*

Tripathi, A., Arora, A., & Bhan, A. (2021). Classification of cervical cancer using Deep Learning Algorithm. *2021 5th International Conference on Intelligent Computing and Control Systems (ICICCS)*, 1210-1218. 10.1109/ICICCS51141.2021.9432382

Tripathy, S. S., Tripathy, N., Rath, M., Pati, A., Panigrahi, A., & Dash, M. (2022). Smart Farming based on Deep Learning Approaches. *2022 2nd Odisha International Conference on Electrical Power Engineering, Communication and Computing Technology (ODICON)*, 1-5. 10.1109/ODICON54453.2022.10010165

Trojovský, P., Dhasarathan, V., & Boopathi, S. (2023). Experimental investigations on cryogenic friction-stir welding of similar ZE42 magnesium alloys. *Alexandria Engineering Journal*, 66(1), 1–14. doi:10.1016/j.aej.2022.12.007

Tsang, Y. P., Choy, K. L., Wu, C. H., Ho, G. T. S., & Lam, H. Y. (2019). Blockchain-driven IoT for food traceability with an integrated consensus mechanism. *IEEE Access : Practical Innovations, Open Solutions*, 7, 188433–188445. doi:10.1109/ACCESS.2019.2940227

Tse, D., Zhang, B., Yang, Y., Cheng, C., & Mu, H. (2018). *Blockchain Application in Food Supply Information Security*. Academic Press.

Tse, D., Zhang, B., Yang, Y., Cheng, C., & Mu, H. (2019). *Blockchain Application in Food Supply Information Security*. Department of Information Systems, City University of Hong Kong.

Tseng, S.-Y., Narayanan, S., & Georgiou, P. (2021). Multimodal embeddings from language models for emotion recognition in the wild. *IEEE Signal Processing Letters*, 28, 608–612. doi:10.1109/LSP.2021.3065598

TuomistoH. L.ScheelbeekP. F. D.ChalabiZ.GreenR.SmithR. D.HainesA.DangourA. D. (2017). Effects of environmental change on population nutrition and health: A comprehensive framework with a focus on fruits and vegetables. *Wellcome Open Res*. doi:10.12688/wellcomeopenres.11190.1

Turing, A. M. (1970). Chapter. In B. Meltzer & D. Michie (Eds.), Machine Intelligence (Vol. 5, pp. 3–23). American Elsevier.

Tzimourta, K. D., Afrantou, T., Ioannidis, P., Karatzikou, M., Tzallas, A. T., Giannakeas, N., Astrakas, L. G., Angelidis, P., Glavas, E., Grigoriadis, N., Tsalikakis, D. G., & Tsipouras, M. G. (2019). Analysis of electroencephalographic signals complexity regarding Alzheimer's Disease. *Computers & Electrical Engineering*, 76, 198–212. doi:10.1016/j.compeleceng.2019.03.018

UCI. (2023, January 7). *Heart disease data set*. Retrieved from https: //archive.ics.uci.edu/ml/datasets/heart+Disease

Uganya, G., Rajalakshmi, D., Teekaraman, Y., Kuppusamy, R., & Radhakrishnan, A. (2022). A novel strategy for waste prediction using machine learning algorithm with IoT based intelligent waste management system. *Wireless Communications and Mobile Computing*, 2022, 2022. doi:10.1155/2022/2063372

Ullah, I., & Mahmoud, Q. H. (2021). Design and Development of a Deep Learning-Based Model for Anomaly Detection in IoT Networks. *IEEE Access : Practical Innovations, Open Solutions*, 9, 103906–103926. doi:10.1109/ACCESS.2021.3094024

Umamaheswari, S., Sreeram, S., Kritika, N., & Jyothi Prasanth, D. R. (2019). BIoT: Blockchain based IoT for Agriculture. In *2019 11th International Conference on Advanced Computing (ICoAC)* (pp. 1-6). IEEE.

Ünal, Z. (2020). Smart Farming Becomes Even Smarter with Deep Learning - A Bibliographical Analysis. *IEEE Access : Practical Innovations, Open Solutions*, 8, 105587–105609. doi:10.1109/ACCESS.2020.3000175

UNCTAD. (2017). The Role of Science, Technology, and Innovation in Ensuring Food Security by 2030. *United Nations Conference on Trade and Development (UNCTAD)*.

Ur Rahman, M., Baiardi, F., & Ricci, L. (2019). *Blockchain Smart Contract for Scalable Data Sharing in IoT: A Case Study of Smart Agriculture*. Department of Computer Science, University of Pisa.

Vanitha, S. K. R., & Boopathi, S. (2023). Artificial Intelligence Techniques in Water Purification and Utilization. In *Human Agro-Energy Optimization for Business and Industry* (pp. 202–218). IGI Global. doi:10.4018/978-1-6684-4118-3.ch010

Vennila, T., Karuna, M. S., Srivastava, B. K., Venugopal, J., Surakasi, R., & B., S. (2023). New Strategies in Treatment and Enzymatic Processes. In *Human Agro-Energy Optimization for Business and Industry* (pp. 219–240). IGI Global. doi:10.4018/978-1-6684-4118-3.ch011

Verma, A. K., Pal, S., & Kumar, S. (2021). Prediction of Different Classes of Skin Disease Using Machine Learning Techniques. In S. Tiwari, M. Trivedi, K. Mishra, A. Misra, K. Kumar, & E. Suryani (Eds.), *Smart Innovations in Communication and Computational Sciences. Advances in Intelligent Systems and Computing (vol. 1168)*. Springer. doi:10.1007/978-981-15-5345-5_8

Verma, A., & Khanna, G. (2016). A survey on digital image processing techniques for tumor detection. *Indian Journal of Science and Technology*, 9(14), 15.

Vigoya, L., Fernandez, D., Carneiro, V., & Nóvoa, F. J. (2021). IoT Dataset Validation Using Machine Learning Techniques for Traffic Anomaly Detection. *Machine Learning*, 10(12).

Vijayabaskar, P. S., Sreemathi, R., & Keertanaa, E. (2018). Crop prediction using predictive analytics. *6th International Conference on Computation of Power, Energy, Information and Communication, ICCPEIC 2017, 2018-January*, 370–373. 10.1109/ICCPEIC.2017.8290395

Vijay, P., Shanthi, S., Revathy, R., & Ohja, S. (2019). Grainchain - Agricultural Supply Chain Traceability and Management technique for Farmers Sustainability Using Blockchain Hyper Ledger. *2019 IEEE International Conference on Blockchain (Blockchain)*, 430-434. doi: 10.1109/Blockchain.2019.000-9

Vincent, P., Larochelle, H., Lajoie, I., Bengio, Y., & Manzagol, P.-A. (2010). Stacked denoising autoencoders: Learning useful representations in a deep network with a local denoising criterion. *Journal of Machine Learning Research*, 11, 3371–3408.

Walch, K. (2020). *How AI can be used in agriculture: Applications and benefits*. TechTarget. https://www.techtarget.com/searchenterpriseai/feature/Agricultural-AI-yields-better-crops-through-data-analytics

Wang et al. (2017). Generative Adversarial Networks: Introduction and Outlook. *IEEE/CAA Journal of AutomaticaSinica, 4*(4), 588–98.

Wang, E. J., Zhu, J., Jain, M., Lee, T.-J., Saba, E., Nachman, L., & Patel, S. N. (2018). Seismo: Blood pressure monitoring using built-in smartphone accelerometer and camera. *Proceedings of the 2018 CHI Conference on Human Factors in Computing Systems*, 1–9. 10.1145/3173574.3173999

Wang, Fan, & Wang. (2021). Comparative analysis of image classification algorithms based on traditional machine learning and deep learning. *Pattern Recognition Letters, 141*, 61-67. doi:10.1016/j.patrec.2020.07.042

Wang, C., & Xiao, Z. (2021). Lychee Surface Defect Detection Based on Deep Convolutional Neural Networks with GAN-Based Data Augmentation. *Agronomy (Basel), 11*(8), 1500. doi:10.3390/agronomy11081500

Wang, H., Zhu, H., Wu, H., Wang, X., Han, X., & Xu, T. (2021). A Densely Connected GRU Neural Network Based on Coattention Mechanism for Chinese Rice-Related Question Similarity Matching. *Agronomy (Basel), 11*(7), 1307. doi:10.3390/agronomy11071307

Wang, L., Xu, L., Zheng, Z., Liu, S., Li, X., Cao, L., Li, J., & Sun, C. (2021). Smart contract-based agricultural food supply chain traceability. *IEEE Access: Practical Innovations, Open Solutions, 9*, 9296–9307. doi:10.1109/ACCESS.2021.3050112

WangP.LinZ.YanX.ChenZ.DingM.SongY.MengL. (2022). *A Wearable ECG Monitor for Deep Learning Based Real-Time Cardiovascular Disease Detection.* arXiv:2201.10083

Wang, S., Liu, Y., Qing, Y., Wang, C., Lan, T., & Yao, R. (2020). Detection of insulator defects with improved ResNeSt and region proposal network. *IEEE Access: Practical Innovations, Open Solutions, 8*, 184841–184850. doi:10.1109/ACCESS.2020.3029857

Wang, T., Xu, X., Wang, C., Li, Z., & Li, D. (2021). From Smart Farming towards Unmanned Farms: A New Mode of Agricultural Production. *Agriculture, 11*(2), 145. doi:10.3390/agriculture11020145

Wang, X., & Li, D. (2006). Value added on food traceability: A supply chain management approach. In *2006 IEEE International Conference on Service Operations and Logistics, and Informatics* (pp. 1019-1024). IEEE. 10.1109/SOLI.2006.329074

Wang, Y., Singgiha, M., Wang, J., & Rit, M. (2019). Making sense of blockchain technology: How will it transform supply chains? *International Journal of Production Economics, 211*, 221–236. doi:10.1016/j.ijpe.2019.02.002

Wang, Y., Xu, C., Park, J.-H., Lee, S., Stern, Y., Yoo, S., Kim, J. H., Kim, H. S., & Cha, J. (2019). Diagnosis and prognosis of Alzheimer's disease using brain morphometry and white matter connectomes. *NeuroImage. Clinical, 23*, 101859. doi:10.1016/j.nicl.2019.101859 PMID:31150957

Wan, J., Al-awlaqi, A. A. H., Li, M., O'Grady, M., Gu, X., Wang, J., & Cao, N. (2018). Wearable IoT enabled real-time health monitoring system. *EURASIP Journal on Wireless Communications and Networking, 2018*(1), 298. doi:10.118613638-018-1308-x

Weegar, R., & Sundström, K. (2020). Using machine learning for predicting cervical cancer from Swedish electronic health records by mining hierarchical representations. *PLoS One, 15*(8), e0237911. Advance online publication. doi:10.1371/journal.pone.0237911 PMID:32822401

Wei, X.-S., Luo, J.-H., Wu, J., & Zhou, Z.-H. (2017). Selective convolutional descriptor aggregation for fine-grained image retrieval. *IEEE Transactions on Image Processing, 26*(6), 2868–2881. doi:10.1109/TIP.2017.2688133 PMID:28368819

Winston, P. H. (1984). *Artificial Intelligence* (2nd ed.). Addison-Wesley.

Woo, S., Park, J., Lee, J.-Y., & So Kweon, I. (2018). Cbam: Convolutional block attention module. *Proceedings of the European conference on computer vision (ECCV)*, 3–19.

World Health Organization. (2021). *Blindness and Vision Impairment*. WHO. https://www.who.int/news-room/fact-sheets/detail/blindness-and-visual-impairment

Wu, J., Gao, Z., & Hu, C. (2009). An Empirical Study on Several Classification Algorithms and Their Improvements. In Z. Cai, Z. Li, Z. Kang, & Y. Liu (Eds.), Lecture Notes in Computer Science: Vol. 5821. *Advances in Computation and Intelligence. ISICA 2009*. Springer. doi:10.1007/978-3-642-04843-2_30

Xiao, C., & Sun, J. (2021). Convolutional neural networks (CNN). *Introduction to Deep Learning for Healthcare, 83-*109. . doi:10.1007/978-3-030-82184-5_6

Xie, C., Sun, Y., & Luo, H. (2019). *Secured Data Storage Scheme based on Block Chain for Agricultural Products Tracking*. Beijing University of Posts and Telecommunications.

Xue, Y. J. (2018). Immature mango detection based on improved YOLOv2. *Transactions of the Chinese Society of Agricultural Engineering, 34*(7), 173-179.

Yadav A. (2020). Digital Shopping Behaviour: Influence of Augmented Reality in Social Media for Online Shopping. *Journal of Multidimensional Research and Review*.

Yang, B.; Gao, Z.; Gao, Y.; Zhu, Y. (2021). Rapid Detection and Counting of Wheat Ears in the Field Using YOLOv4 with Attention Module. *Agronomy, 11*. https://doi.org/11061202 doi:10.3390/agronomy

Yang, Qian, Cricri, Fan, & Kamarainen. (2018). *Object Detection in Equirectangular Panorama*. Academic Press.

Yang, Y., Li, Y., & Fermüller, C. (2015). Robot learning manipulation action plans by watching unconstrained videos from the world wide web. *29th AAAI Conference on Artificial Intelligence (AAAI-15)*. 10.1609/aaai.v29i1.9671

Yi, Z., Zhang, H., & Gong, T. (2017). Unsupervised dual learning for image-to-image translation. ICCV.

Yu, R., Wang, X., & Xie, X. (2022). VTNFP: An Image-based Virtual Try- on Network with Body and Clothing Feature Preservation. *IEEE Xplore*. doi:10.1109/ICCV.2019.01061

Yu, Z., Jung, D., Park, S., Hu, Y., Huang, K., Rasco, B. A., Wang, S., Ronholm, J., Lu, X., & Chen, J. (2020). *Smart traceability for food safety*. doi:10.1080/10408398.2020.1830262

Yupapin, P., Trabelsi, Y., Nattappan, A., & Boopathi, S. (2023). Performance Improvement of Wire-Cut Electrical Discharge Machining Process Using Cryogenically Treated Super-Conductive State of Monel-K500 Alloy. *Iranian Journal of Science and Technology. Transaction of Mechanical Engineering*, *47*(1), 267–283. doi:10.100740997-022-00513-0

Yu, S., Wang, S., Xiao, X., Cao, J., Yue, G., Liu, D., Wang, T., Xu, Y., & Lei, B. (2020). Multi-scale Enhanced Graph Convolutional Network for Early Mild Cognitive Impairment Detection. In *Medical Image Computing and Computer Assisted Intervention—MICCAI 2020* (pp. 228–237). Springer Science and Business Media LLC. doi:10.1007/978-3-030-59728-3_23

Zach, C., Klopschitz, M., & Pollefeys, M. (2010). Disambiguating visual relations using loop constraints. CVPR. doi:10.1109/CVPR.2010.5539801

Zeeshan, M., Member, S., Riaz, Q., Member, S., Bilal, M. A., Shahzad, M. K., Jabeen, H., Haider, S. A. L. I., & Rahim, A. (2022). Protocol-Based Deep Intrusion Detection for DoS and DDoS Attacks Using UNSW-NB15 and. *IEEE Access : Practical Innovations, Open Solutions*, *10*, 2269–2283. doi:10.1109/ACCESS.2021.3137201

Zeiler, M. D., & Fergus, R. (2014). Visualizing and understanding convolutional networks. In *Computer Vision–ECCV 2014* (pp. 818–833). Springer.

Zeng, R., Huang, W., Tan, M., Rong, Y., Zhao, P., Huang, J., & Gan, C. (2019). Graph convolutional networks for temporal action localization. *Proceedings of the IEEE/CVF International Conference on Computer Vision*, 7094–7103. 10.1109/ICCV.2019.00719

Zeng, Y., Cao, D., Wei, X., Liu, M., Zhao, Z., & Qin, Z. (2021). Multi-modal relational graph for cross-modal video moment retrieval. *Proceedings of the IEEE/CVF Conference on Computer Vision and Pattern Recognition*, 2215–2224. 10.1109/CVPR46437.2021.00225

Zhai, Y., Chen, R., Yang, Q., Li, X., & Zhao, Z. (2018). Insulator fault detection based on spatial morphological features of aerial images. *IEEE Access : Practical Innovations, Open Solutions*, 6, 35316–35326. doi:10.1109/ACCESS.2018.2846293

Zhang, F., Li, Z., Zhang, B., Du, H., Wang, B., & Zhang, X. (2019). Multi-modal deep learning model for auxiliary diagnosis of Alzheimer's disease. *Neurocomputing*, 361, 185–195. doi:10.1016/j.neucom.2019.04.093

Zhang, G., Mei, Z., Zhang, Y., Ma, X., Lo, B. P., Chen, D., & Zhang, Y. (2020). A Noninvasive Blood Glucose Monitoring System Based on Smartphone PPG Signal Processing and Machine Learning. *IEEE Transactions on Industrial Informatics*, 16(11), 7209–7218. doi:10.1109/TII.2020.2975222

Zhang, Q., Zheg, X., Hu, W., & Zhou, D. (2017). A Machine Learning-Empowered System for Long-Term Motion-Tolerant Wearable Monitoring of Blood Pressure and Heart Rate With Ear-ECG/PPG. *IEEE Access : Practical Innovations, Open Solutions*, 5, 10547–10561. doi:10.1109/ACCESS.2017.2707472

Zhang, S., Peng, H., Fu, J., Lu, Y., & Luo, J. (2021). Multi-scale 2d temporal adjacency networks for moment localization with natural language. *IEEE Transactions on Pattern Analysis and Machine Intelligence*, 44(12), 9073–9087. doi:10.1109/TPAMI.2021.3120745 PMID:34665720

Zhang, W., Han, J., & Deng, S. (2020). Heart sound classification based on scaled spectrogram and tensor decomposition. *Expert Systems with Applications*, 84, 220–231. doi:10.1016/j.eswa.2017.05.014

Zhang, W., Miao, Z., Li, N., He, C., & Sun, T. (2022). Review of Current Robotic Approaches for Precision Weed Management. *Current Robotics Reports*, 3(3), 139–151. doi:10.100743154-022-00086-5 PMID:35891887

Zhang, X. (2020). Blockchain-based safety management system for the grain supply chain. In *Proceedings of the 2020 IEEE International Conference on Industrial Internet (ICII)* (pp. 847-852). IEEE. 10.1109/ACCESS.2020.2975415

Zhang, Z., Lin, Z., Zhao, Z., & Xiao, Z. (2019). Cross-modal interaction networks for query-based moment retrieval in videos. *Proceedings of the 42nd International ACM SIGIR Conference on Research and Development in Information Retrieval*, 655–664. 10.1145/3331184.3331235

Zhao, J., Mathieu, M., Goroshin, R., & Lecun, Y. (2015). *Stacked what-where autoencoders*. arXiv preprint arXiv:1506.02351.

Zhao, Y., Gong, L., Zhou, B., Huang, Y., & Liu, C. (2016). Detecting tomatoes in greenhouse scenes by combining AdaBoost classifier and colour analysis. *Biosystems Engineering*, 148, 127–137. doi:10.1016/j.biosystemseng.2016.05.001

Zhao, Z.-Q., Zheng, P., Xu, S.-T., & Wu, X. (2019, November). Object Detection With Deep Learning: A Review. *IEEE Transactions on Neural Networks and Learning Systems*, 30(11), 3212–3232. doi:10.1109/TNNLS.2018.2876865 PMID:30703038

Zhao, Z., Zhen, Z., Zhang, L., Qi, Y., Kong, Y., & Zhang, K. (2019). Insulator detection method in inspection image based on improved faster R-CNN. *Energies*, 12(7), 1204. doi:10.3390/en12071204

Zheng, Y., Guo, H., Zhang, L., Wu, J., Li, Q., & Lv, F. (2019). Machine Learning-Based Framework for Differential Diagnosis Between Vascular Dementia and Alzheimer's Disease Using Structural MRI Features. *Frontiers in Neurology*, *10*, 10. doi:10.3389/fneur.2019.01097 PMID:31708854

Zhou, T., Krahenbuhl, P., Aubry, M., Huang, Q., & Efros, A. A. (2016). Learning dense correspondence via 3dguided cycle consistency. CVPR.

Zhu, J., Park, T., Isola, P., & Efros, A. A. (2017*). Unpaired Image-to-Image Translation using Cycle-Consistent Adversarial Networks*. https://doi.org//arXiv.1703.10593 doi:10.1109/ICCV.2017.244

Zhu, N., Liu, X., Liu, Z., Hu, K., Wang, Y., Tan, J., Huang, M., Zhu, Q., Ji, X., Jiang, Y., & Guo, Y. (2018). Deep Learning for Smart Agriculture: Concepts, Tools, Applications, and Opportunities. *International Journal of Agricultural and Biological Engineering*, *11*(4), 32–44. doi:10.25165/j.ijabe.20181104.4475

Zhu, X., Lyu, S., Wang, X., & Zhao, Q. (2021). TPH-YOLOv5: Improved YOLOv5 based on transformer prediction head for object detection on drone-captured scenarios. *Proceedings of the IEEE/CVF International Conference on Computer Vision*, 2778–2788. 10.1109/ICCVW54120.2021.00312

Zilcha-Mano, S., Mikulincer, M., & Shaver, P. R. (2012, October 1). Pets as Safe Havens and Secure Bases: The Moderating Role of Pet Attachment Orientations. *Journal of Research in Personality*, *46*(5), 571–580. doi:10.1016/j.jrp.2012.06.005

Zouka, A., & Hosni, M. (2021). Secure IoT communications for smart healthcare monitoring system. *Internet of Things*, *13*, 100036. Advance online publication. doi:10.1016/j.iot.2019.01.003

Zou, X., Durazzo, T. C., & Meyerhoff, D. J. (2018). Regional Brain Volume Changes in Alcohol-Dependent Individuals During Short-Term and Long-Term Abstinence. *Alcoholism, Clinical and Experimental Research*, *42*(6), 1062–1072. doi:10.1111/acer.13757 PMID:29672876

About the Contributors

P. Swarnalatha is a Professor in the School of Computing Science and Engineering, Vellore Institute of Technology at Vellore, India. She pursued her Ph.D degree in Image Processing and Intelligent Systems. She has published more than 130 papers in International Journals/International Conference Proceedings/National Conferences. She is having 22+ years of teaching experiences. She has filed two Patents and also awarded with Dr. APJ Abdul Kalam Award for Teaching Excellence. She is a senior member of IACSIT, CSI, ACM, IACSIT, IEEE (WIE), ACEEE. She is an Editorial board member/reviewer of reputed International/ National Journals and Conferences. Her current research interest includes Image Processing, Remote Sensing, Artificial Intelligence and Software Engineering.

* * *

C.V. Suresh Babu is a pioneer in Content Development. A true entrepreneur, He floated Anniyappa Publications, a company which is very active in bringing out books related to Computer Science and Management. Dr. C.V. Suresh Babu has also ventured into SB Institute, a centre for knowledge transfer.:= He holds Ph.D in Engineering Education from National Institute of Technical Teachers Training & Research, Chennai along with seven Master degrees in various disciplines such as Engineering, Computer Applications, Management, Commerce, Economics, Psychology, Law and Education. He also has the UGC-NET/SET qualifications in the disciplines of Computer Science, Management, Commerce and Education to his credit. Personal blog: https://sites.google.com/view/cvsureshbabu/.e2f99afb-1a1c-43c5-978b-f2cacc9d88ea

Shiva Chaithanya Goud Bollipelly is a student in the School of Computing Science and Engineering at Vellore Institute of Technology in Vellore, India. He is pursuing a Bachelor of Technology degree in Computer Science Engineering. His current research interests include Data Science, Image Processing, Blockchain Technology, Machine Learning, and Artificial Intelligence.

Sampath Boopathi () completed his undergraduate in Mechanical Engineering and postgraduate in the field of Computer-Aided Design. He completed his Ph.D. from Anna University and his field of research includes Manufacturing and optimization. He published 60 more research articles in Internationally Peer-reviewed journals, one Patent grant, and three published patents.He has 16 more years of academic and research experiences in the various Engineering Colleges in Tamilnadu, India.

Ankita Chaturvedi is an Associate Professor at IIS (deemed to be University), Jaipur and has over 16 years of experience in Teaching, Research, Administration as Department. She is a multifaceted, detail-oriented, and focused professional, with strong teaching experience in shaping and maximizing the potential of individuals toward career growth and self-improvement.. She is an author or Co-author of more than 41 research papers published in national or international refereed journals, 10 chapters in edited books, 3 books with ISBN number and more than 48 conference contributions. She has received several (21) awards in the field of academics and research. Dr Chaturvedi is also on Editorial Board member of various journals. She has been convener of various academic events like international conference, training programmes, Research workshop, Board of Studies, etc.

Megala G. received B.E. and M.E. degrees in Computer Science and Engineering from Anna University in 2009 and 2013 respectively. She is currently pursuing her Ph.D. degree in Computer Science and Engineering from Vellore Institute of Technology, Vellore. She has 8 years of teaching experience and 3 years of research associate. Her field of specialization is cryptosystems, computational theory and compilers. Her research interests include multimedia security, lightweight cryptography, image and video processing, cloud computing and deep learning.

Balaji G. N. is an Associate Professor from the School of Computer Science and Engineering, Vellore Institute of Technology, Vellore. He worked as an Assistant Professor in the Department of IT, CVR College of Engineering, Hyderabad. He graduated from Annamalai University and post-graduated with M.Tech from SRM University. He completed his doctoral research in the Department of CSE, Faculty of Engineering and Technology, Annamalai University under the guidance of Dr. T. S. Subashini and his area of research is Medical Image Analysis. He published his papers in 35 international journals and conferences, including Springer, Elsevier, and Taylor & Francis. He coordinated a UGC-funded research project, Computer Aided Detection and Diagnosis of Diaphyseal Femur Fracture. He is an active editorial member in Austin Cardiology Journal, USA, and in professional bodies like IEEE, ACM, IAENG, ISTE, and EAI. His research interest includes Image Processing, Pattern Recognition, and Computer Vision. He has organized two National workshops and faculty development programs. He is regularly invited to deliver lectures in various programs to impart skills in research methodology to students.

K. Suresh Joesph received his Bachelor's Degree in Computer Science & Engineering from Bharathiar University and a Master's in Computer Science & Engineering from the University of Madras in 1999 and 2003, respectively. He received his Doctoral Computer Science & Engineering degree from Anna University in 2013. Presently he is working as an Associate Professor in the Department of Computer Science at Pondicherry University. His areas of research interest include Services Computing and Image Processing. He has more than 50 research publications in reputed and peer-reviewed journals.

Niha K. is currently working as an Assistant Professor in the Department of Information Security, School of Computer Science and Engineering, Vellore Institute of Science and Technology, India. She was selected by UGC as a Research Fellow with Maulana Azad National Fellowship Award (20152020) to pursue her Doctoral Research. She completed her M.Tech in Computer Science and Engineering from Crescent Institute of Science and Technology, Chennai, India. She completed her B.Tech in Computer Science and Engineering from Avinashilingam University, Coimbatore, India. She has published papers and book chapters on machine learning, deep learning, and Image and signal processing domain in

IEEE, Springer, and Inderscience journals (all Scopus/SCI indexed). She has been selected for Research Excellence Award 2021 by InSc, India. She acted as a reviewer and session co-chair for the IEEE conference and Special Session organizer of the International Conference. She delivered talks on webinars and acted as an organizer for national webinars and workshops. She has published a patent with a grant in her area of research. She is an IEEE Member. Her area of research includes Data mining, Machine learning, Pattern detection, HCI, IoT/IoMT and Deep learning.

A. Kaneswaran received B.Sc Eng Degree with first class honours from University of Peradeniya in 2008 and PhD from Queensland University of Technology (QUT) in 2015. From July 2008 till July 2011, he worked as an Engineer at Sri Lanka Telecom (PLC). He handled new service provisioning process and fault handling process configuration in Operations Support System (Clarity). He worked as a core team member for new CRM system implementation team at SLT. He involved in CRM system implementation, integrations of CRM system with OSS and CRM system with BSS. His PhD research was on "Robust Face Clustering for Real-World Data". His thesis has investigated how to cluster a large number of faces within a multi-media corpus in the presence of large session variation. Findings from his research contribute to improving the performance of both face verification systems and the fully automated clustering of faces from a large video corpus. He obtained most popular thesis (technical research) award from Smart Services Cooperative Research Centre (Smart Services CRC), Smart Services CRC Postgraduate Scholarship, QUT fee Waiver Scholarship (FEEWAIVE) and QUT Write-up Scholarship while pursuing his PhD degree. He obtained Mahapola Higher Education (Merit) Scholarship for the performance in Advanced Level Examination. He is a Member of the IEEE and Associate Member of the Institution of Engineers Sri Lanka (IESL).

Pranav Katte is a pre-final year college student majoring in Computer Science Engineering from Vellore Institute of Technology.

Saifullah Khalid obtained two Ph.D. degrees: one in Electronics and Communication Engineering and another in Electrical Engineering from Institute of Engineering and Technology, Lucknow. He worked at IIT BHU, Varanasi and different Universities before joining the dynamic job of Air Traffic Control officer at Airports Authority of India in 2008. Currently, he is working as a R& D Member at Civil Aviation Research Organization, India. His research interests are in the area of Optimization Algorithms applications for power quality improvement. He has developed three novel optimization algorithms Adaptive Spider Net search Algorithm, Adaptive Mosquito Blood Search Algorithm, and Adaptive blanket body cover search algorithm. Dr. Khalid has published around 100 research papers in various International Journals and Conferences including IEEE, Elsevier, Springer and many more in India and abroad. He is on the editorial board of many International Journals and also in the reviewer's panel of many International Journals (Including IEEE Transactions, Elsevier, Springer, Wiley, etc.). Dr. Khalid has authored four books published by University Science Press, USA.

N. Krishnamoorthy is a faculty member in the Department of Computer Science and Applications (MCA) at the College of Science and Humanities, SRM Institute of Science and Technology, situated in Ramapuram, Chennai, Tamil Nadu 600089, India.

A.V. Senthil Kumar is working as a Director & Professor in the Department of Research and PG in Computer Applications, Hindusthan College of Arts and Science, Coimbatore since 05/03/2010. He has to his credit 11 Book Chapters, 265 papers in International and National Journals, 25 papers in International Conferences, 5 papers in National Conferences, and edited Nine books (IGI Global, USA). He is an Editor-in-Chief for various journals. Key Member for India, Machine Intelligence Research Lab (MIR Labs). He is an Editorial Board Member and Reviewer for various International Journals. He is also a Committee member for various International Conferences. He is a Life member of International Association of Engineers (IAENG), Systems Society of India (SSI), member of The Indian Science Congress Association, member of Internet Society (ISOC), International Association of Computer Science and Information Technology (IACSIT), Indian Association for Research in Computing Science (IARCS), and committee member for various International Conferences.

N.M.G. Kumar is a faculty member in the Department of Electrical and Electronics Engineering at Mohan Babu University, affiliated with Sree Vidyanikethan Engineering College, located in Tirupathi, Andhra Pradesh 517102, India.

Palanivel Kuppusamy holds a Ph.D. in Computer Science & Engineering (2023) from Pondicherry University (A Central University), Puducherry, India. He is a graduate of Engineering (1994) from Bharathiar University, Tamil Nadu, India, and a Post Graduate of Engineering (1998) from Pondicherry University, Puducherry, India. He has over 20 years of diverse professional and teaching experience at Pondicherry University. His research interests include smart education, software architecture, network management & analytics, and technological applications in the higher education sector.

Sharmila L. is working as a Professor and Head in the Department of Computer Science & Engineering at Agni College of Technology, Chennai, India. She received her M.E., and Ph.D degrees in Computer Science and Engineering from Anna University and Sathyabama University. She has secured distinction in both B.E., and M.E. She is an Anna University Rank Holder in PG degree. She is a reviewer for many SCI Indexed Journals like Ambient Intelligence and Humanized Computing (Springer), Journal of Supercomputing, Computer Communications (Elsevier), Microprocessor and Microsystems, Wiley and so on. She has 16 years of Teaching Experience with 6 years of research experience. Her main area of research activity is Data Mining, Medical Image processing, Wireless Networks, Network security, Big data analytics. She has published many research articles in refereed journals like Elsevier and Springer. She has been serving as an Organizing Chair and Program Chair of several International conferences and in the Program Committees of several National / International conferences.

Rohaya Latip is an Associate Professor at Faculty of Computer Science and Information Technology, University Putra Malaysia. She holds a Ph.D in Distributed Database in year 2009 and Msc. in Distributed System in 2001 both from University Putra Malaysia, Malaysia. She graduated her Bachelor of Computer Science from University Technology Malaysia, Malaysia in 1999. She was the Head of Department of Communication Technology and Network in 2017-2022. She served as an Associate Professor at Najran University, Kingdom of Arab Saudi (2012-2013). She is the Head of HPC section in Institute for Mathematic Research (INSPEM)., University Putra Malaysia (2011-2012) and consulted the Campus Grid project and also the Wireless for hostel in Campus UPM project. She is also a Co-researcher at INSPEM. She is the editorial board of International Journal of Computer Networks and

Communications Security (IJCNCS), editorial board of International Journal of Digital Contents and Applications (IJDCA) and editorial board for International Journal of Computer Networks and Applications (IJCNA). Her research interests include Big Data, Cloud and Grid Computing, Network management, and Distributed database. For her research work, she won Gold medal at ICANS 2019, Canada, and two medals at The World Inventor Award Festival (WIAF) 2014 organized by Korea Invention News. She was awarded Gold medal at IMIT-SIC Innovation Expo in 2018, Riau Indonesia, I-RIA 2018 (Best of the best award), Malaysia Technology Expo (MTE2014) and Malaysian Innovation Expo (MiExpo2013). She also won Silver medal at National Design, Research and Innovation Expo (PRPI) 2010 and Bronze medal at National Design, Research and Innovation Expo (PRPI) 2007 and 2006 respectively. She has published more than 80 papers in international and national journals, proceedings and posters.

Krishnaveni M. is an Assistant Professor of Department of Computer Science, Avinashilingam University for Women, Coimbatore, Tamil Nadu, India. She has research experience under Defence projects and worked on disciplines like IoT, Image Processing, Speech Processing, Data Mining, and Computational Intelligence. She has published 4 Books, 6 Book chapters, 1 Monograph and 86 research papers in both national and international level. She has research projects under various funding agencies and acts as an active member of Centre for Machine Learning and Artificial Intelligence and coordinating AI Start-up Programme (Product Development Lab) for the student. She has received awards such as best young teacher award IASTE 2017, best NSS Programme officer award, NYLP 2016, Government of India.

Jennyfer Susan M. B. is a Research Scholar in the Department of Computer Science, Centre for Machine Learning and Intelligence at Avinashilingam Institute for Home Science and Higher Education for Women, Tamil Nadu, India. She has published 1 International Journal, 1 National Conference, 2 International Conferences, 1 Book Chapter and 1 Book Publication. The Research area of interest includes Vision AI, Medical Image Processing and Neural Networks.

Sahil Manoj Chavan is a faculty member in the Department of Electrical Power System at Sandip University, located in Nashik, Maharashtra 422213, India.

Ismail Bin Musirin obtained Bachelor of Electrical Engineering (Hons) in 1990 from Universiti Teknologi Malaysia, MSc in Pulsed Power Technology in 1992 from University of Strathclyde, United Kingdom and PhD in Electrical Engineering from Universiti Teknologi MARA (UiTM), Malaysia in 2005. He is currently a Professor of Power System at the School of Electrical Engineering (formerly known as the Faculty of Electrical Engineering), College of Engineering, UiTM and headed the Power System Operation (POSC) Computational Intelligence Research Group. He has published, over 350 papers in international indexed journals and conferences. He has been given the opportunity to review papers in IEEE Transactions, Elsevier Science, WSEAS, John Wiley, IET and some other publishers. He has chaired more than 20 international conference since 2007. To date, he has delivered keynote speeches at Cambridge University, United Kingdom, Dubai, Korea, China, India and Malaysia. He has also been given opportunity to evaluate research grants at the national and international levels. His research interest includes artificial intelligence, optimization techniques, power system analysis, renewable energy optimization, distributed generation and power system stability. He is a professional engineer and a senior member of International Association of Computer Science and Information Technology (IACSIT), member of Artificial Immune System Society (ARTIST) and member of International Association of

Engineers (IAENG), Hong Kong. To date he has been appointed as the Visiting Professor at UTHM BP, UTHM Pagoh and Lincoln University. He is also one of the Panel Experts for UMP Engineering Programme, besides being appointed as the External Examiner for the Bachelor Degree Programmes at Lim Kok Wing University and Lincoln University and External Examiner for MSc Degree Programme at Universiti Teknikal Malaysia Melaka. He has been appointed as the External Adviser for Universiti Malaysia Terengganu (UMT). He is very grateful and blessed for being the recipient of "The Most Prolific Author Award" of UiTM 2020".

Hema N. is a faculty member in the Department of Information Science and Engineering at RNS Institute of Technology, located in Bengaluru, Karnataka 560098, India.

Satvik Nadkarni is a third year Computer Science Engineering Student studying in VIT Vellore.

Kalyanaraman P. is a Professor in the School of Computer Science and Engineering at VIT University, Vellore, India. He received his Masters' degree in Computer Science from PSG College of Technology, Coimbatore. He has received Doctoral Degree in Computer Science and Engineering from VIT University, Vellore. He has teaching experience of more than twenty five years. His areas of interest include Distributed Computing, E-Learning Systems, Modeling and Simulation and Knowledge Engineering. He is the life member of Computer Science and Engineering and Indian Society of Technical Education.

Subashini P. is working for Department of Computer Science, Avinashilingam University for Women, Tamil Nadu India, from 1994. She also the coordinator of the Centre for Machine Learning and Intelligence sanctioned by Department of Science and Technology. Her research has spanned a large number of disciplines like Image analysis, Pattern recognition, Neural networks, and Computational Intelligence. She has authored and co- authored 4 Book, 4 Book chapters, 1 Monograph, 145 research papers both at international and national level. she has ten sponsored research projects of worth more than 2.54 crores from various Government funding agencies. She also extended her contribution towards various international collaborations with universities from USA, Germany and Morocco.

Venkatesan R. received Bachelor of Engineering degree in Computer Science and Engineering from Park College of Engineering and Technology, Coimbatore and Master of Engineering in Computer Science and Engineering from Sona College of Technology, Salem. He pursued his Ph.D degree in Hyperspectral Image processing from VIT University, Vellore. He has more than 16 years of experience in teaching. He has more than 30 publications in national and international journals and conferences. His current research includes satellite image processing and neural networks. Currently, he is an Assistant Professor in School of Computing, SASTRA University, Thanjavur.

M. Sabarimuthu is a faculty member in the Department of Electrical and Electronics Engineering at Kongu Engineering College, situated in Perundurai, Tamil Nadu 638060, India.

Shivansh Sahai completed class X (ICSE) board in 2018, class XII (ISC) board in 2020 from City Montessori School, Lucknow. Currently pursuing a bachelor's degree (2020-2024) in Computer Science with specialization in IOT from Vellore Institute of Technology Vellore, Vellore and actively working, researching in the field of software development, web scraping and Database operations to build solution for real world problem.

Jonathan Rufus Samuel is currently pursuing a bachelor's degree (2020-2024) in Computer Science Engineering with specialization in IoT from Vellore Institute of Technology Vellore, Vellore. He is actively working and researching in the fields of Software development, Engineering and Planning, Fog and Edge Based Simulation Technologies and MERN applications. He is also an active Open Source contributor, working on Open-Source projects in various fields. Graduated from Bishop Cotton Boys' School, year 2020.

Ramani Selvanambi is an Associate Professor in the School of Computing Science and Engineering at Vellore Institute of Technology (VIT), Vellore, India. He received his B.E in Computer Science and Engineering from Madras University and M. Tech Computer Science and Engineering from Bharathidasan University and Ph.D. in Computer Science and Engineering from Vellore Institute of Technology (VIT), Vellore. He has 13+ years of experience in teaching and 2 years of experience in the Consultancy and Software Industry. He has published about 40 research papers in International Journals on Machine Learning, Nature-Inspired Algorithms, Cyber Security and Health Care. His research interest includes Data Mining, Machine learning, Database Systems, Optimization Techniques and Cyber Security. He is a life member of the Computer Society of India (CSI), IEEE and other technical societies.

Suganthi Shanmugananthan is working as an Assistant Professor in the Department of Genetics and Plant Breeding, Faculty of Agriculture, Annamalai University. She has more than ten+ years of teaching experience and more than fifteen years of research experience. She completed her Under Graduate in 1998, her Postgraduate in 2000, and a Doctoral degree in 2009 at Annamalai University. Her field of research specialization is heterosis breeding and resistance breeding. She has published 35 research articles in International and National Journals and three books and authored three book chapters. She has presented research papers at national and international seminars, conferences, and symposiums.

Prarthana Shiwakoti is an undergraduate student at Vellore Institute of Technology.

Sanjay V. received his B.E. Computer science and Engineering Degree from Adithya Institute of Technology, Coimbatore, India in 2019 and his M.E. Computer science and Engineering Degree from Kumaraguru College of Technology, Coimbatore, India in 2021.He is currently pursuing his Doctoral Research in School of Computer Science and Engineering at Vellore Institute of Technology, Vellore, India. His research interest includes Medical Image processing, Deep Learning and computer vision.

Index

T

U

V

Y

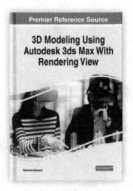

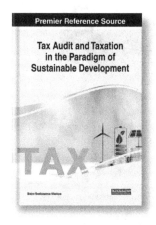

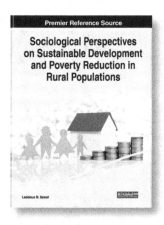

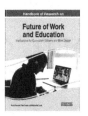

Printed in the United States
by Baker & Taylor Publisher Services